Hellenistic Studies at a Crossroads

Trends in Classics –
Supplementary Volumes

―

Edited by
Franco Montanari and Antonios Rengakos

Scientific Committee
Alberto Bernabé · Margarethe Billerbeck
Claude Calame · Philip R. Hardie · Stephen J. Harrison
Stephen Hinds · Richard Hunter · Christina Kraus
Giuseppe Mastromarco · Gregory Nagy
Theodore D. Papanghelis · Giusto Picone
Kurt Raaflaub · Bernhard Zimmermann

Volume 25

Hellenistic Studies at a Crossroads

Exploring Texts, Contexts and Metatexts

Edited by
Richard Hunter, Antonios Rengakos
and Evina Sistakou

DE GRUYTER

ISBN 978-3-11-055492-2
e-ISBN 978-3-11-034294-9
ISSN 1868-4785

Library of Congress Cataloging-in-Publication Data
A CIP catalog record for this book has been applied for at the Library of Congress.

Bibliographic information published by the Deutsche Nationalbibliothek
The Deutsche Nationalbibliothek lists this publication in the Deutsche Nationalbibliografie; detailed bibliographic data are available in the Internet at http://dnb.dnb.de.

© 2017 Walter de Gruyter GmbH, Berlin/Boston
This volume is text- and page-identical with the hardback published in 2014.
Logo: Christopher Schneider, Laufen
Printing: Hubert & Co. GmbH & Co. KG, Göttingen

♾ Printed on acid-free paper
Printed in Germany

www.degruyter.com

Preface

It has become something of a cliché that the study of Hellenistic poetry has undergone a revolution in the last few decades, and mushrooming international conferences are one of the signs that a subject has been embraced by (most of) the discipline as, if not in the very middle of the mainstream, at least not just curious flotsam or even Callimachean συρφετός. The 2012 Thessaloniki conference, and the volume which now follows, show beyond any doubt that a further sign of 'coming of age' is the sheer variety of subjects and texts which lie open to be reclaimed and which scholars have indeed not been slow to exploit. 'Hellenistic poetry' is no longer (has not been for some time) the 'big three' and the familiar, glib commonplaces about 'learned poetry', but it is the study of a set of widely diffused and long-lived poetic cultures, preserved in papyri, manuscripts and inscriptions, which dip in and out of our sight, but which provide all we know about the transmission of Greek poetry over three centuries and without which much of Roman poetry and imperial Greek culture would remain all but inexplicable.

Hellenistic poetry also offers one powerful litmus-test of the validity of many time-honoured and comforting assertions of how Greek culture changed over time, of whether and how the 'Hellenistic' is indeed different from 'the classical'. One of the strongest trends of recent years has been the recognition that Hellenistic poets were seeking to recreate and restore, as much as they sought change and novelty. If this volume cannot (and should not) pretend to be ground-breaking, it nevertheless celebrates liberation from an excessively narrow scholarly agenda and a real recognition of the size of the task in front of us.

It is in fact the very size of the task which needs emphasising. If Hellenistic studies really stand at a crossroads, the danger is not of taking the wrong path, but rather of not making the best use of all the rich variety of critical opportunities which beckon. It is that variety of both material and methodology that offers genuine hope of increased understanding of extraordinary processes of cultural change and interaction. No area of classical studies can become too inward-looking, too closed up, without running the danger of increasingly repetitive sterility, a danger from which it is younger scholars and graduate students who will most suffer, because they will be urged down paths which lead, not to Vice, but nowhere at all.

All papers assembled in this volume were presented during an international conference held in Thessaloniki (25–27 May, 2012), which was organised by the Department of Classics of the Aristotle University. The conference would never have been materialised without the financial support of the Welfare Foundation for Social and Cultural Affairs (K.I.K.P.E.); heartfelt thanks go to the Vice-President of the foundation, Manos Dimitrakopoulos, who embraced the *Trends in Classics* conference with warmth and enthusiasm. Substantial assistance was provided at various stages by the Aristotle University Research Committee, and the publishing houses D.N. Papadimas and University Studio Press. Our sincere gratitude goes to all of them.

Richard Hunter   Cambridge-Thessaloniki,
Antonios Rengakos   January 2014
Evina Sistakou

Table of Contents

Preface —— V

I. **Genres**

Giulio Massimilla
Callimachus and Early Greek Elegy —— 3

David Sider
Didactic poetry: The Hellenistic invention of a pre-existing genre —— 13

G. O. Hutchinson
Hellenistic Poetry and Hellenistic Prose —— 31

II. **Style and Narrative**

Richard Hunter
Theocritus and the Style of Hellenistic Poetry —— 55

Kathryn Gutzwiller
Poetic Meaning, Place, and Dialect in the Epigrams of Meleager —— 75

Alexander Sens
Narrative and Simile in Lycophron's *Alexandra* —— 97

Annemarie Ambühl
(Re)constructing Myth: Elliptical Narrative in Hellenistic and Latin Poetry —— 113

III. **Aesthetics**

Evina Sistakou
From Emotion to Sensation: The Discovery of the Senses in Hellenistic Poetry —— 135

Filippomaria Pontani
"Your first commitments tangible again" - Alexandrianism as an aesthetic category? —— 157

Évelyne Prioux
The Jewels and the Dolls: Late Hellenistic Ecphrastic Epigrams as Metapoetic Texts —— 185

IV. Scholarship

Marco Fantuzzi
Tragic smiles: When tragedy gets too comic for Aristotle and later Hellenistic readers —— 215

Andrew Faulkner
Philo Senior and the Waters of Jerusalem —— 235

V. Contexts

Annette Harder
Spiders in the Greek Wide Web? —— 259

Ivana Petrovic
Posidippus and Achaemenid royal propaganda —— 273

Silvia Barbantani
"Déjà la pierre pense où votre nom s'inscrit"
　　Identity in context in verse epitaphs for Hellenistic soldiers —— **301**

Bibliography —— 335

Notes on Contributors —— 371

Index —— 375

I. Genres

Giulio Massimilla
Callimachus and Early Greek Elegy

Within Callimachus' poetry, elegy plays a prominent role. Especially his *Aetia* gained him a place in the late 'canons' of the elegists, where we find the names of Mimnermus, Philitas and Callimachus, often preceded by that of Callinus (test. 87 Pf.).[1] Callimachus himself had an influence on the constitution of such lists, since he explicitely proclaims his allegiance to Mimnermus, and probably to Philitas, in the prologue of the *Aetia* (fr. 1, 9–12 M. = Pf.).[2] He expected glory from composing the elegiac *Aetia*, and at the end of the first poem of the collection he begs the Graces to give long-lasting fame to his *elegoi* (fr. 9, 13f. M. = 7, 13f. Pf.).

The elegiac form is very well suited to the contents of the *Aetia*. Callimachus chose to build this most innovatory and experimental work upon a firm traditional base. The elegiac tradition, as a matter of fact, is an important precedent for the great variety of themes and multiplicity of voices that are to be found in the *Aetia*.[3]

The generic versatility of elegy was fully exploited by Callimachus also in other poems, most notably for us in his fifth hymn, *The Bath of Pallas*, a rare example of a hymn in elegiacs and not hexameters.[4] He also composed an independent elegiac epinicion, *The Victory of Sosibius* (fr. 384 Pf.), and one or two elegies that probably celebrated the Cyrenean king Magas and his daughter Berenice (frr. 387–388 Pf.).[5]

We would like to know more about a Callimachean elegy entitled *Grapheion*, since its only surviving couplet contains a harsh criticism of Archilochus (fr. 380 Pf.).[6] We are even more curious about the Callimachean *Ibis*, whose two surviving fragments (frr. 381–382 Pf.) are dubious and do not allow us to say whether

---

[1] The connection between Philitas and Callimachus is already asserted by Propertius, Ovid and Statius, who frequently refer to them as representatives of the same literary tradition: see Massimilla 1996, 209.
[2] Although the interpretation of this passage is much debated, Philitas' relevance to it should not be called into question: see Massimilla 1996, 206–213; Harder 2012 (2), 32–44.
[3] See M. West 1974, 14–18; Harder 2012 (1), 32.
[4] See Bulloch 1985, 31–38.
[5] For a recent discussion of frr. 385–391 Pf., see Chiesa 2009.
[6] On fr. 380 Pf. see Porro 2007, 215; Di Marco 2010. The title *Grapheion* probably means *Archive*. Judging from fr. 380 Pf., we may infer that it dealt with literary questions. We do not know whether it was an elegy proper or a collection of epigrams composed in elegiacs. See D'Alessio 1996 (2), 676 n. 4.

or not the *Ibis* was written in elegiacs like the Ovidian poem bearing the same title.

So Callimachus practised elegiac poetry quite often. But what was his attitude towards the elegiac tradition? I have selected some passages, where we see or may reasonably suppose that Callimachus was inspired by the early Greek elegists. These passages give us an opportunity to explore how Callimachus both imitated and distanced himself from his elegiac predecessors.

Let us start with Tyrtaeus. At the beginning of one of his fragments (fr. 12, 1– 9 W. = 9, 1– 9 G.-P.)[7] we find a long passage, where Tyrtaeus says that he considers all kinds of skills and qualities to be less important than military valour:

οὔτ' ἂν μνησαίμην οὔτ' ἐν λόγῳ ἄνδρα τιθείμην[8]
 οὔτε ποδῶν ἀρετῆς οὔτε παλαιμοσύνης,
οὐδ' εἰ Κυκλώπων μὲν ἔχοι μέγεθός τε βίην τε,
 νικώη δὲ θέων Θρηΐκιον Βορέην,
οὐδ' εἰ Τιθωνοῖο φυὴν χαριέστερος εἴη,
 πλουτοίη δὲ Μίδεω καὶ Κινύρεω μάλιον,
οὐδ' εἰ Ταντανλίδεω Πέλοπος βασιλεύτερος εἴη,
 γλῶσσαν δ' Ἀδρήστου μειλιχόγηρυν ἔχοι,
οὐδ' εἰ πᾶσαν ἔχοι δόξαν πλὴν θούριδος ἀλκῆς.

I would not mention or take account of a man for his prowess in running or in wrestling, not even if he had the size and strength of the Cyclopes and outstripped Thracian Boreas in the race, nor if he were more handsome than Tithonus in form and richer than Midas and Cinyras, nor if he were more kingly than Pelops, son of Tantalus, and had a tongue that spoke as winningly as Adrastus', nor if he had a reputation for everything save furious valour.[9]

Callimachus seems to allude to this passage of Tyrtaeus in his elegy about Acontius and Cydippe, from the third book of the *Aetia* (fr. 174, 44– 48 M. = 75, 44– 48 Pf.). Here Callimachus puts forward his opinion that Acontius, after finally managing to marry Cydippe, would not have given up his first night with her for anything in the world:

---

7 The authorship of the fragment has been doubted on unconvincing grounds (as shown by Prato 1968, 116–138), and is now widely accepted. The fragment's main source is Stobaeus' *Anthology* (4, 10, 1 + 6), that transmits all its 22 couplets: we may well have here an entire poem.
8 Like Prato 1968, 124 and Gerber 1999, 56 I prefer the reading τιθείμην (twice attested in Plato's *Laws*, 629a and 660e) to the reading τιθείην (attested in Stobaeus). M. West 1974, 187 chooses instead τιθείην.
9 The translations into English of the passages from the early Greek elegists are those of Gerber 1999.

οὔ σε δοκέω τημοῦτος, Ἀκόντιε, νυκτὸς ἐκείνης
 ἀντί κε, τῇ μίτρης ἥψαο παρθενίης,
οὐ σφυρὸν Ἰφίκλειον ἐπιτρέχον ἀσταχύεσσιν
 οὐδ' ἃ Κελαινίτης ἐκτεάτιστο Μίδης
δέξασθαι.

I do not think, Acontius, that then you would have swapped that night in which you touched her maiden's girdle for the ankle of Iphiclus, who ran on the corn-ears, or for the possessions of Midas of Celaenae.[10]

Several strong similarities between these two passages suggest that Callimachus is alluding to Tyrtaeus.

1) Both poets begin by putting forward their opinions within negative clauses (οὔτ' ἂν μνησαίμην οὔτ' ἐν λόγῳ ... τιθείμην and οὐ ... δοκέω).

2) Both passages are arranged as catalogues that list inferior attributes in order to emphasize a more precious one. These catalogues are built on anaphoric series of negative particles that tend to occupy the beginnings of the lines.[11]

3) Callimachus seems to take his inspiration from Tyrtaeus also for the content of his passage that looks like a condensed version of the archaic one.

Tyrtaeus' catalogue is quite long and is arranged as a priamel.[12] In vv. 2–8 he lists eight inferior skills and qualities and connects most of them to mythical *exempla*. In v. 9 he also adds a summary reference to all kinds of non-military reputation.[13]

Callimachus shortens the catalogue, by choosing only two of the attributes listed by Tyrtaeus, i.e. fast running and wealth. Besides, while Tyrtaeus refers to "prowess in running" (ποδῶν ἀρετῆς, v. 2) without adding a mythical *exemplum*, Callimachus mentions Iphiclus as the fast runner *par excellence*, whose extraordinary speed over the corn-ears was already referred to in the Hesiodic *Catalogue* (fr. 62 M.-W.).[14] And while Tyrtaeus names both Midas and the king

---

10 The translations into English of the passages from Callimachus' *Aetia* are those of Harder 2012 (1) (with some minor changes).
11 For this kind of anaphoric patterning cf. also Xenoph. fr. 2, 15–17 W. = G.-P., [Thgn.] 701 and 713. See Faraone 2008, 122 n. 14.
12 See Race 1982, 57–59. By contrast, as Race 1982, 104 n. 167 rightly remarks, Callimachus' passage is not a priamel, because there "the climax (νυκτὸς ἐκείνης, 44) *precedes* the foil".
13 See Faraone 2008, 33–35; 100–102.
14 See Schwartz 1960, 585; Reinsch-Werner 1976, 367; Hunter 2005a, 251 = 2008b, 483; Massimilla 2010, 374. Note that Tyrtaeus, after introducing no mythical *exemplum* for fast running in v. 2, mentions Boreas in v. 4, where he possibly refers to fast chariot racing. For this interpretation of θέων, see Prato 1968, 126 f.; Prato 1973 = 2009 (*contra* M. West 1970, 150, who thinks that v. 4 deals again with fast running).

of Cyprus Cinyras as the quintessential rich men (v. 6), Callimachus mentions only Midas.

Callimachus wants us to see that he looks back to Tyrtaeus here. But, by doing so, he also highlights a conspicuous development. While the context of Tyrtaeus' passage was military and paraenetic, the context of his own passage is erotic and aetiological.[15]

Somewhere else in the *Aetia* Callimachus may have in mind a later passage from the same elegy of Tyrtaeus (fr. 12, 37–42 W. = 9, 37–42 G.-P.), describing the glory and the respect enjoyed by the brave soldier, when he has survived war and has gone back to his fellow-citizens:

> πάντες μιν τιμῶσιν, ὁμῶς νέοι ἠδὲ παλαιοί,
>   πολλὰ δὲ τερπνὰ παθὼν ἔρχεται εἰς Ἀΐδην,
> γηράσκων δ' ἀστοῖσι μεταπρέπει, οὐδέ τις αὐτόν
>   βλάπτειν οὔτ' αἰδοῦς οὔτε δίκης ἐθέλει,
> πάντες δ' ἐν θώκοισιν ὁμῶς νέοι οἵ τε κατ' αὐτόν
>   εἴκουσ' ἐκ χώρης οἵ τε παλαιότεροι.

He is honoured by all, young and old alike, many are the joys he experiences before he goes to Hades, and in his old age he stands out among the townsmen; no one seeks to deprive him of respect and his just rights, but all men at the benches yield their place to him, the young, those of his own age, and the elders.

Callimachus possibly echoes these lines in a fragment from the first book of the *Aetia* (fr. 48 M. = 41 Pf.):

> γηράσκει δ' ὁ γέρων κεῖνος ἐλαφρότερον,
> κοῦροι τόν φιλέουσιν, ἐὸν δέ μιν οἷα γονῆα
>   χειρὸς ἐπ' οἰκείην ἄχρις ἄγουσι θύρην.

That old man ages more easily whom the boys love, and they take him by the hand and lead him like their father as far as the door of his house.

Here too we note that, if Callimachus echoes Tyrtaeus, he seems to switch from martial to erotic. He condenses Tyrtaeus' words and imagery and applies them to a paederastic context,[16] that was well represented in early Greek elegy but not (as far as we know) in the poems of Tyrtaeus himself.

---

[15] See Casadio 2007, 25–28; Massimilla 2010, 373.

[16] The paederastic background of Callimachus' fragment can be surmised from the fact that the first part of it (until φιλέουσιν) is quoted in the pseudo-Lucianic *Amores* (48). Such an interpretation of the fragment can also be supported by other considerations: see Massimilla 1996, 318; Harder 2012 (2), 296 f.

It is worth remarking that Tyrtaeus' passage found its way into the Theognidean collection (where the three couplets are conflated into two, vv. 935–938), and was in fact adapted to a different, namely gnomic context, serving as an illustration of the respect enjoyed by the few men who have both virtue and beauty (ἀρετὴ καὶ κάλλος, v. 933 f.).[17]

Indeed, the blend of paederastic and gnomic tones, that transpires in fr. 48 M. = 43 Pf., makes us think above all of the Theognidean *corpus*. As a matter of fact, Callimachus appropriates elsewhere too the gnomic voices of elegiac poets such as Theognis or Solon.[18]

Theognis says that a man's mind must be stronger than his passions (v. 631 f.):

ᾧτινι μὴ θυμοῦ κρέσσων νόος, αἰὲν ἐν ἄταις,
  Κύρνε, καὶ ἐν μεγάλαις κεῖται ἀμηχανίαις.[19]

He whose mind does not control his heart always finds himself in trouble, Cyrnus, and in great perplexity.[20]

Callimachus alludes to this passage of Theognis in his *Victory of Sosibius*, where he praises Sosibius for being attentive to the needs of the people (fr. 384, 53–56 Pf.):

καὶ τὸν ἐφ᾽ οὗ νίκαισιν ἀείδομεν, ἄρθμια δήμῳ
  εἰδότα καὶ μικρῶν οὐκ ἐπιληθόμενον,
παύριστον τό κεν ἀνδρὶ παρ᾽ ἀφνειῷ τις ἴδοιτο
  ᾧτινι μὴ κρε[ί]σσων ἦ νόος εὐτυχίης.

And him we celebrate for his victories, friendly to the people, and forgetting not the poor, a thing so rarely seen in a rich man, whose mind is not superior to his good fortune.[21]

The imitation of the archaic poet draws our attention to the developments brought about by Callimachus. Theognis' words ᾧτινι μὴ ... κρέσσων νόος are now given a different metrical position within the elegiac couplet (v. 56). Further-

---

17 See van Groningen 1966, 356; Ferrari 1987, 183–185; Colesanti 2001, 485 f.; Noussia-Fantuzzi 2010, 64.
18 See Kaesser 2005, 97.
19 The text of v. 632 is corrupt in the manuscripts, where it reads Κύρνε (or κυρναῖ changed into κυρν) καὶ μεγάλαις κεῖται ἐν ἀμπλακίαις. Bergk's emendation Κύρνε, καὶ ἐν μεγάλαις κεῖται ἀμηχανίαις is based on [Thgn.] 646 κείμενος ἐν μεγάλῃ θυμὸν ἀμηχανίῃ. See M. West 1974, 62.
20 As regards θυμοῦ κρέσσων νόος, cf. E. *Med.* 1079 θυμὸς δὲ κρείσσων τῶν ἐμῶν βουλευμάτων, *Teleph. TrGF* 718 θυμοῦ κρείσσονα γνώμην ἔχειν.
21 Translation by Trypanis 1958. On this passage see Fuhrer 1992, 195–199; Weber 2011, 235 f.

more, while Theognis refers to the generic man and says that his mind (νόος) must be superior to his heart (θυμός), Callimachus refers to the rich man (ἀνδρὶ ... ἀφνειῷ) and says that his mind (νόος) must be superior to his good fortune (εὐτυχίῃ).

This last difference is connected to the most conspicuous feature of the *Victory of Sosibius* as a whole, i.e. its being a victory ode composed in elegiacs. On the one hand, the Theognidean diction of our passage is consistent with the elegiac metre of the poem. On the other hand, the praise of great men unspoiled by wealth is a motif to be found in Pindar's victory odes. A passage of *Nemean* Nine (v. 32f.) is particularly close. Here Pindar praises the Aetnaeans as κτεάνων ψυχὰς ἔχοντες κρέσσονας / ἄνδρες ("men who ... have souls superior to possessions").[22]

Elsewhere Callimachus possibly echoes a pentameter of Solon (fr. 18 W. = 28 G.-P.):

γηράσκω δ' αἰεὶ πολλὰ διδασκόμενος

As I grow old I am always learning many things.[23]

We may infer that Callimachus somehow echoed this Solonian line from a scholion to v. 711 of Sophocles' *Antigone* (Call. fr. 678 Pf.):

μὴ αὐθάδη εἶναι ἀντιτείνοντα τοῖς συμβουλεύουσιν· τοῦτο δὲ παρὰ τὸ (τὸ add. A. Nauck) Σόλωνος· 'γηράσκω δ' αἰεὶ πάντα διδασκόμενος'. Καλλίμαχος· (*desinit* L)

(Haemon tells Creon) not to be stubborn in his resistance to the advice of other people. This suggestion conforms to the saying of Solon: "As I grow old I am always learning all". Callimachus: (...).[24]

The scholion to Sophocles is unfortunately incomplete, and the quotation from Callimachus is lost. It would be interesting to know, if not the context, at least the wording of the Callimachean passage. Nevertheless the meager information offered by the scholion allows us to speculate a bit further.

---

[22] Translation by Braswell 1998. Cf. also Pi. *P*. 8, 91f. ἔχων / κρέσσονα πλούτου μέριμναν (quoted by Braswell 1998, 107; "having aspirations superior to wealth", translation by Race 1997). Elsewhere (fr. dub. 346 (a), 2 and (b), 1–3 M.) Pindar apparently praised a certain leader (ἀγη[τ]ῆρα) for being superior to possessions (κτεάν[ων) and for showing a benevolence that delighted the people (λατερπέι). See Vannini 2007, 49–55; D'Alessio 2007, 75–78.
[23] On this fragment see Burzacchini 1995, 78; Noussia-Fantuzzi 2010, 112 and 413f.
[24] Note that, as regards Solon's line, the reading πάντα of the scholion (shared by Tatian, *Adv. Graec.* 35) is certainly inferior to the reading πολλά of all the other sources.

First of all we may note that Solon's line was extremely famous. It is already referred to in Plato (*La.* 188b, 189a, *R.* 536d), and it is quoted in the pseudo-Platonic *Amatores* (133c). Quotations and references grew frequent in the following centuries, and the line became a proverb (nr. 2035 Tosi).[25] Since Callimachus was fond of scattering proverbs throughout his poems,[26] we can imagine that he was particularly interested in Solon's *gnome* because it was also a proverb.

Furthermore Solon's statement, that he keeps learning while growing old, must have appealed to Callimachus because it is consistent with his own views. We are reminded of a famous passage from the prologue of the *Aetia* (fr. 1, 33–40 M. = Pf.), where Callimachus wishes he could shed old age and sing as a cicada, remaining as active as ever (ἐνεργότατος, v. 40).

Also the untiring eagerness to learn is a very Callimachean motif. Particularly telling in this regard is a line of the *Aetia* that occurs in a long fragment probably belonging to the second book (fr. 89, 30 M. = 178, 30 Pf.). During a banquet in Alexandria, Callimachus questions a fellow-guest about a rite performed on his home island, and adds that he likes listening to those who are willing to speak,

οὔατα μυθεῖσθαι βουλομέν[οις ἀνέχων[27]

Pricking up my ears to those willing to tell a story.

The immediate context of these words is missing, but Strabo, who refers to them (9, 438), informs us that here Callimachus qualified his eagerness to learn as a lifelong attitude (πάντα τὸν βίον).[28] Callimachus, as Solon before him, never grows weary of learning. We may say that Callimachus appropriates Solon's voice to validate his own aetiological interests.

As I have said, the setting of Call. fr. 89 M. = 178 Pf. is a banquet. Callimachus outlines this setting in a way that is clearly intended to remind us of another very important constituent of early Greek elegy: the sympotic element.[29]

Elegists state quite often that the good symposiast is a moderate wine drinker (Anacreon fr. 56, 1 G. = fr. eleg. 2, 1 W., Xenophanes fr. 1, 17 f. W. = G.-P., Critias

---

25 See Tosi 2010, 1474 f.
26 See Lelli 2006, 135–185.
27 The line was supplemented so by Pfeiffer 1949, 153.
28 Strabo's testimony led Pfeiffer 1949, 153 to conjecture that the (now missing) second half of the previous hexameter, together with v. 30, formed a sentence meaning "but as long as I live I will not stop pricking up my ears etc.".
29 See D'Alessio 1996 (2), 555 n. 14; Dettori 2004, 41.

fr. 6, 14–27 W. = 4, 14–27 G.-P., *Theognidea* 211 f. = 509 f., 475–478, 837–840).³⁰ In fr. 89 M. = 178 Pf. Callimachus makes use of this motif. ³¹ He says that during the banquet he got along well with his fellow-guest, because this man, just like him, refrained from drinking too much wine (v. 11 f.):

> καὶ γὰρ ὁ Θρηϊκίην μὲν ἀπέστυγε χανδὸν ἄμυστιν
> ζωροποτεῖν, ὀλίγῳ δ' ἥδετο κισσυβίῳ.

> For he too abhorred drinking neat wine with his mouth wide open in large Thracian draughts,³² but enjoyed a small cup.

In the following lines (vv. 13–20) Callimachus develops the motif by equating water and conversation. He says to his congenial fellow-guest (v. 15 f.):

> ἦ μάλ' ἔπος τόδ' ἀληθές, ὅ τ' οὐ μόνον ὕδατος αἶσαν,
> ἀλλ' ἔτι καὶ λέσχης οἶνος ἔχειν ἐθέλει.

> This saying is very true indeed, that wine needs not only a share of water, but also of conversation.³³

As we have seen, the talk Callimachus is going to start, by putting a question to his partner in the conversation, is aetiological and erudite. He wants to learn new things.³⁴

The notion that a banquet must be above all an opportunity to learn is already to be found in the *Theognidea* (vv. 563–566):

> κεκλῆσθαι δ' ἐς δαῖτα, παρέζεσθαι δὲ παρ' ἐσθλόν
> ἄνδρα χρεὼν σοφίην πᾶσαν ἐπιστάμενον.
> τοῦ συνιεῖν, ὁπόταν τι λέγῃ σοφόν, ὄφρα διδαχθῇς,
> καὶ τοῦτ' εἰς οἶκον κέρδος ἔχων ἀπίῃς.

> You should get invited to dinner and sit beside a man of worth who knows every kind of skill. Whenever he says something clever, take note of it so that you may learn and go home with this as profit.³⁵

Callimachus appropriates this topic more explicitly in a fragment from the second book of the *Aetia* (fr. 50 M. = 43 Pf.), that in all likelihood immediately fol-

---

30 See Bielohlawek 1940, 21–29; Colesanti 2007, 252.
31 See Hunter 1996a, 19 = 2008b, 281; Massimilla 1996, 407; Harder 2012 (2), 969.
32 Here the Thracians are referred to as the typical immoderate drinkers.
33 For the value of pleasant conversation at a symposium cf. [Thgn.] 493–496, 1047.
34 See Kaesser 2005, 102 f.
35 Cf. also, in more general terms, Thgn. 31–38. See Levine 1985, 177–180.

lows fr. 89 M. = 178 Pf. Commenting on the same banquet and presenting some new information he acquired in the course of it, Callimachus says (vv. 12–17):

καὶ γὰρ ἐγὼ τὰ μὲν ὅσσα καρήατι τῆμος ἔδωκα
    ξανθὰ σὺν εὐόδμοις ἁβρὰ λίπη στεφάνοις
ἄπνοα πάντ' ἐγένοντο παρὰ χρέος, ὅσσα τ' ὀδόντων
    ἔνδοθι νείαιράν τ' εἰς ἀχάριστον ἔδυ,
καὶ τῶν οὐδὲν ἔμεινεν ἐς αὔριον· ὅσσα δ' ἀκουαῖς
    εἰσεθέμην, ἔτι μοι μοῦνα πάρεστι τάδε.

For certainly everything I put on my head on that occasion, the soft golden oil with fragrant wreaths, immediately faded and died, and everything that went into my mouth and down into my ungrateful belly, of those things too nothing remained until the morning; but everything I admitted to my ears, this only is still with me.

Once more Callimachus picks up a motif from early Greek elegy and, so to say, 'builds' upon it. This time, through a skilful priamel,[36] he develops the 'instructive banquet' theme. Keeping in mind the philosophical discussion about pleasure (ἡδονή),[37] Callimachus says that all the ephemeral pleasures of a banquet, such as exquisite ointments, sweet-smelling garlands and delicious food, have no value when compared to the only long-lasting profit that may ensue from a banquet: the acquisition of new knowledge.

To sum up, the passages we have examined show that Callimachus' attitude towards the elegiac tradition was complex and nuanced. Above all they suggest that Callimachus often adopted the voices of the early Greek elegists in order to highlight the distinctive features of his own poetry.

---

36 See Race 1982, 104 n. 167.
37 See Massimilla 1996, 322.

David Sider
Didactic poetry: The Hellenistic invention of a pre-existing genre

For all that it is almost a cliché that Hellenistic poets were acutely aware of genre —who before Callimachus would or could have boasted of his πολυείδεια?—,[1] discussions, let alone definitions, of didactic poetry as a genre are scarce. Why bother, when it seems so obvious? Look at Aratus and Nicander, whose model was Hesiod, and nothing more need be said. Nonetheless, that will be my aim here. There have of course been many useful studies of classical didactic poetry,[2] some of which offer various classifications (see below); yet I have long felt that insufficient attention has been paid, both by the ancients themselves and by us today, to the *development* of the poems called didactic, although modern terminology and the ancients are not in complete agreement as to what constitutes a

---

[1] Some earlier poets did in fact write in more than one genre, but could have boasted of it only in particular terms, i.e., by specifying "I write poems of type X and Y," as we see at the end of the *Symposium* 223d ὁμολογεῖν αὐτοὺς τοῦ αὐτοῦ ἀνδρὸς εἶναι κωμῳδίαν καὶ τραγῳδίαν ἐπίστασθαι ποιεῖν, καὶ τὸν τέχνῃ τραγῳδοποιὸν ὄντα <καὶ> κωμῳδοποιὸν εἶναι ("They agreed that the same man can know how to compose both comedy and tragedy, and that the skilled tragic poet is also a skilled writer of comedies")—to which one can add that Plato has himself done this within this very dialogue, adding satyrography, as Bacon (1959) shows. Furthermore, since lyric is not considered a genre, Sappho, Stesichorus, Simonides, Pindar, et al. are seen without fuss to write in several genres. This can be seen in Pl. *Laws* 700d (after the Persian wars) ἄρχοντες μὲν τῆς ἀμούσου παρανομίας ποιηταὶ ἐγίγνοντο φύσει μὲν ποιητικοί, ἀγνώμονες δὲ περὶ τὸ δίκαιον τῆς Μούσης καὶ τὸ νόμιμον, βακχεύοντες καὶ μᾶλλον τοῦ δέοντος κατεχόμενοι ὑφ' ἡδονῆς, κεραννύντες δὲ θρήνους τε ὕμνοις καὶ παίωνας διθυράμβοις, καὶ αὐλῳδίας δὴ ταῖς κιθαρῳδίαις μιμούμενοι, καὶ πάντα εἰς πάντα συνάγοντες ("After the Persian wars, there came into existence poets, who, although with some innate talent in the composition of poetry, were yet ignorant as to what was just and right in the realm of the Muse. They began their unmusical lawlessness, acting like Bacchants possessed more than is proper, combining threnodies with hymns and paeans with dithyrambs, imitating songs for the aulos on the lyre, mixing anything with anything"), where the last phrase is regularly taken to mean "mixing together all genres". Plato's terms, it should be noted, refer to songs characterized in the ancient mind very much by occasion, but he clearly does not mean that (e.g.) some singer sang paeonic praise of Apollo at a funeral, but that an element or elements appropriate to one song were noticeably present in another, which entails the idea of genre. See further Effe 1977, 9–26; Rosenmeyer 2006, 428–9.
[2] See, for example, Asquith 2005, Atherton 1997, Cusset 2007, Effe 1977, Erren, 1986, Fabre-Serris 2004, Fakas, 2001, Gale 2004, Horster & Reitz 2005, Hutchinson 2008b and 2009, Kroll 1925, Kruschwitz & Schumacher 2005, Prince 2003, Schiesaro et. al. 1993, Toohey 1996, Volk 2002, Wöhrle 1998.

didactic poem.³ Furthermore, as for what does in fact constitute a didactic poem, this too deserves some further consideration. Accordingly, before we can consider the development of didactic poetry, we must first consider its generic typology, which in turn, for a number of reasons, *also* has its difficulties, if only because if didactic as a form or genre develops, its definition too must be a dynamic one. Any equation with both x_t and y_t, that is, two unknowns, each dependent on time, calls for some tricky calculations. To make matters even more complicated, Hesiod, who must be accounted for in any account of didactic, writes about subjects not altogether easy to gather under one rubric. There is yet another difficulty in all this, but one I would like to dispense with briefly, namely the definition of genre itself.⁴ For the moment at least, although the word has to be used, let us think of it in as untechnical a sense as possible, as if this now-English French word simply meant "kind" (cognate with "genre") or "sort", as we might say that Mime is a *sort* of comedy, without necessarily making any particular technical, generic, or historical claims.⁵ Another area I avoid here is the relationship between didactic poetry and the equally didactic (even if the word is not used in this context) prose that began to flourish in the fifth century.⁶

---

3 It was in fact a conference entitled "Diachrony" in October 2009 in Durham, North Carolina, that first led me to formulate the ideas elaborated here. To that audience, to a second in Moscow in April 2010, and finally to that in Thessaloniki, I owe many useful comments.
4 But see the intelligent and concise discussion in Swales 1990, 36–38.
5 That is, just like εἶδος with its ordinary and more technical meanings. Cf. Kässer 2005, 95, "One of the surprising aspects of ancient literary criticism is the fact that ... a category with the label 'didactic poetry' was never developed". Nonetheless, I am convinced that the composition of so many (largely hexameter) poems on technical subjects could not have occurred without a keen sense that they all belong to the same kind. On the question of the very question of genre applied to ancient texts, see Rosenmeyer 2006. Although he offers many reasons to be skeptical, note his comment that "... despite the reluctance in some quarters to employ the term 'genre', current criticism and theory remain committed to the view that the intelligent discussion of literature, and any response to literature, require some preliminary sorting out of the material available, if only for heuristic ends" (p. 423).
6 In addition to the medical texts that can be reasonably assigned to the fifth century, a number of prose treatises are known to us usually only by title: Sophocles Περὶ Χοροῦ, Polyclitus Κανών (fragments: DK 40 B 1–2), Ictinus on the Parthenon, Theodorus on his own art of sculpture, Simon *Peri Hippikes* (a frag. ed. K. Widdra), Agatharchus on scene painting, and Hippodamus on town planning. Exant are several works by Xenophon, including *Kynegetikos* and *Peri Hippikes* (which freely acknowledges that it incorporates Simon), on which see Hunter 2008a, 170–1. For the audience for these texts, see Fögen 2004, Asper 2007, especially ch. A 3, "Gab es ein Gattungsbewuβtein von Fachtexten in der Antike". For the more precise relationship between individual Hellenistic poems and their prose sources, see Hutchinson 2008a and 2009). D. Fowler 2000, 217, is most sensible on the overarching question of how strict a definition we seek: "We all know that genres are always mixed in practice, but it is often convenient to use a sort of

The nature of Didactic poetry should not be mysterious. Any of us can immediately say that it is poetry that teaches, and, furthermore, we know that there was enough of it in the ancient world to deserve recognition as a distinct, though largely nameless, genre of poetry, although recently Alistair Fowler has preferred to think of didactic poetry as a *mode*, on the grounds that any poetry can teach, a view similar to that of many ancients, as we shall see.[7] This preference for the term mode, although valid and useful enough, cannot do away with the more restrictive way the term is almost universally thought of by classicists. The term genre, then, is certainly the more familiar and still useful starting point, at least. Genres, though, as we know full well, can be as slippery as eels, all the more so when authors engage in *Kreuzung der Gattungen*—an action designed, among other things, to sensitize the reader to the precise nature or genre of the text in hand, turning it, in effect, into a metatext.

After all this, it should come as no surprise that there have been several attempts, both ancient and modern, both to define and to subdivide the genre of didactic poetry. An ancient one is found in the *Tractatus Coislinianus*, which places didactic (here called παιδευτική) poetry within poetry as a whole, and which divides it further into expository (ὑφηγητική) and theoretical (θεωρητική).[8] See fig. 1.

Didactic receives a fuller definition in Diomedes *Ars Gramm*. p. 1.482 Keil: *didascalice est qua comprenditur philosophia Empedoclis et Lucreti, item astrologia ut Phaenomena Arati et Ciceronis et Georgica Vergilii et his similia*.[9]

Effe 1977 analyzes didactic according to the particular aim (*Ziel/Intentionen*) of each author, type one being the most factual, where theme and content are close; that is, the author truly desires to teach. The second is more formal, such as is found in Nicander; while the third calls for going beyond the surface to find the true theme, such as in Vergil's *Georgics*. Effe explicitly ignores any

---

langue/parole distinction, in which individual texts will be mixed, but standing behind them will be Platonic forms of unmixed genres that structure the generic play within the texts". When the composition of the examples examined occur over a long period of time, one can, with Asper 2007, 18 n. 53, apply Saussure's term *identité diachronique*, which the latter first used to express linguistic continuity.

7 A. Fowler 2003.
8 For the text, see Koster 1975, 63–67; for discussions, see Cooper 1922 and Janko 1984.
9 See Effe 1977, 20–1; Volk 2002, 31–2. The word διδασκαλική ("instructional") is never found *simpliciter* in extant Greek with the sense "didactic poetry". Proclus *Chrestomathy* ap. Photius *Bibl*. 239 p. 319b5–7 lists the following kinds of poems designed for miscellaneous occasions (εἰς τὰς προσπιπτούσας περιστάσεις): πραγματικά, ἐμπορικά, ἀποστολικά, γνωμολογικά, γεωργικά, ἐπισταλτικά.

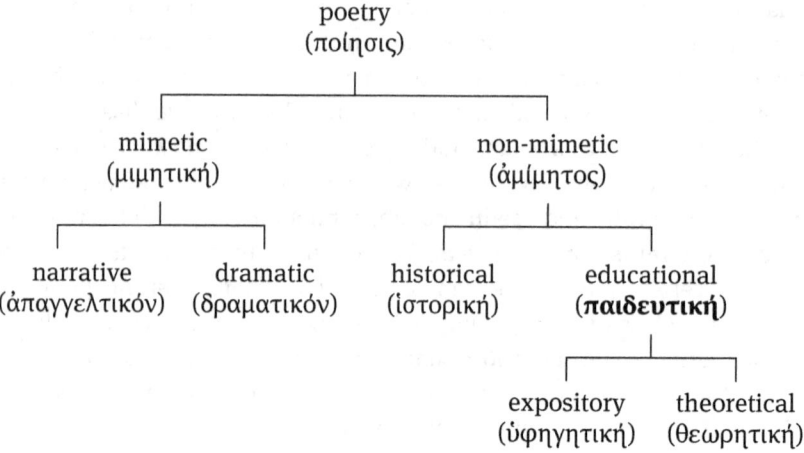

Fig. 1. Poetry's divisions, as laid out in the mss. of the *Tractatus Coislianus*. δραματικόν is divided further into comedy, tragedy, mime, and satyr play.

historical approach to didactic.[10] Volk's criteria for didactic poetry calls for (1) explicit didactic intent (in line with Effe), (2) a teacher-student constellation (such as Hesiod and his brother Perses),[11] (3) poetic self-consciousness, and (4) poetic simultaneity.[12]

I have some difficulties with each of these analyses. For example, Volk's insistence upon having what she calls a teacher-student constellation allows her rather surprisingly to exclude Parmenides from the canon of didactic poets. To this I offer two arguments. First, any scheme that excludes Parmenides is in my mind ipso facto flawed, or at any rate in need of a little flexibility. But second, one could—in fact, I have, elsewhere[13]—argue that what we find here is simply a little literary shifting of personae, where Parmenides has the goddess in the

---

[10] Effe 1977, 34, but he makes up for this in Effe 2005, although starting from Aratus, whereas here I examine what led up to the Hellenistic period.

[11] Cf. Servius ad V. G. proem (p. 129 Thilo-Hagen) *hi libri didascalici sunt, unde necesse est ut ad aliquem scribantur, nam praeceptum et doctoris et discipuli personam requirit, unde ad Maecenatem scribit* [sc. Vergilius], *sicuti Hesiodus ad Persen, Lucretius ad Memium*.

[12] Cf. also D. Fowler 2000, 205: "The primary elements of didactic are [i] a teacher who is usually an explicitly characterized internal speaker, [ii] a body of knowledge that is to be imparted, and [iii] a pupil who may be a figure or figures characterized within the text or may be identified with the general reader" (my square brackets). Note that Fowler ignores [iii] in that he, unlike Volk, is quite ready to consider Parmenides a didactic poet.

[13] Sider 2004. See also D. Fowler 2000, 205, who recognizes that there are elliptical ways to represent the "student".

role of teacher and himself as the student, just as Socrates several times makes up a story in which he is berated by a senior figure fulfilling the role of *didaskalos*, such as in the *Symposium*, where Socrates substitutes himself for his host Agathon and then allows an obviously fictional Diotima (that is, fictional within the dialogue, not just in real life) to chastise him severely. Or as in the (as I think genuine) *Hippias Major*, where Socrates substitutes himself for the philosophically inadequate Hippias and then manufactures an anonymous stranger who castigates him rather than Hippias.[14] Moreover, Effe's starting point of the author's intention is troublesome on its face, as authors notoriously cannot be trusted to reveal all that is on their minds. And yet, as we shall see, it is difficult to get away from authorial intention when talking about didactic, although substituting "authorial persona" for "author" does much to mitigate the problem.

Still, allow for the moment that these objections are groundless, and that not only is each of these three analyses 100% correct, but also allow that they are entirely consistent one with the other. Even so, there remains one common feature I would like to address: most analyses are static, taking for granted that "didactic poetry" was and is one and only one thing; that is, the same poetic genre, from Hesiod on, throughout antiquity and then through Fracastoro's delightful poem on Syphilis, to Josef Eberle's poem on smoking, *Ars Fumatoria*, subtitled *Carmen Didacticum*. My own diachronic study—somewhat different from that of Toohey,[15]—provides a different light on the topic, one which complements the static analyses. It will, among other things, suggest that despite the fact that Hesiod is universally considered the prime example of didactic poetry, this ranking was not developed until long after his death. We shall also consider what was and what was not considered a proper subject for didactic poetry, which often goes unstated. This will allow if not encourage us to return to poets not normally designated didactic to see what instructional message may have been intended.

Since it is now clear that I am interested in how the ancients themselves regarded this kind of poetry, perhaps the first thing to do is look for ways in which the Greeks thought of poetry that taught or from which one could learn, to use

---

14 See Sider 1977/2012.
15 Toohey 1996, 7 ff. (see also Toohey 2005, 19) lists the following stages of development: 1. Oral phase; 2. Hellenistic period, "juxtaposing literate enthusiasms with an oral manner"… "interested more in the trappings of the genre than in instruction"; 3. Cicero (trans. of Aratus) & Lucretius, the latter "invest[ing] the genre with a new seriousness", that of narrative epic; 4. Vergil's *Georgics* & Ovid's *Fasti*, both unique in "confront[ing] the issues of dynastic, political life"; 5. Horace's *Ars Poetica* & 6. Ovid's *Ars Amatoria*—both "didactic epic [as] leisure pursuit" and both "clever, playful, and entertaining artifacts".

intentionally vague descriptions. It may come as a surprise to learn that they never actually used the adjective διδακτικός to modify ποίημα or ποίησις, and in fact it is not clear when the term "didactic poetry", in any language, was first used. The *Oxford English Dictionary* gives 1756 as the earliest occurrence of this adjective applied to a poem in English, but there must have been earlier instances in other languages, although a Latinized *didacticus* does not occur in any of the Medieval Latin dictionaries available to me.[16] Still, we should not do as Bruno Snell did, and deny the existence of a thought solely because we cannot find that the Greeks had a word for it.

What we do find, early on, is that Greek poetry was used for teaching purposes. Indeed, in Aristophanes' *Frogs*, we find the famous line that "poets are the teachers (*didaskaloi*) of men", usually taken out of its context, which plainly gives us the proportion τοῖς μὲν γὰρ παιδαρίοισιν / ἐστὶ διδάσκαλος ὅστις φράζει, τοῖσιν δ' ἡβῶσι ποιηταί, "what teachers are to boys, poets are to men".[17] We are not therefore talking about force-feeding youngsters educational poems, but about grown men learning what is important, in this case, important for the city, from poems. Nor is this notion unique to Aristophanes or a surprise to his audience. Solon and Pindar, for example, are quite forthright about their instructional roles. Note, for example Solon 4.30–1 W:

> ταῦτα διδάξαι θυμὸς Ἀθηναίους με κελεύει,
> ὡς κακὰ πλεῖστα πόλει Δυσνομίη παρέχει.

These things my spirit bids me teach the Athenians, because Lawlessness is furnishing the city with the greatest number of evils.

And in general, one comes away from many of the elegists with the sense that whether in public or in the more private sphere of the symposium they have a message to convey. Here I cite only Tyrtaeus 11.27 W ἔρδων δ' ὄβριμα ἔργα διδασκέσθω πολεμίζειν, although what we really have here is a protreptic to learn how to fight; not actual instruction in fighting. That Theognis meant to instruct is also clear; cf. (inter alia) 35 ἐσθλῶν μὲν γὰρ ἐσθλὰ μαθήσεαι. Back to Aristophanes, though: Who are these poets that can be the teachers of men? In didactic fashion, he catalogues several of them several lines before at 1030–36:

---

16 As noted by Effe 1997, 9, Goethe used the word *didaktische* in his *Über das Lehrgedicht* (1827).
17 Cf. also *Frogs* 686–7 (the parabasis): τὸν ἱερὸν χορὸν δίκαιόν ἐστι χρηστὰ τῇ πόλει / ξυμπαραινεῖν καὶ διδάσκειν, "it is the right thing for the sacred chorus to urge and teach what is useful for the city"; *Ach.* 656–8. See now further Hunter 2009a, ch. 1, and Halliwell 2011, ch. 3.

ταῦτα γὰρ ἄνδρας χρὴ ποιητὰς ἀσκεῖν. σκέψαι γὰρ ἀπ' ἀρχῆς   1030
ὡς ὠφέλιμοι τῶν ποιητῶν οἱ γενναῖοι γεγένηνται.
Ὀρφεὺς μὲν γὰρ τελετάς θ' ἡμῖν κατέδειξε φόνων τ' ἀπέχεσθαι,
Μουσαῖος δ' ἐξακέσεις τε νόσων καὶ χρησμούς, Ἡσίοδος δὲ
γῆς ἐργασίας, καρπῶν ὥρας, ἀρότους· ὁ δὲ θεῖος Ὅμηρος
ἀπὸ τοῦ τιμὴν καὶ κλέος ἔσχεν πλὴν τοῦδ' ὅτι χρήστ' ἐδίδαξεν,   1035
τάξεις, ἀρετάς, ὁπλίσεις ἀνδρῶν;

Consider how the best of the poets have been beneficial from the very beginning:
(i)   Orpheus showed us sacred rites and how to avoid bloodshed;
(ii)   Musaeus (showed us) cures for diseases and oracular responses;
(iii) Hesiod (showed us) the ways to work the land, the seasons, and plows; and
(iv)   the divine Homer—from where did he gain his glorious honor if not that he taught men's strategies, virtues, and fighting?[18]

How didactic is Aristophanes' group? Hesiod presents no problem. Musaeus should qualify, since there are Hellenistic poems on medicine regularly taken as didactic. Orpheus, described here as a religious poet, is a tighter fit by later standards, although Ovid's *Fasti* come to mind;[19] normally when we hear of Orpheus' songs, they concern cosmogonical and cosmological topics that fit more easily into the rubric of didactic. But Homer!? Nobody thinks of *him* as a didactic poet—or rather, hardly anybody nowadays at least. Effe and Volk, for example, would disqualify him on the grounds that (even if they agreed that a moral could be extracted from Homer) there is no express intent to teach.[20] In antiquity, on the other hand, we can point to Xenophanes B 10 D-K: ἐξ ἀρχῆς καθ' Ὅμηρον

---

18 Another list is provided by Isoc. *In Nic.* 43 σημεῖον δ' ἄν τις ποιήσαιτο τὴν Ἡσιόδου καὶ Θεόγνιδος καὶ Φωκυλίδου ποίησιν· καὶ γὰρ τούτους φασὶ μὲν ἀρίστους γεγενῆσθαι συμβούλους τῷ βίῳ τῷ τῶν ἀνθρώπων ("One might cite as examples [sc. of sound advice that is ignored] the poetry of Hesiod, Theognis, and Phocylides, for in fact they [i.e., those who do the ignoring] agree that these men are the best counselors in how men should live"). Also of interest is Hdt. 2.53.1 οὗτοι δέ (sc. Hesiod and Homer) εἰσι οἱ ποιήσαντες θεογονίην Ἕλλησι καὶ τοῖσι θεοῖσι τὰς ἐπωνυμίας δόντες καὶ τιμάς τε καὶ τέχνας διελόντες καὶ εἴδεα αὐτῶν σημήναντες, "these are the ones who produced a theogony, giving the gods their titles, distributing their positions and particular skills, and indicating their appearance"; that is, they taught Greeks what they themselves had invented.
19 See Miller 1980, which further discusses how hymnic elements within the *Fasti*, like parts of Callimachus' hymns, while purporting to give real-time commands to *celebrants* (which would be followed as ordered and repeated on each occurrence of the festival, and thus need not be learned, i.e., remembered) are in fact instructing *readers* in the rituals involved, an elliptical form of didactic. For Orphic cosmogonies as didactic poetry, see Prince 2003, 72–119.
20 For ethical interpretations, see P. Zanker 2004 and Sider, forthcoming.

ἐπεὶ μεμαθήκασι πάντες ("Since all men from the very start have learned from Homer"), Heraclitus B 57 διδάσκαλος δὲ πλείστων Ἡσίοδος ("Hesiod is most men's teacher"), and even Anaxagoras, who is said to have declared that Homer's poetry was on the subject of virtue and justice.[21]

This is all very interesting, but little of this conforms to later views of what constitutes a didactic poem. For one thing, I've included non-hexameter poetry, mostly elegy, but Pindar should be allowed to squeeze in as well.[22] Indeed, according to the pseudo-Platonic *Hipparchus* 228b-e, the Athenian tyrant Hipparchus paid good money to two other lyric poets, Anacreon and Simonides, specifically in order to instruct the townsfolk; note in particular (Hipparchus) ἐπ' Ἀνακρέοντα τὸν Τήιον πεντηκόντορον στείλας ἐκόμισεν εἰς τὴν πόλιν, Σιμωνίδην δὲ τὸν Κεῖον ἀεὶ περὶ αὐτὸν εἶχεν, μεγάλοις μισθοῖς καὶ δώροις πείθων· ταῦτα δ' ἐποίει βουλόμενος παιδεύειν τοὺς πολίτας ("Hipparchus sent a fifty-oared ship to bring Anacreon of Teos to Athens, and he always had Simonides of Ceos at his side, persuading him with lots of money and gifts. He did this in his desire to educate the citizens").

Since this would not work with the less sophisticated country folk, for them Hipparchus erected herms with messages in an elegiac couplet that he composed himself, the hexameter giving the herm's (and the viewer's) location, and the hexameter beginning with an identification of himself as author in a shameless act of self-promotion, followed by a precept illustrating what the *Hipparchus* says of his aim in all this: ἐθαύμαζον αὐτὸν ἐπὶ σοφίᾳ. Two of these "commandments" are quoted here (228ab): Hipparchus fr. 1–2 Diehl:

μνῆμα τόδ' Ἱππάρχου· στεῖχε δίκαια φρονῶν·
μνῆμα τόδ' Ἱππάρχου· μὴ φίλον ἐξαπάτα.[23]

1. This monument erected by Hipparchus: Make your way thinking just thoughts.
2. This monument erected by Hipparchus: Do not deceive a friend.

The generic range of useful/beneficial/instructive poetry is therefore quite wide. Furthermore, the very premise of the *Frogs* is that tragedy can benefit—to which

---

[21] Anaxagoras A 1 = Diog. Laert. 2.11 δοκεῖ δὲ πρῶτος [sc. Anaxagoras], καθά φησι Φαβωρῖνος [fr. 61 Barigazzi] ἐν Παντοδαπῇ ἱστορίᾳ, τὴν Ὁμήρου ποίησιν ἀποφήνασθαι εἶναι περὶ ἀρετῆς καὶ δικαιοσύνης.

[22] See Kurke 1990, an excellent study of "advice" poetry (ὑποθῆκαι).

[23] Although Ps.-Plato says that the hexameter, which announced the viewer's location, is on one side of the herm and the "didactic" pentameter on the other, the one extant stone to contain such an inscription has them together on the right side: *CEG* 304 [ἐ]ν μέσῳ Κεφαλῆς τε καὶ ἄστεος ἀγλαὸς Ἑρμῆς. | [μνῆμα τόδ' Ἱππάρχου· –⏑⏑–⏑⏑–] ("A herm halfway between Kephale and town. This monument erected by Hipparchus...").

one can add Aristophanes himself and his fellow comic poets, who are always ready in their parabases to offer instruction to fellow Athenians.

But this early generous attitude toward instructional poetry, which differs markedly from the Hellenistic one, brings me to my point: didactic has to be seen and judged diachronically. Note, for example, how much ethical and, not entirely a separate matter, religious content determines the matter early on as to what is didactic in this early generous view. Yet when we think about the various poems *now* universally called didactic, none is ethical in content. Note that for all that Lucretius has to say on the fear of death, which admittedly has some transparently ethical implications, his poem famously omits Epicurus' ethical writings. Is this because he never got around to tackling this subject, as used to be thought? Or is it rather that he felt uncomfortable trying to accommodate straightforward ethical matters to what had become by his time a rather restrictive genre?

For your amusement I urge you to read an amusing poem by the American James Russell Lowell written in 1857 entitled *The Origin of Didactic Poetry*, in which a young Athena produces a moral epic so stultifying dull it drives all the other gods from Olympus. His poem ends with a moral spoken by an older and wiser Athena: "The Muse is unforgiving; / Put all your beauty in your rhymes, / Your morals in your living". Lowell's idea may well enunciate the unexpressed Hellenistic attitude that ethics is too boring a subject for didactic poetry. And not only ethics, but history too came in time to be felt to be a subject alien to didactic, although we know that, earlier, poems tracing a particular city's origins, although starting with what we call myth, covered historical events as well.[24]

It is now clear that in the archaic and classical period, there was no clear-cut, or even rough-cut, sense of a didactic genre. Alistair Fowler's *mode* works fine. Aristophanes' phrase in its cut-down version was generally felt to be true: poets are the teachers of men. It is certainly true that Plato in the *Republic* thought that the young were shaped politically and morally by what they saw in the theatre and from the myths they heard, largely in poetic form. Aristotle may have been the first to separate out didactic when in the *Poetics* he famously says that "Homer and Empedocles have nothing in common except their meter, which is why the one is justly called poet and the other physiologist rather than poet", οὐδὲν δὲ κοινόν ἐστιν Ὁμήρῳ καὶ Ἐμπεδοκλεῖ πλὴν τὸ μέτρον, διὸ τὸν μὲν

---

[24] This did not stop the city of Halicarnassus from commissioning a historical poem to be erected in the late second century BC; see Isager and Pedersen 2004, esp. 84 on its possible generic label.

ποιητὴν δίκαιον καλεῖν, τὸν δὲ φυσιολόγον μᾶλλον ἢ ποιητήν. This despite the fact that twice elsewhere in the *Poetics* and again in the *Rhetoric* he illustrates poetic tropes with examples from Empedocles (*Poet.* 1457b23–25, 1461a23–25; *Rhet.* 1373b13, 1407a34); and that in his now-lost work *On Poets*, he calls Empedocles "Homeric" in his poetic use of language; that is, in ways other than meter.[25] We should also note, as Ivana Petrovic reminds me, that, when Socrates proves to Ion that one cannot become a general by reading Homer, implicit is the idea that poetry cannot teach, which would if taken seriously mean that the label didactic is inapplicable to poetry in general.[26]

Aristotle may have been the first person explicitly to separate the useful in poetry from the more poetical, and thus to give us an early adumbration of the didactic genre, but his downgrading of the practical in poetry was not destined to become standard. Even without explicit distinctions, however, it is clear that didactic poetry as a genre was essentially invented in Hellenistic times, and then retrojected backward in time to include only those earlier poets that conformed to Hellenistic notions: *in primis* Hesiod, but also the Presocratics Xenophanes (in his hexameters, not his elegiacs), Parmenides (despite Volk's attempt to exclude him), and Empedocles. Indeed, one would have to say that in many ways Empedocles rivals Aratus for prime didactic poet. Aratus may have been translated more often into Latin, but Empedocles was alluded to and adapted more often, with clear echoes showing up in Lucretius, Ovid, and even Oppian (*Hal.* 1.412–16).[27]

To a certain extent, this Hellenistic invention of what is still the modern view of didactic poetry can be seen most famously in Callimachus' address to Aratus, Ἡσιόδου τό τ' ἄεισμα καὶ ὁ τρόπος, which establishes the important link between "scientific" subject matter and hexameter verse.[28] Aratus, however, did not write

---

25 Aristotle fr. 39.1 Gigon = 65a Rose (Diog. Laert. 8.57) Ἀριστοτέλης ... ἐν δὲ τῷ περὶ Ποιητῶν φησὶν ὅτι καὶ Ὁμηρικὸς ὁ Ἐμπεδοκλῆς καὶ δεινὸς περὶ τὴν φράσιν γέγονε, μεταφορικός τ' ὢν καὶ τοῖς ἄλλοις τοῖς περὶ ποιητικὴν ἐπιτεύγμασι χρώμενος ("Aristotle is his work *On Poets* says that Empedocles is skilled, even Homeric, in expression, making good use of metaphor and all other poetic refinements"). Also laudatory is Aristotle's statement that Empedocles invented rhetoric (fr. 39.2–3 G = 65b–c R).
26 See Pl. *Io* 541b εὖ ἴσθι, ὦ Σώκρατες· καὶ ταῦτά [sc. how to be the best general] γε ἐκ τῶν Ὁμήρου μαθών ("Know this, Socrates: even this I have learned from Homer").
27 See, e.g., Bignone 1929 (Ennius), Sedley 2003 (Lucretius), Hardie 1995 (Ovid), Pascal 1902 (Horace).
28 Callim. *Epigram* 27 Pf. = 56 Gow-Page (*A.P.* 9.507). There is no room here even to survey the large literature on this epigram and its programmatic meaning; cf., e.g., Hunter 2009a, 257–62, which among other things considers the possibility that the word ἔσχατον (if the papyrus reading ἀοιδῶν for ἀοιδόν is adopted) modifies τρόπος.

a poetic treatise *ab ovo*; but translated the prose text of Eudoxus; and translation of prose into verse becomes a Hellenistic hallmark.[29] There is a telling anecdote about how Aratus came to do this, showing the new relationship between prose original and poetic translation. Antigonus the ruler of Pella supposedly simply gave Aratus a copy of Eudoxus with the challenge to put it into verse, so that he, Aratus, would make Eudoxus εὐδοκιμώτερος, which punningly translates as both "more famous" and also as "more Eudoxian".[30] Implicit in this story is the entirely believable idea that Aratus had previously given little thought to astronomy, let alone this particular task, and it is probably fair to extend this to almost all the other composers of didactic poetry. For Aratus, the idea of poetic challenge weighed far more than any educational (that is, didactic) purpose.

It is said that Menecrates of Ephesus, Aratus' teacher, also turned scientific prose into verse (which includes at least Aristotle on bees) in his Hesiodic poem, so Aratus was certainly not the first. Who, though, *was* the first person to versify a pre-existing prose text? Was it Socrates, who whiled away the hours in prison by turning Aesop into verse?[31] In, probably, the fourth century a certain Scythinus was said to have turned Heraclitus into poetry, probably into iambs.[32] It could also be said that the author of the *Hipparchus* snidely suggests that all Hipparchus did was versify his own prosaic thoughts, but an important criterion

---

29 As argued in Sider and Brunschön 2007, 14–15, Eudoxus was Aratus' only prose source and the common view that Aratus went to the treatise *On Weather Signs* (attributed in modern times to Theophrastus) is wrong.
30 Achilles *in Arati Phaenomena*, fragm. p. 77 Maass ὅς (sc. Aratus) παρὰ τῷ βασιλεῖ (sc. Antigono Gonata) γενόμενος καὶ εὐδοκιμήσας ἔν τε τῇ ἄλλῃ πολυμαθείᾳ καὶ <τῇ> ποιητικῇ προετράπη ὑπ' αὐτοῦ τὰ Φαινόμενα γράψαι, τοῦ βασιλέως Εὐδόξου ἐπιγραφόμενον βιβλίον Κάτοπτρον δόντος αὐτῷ καὶ ἀξιώσαντος τὰ ἐν αὐτῷ καταλογάδην λεχθέντα περὶ τῶν φαινομένων μέτρῳ ἐντεῖναι καὶ ἅμα εἰπόντος, ὡς "εὐδοξότερον ποιεῖς τὸν Εὔδοξον ἐντείνας τὰ παρ' αὐτῷ κείμενα μέτρῳ." ("When Aratus, famous (εὐδοκιμήσας) for knowing all sorts of things but for poetry in particular, was at the court of Antigonus, the king urged him to write the *Phainomena*, giving him a copy of Eudoxus' *Katoptron* and asking that he versify what was there laid out in a bare-bones account of the heavens, telling him that "you will make Eudoxus eudoxier by turning his contents into verse").
31 Pl. *Phdo.* 60c-d. Nightingale 1995, 2, includes this passage among others where "Plato mixes traditional genres ... and disrupts the generic boundaries...", but since we do not hear these poems, we should rather consider these as more relevant to Socrates the man than to Plato the author. I thank Suzanne Saïd for the reference to Nightingale.
32 Diog. Laert. 9.16 = Scythinus *FGrHist* 13 T 2 Σκυθῖνον τὸν τῶν Ἰάμβων ποιητὴν ἐπιβαλέσθαι τὸν ἐκείνου λόγον διὰ μέτρου ἐκβάλλειν ("Scythinus the iambic poet took it upon himself to publish a metrical version of Heraclitus' book").

here is versifying someone else's prose. Still, one can see that such versifications were rare until the Hellenistic efflorescence of didactic.[33]

Thus, a preliminary diachronic scheme now suggests itself, each after the first adding something new to what had gone before.

(i) Poets in the Archaic and Classical periods write poems in various meters that, ignoring for the moment the conservative nature of oral poetry, are their own compositions. Although many of these compositions come to be considered "useful" or "beneficial", didactic as such does not exist as a genre until, perhaps, the three presocratic poets led people to view them as Aristotle did. It is no more than a tendency to put much of these into hexameters, a tendency best illustrated by the division of subject matter and verse in Xenophanes.

(ii) The Hellenistic stage: Poets versify preexisting prose treatises, predominately but not entirely, in hexameters.

(iii) In the third stage, the Romans continue to favor hexameters, but innovate in yet another way: translation of a Hellenistic didactic poem, itself depending on a prose text, into Latin. Thus, e.g., Eudoxus > Aratus > Cicero and others.[34]

The situation is of course more fluid than this; in particular, any author in stage ii or iii can return to an earlier form, such as Eratosthenes' *Duplication of the Cube* (ii > i) or Lucretius (iii > ii). In addition, in the ever so didactic section on rivers in his *Hymn to Zeus*, Callimachus is almost certainly versifying his own treatise *On Rivers*, which brings us back to stage i. Furthermore, while formalizing didactic as largely dactylic and technical, there were still deviations, such as some elegiac examples (e.g., Dorotheus of Sidon's astronomical poem) and some others that deviate from the usual run of topics.[35] Even more deviant is Callimachus' elegiac *Aetia*, which, even as Hellenistic poets were formulating a core idea of didactic as a genre, was pushing hard at these inchoate definitions.[36]

And the complex Roman contribution to the genre, which looks back, innovates, and mixes didactic with other genres (*in primis* Ovid's *Metamorphoses*),

---

[33] See appendix, below.

[34] They innovate in many other ways as well of course, and Toohey 2005, 19, is right to speak of a Roman "reinvention".

[35] And perhaps one should note here Posidippus' experiment in didactic epigram; see Sider (2005).

[36] Annette Harder 1998 and 2007 has shown this most clearly; see now Harder 2012, 27–33. For a broader picture of Callimachus' scientific interests, see Sistakou 2009b.

can only be hinted at here, in large part because of their great inventiveness. For in addition to a number of poems that fall squarely into didactic, there are some that do much to extend the boundaries. Examples of the former would certainly include Lucretius, who, in ways we are continuing to learn as new parts of Epicurus' papyri of his Περὶ Φύσεως are published, translated his master's prose into verse.[37] Nonetheless, anyone who has read any significant amount of Epicurus' unexciting prose will see that Lucretius has done far more than merely translate as he accommodates Epicurean content to Empedoclean poetics. Vergil's *Georgics* should probably also be included in this first group, however much he artfully avoids quoting Hesiod directly while evoking a thoroughly Hesiodic flavor.[38] Other Roman examples, however, take great delight in playfully transgressing generic boundaries, such as Horace's *Ars Poetica*, which is a triumph of self-reflexive examination, a poetic form used later by Karl Shapiro.[39] The very word *ars* in the title, clearly evoking the prosaic τέχνη that accompanied many earlier Greek prose treatises, declares its intentions, just as Ovid used it later in his *Ars Amatoria*, which pretends to be versification of preexisting Greek love manuals, such as that of Philainis.[40] Horace's *Ars Poetica* is his own composition, however, in that, in a way reminiscent of Hesiod, for all that it draws on Hellenistic prose treatises on the nature of poetry, it is meant to represent Horace's own views on the matter. In form, it may not differ from Horace's two literary epistles, but this is in harmony with the ease with which Romans slipped between didactic and other genres. A test case for all this is Ovid's *Metamorphoses*, which many modern scholars do not regard as at all didactic. I think, though, that an original reader would have no doubts. It opens with a declaration of purpose that cannot but recall to its learned audience such Hellenistic didactic epics as Nicander's *Heteroioumena*, Antigonus' *Alloioseis* and, even more so, Didymarchus' *Metamorphoses*. These Hellenistic poems of mythical transformations, however, it is probably safe to assume, were, however artful in the details, versifications of preexisting prose handbooks of mythological transformations, such as we see in Apollodorus; that is, one story follows another, with only the weakest link (perhaps a chronological one) between them, whereas Ovid separates himself from his predecessors by alluding to the proem of Callimachus' *Aetia*, itself a sort of concatenation of mythical tales, where Callimachus defends himself against the charge that he has not

---

37 See Sedley 2003.
38 See Wender 1979.
39 Shapiro 1945. Cf. vv. 43–45: "Perhaps Lucretius felt that through the means | of language highly charged, more could be said | of his philosophy than prose could prove."
40 See Vessey 1976.

written an ἄεισμα διηνεκές, "a continous poem", presumably a long poem such as an epic of any sort, Homeric or Hesiodic. He defends himself not by claiming that he has done so, but rather by saying that a poem can be good without being long. Ovid, therefore, who weaves many Roman *aetia* into his own *Metamorphoses*, proclaims that he will one-up Callimachus by composing a *perpetuum carmen*, and whatever else the *Metamorphoses* turns out to be, in the first four lines it fairly clearly declares itself a didactic poem, as it narrates a cosmogony of a general sort overlaid with unmistakable Empedoclean allusions. (I say little here about the 404-line Empedoclean didactic epyllion embedded within book 15 and put into the mouth of Pythagoras, except to note that it is in perfect accord with what I have been calling the general playfulness of Roman poets with the didactic genre.)[41] Note too that just as Callimachus' *Aetia* IV ends with a metamorphosis in the form of a catasterism that supposedly took place in historical times—that of Queen Berenice's lock of hair—so too does Ovid end his *Metamorphoses* with the assumption into heaven of Julius Caesar.

But how innovative was Ovid in composing his didactic *perpetuum carmen*? In one way, Ovid's poem is the most daring experiment in genre, as it starts with an old-fashioned Hesiodic- and Empedoclean-style didactic poem, which then elliptically announces that it will be Callimachean as well, but which also in the course of its development assumes the mantle of Vergil as it takes us through the birth and history of Rome. In another way, however, I would say that it is in fact not all that innovative, because from the very start what we now call didactic has always been ready to incorporate various genres within itself.

A case could be made for Hesiod's having done just this in both his extant poems. In the *Works & Days*, it is easiest here to limit ourselves to the first 382 lines, but what I have to say can be extended to the whole poem. First, we should read Hesiod's proem as we read other epic authors, and observe that that by a purely formal analysis, the subject is Zeus. That is, if you ask an experienced classicist for the subject of the *Works and Days*, he or she would probably smile and say "works and days". But suppose you were to show this to a young classicist, one who has read Homer, Vergil, and a few other opening passages of epic along with some hymns, but one miraculously ignorant of Hellenistic poetry. This person would analyze Hesiod's opening four lines formally and say that the subject of the poem was clearly going to be Zeus:

Μοῦσαι Πιερίηθεν ἀοιδῇσι κλείουσαι,
δεῦτε Δί' ἐννέπετε, σφέτερον πατέρ' ὑμνείουσαι.

---

41 See Hardie 1995.

ὅν τε διὰ βροτοὶ ἄνδρες ὁμῶς ἄφατοί τε φατοί τε,
ῥητοί τ' ἄρρητοί τε Διὸς μεγάλοιο ἕκητι.

> Muses of Pieria, famed for your song, hither come and speak of Zeus, hymning your father. Thanks to him, mortal men are either famous or not, spoken of or not, for the sake of great Zeus.

Although these lines are often taken as or at least thought of as a (theoretically) detachable Zeus-hymn,[42] it can easily be argued that this is indeed precisely what the poem is about—not Zeus in all his aspects, but as Hesiod reveals, Zeus in his role of judge of human actions—Zeus δικηφόρος, as Aeschylus calls him in the *Agamemnon* (525–6). Briefly, then, 11–41 is on Strife (ἔρις), in general (two kinds) and then as it pertains to Hesiod and his brother as they contest over their inheritance (= means of livelihood); cf. 35–6 ἀλλ' αὖθι διακρινώμεθα νεῖκος / ἰθείῃσι δίκῃς, αἵ τ' ἐκ Διός εἰσιν ἄρισται ("But let us decide our differences right now with straight judgement, which come best from Zeus"). Next come 42–89 on Livelihood (βίος) hidden by gods, esp. Zeus (42), as illustrated by the story of Prometheus and Pandora. It is Zeus who allowed us to have Hope. Next 106–201: The Races of men, all but the first under the control of Zeus (138, silver; 143, bronze; 158, heroes; 169, iron; 180, the generation to come). This is followed by 202–212: the Fable of hawk and nightingale. The next long section can be broken down into (i) 213–247: Justice and hybris, overseen by Zeus (238–247) (ii) 248–273: Rant against princes: Zeus observes and punishes (253) those whose wrongdoing he has heard from Dike; (iii) 274–382: Back to Perses. Zeus gave Dike to men (276, 281). Live right. Rules of behavior. This is the end of the tight Zeus section, but 383 to the end—in other words, The Works (383–764) & Days (765–828)—, containing details of proper/just (agricultural) living/livelihood, which the first part of the poem tells us that all this depends on Zeus. In other words, this traditional title may be missing the point. A better title would be the *Zeusiad*.[43] But all these several genres—parable, fable, rant, exhortation, etc.—fit so comfortably within Hesiod's poem that we have no problem seeing it as a unit with its own generic title of didactic, albeit one that is very much ethical in purpose, despite what later ages thought of ethical didactic poetry (as I said earlier). Didactic poetry, in other words, as it was understood

---

42 Cf., e.g., Fakas (2001), 11–18; Rousseau (1996) 93–4, who speaks of "la transition entre cet éloge et le développement qui suit".

43 With this hasty Zeus-focused analysis, cf. Clay 2009, 72–3, "the changing faces of Zeus must be mapped over the course of the poem; for the role that Hesiod ascribes Zeus modulates ...". For a complex and sophisticated analysis of how Hesiod may or may not be considered a didactic poet, see Nelson 1998, 48–58.

from the Hellenistic age onward, is a type that purports to teach (Effe's "intention" again), but on a formal level can be a congeries of subtypes each capable of bearing its own generic label if found elsewhere.

A natural stopping point for the genre would have been Ovid's *Remedia Amoris*. Here we find not only a counter-didactic, in that Ovid is trying to provide an antidote for the learning he had supplied earlier in the *Ars Amatoria*, which was, it seems, altogether too successful. Its readers now have too many women in pursuit.[44] Of all the countermeasures Ovid offers, my favorite way of immersing oneself in the study of agricultural matters (*studium colendi*,169), which suggests a scene in which a person reads one didactic poem, the *Remedia Amoris*, only to be told to read a second didactic poem, *The Works and Days*, in order to counter the effects of yet another didactic poem, *The Ars Amatoria*.[45] This did not turn out to be the stopping point for didactic poetry, but it seems a natural place to end this discussion on didactic poetry.[46]

APPENDIX

Hellenistic didactic poems

Only three long ones are extant, one by Aratus and two by Nicander, but several short poems seem complete, such as those of Archimedes and Eratosthenes. Most, though, are quite fragmentary, if not known only by title. Nonetheless, even a list as sketchy as this demonstrates the great popularity of didactic in the Hellenistic period. Works in dactylic hexameter (or assumed so in the lack of evidence to the contrary) are unmarked; elegiac works are so indicated. For a more detailed survey of this material, see Harder 2011, 176–85. CA = *Collectanea Alexandrina*; SH = *Supplementum Hellenisticum*.

> Aglaias (medical, elegiac, SH 18)
> Alexander Aitolos
> Alexander of Ephesos, *Phainomena* (SH 20), geographical (SH 23–28)
> Anacreon, *Phaenomena*, eleg. (CA 130)
> Antigonus, *Alloiosis* (SH 50)

---

[44] For Ovid's generic games in this poem, see Fréchet 2006.
[45] The passage on how to farm extends from vv. 169 to 197, touching on topics such as plowing and planting, fruit trees, goats, cattle, and grapes. A mention of bees calls Vergil to mind as well.
[46] But not before I thank Richard Hunter for his comments, as well as many others who have heard one or another form of this talk over the past few years in Durham (North Carolina), Moscow, and Thessaloniki, as well as my students in New York and Venice.

Didactic poetry — 29

Anubion, astrological elegies
Aratus, *Phainomena (tr. > Lat. by Cicero. Ovid, Avienus, and Germanicus); Iatrika
Archelaus Chersonites, mirabilia SH 125–9
Archimedes, Problema (SH 201)
Archestratus, Hedypatheia (food, SH 132–92)
Boius, Ornithogonia (tr. > Lat. by Aemilius Acer)
Caecalus, Halieutica SH 237
Callimachus Aetia, eleg.
Callimachus Junior, On Islands (SH 309)
Damocrates Servilius, medical, iambics, ed. Vogt, forthcoming
Didymarchus, Metamorphoses (SH 378 A)
Dorotheus of Sidon, astronomical elegy, ed. Pingree
Eratosthenes, Hermes, Duplication of the Cube (CA 58ff)
Eudemus, medical (SH 412
Euthydemus, on dried fish (SH 455)
Hegesianax, Phainomena (SH 465–70, CA 8–9)
Heliodorus, medical (SH 471)
Hermesianax, Leontion (catalogue poem; CA 98–106)
Hermippus, Phainomena (SH 485–90)
Menecrates of Ephesus, Erga, Bee Keeping (SH 542–50)
Mnesitheus, On Wine, in iambics (fr. 41 Bertier)
Neoptolemus, Trichotonia (?) (CA 27)
Nicaenetus, Catalogue of Women (CA 2)
Nicander, *Theriaka, *Alexipharmaka, Heteroioumena, Georgica, Melissourgica Ophiaca
Nicomachus, On Painters, elegies
Numenius, Theriaca, Halieutika (SH 568–94)
Orus, medical
Pancrates of Argos, Thalassia Erga (SH 598–600)
Parthenius, Metamorphoses (SH 636–7)
Pausanias of Damascus, geography, in iambics (perh. = Ps.-Scymnus)
Periander, physician who wrote verse (Plut. Apophth.Lac. 218 f)
Petrichus, on snakes (Pliny NH 20.96, 22.40; schol. in Nicand. Ther. 226)
Philo of Tarsos, medical (SH 690)
Polycratus of Mende, Sicelica, natural science ([Arist.] Mirab. 840b32)
Posidippus of Pella, didactic epigrams
Posidonius of Corinth, Halieutika (SH 709)
Sosicrates (or Sostratos), Ἠοῖοι, Cynegetica (SH 732, 735)
Satyrus, on stones (SH 717–19)
Simias, on the names of months (fr. 8 CA)
Sminthes, Phainomena (SH 729)
Theodorus, Metamorphoses (SH 749)
Theodotus, On the Jews (SH 757–764)
Timachidas, Deipna (SH 769–773)
Timaristus, flowers (Pliny NH 21.105)
Timon of Phlius, Indalmoi (= Phainomena; elegiacs, SH 841–4)
Zenothemis, on stones (SH 855–858)

G. O. Hutchinson
Hellenistic Poetry and Hellenistic Prose*

Hellenistic poetry was written and read in a context formed partly by contemporary prose. The prose was not a mere artless repository of abstruse technicalities and erudition: it too was writing, and the interaction of poetry and prose should be considered in this light. That has been little done hitherto. Kathryn Gutzwiller's *Guide* (2007) and, later, the Blackwell's *Companion* (2010) performed the great service of bringing Hellenistic poetry and prose together. We now need to think more about their relationship.[1]

What follows will only look at a few aspects. The aim will be merely to suggest the existence of a context relevant to the poetry, which makes us notice points and angles we might otherwise have missed. To suggest its existence and relevance, the most effective means will be particular passages; we will spend most time on them, but specific intertextualities between passages will not be alleged. The direction of causation is a problem too, when so much has been lost, when chronology can be uncertain, and when the usual 'Hellenistic period' is uncomfortably extended in time. We will most often have to rest content, like many physicists and modern historians, with a group of phenomena which look to be related in some way; dating will be kept in mind throughout.

In general, poetry and prose are much interested by each other in this 'period'. Obvious examples are didactic poetry reworking didactic prose, or Callimachus and Apollonius exploiting and even epitomizing local historians; but the interest is seen the other way round as well. An illustration is seen in the different use to which two first-century writers put the same piece of poetry in their own prose.

Phld. *De Morte* col. xxxviii 3–14 Henry ἔνιοι δ' οὕτως | εἰσὶν τὸν ἀνθρώπινον βίον †παρω‹ι›-κηκό|τες†, οὐ χυδαῖοι μόνον ἀλλὰ καὶ τῶν φι|λοσοφεῖν δὴ λεγομένων, ὥστε καὶ δι|ατ‹άτ›τονται τοσαῦτα μὲν ἔτη διατρί|ψειν Ἀθήνησιν φιλομαθοῦντες, τοσαῦτα δέ ... τοσαῦτα δέ ... τὰ δὲ λοιπὰ με|τὰ τῶν γνωρίμων. ἄφνω δ' ἄφαντον | προσέβα μακρὰς ἀφαι-ρούμενον ἐλπί|δας τὸ χρεών.

But some, not just ordinary people but some of those called philosophers, have †taken up residence by† human life in such a way that they actually arrange to spend so many years

---

* Much gratitude is owed to the conference organizers Professor Rengakos and Professor Sistakou for carrying the event on, in the most friendly fashion, amid very difficult circumstances.
1 Gutzwiller 2007, Clauss/Cuypers 2010; note in the latter Cuypers 2010, Gowing 2010. Only a very limited number of scholarly works is mentioned in what follows: mostly editions, to help orientate the reader, and recent items, from which more bibliography can be found.

studying in Athens, so many [doing this], so many [doing that], and the rest of their years with their friends. And suddenly, there has arrived unseen, removing their extended hopes, necessity.

D.S. 16.92.3–93.2 ... ἤρξατο λέγειν τόδε τὸ ποίημα· ' ... ἄφνω δ' ἄφαντος προσέβα | μακρὰς ἀφαιρούμενος ἐλπίδας | θνατῶν πολύμοχθος Ἀίδας.' καὶ τὰ τούτων ἐφεξῆς προσςυνεῖρε ... τηλικαύτης δ' οὔςης περὶ αὐτὸν ὑπεροχῆς καὶ πάντων ἐπαινούντων ἅμα καὶ μακαριζόντων τὸν ἄνδρα, παράδοξος καὶ παντελῶς ἀνέλπιστος ἐφάνη κατὰ τοῦ βασιλέως ἐπιβουλὴ καὶ θάνατος.

[The tragic actor] began to recite this passage: ' ... suddenly, there has arrived unseen, removing the extended hopes of mortals, Hades full of suffering.' He added on what follows ... With so much excess going on about Philip [cf. 16.92.5], with everyone praising him and congratulating him, surprisingly and quite unexpectedly there appeared against the King conspiracy and death.

Philodemus (a writer of both poetry and prose) slips the poetry, without explicit citation, into the texture of his own exposition; he conspicuously replaces the poet's fiction of a god Hades with, not a word for his subject death, but τὸ χρεών: less personified and direct, but argumentatively telling. The story about the quote before Philip's death will have preceded Philodemus; but Diodorus spells out the unexpected application of the poem by then 'translating' it into his own prose. His version is rich in pairs, but moves from the elaborate genitive absolute of good fortune to the decisive and unmythologized θάνατος, separated from the predicative adjectives and like Ἀίδας in the poem ending the sentence.[2]

Parthenius' Ἐρωτικὰ παθήματα is a work based on transposition between poetry and prose: from Hellenistic poetry to Parthenius' Hellenistic prose to Gallus' Latin poetry. The process is highlighted when Parthenius quotes some of his originals, including poetry by himself; the very fact of the quotations suggests that Parthenius is not merely concerned with brevity as a practical goal (ὅτι

---

[2] Notes on the passage of Philodemus: Henry 2009a, 87, 89. It seems implausible both that παροικέω with the accusative can mean 'live in a place as a non-citizen' and that it can convey 'be foreign to' (cf. Henry 2009a, 87); Ph. Confus. 80–1 comes closest to a support, but is insufficient as well as allegorical. The perfect would be very curious. The position of οὐ χυδαῖοι κτλ. tells against a neutral 'settle in'. One possibility might be παρεωρακότες (corrupted via -εωρηκότες?), 'have overlooked' (the nature of); cf. for the perfect e.g. Plb. 4.14.7, 39.6.4, D. S. 12.12.3. On Philodemus' own prose writing cf. Henry 2009b, esp. 102. Didactic poetry and prose (actually two-way traffic): Hutchinson 2009, and 2008, ch. 10. Wirth 1993, 4 n. 6, 52 sees pointers to Augustus in Diodorus; but it seems fairly clear that his work was largely written before Actium (note the treatment of Alexandria). He should be regarded as a Hellenistic writer, for what the category is worth. 'Fiction' is capaciously used in this piece for elements which are separated from the world of the reader, either by conflicting with the rules of reality familiar in that world, or by involving specifics which are known to be invented.

πλεῖϲτα ἐν βραχυτάτοιϲ, he modestly states). And a leading poet would seem unlikely to have circulated a purely utilitarian reminder.³

The relation of poetry and prose was the subject of lively theoretical debate. The subject has been discussed by others, and will not be dwelt on here. It is enough to notice that artistry in prose could be allowed for even in theoretical discussion of what distinguishes poetry: so

> Phld. *Poem.* 5 col. xxix 23–xxx 6 ... διέψευϲται ... καὶ | τῶι τὸ κεκρατημένωϲ | τί π[οτ'] ἐϲτὶν ἀγνοεῖϲθαι, | τό τ[ε κ]α[λ]ῶϲ μηδὲν ἧττον, | καὶ τῶι καὶ πεζοῦ λόγου | ποιοῦ τινοϲ κοινὴν [ἀ]|ρετὴν αὐτὴν εἶναι κἂν | λέγειν ἐνίουϲ.
>
> [This view] is mistaken ... also because it is not known what on earth 'effectively' (?) or 'beautifully' means, and because some would say it was a virtue of a certain kind of prose writing too.

Artistry in prose is naturally presupposed in rhetoric, a theoretical area much developed in the Hellenistic 'period', from Aristotle on.⁴

In the very elements of what determines genre and the division between poetry and prose, the beginning of the Hellenistic period sees some striking developments. Hegesias (iv-iii BC) inaugurates a way of writing prose that usually limits the rhythm at the end of phrases in the sentence, and is seen by critics as breaking the sentence up into neat entities. Cf. e. g. Cic. *Brut.* 287 *at quid est tam fractum, tam minutum, | tam in ipsa quam tamen consequitur concinnitate puerile?* |, *Orat.* 230 *sunt etiam qui illo uitio quod ab Hegesia maxime fluxit | infringendis concidendisque numeris | in quoddam genus abiectum incidant uersiculorum simillimum.* | The conception reduces the gap between poetry and prose; but it also bears affinities to the tightening up of metre within poetry. It is important for the impact of Callimachus, in particular, that his imaginative explorations in content and language are bound into strictly organized lines, within which each part has its own constraints, especially over ending. The effect is not so uniformly fragmented, either in the fragments of Hegesias or in Callimachus, as Cicero suggests for Hegesias; but e.g. Call. *H.* 6.27 will bring out the sense of elegant sub-division: ἐν πίτυϲ, ἐν μεγάλαι πτελέαι ἔϲαν, ἐν δὲ καὶ

---

3 For some recent discussion related to these topics, since the fundamental edition Lightfoot 1999, see Biraud/Voisin/Zucker 2008, 22–43 and Zucker 2008, esp. Billault 2008*b* and Spatafora 2008.

4 On text and meaning cf. Mangoni 1993, 300–302. On the Hellenistic discussion of poetry and prose, cf. Mangoni 1988, Gutzwiller 2010; ideas of rhetoric: e. g. Longo Auricchio 1985; Chandler 2006; Erbì 2009 and 2010.

ὄχναι. There is likely to be some contextual link between the developments in both spheres.[5]

The possibility of a link is confirmed by developments in Latin. Cicero, as I argue elsewhere, is the first, or first significant, Latin writer to adopt Hellenistic prose-rhythm. He also effects, and may be the first significant Latin writer to effect, tighter limitations in hexameter poetry. These are not the same as the Callimachean limitations, but display the same kind of desire for constriction (so even in the *Aratea* lines usually end with words of two or three syllables, except for Greek names, and Hermann's Bridge is usually observed). Later than the start of these practices by Cicero, his antagonist Calvus forges a more unexpected alliance: not between Hellenistic tendencies in prose and in poetry, but between Callimachean aesthetics and Attic oratory of the fourth century. Cf. e.g. Cic. *Brut.* 284 *tum Brutus 'Atticum se' inquit | 'Caluus noster dici oratorem uolebat: | inde erat ista exilitas | quam ille de industria | consequebatur.'* | and e.g. Catullus 50 (note perhaps Calvus *FRP* 35 *durum rus fugit et laboriosum*), Hor. *Sat.* 1.10.19. Not that either Atticism or Asianism is a Roman invention, in my opinion: Latin oratory recreates a controversy of Hellenistic prose.[6]

But can we really find a relation between Hegesias, a by-word (among his critics) for tastelessness, and Callimachus, a by-word (among his fans) for refinement? Even Hegesias' style could be praised (Cic. *Att.* 12.6.1 *huc aurum si accedit —sed quid loquor? tu uidebis. habes Hegesiae genus, quod Varro laudat*); and refinement may be a more positive way of looking at what Hegesias' critics call puerile neatness. He would not have been attacked so much unless he had many admirers, whose viewpoint was naturally positive.

---

5 Rhythmical writing includes the inscriptions of Antiochus I of Commagene (i BC; for recent evidence cf. Crowther/Facella 2003, Wagner/Petzel 2003) and *I.Thrac.Aeg.* 205, an aretalogy of Isis (second half of ii BC to early i BC; text Loukopoulou *et al.* 2005; cf. recently Hunter 2006, 57–61 (brings into relation with poetic texts on Isis), Papanikolaou 2009 (also discusses rhythm in Hellenistic texts generally)). See further Winterbottom 2011, 262–265 and 275 on prose-rhythm in the Hellenistic and early Imperial periods. On Hegesias' date cf. Jacoby 1930, 529 ('wohl ungefährer zeitgenosse des Timaios'); he will not be later than Callimachus (Cic. *Brut.* 286f. makes it sound as though there is no long gap between the activity of Charisius and Demochares (Demosthenes' nephew) and of Hegesias, who begins later than Charisius). | in prose not preserved on papyrus indicates a rhythmical close.

6 On *FRP* 35 see Hollis 2007, 79; *durum rus* could still have had some metapoetic point. Note that Catullus 50 itself draws on Apollonius Book 3: see Hutchinson 2012, 74. Prose-rhythm in Cicero: Hutchinson 1995; for his place in the introduction of prose-rhythm and the role of Greek rhetors in its spread, see Hutchinson 2013, 233–8. View of Asianism etc. as Roman invention: Wisse 1995, followed by e.g. Papanikolaou 2009, 64, Spawforth 2012, 20–1.

The matter, though, may be more involved. Agatharchides' assault on Hegesias, itself an animated specimen of Hellenistic prose, at one point attacks Hegesias' transference of language:

Agatharch. *GGM* i.121 Müller (fr. 21 Burstein) 'τῆc μὲν πόλεωc καταcκαφείcηc | ... αἱ δὲ γυναῖκεc μετήχθηcαν | εἰc Μακεδονίαν, | τὴν πόλιν θάψαcαί τινα τρόπον. | [Hegesias *FGrHist* 142 F 16]' ἕτερον ὅμοιον· 'ἡ δὲ φάλαγξ τῶν Μακεδόνων | εἰcβιαcαμένη τοῖc ὅπλοιc | ἐντὸc τείχουc τὴν πόλιν ἀπέκτεινεν. | [F 17]' ἐκεῖ μὲν ταφὴ πόλεωc, ἐνταῦθα δὲ θάνατοc· λοιπὸν ἐκφορὰν δεῖ προcθέντας ἐπιγράμματι χρήcαcθαι καὶ παντελὴc ἡ πρᾶξιc.

'When the city was razed to the ground ... the women were transported to Macedonia, when they had so to speak buried the city.' And a similar bit: 'The Macedonian phalanx forced its way by arms inside the wall and killed the city.' There we had the burial of a city, here we have its death. So we just need to add the carrying out of the body and have an epitaph and the job is complete.[7]

Yet the assimilation of the destruction of a city to the death and funeral of a person appears in Callimachus too, but with the person as the reality. Arsinoe's deified sister sees from afar what is in fact Arsinoe's pyre:

ἀπὸ δ' αὔγαcαι ...
τ]ίc ἀπώλετο, τίc πολίων ὁλόκαυτοc α[ἴ]θει.
ἔνι μοι φόβοc. ἀλλὰ ποτεῦ· νότοc αυ[,]
νότοc αἴθριοc. ἦρά τι μοι Λιβύα κα[κοῦται;
    (fr. 228.47–51 Pfeiffer = fr. 16 Lelli)

[the sister speaks to Charis] Look forth and see which city has perished, which city is blazing burned whole. I feel fear. Go on, fly. A south wind ... , a clear south wind. Is my Libya being wronged?

Here the assimilation of the burial of the person and the destruction of the city is part of a character's erroneous imagining; and the whole scene is part of an elaboration of poetic worlds which takes fiction to a memorable point. There are important differences, then, from the prose. But there is also a connection; and the short units and anaphora of this speech may strengthen the affinities with contemporary rhetoric (see below). Knowledge of the prose at any rate helps one perceive more keenly the extremity in the poetry, and realize the more through comparison with the prose its ambitious grandeur of conception.[8]

---

7 See Burstein (1989) for Agatharchides, though there is no Greek text.
8 On the passage cf. Lelli 2005, 183 (style), 185 (difference from Hom. *Il.* 22.409–411; 'l'intera città' should not imply that Philotera knows which city). Callimachus' handling of divine perception enables a gradual approach to Philotera's knowledge of her sister's death. The pattern has similarities with that in Hom. *Il.* 22.447–467 (Andromache); the role of the messenger

It is rewarding to compare Hellenistic poetry and Hellenistic prose on related material, even when the features concerned are less distinctive. Let us take first a passage from a speech by Hegesias; Hegesias' oratory, known through Rutilius' adaptation of Gorgias' manual, is less dwelt on by scholars than his history of Alexander.

> Rut. Lup. 1.7 pp. 156, 158 Barabino item Hegesiae: 'miseremini mei, iudices, quem coniurata tanta uis inimicorum oppugnat; miseremini solitudinis, cui ne in summo quidem tempore periculi liberos adhibere ad communem calamitatem deprecandam licitum est; miseremini senectutis, quae me etiam sine ceteris malis grauiter defatigat.'

Likewise this passage of Hegesias: 'Pity me, men of the jury, as I am assailed by so large a conspiracy of my enemies; pity my isolation [i.e. childlessness], as I have not been vouched safe even in extreme danger to use offspring in begging to avert a disaster shared with them; pity my old age, as it wearies me grievously even without my other misfortunes.

The emotive extremity of the repeated *miseremini* goes beyond Attic oratory; it is picked up in Cicero (cf. *Flac.* 106 *miseremini familiae, iudices,* | *miseremini fortissimi patris,* | *miseremini fili* |), and Seneca extends the device through Phaedra's rising appeal to Hippolytus: *Phaed.* 623 *miserere uiduae*, 636 *miserere, pauidae mentis exaudi preces*, 671 *miserere amantis*.[9]

In a moment, this passage will be related to a passage of Hellenistic poetry; but to that passage of poetry another passage of Hellenistic prose can also be compared. In Polybius' overwhelming account of Achaeus' capture and death, the surprise of this powerful rebel's fall is dramatized within the account through the response of his enemy Antiochus III:

> . . . εἰς τοιαύτην ἀφασίαν ἦλθε διὰ τὸ παράδοξον ὥστε πολὺν μὲν χρόνον ἀποσιωπῆσαι, τὸ δὲ τελευταῖον συμπαθὴς γενέσθαι καὶ δακρῦσαι. τοῦτο δ' ἔπαθεν ὁρῶν, ὡς ἔμοιγε δοκεῖ, τὸ δυσφύλακτον καὶ παράλογον τῶν ἐκ τῆς τύχης συμβαινόντων. Ἀχαιὸς γὰρ ἦν Ἀνδρομάχου μὲν υἱός τοῦ Λαοδίκης ἀδελφοῦ τῆς Σελεύκου γυναικός, ἔγημε δὲ Λαοδίκην τὴν Μιθριδάτου τοῦ βασιλέως θυγατέρα, κύριος δ' ἐγεγόνει τῆς ἐπὶ τάδε τοῦ Ταύρου πάσης. δοκῶν δὲ τότε καὶ ταῖς αὐτοῦ δυνάμεσι καὶ ταῖς ὑπεναντίων ἐν ὀχυρωτάτωι τόπωι τῆς οἰκουμένης διατρίβειν, ἐκάθητο δεδεμένος ἐπὶ τῆς γῆς, ὑποχείριος γενόμενος τοῖς ἐχθροῖς, οὐδέπω γινώσκοντος οὐθενὸς ἁπλῶς τὸ γεγονὸς πλὴν τῶν πραξάντων.
>
> (8.20.9 – 12)

---

connects the pattern more closely to Plb. 8.21.4 – 5 (Laodice, cf. below), of course without Callimachus directly affecting Polybius. The element of grandeur in Hellenistic poetry: Porter 2011; add Netz 2009, 54 – 8 for big and small. Wilamowitz 1924, i.196 writes on this poem, 'Wer kann leugnen, daß Kallimachos hier einmal etwas Grandioses geschaffen hat.' (he brings in Rubens's cycle for Maria de' Medici; the 'einmal' is a pity).

9 Jacoby misses out Rut. Lup. 1.11; other extracts *FGrHist* 142 F 27 – 29. On Rutilius, cf. Hutchinson 2013, 16, 235.

... he was so reduced to speechlessness by the extraordinary nature of the sight that for a long time he kept silent, and finally felt sympathy and wept. He was subject to these emotions because, in my opinion, he saw how hard it is to avoid events produced by fortune and how they counter expectation. Achaeus was the son of Andromachus, the brother of Laodice the wife of Seleucus; he had married Laodice the daughter of king Mithridates; he had become master of all the land on this side of the Taurus mountains. At that moment his own and his enemies' forces thought he was in the most secure place in the world. He was actually sitting tied up on the ground, in the control of his enemies; absolutely no one besides those who had done the deed was yet aware of what had happened.

Antiochus' distress is temporary: he puts Achaeus to a humiliating death. Polybius' main point is the remarkable turn of fortune: Polybius could himself be called in some respects a tragic historian, but the historian sees through tragedy to a pragmatic wisdom. The moment is none the less intense. In the resonant detailing of Achaeus' royal lineage and marriage and the range of his power is conveyed, with some embedded focalization through Antiochus, the abrupt change to Achaeus' present powerlessness and degradation.[10]

In Apollonius, Phineus makes his appeal to the Argonauts:

' ... χραίςμετέ μοι, ῥύςαςθε δυςάμμορον ἀνέρα λύμης ...
οὐ γὰρ μοῦνον ἐπ' ὀφθαλμοῖςιν Ἐρινύς
λὰξ ἐπέβη, καὶ γῆρας ἀμήρυτον ἐς τέλος ἕλκω·
πρὸς δ' ἐπὶ πικρότατον κρέμαται κακὸν ἄλλο κακοῖςιν ...
       οὐδ' ὀθνεῖοι ἀλαλκήςουςιν ἐόντες,
εἰ δὴ ἐγὼν ὁ πρίν ποτ' ἐπικλυτὸς ἀνδράςι Φινεύς
ὄλβωι μαντοςύνηι τε, πατὴρ δέ με γείνατ' Ἀγήνωρ,
τῶν δὲ καςιγνήτην, ὅτ' ἐνὶ Θρήικεςςιν ἄναςςον,
Κλειοπάτρην ἕδνοιςιν ἐμὸν δόμον ἦγον ἄκοιτιν.'
                                                        (2.218–239)

' ... Defend me, rescue a most wretched man from this brutality ... Not only has the Erinys trodden on my eyes with her foot, and not only do I drag an interminable old age to its close; besides, a most bitter further woe hangs over the other woes ... Nor will I be defended by people who are unrelated to me, if I am indeed the Phineus once famous among men for good fortune and prophecy, Agenor's son, who, when I was reigning among the Thracians, paid bride-gifts and took the Boreadae's sister Cleopatra to my house as my wife.'[11]

---

[10] The account is discussed by McGing 2010, 26 f.; he rightly stresses a Homeric element, but does not mention *Iliad* 24, and in other ways assimilates too closely to Homer (the details of Achaeus' family, etc., on which see Walbank 1957–79, ii.96, are not really a Homeric character sketch). Still more recent overview of Polybius: Dreyer 2011. For tragedy and history in Polybius and elsewhere, see Schepens 2005, Van der Stockt 2005, Rutherford 2007.
[11] Matteo 2007, 171, following Vian/Delage 2002, 187, takes ἐς τέλος with ἀμήρυτον; that sounds contrived in this author, and her objection to the alternative is too literal-minded. In 222 (2007,

At the beginning here, Apollonius does not go to Hegesias' extreme of repeating the same imperative three times; he has two imperatives, close in meaning, but they are combined in an asyndeton which departs from Homeric norms. (Callimachus' *Hymn to Delos* is less restrained: Leto's part is marked by repeated imperatives: 118 f. ἀλλὰ cὺ μεῖνον, | μεῖνον, 150 f. cώιζεο χαίρων, | cώιζεο, 214 γείνεο, γείνεο, κοῦρε.) Wearying age is the third of the *mala* suffered by Hegesias' speaker; but it is only the second of Phineus' κακά. The climax of his woes, the Harpies, take us beyond familiar reality into the fiction of poetic mythology. At the end of the speech, he explains that the Boreadae will rescue him, and indicates his connection to them. At the same time, the character is showing the Argonauts his prestigious status (cf. S. *Ph*. 261–263), and character and author are bringing out the pathos and the magnitude of his fall (note ὁ πρίν ποτ' ἐπικλυτὸς ἀνδράcι Φινεύc and ὅτ' ἐνὶ Θρήικεccιν ἄναccον). As in the Polybius, specifics of lineage, marriage, and power drive home the change. The Argonauts, like Antiochus, weep. The prose helps one to see the tragic intensity and oratorical strength of this speech in Apollonius.[12]

Two more passages, not connected with each other, may be appended to close this part. Another extract in Rutilius brings out Hegesias' interest in extremes of emotion, and enables us to glimpse his power as a writer:

> Rut. Lup. 2.10 p. 196 Barabino (ἀπορία) *item Hegesiae:* 'non haec est, ut uulgari uerbo appellatur, calamitas. quid igitur? quod proprium <nomen> imponam nescio, nisi illud unum, tantam esse aerumnae magnitudinem ut omnem Fortunae superbissimam crudelitatem ingens miseria superarit.'

> Likewise this passage of Hegesias: 'This is not, as the standard term has it, a disaster. What is it, then? I do not know what name to give it that would be right—save to say that the immensity of distress is so great that the huge affliction has surpassed all the most haughty cruelty of Fortune.'

The Peneius' reply to Leto's appeal in Callimachus' *Hymn to* Delos displays a sudden shift from sorrowful evasion to magnanimous daring.

> 'Λητοῖ, Ἀναγκαίη μεγάλη θεός ...
>   τί μήcομαι; ἦ ἀπολέcθαι
> ἡδύ τί τοι Πηνειόν; —ἴτω πεπρωμένον ἦμαρ·
> τλήcομαι εἵνεκα cεῖο, καὶ εἰ ...
> ἠνίδ' ἐγώ· τί περιccά; κάλει μόνον Εἰλείθυιαν.'
>   (122, 127–132)

171–2) she takes πρόc as governing κακοῖcιν, 'in addition to': a rare sense in Homer, and unpromising with this initial πρὸc δέ.

12 Phineus: Hutchinson 2008, 82–3, with literature in 83 n. 37.

'Leto, Necessity is a great goddess. ... What am I to do? Would it be a pleasure for you that Peneius should perish? —Let the fated day come! I will endure for your sake, even if ... Look, here I am. Why say anything superfluous? Just call Eileithyia.'

The climax of the first part is marked by short units in asyndeton (127–128*a*). The shift to the second happens with asyndeton and a short unit; the climax of the second part is again marked by short units in asyndeton, with a self-reflexive τί περισσά;. Here one part of the stylistic context for the reader is likely to be the brevity of units and the asyndeton sometimes found in Hegesias (so *FGrH* 142 F 24) and taken to an extreme in this poetic rhetoric. The prose helps us to see in the passage, not parody, but noble gestures, within a poetic world that takes fiction to its furthest point and toys with it: fleeing places, including rivers, and a god that can be destroyed, like his river. The treatment of Thebes as a person in 87–98 of the hymn is much more fully realized and mythological than the treatment of Thebes (?) as a person in Hegesias' language (F 16, 17, above).[13]

Likenesses, then, and difference are to be seen in the rhetorical and emotive writing of Hellenistic prose and poetry. The prose encourages us to see more emotion and elevation in the poetry, but also brings out distinctive aspects of poetic worlds. The worlds of poets and prose authors come closer in meta-literary discussion which involves the writer; it would be more illuminating, however, to go beyond just the discussion of literature and talk about ego-language, that is first-person language applied to the writer. The unlovely term 'ego-language' is twisted from the term 'ego-documents' used by modern historians. But an ego-document is the sort of work, such as a diary, which you would expect to be focused on the person that produced it. The Hellenistic 'period' shows us ego-language expanding into unexpected areas or expanding with unexpected breadth. There had of course been plenty of ego-language before. But utterances by the author or even inclusion of the author as character (cf. Cratinus' *Pytine*) fit in with the concerns and conventions of Old Comedy; a mime about the author and his work like Herodas 8 seems more of a surprise (from what we can tell of mime; Laberius' prologue, fr. 90 Panayotakis, is a very different matter). Herodotus' history is full of brief comments by the author, with free use of the first-person pronoun and first-person verbs; but the copious first-person expatiations which interrupt Polybius' narrative would very much surprise us in Herodotus or Thucydides. The point is about generic experiment and freedom rather than about understanding of the individual (one could likewise contend that 'realism' in Hellenistic sculpture is primarily a matter of artistic genre). We can look now

---

13 On the punctuation of 128 f., see Mineur 1984, 146. Particularly in view of the prose, I would now modify the account at Hutchinson 1988, 38.

at resemblances and divergences in the use of ego-language in Hellenistic poetry and prose.[14]

The ego-language of this literature often appears in contexts of antagonism, where the writer, or better the literary construction formally identified with the writer, is in conflict with other persons. We might at first think that there could be little common ground between the elegant indirectness of poetry and the ferocious polemic and uninhibited self-assertion of prose (Polybius and, in the Imperial period, Galen could come to mind). But the picture in prose is more complicated. Hipparchus, for instance (ii BC), writes against Aratus from a position of superior expertise; but he is acutely conscious of how invidious and self-glorifying his procedure could seem, and justifies himself with the aid of his addressee:

θεωρῶν δ' οὖν <ἐν> τοῖc πλείcτοιc καὶ χρηcιμωτάτοιc διαφωνοῦντα τὸν Ἄρατον πρὸc τὰ φαινόμενα καὶ γινόμενα κατ' ἀλήθειαν ... ἔκρινα, τῆc cῆc ἕνεκα φιλομαθείαc καὶ τῆc κοινῆc τῶν ἄλλων ὠφελίαc, ἀναγράψαι τὰ δοκοῦντά μοι διημαρτῆcθαι. τοῦτο δὲ ποιῆcαι προεθέμην οὐκ ἐκ τοῦ τοὺc ἄλλουc ἐλέγχειν φανταcίαν ἀπενέγκαcθαι προαιρούμενοc— κενὸν γὰρ καὶ μικρόψυχον παντελῶc ... —ἀλλ' ἕνεκα τοῦ μήτε cὲ μήτε τοὺc λοιποὺc τῶν φιλομαθούντων ἀποπλανᾶcθαι τῆc περὶ τὰ φαινόμενα κατὰ τὸν κόcμον θεωρίαc.

(1.1.5–6)

I observed that in most matters, and those of greatest use, Aratus does not match the phenomena and what really happens. So I decided, for the sake of your study and the advantage of people in general, to write down the mistakes which I thought had been made. I resolved to do this not with the intention of winning prestige by refuting others—that would be completely pointless and small-minded ... —but rather so that neither you nor others who study such matters should not wander erroneously from the observation of phenomena in the sky.

We can actually find resemblances between prose and poetry in modes of engagement with an opponent. Here is Philodemus:

χα[ρ]ιζόμεθα δὲ ǀ[τ]ἀνδρὶ καὶ τὸ πλῆθοc τῶν ǀ κεφαλαίων δι' ὧν ὡc ἐλέγǀχων περ[ι]ίcταται τὴν δό̣ǀξαν ἡμῶν· οὐδ' ἂν ἐ[μ]νή̣ǀcθημ̣[εν] μὰ τοὺc θε[οὺc αὐ]ǀτῶν. τί γὰρ ἔμελλον; ... ἐρωτ[ῶ] γάρ, ὦ βέλτιcτ' Ἐǀφεc<ί>ω[ν] τῶν ἁπάντων, τί̣ǀνα τα̣[ῦτ'] ἔcτιν τοῖcδε ἐν τῆι φιλοǀcοφίαι τῆι καθ' ἡμᾶc ἀνεǀǀ[cτραμ]μένοιc; (Phld. Rhet. 2 P. Herc. 1672 col. viii 30–ix 7)

I forgive the man too the abundance of arguments through which he surrounds my view, thinking he is refuting it; I wouldn't have mentioned them, by the gods. Why should I have? ... I ask you, best of all the Ephesians, what are those things to these men who are engaged in our sort of philosophy?

---

14 For ego-documents cf. Dekker 2002, Fulbrook and Rublack 2010.

The opponent is contrasted with the writer. He heaps up arguments in aggressive attack; but the writer is not bothered. He counters with a suave, formally laudatory address, which accompanies a pressing question. Here is Callimachus:

' ... τεῦ μέχρι τολμᾶιc; οἱ φίλοι cε δήc[ουcι ...
ὡc ὑγιείηc οὐδὲ τῶιγυχι ψαύειc ... ' ...
'ὦ λῶιcτ', ...
τίc εἶπεν ...
"cὺ πεντάμετρα cυντίθει, cὺ δ' ἡ[ρῶιο]ν ..." ;
δοκέω μέν, οὐδείc ... '

(Ia. 13.19–33)

' ... How far will your audacity go? Your friends will put you in a straitjacket. You don't touch sanity even with your fingernails ...' ... 'My excellent fellow ... who said ... "you, compose pentameters; you, the hexameter ..."? No one, I believe ...'

The opponent has heaped up objections to Callimachus' crazily mixed-up work, and ends with an aggressive question and aggressive insult. Callimachus counters with an urbane address and, before long, a pressing question. The scene is more of a fictionalized dialogue than in Philodemus; but, as we shall see, such a form creates less of a distance from prose, and philosophical prose, than other types of fiction that we have observed.[15]

Comparable too is Theocritus' depiction of his attempts to get patronage in poem 16. People's refusals are combined in an unfriendly heap of remarks, which end with rudeness unpleasantly trying to be funny. The writer then in his poem replies to them all, with a polite address (cf. 22.145) and a pointed question.

...
'οὗτοc ἀοιδῶν λῶιcτοc, ὃc ἐξ ἐμεῦ οἴcεται οὐδέν.'
δαιμόνιοι, τί δὲ κέρδοc ὁ μυρίοc ἔνδοθι χρυcόc
κείμενοc;

(16.21–3)

... 'The best poet is the one who gets nothing from me.' Gentlemen, what good is boundless gold lying indoors?

Studied obliqueness is seen in a passage of Philodemus where the writer is not confronting an adversary but talking about philosophers and others who live abroad.

---

15 For the Philodemus, see Longo Auricchio 1977, 164–7; also Chandler 2006, 43–4.

καὶ ταῦ|τα μὲν ἐγὼ λέγω περὶ | τῶν φιλοcόφων αὐτῶν | ἀπολ[ογ]ούμενοc· ἕτεροc δ' ἴcω[c
ἀγρ]οικότεροc κἂν | εὔξα[ιτο] τῶν ῥητόρων | πολλοὺc ἐπὶ ξ[έ]νηc ἀ|ναγκάζεcθαι καταβι|οῦν
ὡc βέλτιο[ν] οὕτω δι|αξουcῶν τῶν ὅθεν εἰcὶ | πόλεων ἢ καθ' ἃc ἀν[α]|cτρέφονται.
(*Rhet*. P. Herc. 1078/1080 ii.145 – 6 Sudhaus fr. III 15 – 26)

Now I say this about the philosophers themselves in defence; but someone cruder than myself would perhaps actually pray that many rhetoricians would be forced to live abroad: the cities they came from would get on better than the ones they frequented.

The writer emphasizes his own kindly intent towards one subset of the set of expatriate intellectuals (philosophers), but communicates a wittily disagreeable remark on another subset (rhetoricians or orators), while ascribing it to a contrasted speaker (ἐγώ … ἕτεροc δ'), a hypothetical man less refined than himself. He further distances it with a 'perhaps'.

Callimachus' olive proceeds in a parallel way, though against her antagonist the laurel, who has been unsubtly abusive.

'ὦ πάντα καλή, τῶν ἐμῶν τὸ κ[άλλιcτον]
ἐν τῆι τελευτῆι κύκνοc [   ]
ἤειcαc …
ἐγὼ μὲν οὔτε χρηcτὸν οὔτε cε γρύζω
ἀπηνὲc οὐδέν· ἀλλά μοι δύ' ὄρνιθεc
ἐν τοῖcι φύλλοιc ταῦτα τινθυρίζουcαι
πάλαι κάθηνται, κωτίλον δὲ τὸ ζεῦγοc. … '
(*Ia*. 4.45 – 63)

'You who are beautiful in all ways, you sang of the most beautiful of my features at the end, like a swan… I myself mutter nothing about you, good or harsh; but two birds have long been sitting in my branches twittering as follows, the pair of chatterers …

She opens with smooth praise (not to say oleaginous: cf. D.H. *Dem*. 20 i.171.5 – 8 Usener-Radermacher). She then contrasts herself (ἐγὼ μέν), coolly neutral, with two birds in her branches, unrestrained chatterboxes who will turn out to be much more outspoken against the laurel and for the olive. In both authors, the ego-language involves indirectness; but in Callimachus even the first person is not formally the writer. Philodemus merely introduced a hypothetical figure in one sentence; in Callimachus we have fiction within fiction within fiction. The poem creates a story of conflict between the writer, a rival, and someone who interrupts them; the writer distances the conflict by creating (retelling) a fable; a character in the fable distances her reply by creating some further speakers.[16]

---

16 The poem has an additional relation with prose through encomium: cf. Pl. *Smp*. 177b4 – 7 (praise of salt etc.), Radermacher 1951, 130 – 1, Russell and Wilson 1981, 229 – 230; P. Oxy. XVII

Despite the connections, there remain significant differences to be drawn between poetry and prose in this area. Archimedes and Polybius may not be average prose-writers in their self-confidence: both are writing from the pinnacle of their respective professions (like Galen after them). We can see, though, an element of convention in their procedures. The robustness with which they and others assert themselves would seem unlikely to occur in Hellenistic poetry. Patterns, and so conventions, can be discerned in, for instance, the following three passages, from Archimedes and Heraclides Creticus in the third century and Polybius in the second.

Archim. *Aren.* 1.1–3 ii.216 Heiberg Οἴονταί τινες, βαcιλεῦ Γέλων … ἐντί τινες δὲ οἳ … ὑπολαμβάνοντι. . . . ἐγὼ δὲ πειραcοῦμαί τοι δεικνύειν δι' ἀποδειξίων γεωμετρικᾶν αἷc παρακολουθήcειc ὅτι τῶν ὑφ' ἀμῶν κατωνομαcμένων ἀριθμῶν … ὑπερβάλλοντί τινεc οὐ μόνον τὸν ἀριθμὸν τοῦ ψάμμου τοῦ κτλ.

Some think, King Gelon [that the number of grains of sand in the world is infinite]; there are those who suppose [that the number is finite, but exceeds any expressed number]. But I will try to show you, through geometrical proofs which you will understand, that some of the numbers I have expressed not only exceed the number of grains of sand [of a body equal to the world] …

Heraclid. Cret. fr. III.1–5 Pfister, Arenz τάχα δὲ φήcουcίν τινεc ἡμᾶc ἀγνοεῖν τὴν Θετταλίαν τῆc Ἑλλάδοc καταριθμοῦντεc, ἄπειροι τῆc τῶν πραγμάτων ὄντεc ἀληθείαc. … ἡ δὲ καλουμένη νῦν Ἑλλὰc λέγεται μέν, οὐ μέντοι ἐcτί. τὸ γὰρ ἑλληνίζειν ἐγὼ εἶναί φημι οὐκ ἐν τῶι διαλέγεcθαι ὀρθῶc ἀλλ' ἐν τῶι γένει τῆc φωνῆc· αὕτη <δ'> ἐcτὶν ἀφ' Ἕλληνοc. ἡ δὲ Ἑλλὰc ἐν Θετταλίαι κεῖται. ἐκείνουc οὖν ἐροῦμεν τὴν Ἑλλάδα κατοικεῖν καὶ ταῖc φωναῖc ἑλληνίζειν.

Perhaps some will say that I am ignorant in classing Thessaly as part of Hellas, unacquainted as they are with the truth about these matters. … What is called Hellas is said to be Hellas, but is not. For I say that 'Hellenic' speech does not lie in correct utterance but in the type of dialect; the dialect comes from Hellen. And Hellas is in Thessaly. It is people living there that I will say live in Hellas, and produce Hellenic speech.

Plb. 22.18.2–7 (cf. 3.6.1–3) καίτοι γ' οὐκ ἀγνοῶ διότι τινὲc τῶν cυγγραφόντων περὶ τοῦ <   > Ῥωμαίοιc πολέμου πρὸc Περcέα, βουλόμενοι τὰc αἰτίαc ἡμῖν ἐπιδεικνύναι τῆc διαφορᾶc, πρῶτον μὲν ἀποφαίνουcι … ἐξ ὧν ἔνιοί φαcι φῦναι Περcεῖ τὸν πρὸc Ῥωμαίουc πόλεμον. ἐγὼ δέ φημι κυριώτατον μὲν εἶναι καὶ τοῖc cυγγράφουcι καὶ τοῖc φιλομαθοῦcι τὸ γινώcκειν τὰc αἰτίαc … · cυγκέχυται δὲ ταῦτα παρὰ τοῖc πλείcτοιc τῶν cυγγραφέων διὰ τὸ μὴ κρατεῖcθαι τίνι διαφέρει πρόφαcιc αἰτίαc καὶ πάλιν προφάcεωc ἀρχὴ πολέμου. καὶ νῦν δὲ τῶν πραγμάτων αὐτῶν προcυπομιμνηcκόντων ἠνάγκαcμαι πάλιν ἀνανεώcαcθαι τὸν αὐτὸν λόγον.

2084 (iii AD) on the fig (rightly mentioned by Kerkhecker 1999, 102 n. 20), cf. LXVIII 4647 on the horse.

> I am not unaware that some who have written on the war < > the Romans against Perseus, want to show us the causes of the conflict, and so point first to ... From these things, say some, came Perseus' war against the Romans. But I say that it is certainly fundamental for both writers and those who study these matters to know the causes ... but these matters are confused in most writers through a failure to grasp the difference between ground and cause and again between ground and the beginning of a war. And now, at the prompting of the events themselves, I have been compelled to renew once more the tenor of the same points.[17]

The basic pattern 'some ... but I say' is visible in all three; it goes back before the third century (cf. especially [Hp.] *Nat. Hom.* 2.1–3 *CMG* i.1.3, Isoc. *Panath.* 131–2). The variations are of interest, and show modifications even in these authors. Archimedes' ἐγὼ δὲ πειρασοῦμαί τοι δεικνύειν injects an element of modesty; δι' ἀποδείξιων γεωμετρικᾶν indicates that πειρασοῦμαι is occasioned by the tactics of self-presentation rather than by actual doubt. Polybius makes his aggression seem less objectionable by beginning from agreement over the importance of what other authors are attempting. Heraclides makes the statement of τινές merely a possibility; at the same time, the τινές are endowed with enough substance to be called ἄπειροι τῆς τῶν πραγμάτων ... ἀληθείας. In the prologue to his *Aetia*, Callimachus gives his antagonists more substance: they are not only called νήϊδες ... Μούςης, but are furnished with the colour of figures derived from mythological fiction—Telchines. But Callimachus does not mark out his own opinion and practice with a resounding 'but I say', even though he separates himself from others in poetic images. The poetic fiction of an encounter with Apollo ascribes the authority to the god. The indirectness is not due to a lack of expertise on the subject-matter: Callimachus, from his viewpoint, is well-equipped with understanding and experience. The difference is to do with genre, with the interval between Hellenistic prose and poetry.[18]

The plausibility of such generic difference can be seen from a fragment of Callimachus' own prose.

ἐν τῆι συναγωγῆι τῶν ποταμῶν ὁ Καλλίμαχος γελᾶν φηςὶν εἴ τις θαρρεῖ γράφειν τὰς τῶν Ἀθηναίων παρθένους ἀφύccεcθαι καθαρὸν γάνος Ἠριδάνοιο [*SH* 1180], οὗ καὶ τὰ βοσκήμα-

---

[17] On the *Sand-Reckoner* see Netz 2009, 30–3. On the passage of Heraclides see Ballati 2001, 54–62. γένει may suggest 'race' or 'origin' as well, on the basis of fr. III.2; but Pfister's 'besteht ... in ihrer ererbten Übernahme' (*sc.* der griechischen Sprache) (1951, 53) ignores the narrower sense of ἑλληνίζειν and φωνή here which III.2 and III.6 imply (cf. 1951, 221–2), as does the comment of Arenz 2006, 223. On Heraclides' date, cf. Arenz 2006, 49–83.
[18] The Hippocratic treatise should be dated 420–400 BC, according to Jouanna 1975, 59–61; ἐγὼ δέ φημι there is forcefully cited by Gal. i.247 Kühn. On the question of authority cf. Hunter 2008a, 168–75. For the syntax of Call. fr. 1.2 see Harder 2012, ii.16–17.

τα ἀπόσχοιτ' ἄν.

(fr. gramm. 458 Pfeiffer)

In his work gathering together rivers Callimachus says he laughs if someone has the confidence to write that the girls of Athens draw the pure liquid of the Eridanus: even animals would keep away from it.

Here Callimachus appears in the guise of a prose-writer mocking ill-informed poetic idealization. The turn is found in earlier prose: cf. Hdt. 4.36.2 γελῶ δὲ ὁρῶν γῆc περιόδουc γράψανταc πολλοὺc ἤδη καὶ οὐδένα νόον ἐχόντωc ἐξηγηcάμενον ... ἐν ὀλίγοιcι γὰρ ἐγὼ δηλώcω ... In Satyrus' prose dialogue on the life of Euripides (iii BC), a character describes an aspect of Euripides' poetry as laughable:

πρὸc ὅλον δὲ | τὸ φῦλον δ[ι]ε|τέλει μαχόμε|νοc ἐν τοῖc ποιήμαcιν. | (B) νὴ γελοίωc γε· | τί γὰρ ἄν τιc εὐ|λογώτερο[ν] | διὰ τὴν φθα|ρεῖcαν ψέγοι | τὰc γυναῖκαc | ἢ διὰ τὸν φθεί|ραντα τοὺc ἄν|δραc;

(Satyr. F 6 Schorn fr. 39 col. xiii 18–31)

'He went on attacking the whole sex in his poems.' 'Ridiculous of him! Why would it be more reasonable to abuse women because of the woman seduced than men because of the man who seduced her?'[19]

When in *Hymn* 1 Callimachus' poetry assails the opinion of earlier poets (Homer in particular), he calls anyone who acted in the way they supposed very foolish, and uses himself to bring out their implausibility; but he does not deploy the language of open mockery against the poets themselves.

δηναιοὶ δ' οὐ πάμπαν ἀληθέεc ἦcαν ἀοιδοί·
φάντο ...
τίc δέ κ' ... ὃc μάλα μὴ νενίηλοc; ...
ψευδοίμην ἀΐοντοc ἅ κεν πεπίθοιεν ἀκουήν.

(*H.* 1.60–65)

The poets of old were not at all truthful: they said ... Who would ... unless he was very foolish? May I tell lies that would persuade the ear of my listener.

An 'I laugh' of the kind found in the prose fragment is hard to imagine in Callimachus' poems.

---

[19] This seems to be the only example of νή ... γε with one word between other than Δία; νή usually accompanies a god's name or the like. Hunt's νή <Δία> γε would give a pattern like e. g. Pl. *Phdr.* 263d4 νὴ Δία ἀμηχάνωc γε ὡc cφόδρα, Aesch. 1.28 νὴ Δία καλῶc γε. Cf. Schorn 2004, 305. Discussion of Satyrus, including the role of the passages on women: Knöbl 2010.

Another comparison shows both kinship and dissimilarity. Polybius writes, on historians' claims of unnatural phenomena with regard to sacred objects and places:

ἐγὼ δὲ πρὸc τὰc τοιαύταc ἀποφάcειc τῶν ἱcτοριογράφων οὐκ οἶδ' ὅπωc παρ' ὅλην τὴν πραγματείαν ἐναντιούμενοc καὶ δυcαναcχετῶν διατελῶ. δοκεῖ γάρ μοι τὰ τοιαῦτα παντάπαcι παιδικῆc εὐηθείαc ...

(16.12.5 f.)

But I somehow in the whole work carry on contradicting such declarations by historians and getting really annoyed. For such remarks as ... seem to me of absolutely childish silliness.

The οὐκ οἶδ' ὅπωc and the δυcαναcχετῶν add to the stance an element of confessedly personal response, which makes the vehemence more sympathetic to the reader. (The same end is pursued in what follows: a little pious blurring, Polybius avers, can be pardoned.) Callimachus' *Epigram* 28 Pfeiffer incorporates a stance on literature into what is presented as a personal way of seeing things:

Ἐχθαίρω τὸ ποίημα τὸ κυκλικόν, οὐδὲ κελεύθωι
  χαίρω τίc πολλοὺc ὧδε καὶ ὧδε φέρει.
μιcέω καὶ περίφοιτον ἐρώμενον, οὐδ' ἀπὸ κρήνηc
  πίνω· cικχαίνω πάντα τὰ δημόcια.

(1–4)

I loathe the cyclic poem; I do not enjoy a road that takes many people now here, now there. I detest a boy that goes from lover to lover; I do not drink from a fountain. Everything that is for the public makes me feel sick.

The position on roads and fountains sounds particularly idiosyncratic; the final verb goes outside the usual poetic vocabulary to convey an almost physical revulsion. The approach to literature is familiar to readers of Callimachus' wider *œuvre* as no mere subjectivity; but this epigram goes on to play with the general outlook in a specific amorous situation, and that situation emerges as the real centre of the speaker's concerns. The move is one possible in at least this particular genre of Callimachus' poetry, and some others (so *Iambus* 3); but such sliding between pronouncement and play is less easy to conceive of in what we know of Hellenistic prose. It could be added that παντάπαcι παιδικῆc εὐηθείαc is more akin to the language of the Telchines (cf. fr. 1.6 παῖc ἅτε) than to Callimachus' first-person attacks.

The play possible in poetry can be illustrated by juxtaposition of Callimachus with the other end of Archimedes' Ψαμμίτηc, the beginning of which was quoted earlier:

ταῦτα δέ, βασιλεῦ Γέλων, τοῖϲ μὲν πολλοῖϲ καὶ μὴ κεκοινωνηκόντεϲϲι τῶν μαθημάτων οὐκ εὔπιϲτα φανήϲειν ὑπολαμβάνω, τοῖϲ δὲ μεταλελαβηκότεϲϲιν καὶ περὶ τῶν ἀποϲτημάτων καὶ τῶν μεγεθέων τᾶϲ τε γᾶϲ καὶ τοῦ ἁλίου ... πεφροντικότεϲϲιν πιϲτὰ διὰ τὰν ἀπόδειξιν ἐϲϲεῖϲθαι.
(*Aren.* 4.20 ii.258 Heiberg)

All this, King Gelon, I imagine will not seem easy to believe to most people, who have not had a share in mathematics; to those that have partaken in it, and thought about the distances and sizes of earth and sun ... I imagine it will be plausible, because of the proof.

We have already seen Callimachus' separation of himself from others; in fr. 75.44–9 Pfeiffer, Harder = 174 Massimilla he presents an implicit division between those who do not know and those who know and so would share his own apparently extreme opinion:

οὔ ϲε δοκέω τημοῦτοϲ, Ἀκόντιε, νυκτὸϲ ἐκείνηϲ
 ἀντί κε τῆι μίτρηϲ ἤψαο παρθενίηϲ
οὐ ϲφυρὸν Ἰφίκλειον ...
 οὐδ' ἃ Κελαινίτηϲ ἐκτεάτιϲτο Μίδηϲ
δέξαϲθαι· ψήφου δ' ἂν ἐμῆϲ ἐπιμάρτυρεϲ ε̣ι̣ε̣ν
 οἵτινεϲ οὐ χαλεποῦ νήϊδέϲ εἰϲι θεοῦ.

I do not think that then, Acontius, you would have taken in exchange for that night when you touched the virgin's girdle the ankle of Iphiclus ... or the possessions of Midas of Celaenae. Witnesses to the view I am voting for would be all who are not ignorant of the harsh god.[20]

But this type of knowledge is not so self-evidently preferable to ignorance as the kind of which Archimedes speaks; in Archimedes the mental state springs from mathematical proof. In Callimachus χαλεποῦ suggests an unwelcome sort of knowledge, and calls to mind *Epigr.* 43.6 Pfeiffer φωρὸϲ δ' ἴχνια φὼρ ἔμαθον; νήϊδεϲ perhaps suggests the possibility of a desirable kind of knowledge, as in A.R. 3.932–937:

ἀκλειὴϲ ὅδε μάντιϲ, ὃϲ οὐδ' ὅϲα παῖδεϲ ἴϲαϲιν
οἶδε νόωι φράϲϲαϲθαι ...
ἔρροιϲ, ὦ κακόμαντι, κακοφραδέϲ, οὐδέ ϲε Κύπριϲ
οὔτ' ἀγανοὶ φιλέοντεϲ ἐπιπνείουϲιν Ἔρωτεϲ.

---

[20] The dots under εϲ are based on my reading of the papyrus in 2003 with ultra-violet light; ε̣ι̣ε̣ν is very hard to see. Massimilla 2010 uses more dots in his edition of the fragment than Harder 2012 or than Fowler 2000, 370–3. My own preference would be for wielding the pepper-pot more liberally still.

> This prophet deserves no fame: he does not know how to consider in his mind what even children know. Curse you, bad prophet with bad sense! Aphrodite and the gentle Erotes do not love you and inspire you.

An element of humour as well as pathos comes into Callimachus' passage; such toying with the reader goes beyond the ego-language of extant Hellenistic prose. The sense of game is still more evident in *Epigr.* 29.3–4:

> καλὸс ὁ παῖс, Ἀχελῶιε, λίην καλόс· εἰ δέ τιс οὐχί
> φηсίν, ἐπιсταίμην μοῦνοс ἐγὼ τὰ καλά.

> The boy is beautiful, Achelous, exceedingly beautiful. If someone says he isn't—well, may I be the only one to know about what is beautiful.

The last sentence must sound paradoxical; hence the passage will sport not just with exclusive cultic knowledge (cf. lines 1–2 οὐδ' Ἀχελῶιοс | κείνου τῶν ἱερῶν αἰсθάνεται κυαθῶν), but with the writer's wish that his opinions should be accepted.[21]

Even these few passages are enough to indicate that Hellenistic poetry and prose can rewardingly be compared and contrasted. The more extensively this subject were considered, the more complicated and enlightening it would become. The poetry has been seen to part from prose especially in the area here designated as 'fiction'. But precisely in this area the relation of poetry and prose becomes more complex in these centuries. Any general confinement of fiction to poetry would be made problematic by, for example, Callimachus' citation of Xenomedes as his surprising source for the story of Acontius and Cydippe; in that passage the Telchines too turn out to appear in Xenomedes as well as in choral lyric. Novels may well exist by the end of this 'period'. From the third century on, declamation extends, beyond Antiphon and Isocrates, the fictional expansion of history and mythology as a focus of rhetorical activity. Philosophy continues the creation of worlds remote from the familiar, and elaborates the attempt to show them false or true. Mathematics can build up constructions on the basis of postulates which are not necessarily known to be true but are posited.[22]

---

[21] On χαλεποῦ cf. Harder 2012, i.630–1, including Hunter's comment.
[22] Declamation: already *BKT* vii.4–13 (P. Berol. inv. 9781 (iii BC); Russell 1983, 3–4, 107), reply to Demosthenes against Leptines. Cf. Cribiore 2001, 231–8. On questions of fiction and Hellenistic prose cf. Whitmarsh 2010; for fiction and Hellenistic poetry cf. notably Payne 2007. On the postulates in Archimedes' *On the Sphere and the Cylinder* (Netz/Noel/Tchernetska/Wilson, 2011, ii.191 col.ii 14–17, 193 col. i 25–col.ii 33) cf. Netz 2004, 40. Scholars concerned with worldbuilding could in general give more consideration to mathematics and science: cf. Werth 1999, 180–209, Gavins 2007, 168f.

The complicated relations that can exist between fiction in Hellenistic poetry and fiction in prose can be illustrated from one final juxtaposition; the piece of prose could have been written before or after, say, the death of Philip. Theocritus poem 7 has well been linked with dialogue, but only with Platonic dialogue. And yet much had happened to dialogue since Plato; we can see this from Cicero, for whom Aristotle and Heraclides Ponticus offer important possibilities. It would generally be agreed that Theocritus 7 in some way or other toys with an inexplicit link between the narrator Simichidas and the author Theocritus. Some dialogues of Plato offer significant examples for the unusual set-up of a first-person narrative; the narrator is clearly not the author. The position becomes more intriguing with a division between Aristotelian dialogue, where the author is the main speaker, and Heraclidean dialogue, where the author is often present but does not speak, or the work is set in a past before the author.[23]

A papyrus of a dialogue is now ascribed by scholars to Heraclides, with probability; the dialogue is set in the sixth century BC. The following will be part of the opening:

ἐγὼ δὲ καταμείνας, | ἤδη Πιcιcτράτου τυραννγ[ο]ῦν|τοc ἀποδημίαν ἐντεῦθεν | ποιηcάμενοc ἐν Ἰωνίαι μετὰ | Cόλωνοc διέτριβον. χρόνωι δέ ... ἐπανῆλθον Ἀθήναζε. κατέ|λ<ε>ιπον μὲν οὖν ἐνταῦθα παῖ|δα Θραcύβουλον τὸν Φιλο|μήλου· κατειλήφειν δὲ μειρἀκ[ι]ον ἤδη μάλα καλὸν κἀγα|θὸν καὶ τὴν ὄψιν καὶ τὸν τρόπον πολὺ διαφέροντα τῶν | ἡλικιωτῶν ... πάντας δὲ ὑπερέ|βα<λ>λεν ἱπποτροφίαιc καὶ κυ|νηγίαιc καὶ ταῖc ἄλλαιc δαπά|[ν]αιc. ᾖ[ιε]βέ- βλητο δ' ἐν τῆι πό|λ[ε]ι τῆc νεωτέραc τῶν τοῦ | {τοu} Πιcιcτράτου θυγατέρων | ἐρᾶν ἰδὼν ἀρρηφοροῦcαν. Ἀγνόθεοc οὖν ὁ πάππος αὐ|τοῦ ... , τραχυνθείc τί μοι δοκεῖ πρὸc αὐτόν, καλεῖ μ' | εἰc οἶκον ... κἀγὼ μάλα προθύμωc | ἐβάδιζον. καὶ γὰρ ἦν ἐν ἡδονῆι μοι τὸ cυνδια- τρίβειν Ἀγνο||[θέωι.

(CPF 56 1 fr. A col. i 5–ii 1; Heraclid. Pont. fr. 155 Schütrumpf, without text)

I had remained in Athens; but when Peisistratus was tyrant, I travelled away from Athens and lived in Ionia with Solon. But eventually ... I returned to Athens. I had left Thrasybulus son of Philomelus there as a boy. I found him as already a youth, very much a noble, greatly different from the people of his age in his appearance and his character ... He excelled all

---

23 On Plato and Theocritus 7 cf. Hunter 1999, 145f.; Billault 2008a (stresses *Symposium*). Relation of Simichidas and Theocritus: Hutchinson 1988, 203–212, Hunter 1999, 146, etc. The chronology of Heraclides raises difficulties; but the evidence has perhaps not been evaluated rightly. Heraclides would seem to have been taught by Plato, but also by Aristotle (Sotion (Διαδοχαί) fr. 17 Wehrli (Heraclid. Pont. fr. 3 Wehrli = fr. 1.86 in Schütrumpf *et al.* 2008); he would thus have been some years younger than Aristotle, who was born 384 BC. One may consequently doubt the story of his being put in charge of the Academy while Plato was in Sicily, at latest 361/0 BC (*Suda* η 461.18–19 Adler (Heraclid. Pont. fr. 2 Wehrli = fr. 3 Schütrumpf)). It would be strange to prefer the *Suda* here to Sotion. Some discussions: Wehrli 1968, 58–61, 1978, 49–51, Gottschalk 1980, 2–6, Dillon 2003, 204–5, Mejer 2009, 27–9. On Heraclides and dialogue see Fox 2009.

others in his horse-keeping, hunting, and other forms of expenditure. He had been spoken ill of in the city: it was said that he was in love with Peisistratus' younger daughter, whom he had seen acting as *arrephoros*. So his grandfather, cross with him, I think, invited me to the house … I proceeded there very gladly: it was a pleasure for me to spend time with Hagnotheus.[24]

The dialogue that ensued must have involved interplay between the older narrator and the youthful Thrasybulus which exploited their difference in age.

As throughout the present piece, a specific intertextuality is not suggested; but the potential significance of dialogue for the poem seems to be enhanced by the eager walking of the narrator to the house of a friend who has invited him, and by the exceptional and love-lorn youth who seems a focus of attention. One may note in Theocritus, for instance:

ἦ μετὰ δαῖτ' ἄκλητος ἐπείγεαι … ; (24)

Are you hurrying off to a feast without an invitation … ?

ἦ γὰρ ἑταῖροι
ἀνέρες … Δαμάτερι δαῖτα τελεῦντι … (31 f.)

Friends of mine are presenting … Demeter with a feast . …

κἠμὲ λέγοντι
πάντες ἀοιδὸν ἄριστον· ἐγὼ δέ τις οὐ ταχυπειθής … (37 f.)

Everyone says I am the best singer; but I am not one to be quickly convinced.

'τάν τοι' ἔφα 'κορύναν δωρύττομαι, οὕνεκεν ἐσσί
πᾶν ἐπ' ἀλαθείαι πεπλασμένον ἐκ Διὸς ἔρνος. … ' (43 f.)

'I present the stick to you', he said, 'as you are a shoot completely fashioned for truth by the god of the sky … '

Cιμιχίδαι μὲν Ἔρωτες ἐπέπταρον· ἦ γὰρ ὁ δειλός
τόσσον ἐρᾶι Μυρτοῦς ὅσον εἴαρος αἶγες ἔρανται. (96 f.)

The Erotes have sneezed in favour on Simichidas, who, poor man, desires Myrto as much as the goats desire spring.

The papyrus also helps to bring out the importance of age in the meeting between Simichidas and Lycidas.

---

24 On text and authorship see Haslam 1992, 199–203, 211–214 (strengthened from Haslam 1983, 93, 94 f.; cf. Heraclid. Pont. frr. 144 f. Wehrli = 28 f. Schütrumpf), Dorandi 2009, 17–19. For *arrephoroi* cf. Parker 2005, 219–223. In other versions, Thrasybulus (or Thrasymedes or a young man) is certainly in love with the daughter, as Hagnotheus evidently supposes here; cf. D.S. 9.37.1, V. Max. 5. 1 *ext.* 2 , Polyaen. 5.14, [Plu.] *Apophth. Reg.* 189c.

The prose literature of the Hellenistic 'period' was abundant and diverse; it has emerged that even what has survived will repay the attention of scholars interested in the poetry. The literary and cultural context for the poetry is enriched; and aspects and features of the poems are brought into sharper relief. Often what could have been observed within the poetry itself, or had actually been observed there, becomes more clearly visible. The study of Hellenistic poetry stands to gain when its students realize the importance of being (as it were) prosaic.

II. Style and Narrative

Richard Hunter
Theocritus and the Style of Hellenistic Poetry*

Of the major poets of the third century it is perhaps Theocritus who most invites us to reflect upon what we think we know about Hellenistic poetry and upon the usefulness, or otherwise, of the label itself. Theocritus was not—as far as we know—a scholar-poet, that figure identified by Rudolf Pfeiffer (1955, 69) as 'the feature of the Hellenistic age';[1] there is, moreover, no reason to associate many of his poems with any particular situation of patronage, however clearly the Ptolemaic world looms in the background of several of them. On the other hand, it is his poetry which has given particular impetus to some of the ideas about Hellenistic poetry which have been most influential in modern scholarship—the appeal to the ordinary and the everyday, 'Kreuzung der Gattungen', the dominance of the miniature over the grand structures of epic, the interest in poetic and reconstructive dialect, and so forth. In this essay I want to use one poem in particular, *Idyll* 16, to explore some of the phenomena that we think of as most characteristic of the poetry of the third century.

I choose to revisit *Idyll* 16, the *Charites*, for a number of reasons. First, because there is every reason to suppose that it has nothing to do with Alexandria, and is therefore not an example of 'Alexandrian poetry', as that phrase is most commonly used. Secondly, of course, because it is one of the most intriguing and puzzling of the poems which survive to us from the earlier part of the century. It has recently been argued (Willi 2004) that we can see here poetry in transition: Theocritus has written in a new form but preserved poetry's traditional social function of protreptic advice; it was to be left to Callimachus to change both form and function, the latter in the direction of a purely aesthetic function, 'art for art's sake'.[2] It matters less for present purposes that I cannot share this view of Callimachus' poetry, than that *Idyll* 16 continues to attract attention as marking a new stage in the Greek poetic tradition. From another perspective, *Idyll* 16 has recently been the subject of interesting work which seeks to link it

---

* An earlier version of this essay formed part of the opening lecture to the 2012 Thessaloniki conference; I have not sought to remove all marks of its origin in an oral presentation for a specific occasion.
1 Much might be thought to hang on whether the writing of prose treatises, as well as poetry, was thought to be a necessary criterion for classification as a 'scholar-poet'.
2 For this as a view of *Idyll* 16, however, cf., e.g., Fabiano 1971, 519 n. 7. Sistakou 2008a, 42–4 offers a clear account of the poetics of *Idyll* 16.

very closely to a historical context—something which, I think, scholars of Hellenistic poetry still try to do less often than they should, perhaps because they know in their hearts that, where the burden of proof is so heavy, such arguments have traditionally failed to carry conviction. Thus, José González (González 2010) has seen a traditional social function in *Idyll* 16—Theocritus revives the poetic voice of Theognis, a poet associated in some traditions with Sicily, to lecture and cajole his Syracusan fellow-citizens about the terrible state into which their city has fallen. For Malcolm Bell, on the other hand (Bell 2011), Theocritus joins his bucolic voice to the hopes of the young Hieron to rescue Syracuse from the agrarian crisis which besets it; we have nothing less than 'a political and economic program for the new leader'.[3] Much here would demand discussion on another occasion, but for the present I will focus on some very traditional critical criteria, to see if we can pick out features that we might wish to label 'Hellenistic', and whether that label helps or hinders understanding.

First, structure. It is clear, and generally recognized,[4] that the poem falls into two halves, with something of a fresh start at v. 58:

ἐκ Μοισᾶν ἀγαθὸν κλέος ἔρχεται ἀνθρώποισι,
χρήματα δὲ ζώοντες ἀμαλδύνουσι θανόντων.

Theocritus 16.58–9

From the Muses comes excellent renown to men, but the living waste away the possessions of the dead.

ἐκ Μοισᾶν with which this second part of the poem begins—starting 'from the Muses' is a good move for any poet in any section of his song—takes us back to the opening quatrain:

αἰεὶ τοῦτο Διὸς κούραις μέλει, αἰὲν ἀοιδοῖς,
ὑμνεῖν ἀθανάτους, ὑμνεῖν ἀγαθῶν κλέα ἀνδρῶν.
Μοῖσαι μὲν θεαὶ ἐντί, θεοὺς θεαὶ ἀείδοντι·
ἄμμες δὲ βροτοὶ οἵδε, βροτοὺς βροτοὶ ἀείδωμεν.

Theocritus 16.1–4

It is always the task of the daughters of Zeus, always of singers, to hymn the immortals, to hymn the glorious deeds of excellent men. The Muses are goddesses, goddesses sing of gods; we here are mortals, let us mortals sing of mortals.

---

3 Bell also draws suggestive connections between Theocritus' bucolic poems and the 'pastoral' art of third-century Sicily.
4 An exception here is Meincke 1965, 34–5 who appears to place the major break in the poem after v. 70; this cannot, I think, be correct. On the sequence of thought in vv. 68ff cf. below p. 73–4.

Both halves of the poem thus begin with the Muses, just as ἀγαθὸν κλέος in v. 58 picks up ἀγαθῶν κλέα ἀνδρῶν in v.2. This second part of the poem itself is bounded in ring composition:

> τί γὰρ Χαρίτων ἀγαπητόν
> ἀνθρώποις ἀπάνευθεν; ἀεὶ Χαρίτεσσιν ἅμ' εἴην.
> Theocritus 16.108–9
>
> What is desirable for men apart from the Graces? May I always be together with the Graces.

ἐκ Μοισᾶν ... ἀνθρώποισι (v. 58) is picked up by ἀνθρώποις ... Χαρίτεσσιν (v. 109), with variation between the two sets of goddesses with whom the poem has been concerned. There is of course no 'clean break' between the two sections of the poem: the transitional verse, 'From the Muses comes excellent renown to men' (v. 58), also summarises the immediately preceding section on the 'benefits' conferred by Simonides and Homer on the characters (real and fictional) about whom they wrote; moreover, the 'formal' break after v. 57 is by no means the only important structural moment within the poem. Nevertheless, it is not always appreciated just how neat is the formal division between the two 'halves' of the poem. If we include the opening quatrain in the first part, then the division is into 57 and 52 verses, or if we separate off the opening quatrain, as there seems every reason to do—among which will be both the very distinctive style of vv. 1–4 and the fact that we then have one part beginning with the Charites and the second with the Muses—we have 53 and 52 verses respectively, all but a complete equality. Are these figures simply the kind of accident which happens? Perhaps, but along with the 'materiality' of poetry—poems figured as unloved papyrus rolls etc—which is so central to *Idyll* 16, we ought perhaps also consider whether the stichometric habit has here encouraged an attention to neat divisions, as part of an *epideixis* of what poetry is or can be, and this is one manifestation of a set of such phenomena which become important in the Hellenistic period; we think, for example, of pattern poems ('*technopaignia*'), acrostics, the organization of poetry books and so forth.[5] We will want to associate these phenomena with the writing habit, though their roots in archaic and classical verse require careful attention;[6] it would, above all, be very nice to know just how such formally marked structures were 'felt'. Be that as it may, if this structural analysis is on the right lines, then the neat division of *Idyll* 16 is a special case within a general tendency of Theocritean poetry. *Idyll* 17 falls into verse paragraphs of

---

[5] Bing 1988 remains a valuable guide in these areas; on pattern-poems, acrostics etc cf. Luz 2010.
[6] Relevant here is Faraone 2008.

roughly (though certainly not exactly) equal lengths;[7] a case has recently been made for a very neat triptych structure of 72–28–72 for *Idyll* 24;[8] the main body of *Idyll* 18 falls into ten-verse paragraphs, and similar structures may be found in the *Hymns* of Callimachus.[9]

What is true of the second part of the poem is also true of the poem as a whole. ἀνθρώποις in the final verse does not just take us back to v. 58, but also picks up the repeated βροτοί of v. 4. More is going on here than just the formal device of ring-composition. As is well known, the closing prayer to the Graces of Orchomenos in vv. 104–9 reworks the opening of Pindar's *Olympian* 14 for a victor from Orchomenos:

> Καφισίων ὑδάτων
> λαχοῖσαι αἴτε ναίετε καλλίπωλον ἕδραν,
> ὦ λιπαρᾶς ἀοίδιμοι βασίλειαι
> Χάριτες Ἐρχομενοῦ, παλαιγόνων Μινυᾶν ἐπίσκοποι,
> κλῦτ', ἐπεὶ εὔχομαι· σὺν γὰρ ὑμῖν τά <τε> τερπνὰ καί
> τὰ γλυκέ' ἄνεται πάντα βροτοῖς,
> εἰ σοφός, εἰ καλός, εἴ τις ἀγλαὸς ἀνήρ.
> οὐδὲ γὰρ θεοὶ σεμνᾶν Χαρίτων ἄτερ
> κοιρανέοντι χοροὺς
>   οὔτε δαῖτας·
>   Pindar, *Olympian* 14.1–9

> Controllers of the waters of Kephisos, dwellers in a place of fine horses, O Graces, queens, celebrated in song, of shining Orchomenos, guardians of the ancient Minyans, hear when I pray. With you come all things pleasant and sweet for mortals, whether a man be wise, or handsome, or of glittering fame. Not even the gods organize dances or feasts without the holy Graces.

Theocritus' opening distinction between gods and men is in fact, as we now see, repeated at the end of the poem, but implicitly, through evocation of that same distinction within a model text. This is sophisticated, allusive poetry which makes demands upon us: ἀνθρώποις in v. 109 is anything but a mere line-filler.

---

[7] One division would be 1–12 (proem), 12–33 (Soter, 21 verses), 34–57 (Berenice, 24), 58–76 (Cos), 77–94 (Ptolemy's power, 18), 95–120 (wealth, 26), 121–34 (piety, 14), 135–7 (envoi, 3); various subdivisions within this structure are readily identifiable.
[8] Cf. Bernsdorff 2011. A perhaps more obvious division is into 1–63 (Heracles and the snakes), 64–102 (Teiresias), 103 to the end (Heracles subsequent education and career), i.e. 63–39–70 verses, or (more likely?) 1–63, 64–102, 103–(??)166 (Heracles' education and early career), 167–172 (hymnic envoi and prayer for victory).
[9] Cf. Hunter 1996b, 155–6.

As for the initial quatrain itself, this falls—as do the three quatrains of the proem to *Idyll* 17[10]—into paired couplets; the couplets in this instance are held together by rhythmical identity and difference from each other (vv. 3–4 are *spondeiazontes* and share an identical pattern of syllables per word throughout the verse), and by the mannered verbal repetitions and parallelisms which they display.[11] In running through the three classes of gods, (epic) heroes (ἀγαθοὶ ἄνδρες), and ordinary mortals (βροτοί), as also does the proem of *Idyll* 17 (though to somewhat different effect), the proem to *Idyll* 16 repeats with variation the same priamel-like function as the opening of Pindar's *Second Olympian*, and the following τίς question in v. 5 perhaps makes it not impossible that Theocritus was here actually reworking that grand opening for a Sicilian patron:[12]

ἀναξιφόρμιγγες ὕμνοι,
τίνα θεόν, τίν' ἥρωα, τίνα δ' ἄνδρα κελαδήσομεν;
                              Pindar, *Olympian* 2.1–2

Hymns, masters of the lyre, which god, which hero, which man shall we celebrate?

Theocritus' choice of βροτοί for emphasis in v. 4 will have been influenced by, and evoke, the Homeric tendency to use this form to refer purely generally to (ordinary) 'mortals' of any time; 'mortals' also introduces the central theme of the poem—the power of the poet to offer immortal κλέος, such as that already achieved by the ἀγαθοὶ ἄνδρες. Hanging over the opening fifteen verses of the poem are Homer's deprecatory οἷοι νῦν βροτοί εἰσι (*Iliad* 5.304, 12.383, 449, 20.287) and οἳ νῦν βροτοί εἰσιν ἐπιχθόνιοι (*Iliad* 1.272), a memory with particular bite in v. 15, τίς τῶν νῦν τοιόσδε;, which picks up the question of vv. 5–7 after the parenthesis of vv. 8–12.[13] Theocritus' complaints about 'men of the present day' turn out to have Homeric precedent: both look back to a lost time of heroic deeds (ὡς

---

10 Cf. Hunter 2003, 93–4.
11 These parallelisms would be increased were we to emend ἀείδοντι in v. 3 to the subjunctive ἀείδωντι. I am not aware that this has ever been suggested; Austin 1967, 3 paraphrases the verse as 'Let gods hymn gods ...', but does not suggest the emendation. In favour of the transmitted text, it may be argued that the poet is describing what the Muses *do* (habitually), as in the opening of Hesiod's *Theogony*, whereas the subjunctive is appropriate for the human poet at the start of a new song.
12 For other aspects of the opening quatrain cf., e.g., Gutzwiller 1983, 217–19, Fantuzzi 2000, 142–5.
13 The first half of v. 15 is more usually associated with Simonides fr. 10 Poltera (= *PMG* 506), cf. Gutzwiller 1983, 222–3, Vox 2002, 199–200 (adducing the contextual appropriateness of the Simonidean poem); I see no difficulty in the Theocritean question evoking both Homer and Simonides.

πάρος, v. 14), but—unlike his epic model—Theocritus will be able to express the hope that such days may yet return.

There is, of course, particular point in creating a neat stichometric division within *Idyll* 16, as one of the differences between the two parts is that whereas the first one illustrates the power of poetry from the great figures of the past (Simonides, Homer), the second focuses on the present and future and on what Theocritus himself could do for a worthy patron; present and future possibilities are indeed to be equal to those of the past. Both halves also move from the allegedly current distorted relations between poet and patron (vv. 5–21, 60–5) to an imagined ideal. Theocritus offers Hieron the same or even more in fact than the patrons of the past. A particular effect here is the replay of vv. 36–9 in the poet's wishes for peace in Sicily in the second half of the poem:

πολλοὶ δὲ Σκοπάδαισιν ἐλαυνόμενοι ποτὶ σακοὺς
μόσχοι σὺν κεραῇσιν ἐμυκήσαντο βόεσσι·
μυρία δ' ἂμ πεδίον Κραννώνιον ἐνδιάασκον
ποιμένες ἔκκριτα μῆλα φιλοξείνοισι Κρεώνδαις·

Theocritus 16.36–9

Many were the calves which lowed as they were driven to the stalls of the Scopadae, together with the horned cattle; countless the splendid sheep which shepherds pastured for the hospitable Creondae over the plain of Crannon.

αἱ δ' ἀνάριθμοι
μήλων χιλιάδες βοτάναι διαπιανθεῖσαι
ἂμ πεδίον βληχῷντο, βόες δ' ἀγεληδὸν ἐς αὖλιν
ἐρχόμεναι σκνιφαῖον ἐπισπεύδοιεν ὁδίταν·
νειοὶ δ' ἐκπονέοιντο ποτὶ σπόρον, ἁνίκα τέττιξ
ποιμένας ἐνδίους πεφυλαγμένος ὑψόθι δένδρων   95
ἀχεῖ ἐν ἀκρεμόνεσσιν· ἀράχνια δ' εἰς ὅπλ' ἀράχναι
λεπτὰ διαστήσαιντο, βοᾶς δ' ἔτι μηδ' ὄνομ' εἴη.

Theocritus 16.90–7

May numberless thousands of sheep, fattened by pasturing, bleat over the plain, and cattle moving in herds towards their home stalls speed the evening traveller on his way. May the fallow fields be worked for sowing, while high up in the trees the cicada watches the shepherds in the sun, and trills in the branches. May spiders weave delicate webs over weapons, and not even the name of the war-cry remain.

Some of the correspondences may be simply set out in schematic form: πολλοί ... μυρία ~ ἀνάριθμοι ... χιλιάδες, ἐλαυνόμενοι ποτὶ σακοὺς ~ ἀγεληδὸν ἐς αὖλιν | ἐρχόμεναι, ἂμ πεδίον ~ ἂμ πεδίον, ἐμυκήσαντο (cattle) ~ βληχῷντο (sheep), ἐνδιάασκον | ποιμένες ~ ποιμένας ἐνδίους;[14] σκνιφαῖον in v. 93 spells out what

---

14 This last case calls particular attention to itself as (cf. Gow ad loc.) v. 38 seems to offer the

is implied in the action of vv. 36–7. The replay, and indeed *auxêsis*, of the first passage in the second is reinforced by a reworking of part of Bacchylides' famous encomium of peace from a paean to Apollo Pythaieus at Asine:

ἐν δὲ σιδαροδέτοις πόρπαξιν αἰθᾶν
ἀραχνᾶν ἱστοὶ πέλονται,

ἔγχεα τε λογχωτὰ ξίφεα
  τ' ἀμφάκεα δάμναται εὐρώς.
<–∪– – –∪– – –∪–
  –∪∪–∪∪– –>
χαλκεᾶν δ' οὐκ ἔστι σαλπίγγων κτύπος κτλ.
                  Bacchylides fr. 22 + fr. 4, vv. 69–75 Maehler

Over the iron shield-grips lie the webs of reddish spiders, and rust eats away at the sharp spears and double-edged swords ... no sound is heard from the bronze trumpets ...

Bacchylides was another encomiast of the first Hieron, but—more significantly in the present context—he was Simonides' nephew, and in setting himself to write 'Simonidean' verse as a 'Bacchylides' for Hieron II, Theocritus here tropes literary affiliation and imitation in genealogical terms; the trope was to become much more familiar in Roman poetry.[15]

After structure, style. A case can be made, I think, that, for all our proper interest in Callimachean programmatics, the slender Muse and the tiny drop of pure water, and the very welcome recent concern with possible links between Hellenistic poetry and the kind of euphonist criticism about which we are constantly learning more from the papyri of Philodemus,[16] there still remains much to be done in determining how the styles of Hellenistic poetry differed from what went before.[17] The history of style is, of course, very difficult to trace, not least because 'style' is hardly separable from form and meaning, but there is no area of Greek, and specifically Hellenistic, poetics which remains as under-examined and as important. The remarks which follow will, of course, hardly make a dent in the surface.

---

only example of ἐνδιάω used transitively. In vv. 94–6 a reminiscence of Plato, *Phaedrus* 259a, with its repeated reference to the middle of the day, is possible; ἐνδιάω and related words are standardly associated in ancient lexica with midday, cf. the scholia on vv. 94–7b, Gow on v. 38, and the scholia on *Odyssey* 4.450. There may be a memory of one or both of these passages at [Theocritus] 25.85–99.
15 Cf., e.g., Hardie 1993, Chapter 4.
16 Helpful orientation in Gutzwiller 2010, 346–54.
17 Any full account would, of course, have to give due acknowledgement to the important work which has been done, such as that of Marco Fantuzzi on the style of Apollonius' *Argonautica*.

That *Idyll* 16 contains almost a potpourri of stylistic levels is familiar critical territory,[18] and it might be thought that a poem probably (though not certainly) entitled Χάριτες by its author would have style as a central concern, for χάρις and χάριτες are important terms in the ancient stylistic vocabulary. It is noteworthy that the discussion of χάριτες in Demetrius, *On style* gives a prominent place to both Sophron, the Syracusan mime-poet, and to the use of proverbs (156), and this will remind us that the marvellously inventive description of the poet's Χάριτες in vv. 5–21 is itself full of χάρις. Stylistic levels are, however, a crucial vehicle of poetic meaning throughout the poem. Consider Theocritus' demonstration of the power of Homeric poetry:

οὐδ' Ὀδυσεὺς ἑκατόν τε καὶ εἴκοσι μῆνας ἀλαθείς
πάντας ἐπ' ἀνθρώπους, Ἀΐδαν τ' εἰς ἔσχατον ἐλθών
ζωός, καὶ σπήλυγγα φυγὼν ὀλοοῖο Κύκλωπος,
δηναιὸν κλέος ἔσχεν, ἐσιγάθη δ' ἂν ὑφορβός
Εὔμαιος καὶ βουσὶ Φιλοίτιος ἀμφ' ἀγελαίαις   55
ἔργον ἔχων αὐτός τε περίσπλαγχνος Λαέρτης,
εἰ μή σφεας ὤνασαν Ἰάονος ἀνδρὸς ἀοιδαί.

Theocritus 16.51–7

Not even Odysseus, who wandered through all men for one hundred and twenty months and went alive to furthest Hades and escaped from the cave of the murderous Cyclops, would have secured long-lasting renown, and the swineherd Eumaeus and Philoitios whose task was the herds of cattle and great-hearted Laertes himself would have been covered in silence, had not they benefited from the songs of a man of Ionia.

Odysseus 'wandered through all men for one hundred and twenty months'; here we have, I think, a rewriting, or perhaps explanatory gloss, on the opening of the *Odyssey* (ὃς μάλα πολλὰ | πλάγχθη ... πολλῶν δ' ἀνθρώπων κτλ.). It is perhaps not accidental that the opening of the *Odyssey* may also be evoked in Pindar's *Seventh Nemean*, a poem which is very important to *Idyll* 16:[19]

σοφοὶ δὲ μέλλοντα τριταῖον ἄνεμον
ἔμαθον, οὐδ' ὑπὸ κέρδει βλάβεν·
ἀφνεὸς πενιχρός τε θανάτου παρὰ
σᾶμα νέονται. ἐγὼ δὲ πλέον' ἔλπομαι   20
λόγον Ὀδυσσέος ἢ πάθαν
    διὰ τὸν ἁδυεπῆ γενέσθ' Ὅμηρον·

---

18 Cf., e.g., Fabiano 1971, 519–20.
19 V. 63 φιλοκερδείηι βεβλαμμένον ἄνδρα seems to pick up οὐδ' ὑπὸ κέρδει βλάβεν in *Nemean* 7.18; on various aspects of the use of *Nemean* 7 in *Idyll* 16 cf. Sbardella 2004.

ἐπεὶ ψεύδεσί οἱ ποτανᾶι <τε> μαχανᾶι
σεμνὸν ἔπεστί τι· σοφία
    δὲ κλέπτει παράγοισα μύθοις. τυφλὸν δ' ἔχει
ἦτορ ὅμιλος ἀνδρῶν ὁ πλεῖστος.
                                    Pindar, *Nemean* 7.17–24

The wise understand the wind which will come on the third day, and they are not damaged by pursuit of profit, for rich and poor alike go to the tomb of death. I think that Odysseus' story has become greater than his suffering, as a result of sweet-voiced Homer; upon his lies and winged art there is something magnificent, and his skill deceives and leads men astray with stories. The vast majority of men have a blind heart.

Although the power of poetry is a ubiquitous theme in Pindar, the scholia (III 120–1 Drachmann) on this famous passage give a clear idea as to why it is particularly important for *Idyll* 16:

Intelligent men should not be deluded by their present wealth, but should take thought for what comes after and do something worthy, so that, afterwards also, they may be hymned and have immortal renown (εὐδοξία). Both the rich and the poor die, and therefore it is necessary to give thought to one's future renown. ... Men must not be mean (φιλοκερδεῖς), but offer pay (μισθός) to poets, so that they may have an eternal memorial of their virtue.
                                    Scholium, Pindar, *Nemean* 7.17

Poets are able to magnify and increase ordinary deeds; therefore you too should give thought to being hymned.
                                    Scholium, Pindar, *Nemean* 7.20

This gloss on Pindar's argument could well stand also as a gloss on much of *Idyll* 16. Should we therefore leap to the conclusion, as we tend to do in such situations, that Theocritus' reworking of Pindar (or indeed of any archaic poet) is influenced by contemporary or near-contemporary scholarship (of various intellectual levels)? What are the rules for determining when this approach is correct and when it is misleading? All reading and creative imitation is after all, to a greater or less extent, and with greater or lesser degrees of self-consciousness, a product of the educational and cultural context of the later reader and/or writer. In this case, some may think it significant for Theocritus' difference from, say, Callimachus that we are here not dealing with the intrusion of rare (scholarly) glosses in the Theocritean text, but rather with broad structures of meaning in an earlier text.

This Pindaric passage has been the subject of much debate and bibliography in modern times, and this is not the place to add to that.[20] There is, however, no

---

20 Fränkel 1960b, 360–1 is an important contribution, cf. Most 1985, 149.

good reason to doubt that Theocritus would have understood Pindar to be saying that the power of Homer's poetry, its σεμνότης, had given the story of Odysseus a greater circulation and renown than would be commensurate with what he actually 'suffered'; πλέον' ... λόγον Ὀδυσσέος ἢ πάθαν in v. 21 alludes to and trumps πολλά ... πάθεν ἄλγεα in *Odyssey* 1.4.[21] Theocritus then chooses the two most extended, but also most 'fabulous', episodes of that λόγος, the Underworld and the Cyclops' cave, to make the related point that no one would ever have heard even of Odysseus, had it not been for Homer; whether or not the memory of *Nemean* 7 also encourages us to entertain a doubt about the reality of those adventures—look what a poet can do for you!—may be debated. What is clear, however, is that the style of Theocritus' rewriting of the opening of the *Odyssey*, 'Odysseus wandered through all men for one hundred and twenty months', also contributes to the point that Theocritus is making. One ancient explanation of Pindar's description of Homer's (and Odysseus') ποτανὰ μαχανά (*Nemean* 7.22) is that the Homeric poems 'exalt and raise up (ὑψοῖ καὶ μετεωρίζει) the virtuous deeds of those who are hymned' (III 121.9 – 10 Drachmann). The language of ὕψος is suggestive here, because the *akribeia* of 'wandered for one hundred and twenty months' is very far from any ancient notions of stylistic grandeur or sublimity; Theocritus' phrase is, in fact, as prosaic a gloss on the opening of the *Odyssey* as one could imagine, and that perhaps is the point. The σεμνότης of Homeric verse can turn the bald facts and numbers of 'what happened' into something memorable. Theocritus here takes Odysseus' own echo of the opening of the poem,

> ἀλλ' ὅδ' ἐγὼ τοιόσδε, παθὼν κακά, πολλὰ δ' ἀληθείς,
> ἤλυθον εἰκοστῶι ἔτεϊ ἐς πατρίδα γαῖαν
>
> Homer, *Odyssey* 16.205 – 6
>
> I am that man as you see him, having suffered misfortunes and wandered much, and I have returned to my fatherland in the twentieth year,

and surpasses it. Mortals count up and reckon, because our time is painfully finite and ever-diminishing; Muses operate across much larger and much more impressionistic vistas of time and space. The tedious detail of τὸ ἀκριβές matters to us in ways in which it cannot matter to higher powers. So too, Philoitios' 'job' (the very prosaic ἔργον ἔχων) was looking after the cattle (vvv. 55 – 6); Homer could make something wonderful even of so banal a phrase and of such unpromising material. Whether we can move from these examples

---

[21] Although associating πάθα with *Odyssey* 1.4, Fränkel (previous note) thought the most important passage for Pindar here was *Odyssey* 11.363 – 76 (Alcinous' intervention).

to speculations about the critical discussions of Homeric, and more generally poetic, style which were available to Theocritus is (again) a matter for further discussion.

As for περίσπλαγχνος Λαέρτης, commentators rightly look to *Odyssey* 24.365 where the poet calls Laertes μεγαλήτωρ; the *hapax* περίσπλαγχνος, a formation of a relatively common type found, e.g., in medical texts as well as in poetry, is here used, as with the previous examples, to illustrate what a poet can do for you. It is, however, not just the epithet μεγαλήτωρ which is at issue here.[22] In Homer the epithet introduces the passage in which Laertes is bathed and given a splendid cloak, and Athena—acting, so Theocritus might observe, like Homer or another encomiastic poet—restores his physical beauty so that he looks like the immortal gods and becomes an object of θαῦμα to those around him (*Odyssey* 24.365–74); Laertes then proceeds to recall a glorious deed of his youth. The transformation of Odysseus' father from the pitiful sight he presented when Odysseus first saw him at 24.226–31 (and cf. 11.187–96) becomes a paradigm case of what a poet, and poetic style, can do for you. The power of style at which Theocritus hints finds a later resonance in Dionysius of Halicarnassus' famous comparison (*De compositione verborum* 4.12) of the power of verbal arrangement (σύνθεσις) to Homer's Athena who could give Odysseus different appearances, from the lowly to the magnificent, at different times; word arrangement too, claims Dionysius, can make ideas (νοήματα) expressed in the selfsame words either 'ugly and low and beggarly' or 'lofty (ὑψηλά) and rich and beautiful'. Though Dionysius is extolling verbal arrangement rather than style and lexical choice, it is (again) at least worth wondering whether there is any shared background for poet and critic here, or whether (as so often) we have a foreshadowing of a critical notion within poetry itself.[23]

An earlier passage of *Idyll* 16 operates through a related stylistic effect. Like Pindar in *Nemean* 7 (cf. above), Theocritus uses the universality of death as a reason to employ poets:

---

[22] Gow on v. 55 tentatively suggested that Theocritus in this passage was thinking of the scene in which 'Odysseus and Telemachus, attended by Eumaeus and Philoetius, go to visit Laertes'; this is surely correct.

[23] Behind Dionysius here lies, of course, a rich tradition, cf. Isocrates, *Panegyricus* 8 (criticized at 'Longinus', *On the sublime* 38.2–3). For a not dissimilar phenomenon cf. Strabo 1.2.9 where Homer's alleged practice of adding myth to 'historical fact' is illustrated by three Homeric descriptions of beautification or the creation of brilliant artefacts.

> Μοισάων δὲ μάλιστα τίειν ἱεροὺς ὑποφήτας,
> ὄφρα καὶ εἰν Ἀίδαο κεκρυμμένος ἐσθλὸς ἀκούσῃς, 30
> μηδ' ἀκλεὴς μύρηαι ἐπὶ ψυχροῦ Ἀχέροντος,
> ὡσεί τις μακέλαι τετυλωμένος ἔνδοθι χεῖρας
> ἀχὴν ἐκ πατέρων πενίην ἀκτήμονα κλαίων.
>
> Theocritus 16.29–33

> [The best use of wealth is] most of all to honour the holy prophets of the Muses, so that even when you are hidden in Hades your reputation will be an excellent one, and you will not mourn, fameless, beside chilly Acheron, like a poor man from a poor family, the palms of his hands hardened by use of the mattock, who bewails his empty poverty.

Some recent criticism, picking up a hint from Gow, has wanted to see Sappho 55 Voigt behind Theocritus' reference to the unknown peasant languishing in Hades:[24]

> κατθάνοισα δὲ κείσῃ οὐδέ ποτα μναμοσύνα σέθεν
> ἔσσετ' οὐδὲ +ποκ'+ ὕστερον· οὐ γὰρ πεδέχῃς βρόδων
> τῶν ἐκ Πιερίας· ἀλλ' ἀφάνης κἀν Ἀίδα δόμωι
> φοιτάσῃς πεδ' ἀμαύρων νεκύων ἐκπεποταμένα.
>
> Sappho fr. 55 Voigt

> When you are dead, you will lie there, and in future time there will be no memory of you, for you have no share in the roses of Pieria. Unnoticed in the house of Hades when you have flitted away, you will go here and there amidst the insubstantial dead.

The theme is, however, a common one, and, however close in thrust the two passages may be, there seems no particular reason to think of Sappho here. Given what immediately follows in *Idyll* 16, we might rather think of Simonides' θρῆνοι,[25] and that at least would be in keeping with the principal intertexts of the poem. Horstmann, however, tentatively suggested that behind this passage lay Achilles' famous exchange with Odysseus in the Underworld:[26]

> "σεῖο δ', Ἀχιλλεῦ,
> οὔ τις ἀνὴρ προπάροιθε μακάρτερος οὔτ' ἄρ' ὀπίσσω·
> πρὶν μὲν γάρ σε ζωὸν ἐτίομεν ἶσα θεοῖσιν
> Ἀργεῖοι, νῦν αὖτε μέγα κρατέεις νεκύεσσιν 485
> ἐνθάδ' ἐών· τῷ μή τι θανὼν ἀκαχίζευ, Ἀχιλλεῦ."
> ὣς ἐφάμην, ὁ δέ μ' αὐτίκ' ἀμειβόμενος προσέειπε·
> "μὴ δή μοι θάνατόν γε παραύδα, φαίδιμ' Ὀδυσσεῦ.

---

24 Cf., e.g., Griffiths 1979, 29 n. 55, Sbardella 1997, 137–9.
25 Acosta-Hughes 2010a, 183 associates vv. 40–3 with the θρῆνοι.
26 Horstmann 1976, 126 n. 55.

βουλοίμην κ' ἐπάρουρος ἐὼν θητευέμεν ἄλλωι,
ἀνδρὶ παρ' ἀκλήρωι, ὧι μὴ βίοτος πολὺς εἴη,   490
ἢ πᾶσιν νεκύεσσι καταφθιμένοισιν ἀνάσσειν."
                                Homer, *Odyssey* 11.482–91

'No man, Achilles, is more fortunate than you, either from times past or in the future. Before, when you were alive, we Argives honoured you equally to the gods, and now again you hold mastery over the dead down here. Therefore, Achilles, do not grieve at death.' So I spoke, and he replied: 'Do not try to console me for death, glorious Achilles. I would rather be a bonded workman to another man, an impoverished peasant without much livelihood, than rule over all the lifeless dead.'

Theocritus' point is of course, as Kathryn Gutzwiller points out,[27] different from Achilles', but we may at least be encouraged to speculate further in this direction by the fact that v. 30 begins with a verbal repetition of another verse from *Odyssey* 11 (v. 211); the *Nekuia* does seem to have been in Theocritus' mind here. The poor man, 'the palms of his hands hardened by use of the mattock', will then be an expansive gloss, with characteristic Theocritean earthiness, upon Achilles' ἐπάρουρος, which is glossed in the scholia either as γεωργός or as ἐπίγειος καὶ ζῶν. So too, it will be Achilles' ἀνὴρ ἄκληρος, glossed in the scholia as πένης, κλῆρον καὶ οὐσίαν μὴ ἔχων, which is the starting-point for Theocritus' ἀχὴν ἐκ πατέρων.

There are two other reasons for seeing Achilles' words behind this passage, and both may be classed as stylistic. The closest verbal model for these verses in Homer is not in *Odyssey* 11, but rather in the famous simile of *Iliad* 23, in which Achilles' attempts to escape the river-god are compared to a man clearing an irrigation channel:

ὡς δ' ὅτ' ἀνὴρ ὀχετηγὸς ἀπὸ κρήνης μελανύδρου
ἂμ φυτὰ καὶ κήπους ὕδατι ῥόον ἡγεμονεύηι
χερσὶ μάκελλαν ἔχων, ἀμάρης ἐξ ἔχματα βάλλων·
τοῦ μέν τε προρέοντος ὑπὸ ψηφῖδες ἅπασαι   260
ὀχλεῦνται· τὸ δέ τ' ὦκα κατειβόμενον κελαρύζει
χώρωι ἔνι προαλεῖ, φθάνει δέ τε καὶ τὸν ἄγοντα·
ὣς αἰεὶ Ἀχιλῆα κιχήσατο κῦμα ῥόοιο
καὶ λαιψηρὸν ἐόντα· θεοὶ δέ τε φέρτεροι ἀνδρῶν.
                                Homer, *Iliad* 21.257–64

---

27 Gutzwiller 1983, 226 n. 55; cf. also Kyriakou 2004, 238 n. 32.

As when a man working on irrigation directs water from a dark spring through his plants and fruit, by working with a mattock and throwing muck out of the channel. As the stream flows forward, all the pebbles roll down and the swift-flowing water gurgles as it runs down the slope and catches up with the gardener. Just so did the river's wave ever catch up with Achilles, swift as he was: gods are more powerful than men.

The style of this famous simile, which contains the only occurrence of μάκελλα in Homer, is discussed in the scholia in terms of a move by Homer from his grand style to a much plainer manner (τὸ ἰσχνόν);[28] Theocritus, in running together two scenes involving Achilles, has made the language as plain as possible, including the only instance of τυλόω in poetry, to reinforce the warning about what happens to those who do not give thought to how poets can benefit them. The second reason for thinking of Achilles in this passage of *Idyll* 16 derives from another aspect of style. Odysseus' attempted consolation to the hero, μή τι θανὼν ἀκαχίζευ, Ἀχιλλεῦ, will certainly have evoked the familiar connection between Achilles' name and ἄχος (cf., e.g., AT-scholia on *Iliad* 1.1 h Erbse), and these sounds seem strangely persistent in this Theocritean passage: ἀκλεής, Ἀχέροντος, ἀχήν, ἀκτήμονα. ἀχήν, which does not otherwise appear in literature (cf. Gow ad loc.), may in fact have been chosen to activate or reinforce a connection with Achilles and ἄχος.

The very variety of Theocritus' engagement with, and reproduction of, the poetry of the past, even within a single poem, and the lesson for the study of Hellenistic poetry more generally that this carries, does not need to be laboured at length, but another example, where it is again Achilles who carries the weight of the past, may suggest something of the range of phenomena which the Theocritean text has to offer.

As is well known, in his account in *Idyll* 14 of the disastrous party which revealed to him that his girlfriend's mind was on someone else, Aischinas uses two Achillean similes in very quick succession:

ἁ δὲ Κυνίσκα
ἔκλαεν ἐξαπίνας θαλερώτερον ἢ παρὰ ματρί
παρθένος ἑξαετὴς κόλπω ἐπιθυμήσασα.
τᾶμος ἐγώ, τὸν ἴσαις τύ, Θυώνιχε, πὺξ ἐπὶ κόρρας
ἤλασα, κἄλλαν αὖθις. ἀνειρύσασα δὲ πέπλως   35
ἔξω ἀποίχετο θᾶσσον. 'ἐμὸν κακόν, οὔ τοι ἀρέσκω;
ἄλλος τοι γλυκίων ὑποκόλπιος; ἄλλον ἰοῖσα
θάλπε φίλον. τήνωι τεὰ δάκρυα; μάλα ῥεόντω.'
μάστακα δοῖσα τέκνοισιν ὑπωροφίοισι χελιδών

---
28 Cf. Hunter 2009a, 158–60.

ἄψορρον ταχινὰ πέτεται βίον ἄλλον ἀγείρειν·   40
ὠκυτέρα μαλακᾶς ἀπὸ δίφρακος ἔπτετο τήνα
ἰθὺ δι' ἀμφιθύρω καὶ δικλίδος, ᾇ πόδες ἆγον.

Theocritus 14.31–42

Kyniska suddenly burst into tears, more violently than a six year-old girl crying for her mother's lap. Then I—you know what I'm like, Thyonichus—punched her on the temple with my fist, and then gave her another one. Gathering up her dress, she took off as fast as she could. 'Wretch, don't you like me? You prefer some other lover? Be off and keep your new friend warm! Are your tears for him? Let them flow down big as apples!'. The swallow gives her young under the roof a morsel to eat and swiftly flies back off to gather more nourishment; more quickly than that did Kyniska fly off her soft seat, straight through the porch and the door, wherever her feet took her.

The first of these similes goes back of course to Achilles' address to Patroclus at the opening of *Iliad* 16:

τίπτε δεδάκρυσαι Πατρόκλεις, ἠΰτε κούρη
νηπίη, ἥ θ' ἅμα μητρὶ θέουσ' ἀνελέσθαι ἀνώγει
εἰανοῦ ἁπτομένη, καί τ' ἐσσυμένην κατερύκει,
δακρυόεσσα δέ μιν ποτιδέρκεται, ὄφρ' ἀνέληται;
τῇ ἴκελος Πάτροκλε τέρεν κατὰ δάκρυον εἴβεις.

Homer, *Iliad* 16.7–11

Why are you crying, Patroclus, like a young girl who runs to her mother and begs to be picked up, tugging at her dress and holding her back as she tries to hurry off, and as she cries she looks at her until she is picked up? Like her, Patroclus, you are shedding womanly tears.

In his note on v. 33 Gow observes 'There is some force in the criticism that ἑξαετής is old for such behaviour'. If we ask why Theocritus introduced this change in his model, a number of answers might come to mind, but—as often—we could do worse than begin with the Homeric scholia. The bT-scholia on the simile of *Iliad* 16 note how the poet uses similes to enable him to include all ages of females in his poem and how he here 'takes a banal (εὐτελές) event and represents it with grandeur and envisionment (μεγαλοπρεπῶς καὶ μετ' ἐναργείας)'. At one level this is merely a specific instance of the standard ancient view that similes aid *enargeia*,[29] but I am sure that many modern readers of Homer will gladly concur with the particularly memorable power of this 'realistic' image. Why did Theocritus replace the unspecific Homeric κούρη νηπίη by the more specific παρθένος ... ἑξαετής? For Dover, to some extent echoing (I do not know whether deliberately) the Homeric scholia, Theocritus' image is 'a

---

29 Cf., e.g., Nünlist 2009, 291.

much less vivid picture of everyday life', though he says nothing as to whether he thinks this was simply Theocritus' lack of competence or whether it served some artistic purpose.[30] There would of course be much more to say about why Aischinas is made to appropriate an Achillean voice, but I want to ask a simpler question: can we be sure that Theocritus did not make his character use the specific (or, in Greek, ἀκριβές) epithet ἑξαετής precisely to increase the image's vividness, to out-Achilles Achilles, if you like? How secure are our judgements about ancient stylistic effects? Theocritus poses, as is well known, some of the thorniest problems in this area: to move from the micro- to the macro- level, how many modern readers are sure they understand the stylistic level of the Adonis-hymn in *Idyll* 15 and the purpose of that level.

We may well think that, leaving everything else aside, the image of the crying girl is much more powerful when used, as in Homer, of a man than, as in Theocritus, to describe an older female, but the narrative situation hardly allowed that in the case of Theocritus. There is, in any case, obvious humour in the Iliadic echoes: a lovers' spat at a party is improbably made as portentous as the story of the *Iliad* and, particularly, as tragic as the story of Achilles and Patroclus. The following verses in which Aeschinas twice hits Kyniska have been compared to the violence sometimes exercised against women in New Comedy, but what seems more likely is that we have here a version of Achilles' anger when faced with the prospect of losing *his* girl in *Iliad* 1, an anger that puts him on the point of running Agamemnon through. 'You know what I'm like' (v. 34) functions (*inter alia*) as a kind of reference back to that scene: yes, we all do know the model text here—and Achilles' emotional character was probably the most notorious of any literary figure. Not for Aischinas, however, the indecision of the Homeric scene—he just let Kyniska have it ... Not for nothing, too, has Theocritus placed *antilabe* in each of the first three verses of *Idyll* 14[31]—it is these verses which mark how the hexameter of epic poetry has been brought down to the level of mime.

The source of Aischinas' second Achillean image is Achilles' account of his own labours in *Iliad* 9:

οὐδέ τί μοι περίκειται, ἐπεὶ πάθον ἄλγεα θυμῶι
αἰεὶ ἐμὴν ψυχὴν παραβαλλόμενος πολεμίζειν.
ὡς δ' ὄρνις ἀπτῆσι νεοσσοῖσι προφέρηισι

---

30 Griffiths 1979, 114–15 argues that this 'literary posturing' by Aischinas cuts a very poor figure, as indeed do other Theocritean lovers: 'He has only the dimmest grasp of what his [Achillean] images mean ...'; for a very different approach cf. Burton 1995, 49–52.
31 There is a similar phenomenon at the head of *Idyll* 15.

μάστακ' ἐπεί κε λάβῃσι, κακῶς δ' ἄρα οἱ πέλει αὐτῆι,
ὣς καὶ ἐγὼ πολλὰς μὲν ἀΰπνους νύκτας ἴαυον,   325
ἤματα δ' αἱματόεντα διέπρησσον πολεμίζων
ἀνδράσι μαρνάμενος ὀάρων ἕνεκα σφετεράων.
                                                Homer, Iliad 9.321–7

Nor do I gain any advantage from the fact that I have suffered grievously in my spirit, always putting my life at risk in war. Like a bird which brings its flightless chicks whatever morsel it finds, but itself goes without, so I have passed through many nights without sleep and endured blood-filled days of warfare, fighting with men over their women.

Again, there would be much to say about Theocritus' turning of this image into a paratactic simile: when we remember the surrounding context in Homer we note (with a smile) that Aischinas' subsequent counting of the days suggests an eroticization of Achilles' 'I have passed through many sleepless nights' (v. 325)—no doubt Aischinas really had, whereas Achilles' 'I have spent (many) blood-filled days in warfare' (v. 326) is probably somewhat remote from Aischinas' experience. Achilles may fight with men 'over' women, but we have just witnessed Aischinas fighting 'with' women. Here, however, I want merely to draw attention to one stylistic feature of Theocritus' reworking. V. 39 begins with the same Homeric gloss as stands in necessary enjambment at the head of *Iliad* 9.324, μάστακα.[32] Nevertheless, the Theocritean reworking precisely inverts every element of the corresponding Homeric utterance; the matter may be set out in a table, with the elements numbered as they appear in their respective texts:

Theocritus		Homer	
μάστακα	1	μάστακα	5
δοῖσα	2	προφέρῃσιν	4
τέκνοισιν	3	νεοσσοῖσι	3
ὑπωροφίοισι	4	ἀπτῆσι	2
χελιδών	5	ὄρνις	1

Is this an accident (we can hardly doubt that such accidents do happen)? Would such *uariatio* (deliberate or not) surprise us at an earlier date? Is a dichotomy in such matters between 'accident' and 'design' a misleading one—are things rather more complicated than that? Are such things only possible in a poetry which re-

---

32 Three interpretations of Homeric μάστακ' at *Iliad* 9.324 seem to have had ancient currency, cf. the scholia ad loc., Gow on Theocr. 14.39: 'a mouthful, morsel', 'a locust' (both understanding μάστακα), and 'with the mouth' (understanding μάστακι, accepted by, e.g., Hainsworth ad loc.). Theocritus' μάστακα allows only the first two interpretations, and the first is, as far as I know, universally accepted by modern editors and translators; I am not convinced that Theocritus' usage here is a strong case of overt interpretation within a poem of a disputed Homeric word, but this is an area where differences of opinion are certainly possible.

lies upon writing and expects reception through reading? The Theocritean text, of course, abounds in patterns and echoing repetitions of all kinds, and not just in the bucolic poems (as usually understood).

Another poem of Pindar which has long been seen to have a special importance for *Idyll* 16 is the *Second Isthmian*, also for a Sicilian victor. It is, after all, in this poem that Pindar complains that the Muse of old was 'neither φιλοκερδής nor ἐργάτις', whereas today the watchword is χρήματα χρήματ' ἀνήρ. The scholia spin a story about how this poem was prompted by the μικρολογία of a patron, but also—more interestingly—interpret Pindar's reference to the avaricious Muse as a reference to Simonides and cite iambics of Callimachus (fr. 222 Pf.) which echo this Pindaric passage in an explicit reference to the Cean poet; if nothing else, the Callimachus fragment suggests the familiarity of the Pindaric passage and its probable link to Simonides in the third century. Reference to *Isthmian* 2 may in fact be able to help with a difficult passage of *Idyll* 16, in a way which is perhaps exemplary for the poetry of the third century.

Not far into the second part of the poem Theocritus dismisses the potential patron who does not want to part with his money:

χαιρέτω ὅστις τοῖος, ἀνήριθμος δέ οἱ εἴη
ἄργυρος, αἰεὶ δὲ πλεόνων ἔχοι ἵμερος αὐτόν· 65
αὐτὰρ ἐγὼ τιμήν τε καὶ ἀνθρώπων φιλότητα
πολλῶν ἡμιόνων τε καὶ ἵππων πρόσθεν ἑλοίμαν.

Theocritus 16.64–7

Farewell to such a man—let him have measureless silver and ever be possessed by desire for more. For myself, I would choose honour and the friendship of men in front of many mules and horses.

Here Theocritus puts the old hymnic/rhapsodic structure χαῖρε ... αὐτὰρ ἐγὼ to brilliant (and ?? very Hellenistic) new use.[33] Whereas χαῖρε is used to 'hail' the deity who has just been the object of song, with a sense that he or she 'appears' in response to the power of the rhapsode's hymn,[34] χαιρέτω dismisses the mean patron out of hand, as the poet moves on to a worthy subject of song; this is clearly an important structural moment in the poem, and one that cuts across the formal division I was considering earlier. Moreover, the wish (or curse) that such a patron should suffer from unquenchable desire for money (like Erysichthon for food) is a corresponding inversion of the closing hymnic request to

---

33 Cf., e.g., González 2010, 100. Acosta-Hughes 2010a, 185 wants Simonides fr.eleg. 11.19–20 W to be the specific model here, but there seems nothing to activate such specific reference. On the transitional formula αὐτὰρ ἐγώ cf. further Hunter 2003, 103 with earlier bibliography.
34 Cf. García 2002.

the god who has been praised for ἀρετή and/or ὄλβος, a request that Theocritus also reworks at the end of *Idyll* 17, as Callimachus does at the end of the *Hymn to Zeus*.³⁵ This poet has now risen above such considerations. Theocritus is here, *inter alia*, exploring the relation between 'modern' encomiastic poetry and traditional hymnic poetry. What follows has been described as a 'baffling' transition:³⁶

> δίζημαι δ' ὅτινι θνατῶν κεχαρισμένος ἔλθω
> σὺν Μοίσαις· χαλεπαὶ γὰρ ὁδοὶ τελέθουσιν ἀοιδοῖς
> κουράων ἀπάνευθε Διὸς μέγα βουλεύοντος.   70
> οὔπω μῆνας ἄγων ἔκαμ' οὐρανὸς οὐδ' ἐνιαυτούς·
> πολλοὶ κινήσουσιν ἔτι τροχὸν ἄματος ἵπποι·
> ἔσσεται οὗτος ἀνὴρ ὃς ἐμεῦ κεχρήσετ' ἀοιδοῦ κτλ.
>   Theocritus 16.68–73

I am looking for the mortal to whose house I may come as a welcome guest (κεχαρισμένος) in company with the Muses, for the ways are difficult for singers without the daughters of great-counselling Zeus. Not yet have the heavens wearied of leading round the months and years; often still shall the horses set the wheel of the day in motion. There will come the man who will need me to be his singer ...

Gow glosses the reference to the Muses as 'in plain prose it appears to mean no more than that it is useless for a poet to travel unless he carries his inspiration with him' (n. on 69f.), a rather lame explanation which, however, is in its essence taken over by Dover. The image of the ὁδοί of poetry is of course ubiquitous, but it is important that Theocritus is looking for a worthy patron, someone who—as he will go on to say—has the deeds of an Achilles or an Ajax to his credit; it is to such a man that one makes journeys 'with the Muses'. In the *Second Isthmian* Pindar uses the 'journey' metaphor in a similar manner:

> οὐ γὰρ πάγος οὐδὲ προσάντης
>   ἁ κέλευθος γίνεται,
> εἴ τις εὐδόξων ἐς ἀν-
>   δρῶν ἄγοι τιμὰς Ἑλικωνιάδων.
>   Pindar, *Isthmian* 2.33–4

There is no hill, nor is the path steep, if one brings the honours of the maidens of Helicon to the homes of famous men.

---

35 Cf. Hunter 2003, 197–8.
36 Griffiths 1979, 35. For other aspects of this transition cf. Hunter 1996, 105.

The interpretation of these verses is (inevitably) disputed, but it is not hard to believe that Theocritus understood them as does the scholiast: 'For those who are praising glorious men the road (ὁδός) is not rough (τραχεῖα), but the opposite—easy and gentle, for they themselves (i.e. the subjects of song) provide the starting-points (ἀφορμαί) for praise' (scholium on v. 33, p. 219 Drachmann). If Theocritus has found *his* ἀφορμή in this passage,[37] then his 'Muses' will be songs in praise of great deeds (a meaning which also suits the reprise in v. 107): if there are no great deeds to praise, then poets really do find the going tough, but Theocritus is confident enough that there is still time for a worthy patron to arise. Behind both Pindar and Theocritus may of course lurk Hesiod's steep path towards virtue (*WD* 286–92): the patron will have to work very hard for the successes which manifest his ἀρετή, but it is those successes which make the way easy for poets.

The language of Hellenistic poetry thus leaves us with much to do, and much that leads to frustration. If only we could more often be sure of our stylistic sense: when in v. 75 of *Idyll* 16 Theocritus describes the plain of Troy as 'the plain of Simois, where is the tomb of Phrygian Ilos', is it important that Homer never says 'the plain of Simois' and never uses the singular Φρύξ, that in Homer the Phrygians are, in any case, quite distinct from the Trojans (a fact commented upon by the Homeric scholia),[38] and that to make the eponymous hero of Ilion a 'Phrygian' might in some circumstances be highly loaded (cf. Callimachus, *Hymn to Athena* 18 of Paris),[39] and that ἠρίον occurs only once in Homer (of the mound which Achilles 'devised' for himself and Patroclus, *Iliad* 23.126) and only here in our corpus of Theocritus? Was Theocritus thinking of the opening of *Iliad* 6 in which the plain of Troy, the Simois (in the genitive in the same *sedes*), and a heroic exploit of Ajax all come together? So many questions …

---

37 Perrotta 1925, 21 illustrates this Theocritean passage from *Olympian* 1.109–11, where there seems indeed to be a similar thought: Olympian success by the victor will offer the poet an ἐπίκουρον … ὁδὸν λόγων.
38 Cf. bT- scholia on *Iliad* 10.415.
39 Cf. Bulloch's note ad loc.

Kathryn Gutzwiller
Poetic Meaning, Place, and Dialect in the Epigrams of Meleager

After discussing what Gow and Page call the "tiresome and insoluble problem" of dialect in the *Greek Anthology*, they conclude that "it is some consolation ... to reflect that vagaries of dialect affect neither the meaning nor, to a modern reader, the poetical value of the poems."[1] It is one of the important trends in epigram studies, partially stimulated by the publication of the Milan Papyrus,[2] to question such asserted lack of poetic meaning attaching to the dialects found in Hellenistic literary epigrams. In particular, Alexander Sens has shown that the Doric dialectal forms found in the Posidippus papyrus have specific cultural and literary purposes. He suggests that Posidippus' use of Doric in the statues section connects to the Doric background of the sculptors and in the equestrian section to the Macedonian heritage of the Ptolemaic victors.[3] He further argues, also with reference to Asclepiades, that dialect was sometimes used to mark a speaker's native speech patterns or to signal reliance on certain literary traditions, such as Doric epinician.[4] The corpus of 125 epigrams by Meleager, composed in late second and early first centuries B.C. and incorporated into his *Garland* of earlier epigrammatists, offers another useful benchmark for assessing dialect use in Hellenistic literary epigrams. My analysis will show that, in addition to the types of dialect use found in Asclepiades and Posidippus, choice of dialect may also point to the most likely place of composition and the most likely first readers.[5]

Like most of the earlier epigrams transmitted through the *Garland*, Meleager's poems can generally be classified as either Attic-Ionic or Doric. Throughout the corpus, the underlying, or unmarked, dialect is koine Attic, which is a slightly ionicized form of Attic. Intermingled in many epigrams, however, are other dialectal forms. In some cases only minor intrusions of one or two words appear within

---

1 Gow-Page 1965, 1.xlvii.
2 P.Mil.Vogl. VIII 309. The *editio princeps* was edited by Bastianini and Galazzi, and the *editio minor* by Austin and Bastianini.
3 Sens 2004; cf. Guichard 2005. See too Hunter 2005c, 190–96, who argues that Doric dialect in early Hellenistic poetry may act as a marker of the Macedonian heritage of the Ptolemies.
4 Sens 2004; 2011, lxv–lxxii; cf. Sens forthcoming, on the Anacreontea.
5 The corpus used for my analysis consists of those epigrams attributed only to Meleager (see Table 1); poems with ambiguous attribution to both Meleager and another poet have been excluded. For dialect in Meleager, see also Ouvré 1894, 155–67.

the dominant dialect, but in other cases the presence of non-Attic forms is extensive enough to produce a distinct dialectal coloring, usually Doric but selectively also Ionic.⁶ In fact, dialect mixture was part of the heritage from inscribed epigrams of the archaic and classical age, where epic forms sometimes appear within the dominant dialect and the names of individuals often retain the original dialectal spelling.⁷ In addition, Hellenistic epigrammatists were undoubtedly influenced by a new poetic aesthetic involving inclusion of choice words and mixture of dialect forms.⁸ Most expressly, Callimachus in his *Iambi* defended his use of Ionic, Doric, and a mixture of dialects as a feature of his πολυείδεια (τοῦτ' ἐμπ[έ]πλεκται καὶ λαλευς[..]..['Ιαστὶ καὶ Δωριστὶ καὶ τὸ σύμμικτον[, fr. 203.17–18).⁹

Despite these inscriptional and literary precedents, however, there has been a long editorial tradition of regularizing the dialects within the epigrams of the Greek Anthology. Certainly it is true, as confirmed by dialectal variation between the manuscript sources and in a few papyri, that the transmission of dialect was subject to error or deliberate alteration.¹⁰ My work in editing and commenting on Meleager has convinced me, however, that the Palatine Codex is, in general, our most reliable source for dialect usage; not only Planudes but also the corrector in

---

6 In *AP* 12.92.7 = 116.7 *HE*, the transmitted ὑποκαόμενοι is the classical Attic form rather than koine Attic, but this is an exceptional usage.

7 In examining early inscriptional epigrams of Attic authorship, Buck 1923, 134 attributed non-Attic η to epic influence and non-Attic ᾱ to that of choral lyric. See too Mickey 1981 and Kaczko 2009, 91–94, on the inclusion of non-local forms in inscriptions written in the author's own dialect.

8 Kaczko 2009, 95 points out that Hellenistic epigrammatists shared a taste for the *Kunstsprachen* found in other genres, stating that "the use of dialect forms must have been perceived as means to 'embellish' a poetical text."

9 Note that Callimachus' choice of ἐμπ[έ]πλεκται anticipates Meleager's use of πλέκειν for the intertwining of poets in his *Garland* (*AP* 4.1.5, 9, 18, 25; 12.257.6), for weaving a garland for a female love (*AP* 5.147), and for his intertwining of different boy loves in his own poetry (*AP* 12.165.4; 12.256.3, 5). For Meleager, interweaving became a symbol of poetic composition on many levels.

10 A good example of inconsistent readings in the sources is offered by *AP* 7.164 = 21 *HE* by Antipater of Sidon, an epitaph for a woman from Samos. Ionic endings appear in the version transmitted in the Palatine Codex, while line ends preserved in P.Oxy. 662 of the Augustan age preserve three variants. Of these παρθ]ενίαν (παρθενίης in P) and ποίαν (ποίην in P) are uncertainly Attic or Doric, while νεότατι (νεότητι in P) is clearly Doric. The Antipater epigram is a close variation of an epitaph in Ionic dialect by Leonidas of Tarentum that immediately precedes in both the papyrus and the Palatine Codex (*AP* 7.163 = 70 *HE*). Since it is logical for an epitaph for a Samian woman to be in the Ionic dialect of her homeland, an editor might reasonably assume that the non-Ionic forms in the papyrus have resulted from ancient scribal error. Here the manuscript has likely preserved the correct forms, but the example shows how easily and how early mistakes entered the tradition.

the Palatine sometimes introduced variants as conjectures in order to produce consistency in a poem's dialect. We should remember that Planudes' selection of epigrams was the source for all published versions of the Greek Anthology from the *editio princeps* of 1494 up to Brunck's edition in 1772, which was the first to include the additional epigrams from the Palatine; consequently, Planudes' editorial choices have influenced the textual tradition in subtle ways that have had an impact up to the present. The editors who came after Brunck were slow to recognize the Palatine's independent status as the oldest and best manuscript, and the impulse to emend away dialectal inconsistencies continued without hesitation until Gow-Page's edition. Gow and Page were considerably more willing to follow the manuscripts in admitting dialectal variation within a single epigram, although they still print some dialectal forms conjectured by earlier scholars and a few of their own proposal. The Doric examples from the Posidippus papyrus make it clear, however, that the dialect mixtures found in Hellenistic epigrams do, in aggregate, reflect the stylistic preferences of the author. Although certainty about the authorial authority for any particular form is elusive, patterns of usage and meaningful allusion may act as guides for assessing the purposes of dialect in literary epigram.

Meleager's dialect usage is more restricted than that of third-century poems composed in a literary adaptation of a dialect, such as Theocritus' Doric and Aeolic poems, Callimachus' Doric hymns (5 and 6), and Herodas' Ionic *Mimiambi*. Its main features are easily summarized. By far the most common indicator of Doric is ᾱ for original /a:/, which frequently occurs in endings.[11] Ionic forms, which may be considered epic-Ionic for forms that appear in archaic epic, are often indicated simply by η replacing Attic long α as after ε, ι, and ρ. Other indicators of Ionic or epic-Ionic are uncontracted endings, typically -εος for Attic -ους in the genitive singular of third declension -s stems, -εω for Att. –ου in the genitive singular of masculine ᾱ stems, and -εων for Attic -ῶν in the genitive plural of all ᾱ stems. The choice between the Ionic forms μοῦνος and ξεῖνος or the Attic μόνος and ξένος is based at least partly on metrical convenience. Certain words with the contraction ευ for εο, such as so σεῦ and μεῦ (Attic σοῦ, μοῦ), are uncertainly Ionic or Doric,[12] since they occur in Hellenistic inscriptions written in both dialects. I attribute them to either Ionic or Doric in accordance

---

[11] Rarely other Doric forms appear, such as the preposition ποτί in *AP* 12.86.3 = 18.3 *HE*.
[12] Buck 1955, §42.5 notes that the contraction ευ from εο (Att. ου) does not appear in Ionic inscriptions until the fourth century B.C. The same contraction ευ is typical of the "middle" Doric inscriptions of the Aegean area in the Hellenistic era, and is particularly strong in Rhodes, Cos, and Cnidos; see Bubeník 1989, 102–6. For the phenomenon in Theocritus, see Molinos Tejada 1990, 88–96.

with the dialect of the surrounding forms. Another category consists of epic forms that have disappeared from later dialects and survive only as part of the poetic tradition. These are the endings -ῃσι (ν) for the dative plural of ᾱ stems, -οισι(ν) for the dative plural of o stems, -οιο for the genitive singular of o stems, and -εες (Att. -εῖς) for the nominative plural of third-declension adjectives of the –ης/ες class. Poetic forms like χρύσειος occur only occasionally to give an epic flavor. In the texts quoted below, Doric forms are underlined, Ionic ones are in bold, and epic forms are italicized.

We should keep in mind that the period from the first half of the third century to the end of the second century B.C. saw the progressive adoption of Attic koine throughout the Greek-speaking world at the expense of local dialects, though at different paces in different locations. Bubeník has compiled statistics on the diminution in non-Ionic dialects throughout the Greek world in the Hellenistic period.[13] It may be, then, that Meleager's limited dialectal use (in comparison with earlier Hellenistic epigrammatists) reflects, in part, the written (and spoken?) linguistic practices of his own lifetime. I will argue that although Meleager's use of dialect sometimes reflects the dialectal preferences of the immediate audience for which it was composed, the poet also employs dialect for literary purposes, as did his epigrammatic predecessors. It can be shown in many instances that the dialect forms transmitted in manuscript are chosen for a specific purpose, including the following: to signal the linguistic ambiance of a person or place mentioned in the epigram,[14] to support the historical circumstances of the poem's dramatized setting, or to make allusion to poetic models and traditions. As will be shown below, the general pattern of Doric versus Attic-Ionic in Meleager's arrangement of his epigrams within the *Garland* also correlates, to a not insignificant degree, with the probable place of composition.

That dialect in Meleager has poetic significance is evident from the proem to the *Garland*, *AP* 4.1 = 1 *HE*. I quote here the opening (1–6), a middle section (42–48), and the conclusion (53–58):

---

[13] Bubeník 1989. Horrocks 2010, 79–123 usefully surveys the rise of koine, stressing its local varieties; on so-called "Doric koines," see 87–88. My own quick survey of the first 300 epitaphs in Peek 1955 confirms this pattern of progressive diminution of dialect in inscribed verse epitaphs during the last three centuries B.C.

[14] The use of dialect to show respect to a person or place has roots in inscriptions of the archaic and classical ages; see Mickey 1981, 44 with notes 23–24; Kaczko 2009, 93–94. Buck 1913, 135–37 points out that an artist's native dialect or alphabet often appears in his signature, whereas the dialect of the epigram itself is typically that of the local area or of epic; as an example, see 388 *CEG*.

Μοῦσα φίλα, τίνι τάνδε φέρεις πάγκαρπον ἀοιδάν
  ἢ τίς ὁ καὶ τεύξας ὑμνοθετᾶν στέφανον;
ἄνυσε μὲν Μελέαγρος· ἀριζάλῳ δὲ Διοκλεῖ
  μναμόσυνον ταύταν ἐξεπόνησε χάριν·
πολλὰ μὲν ἐμπλέξας Ἀνύτης κρίνα, πολλὰ δὲ Μοιροῦς   (5)
  λείρια, καὶ Σαπφοῦς βαιὰ μέν, ἀλλὰ ῥόδα,
...
φοίνισσάν τε νέην κύπρον ἀπ' Ἀντιπάτρου·
καὶ μὴν καὶ Συρίαν σταχυότριχα θήκατο νάρδον
  ὑμνοθέταν Ἑρμοῦ δῶρον ἀειδόμενον
ἐν δὲ Ποσείδιππόν τε καὶ Ἡδύλον, ἄγρι' ἀρούρης,   (45)
  Σικελίδεώ τ' ἀνέμοις ἄνθεα φυόμενα·
ναὶ μὴν καὶ χρύσειον ἀεὶ θείοιο Πλάτωνος
  κλῶνα, τὸν ἐξ ἀρετῆς πάντοθι λαμπόμενον.
...
τάν τε φιλάκρητον Θεοδωρίδεω νεοθαλῆ
  ἕρπυλλον, κυάνων τ' ἄνθεα Φανίεω,
ἄλλων τ' ἔρνεα πολλὰ νεόγραφα· τοῖς δ' ἅμα Μούσης   (55)
  καὶ σφετέρης ἔτι που πρώιμα λευκόια. —
ἀλλὰ φίλοις μὲν ἐμοῖσι φέρω χάριν· ἔστι δὲ μύσταις
  κοινὸς ὁ τῶν Μουσέων ἡδυεπὴς στέφανος.

2 ὑμνοθέταν P 47 χρύσειον apogr.: -σιον P 53 φιλάκρητον apogr.: φαλ- P 54 ἕρπυλλον apogr.: -υλον P

Dear Muse, to whom do you bring this all-fruited song? Who has made a garland of poets? Meleager accomplished the deed and completed this work as a charming gift and a memento for illustrious Diocles. In it he plaited the many white lilies of Anyte, the many Madonna lilies of Moero, and Sappho's bouquet, small yet of roses.

... and [he put in it] new red henna from Antipater. He also placed in it Syrian spikenard topped with grainlike ears, a poet celebrated as Hermes' gift [Hermodorus], and in it both Posidippus and Hedylus, wild flowers of the cultivated field, and Sicelides' flowers that blossom with the winds. So too [he included] a golden branch of the ever divine Plato, the one who gleams forth everywhere from excellence.

... [mixing in] the newly blossoming thyme, fond of wine, of Theodoridas, and the cornflower blooms of Phanias, and the many recently composed shoots of others. Together with these he placed the perhaps still early-blooming white violets of his own Muse. I bring it as a charming gift to those dear to me, but the sweet-voiced garland of the Muses exists for their devotees as a common possession.

The proem opens by asking the Muse to name both the recipient and the creator of the garland of poets she brings. In reply, the Muse identifies the maker of the anthology as Meleager and dedicatee of his gift as illustrious Diocles. There follows a section of 52 lines listing many of the poets whose epigrams are anthologized in the *Garland* with comparison of each to a plant or flower. The final entry in the catalog is Meleager's own white violets (55–56), and in a final couplet, with framing echoes of the opening four lines, the Muse purports to bring the garland to her friends, that is, to other poets, while asserting that the collection will also exist as a common possession for others.

The dialect mixture in the proem is complex and surely meaningful. The first two couplets are heavily doricized. Not only is there a series of Doric ᾱ's for η's (φίλα,¹⁵ τάνδε, ἀοιδάν, ἄνυσε, ἀριζάλῳ,¹⁶ μναμόσυνον, ταύταν), but the genitive plural in -ᾶν for Attic -ῶν used in the rare noun ὑμνοθετᾶν (with the necessary change of the Palatine's accusative to the circumflex) is a traditional marker of poetic Doric that occurs elsewhere in Meleager's epigrams only in repetition of this word.¹⁷ In other words, the dialect in the opening lines of the *Garland* is strongly marked as Doric. This distinctive use of dialect in the proem prompts us to ask who is being represented by the voices of the questioner and the Muse. In a papyrus bookroll, a title and author's name were often written at the beginning, as in the σύμμεικτα ἐπιγράμματα collection by Posidippus on a third-century B.C. papyrus (P.Petrie II 49a = 961 *SH*). In the proem to the *Garland*, however, an imagined reader solicits the very information that an actual reader would expect to find in this place in the bookroll. The Muse who responds should be understood, I suggest, as the poetic voice of the collection itself.

---

15 Μοῦσα, modified by Doric φίλᾱ, is a dialectally ambiguous form. Μοῦσα is proper Attic-Ionic, while Doric Μῶσα is found in Alcman (e. g., 8.10, 14(a).1, 28.1 *PMG*), in the epigrammatist Theodoridas (*AP* 13.21.3 = 15.3 *HE*), and in the bucolic scholiasts (*Id*. 1.9a Wendel). The long vowel resulting from compensatory lengthening of /o/ in the original ending *-ontya has, however, a more complicated history in Doric. Buck 1955, §25 notes that secondary /o:/ became either ω or ου in some Doric dialects (those called "middle" Doric dialects; see Bubeník 1989, 90–109), namely Argolic (§25b-c, 250.1), Megarian (§257.1), Rhodian (§261.1), Coan (§265.1), and Theran (§268.1). The papyri and manuscripts of Theocritus' bucolic poems vary between Μοῖσα and Μοῦσα, and Μῶσα appears only in some manuscripts of *Idyll* 1 (Gow 1952, ad *Id*. 1.9; Molinos Tejada 1990, 56–58). That Μοῦσα was sometimes understood as Doric (especially, perhaps, in bucolic poetry) is suggested by Herodianus (περὶ κυρίων καὶ ἐπιθέτων καὶ προσηγορικῶν μονόβιβλον 3.2.1), who states that Μοῦσα is the Attic, Ionic, and Syracusan form (Ἀττικοὶ δὲ καὶ Ἴωνες καὶ Συρακούσιοι μοῦσα, Λάκωνες μῶσα). The attribution of μοῦσα to the Doric-speaking Syracusans is likely connected to the presence of the form in Theocritus (note particularly Μουσάων in Theoc. *Id*. 17.115, with Doric ending among other Doric forms, and Μοῦσαν δ' ὀθνείαν οὔτιν' ἐφελκυσάμαν, "nor did I drag in my wake any foreign Muse," [Theoc.] *AP* 9.205.4 = *epigr*. 27.4 Gow (note the Doric verb ending in the same line), in a statement of the poet's Syracusan heritage. This ambiguity in the grammatical tradition makes it possible to interpret Μοῦσα φίλα as entirely Doric. My thanks to David Sider for discussion on this point.

16 An epic word usually given the Attic-Ionic spelling with -η- in literature, even in Callimachus' Doric-colored celebration of Berenice as one of the Graces (*AP* 5.146.3 = 15.3 *HE*). The Doric form appears, however, in Antipater's epigram on the seven sages (*AP* 7.81 = 34 *HE*).

17 The genitive plural -ᾶν in ᾱ stems appears in old lyric, in Theocritus, and in the stricter forms of Doric attested in Hellenistic inscriptions; see Molinos Tejada 1990, 84–85; Bubeník 1989, 82–84.

The Charites in Theocritus' *Idyll* 16 provide an earlier example of the personification of an author's poetry as divine figures, and in *AP* 5.215 = 54 *HE* Meleager uses the phrase "my suppliant Muse" to refer to the very plea he is making in that epigram. The Muse of the proem represents the creative force behind the garland she brings; it is she who knows the intentions of the anthologizer, the list of poets collected there, and the specific plant that characterizes each.

Why, then, does the imagined or internal reader pose this initial question in Doric? The reader seems to have a special relationship to the Muse, as a poet would, since the address to Μοῦσα φίλα anticipates the concluding reference to the Muse's "friends" (φίλοι, 57) to whom she brings Meleager's garland as a gift. The Doric dialect may reflect the solemn style of hymn or the tradition of lyric song, like the Doric coloring in three epigrams by Meleager addressed to deities—Aphrodite (*AP* 12.86 = 18 *HE*), Eros (5.180 = 8 *HE*), and Dionysus (12.119 = 20 *HE*).[18] There is, however, an additional and not mutually exclusive possibility. As Meleager tells us in three self-epitaphs (*AP* 7.417–19 = 2–4 *HE*), after his formative years in his "Attic" Gadara "among the Assyrians" (7.417.2) and his youth spent in Phoenician Tyre, he lived his later years as an adopted citizen of Cos. Since these self-epitaphs were included in the *Garland*, it is all but certain that the formation of the anthology was a product of his years in Coan residence. Hellenistic Cos was particularly fond of its Doric heritage, as well as its illustrious literary past, and its inscriptions show an unusually persistent use of Doric forms well into the first century B.C.[19] It is natural, then, that this internal reader, the one that Meleager projects as an early or first reader, would represent the voice of a contemporary Coan speaking the mild Doric found in the inscriptions of his island home.

Although in the second couplet the Muse politely responds in Doric to the specific question asked in Doric, for a fuller description of the garland of over forty epigrammatists she switches to Attic, though with a significant admixture of epic, Ionic, and occasional Doric forms. At the end of the proem, she names the anthology a "common" garland of the Muses, and here the plural form Μουσέων with its epic-Ionic ending stands for the poetry of the various epigrammatists while the word "common" (κοινός) at least hints at a core form of

---

[18] For this now well-accepted view for the presence of Doric (more precisely, non-Attic-Ionic) ᾱ in tragic song and at times in early epigrams, see Buck 1923, 134–36. Mickey 1981, 44–45 cites Doric ᾱ's in words referring to deities in Attic inscriptions of the sixth and early fifth centuries, and points out that this vocalism "had a high-style solemnity" that was "particularly appropriate for references to deities" (44).

[19] Bubeník 1989, 97–98 charts the ratio of Doric to koine forms in Coan inscriptions of the Hellenistic period. For a survey of Cos' literary history, see Sherwin-White 1978, 15–19.

Greek underlying all their linguistic differences. I believe that the marked dialectal forms within her catalog were intended to fit the literary associations of the poet being described. Some are epic forms that celebrate the heroic status of certain authors, such as the "golden bough of always divine Plato" (χρύσειον ἀεὶ θείοιο Πλάτωνος | κλῶνα, 47–48), where χρύσειον is the epic form and θείοιο has an old epic ending. In other instances, use of Ionic or Doric highlights the linguistic associations of a poet's place of origin and/or literary tradition. Doric appears in connection only with two poets. Hermodorus, of unknown origin, is called "Syrian spikenard" (Συρίαν ... νάρδον, 4), where Συρίαν is probably to be read as Doric rather than Attic because of the unmistakably Doric ὑμνοθέταν (46) that follows in apposition.[20] The other poet associated with Doric is the Syracusan Theodoridas (53–54). His plant is ἕρπυλλον, "tufted thyme," which receives the Doric form of the article τάν, occurring only here in the proem. The Ionic η in φιλάκρητον and the Ionic genitive ending in Θεοδωρίδεω produce a mixed dialectal coloring for the couplet, but the Doric τάν at the line beginning provides the more deliberate dialectal choice. Like other literary epigrammatists, Meleager uses only the Ionic form of ἄκρητος, and neither the Doric or Attic genitive of the patronymic would fit the meter. While Theodoridas' anthologized epigrams are partly in Doric and partly in Attic-Ionic, Meleager apparently intends to honor his Syracusan origin with the Doric form of the article.

Grouped together in a single couplet (45–46) are Posidippus, Hedylus, and Asclepiades, the important trio of third-century practitioners of erotic-sympotic poetry in the Ionic tradition of Anacreon. The first two are called "wild flowers of the field" (ἄγρι' ἀρούρης) where η after ρ marks the noun as Ionic. Despite his origin in Macedonian Pella, the cosmopolitan Posidippus composed his erotic epigrams with an Ionic flavor, as did Hedylus who is said to have been from Samos or Athens (Ath. 7.297 A).[21] Asclepiades, who is identified with anemones, is referred to as Sicelides, as he is in Hedylus 6.4 *HE* (= Ath. 11.473 A). He receives the same patronymic in Theocritus' *Idyll* 7, where the Doric accusative ending in -ίδαν (40) fits the word's reference to Sicily.[22] Meleager, like Hedylus before him, uses the Ionic genitive Σικελίδεω, which perhaps acknowledges both Asclepiades' origin from Ionic-speaking Samos and his poetic preservation of the Ionic dialectal tradition.

---

20 Accenting the form as the accusative singular is the simpler choice, though the genitive plural in -ᾶν, as in 2, remains a possibility ("the Syrian spikenard among poets").
21 See Gow-Page 1965, 2.289.
22 Sens 2011, xxxi discusses the possibility that Asclepiades lived with his family on Sicily during the Samian exile.

Specifically Ionic forms also appear with reference to both Antipater and Meleager, who are connected through their residency in Phoenicia. Antipater is called a Sidonian in the lemmata, though Meleager acclaimed him a native of Tyre (AP 7.428.13–14 = 122.13–14 HE). His plant is henna (κύπρον), which is labeled both φοίνισσαν (the poetic and common koine form of the adjective), meaning ambiguously "red" or "Phoenician," and, with Ionic ending, νέην, "new," apparently to indicate the recentness of his epigrams (42). Similar dialectal treatment is afforded the anthologist, who was born in Syrian Gadara and lived as a young man in Tyre. When the *Garland*'s Muse identifies Meleager's white violets as those belonging to "his own Muse" (Μούσης ... σφετέρης, 55–56), she uses a Ionic ending for the possessive adjective, which here has a specialized epic/poetic reference to the singular ("his own"). Although the inscriptional evidence from Sidon and Tyre is thin for the Hellenistic period, it is generally consistent with the accepted view that the standard Greek used there was the ionicized Attic introduced by the Macedonians after Alexander's conquest.[23] Although the dialect mixture in the proem is complex, it is far from random, since Doric dominates the conversation in the first two couplets and Ionic-Attic with an admixture of meaningful epic, Doric, and Ionic forms prevails in the list of epigrammatists. The proem surely sets a template for the use of dialect in Meleager's own epigrams as in the epigrams of the other anthologized poets, where a dialectal mixture occurs within epigrams and sequentially from one epigram to the next.

My supposition that the Doric at the opening of the proem reflects the dialect of the reading community at the time and place the *Garland* was produced, that is, the island of Cos circa 100 B.C., can be strengthened by examining where Doric forms tend to cluster in other Meleager epigrams. A distinctive Doric coloring is found in three types of epigrams—poems likely composed with the assembly of the *Garland* in mind, epitaphs for Meleager himself or for his acquaintances (likely written during his later period), and epigrams that mention Cos. In Table 1, Meleager's epigrams are grouped into the categories of *erotica* (by far the largest), *anathematica*, *epitaphica*, and those called *epideictica* for lack of a better name. The smaller groups of dedications and epitaphs come from Books 6 and 7 of the Palatine Anthology and the epideictic poems from Book 9 or Planudes (*AP* 16), while the larger group of erotic poems was divided by the Byzantine editor Cephalas into the heterosexual Book 5 and the pederastic

---

[23] On the development of Hellenistic koine as a shared form of communication among Greek immigrants to the East, see Bubeník 1989, 55–56; Horrocks 2010, 80. The inscriptions from Tyre are published by Rey-Coquais 2006; verse inscriptions from Sidon are collected in Merkelbach-Stauber 1998–2004.

Table 1: Epigrams by Meleager grouped in the approximate order of their occurrence in the books of the Greek Anthology (by *AP* numbers), with dialect designation.
A-I = Attic-Ionic, D = Doric, d = minor Doric.

Proem 1. 4.1	D, A-I	Proem 1. 4.1	D, A-I
erotica		39. 12.41	A-I
2. 12.49	D	40. 12.47	A-I/d
3. 5.136	D (Heliodora)	41. 12.48	A-I
4. 5.137	D (Heliodora)	**42. 12.23**	**A-I/d (Myiscus)**
5. 5.139	D (Zenophila)	**43. 12.101**	**A-I/d (Myiscus)**
6. 5.140	A-I (Zenophila)	**44. 12.106**	**A-I (Myiscus)**
7. 5.141	D (Heliodora)	45. 5.151	A-I (Zenophila)
8. 5.143	A-I (Heliodora)	46. 5.152	A-I (Zenophila)
9. 5.144	D (Zenophila)	**47. 12.109**	**A-I**
10. 5.147	A-I (Heliodora)	**48. 12.110**	**A-I (Myiscus)**
11. 5.148	D (Heliodora)	49. 5.154	A-I
12. 5.149	D (Zenophila)	50. 5.155	A-I (Heliodora)
		51. 5.156	A-I
13. 12.52	D	52. 5.157	A-I/d (Heliodora)
14. 12.53	D (Phanion)	**53. 12.113**	**A-I/d**
		54. 12.114	A-I
15. 12.54	A-I	**55. 5.96**	**A-I**
16. 12.56	A-I/d	56. 5.57	A-I
17. 12.57	A-I/d	57. 5.160	A-I/d
18. 12.59	**A-I (Myiscus)**	58. 5.163	A-I (Heliodora)
19. 12.60	**A-I**	59. 5.165	A-I (Heliodora)
20. 12.63	**A-I**	60. 5.166	A-I (Heliodora)
21. 12.65	**A-I (Myiscus)**	61. 12.117	A-I
22. 12.68	A-I	62. 12.119	D (Dionysus)
23. 12.70	**A-I (Myiscus)**	63. 12.122	A-I
24. 12.72	A-I	64. 12.125	A-I
25. 12.74	A-I	65. 12.126	A-I/d
26. 12.76	A-I/d	66. 12.127	A-I/d
27. 12.78	A-I/d	**67. 12.128**	**A-I**
28. 12.80	A-I	68. 12.132	A-I
29. 12.81	A-I/d	69. 12.133	A-I/d
30. 12.82	A-I	70. 5.171	D (Zenophila)
31. 12.83	A-I/d	71. 5.172	A-I/d
32. 12.84	A-I	72. 5.173	A-I/d
33. 12.85	A-I	73. 12.137	D
34. 12.86	D (Aphrodite/Eros)	74. 5.174	A-I (Zenophila)
35. 12.92	A-I	**75. 12.141**	**A-I**
36. 12.94	**A-I (Myiscus)**	**76. 12.144**	**A-I (Myiscus)**
37. 12.95	**A-I**	77. 12.147	A-I/d (Heliodora)
38. 12.33	A-I	78. 5.175	A-I

Proem		Proem	
1. 4.1	D, A-I	1. 4.1	D, A-I
79. 12.154	A-I (Myiscus)	107. 12.256	A-I (Myiscus and others)
80. 5.176	A-I		
81. 5.177	A-I/d (Zenophila)	*anathematica*	
82. 5.178	A-I (Zenophila)	108. 6.162	A-I
83. 5.179	A-I	109. 6.163	A-I
84. 5.180	D		
85. 5.182	A-I	*epitaphica*	
86. 5.184	A-I	110. 7.79	I, A (Heraclitus)
87. 5.187	A-I	111. 7.182	D (Cleariste)
88. 12.157	A-I	112. 7.207	A-I/d (Phanion's hare)
89. 12.158	A-I/d	113. 7.417	D (Meleager on self)
90. 12.159	A-I (Myiscus)	114. 7.418	D (Meleager on self)
91. 5.190	A-I	115. 7.419	A-I (Meleager on self)
92. 5.191	A-I	116. 7.421	A-I, D (Meleager on self)
93. 5.192	A-I	117. 7.428	D (Antipater of Sidon)
94. 5.195	D (Zenophila)	118. 7.461	A-I
95. 5.196	A-I	119. 7.476	D (Heliodora)
96. 9.16	A-I	120. 7.195	A-I/d
97. 5.197	A-I	121. 7.196	A-I/d
98. 5.198	A-I	122. 7.535	A-I
99. 5.204	A-I		
100. 5.208	A-I, D	*epideictica*	
101. 12.164	A-I	123. 9.331	A-I
102. 12.165	A-I	124. 16.134	D
103. 5.212	A-I		
104. 12.167	A-I (Myiscus)	*finis*	
		125. 12.257	D (coronis)
105. 5.214	D (Heliodora)		
106. 5.215	D (Heliodora)		

Book 12. We can reconstruct in a general way much of the original sequence of epigrams in Meleager's *erotica*, because Cephalas kept the majority of the epigrams in their thematically arranged *Garland* order. My ordering matches poems from Books 5 and 12 in an approximation of the original arrangement.[24] Epigrams with a Doric coloring are labeled D, and those in Attic koine with the inclusion of some specific Ionic forms are labeled A-I, while the addition of /d indicates only a minor Doric presence, often as little as a single word. These cat-

---

24 Details can be found in Gutzwiller 1998, 277–322.

egories are of course without computational rigor, since it is not possible to quantify for every poem the amount of dialect that determines categorization nor to compensate for errors in transmission that undoubtedly exist in some epigrams. Nevertheless, I believe that general patterns can be reliably observed.

Among the other epigrams composed for the assembled *Garland*, the most obvious is *AP* 12.257 = 129 *HE* (no. 125):

> ἁ πύματον καμπτῆρα καταγγέλλουσα κορωνίς,
>   οἰκουρὸς γραπταῖς πιστοτάτα σελίσιν,
> φαμὶ τὸν ἐκ πάντων ἠθροισμένον εἰς ἕνα μόχθον
>   ὑμνοθετᾶν βύβλῳ τᾷδ' ἐνελιξάμενον
> ἐκτελέσαι Μελέαγρον, ἀείμνηστον δὲ Διοκλεῖ
>   ἄνθεσι συμπλέξαι μουσοπόλον στέφανον.
> οὖλα δ' ἐγὼ καμφθεῖσα δρακοντείοις ἴσα νώτοις,
>   σύνθρονος ἵδρυμαι τέρμασιν εὐμαθίας.
> 4 ὑμνοθέταν P

> I, the *coronis* who announce the final turn, a most trustworthy guardian of the written page, I certify that the one who rolled up in this papyrus the effort of all poets gathered into one, Meleager, has completed his task and that he has plaited from flowers a Muse-tending garland, always to be remembered, for Diocles. Curled up tightly like the coil of a snake's back, I sit enthroned at the finish line of his great learning.

Here the *Garland*'s *coronis*, a mark of punctuation used to signal the end of a literary work, speaks with Doric intonation to declare that Meleager has reached the finish line of his labor. The Doric dialect is highlighted by the initial article ἁ and continues in the second couplet with the long α's in φαμὶ, τᾷδ', and ὑμνοθετᾶν, undoubtedly here to be accented as Doric genitive plural. This last, a rare synonym for ποιητής appearing in the *Garland* in the opening and closing poems (also in 7.428.16), seems to be for Meleager a signature designator of Doric, perhaps suggesting that Doric has a special poetic quality. Given the metaphor of athletic achievement in reference to the "final turn," the Doric forms may also remind the reader of lyric epinician. At the same time, the parallel in the second and third couplets to the opening two couplets of the proem associate this final use of Doric with Meleager's first use of Doric.

Other Doric colored-epigrams cluster in the opening and closing sequences of the erotic section, which are also places where we are likely to find poems composed or edited for their *Garland* position. It is significant that eight of the eleven poems in the opening sequence of *erotica*, my nos. 2–12 in Table 1, a group connected programmatically by the themes of wine, song, and garlands,[25]

---

[25] Gutzwiller 1997, 172–88; cf. Höschele 2009a, 104–20 and similarly in German 2010, 197–213.

and the last two Meleager epigrams in the *erotica*, nos. 105 and 106, are Doric-colored. All these epigrams, apart from the first, feature Meleager's two favorite female loves, Heliodora and Zenophila. Although some epigrams for Heliodora and Zenophila are in Attic-Ionic, the dominance of Doric epigrams at the beginning and end of the *erotica* strongly suggests that at least these poems were composed or edited in association with the *Garland*'s assemblage on Cos. Also significant is the heavy presence of Doric in Meleager's epitaph for Heliodora (*AP* 7.476 = 56 *HE*), in his epitaph for his anthologized compatriot Antipater (*AP* 7.428 = 122 *HE*), who was alive ca. 100 B.C., and to a lesser extent but prominently in three of his four self-epitaphs (AP 7.417–18, 421 = 2–3, 5 *HE*). These were quite likely composed in later life when Meleager was living on Cos.

To give a taste of these Doric-colored epigrams, I include one on Heliodora and one on Zenophila from the introductory sequence and another on Heliodora from the end:

AP 5.137 = 43 *HE* (no. 4)
ἔγχει τᾶς Πειθοῦς καὶ Κύπριδος Ἡλιοδώρας
  καὶ πάλι τᾶς αὐτᾶς ἁδυλόγου Χάριτος.
αὐτὰ γάρ μί' ἐμοὶ γράφεται θεός· ἇς τὸ ποθεινὸν
  οὔνομ' ἐν ἀκρήτῳ συγκεράσας πίομαι.

Pour a cup for Persuasion and Cypris, both Heliodora, and again for the same girl, a sweet-speaking Grace. For I consider her to be a single goddess, whose beloved name I will drink, mixed in unmixed wine.

AP 5.139 = 29 *HE* (no. 5)
ἁδὺ μέλος, ναὶ Πᾶνα τὸν Ἀρκάδα, πηκτίδι μέλπεις,
  Ζηνοφίλα †λιγίαν† · ἁδὺ κρέκεις τι μέλος.
ποῖ σε φύγω; πάντη με περιστείχουσιν Ἔρωτες,
  οὐδ', ὅσον ἀμπνεῦσαι, βαιὸν ἐῶσι χρόνον.
ἢ γάρ μοι μορφὰ βάλλει πόθον ἢ πάλι μοῦσα
  ἢ χάρις ἢ – τί λέγω; πάντα· πυρὶ φλέγομαι.
1 ἁδὺ P,*Suda*: ἡδὺ Pl 2 λιγίαν P: ναὶ Πᾶν' Graefe 5 μορφᾷ P: -ἢ Pl

Sweet is the song, by Arcadian Pan, you sing to the harp, Zenophila, ...; sweet is the song you pluck. How am I to flee you? Everywhere Erotes revolve around me, and do not allow me a little time just to breathe. For it's your beauty that arouses my desire, or maybe your music, or your charm, or—What am I to say? It's all of you. I'm on fire.

AP 5.214 = 53 *HE* (no. 105)
σφαιριστὰν τὸν Ἔρωτα τρέφω· σοὶ δ', Ἡλιοδώρα,
  βάλλει τὰν ἐν ἐμοὶ παλλομένην κραδίην.
ἀλλ' ἄγε συμπαίκταν δέξαι Πόθον· εἰ δ' ἀπὸ σεῦ με
  ῥίψαις, οὐκ οἴσω τὰν ἀπάλαιστρον ὕβριν.
2 παλλομένην κραδίην P: –ναν ... ίαν C

I nurture Eros as ballplayer. To you, Heliodora, he tosses the quivering heart within me. Come now, accept Desire as your playmate. If you cast me aside, I won't put up with your unsportsmanlike arrogance.

In 5.137 the pronouns and adjectives referring to Heliodora or the goddesses with which she is identified all have Doric ᾱ's, while the name Heliodora is ambiguously Attic or Doric but would most naturally be read as Doric in the context. Interestingly, the adjective ἀκρήτῳ, as always in Meleager, is in the Ionic form with η. Is this consistency of form just a remembrance of Homer's use of the word, or does it point to a metapoetic play on the mixing of the name Heliodora into "unmixed" wine, standing for the purer Ionic tradition of the erotic/sympotic poetry practiced by Anacreon and Asclepiades?[26] In 5.139 Zenophila, whose name is unambiguously Doric, is associated, as a singer and a harp player, with a bucolic ambiance through the echo, in the repeated ἁδὺ ... ἁδὺ, of the opening of *Idyll* 1 and in the Doric form μορφά in line 5. In 5.214, from the close of the *Garland*'s *erotica*, Meleager reworks a famous Anacreon poem (358 *PMG*) in which Eros strikes the poet with a purple ball, inviting him to play with a girl from Lesbos. In direct contrast to the Ionic in his Anacreontic model, Meleager gives his epigram Doric coloring, marked by four terminations in -αν supplemented by σεῦ. The Ionic endings in the phrase παλλομένην κραδίην (modified by the Doric article τάν) are changed to Doric by the Palatine corrector. Nevertheless, the epic-Ionic forms should be preserved, being an allusion to *Iliad* 22.461, where Andromache, fearing Hector's death, rushes forth "quivering in her heart" (παλλομένη κραδίην).[27]

Some Doric coloring also appears in two epigrams, *AP* 12.52–53, which occur in a transitional section between the programmatic opening sequence of the *erotica* and the larger body of epigrams beginning with pederastic poems:

AP 12.52 = 81 *HE* (no. 13)
οὔριος ἐμπνεύσας ναύταις Νότος, ὦ δυσέρωτες,
  ἥμισύ μευ ψυχᾶς ἅρπασεν Ἀνδράγαθον.
τρὶς μάκαρες νᾶες, τρὶς δ' ὄλβια κύματα πόντου,
  τετράκι δ' εὐδαίμων παιδοφορῶν ἄνεμος·
εἴθ' εἴην δελφίς, ἵν' ἐμοῖς βαστακτὸς ἐπ' ὤμοις
  πορθμευθεὶς ἐσίδῃ τὰν γλυκύπαιδα Ῥόδον.
2 ψυχᾶς apogr.: ψυχὰς P 4 παιδοφορῶν apogr.: παιδοφόρων P

---

[26] For the thematic use of mixing imagery in Meleager, Höschele 2010, 184–87.
[27] The phrase, in the Homeric form with accusative of respect, repeats only once in extant Greek before Meleager, in Mosch. *Eur.* 17.

Blowing favorably for sailors, the South Wind, unhappy lovers, has carried off Andragathus, half of my soul. Thrice blest are ships, three times happy are the sea's waves, and four times fortunate the wind that carries a boy. If only I were a dolphin so that he might be borne on my shoulders, conveyed within sight of Rhodes with its sweet boys.

AP 12.53 = 66 HE (no. 14)
εὔφορτοι νᾶες πελαγίτιδες, αἳ πόρον Ἕλλης
  πλεῖτε καλὸν κόλποις δεξάμεναι Βορέην,
ἤν που ἐπ' ἠιόνων Κῴαν κατὰ νᾶσον ἴδητε
  Φάνιον εἰς χαροπὸν δερκομέναν πέλαγος,
τοῦτ' ἔπος ἀγγείλαιτε, καλαί· νόει ὥς με κομίζει
  ἵμερος οὐ ναύταν, ποσσὶ δὲ παιζοπόρον·
εἰ γὰρ τοῦτ' εἴποιτ' εὐάγγελοι, αὐτίκα καὶ Ζεὺς
  οὔριος ὑμετέρας πνεύσεται εἰς ὀθόνας.

5 ἀγγείλαιτε Scaliger, ἀγγείλατε P καλαί· νόει ὡς conieci: καλη· νοες ως P: καλαὶ νέες, ὥς Meineke 6 παιζοπόρον P: πεζ- Scaliger 7 εὐάγγελοι Piccolos: εὐ**τελοι P

Well-laden seaworthy ships, you that have taken fair Boreas into your sails/bosoms and sail the strait of Helle, if you should see somewhere on the shores of the Coan island Phanion gazing out at the bright blue sea, announce this, lovely ones: Know that desire conveys me, not as a sailor, but bringing boys by foot. For if you speak so, bringing good tidings, straightway Zeus too will breathe into your sails with favor.

These poems share a theme of travel toward one of the two main Doric islands of the Aegean—Rhodes and Cos—and are linked as a pair by framing verbal echoes. In *AP* 12.52 the lover complains that the South Wind has snatched away his boy love and wishes that he were a dolphin in order to convey Andragathus to Rhodes. Doric forms (μευ, ψυχᾶς, ἅρπασεν, νᾶες, τάν) include the article that modifies Rhodes, which was the epicenter for the development of the Doric koine used in official documents and inscriptions in the central Aegean.[28] In the second poem (*AP* 12.53), the speaker asks ships sailing south from the Bosporus under the force of Boreas, which is given an Ionic ending as the wind coming from the Ionic Hellespont (Βορέην), to carry a message of his overland route to Phanion, who watches for him on the shore of the Coan island, Κῴαν ... νᾶσον, a phrase with the Doric form of the noun modified by an adjective with an uncertain Doric or Attic ending. Meleager perhaps composed both of these epigrams during a period of relocation from the East into the Aegean region, and Phanion in another epigram mainly in Attic-Ionic (*AP* 7.207 = 65 *HE*) receives a Doric article (ἁ ... Φάνιον, 3–4),[29] supporting the possibility that she was Coan. In the

---

[28] Horrocks 2010: 87. Bubeník 1989: 94–95 points out that Doric koine was the norm in Rhodian inscriptions into the first century B.C.
[29] In the Palatine and in Planudes after correction.

context of his collection, however, these two poems separate the initial sequence on Heliodora and Zenophila, with its Doric poems, from the main body of erotic epigrams where Attic-Ionic dominates (see Table 1). Since it is in not possible to travel to Cos by foot, it seems significant that the manuscript in 12.53.6, where Scaliger's redundant πεζοπόρον is usually printed, reads παιζοπόρον (echoing παιδοφορῶν in 12.52.4), to mean "desire conveys me, not as a sailor, but bringing boys by foot." The manuscript reading makes sense if it is taken metapoetically (ποσσί = verses) as a reference to pederastic epigrams that the poet is bringing to Cos, namely those in the next section of the *erotica*.

It is surely significant that in the long run of the *erotica* between the opening and closing sequences (nos. 15–104)—the great majority of poems—are, with only a few exceptions, in Attic-Ionic, either purely so or with a minor Doric presence.[30] Practically all the pederastic poems occur here, and a fair number can be shown to have a Tyrian association. The evidence comes from *AP* 12.256 = 78 *HE* (no. 107), which occupied an unknown *Garland* position; it contains a list of seven boys who participate in a ritual for Aphrodite in her sacred grove at Tyre, including Meleager's first love Myiscus, who is singled out for special praise as the last in the list. If we seek out the other epigrams that mention Myiscus, which are twelve, and the additional epigrams that mention the other boys listed in 12.256, which are seven, and the additional epigrams that mention a person associated with one of these boys, which are three, then we have a total of 23 poems (including 12.256) that can be reasonably situated at Tyre.[31] They are marked in bold in Table 1. This relatively certain placement of approximately a quarter of Meleager's Attic-Ionic epigrams at Tyre provides a strong indication that the great majority of the epigrams in this central section of the *erotica* come from Meleager's Tyrian period. Dialect in literary epigram, imitating the mixture of koine and local dialect often found in Hellenistic inscriptions, surely does at times offer a clue to the geographical setting of the poem and perhaps even to the specific audience for which it was composed.

---

30 I categorize only six of this group of one hundred epigrams as strongly Doric-colored. In each of these, the Doric is explained by the subject matter, since three concern deities (nos. 34, 62, 84), one is in mock hymnal style (no. 73), and two concern Zenophila (nos. 70, 94). I categorize a seventh epigram (5.208 = no. 100) as Attic-Ionic with a significant Doric admixture (A-I, D) because there Meleager imitates in Doric a saying of Epicharmus (quoted in Pl. *Ax.* 366c).
31 Myiscus is mentioned in *AP* 12.23, 12.59, 12.65, 12.70, 12.94, 12.101, 12.106, 12.110, 12.144, 12.154, 12.159, and 12.167, as well as 12.256. The other boys in 12.256 are mentioned in *AP* 12.41, 12.60, 12.63, 12.95, 12.109, 12.128, 12.141 (as well as in 12.94 counted in the Myiscus list). Timarion, who is associated with the boy Diodorus from 12.256, appears also in *AP* 5.96, 5.204, and 12.113. See Gutzwiller 2013, 51–53.

Meleager's fewer epigrams preserved in other books of the *AP* show similar reasons for dialect use. As pointed out above, the partial use of Doric in his self-epitaphs (*AP* 7.417–19, 421) and the more intensive use in the epitaph for Antipater of Sidon (*AP* 7.428) and in that for Heliodora (*AP* 7.476) likely reflect composition in a Coan environment. There may, however, be other, or additional, reasons for the dialect choice. If Heliodora's name, like Zenophila's, points to a Doric homeland, then the dialect may honor her heritage (perhaps Cos); at the same time, the form given the epigram as a first-person lament blends epitaphic purpose with the tradition of Doric lyric song. In his playful epitaph for Antipater, Meleager imitates Antipater's own enigmatic epitaphs and chooses to imitate as well the Doric dialect that dominates in the two that immediately precede his own epitaph for that poet (*AP* 7.426–27 = 31–32 *HE*). Likewise, Meleager's epigram on Niobe (*AP* 16.134 = 128 *HE*) is heavily doricized as are the two earlier epigrams on the same subject, although Niobe herself has no connection with Doric areas. The earliest, by Theodoridas of Syracuse, (*AP* 16.132 = 18 *HE*) was composed in the poet's native dialect, and that dialect was preserved in the apparent imitation by Antipater of Sidon (*AP* 16.133) and then in Meleager's imitation of his two predecessors.[32] The heavy use of Doric in Meleager's epigram on a bride who died on her wedding night (*AP* 7.182 = 123 *HE*) may reflect the local dialect in her place of burial or, particularly since the poem reads more like a pathetic narrative of her death rather than an epitaph, some literary tradition of lament, even perhaps a direct reminiscence of Erinna's *Distaff* and her epitaphs for Baucis who died shortly after marriage (*AP* 7.710, 712 = 1–2 *HE*).[33] None of this gives adequate reason, however, to change her name from the Attic-Ionic Κλεαρίστη, found in both the Palatine and Planudes, to the Doric form, as editors have typically done. Inscribed epitaphs, which offer the generic model for the Cleariste epigram, often preserve the original dialectal form of a deceased person's name in contrast to the principal coloring of the inscription.[34]

---

[32] See Gutzwiller 2002, 107–9, with an argument for the Sidonian's authorship (esp. n. 32); in agreement on the authorship is Argentieri 2003, 153–54.
[33] The *Distaff* is in Doric with admixture of Aeolic forms (apparently with allusion to Sappho), and the epitaphs are heavily Doric-flavored.
[34] Morpurgo Davies 2000, 27 provides an instructive example of name consistency despite dialect mixture produced by developments within late Hellenistic koines. An Arcadian inscription dated to the end of first century B.C. or the early first century A.D honoring one Ἐπιγόνη (*IG* V (2) 268) starts in Doric koine with ᾱ's for η's and concludes in formal Attic. The name of the celebrant, however, never varies from its Attic-Ionic form. Similarly, Sens 2004, 73 points out that the name of the deceased in Posidippus 47 Austin-Bastianini (Ὀνασαγορᾶτιν) is the only Doric form in the epitaph.

Meleager's most striking use of the Ionic dialect occurs in his epitaph for the philosopher Heraclitus of Ephesus (*AP* 7.79 = 121 *HE*):

ὤνθρωπ', Ἡράκλειτος ἐγὼ σοφὰ **μοῦνος** ἀνευρών.
  – φαμί. τὰ δ' ἐς πάτραν **κρέσσονα** καὶ σοφ**ίης**·
λὰξ γὰρ καὶ **τοκέωνας**–. –ἰὼ ξένε, δύσφρονας ἄνδρας
  ὑλάκτευν. —λαμπρὰ θρεψαμένοισι χάρις.
– οὐκ ἀπ' ἐμεῦ; —μὴ **τρηχύς**, ἐπεὶ τάχα καὶ σύ τι πεύσῃ
  τρηχύτερον πάτρας. χαῖρε. – σὺ δ' ἐξ Ἐφέσου.

1 ὤνθρωπ' P: ὤνθρωφ' Reiske Ἡράκλειτος scripsi: Ἡράκ- P **2** κρείσσονα P: κρέσσονα C (ει scripto supra) **3** τοκέωνας, ἰὼ Headlam: τοκέων ἀσίωι P **5** ἀπ' ἐμεῦ C: ἀτομεῦ P καὶ apogr.: μαι P

Good man, I am Heraclitus who discovered wise precepts all by myself.
  —I agree, but one's community is greater than even wisdom,
Since kicking your own parents—.—Hey stranger, it was foolish men
  I used to bark at. —Your gratitude to your nurturers is clear.
—Get away from me.—Don't be rough, or perhaps you'll learn something
  rougher than your fatherland did. Bye now.—So *you*'re from Ephesus.

Contrary to Page's assertion that the poem's dialect is "more thoroughly mixed than usual,"[35] this epitaph for a famous Ionian philosopher, as transmitted in the Palatine Codex, presents a marked—and meaningful—number of Ionic forms: ὤνθρωπ', Ἡράκλειτος, μοῦνος, ἐς, κρέσσονα,[36] σοφίης, τοκέωνας, ὑλάκτευν,[37] ἐμεῦ, τρηχύς, τρηχύτερον. The proper division of speech between the dead philosopher and his interlocutor has proved a difficulty for interpreters of the poem,[38] and I suggest that the variance between Ionic and non-Ionic forms aids the reader's reconstruction of the exchange between the two.

In the opening words the deceased philosopher addresses a passerby to give, in epitaphic form, his name and the reason for his fame. Jacobs pointed out long ago that in P's ὤνθρωπ' (1) reflects the psilosis of old East Ionic, as befits Heraclitus' speech.[39] Although most editors have rejected Jacobs' observation and print Attic ὤνθρωφ', it strains credulity that the scribe would either intentionally emend to old Ionic or make a mistake that accidentally results in the cor-

---

35 Gow-Page 1965, 2.672
36 κρέσσων, though found in some other dialects, should here be considered Ionic; epic and old Attic have κρείσσων, later Attic κρείττων, and Doric κάρρων.
37 P's scribe first wrote the infinitive ὑλακτεῖν and then self-corrected to the Ionic imperfect, which was surely the form in the archetype.
38 The division of speakers has been clarified by West 1967, with additional improvements by Lloyd-Jones 1968, though neither notes the dialect variance.
39 Jacobs 1794–1814, 12.384–85.

rect dialectal form.⁴⁰ In my view, it is only reasonable to accept the Ionic form of the vocative and correct what must then be an error, by printing the following name in its proper old Ionic form Ἡράκλειτος. The passerby replies, accepting Heraclitus' claim to fame as a philosopher but criticizing his neglect of political affairs and accusing him of attacking his parents. As transmitted, the passerby's first speech begins with non-Ionic (φαμί, πάτραν) before slipping into Ionic (κρέσσονα, σοφίης, τοκέωνας). The result of the mixture is to obscure his city of origin. Just as Heraclitus' refusal to participate in the governing of Ephesus had become a standard part of his biography,⁴¹ so too the accusation of parental abuse seems to descend from the Ionian tradition of iambic verse. In Leonidas' epitaph for Hipponax of Ephesus (*AP* 7.408.3 = 58.3 *HE*), anthologized in Meleager's *Garland*, the iambic poet was said to have 'barked even at his parents' (ὁ καὶ τοκέωνε βαΰξας, 7.408.3 = 58.3 *HE*). Headlam has shown that the corrupt text of the Hipponax epitaph actually preserves the correct form of the rare old Ionic word τοκέων with its proper accent and that the same word similarly accented (though obscured by the scribe's word division) appears also in Meleager's epitaph for Heraclitus.⁴² Meleager has clearly adapted the old Ionic form of the word from Leonidas' poem, making it the impetus for Heraclitus' defensive reaction to the passerby's accusation. Without a clear denial of criticizing his parents, he admits only to "barking at foolish men," with replacement of the verb βαΰξας from the Hipponax epitaph with the synonym ὑλάκτευν (with an Ionic ending). The synonym makes reference to Theodoridas' epitaph for Heraclitus (*AP* 7.479 = 16 *HE*), where the philosopher is called θεῖον ὑλακτητὴν δήμου ... κύνα (6), "divine dog who once barked at the people." This is the criticism that Heraclitus expects and takes pride in.

The passerby then remarks ironically (note the epic ending on θρεψαμένοισι), "your gratitude to your nurturers is clear."⁴³ The non-Ionic and presumably Attic form λαμπρά could be translated either "splendid" (with irony) or "clear" (sarcastically), with a play on Heraclitus' famed obscure manner

---

40 The corrector in P made no attempt to change the form.
41 When the Ephesians asked Heraclitus to be their lawmaker, he refused on the basis of their defective constitution and went off to play knucklebones with children, saying that "it is better to do this than to engage in civil life with you" (κρεῖττον τοῦτο ποιεῖν ἢ μεθ' ὑμῶν πολιτεύεσθαι, Diog. Laert. 9.3; cf. Lucian *Vit. auct.* 14). Meleager's first pentameter seems a version of Diogenes' quotation, and the passerby's attempted accusation of parental abuse may be derived from Heraclitus' (philosophically motivated) preference for the company of boys over the serving in government with their fathers.
42 Headlam 1901.
43 The epic ending on θρεψαμένοισι heightens the mocking tone.

of expression.⁴⁴ The disgruntled philosopher then tells his hostile interlocutor to leave, again in Ionic (ἐμεῦ), and the second voice now replies with Ionic vowel tones, giving τρηχύς and τρηχύτερον harsh η's to enhance the meaning though the sound. Only then does Heraclitus realize that his supposedly "foreign" interlocutor (Attic ξένε, 3) must be from Ephesus, one of those δύσφρονας ἄνδρας he despised and abused. The ending of the poem thus plays on the tradition of associating abusive moral criticism with Ephesus, perhaps even recalling Callimachus' resistance in *Iambus* 13 to his critic's insistence that as iambographer he should "go to Ephesus" (fr. 203.12, 64). Meleager's use of Ionic in this epigram not only supports the characterization he gives the famed philosopher but also provides clues to the division of speech and the proper understanding of the poem.

As a complement to Sens's work on dialect in the third-century epigrams of Posidippus and Asclepiades, this survey of dialect in Meleager offers a case study of the use of dialect in the later Hellenistic age. The need remains for a more systematic overview of dialect in the literary epigrammatists, a task that requires careful attention to manuscript and papyrological sources and correlation with the inscriptional evidence. Even before such a thorough study, it is clear that dialect choice contributes to the formation of an epigrammatist's poetic self-representation. Asclepiades' use of Ionic mimics not just his local dialect as a Samian (if that), but it also establishes his debt to the love poetry of Ionians like Mimnermus and Anacreon. Likewise, Nossis' Doric provides aural realism for her female community in Epizephyrian Locri, and ultimately distinguishes her voice from that of her admired Sappho (*AP* 7.718 = 11 *HE*). Leonidas of Tarentum, a wandering poet, offers a more complex picture. He writes in strong Doric for Cretans (*AP* 6.289 = 42 *HE*, 7.448–49 = 12–13 *HE*) and strong Ionic for a Samian buried on Paros (*AP* 7.163 = 70 *HE*), but when speaking in his own voice (*AP* 6.300, 302 = 36–37 *HE*), he avoids his native Doric. In his self-epitaph for a burial far from his homeland (*AP* 7.715 = 93 *HE*), it is the Ionic ending in the opening phrase πολλὸν ἀπ' Ἰταλίης, "far from Italy," that poignantly emphasizes his separation from Tarentum, to be made permanent by death. As the anthologizer of these many dialectal voices, Meleager authenticates through dialect his own poetic self-representation. In his autobiographical epitaphs, he is presented as an Attic-speaking Syrian, who writes Attic-Ionic love poetry while resident in polyglot Tyre and who comes to live his later years as a

---

44 Called a "riddler" by Timon (αἰνικτής, 817.2 *SH*), Heraclitus was nicknamed "dark" (σκοτεινός, Strab.14.1.25). The play on λαμπρά is evident from anon. *AP* 9.540, where his writings are said to be "darkness without light" (σκότος ... ἀλάμπετον, 3), although an interpreter may make them "brighter than the gleaming sun" (φανεροῦ λαμπρότερ' ἠελίου, 4).

citizen of Cos (where perhaps he celebrates more lasting relationships with women who have Doric, or specifically Coan, associations). On Cos he creates a magnificent garland of poets who compose in different dialects and, like Callimachus in the *Iambi*, mingle dialects, and he sets there his own *poikilia* of dialect use, framed at the start by the Doric tones of his first, imagined reader and the answering Muse of the *Garland* and at the end by the Doric-colored words of the *Garland*'s *coronis*. Whatever else this highlighting of Doric may mean, it surely celebrates the poetic heritage of the island of Cos, once the homeland of Philitas and then the residence of Theocritus, the only other poet known to have used the word ὑμνοθέτη/ας (*AP* 7.661.4 = 10 *HE*).

Alexander Sens
Narrative and Simile in Lycophron's *Alexandra*[1]

Commenting on the simile of *Iliad* 2.87–93, in which the Homeric narrator compares the mustering Greek forces to bees, the A and bT scholia point out that in describing the swarms as ἔθνεα, the poet has used a word appropriate to the Greeks themselves, since the proper word for the groups of bees would have been σμήνεα (πρὸς τοὺς εἰκαζομένους Ἕλληνας, ἐπεὶ σμήνεα ἔδει. πρώτη δὲ αὕτη παραβολὴ τῷ ποιητῇ). The scholia further observe that the bee is affiliated with the art of poetry through its toil, sweetness, and composition of the hive (συγγενὲς δὲ ποιητικῇ τὸ ζῷον διὰ τὸν μόχθον καὶ τὸ γλυκὺ καὶ τὴν σύνθεσιν τοῦ κηρίου). In the context of a discussion of the literary merits of the simile —for the scholia go on to remark on the relevance of the comparison of the soldiers to creatures armed with stings, obedient to their leaders and set on a common goal—the seemingly irrelevant remark about the relationship of bees to poetry suggests an ancient critical understanding of the simile as a potentially analogical, metatextual moment at which the poet does not merely display his artistry, but also reflects upon it.

This ancient critical understanding of similes as a lens into the poet's artistic project seems to be reflected in Hellenistic poetry.[2] This paper focuses on the relatively few similes in Lycophron's *Alexandra*, in which a messenger reports to Priam the lengthy prophecies uttered by Cassandra on the occasion of Paris' departure from Troy. The predominant mode of both the messenger's frame and Cassandra's prophecy is metaphorical and metonymical, which is to say that the human beings, gods, and objects mentioned in the poem are for the most part *identified as* rather than compared to other creatures and things,[3] and in this sense the few similes that do appear in the poem are heavily freighted.[4] Al-

---

[1] I am profoundly indebted to Charles McNelis for his many contributions to this paper, some details of which descend from our collaborative, in-progress study of the *Alexandra* as a work of literature, and are included here with his generous permission.
[2] See especially Hunter 1993b, 129–38 on Apollonius' similes. For Lycophron's engagement with Homeric scholarship, cf. Rengakos 1994.
[3] The scholia frequently treat Lycophron's metaphors as similes with the ellipsis of the comparing adverb ὡς (cf. Σ Lyc. 184c, 214, 328a, 384, 395b Leone λείπει τὸ ὡς); see p. 102 with n. 2.
[4] Similes occur at 15, 76, 121, 182, 252, 293, 387, 598, 755, 789–90 (two), 1110–11, 1375, 1427, 1429, 1430, 1432–3. This paper does not aim to discuss all of them thoroughly, though it touches on the great majority.

though the poem has usually been treated as a literary-historical curiosity, in recent years scholars have increasingly come to appreciate the ways in which it engages with and comments on the literary tradition that represents the poet's past and his character Cassandra's future.[5] The poem's similes offer a particularly clear lens through which to assess this engagement.

As a free-standing messenger's speech in which the speaker reports verbatim Cassandra's long prophecy about the Trojan War and its aftermath, the *Alexandra* sits at the boundary between epos and tragedy,[6] and its similes reflect the influence of both genres in their content and style. Homeric similes may either be long, consisting of syntactically free-standing narrative, or short comparisons of merely a few words, without a finite verb, and the scholia as well as Demetrius *On Style* (*Eloc.* 80, 89, 274) draw a terminological distinction between the former, which they call παραβολαί, and the latter, which they call εἰκόνες or εἰκασίαι: thus in their discussion of the bee-simile with which I began, the scholia note that it is the poem's first παραβολή, despite the fact that there are several shorter comparisons in the first book.[7] On the other hand, the similes of tragic dialogue and monologue, including messenger speeches, usually consist of short, grammatically interdependent phrases.[8] The *Alexandra* follows suit. Though a number of its similes engage closely at the level of content and language with longer Homeric parabolae, all of them take the form of short comparisons: none occupies more than two verses or constitutes a grammatically independent clause with a separate verbal idea. In this sense, the similes of the *Alexandra* formally resemble tragic similes and the short εἰκόνες of epic. Although most are introduced by οἷα, ὁποῖα, ὡς and ὥστε, two are marked by postpositive δίκην (596, 1375), a word that does not serve to introduce comparisons in epic but commonly does so in tragedy. In this case, at least, the interaction of form and content mirrors that of the poem's generic influences more broadly.

As is widely recognized,[9] Homeric similes compare the heroic events of the narrative to activities familiar to the contemporary audience, often involving encounters between humans and the natural word, including wild animals, which

---

5 See for example the papers in Cusset/Prioux 2009.
6 Fusillo 1984.
7 Snipes 1988, 206–8. For a survey of ancient discussions of simile and metaphor, see McCall 1969.
8 See De Jong 1991, 87–94, 193–4. The similes in Sophoclean trimeter are sometimes longer, and though those in the complete plays are all under a few lines in length, the fragments preserve several longer examples (F 149, F 659, F871); see C. Hahnemann in Ormand 2012, 177–80.
9 For an overview of Homeric similes, see Edwards 1991, 24–41.

are regularly represented either as engaging in attacks on their domestic counterparts or as the objects of the hunt.[10] A number of similes describe violent weather, including lightning, storms, and floods, that adversely affect the human world, while others feature agriculture and technology that reflect efforts by humans to control nature. Thus, as the ancient scholia and Eustathius collectively acknowledge, with respect both to the actions, creatures and objects they describe and the language and style with which they do so, the similes of the *Iliad* and *Odyssey* reflect a world distinct from and more familiar than the distant heroic universe depicted in the narrative, and thus provide not only amplification (*auxesis*) and adornment (*kosmos*), but also vividness (*enargeia*) and clarity (*sapheneia*).[11]

Lycophron's similes engage in interesting ways both with specific Homeric models, and, in several places, seem to reflect a familiarity with the ancient exegetical discussion of them.[12] As has already been observed, at an obvious level, one of the reasons that similes are infrequent in the *Alexandra* is that Cassandra's basic prophetic mode is to identify human beings metaphorically, principally by treating them as animals. In a number of cases, these metonyms have their origin in what were similes in Lycophron's models. For instance, the identification of Odysseus' men as mullets in Cassandra's account of the Laestrygonian attack rewrites the Odyssean simile describing the attack, in which the narrator compares the men to fish: 644–5 οἳ πάντα θρανύξαντες εὔτορνα σκάφη / σχοίνῳ κακὴν τρήσουσι κεστρέων ἄγρην ("an evil din arose of men dying and ships being broken up at the same time; and piercing them like fish they carried off their unpleasant catch"), cf. *Od* 10.124 ἰχθῦς δ' ὣς πείροντες. More broadly, it cannot be coincidental that the two animals with which Cassandra most often identifies Greek and Trojan heroes are wolves and lions,[13] and that these are also two frequent points of comparison in Homeric animal similes.[14] On the other hand, neither these predators nor the raptors that serve as points of com-

---

10 See Edwards 1991, 34–7.
11 Snipes 1988, 208–11, 215; Richardson 1980, 279.
12 Because the exegetical bT-scholia, though having roots in the Hellenistic period, came into their current form at a later period (cf. Schmidt 2002, 17–77), great caution is necessary in asserting the direct relationship of the views they report to individual passages of Hellenistic poetry, but where there is an identifiably close correlation of Homeric exegesis and poetic practice, the similarity is at least suggestive of an engagement with Hellenistic ideas.
13 For animal metaphors in the *Alexandra*, see Cusset 2011.
14 On lion similes, see now Alden 2005; there are four wolf similes, for which cf. Scott 1974, 71, Janko 1992, 338 (on *Il.* 16.156–63). For a convenient list of the topics covered in Homeric similes see Lee 1964, 65–73.

parison in Homeric bird similes appear in the similes of the *Alexandra*.[15] Instead, with a few notable exceptions, the animals that appear in Cassandra's similes do not have Homeric counterparts, and in some cases seem to represent pointedly humble departures from the macrofauna in the similes of the *Iliad* and *Odyssey*. Thus, for example, in his travels from Samothrace to the Troad, Dardanus is compared to a κέπφος, a bird whose name was associated with lightness and fragility.[16] Here some caution is necessary, since Homeric similes are highly variable, and occasionally compare warriors even to lowly creatures like worms (see *Il.* 13.654). But when, for instance, Cassandra compares the unparalleled underground journey of Proteus to that of an animal called the σιφνεύς (121), the very obscurity of the creature may stand as a self-referential reflection on the poetics of the *Alexandra* itself, especially in the case of a god who immigrates from Calchidice to Alexandria and whose journey along an untrod path (ἀστίβητον οἶμον) instantiates the originality that was an obvious Hellenistic esthetic desideratum.[17] At the very least, the difficulty of identifying the σιφνεύς—a creature whose identification with the mole-rat, ἀσπάλαξ, is explicitly treated as pure speculation in the lexicographical tradition[18]—stands at odds with the *sapheneia* that ancient critics thought similes contributed to the epic narratives. Beyond this, moreover, it may instantiate the poetic novelty that the untrod byway represents in the *Aetia* prologue and elsewhere.[19]

Although ancient critics recognized that the world depicted in Homeric similes stands at a distance from the heroic narrative, they also understood the boundaries between them to be permeable.[20] The phenomenon of "interaction" between simile and narrative is a common feature of much Greek poetry,[21] but is particularly striking in the *Alexandra*, since the metaphorical character of Cassandra's prophetic language effaces the distinctions between the subject matter of the simile and of its narrative context. That is, in a narrative that regularly re-

---

15 Avian similes in the *Alexandra* feature sea-birds (76 κέπφος, 387 κήρυλος, 789 καύηξ).
16 Dionys. de av. 2.10, Hsch. κ 2242 εἶδος ὀρνέου κουφοτάτου ... ὃ εὐχερῶς ὑπὸ ἀνέμου μετάγεται; Thompson 1895, 71. The bird could be used metaphorically of foolish humans, cf. Olson 1998, 273 (on Ar. *Pax* 1067).
17 The composition of poetry is commonly represented as a voyage, and the untrod path serves as a metaphor for poetic innovation at Call. fr. 1.27–8; see Massimilla 1996, 219–221 (cf. Pi. *Pae.* 7b.11–14 [fr. 52 h.11–14 S–M]).
18 *EM* p. 715.8 Kallierges σιφνεύς: σημαίνει (ὡς οἶμαι) τὸν ἀσπάλακα; cf. Sud. σ 509 σιφνεύς: ὄνομα κύριον.
19 For the relationship of the image of the path of song in the messenger's prologue to the opening of the *Aetia*, cf. Durbek 2006.
20 Cf. Σ^A *Il.* 16. 364; Σ^A *Il.* 18.219–21; Snipes 1988, 214–15.
21 See Silk 2006. For Porphyry's treatment of the phenomenon, see Richardson 1980, 280–81.

fers to humans as animals, similes that compare humans to other animals stand in a different, and more interconnected, relationship to the narrative than do Homeric similes. This fact provides Lycophron opportunities for manipulating the boundaries between narrative and simile. For example, Cassandra opens her account of Diomedes' settlement of Italy by reporting the transformation of his companions into birds, observing that the hero will settle Italy, having watched the "bitter, winged, bird-mixed destiny of his companions, who will praise the life of the sea, like fishermen, made to resemble in their body swans with beautiful eyes" (594–7):

> ὁ δ' Ἀργυρίππαν Δαυνίων παγκληρίαν
> παρ' Αὐσονίτην Φυλαμὸν δωμήσεται,
> πικρὰν ἑταίρων ἐπτερωμένην ἰδὼν
> οἰωνόμικτον μοῖραν, οἳ θαλασσίαν
> δίαιταν αἰνήσουσι *πορκέων δίκην*,
> κύκνοισιν *ἰνδαλθέντες* εὐγλήνοις δομήν.
>
> And he will found Agyrippa, estate of the Daunians beside Ausonian Phylamos, having seen the bitter bird-mixed fate, endowed with wings, of his companions, who will praise the life of the sea like fisherman, resembling fair-eyed swans in their bodies.

The narrative describes the transformation of the companions in terms that emphasize their liminal position between humans and animals: the companions will have a fate that is οἰωνόμικτον, "bird mixed." In its context the simile plays on the usual practice of epic similes that compare humans to animals or to other humans engaged in non-martial activities, including fishing (cf. *Il.* 16.406–8): here, humans literally transformed into animals are compared to humans engaged in a quotidian professional activity. But what makes the passage interesting is that Cassandra goes on to describe the appearance of the transformed companions in language that metatextually suggests a simile. In predicting that the companions will "resemble" swans in their form, Cassandra uses the verb ἰνδάλλομαι, a word that, though used in early epic of perception and expectation, comes in Hellenistic poetry to mark similitude, as in Theocritus 22.39, where the pebbles visible in Amycus' pellucid spring are said to "resemble crystal or silver" (λάλλαι κρυστάλλῳ ἠδ' ἀργύρῳ ἰνδάλλοντο; cf. Euph. fr. 50.3).

The blurring of the boundaries between narrative and simile is also obvious, and striking, in Cassandra's account of the death of Locrian Ajax in 387–97. The passage, which follows the basic contours of the version told in the *Odyssey* (4.499–511), opens by juxtaposing animal metaphor and simile: τὸν δ' οἷα δύπτην κηρύλον διὰ στενοῦ αὐλῶνος οἴσει κῦμα γυμνήτην φάγρον ("him a denuded *fagros* [a carnivorous fish] the wave will bear through the strait like a *kerylos* gone underwater." The oddness of the juxtaposition of simile and metaphor led at least one ancient critic to suppose that οἶα should be understood *apo koinou* with φάγρον, so that Ajax is compared to both rather than identified with one and compared to the other,[22] but such a view does violence both to the language and to Lycophron's usual practice. For our purposes, however, what matters more is that within a few verses the simile is picked up in the metaphorical language of the narrative, when Ajax, taking shelter on the Gyrae rocks is treated as a bird drying its wings (390–1 Γυραῖσι δ' ἐν πέτραισι τερσαίνων πτερὰ / στάζοντα πόντου δευτέραν ἄλμην σπάσει). A fragment of Archilochus contains a simile in which the point of comparison is a *kerylos* flapping its wings on a rock (fr. 41 West κηρύλος / πέτρης ἐπὶ προβλῆτος ἀπτερύσσετο, preceded in Σ Arat. 1009 by ὥστε). The Aratus-scholia that cite it explain that birds do this either out of pleasure or to dry their wings. Although it seems that the former was the case in the Archilochean context, and although the image of a seabird drying its wings would have been readily available from an observance of nature rather than literature, the highly literary character of the *kerylos* (cf. Thompson 1895, 80) makes it possible that Lycophron has combined a simile featuring the bird with a narrative that evokes an archaic simile in which the creature appears. Whatever the case, the comparison of Ajax to the grand *kerylos* (a creature described as a "sacred bird" by Alcman *PMG* 26), gives way at the end of the passage, after Poseidon's violent intervention, to a significantly different, and much more humble ornithological identification: in line 395, Ajax is called a boastful cuckoo, a bird notorious for its cowardice since Anacreon (cf. *PMG* 437).

A remarkable passage toward the end of Cassandra's prophecy intertwines narrative and simile at the grammatical level. In 1426–34, Cassandra's account of the Persian Wars combines four similes in a single long sentence:

κύφελλα δ' ἰῶν τηλόθεν ῥοιζουμένων
ὑπὲρ κάρα στήσουσι Κιμμερός θ' ὅπως,
σκιὰ καλύψει πέρραν, ἀμβλύνων σέλας.
Λοκρὸν δ' ὁποῖα παῦρον ἀνθήσας ῥόδον
καὶ πάντα φλέξας ὥστε κἄγκανον στάχυν   1430
αὖθις παλιμπλώτοιο γεύσεται φυγῆς,
μόσσυνα φηγότευκτον, ὡς λυκοψίαν
κόρη κνεφαίαν, ἄγχι παμφαλώμενος,
χαλκηλάτῳ κνώδοντι δειματουμένη.

And a cloud of arrows whizzing from afar they will put overhead, and like Cimmerian darkness, blotting the light, a shadow will cover the sun. And having bloomed for a brief time like a Locrian rose and having burned everything like dry grain, he will taste of back-sailing

---

[22] Σ Lyc. 387b, p. 75 Leone: ἀπὸ κοινὸν τὸ οἶα· οἶα γυμνὸν φάγρον, ὅ ἐστιν ἰχθὺν θαλάσσιον [sic].

flight, gazing up close at the oak-built bulwark, like a girl at the dark gloaming, frightened by the bronzed-edged blade.

The density of similes in this passage is unparalleled in the poem, and constitutes a rhetorical climax at the conclusion of Cassandra's treatment of the hostility between Europe and Asia, immediately before the culmination of the prophecy in the coming of Alexander the Great and the Romans. The first and last similes feature images of darkness in a way that emphasizes the Persians' change of fortune. The first, in which the arrows of the Persians cover the sun "like Cimmerian darkness ... blotting out the light" alludes to Dieneces' famous response to the prospect of Persian arrows darkening the sky (Hdt. 7.226). At the end of the sentence, however, the Persians in their retreat from the Greek fleet are likened to a girl afraid of the dark, and thus implicitly very different from the unfazed Dieneces of Herodotus' account.[23]

This thematic link between the opening and closing simile is underscored by the way in which in both cases the word order confounds the distinction between tenor and vehicle. In the first, the simile Κίμμερός θ' ὅπως alludes to the description of the misty and dark land of the Cimmerians as it is described at *Od.* 11.14–19. Whether one assumes Κίμμερος (δνόφος) or the like or understands κίμμερος as a substantive (cf. *EM* 513.50–3 ἔνιοι δὲ Κεμμερίων· κέμμερον γὰρ λέγουσι τὴν ὀμίχλην), the important point is that the masculine participle ἀμβλύνων modifies it rather than σκιά, so that main clause has been grammatically interposed within the simile. Similarly, in the final simile, two participial clauses—one referring to the Persian, the other to the little girl—are arranged in such a way as to create an interlocked arrangement of clauses belonging to narrative and the simile. Thus the simile ὡς λυκοψίαν / κόρη κνεφαίαν illustrates the meaning of μόσσυνα φηγότευκτον ... ἄγχι παμφαλώμενος, but is subsequently picked up again and further developed in the final verse χαλκηλάτῳ κνώδοντι δειματουμένη, a phrase that, though grammatically referring to the girl, is equally applicable to Xerxes and the Persian army. Thus the word order, in which elements of the narrative alternate with elements of the simile, contributes to a blurring of the boundary between comparison and metaphor that runs through the entire poem.

---

23 The central two similes, for their part, use agricultural images, the first denoting freshness, the second desiccation—an opposition underscored by the placement of ῥόδον and στάχυν at the ends of successive lines. Xerxes' military vigor will be temporary (παῦρον), and, like that of the crops he burns, soon be gone.

The phenomenon is illustrated in an especially complex way in 180–2, where Cassandra foretells the response of the Greeks to Paris' theft of Helen. There, she predicts that Paris' return will rouse a swarm of wasps:

χὼ μὲν παλιμπόρευτον ἵξεται τρίβον,
σφῆκας δαφοινοὺς χηραμῶν ἀνειρύσας,
ὁποῖα κοῦρος δῶμα κινήσας καπνῷ

And he will come on his return path, having drawn from their hides the murderous wasps, like a boy disturbing their home with smoke.

The passage engages closely with a Homeric simile in which the narrator compares the Myrmidons preparing for battle to wasps roused from their nests by children, *Iliad* 16.259–65:

αὐτίκα δὲ σφήκεσσιν ἐοικότες ἐξεχέοντο
εἰνοδίοις, οὓς παῖδες ἐριδμαίνωσιν ἔθοντες   260
αἰεὶ κερτομέοντες ὁδῷ ἔπι οἰκί' ἔχοντας
νηπίαχοι· ξυνὸν δὲ κακὸν πολέεσσι τιθεῖσι.
τοὺς δ' εἴ περ παρά τίς τε κιὼν ἄνθρωπος ὁδίτης
κινήσῃ ἀέκων, οἳ δ' ἄλκιμον ἦτορ ἔχοντες
πρόσσω πᾶς πέτεται καὶ ἀμύνει οἷσι τέκεσσι.

Immediately they poured out like wasps on the road, which children customarily stir up, always mocking them, wasps that have their houses on the road. Fools, they cause shared trouble for many. But if any traveler passing by disturbs them unwillingly, each of them flies out with a fearless heart and defends his children.

In 180–1, Lycophron converts what is a simile in his model to a metaphor by simply identifying the mustering Greeks as wasps. In 182, however, Cassandra reintroduces the formal features of the model by briefly comparing Paris to a boy who has disturbed a house with smoke. As the Homeric simile makes clear, the δῶμα in question must be that of the wasps, and there is thus complete slippage between simile and metaphor: the Greeks are both metaphorically identified with wasps and, via the simile comparing Paris to a boy who has disturbed a hive, implicitly compared to them as well.

Ancient scholarship was regularly interested in, and frequently comments upon, the point or points at which the simile connects to the surrounding narrative.[24] On the wasp simile, the bT-scholia note that like the Greek forces insects rush from their hives with a common mind, full of anger. In reworking the simile as he has, Lycophron creates an additional *Gleichnispunkt* absent from his

---

24 Snipes 1988, 211–13; Edwards 1991, 30–4.

model: whereas in the Homeric simile the anthropomorphizing reference to the wasps' houses has little connection to the narrative, here it constitutes a thoroughly relevant evocation of Paris' meddling in the affairs of Menelaus' household. At the same time, however, in constructing the simile as he has, Lycophron may be engaging with features of the passage that ancient criticism found problematic. The scholia report that verse 261 was athetized by Aristophanes of Byzantium, followed by Aristarchus, on the ground that ἐριδμαίνωσιν ἔθοντες and αἰεὶ κερτομέοντες are tautologous and that Homer elsewhere exclusively uses κερτομέω of words rather than deeds. Moreover, the bT-scholia report that some critics read ἔχοντες at the end of 261, so that the roadside homes became those of the children. We cannot know whether Lycophron, who probably composed the *Alexandra* in the first half of the second century,[25] was specifically responding to a critical position. Still, seen against this backdrop, the structure of the simile is significant. Lycophron has included in the comparative part of the sentence precisely the material that some scholars explicitly found problematic in the Homeric simile. In so doing, he has avoided the ambiguous (and, from the standpoint of Aristophanes, linguistically problematic) provocation suggested by κερτομέοντες and replaced it with the clear and specific act of smoking the wasps from their nest, while simultaneously making clear that the "house" in question is that of the wasps rather than the boy.

A similarly close engagement with Homeric models is evident in Cassandra's account of the destruction of Troy. In 249–53, she vividly envisions the land ravaged by Greek soldiers, whom she compares to a field of wheat:

Καὶ δὴ καταίθει γαῖαν ὀρχηστὴς Ἄρης,
στρόμβῳ τὸν αἱματηρὸν ἐξάρχων νόμον.   250
ἅπασα δὲ χθὼν προὐμμάτων δῃουμένη
κεῖται, *πέφρικαν δ' ὥστε ληίου γύαι
λόγχαις ἀποστίλβοντες.*

And dancer Ares burns the land, striking up the bloody tune with his trumpet-shell. And the whole earth lies destroyed before my eyes, and they shudder like fields of crop, flashing with their spears.

---

25 In two passages, Cassandra predicts the coming power of the Romans in enthusiastic terms, and scholars have abundantly debated whether these are likely to have been written in Alexandria in the early years of the third century; S. West (especially West 1984) has argued for the view that they are interpolations. Charles McNelis and I (McNelis/Sens 2011) have elsewhere argued that these passages are carefully integrated in and essential to the larger argument of the poem, and that they suggest a date later than the lifetime of the Lycophron of Chalcis who was in charge of comedy in the Alexandrian library.

The simile picks up an idea that ancient scholarship identified as implicit in *Il.* 13.339 (ἔφριξεν δὲ μάχη φθιϲίμβροτοϲ ἐγχείῃϲι), where the narrator describes the battle as "shuddering" with spears. The bT-scholia observe that the image is "a metaphor close to a simile" that simultaneously captures the elevation of spears and their movement, "for something like the movement of wheat-ears takes place." Lycophron here makes explicit what the scholia identify as the implicit point of the Homeric image, namely that the movement of spears on the battlefield resembles that of ears of wheat. At the same time, the simile picks up the use of the verb φρίσσω in explicit connection to a field in the simile of *Il.* 23.598–9, where the narrator compares the warming of Menelaus' heart to dew on ears of wheat in the field (περὶ ϲταχύεϲϲιν ἐέρϲη / ληΐου ἀλδήϲκοντοϲ, ὅτε φρίϲϲουϲιν ἄρουραι). Cassandra's use of the verb thus conforms closely to and mimics Homeric practice, in that she applies it in the narrative metaphorically to spears, and, within the simile, to ears of grain.[26]

The context in which Lycophron's wheat simile occurs requires further consideration. It falls in the heart of a synoptic overview of the Trojan War that is framed by allusions to the beginning and end of the fighting in the *Iliad*. The narrative opens, in 243–8, with a prediction of the Greek arrival on Trojan soil:

Καὶ δὴ ϲτένει Μύρινα καὶ παράκτιοι
ἵππων φριμαγμὸν ᾐόνες δεδεγμέναι,
ὅταν Πελαϲγὸν ἅλμα λαιψηροῦ ποδὸς   245
εἰς θῖν' ἐρείϲαϲ λοιϲθίαν αἴθων λύκοϲ
κρηναῖον ἐξ ἄμμοιο ῥοιβδήϲῃ γάνοϲ,
πηγὰϲ ἀνοίξαϲ τὰς πάλαι κεκρυμμέναϲ.

And Myrina growns and the shores of the sea that have received the whinnying of horses, when having propped the Pelasgic leap of his swift foot on the shore, the burning wolf will make gush from the sand the water of a spring, opening streams long concealed.

Though this event clearly lies outside the scope of the *Iliad* itself, Cassandra's narrative allusively equates it with the initial mustering and enumeration of Greek and Trojan forces in that poem. First, the reference to Myrina in 243 evokes the initial introduction of Hector and the marshaling of the Trojans at the raised ground that is said to be called the "tomb of much-gamboling Myrina" by the

---

[26] Similarly, at 1429 Λοκρὸν δ' ὁποῖα ταῦρον ἀνθήϲαϲ ῥόδον, the participle of ἀνθέω is appropriate to the narrative in the metaphorical sense "having flourished" (LSJ s.v. II), and to the simile in the literal sense "having flowered."

immortals (*Il.* 2.811–14).²⁷ Second, Cassandra's reference to the groaning of that same place recalls the lamentation of the earth under Greek feet at the same narrative point in the epic: at *Il.* 24.780–5 the narrator compares the groaning of the earth (781 γαῖα δ' ὑπεστενάχιζε) to the sound made when Zeus lashes the land around Typhoeus. Thus Cassandra's overview of the fate of her homeland tendentiously associates the arrival of the Greeks in Troy with the moment at which combat operations are about to commence in the *Iliad*. Her vision of the fall of the city, moreover, concludes with a vivid image of the mourning of women:

> οἰμωγὴ δέ μοι
> ἐν ὠσὶ πύργων ἐξ ἄκρων ἰνδάλλεται,
> πρὸς αἰθέρος κυροῦσα νηνέμους ἕδρας,   255
> γόῳ γυναικῶν καὶ καταρραγαῖς πέπλων
> ἄλλην ἐπ' ἄλλῃ συμφορὰν δεδεγμένων.

Wailing appears in my ears from the tops of the towers, reaching the windless seats of the air, from the lamentation of women and the rending of robes, receiving one misfortune after another.

Such lamentation finds its counterpart in the *Iliad* in the aftermath of Hector's death (22.405–515), where Hecuba and Andromache lament the fallen hero (cf. 430 ἐξῆρχε γόοιο, 476 γοόωσα), and more importantly, in the final events of the epic, where Andromache, Hecuba and Helen lead the lamentation (24.723, 747, 761 ἐξῆρχε γόοιο) for Hector in turns. In the *Alexandra*, therefore, the overview of the war is framed by references to the beginning of Trojan conflict and to the aftermath of the last battlefield death in the poem.²⁸

In this highly "Homeric" context, Lycophron's wheat simile exemplifies one of the principal functions of epic similes as they were understood in the exegetical tradition. As noted above, in the view of ancient critics, Homeric similes, in addition to contributing adornment, amplification and clarity, provided vividness, *enargeia*. Unlike all but a few similes in Homer, the similes of the *Alexandra* are explicitly focalized by a particular speaker, Cassandra, rather than by the anonymous narrator. The passage into which the wheat simile is embedded explicitly underscores the vividness with which the images of the fall of Troy appear in her perceptions: the simile is preceded by reference to her vision of

---

27 The phrase παράκτιοι / ἵππων φριμαγμὸν ἠόνες δεδεγμέναι evokes the connection to horses implied by the Homeric epithet πολυσκάρθμοιο, which ancient critics connected to the claim that Myrina was the name of an Amazon (cf. Str. 12.8.6).
28 The link between the two passages is reinforced by the appearance of the perfect participle of δέχομαι in each of them (244, 257).

the whole land lying destroyed "before her eyes" (251 προὐμμάτων) and followed by reference to the sounds of lamentation appearing "in [her] ears" (ἐν ὠσὶ ... ἰνδάλλεται). The claim that the speaker has a vivid perception of the events he or she describes is a feature of both prophecy and messenger speeches,[29] and it is not provable that Lycophron had ancient discussions of the role of similes specifically in mind, but it is at least possible that he did. In any case, whether by accident or not, the wheat simile clearly fulfills one of the roles that ancient scholarship ultimately ascribed to its Homeric predecessors.

In several cases, similes appear in marked pairs, as they often do in Homer.[30] Thus, for example, the comparison of the shipwrecked Locrian Ajax to a *kerylos* that we considered earlier finds a complement in the simile in which Cassandra treats Odysseus, at the moment his raft is destroyed by Poseidon, as "like the unfledged offspring of the wife of the *kerylos*," a reference to the ancient view that the *kerylos* and the *halcyon* were different sexes of the same bird (cf. 750 with Σ ad loc, p. 151 Leone). More interesting, however, is the pair of insect-similes that frame Cassandra's account of the military conflict. We have already considered the simile comparing the Greeks roused by Paris's return to Troy with Helen to wasps. This simile, marking the initial Greek response to Paris' actions, finds a complement in Cassandra's account of Hector's accomplishments in the war in 283–97:

οὐ μὴν ἀνατεί γ' οὐδ' ἄνευ μόχθων πικρῶν
πένθους θ' ὁ λῃστὴς Δωριεὺς γελᾷ στρατός,
ἐπεγκαχάζων τοῦ δεδουπότος μόρῳ,   285
ἀλλ' ἀμφὶ πρύμναις τὴν πανυστάτην δραμὼν
πεύκαις βίου βαλβῖδα συμφλεχθήσεται,
καλῶν ἐπ' εὐχαῖς πλεῖστα Φύξιον Δία
πορθουμένοισι κῆρας ἀρκέσαι πικράς.
τότ' οὔτε τάφρος οὔτε ναυλόχων σταθμῶν   290
πρόβλημα καὶ σταυροῖσι κορσωτὴ πτέρυξ,
οὐ γεῖσα χραισμήσουσιν οὐδ' ἐπάλξιες·
ἀλλ' ὡς μέλισσαι συμπεφυρμένοι καπνῷ
καὶ λιγνύος ῥιπαῖσι καὶ γρυνῶν βολαῖς,
ἄφλαστα καὶ κόρυμβα καὶ κληδῶν θρόνους   295
πυκνοὶ κυβιστητῆρες ἐξ ἐδωλίων
πηδῶντες αἱμάξουσιν ὀθνείαν κόνιν.

Not without punishment or bitter toils and grief will the Dorian brigand army laugh, mocking his fate when he has crashed to the ground, but about the sterns it, along with the pine

---
[29] For vividness in messenger speeches, cf. Barrett 2002, 31–4.
[30] Edwards 1991, 39–40.

ships, will be incinerated with torches as it runs its final life's lap, calling greatly in its prayers to Zeus of Flight, to ward off bitter fate from them as they are being sacked. Then neither trench nor bulwark of naval stations nor palisade terraced with stakes nor cornice nor battlements will defend them. But like bees disturbed by smoke and blasts of flame and hurling of firebrands numerous divers leaping from the decks to the stern- and prow-beaks and the benches will bloody the foreign dust.

In this passage, Cassandra pointedly corrects the Homeric narrator's description of Greek soldiers mocking the dead body of Hector (cf. *Il.* 22.370–5).[31] After lamenting his loss, she observes, anachronistically, that the Greek army will not get away with laughing at Hector without punishment, since they will not be protected by military defenses when their ships are burnt, but will bloody the dirt by leaping from their ships "like bees disturbed by smoke." This simile picks up and subverts Asius' comparison of the Greek defenders Polypoetes and Leonteus to bees or wasps who refuse to abandon their home in defense of their children (*Il.* 12.167–72). Instead of a simile suggesting steadfastness, however, Lycophron associates the Greek would-be defenders with bees routed by smoke.[32] In the *Alexandra*, then, the paired insect-similes frame the major hostilities of the *Iliad*, and mirror the trajectory of the narrative as a whole, in which the Greeks' aggression towards Troy gives way to misfortune in victory.

As a final example of the way similes interact with the narrative of the *Alexandra*, let us consider the two similes that occur in Cassandra's account of the moment of Agamemnon's death and of her own. The two parts of the poem in which she discusses this event are separated by several hundred verses but are closely related to one another by language and theme: the first is an extended account of the unhappy end to Agamemnon's homecoming, and the second a brief summary of the murder in a reference to Orestes in the dialectical account of East-West hostilities. In the latter (1374–5), Cassandra describes Orestes as "the son of the one killed in nets like a mute fish" (ὁ δεύτερος δέ, τοῦ πεφασμένου κέλωρ / ἐν ἀμφιβλήστροις ἔλλοπος μυνδοῦ δίκην). That description is a reworking of Clytemnestra's account of the murder in Aeschylus' *Agamemnon* (1381–2), where she notes that she threw around her husband "a boundless net, like one for fish" (ἄπειρον ἀμφίβληστρον, ὥσπερ ἰχθύων, / περιστιχίζω, πλοῦτον εἵματος κακόν). In the *Agamemnon*, however, the comparative clause calls attention to the metaphorical character of Clytemnestra's ἀμφίβληστρον, an image that is explained by πλοῦτον εἵματος κακόν: the robe is a boundless net, *like* one for fish, and the implication that Agamemnon is himself like a

---

[31] McNelis/Sens 2011, 70–1.
[32] McNelis/Sens 2011, 72.

fish is only secondary. Lycophron's Cassandra picks up the implication and makes it concrete. In her simile, Agamemnon is killed in the net, "like a mute fish." Given the ancient etymology of ἔλλοψ as derived from ἴλλεσθαι and ὄψ (i. e. "with voice blocked," "mute"),³³ the phrase is something of an erudite *figura etymologica*; beyond the learned point, the expression as a whole picks up on and develops an idea that runs through Cassandra's earlier, more extended account of her own death by the side of her alleged consort Agamemnon.

Cassandra begins that narrative by relating Agamemnon's attempts to escape the hard-to-exit bonds of Clytemnestra's garment. The obviously self-referential character of Cassandra's engagement with the fate of her Aeschylean literary predecessor is underscored by the fact that the language of verses 1099 – 1100 recapitulates the language with which the messenger describes his own reporting of Cassandra's prophecies in the prologue. Thus the prediction that Agamemnon will fail in his attempt to find a way out of τὰς δυσεξόδους ... κελεύθους of the "throttling noose" (i. e. robes) cast upon him by Clytemnestra picks up the messenger's claim that he will move to the "escape routes of slanted words" (14 – 15 ἄνειμι λοξῶν ἐς διεξόδους ἐπῶν, / πρώτην ἀράξας νύσσαν, ὡς πτηνὸς δρομεύς "I will proceed to the throughways of slanted words, having struck the starting gate, like a winged runner").³⁴ But what matters more for our immediate purposes is that Cassandra focuses on Agamemnon's lack of perception. Most obviously, she underscores his blindness as he attempts to grope his way free, but more subtly, the passage evokes and responds to Agamemnon's own account of his death in the *Odyssey*, and in so doing, underscores his deafness. In 1118 – 19, Cassandra's reports that she will cry out for Agamemnon, her husband and master, as her soul flees to the Underworld:

βοῶσα δ' οὐ κλύοντα δεσπότην πόσιν
θεύσω κατ' ἴχνος ἠνεμωμένη πτεροῖς

Calling for my master-husband who does not hear me, I will run following in his track, raised aloft by my wings.

---

33 See Olson/Sens 2000, 61.
34 The phrase ὡς πτηνὸς δρομεύς, the only simile in the messenger's frame, plays on the conventions messenger speeches in drama, where it is conventional to observe that the speaker has arrived with all possible haste (e.g. A. *Pers.* 247, S. *Ant.* 223 – 4; E. *Hipp.* 1151 – 2). The *Alexandra*'s characterization of its messenger as a "winged runner" (ὡς πτηνὸς δρομεύς) in making the running figurative rather than literal, evokes the *mise-en-scene* of dramatic messenger speeches (cf. 1461 where the messenger claims to have arrived παλίσσυτος ποσίν). The image of running reappears in the epilogue in a different, figurative sense, in the messenger's expressed wish that events turn out better than Cassandra has predicted (1472 – 3 δαίμων δὲ φήμας εἰς τὸ λῷον ἐκδραμεῖν / τεύξειεν).

The point of verse 1118 only becomes fully intelligible when read against the account Agamemnon's shade gives of his death in the *nekyuia*, where he reports that as he lay dying amidst the mixing bowls and tables of his dining room, he heard the voice of Cassandra as Clytemnestra was killing her (*Od.* 11.421–3):

οἰκτροτάτην δ' ἤκουσα ὄπα Πριάμοιο θυγατρὸς
Κασσάνδρης, τὴν κτεῖνε Κλυταιμνήστρη δολόμητις
ἀμφ' ἐμοί

I heard the most pitiable voice of Priam's daughter Cassandra, whom Clytemnestra was killing by my side.

Both the Homeric Agamemnon and Lycophron's Cassandra describe the same mythological moment, but in contrast to the Odyssean Agamemnon, Lycophron's is complete insensate and helpless, without the ability even to hear, see, or speak at the moment of his death; and though he is said to have witnessed the bitter housekeeping of his serpent-wife, his vision is couched as a past act (ἰδών).

By stark contrast, Cassandra's own fate is represented via a simile that evokes the deaths of Homeric warriors (1110–12). The phrase ῥήξει ... τένοντα finds close parallels in the *Iliad* (5.307 θλάσσε δέ οἱ κοτύλην, πρὸς δ' ἄμφω ῥῆξε τένοντε; 16.587 ῥῆξεν δ' ἀπὸ τοῖο τένοντας) while the noun μετάφρενον, which denotes the space between the shoulders, is used regularly in that poem of warriors, including Patroclus, killed by a blow from behind (e.g. *Il.* 16.791, 806). Moreover, the substance of the simile reworks, from a different perspective, Homeric comparisons of dying warriors to falling trees, such as those describing the death of Asius at *Il.* 13.383–81 and of Sarpedon at *Il.* 16.482–4. At the same time, Lycophron's engagement with Homeric passages is mediated by a more specific reworking of Sophocles, *Electra* 97–9 μήτηρ δ' ἡμὴ χὼ κοινολεχὴς / Αἴγισθος ὅπως δρῦν ὑλοτόμοι / σχίζουσι κάρα φονίῳ πελέκει ("My mother and her bedmate Aegisthus split his head with a bloody axe like woodcutters splitting an oak"). But whereas, in the Sophoclean passage, Electra describes the death of her father at the hands of Clytemnestra and Aegisthus, here, by contrast, only the killing of Cassandra is so described. Thus, by couching her demise in epic terms, Lycophron's narrative juxtaposes Agamemnon's insensate haplessness to the sort of epic death that his Homeric counterpart wishes he had had, and distinguishes Cassandra's heroicized death from Agamemnon's pathetic victimhood.

Annemarie Ambühl
(Re)constructing Myth: Elliptical Narrative in Hellenistic and Latin Poetry

1. Introduction

Innovative experiments with narrative form and their self-conscious advertisement by the narrator have long been defined as one of the hallmarks of Hellenistic poetry.[1] Hellenistic poetics are indeed communicated not only through explicitly programmatic passages such as the Prologue to Callimachus' *Aetia*, but also mirrored in the ways how stories are told. In recent years, this line of research has been pursued more systematically, as critical tools derived from narratology or reader response theory have been applied to Hellenistic poetry and to Latin texts that adapt and develop Hellenistic narrative techniques.[2] Special attention has been paid to the intricate plots of these poems that often feature 'gaps' in the narrative and thereby invite the readers' active participation in the process of interpretation. There have interesting analogies been drawn between reader or viewer supplementation in interpreting texts and visual art,[3] and especially with regard to the genre of epigram the crucial role of reader participation has been stressed.[4]

In my paper I will address a specific issue related to this general approach by focusing on ellipses in mythological narratives and looking for ways how such 'gaps' can be filled in. After giving a preliminary overview of various types of elliptical narrative based on a sample of Hellenistic texts that anticipate and/or frustrate audience expectations through narrating myths in a highly selective, elliptical way, I will then compare and contrast them with some Latin examples taken from Catullus, in order to investigate whether he employs ellipses in a manner similar to his Hellenistic predecessors. I will argue that the omission

---

[1] I would like to thank the organizers for the wonderful Thessaloniki conference and the audience for the stimulating discussion. The original character of an oral presentation has been retained in the revised version of the paper.
[2] For an overview see the respective articles on the Hellenistic poets in the three hitherto published volumes of *Studies in Ancient Greek Narrative* (de Jong/Nünlist/Bowie 2004; de Jong/Nünlist 2007; de Jong 2012). Specifically on the narrator's role in Hellenistic poetry see Morrison 2007, on Callimachus see also Harder 1990.
[3] Zanker 2004, 72–102 (Chapter 3: Reader or Viewer Supplementation).
[4] Meyer 1993 and 2005. On the concept of '*Ergänzungsspiel*' in epigrams see also Bing 1995.

of certain key elements is signaled within his collection of longer poems by metaliterary markers such as similes that reflect on the creative process of composing. The displacement of motifs from one poem to another establishes cross-connections within a book of poetry that guide its reception and help to create the impression of an aesthetic whole.

2. Elliptical narrative in Hellenistic poetry: A preliminary overview

For the present purpose I focus on small-scale compositions with mythological subject matter that have often been classified as epyllia in modern scholarship.[5] I will however refrain from discussing fragmentary texts, because there the narrative structure cannot be studied on a larger scale and many details inevitably must remain a matter of speculation. Of course, in order to get a more complete picture, the range of samples should also be extended in the other direction to include possible precedents of Hellenistic narrative, for instance in archaic Greek lyric with its highly selective way of telling myths.[6] In view of the limited space, I will have to leave open this 'gap' in my own narrative.

First, I shall define what I mean by elliptical narrative. In strictly narratological terms, an ellipsis is a special case of the temporal ordering of the story whereby an event is explicitly or implicitly passed over so that no story-time corresponds to the fabula-time; the resulting gap in the narrative may or may not be filled in later by a completing analepsis.[7] In Hellenistic poetry, where myths often

---

[5] For the problems connected with and possible approaches to the 'genre' of epyllion I refer to my discussion in Ambühl 2010a and the recently published *Brill's Companion to Greek and Latin Epyllion and Its Reception* (Baumbach/Bär 2012a), which exhibits a very broad approach to the concept by including examples from archaic Greek poetry to the eighteenth century (for their criteria see the introduction by Baumbach/Bär 2012b).

[6] See Morrison 2007 on the narrator in Archaic and Hellenistic poetry and generally on the Hellenistic reception of Archaic lyric Acosta-Hughes 2010a; see now also Luz 2012 on Pindaric narrative technique in Hellenistic epyllion.

[7] See the definitions in Genette (1980, 43, 51f.), who also notes the related phenomenon of paralipsis (i.e. delay), and Bal (2009, 100–102), who draws attention to the reader's role (102: "How are we to become aware of these ellipses, which can, apparently, be so important that it seems worth the trouble to look for them?"); cf. also Iser's term *'Leerstelle'* (1994, esp. 284–327). On the application of the concept to ancient Greek narrative see the glossary, the introduction and the epilogue in de Jong/Nünlist (2007, xi–xiii, 6, 12, 517f.) and the articles on Apollonius (Klooster 2007a, 77f.), Callimachus (Harder 2007b, 94–96), and Theocritus (Klooster 2007b, 106f.). I am happy to find that Schmitz in his chapter on *Idyll* 25 in Baumbach/Bär (2012a), which

are told in a non-linear fashion, ellipsis obviously plays an important role. It can be related to the selection of a comparatively small episode from a larger mythological context, a narrative strategy which Evina Sistakou has called "snapshots of myth".[8]

In a broader sense, ellipses not only affect the temporal structure of the narrative, but extend to the level of content and the interaction with the audience, insofar as crucial pieces of information are left out and are to be supplied by the reader. Of course, not every missing piece needs to pose a problem at all, as readers—depending on their degree of familiarity with earlier texts—can rely on resources of knowledge which will enable them to supplement specific details of certain myths or familiar mythological patterns. In the case of mimetic-dramatic compositions like certain of Theocritus' *Idylls* or the *Megara* ascribed to Moschus, where the identity of the speaking characters and the situation they find themselves in are being revealed only gradually, the audience may have been given additional clues through a performance or paratextual means. A familiar intratextual technique to compensate for ellipses is to introduce a second myth through a digression or an ecphrasis by way of analogy or contrast, as for example in Moschus' *Europa* or in Catullus' poem 64. Curiously, however, in Moschus' *Europa* the ecphrasis does not seem to illustrate the main story, as is usually the case, but rather the other way round, since chronological displacements and ellipses occur in the three scenes of the ecphrasis of the myth of Io on the flower basket (37–62), but not in the framing story of Europa, which is told in a rather straightforward fashion.[9]

There are however also cases where the ellipsis forms a built-in part of the narrative structure which is deliberately not compensated for. As often, it is Callimachus' self-conscious narrator who explicitly draws attention to this aspect of his story-telling, when in the introductory elegy to the third book of the *Aetia*, the *Victoria Berenices*, he cuts short the story of how Heracles overcame the Nemean lion and tells the reader to supply himself the missing part of the narrative (54 h.1f. Harder = fr. 57.1f. Pfeiffer = SH 264.1f.):[10]

I read after completing my manuscript, shares a similar narratological approach in exploring reader-responses to ellipses in Hellenistic poetry (esp. 265–268, 273–275, 279f.).
8 Sistakou 2009a.
9 On narrative anachrony in Moschus' ecphrasis see Petrain 2006, esp. 249–256; on the 'rhetoricisation' of the ecphrasis see Fantuzzi/Hunter 2004, 215–224 (esp. 223: "The *ekphrastic* description itself now functions as a rhetorical figure, a kind of simile writ large") and Fernandelli 2008, 12–15. On the elliptical character of the ecphrasis in Catullus 64 see below.
10 Text and translation according to Harder 2012, 1.212; see the commentary *ibid.* 2.471–473 and Harder 2007b, 94: "[...] the way in which the ellipsis is brought to the narratee's attention

αὐτὸς ἐπιφράσσαιτο, τάμοι δ' ἄπο μῆκος ἀοιδῆι·
ὅσσα δ' ἀνειρομένωι φῆ[σ]ε, τάδ' ἐξερέω·

he [sc. the reader] may find out for himself and cut short the length of the song, but all that he [sc. Heracles] said to him [sc. his host Molorcus] in answer to his questions I shall tell: ...

A narrative ellipsis on an even larger scale is to be found in the poem *Heracles the Lion-Slayer*, transmitted as nr. 25 in the Theocritean corpus.[11] Here the apparent main theme, the cleaning of Augias' stables, is not even explicitly mentioned and instead replaced by an apparently more heroic tale by Heracles himself about how he overcame the Nemean lion. Moreover, on the level of the narrative Heracles does not disclose his identity to the other characters within the story, who remain in the dark, although they guess who the unknown hero might be. The external readers thus enjoy a privileged position with regard to their superior knowledge about the identity of the hero, but they are cheated of the tale they were originally tricked into expecting.

Yet the concept of audience expectation can be deceptive and distract from the possibility that the author may have introduced innovative or even conflicting variants. Especially intriguing are borderline cases where the *re-construction* of an existing myth ends and the *construction* of a new myth begins, cases where the poet-narrator and the audience work together to create a new version or an unusual interpretation of a familiar story.[12] A similar problem exists with the

---

enables those who wish to do so to add the information left out and to fill in the gaps in the poem." On the function of the '*Abbruchsformel*' in the context of the whole episode and possibly even in comparison to the *Hecale* see also Ambühl 2004, 42. In a new fragment from the *Victoria Berenices* (54a Harder: Harder 2012, 1.200f., 2.413–420), there occurs the phrase 'οὐκ ἐρέω' (15), which might suggest that the narrator's elliptical way of telling stories was mirrored in the introductory frame.

11 For a fuller discussion I refer to Ambühl 2010a, 160–163; see also Hunter 1998 (= 2008); Fantuzzi/Hunter 2004b, 210–215; Hunter 2004a, 88f. ("There is in fact no real parallel in Greek narrative poetry for such a chronologically linear account in which we are merely given excerpts from 'the full story', each of which is, however, itself detailed and coherent"); Zanker 1996 and 2004, 89–95 (a comparison with analogous strategies in Hellenistic art); Sistakou 2009a, 298, and recently Schmitz 2012 (see note 7 above), esp. 267: "How, then, is the reader invited to (re-)construct a coherent and continuous narrative from the bits and pieces in our poem?"; 279: "[...] our poem is a meditation on different manners of storytelling and on readers' ways of making sense of narrative ellipses."

12 Cf. the perceptive remarks in Hunter 1996b, 65 (on Theocritus *Id.* 22): "[...] it begins as though it were familiar [...] which does not mean that we should assume that it *was* familiar. [...] Hellenistic narrative [...] also experiments not only with how the reader's knowledge can be exploited, but with how that knowledge can actually be constructed. A technique of elliptical narrative suggests that what we are hearing or reading follows a well-known story (which may,

concept of 'future reflexive' in so-called 'prequels': How much has to be filled in from our knowledge of earlier texts and to what extent is the future of mythical characters like Callimachus' Theseus, Apollonius' Medea, Theocritus' young Cyclops or his newly-wed Helen still open for a new reading?[13]

After this inevitably elliptical overview, in the main part of my paper I am now going to focus on cases of reader supplementation that involve not just one text and its intertextual referents but that are based on connections across poems within a book. Due to the loss of many Hellenistic poetry books and the uncertainties of transmission, hard cases are difficult to establish, but there might be some examples of mythical narratives that are to be read as companion pieces. If we read Callimachus' *Hymns* as a carefully designed collection, we discover that episodes from the childhood stories of Apollo and Artemis in *Hymns* 2, 3 and 4 have been displaced from one hymn into the sibling's.[14] The parallel stories about Tiresias in *Hymn* 5 and Erysichthon in *Hymn* 6 raise the issues at stake into even sharper relief, as the audience is given clues for evaluating the respective degrees of innocence or guilt and the appropriateness of the reactions of the goddesses Athena and Demeter through comparison and contrast; the diptych thus mutually explains each other. The formally and thematically closely related, but relatively more 'isolated' poems by Theocritus on Pentheus (26) and by Catullus on Attis (63) are much more ambivalent on these points, as crucial information about the motivation of the human offenders and the punishing gods is

---

of course, also be true); such a technique invests the narrative with a 'surface authority', which his however meant to be understood for what it is, namely an internally generated 'authority' independent of the existence of external witnesses. [...] Thus both the technique and the subject acquire a seal of hallowed antiquity; it would, however, be very naive to assume that all is as it seems." Again, Schmitz 2012 (on *Id.* 25) reaches similar conclusions as the present paper (275): "This would mean that our poem invited its readers not so much to remember a canonical version as to *construct* or *imagine* what such a version would have been like. [...] Its parts suggest a total which is more complete, yet this 'unabridged' version exists only as a mental image in the mind of the readers."
13 On the concept of 'future reflexive' see Barchiesi 1993 (= 2001) and the discussions in Ambühl 2005, 23–30, and Sistakou 2008a, 29–37; on Theocritus see also Klooster 2007b, 103 f.
14 In Ambühl 2005, 233–235, 275–284, 309–323, I interpret this phenomenon as cross-textual sibling rivalry. On the cross-connections between the *Hymn to Delos* and the surrounding hymns see Ukleja 2005. Callimachus' *Aetia* as a catalogue-poem has a much more continuous narrative structure (see recently Hutchinson 2008, 42–65; Harder 2012, 1.2–56). One might perhaps also consider the poems on Heracles in the Theocritean corpus (13, 24, 25) as a kind of 'sequential biography', although the evidence for an author-designed collection is more problematic in this case. For the present purpose I do not take into account epigram books, as they do not feature extensive mythical narrative. On Hellenistic and Roman poetry books in general see Hutchinson 2008.

lacking; the readers are left with an uneasy feeling precisely because the narrator omits crucial details and refuses to interpret the myth he is telling.[15]

3. The forgotten apple: Creating and reflecting elliptical narrative in Catullus' longer poems

With the last example we have moved to Latin poetry and to an author with undoubted affinities to Hellenistic poetics, Catullus. The close interconnections between his longer poems 61 to 68, his most 'Alexandrian' compositions, have often been stressed, and the view that these poems make up a single book of poetry carefully designed by the author himself is certainly attractive, even if it cannot be proved conclusively.[16] Based on this hypothesis I am proposing a reading that actively involves reader supplementation by establishing links between different poems in a sequential reading and re-reading of the book.

My first case study is poem 64 and its surroundings. Poem 64, Catullus' specimen of the fashionable genre of miniature epic, is perhaps even more re-

---

[15] This remains the case even if we take into account Euripides' *Bacchae* as a crucial intertext of both poems. On Theocritus 26 see e.g. Hutchinson 1988, 160–162 (162: "narrative and narrator are in discord"), Cairns 1992 and Ambühl 2005, 215–221 (with further literature). On Catullus 63 and its possible Hellenistic models, among them Theocritus 26 and Callimachus' *Hymns*, see Hutchinson 1988, 310–314, Fantuzzi/Hunter 2004, 477–485, and especially Harrison 2005 and Harder 2005 (592: "One may also observe that the story is not told in full and that some information is left out, again a feature well-known from Hellenistic narrative.").

[16] Generally on poems 61–68 see the commentary by Godwin 1995 and Syndikus 2001. On the longer poems as a group with close formal and thematic connections see especially Lieberg 1958; Putnam 1961; Most 1981; Block 1984; Schmidt 1985, 29–33, 87–101; Arkins 1999, 45–88. On the history of the debate see Skinner 2007b and Gaisser 2009, 22–44; see also note 30 below on alternative groupings. Holzberg (2002, 49–54, 111–172) has some interesting ideas on thematic connections between the longer poems, although I do not agree with his overall comic-ironical reading; Höschele 2009 has recently offered stimulating thoughts on the intertextual (especially Callimachean) interrelations between the poems around *c*. 66. On the Roman Alexandrianism of the central poems see Newman 1990, 204–247; generally on Catullus' reception of Callimachus and other Hellenistic poets see Clausen 1970; Hutchinson 1988, 298–325; Fantuzzi/Hunter 2004, 474–485; Nauta/Harder 2005 (on poem 63); Knox 2007; Acosta-Hughes/Stephens 2012, 214–233. Nelis' opening chapter in Du Quesnay/Woodman 2012 emphasizes the political dimension of Catullus' Alexandrianism (I thank the author for letting me read it in advance of publication); see also the contributions by Woodman on *c*. 65, Du Quesnay on *c*. 66 and Gale on *c*. 68 in the same volume.

markable for what it does *not* tell than for what it *does* tell:¹⁷ It is not a poem about the Argonauts nor about Medea, as the beginning would make us believe, but instead a poem on the wedding of Peleus and Thetis, a marriage which perhaps here is not doomed to fail; only as we read on, we discover that although Medea is never mentioned explicitly, she plays a crucial hidden role, for not only Peleus and Thetis, but also Theseus and Ariadne in the ecphrasis of the wedding coverlet replay the story of Medea and Jason from Apollonius.¹⁸ In apparent contrast to the *Argonautica*, however, the Argo is emphatically presented as the first ship, were it not for the notorious chronological contradiction with the myth told within the ecphrasis that seems to presuppose earlier seafaring.¹⁹ Or, since in contrast to the standard procedure of ecphrasis the narrator does not mention where the coverlet on the wedding couch came from nor by whom it was made, is the ecphrasis not to be read as an analepsis of events prior to the main narrative, but as a prolepsis, a divine prophecy of events that from the point of view of the internal audience still lie in the future?²⁰ The ecphrasis would then be analogous to the song of the Fates, but just as the ecphrasis, the song, too, stands in a precarious relationship to the framing story, for it hinges again on a major ellipsis that has been called the "unstated climax" of Catullus 64: The missing link between the wedding of Peleus and Thetis and the Trojan War should have been the apple thrown by Eris that provokes the beauty contest among the three goddesses, which is finally decided by the judgment of Paris and thus forms the origin of the Trojan war.²¹ But just as the narrative

---

17 The bibliography on *c.* 64 is almost as labyrinthical as the poem itself; in the following I quote only a few key publications. The monograph by Schmale (2004) gives a well-balanced overview of the issues involved in the interpretation of the poem, while Trimble (2012) reviews the history of scholarship from the perspective of Catullus 64 as the 'perfect epyllion'. The substantial study by Fernandelli (2012) on the poem and its reception in Virgil appeared too late to be taken into account in the argument of the present paper. See also the essay by Damien Nelis in this volume.
18 On the reception of Apollonius' *Argonautica* see esp. Clare 1996 and DeBrohun 2007. Of course, also the tragic Medea's from Euripides and Ennius lure in the background; on Catullus' complex intertextual strategies see Thomas 1982 (= 1999); Zetzel 1983 (= 2007); Gaisser 1995, 580–587 (= 2007, 219–227); Schmale 2004, 53–76.
19 On the chronological contradiction see esp. Weber 1983; Gaisser 1995, 580–608 (= 2007, 219–251); O'Hara 2007, 34–41.
20 This solution has notably been proposed by Harrison 2001, 84–87; but cf. also Theodorakopoulos 2000, 126 with n. 26; O'Hara 2007, 37 with n. 8. On the striking omissions in Catullus' introduction of the ecphrasis see esp. Gaisser 1995, 588–591 (= 2007, 228–232).
21 Townend 1983, esp. 26–29; apart from this "major omission", he points out further lacunae and aposiopeses in poem 64. On the literary and iconographic sources for the Apple of Discord see also Littlewood 1968, 149–151. Although most extant literary sources are later than Catullus,

breaks off directly after the song of the Fates right before this crucial moment, the ecphrasis, too, breaks off just before the despairing Ariadne gets to see Bacchus who has come to rescue her.

The disproportionately numerous ellipses in this miniature epic have such a huge impact on the interpretation of the poem that scholarship is still divided on the issue whether it should be read in an optimistic or a pessimistic way, a question which perhaps will never be resolved and probably is not meant to be resolved at all.[22] As a possible way out of this dilemma, recent narratological studies have pointed out that the ambiguities in the text are closely bound up with the voice of the narrator, who plays an ambivalent role and at times even acts as an unreliable narrator who leads the audience astray;[23] his elliptical way of telling stories can thus be seen as one of his defining characteristics. It remains to be seen whether this is limited to poem 64 or constitutes a defining trait of the authorial voice in Catullus' longer poems. In most cases the ellipses are not signaled explicitly in the text, but sometimes the narrator hints at different versions of the myth, mostly through subtle intertextual references that are to be deciphered by the *lector doctus*. But what is the reader to make of these intertextual signposts? Should we follow the path the narrator proposes for us and ignore the diversions, or should we just on the contrary follow the sidetracks in order to avoid the hidden gaps and traps the narrator has laid out for us on the way? I would indeed suggest that the reader is meant not only to look to other versions of the myth by earlier poets in order to detect and fill in the gaps, but also to look beyond the boundaries of the poem in its setting within the book.

I agree with Townend (*ibid.*, 27) that Catullus' audience was probably familiar with the apple (for a further argument for this reading see below).

22 Bramble 1970 bases his pessimistic reading on the structural ambiguities; similarly Curran 1969, 181: "Catullus goes out of his way to bring in the less pleasant aspects of the Peleus story by means of direct statement, allusion, and suppressions of detail so violent that they call attention to what is being glossed over." Cf. Stoevesandt 1994/1995, 195 (with further references) and the overview of pessimistic vs. optimistic readings in Schmale 2004, 26–31.

23 Gaisser 1995 (= 2007) is a fundamental study of the "competing views and voices" in poem 64; on its intratextual labyrinth see Theodorakopoulos 2000; on the narrator and his conflicting relationship with the literary tradition see DeBrohun 2007, esp. 294f. O'Hara (2007, 33–54) points out that the inconsistencies are effects controlled by the poet. Schmale 2004 also bases her interpretation on narratology and intertextuality, whereas the narratological analysis by Bartels (2004, 17–60) is mainly confined to a technical level. On the narrator and narration in Catullus 64 see now also Fernandelli (2012, esp. 418–473, and the index s.v. *ambiguità, brevità, complessità, incongruità, inversione, ironia, narrazione frammentata, paradossi, selettività, sorpresa*).

Interestingly, at least two of the major gaps in the narrative of poem 64 are partially compensated for in the surrounding poems. The Trojan War anyway forms an important thematic link between most of the longer poems, but it is precisely in the framing poems of the 'book' that the judgment of Paris surfaces in close connection with weddings.[24] In poem 61, the bride is compared to Venus appearing before Paris (61.16–20):[25]

> *namque Iunia Manlio,*
> *qualis Idalium colens*
> *uenit ad Phrygium Venus*
> *iudicem, bona cum bona*
>   *nubet alite uirgo,*

> For Junia is marrying Manlius,
> just like she who dwells on Idalium,
> Venus when she went to her Phrygian
> judge, a good virgin
>   with good auspices.

In poem 68, the consequence of the judgment of Paris, the abduction of Helen, results in the Trojan War and the death of Laodamia's husband, a myth we will shortly return to (68.87 f.):

> *nam tum Helenae raptu primores Argiuorum*
>   *coeperat ad sese Troia ciere uiros,*

> For at that time, with the stealing of Helen, Troy had begun
>   to draw to itself the leaders of the Argives, ...

In a similar way, the abrupt ending of the ecphrasis with the arrival of Bacchus, that leaves the story of Ariadne in an elliptical state, finds a kind of sequel in the *Coma Berenices*, where the lock's reference to the catasterism of Ariadne's crown completes the unfinished narrative of the ecphrasis in poem 64 (66.59–62):[26]

---

24 On the framing function of the references to the Trojan War in the longer poems see also Holzberg 2002, 121. Moreover, the reference to the origin of the Trojan War in *c.* 61.16–20 is internally mirrored by a reference to Penelope and Telemachus near the end of the poem (61.219–223).
25 In this and all the following quotes, the Latin text of Catullus is from Mynors 1958 (except where variant readings are stated); the translations are taken from Godwin (1995) and sometimes from Green (2005), with slight adaptations.
26 See e.g. Höschele 2009, 140 f.

> [...] uario ne solum in lumine caeli
>> ex Ariadnaeis aurea temporibus
> fixa corona foret, sed nos quoque fulgeremus
>> deuotae flaui uerticis exuuiae,
>
> ... lest in the sparkling light of the sky
>> the golden crown from Ariadne's temples
> should alone have its fixed place, but rather that we also should shine,
>> votive spoils from a blonde head, ...

Third, a more oblique connection: Might it not be the case that the missing apple from the mythical wedding feast in poem 64 unexpectedly rolls forth at the end of poem 65 from the lap of the girl who has forgotten that it lay hidden there (65.19–24)?

> ut missum sponsi furtiuo munere malum
>> procurrit casto uirginis e gremio,
> quod miserae oblitae molli sub ueste locatum,
>> dum aduentu matris prosilit, excutitur,
> atque illud prono praeceps agitur decursu,
>> huic manat tristi conscius ore rubor.
>
> like an apple, sent to a girl by her betrothed as a secret gift,
>> which rolls out of her chaste virginal lap;
> the poor girl had put it under her soft clothes and forgotten it,
>> and when she leaps up at the arrival of her mother it is shaken out.
> The apple falls right down and keeps on rolling,
>> and a self-conscious blush flows over her sad face.

This intriguing simile has provoked a lot of scholarly discussion, and the possible relationships between *comparandum* and *comparatum* have been construed in various ways; especially attractive is a metaliterary reading, which however has been confined to poem 65 itself and its accompanying piece, Catullus' version of Callimachus' *Coma Berenices* (66), in the sense that one or both of these poems are represented by the gift of the apple.[27] Additionally, I would sug-

---

27 For metaliterary readings of the simile see Johnston 1983; Block 1984, 49f., 56; Laursen 1989; Hunter 1993, 180 (= 2008b, 207); Formicola 2003, 195–201; Skinner 2003, 13–19; Sweet 2006, 93–96; Clarke 2008, 140–14; Höschele 2009, 143–146; Woodman 2012, 136, 143, 149–151, who links the apple in the simile via a Pindaric allusion to the *dulcis Musarum ... fetus* (3) from the beginning of the poem and also to the 'apple-loving' Philo-mela implied in the nightingale simile (13f.). Intratextually, the girl (20: *uirginis*), too, is associated with the Muses in 65.2 (*doctis ... uirginibus*); these on their turn recall the singing Parcae from the wedding in poem 64 (303–383), who in Catullus replace the traditional hymn of the Muses (cf. Schmale 2004, 222f.).

gest that within the (secondary) context of a collection of poems the simile might also refer back to the preceding poem, the more so as the death of Catullus' brother at Troy (65.5–8) and the simile of the nightingale's lament (13f.) with its intertextual references to Penelope's lament in Homer's *Odyssey* (19.518–523) have already reactivated the myth of the Trojan War in the mind of the readers. Once such a connection between the two apples has been drawn, the reference to the girl forgetting about the apple (*oblitae*) can also be read as a sly comment by the auctorial narrator on his own apparent 'forgetting' about the crucial apple in poem 64 and thus as a hint for the attentive reader.[28] So even if poem 64 demonstrates very successfully that old stories can assume new meanings if certain key-elements are omitted and the remaining parts are assembled in unexpected ways, at the same time the readers are encouraged to re-import the missing elements back into the text by establishing cross-connections within the book.[29]

My second example from Catullus illustrates a closely related variant of elliptical narrative, that is the implicit use in one poem of a myth that surfaces explicitly in a subsequent poem. Here I focus on Catullus' use of the myth of Protesilaus and Laodamia in poems 65, 66 and 68, which according to another reconstruction hypothesis open Catullus' 'Callimachean' book comprising poems 65 through 116.[30] Regardless of the controversial issue whether poem

---

[28] The themes of memory and forgetting had already played a crucial role in the story of Ariadne and Theseus contained in the ecphrasis of poem 64: cf. the comments by the narrator-focalizer and by Ariadne on the forgetful and faithless Theseus (64.58: *immemor*; 123: *immemori ... pectore*; 135: *immemor*), Ariadne's curse (200f.) and its fulfillment (207f.: *ipse autem caeca mentem caligine Theseus / consitus oblito dimisit pectore cuncta*; 238–240; 247f.: *mente immemori*), and Theseus' neglect to obey his father's command to set white sails (321f.: *tum vero facito ut memori tibi condita corde / haec vigeant mandata, nec ulla oblitteret aetas*); on a metaliterary level, Theseus' (in)voluntary forgetfulness may also hint at the *other* version implied in the second tableau which Ariadne cannot see, Bacchus getting rid of his rival in love (cf. Gaisser 1995, 596 = 2007, 237; Schmale 2004, 191–199). Even more explicitly programmatic is the narrator's self-reproach for his failure to continue the 'original' story-line (64.116f.: *sed quid ego a primo digressus carmine plura / commemorem ...*), which can also be read as a self-conscious comment on the complicated elliptical relationship between the framing narrative and the ecphrasis. Needless to say that also poem 65 centers on forgetting (e.g. 65.5: *Lethaeo gurgite*) vs. commemorating the dead through poetry (cf. Fantuzzi/Hunter 2004, 475; Sweet 2006; Clarke 2008; Woodman 2012).
[29] Cf. Hunter 2006, 89: "There is a network of similarities and analogies, and an exploration of what is at stake in this network, which run through Catullus' 'longer elegies' (Poems 65–8) or, perhaps, through all of Poems 61–8; the closing simile of Poem 65 does not stand alone."
[30] See again Skinner 2007b. Among scholars who divide the longer poems into *c*. 61–64 and *c*. 65–68 as the introductory sequence of an elegiac *libellus* comprising also the epigrams (69–116)

68 constitutes a single elegy or is to be divided into two separate poems, in any case the close intratextual links between the different parts of poem 68 are reinforced through its intertextual links to poems 65 and 66, the introductory epistle and Catullus' translation of the *Coma Berenices*, while poem 67 can be read as a burlesque variation on the theme.[31] In contrast to poem 68, in poem 66 the myth of Protesilaus and Laodamia does not appear on the surface of the text, but Berenice's grief for her absent brother-husband (66.21f.) implicitly re-enacts the tragedy of the mythical couple (as well as Catullus' personal tragedy), only this time with a happy ending—at least for the royal couple, although not for the speaking lock who still longs for her queen. This association, which may already have been suggested in Callimachus,[32] is made more explicit by Catullus through cross-references to poem 68. This latter poem, which is often seen as a forerunner of Latin love elegy,[33] exhibits an intricate ring-composition, but perhaps the most remarkable fact about its unusual narrative structure is that it seems to be construed around a series of gaps, with at its very centre the void left by the death of Catullus' brother, a theme taken up from poem 65. In addition, also the allegedly autobiographical love story that forms the inner frame is told in a highly elliptical manner, as the foot of the beloved is left suspended on the threshold for more than fifty lines, which are then filled by a series of mythical comparisons and similes; to quote a memorable phrase by Denis Feeney: "The beloved herself is a gap, a vacancy to be filled with analogies [...]."[34] In my view, it is precisely this elliptical structure that invites the reader to fill in the gaps in order to construct (or re-construct) a potential narrative and thereby also to look beyond the boundaries of poem 68 back to the preceding poems.

Both the main themes of poem 68, the death of Catullus' brother at Troy and Catullus' furtive love affair with his divine beloved, are mirrored in the mythical couple Protesilaus and Laodamia. Through the association of Catullus' deceased brother who is buried at Troy with Protesilaus, the first Greek hero fallen at Troy, Catullus' poetic persona is turned into a grieving Laodamia, while his love, too,

---

and marked by opening and closing references to Callimachus are King 1988, Holzberg 2002, Skinner 2003, and Hutchinson 2008, 64f., 109–130, 256–258; see also Hutchinson 2012 for a reading of the corpus arranged by the subject of male and female desire.

31 On the problems involved in the interpretation of poem 68 and the history of scholarship see recently Theodorakopoulos 2007, 315f. I personally prefer a 'unitarian' reading. On the close connections between the poems around the *Coma Berenices* see Clausen 1970; Puelma 1982, 230–235 (= 1995, 369–374); Höschele 2009.
32 So Pelliccia 2010/2011, 187–194.
33 For a brief overview see Miller 2007, 410–413; on some of the issues involved see also Döpp 2005.
34 Feeney 1992, 43 (= 2007, 444).

is compared to Laodamia's passionate love for Protesilaus that was to end so tragically. Scholars have pointed out the ambiguities and dark hints evoked by the precarious relationship between the mythical paradigm and the surrounding love story.[35] The passages about Laodamia can however be read not only as an extended simile, but also as fragments of a mythical narrative. Catullus' story apparently breaks off with the death of Protesilaus and the abyss of grief into which Laodamia is plunged. Yet there are two further elements of the story that seem to have originated in Euripides' *Protesilaus* or perhaps in a later version of the myth and that are in any case presupposed by Propertius (1.19) and Ovid (*Heroides* 13; cf. *Remedia Amoris* 723f.), so that we may assume that Catullus' readers could also have been familiar with them.[36] These are Protesilaus' return from the underworld that he has been granted for just one day in order to meet his wife Laodamia, and the statue she fabricates in his likeness after she has lost him for the second time, the destruction of which ultimately leads to her suicide.[37] In a poem that is construed around gaps in such a self-conscious manner, the omission of these crucial parts of the myth is certainly not a coincidence. Of course it cannot be excluded that Catullus may not have wanted the reader to import these elements into his story, but I am going to argue that the boundaries of meaning cannot be limited in such a narrow way and that just on the contrary the apparently missing elements fulfill an important role in the texture of the poem.[38]

---

35 Besides Feeney 1992 (= 2007), on the crucial but ambiguous role of similes and mythical paradigms in poem 68 see MacLeod 1974, 82–88; Lyne 1980, 52–61 and 1998, 204–209; Sarkissian 1983; Hubbard 1984; Hutchinson 1988, 314–322; Clauss 1995; Godwin 1995, 204–207; Kennedy 1999; Miller 2004, 31–59; Hunter 2006, 102–108; Theodorakopoulos 2007, 323–326; Öhrman 2009; Gale 2012, who adduces Agamemnon, Clytemnestra and Helen from Aeschylus' *Agamemnon* as a further intertextual paradigm.
36 For the various transmitted versions and attempts at reconstructing a literary genealogy of the myth see Lieberg 1962, 209–246; Jacobson 1974, 195–212; Sarkissian 1983, 17f., 42–44; Lyne 1998; Skinner 2003, 54–57; Pelliccia 2010/2011, 175–198. Bettini (1999, esp. 9–14) offers a stimulating discussion of related story types involving the portrait of an absent lover; see also Hardie 2002, esp. 132–137. I disagree with Lefèvre's (1991) hypothesis that Catullus has translated an 'original' Hellenistic elegy on Laodamia. The fragments of Laevius' *Protesilaodamia* (Courtney 2003, 130–135) are too scanty to allow any conclusions regarding his treatment of these aspects of the myth (in fr. 18 Courtney, Laodamia perhaps addresses Protesilaus' ghost, but Courtney *ibid.* 133f. is sceptical); on the possible allusion to Laevius' title in Catullus 68.74 see Hinds 1998, 78.
37 This is the sequence of events according to Hyginus (*fab.* 103–104), who perhaps reflects Euripides' tragedy.
38 Lyne (1998, 208f.) argues that Catullus deliberately excludes all references to the lovers' reunion from his version; cf. also the brief remark in Hutchinson 1988, 316. I rather agree with Sarkissian, who identifies an allusion at least to the second missing motif (1983, 44; see also n.

I therefore suggest that both of the missing motifs are echoed at a crucial turning point of poem 68, the moment when the beloved appears, who is on the surface of the text associated with a goddess and with the bride Laodamia entering Protesilaus' house (68.70–75):

> *quo mea se molli candida diua pede*
> *intulit et trito fulgentem in limine plantam*
> *innixa arguta constituit solea,*
> *coniugis ut quondam flagrans aduenit amore*
> *Protesilaeam Laudamia domum*
> *inceptam frustra, …*

> Hither my radiant goddess brought herself with delicate foot
> and set her shining sole on the well-rubbed threshold,
> leaning on it with a squeak of her sandal,
> just as once, burning with love for her husband,
> Laodamia came to the house of Protesilaus,
> a house begun in vain, …

The beloved's marble-white, shining appearance and especially the static position wherein she is kept until the intervening mythical paradigm has been brought to its conclusion evoke a statue and thus associate her not only with Venus but also with the image of Protesilaus.[39] Moreover, her sudden epiphany also recalls the second missing element, the unexpected return of Protesilaus as a ghost or even in full flesh.[40] This association can be read as a further dark hint

---

40 below): "[…] we must assume that the readers of poem 68 also knew this version of the story. Indeed although neither Laodamia's suicide nor the image are mentioned explicitly in 68, the phrase *flagrans amore* with which she is introduced obliquely hints at both."

39 In the immediately following passage, Skinner (1984, 140 f.; 2003, 12 f.) identifies in the invocation of the *Rhamnusia virgo* (68.77) an allusion to the cult statue of Nemesis resembling Venus (and carrying an apple branch …). In the corresponding passage 68.131–134, the beloved is even more clearly associated with Venus. Readers of the collection may also recall the simile in the ecphrasis in poem 64.61, where Ariadne is compared to the statue of a Maenad.

40 While I argue that both of these motifs have been transferred from Protesilaus to Laodamia, Sarkissian sees in the phrase *flagrans amore* (68.73) a direct allusion to Laodamia's suicide on the pyre (1983, 19): "This is surely a *double-entendre* intended to remind the reader of the Laodamia who actually burns in the fire in which her father has destroyed the image of Protesilaus. Thus without actually introducing it into the poem, the poet calls attention to the strangest variation of the myth, and the simile takes a sinister turn." Similarly Hunter 2006, 107 f.; Öhrman 2009, 51 (although later on [55] she denies any obvious allusions to Laodamia's suicide or Protesilaus' return from the dead along with Lyne [see note 38 above]). Janan (1994, 127 f.) associates the "shiny-pale" foot of the beloved in poem 68 (71: *fulgentem … plantam*) with

by the narrator that such an unequal match is bound to fail and that his furtive love may last not much longer than one happy day, just as the mythical lovers' brief reunion (68.147 f.):[41]

> *quare illud satis est, si nobis is datur unis*
> *quem lapide illa dies candidiore notat.*
>
> So it is enough, if to me alone is given
> the day which she marks out with a whiter stone.

In a similarly ominous manner, Laodamia's suicidal despair at the loss of her husband (68.84: *posset ut abrupto uiuere coniugio*; 106 f.: *ereptum est uita dulcius atque anima / coniugium*) seems to be recalled in the final line of the poem, where the narrator's joy of life is equated with his beloved's life (160: *lux mea, qua uiua uiuere dulce mihi est*).[42]

Finally, I would like to read the elements from the myth of Protesilaus and Laodamia that can be projected onto the narrative of poem 68 on a further, metaliterary level. Both poem 65 and the beginning of 68 reflect on the relationship between grief and the production of art. In poem 65, Catullus states in reply to Hortalus' request that due to his grief for his brother he is not able to produce a poem of his own, only to re-produce a poem by Callimachus—although his sophisticated adaptation and of course also the highly metaphorical poem 65 itself clearly show this to be a modest understatement. As in poem 65, at the beginning of poem 68 Catullus again regrets in a sort of *recusatio* that he is unable to fulfill a friend's request for a poem. But whereas in poem 65 he claims to have lost his creative powers and to have to resort to a translation, here he states that in addition to his grief he misses his library during his stay at Verona and therefore is not able to reproduce playful erotic poetry in the Hellenistic style

---

the pale foot of Catullus' dead brother in poem 65 (6: *pallidulum ... pedem*)—another ghostly presence.
41 Sarkissian (1983, 30 f.) puts a slightly different emphasis on the motif (on lines 131–134): "Both come to their lovers for brief periods of intense love and joy, but are also soon to depart, Protesilaus permanently back to the Underworld, Lesbia occasionally to her *furta* (137). [...] Lesbia did stay longer than the three hours or single day allotted to Protesilaus, although to Catullus the period of time was still relatively and unbearably brief."
42 Lyne (1998, 206 n. 28) accepts this proleptic association; "but still the suicide is not actually described, still Laodamia is on the brink of tragedy" (*ibid.* 208). Öhrman (2009) suggests a different effect of foreshadowing through hints at an alternative ending to the myth (and to Catullus' own adulterous affair), where Laodamia's excessive passion would be tamed and turned into a lasting marital relationship.

(1–40), but instead goes on to write a purportedly autobiographical poem about his own sorrows.

In view of the close correspondences between the two poems, if in poem 68 the death of his beloved brother assigns to Catullus the role of a grieving Laodamia, could the poet not already in poem 65 implicitly associate himself with Laodamia by alluding to the one element of the myth that easily evokes metaliterary associations, namely her reproduction of an image of Protesilaus? Both Laodamia and Catullus create an artifact of their grief which however cannot satisfy their desire for the absent beloved. Just as the statue made by Laodamia, the eternal dirge Catullus promises his brother only serves to highlight the permanent absence by conjuring up a vain presence (65.10–12):[43]

> *numquam ego te, uita frater amabilior,*
> *aspiciam posthac? at certe semper amabo,*
> *semper maesta tua carmina morte canam,*

> Shall I never, brother dearer to me than life,
> see you again? But for sure I will always love you,
> always sing songs that are saddened by your death, ...

Perhaps a further hint at such a metapoetic reading can be found in the concluding simile of the girl with the apple (65.19–24), to which I return once again. The obvious intertextual referent for the simile is the apple from Callimachus' episode of Acontius and Cydippe in *Aetia* 3, which bears the inscribed oath that Cydippe reads aloud and thus inadvertently swears to marry Acontius.[44] This inscribed apple which has been turned into a simile representing elegiac poetry indeed appears to be an ideal intertextual medium for metaliterary significations.[45] But curiously, it is precisely an element of the simile *not* found in the

---

[43] A similar complex of love, death, grief and poetry is associated with the prototype of the elegiac poet, Orpheus, and his dirge for Eurydice (cf. Ambühl 2010b on some passages from Hellenistic and Latin poetry and beyond); Barchiesi (1993, 364 = 2001, 126) notes that Virgil has adapted the nightingale simile from Catullus 65.13f. in his Orpheus story in *Georgics* 4.511–515.
[44] On Acontius and Cydippe in Callimachus see Harder 2012, 1.231–247, 2.541–659. Many commentators have noted the reference to Callimachus, combined with a reference to Sappho: e.g. Kroll 1968, 198f. *ad* 19; Clausen 1970, 93; Johnston 1983; Hunter 1993 (= 2008b) and 2006, 88f., 101f.; Formicola 2003; Skinner 2003, 15–18; Acosta-Hughes 2010a, 76f. and 2010b, 9–11; Acosta-Hughes/Stephens 2012, 227f. Woodman 2012, 149–151, brings in Pindar instead (see note 27 above).
[45] See Barchiesi 1993, 363–365 (= 2001, 126f.) and generally on Acontius' apple Rosenmeyer 1996. I only mention in passing Catullus' (fragmentary?) poem 2b, where the lyrical 'I' compares something to the golden apple that loosened Atalanta's virginal girdle to her own satisfaction (*tam gratum est mihi quam ferunt puellae / pernici aureolum fuisse malum, / quod zonam soluit*

story of Acontius and Cydippe that is closely paralleled by an element of the myth of Laodamia missing from Catullus 68:[46] While according to Aristaenetus (1.10.39) Cydippe immediately throws away the apple after reading the message, in the simile of the apple in Catullus 65, the girl who is surprised by her mother inadvertently reveals her secret love token; therefore, it will probably be taken away from her against her will, just as Laodamia is caught by her father while hugging or even making love to the statue of Protesilaus on their marriage bed —angrily, he takes the waxen image from her and burns it on a pyre, onto which Laodamia then throws herself.[47]

Here again, we might draw an associative connection to the first part of the outer frame, where Catullus reflects on the genesis of the very poem we are reading by 'quoting' from his friend's letter (68.5–10):

quem neque sancta Venus molli requiescere somno
  desertum in lecto caelibe perpetitur,
nec ueterum dulci scriptorum carmine Musae
  oblectant, cum mens anxia peruigilat:
id gratum est mihi, me quoniam tibi dicis amicum,
  muneraque et Musarum hinc petis et Veneris.

..., you, whom neither holy Venus allows to rest in soft sleep,
  abandoned on your bachelor bed,
nor do the Muses delight you with the sweet song of writers of old,
  while your anxious mind keeps wakeful:
this is welcome to me, since you call me your friend
  and ask me for gifts of the Muses and of Venus.

---

diu ligatam). Here, too, the apple is a love token (cf. Littlewood 1968, 152f.), but unfortunately, any metaliterary significations are difficult to establish, although it is intriguing that Catullus' 'I' again compares himself to a female figure like (among others) Procne (and through the intertextual implication also Penelope) and the nameless girl in 65, Berenice and the lock in 66, and Laodamia in 68. On the problems involved in the textual transmission see recently Tar 2005b, who argues that 2b is a complete poem.

46 Cf. Kroll's note (1968, 198f. *ad* 19): "Aber der eigentliche Vergleichspunkt, das Fortrollen des Apfels, stammt anderswoher." Similarly Syndikus 2001, 198; Woodman 2012, 150f.: "[...] the essential points of contact between Catullus' scene and the Acontius and Cydippe story are missing."

47 The sources for the simulacrum are conveniently collected in Pelliccia 2010/2011, 177 with n. 86, 186 with n. 107. Compare Catullus' description of Laodamia's sexual passion for her living husband in 68.81–83 (... *coniugis ante coacta noui dimittere collum, / quam ueniens una atque altera rursus hiems / noctibus in longis auidum saturasset amorem*, ...). The hopes of Laodamia's father for a grandchild are thwarted, unlike the old man's in the simile in 68.119–124 (cf. Sarkissian 1983, 29). In the discussion, Richard Hunter suggested a further parallel with the impotent first husband of the wife in poem 67 who would be as inert in bed as a statue.

The reference to the friend's involuntary celibacy has often been explained biographically, either as lovesickness for a lost mistress or as an innuendo at a desired homoerotic relationship with Catullus himself.[48] In view of the prominent role the myth of Laodamia will play in the rest of the poem, we might also look for an intrinsically poetic motivation:[49] Catullus may already at this point construe his friend's plight as that of a second Laodamia turning and tossing in her empty bed until she finally comes up with the statue of her husband as a temporary relief;[50] again there seems to be a parallel and/or contrast between material and literary artifacts implied, as Catullus' friend asks him for a poetic as well as an erotic gift as a solace—perhaps to be combined in a love-poem about Laodamia's love-sickness.

The concept of a statue as an inadequate substitute for a living person recurs once again in poem 68. In two corresponding passages from the frame, the immortalizing power of poetry is stressed and contrasted with an imaginary portrait inscribed with Allius' name that after his death will be covered by cobwebs and rust (68.48–50; 151 f.):

> *notescatque magis mortuus atque magis,*
> *nec tenuem texens sublimis aranea telam*
> *in deserto Alli nomine opus faciat.*

---

48 On the various interpretations of these lines see recently Theodorakopoulos 2007, 316–318. Cf. the related passage 68.27–30: *quare, quod scribis Veronae turpe Catullo / esse, quod hic quisquis de meliore nota / frigida deserto tepefactet membra cubili, / id, mi Alli, non est turpe, magis miserum est.* In line 28, I understand *hic* as a reference to Catullus' friends left behind at Rome (on the problems involved see Skinner 2003, 146–151; Lowrie 2006, 121–123; Theodorakopoulos *ibid*. 319 f.); in line 30, I accept Schöll's conjecture *mi Alli* (as does Godwin 1995) instead of Lachmann's *Mani* (as in Mynors 1958) in order to maintain consistency of the addressee throughout poem 68 (on the textual transmission see the summary in Theodorakopoulos *ibid*. 315 f.).
49 Kroll (1968, 220 *ad* 6) and Fordyce (1961, 345 *ad* 6) quote Laodamia's words in Ovid *Her*. 13.107 as a parallel (*aucupor in lecto mendaces caelibe somnos*), which not only proves that "Ovid read 68 A and B as strongly interrelated" (Lowrie 2006, 116 n. 5), but perhaps also that Catullus wanted his readers to draw such a connection (so also Casali 1996).
50 This motif, too, finds an echo in the *Coma Berenices*, where the lock recalls how Berenice wept in her empty bed (66.21 f.: *et tu non orbum luxti deserta cubile, / sed fratris cari flebile discidium?*; cf. 31 f.: *an quod amantes / non longe a caro corpore abesse uolunt?*). Moreover, in an intriguing passage from Aeschylus' *Agamemnon* (408–426), a play which is adduced as an important intertext for Catullus 68 by Gale 2012 (though she does not mention the present passage), the chorus speaks of traces (either footprints or bodily impressions left behind in the marriage-bed), statues and dreams that torment Menelaus who still longs for Helen (cf. Bettini 1999, 14–17), a complex of images which seems to be recalled in various passages from Catullus 68.

[…]
ne uestrum scabra tangat rubigine nomen
 haec atque illa dies atque alia atque alia.

  … and being dead may he yet grow more and more famous,
nor, weaving her fine-spun web, let the lofty spider
  make her work over Allius' neglected name.
[…]
  … so that this day and the next, and then another and then another
  may not touch your name with scabrous rust.

While in the first passage we might imagine a dust-covered sarcophagus or portrait bust with Allius' epitaph inscribed on it, the rust in the second passage rather points to a statue made from metal that may also recall the statue of Protesilaus made by Laodamia as a token of memory.[51] But whereas the fragile waxen image of Protesilaus perishes in the fire and even more solid material monuments will decay in the course of time, Catullus' poem and the friend celebrated in it will live forever.[52]

4. Conclusion

In the preceding examples from Catullus' longer poems we have come across two different kinds of elliptical narrative. The one compensates for ellipses on the level of the content by activating the audience to fill in missing elements of the respective myths in one poem from another. The second kind operates on a metaliterary level through reflecting elliptic narrative as a way of commenting on the creative processes of the composition and reception of poetry. Catullus explicitly reflects on the effects he expects his poems to have on the audience also in his shorter poems. Here the lyrical 'I' not only addresses individual readers such as the dedicatee Cornelius Nepos in the opening poem or Furius and Aur-

---

[51] E.g. Clauss 1995, 240 (on 49f.): "The image conjures up a statue or bust identified by a *titulus*." Kroll (1968, 240 *ad* 151) thinks of metallic letters on an inscription. Clauss (*ibid*. 240–242) discusses further metapoetical implications of these lines with reference to Poliakoff 1985; for echoes of Theocritus 16 see Hunter 2006, 103.
[52] The (self-)comparison of the poet with an artisan and of his poems with the plastic arts, especially with statues, has been a well-known poetological topos since archaic Greek poetry, where also often the superiority of poetry over material artifacts is implied (cf. Nünlist 1998, 119–125; on the dialectics involved see Fowler 2000b, esp. 200 on Catullus). Lowrie (2006, 124–131) points out the ironies involved in Catullus' references to the written and the spoken name in poem 68; in line 50, the actual name is blurred by the elision, whereas in line 152 the repeated *alia* seems to conjure up the missing name through assonance.

elius in the notorious poem 16, which at the same time comments on and enacts abusive and arousing sexual language, but in a tantalizing scrap the 'I' also speaks to his anonymous future readers (14b):

> *Si qui forte mearum ineptiarum*
> *lectores eritis manusque uestras*
> *non horrebitis admouere nobis,*
>
> If maybe there are some of you who will read my ineptitudes,
> and won't recoil from reaching out and laying hands upon us ...

Here we get a glimpse of Catullus' slightly self-ironical reflection on the reception of his poems.

In the longer poems similar strategies are employed in a more complex, enigmatic way. The dense web of cross-textual (re-)constructions of and metaliterary reflections on elliptical narrative which I have tried to establish through a sequential reading of Catullus' longer poems does not seem to have close analogies in existing Hellenistic poetry, except perhaps in Callimachus' *Hymns* where instances of a self-conscious use of cross-references within a collection of poems can be observed, although there can of course no conclusive results be drawn on such a slight base.[53] But at least in this respect, Catullus appears not only as an heir to Hellenistic narrative techniques, but also as an important forerunner of the Latin love elegists, who in their books of elegies encourage the reader to create a story out of fragmentary "snapshots of a love affair".[54] Similarly, Catullus' longer poems when read in sequence create a sense of a fragmented but somehow coherent mythological narrative, a narrative reflected through shattered pieces of glass that the readers are supposed to put together in order to construct a mosaic.

---

[53] See also Benjamin Acosta-Hughes' paper in this volume, who even suggests a cross-textual link between the *Hecale* and the *Aetia*.
[54] On the narratology of fragmented stories in Latin love elegy (although not in Catullus) see Liveley/Salzman-Mitchell 2008, especially the contribution by Salzman-Mitchell 2008 (the quote is from her title).

III. Aesthetics

Evina Sistakou
From Emotion to Sensation: The Discovery of the Senses in Hellenistic Poetry

> O sunken souls, slaves of sensation.
> H. More, *Psychodia Platonica* (1642)

This verse from a poem called *Psychodia Platonica: or A Platonicall Song of the Soul*, written by the theologian and Neoplatonic philosopher Henry More (1614–1687), records the second earliest occurrence of the word 'sensation' in English–the first is found in a treatise by the physician and anatomist Helkiah Crooke in 1616. These beginnings contextualize the word 'sensation' within physical science and philosophy; it is these contexts (among several others) that may, ideally, be taken into account before discussing the other half of the title, namely 'emotion'. The present study may be subsumed under the umbrella of emotion studies, which involve a series of disciplines, such as philosophy, linguistics, neuroscience, psychology, social sciences, anthropology and ethics. Both scale and skill do not allow for an interdisciplinary approach here. Therefore, the role of emotions in literature will only be treated as a means of understanding the aesthetic principles underlying Hellenistic poetry and poetics. But before moving to the core argument of my paper, a short digression on the notions of 'emotion' and 'sensation' is neccessary.[1]

Emotion is a huge topic, and Aristotle, as usual, provides an ideal point of departure for its exploration. In the *Rhetoric* he explains the ways in which the orator stirs the emotions of his audience to enhance persuasion; within this context he asserts that emotions (πάθη), such as anger (ὀργή), pity (ἔλεος), fear (φόβος) and their opposites, have the power to alter the judgments of men, and remarks that emotions are always followed by either pain (λύπη) or pleasure (ἡδονή) (*Rh.* 1378a.19–22).[2] A first observation deals with the conception of emotion as a passive state of the soul, a πάθος or πάθημα.[3] A second with the distinction between emotion and its effect of pain or pleasure, termed elsewhere

---

[1] For a fascinating introduction to emotion from Aristotle to the present day, see Konstan 2006, 3–40. A general overview of emotions in Greek philosophy in Fitzgerald 2008.
[2] A nice introduction to the emotions in Aristotle's *Rhetoric* is offered by Leighton 1982.
[3] As opposed to ποίημα 'deed, act' (*LSJ*) in Plato, *Sph.* 248b, *R.* 437b. For the history of the Greek term πάθος and its three possible translations into English as 'emotion', 'affect' and 'passion', see Fitzgerald 2008, 2–5.

αἴσθησις (e.g. Aristotle, *On the Soul* 414b.4).[4] On the whole, Aristotle reinforces the cognitive nature of emotions, i.e. their direct association with rationale, judgment and knowledge; moreover, he maintains that emotions always involve moral evaluation and should be construed within the social circumstances that generate them.[5]

Emotion is of primary importance to Aristotle's theory of poetry too. The key concepts of the *Poetics*, μίμησις and πρᾶξις, as also the interdependence between action and character, presuppose the representation of emotions in tragedy in accordance with the logical structuring of the plot and the ethical profile of the characters. But the core of his argument concerns not dramatic emotions as such, but the emotive impact of tragedy upon the audience. I refer of course to the much debated statement that the tragic poet's ability to inspire strong emotions, namely pity and fear, results in the emotional purification, the *katharsis*, of the audience (*Po.* 1449b.27–28).[6] Thus, given the cognitive nature of emotion in Aristotle's thought, the pleasure obtained by a tragic performance satisfies the human desire for knowledge and is not merely a sensual experience.[7]

The power of (poetic) speech to emotionally affect the souls of the listeners is sketched out with greater precision by the sophist Gorgias (*Encomium of Helen* fr. 11 D-K, transl. D.A. Russell): *Those who hear poetry feel the shudders of fear* (φρίκη περίφοβος), *the tears of pity* (ἔλεος πολύδακρυς), *the longings of grief* (πόθος φιλοπενθής). *Through the words, the soul experiences* (ἔπαθεν ἡ ψυχή) *its own reaction to successes and misfortunes in the affairs and persons of others.* I consider Gorgias' passage to be vital in another sense too: in that it explicitly states, through a verb denoting motion (εἰσῆλθε), that emotion (φρίκη, ἔλεος,

---

[4] It is noteworthy that *LSJ* translates αἴσθησις as 'sense-perception, sensation', a translation that matches, at least partly, my own apprehension of the modern term 'sensation'. Potentially relevant to the present argument is another use of αἴσθησις in a passage from the *Poetics* where it denotes the stage-effects as concomitants of poetry proper (*Po.* 1454b.16).

[5] For a cognitive interpretation of emotion in Aristotle, see Fortenbaugh 2002 and Nussbaum 1996.

[6] A comprehensive analysis of tragic emotions in the *Poetics*, also in comparison with other conceptions of emotion in the *Rhetoric* and elsewhere in Aristotle, in Belfiore 1992, 177–253 and more recently in Munteanu 2012; on the role of emotion in Aristotle's aesthetics, see Halliwell 1996, 168–201.

[7] Munteanu 2012, 22 rightly points out that "the term 'mimetic' instead of 'aesthetic' captures the Aristotelian and Platonic understanding of the emotions caused by tragedy", due to the emphasis placed on the mimetic, representational aspects of poetry and not the sensual ones. Yet in the *Republic* (605a-607a) Plato views poetic imitation as being far removed from cognition and truth and stresses the fact that poets nourish desire, pleasure and pain in their listeners' souls instead of teaching them something useful for government and human life.

πόθος) is transferred from the characters into the souls of the listeners. In other words, that the characters' fictive emotions, emotions alien to the listener's life (ἐπ' ἀλλοτρίων πραγμάτων καὶ σωμάτων), become his own experiences (ἴδιόν τι πάθημα).[8]

Gorgias thus inextricably links the emotions expressed in a literary work with the extra-textual emotions of the audience; in effect, he maintains that the emotive response is only possible if the characters themselves are shown to 'feel' strong emotions. Along the same lines, the Platonic Ion, a rhapsode of Homeric poetry, demonstrates that to make his performance highly effective he must be overcome with the emotions of the passages recited (*Ion* 535c-e, transl. D.A. Russell): *When I recite a pathetic passage* (ἐλεινόν τι λέγω), *my eyes fill with tears; when it is something alarming or terrifying* (φοβερὸν ἢ δεινόν), *my hair stands on end in terror and my heart jumps...I can see the people from up on the platform, weeping* (κλάοντας) *and looking fierce* (δεινὸν ἐμβλέποντας) *and marvelling at the tale* (συνθαμβοῦντας τοῖς λεγομένοις). Socrates responds by attributing the ability of the rhapsode, and by extension of the poet, to re-enact intense emotions not to artistic knowledge but to inspiration, the so-called ἐνθουσιασμός (*Ion* 535e-536d).[9]

The question of emotion in art and literature raises significant issues. *Whose emotions are implied?* Those pertaining to the audience, as Aristotle suggests, or to the artist/author, as Ion persuasively argues, or to the work of art itself? *What is their effect?* Enchantment says Gorgias, thrill and marvel affirms Ion, pain and pleasure argues Aristotle. *To what end?* Aristotle's answer is *katharsis*, Gorgias opts for persuasion. But what do the abovementioned passages from the classical era have to do with Hellenistic poetics? What do Hellenistic poets have to say about the emotive role of poetry? The matter is usually suppressed in their most often quoted poetological declarations. We may say, though, without pushing the point, that Callimachus in his *Prologue* views slenderness, lack of bombast, absence of ἐνθουσιασμός as the quintessence of the new poetics; that Theocritus' *boukoloi* pursue sweetness (ἡδύτης) as the ultimate goal of poetry; that Apollonius' persona in the *Argonautica*, the mythic poet Orpheus, has a soothing, en-

---

8 For a classical analysis of Gorgias' aesthetic theory from the viewpoint of its emotional impact on human psychology, see Segal 1962.
9 In *Phaedrus* 245a Socrates explains how the poet's soul is possessed by madness (μανία) when he falls under the spell of the Muses. Several centuries later [Longinus] makes the same connection between emotion and poetic madness by noting that 'strong and inspired' emotion (τὸ σφοδρὸν καὶ ἐνθουσιαστικὸν πάθος) is a vital, albeit not indispensable, source of sublimity (*On the Sublime* 8.1–4).

chanting effect (ἠρεμέοντες κηληθμῷ) upon the listeners of his song. None of these poets seems to link emotion, πάθος, to any of the agents of poetry.[10]

At the opposite end of the spectrum there is 'sensation', a notion deriving from natural science and psychology which denotes the operation of the senses, the impressions received by the organs of sense and hence perception by means of the senses. Sense-perception, αἴσθησις, is a psychological category in Aristotle, characteristic of both men and animals, as argued in his treatises *On the Soul* and *On Sense and Sensibilia*.[11] In regard to poetry sense-perception is considered a negative feature. Αἴσθησις, denoting probably sensation during performance, is found only once in the *Poetics* where it is regarded as a necessary evil of the poetic art (*Po.* 1454b.16 τὰς ἐξ ἀνάγκης ἀκολουθούσας αἰσθήσεις τῇ ποιητικῇ 'the appeals to the senses are the necessary concomitants of poetry').[12] Sensation in Aristotle accounts for the lower type of pleasure that stems not from the mimetic but from the sensual aspects of poetry, such as the visual presentation of tragedy in the theatre or the music accompanying its lyrical parts.

The exploration of the senses, and not of the emotions, during the aesthetic process would have been an anathema to Aristotle. Considering his view of ὄψις the spectacle may be a powerful concomitant of the tragic performance but secondary in comparison to the structure of the tragic plot itself (*Po.* 1453b.1–11). Thus, according to Aristotle's aesthetic scheme, if ὄψις appeals to the senses exclusively through 'cheap' visual effects in the theatre (probably implied by the term τὸ τερατῶδες), it produces sensations in the audience but not genuine emotions as the tragic πρᾶξις does. It would be too superficial to presume that this view applies only to drama. In effect, in devaluating ὄψις Aristotle shifts the focus from the sensual to the cognitive pleasure of poetry.[13] A point reinforced by the fact that "in Aristotle's view, emotions are not blind animal forces, but intelligent and discriminating parts of the personality, closely related to beliefs of a certain sort, and therefore responsive to cognitive modification."[14] In highlighting the cognitive and ethical aspects of emotion, Aristotle at the

---

10 A notable exception: Parthenius highlights emotion as a vital component of his *Erotika Pathemata*. Lightfoot 1999, 220–221 and 367–368 takes a somewhat different view in interpreting παθήματα as symptoms of the pathology of love and not as mere emotions; however, the numerous occurrences of the term πάθος or πάθημα in Parthenius' summaries suggest that he considers it to be a synonym for the passion of love, a strong emotion in itself (on the point cf. Lightfoot 1999, 401–402).
11 For sense-perception in Aristotle, see Everson 1997.
12 On sensation as the lowest type of pleasure as deriving from tragedy, see Halliwell 1998, 66–69.
13 On the cognitive demands of poetry on poets and audiences in Aristotle, see Heath 2009.
14 Nussbaum 1996, 303.

same time rejects sensual pleasure as the aim of poetry.[15] He claims that experiencing art is a process of understanding and learning; therefore, form, colour, texture or rhythm, i.e. sense-perceptions stemming from art that do not exploit the cognitive capacity of the audience, are irrelevant to the true nature of poetics.[16]

This is the key to the interpretation of 'emotion' and 'sensation' in the present paper. My claim is that, instead of pursuing πάθος, i.e. instead of adhering to the principles introduced by Aristotle, several Hellenistic poets exploit the senses to create aesthetic impressions. During the laborious process of transforming emotion to sensation, Hellenistic aesthetics is characterized by two parallel tendencies, as I shall argue below: the deconstruction of 'classical' emotions in plot-based genres and the evocation of the senses for the creation of aesthetic effects in both mimetic and descriptive contexts. Examples shall be drawn from the entire range of Hellenistic poetry and are deliberately not confined to a sole genre or poet; for methodological reasons, the focus is first on the representation of emotions/sensations within the poems, and eventually on the aesthetic evaluation of this representation.[17]

1. Emotions revisited

> The first and the simplest emotion
> which we discover in the human mind is curiosity.
> E. Burke, *On the Sublime and Beautiful* (1756)

Emotions depend on genre and gender, and words or actions of particular characters, as well as their ethical standards, are defined by them.[18] For Aristotle, to quote once more his authoritative statements about aesthetics, character is a complex dramatic construct and does not imply any 'actual' individual. Thus, in epic the male hero is expected to comply with the heroic values and express

---

15 By presupposing the dichotomy between sense and knowledge in the human soul as expressed in *On the Soul* (431b.21–23): ἢ γὰρ αἰσθητὰ τὰ ὄντα ἢ νοητά, ἔστι δ' ἡ ἐπιστήμη μὲν τὰ ἐπιστητά πως, ἡ δ' αἴσθησις τὰ αἰσθητά.
16 For an in-depth analysis of Aristotle's distinction between the function of sense and that of cognition and the pleasure of art, see Halliwell 1998, 66–69.
17 In my discussion of Hellenistic poetry, I use the following translations: for Callimachus Nisetich 2001; for Apollonius' *Argonautica* Hunter 1993a; for Theocritus Gow 1950; for Moschus and Bion Edmonds 1912 with modifications.
18 On how genre and gender influence the representation of emotions in ancient literature and art, see the excellent collective volume by Munteanu 2011.

corresponding emotions which motivate specific speech and action—and the same holds true for the σπουδαῖοι or φαῦλοι of tragedy and comedy respectively. Despite the Alexandrian penchant for ποικιλία, the so-called 'crossing' between genres, characters that are expected to display typical emotions can be found within traditional generic forms.

Apollonius' *Argonautica* provides cogent evidence for this.[19] Jason may not have the status of an Achilles or an Ajax (as regards for example the emotions of anger or shame), yet he often shares intense feelings with other characters in the epic: when Herakles is left behind in Mysia, a fierce quarrel breaks out (κρατερὸν νεῖκος), Telamon, blinded by folly (ἀασάμην), is seized by wrath (ἕλεν χόλος) that causes bewilderment (ἀμηχανίῃσιν ἀτυχθείς), frustration (βαρείῃ ἄτῃ θυμὸν ἔδων) and grief (ἀνιηθείς) to Jason, until forgiveness is offered and concord restored (1.1289–1343);[20] the passage of the Argo through the Symplegades, a terrifying experience for the Argonauts (ὀκρυόεντος ἀνέπνεον ἄρτι φόβοιο), is followed by Jason's speech on his fear (περισσὸν δεῖμα, δείδι' ἑταίρων, τάρβος) about his comrades (2.607–648); grief, a feeling dwelling in Jason's heart from the onset of the enterprise (1.297 ἐπ' ἄλγεσιν ἄλγος), marks all the crucial stages of the voyage (e.g. when the Argonauts lament for Idmon and Tiphys in 2.835–863); Jason also experiences joy, once he receives a good omen (1.1104 κεχαρημένος) or help from Medea (3.1148 κεχαρμένος); elsewhere he feels gratitude (3.973 τίσαιμι χάριν) or shame towards the gods (4.1316 δαίμονας αἰδεσθείς).[21] A variety of emotions is expressed by Herakles, the representative of archaic epic, several Argonauts such as Idas and Tiphys, the tyrannical king Aietes and others. Females in the *Argonautica* are even more susceptible to emotion than males. Alkimede, Jason's mother, is given over to lamentation and woe upon the departure of the Argo supported by other Thessalian women (1.247–293); more nuanced is the role of Chalkiope, a mother/daughter/sister figure, who is involved in complex emotional relations with other char-

---

[19] For a critical overview of the studies about 'character' in the *Argonautica*, see Glei 2008, 6–15.
[20] Mori 2005 argues that in privileging self-control over excessive anger, Jason becomes a new type of epic hero and hence Apollonius, by promoting reconciliation and harmony in the episode with Telamon, rejects traditional epic quarrels. On anger in the *Argonautica*, see Manakidou 1998; on the deconstruction of 'heroic anger' in the face of Jason, see Fantuzzi/Hunter 2004, 104–117.
[21] Character and emotion are inextricably woven together, especially in plot-based genres; for a detailed discussion of both, also in interaction with the status of male heroism, see Beye 1982, 77–99, Clauss 1993 and the very convincing analysis of the epic character in the *Argonautica* by Hunter 1993b, 8–15.

acters in the epic (e.g. in 3.669–739); Hypsipyle, and, above all, Medea, become victims of the most powerful emotion—love.

What can be inferred from this rough sketch of the emotions in the *Argonautica*? First, that (at least) Apollonius does not refrain from depicting strong emotions. Yet, secondly, that he dramatically modifies conventional epic emotion. Jason's anger and fear, joy and shame, his 'heroic' emotions lack coherence, depth and hence moral underpinning. The attempt to treat Jason and the Argonauts as 'real people' with a credible psychology has rightly been rejected:[22] as textual heroes, trapped in their literary history and incorporating a pastiche of previous heroic behaviours, they convey only fossilized, fractured emotional states. On the other hand, emotion bordering on human passion is dislocated, once transferred not only from male to female, but also, on a generic level, from epic to tragedy in the *Argonautica*.[23] Ἔρως is the matrix from which the moral dilemmas and the ensuing emotions of Medea, the tragic heroine, arise.[24] In experiencing a wide range of emotions from shame to fear, from grief to joy, from agony to despair, Medea is given the finest psychological profile in all Alexandrian poetry. It is through this heroine that Apollonius subsumes emotion under the category of the erotic rather than the heroic, a trend pervading Hellenistic aesthetics on the whole.[25]

Fossilization and dislocation are not the only strategies employed in the treatment of Hellenistic emotion. Another, very significant one, is detachment. Theocritean bucolic offers striking examples of how emotion can be moderated and restrained through distancing. A test case is *Idyll* 1, where the bucolic frame minimizes the impact of the emotions depicted within the framed narratives.[26]

---

[22] The non-Aristotelian conception of character in the *Argonautica* is reinforced by a) the reduction of direct speech which renders the characters less dramatic and b) the un-Homeric setting in which less credible characters move (Hunter 1993b, 13). For the contrasting, realistic reading of Jason, see Clauss 1993, 24–25.
[23] Females acquire key roles in Hellenistic poetry, and it is noteworthy that their characterization is achieved through direct speech: cf. e.g. the emotional monologues of Callimachus' Hekale or the affective dialogue between Alkmene and Megara in Moschus' *Megara*. Both poems have a special affinity with tragedy too: as Fantuzzi/Hunter 2004, 195–196 note in regard to the epyllia "the boundaries between *mimesis* and *diegesis* are breaking down".
[24] For a thorough analysis of Medea and the conflicts of love, see Vian 1995, 39–48.
[25] Conspicuous examples of erotic emotion in excess include Theocritus' Simaitha from *Idyll* 2, Peisidike from Apollonius' *Lesbou ktisis* and several minor erotic heroines treated by Euphorion and Parthenius. On Hellenistic love, see Rohde 1960, 12–177 and on erotic suffering as a neoteric feature, see Johnson 2007, 180–186; the shift from the heroic to the erotic is also evident in the Hellenistic depiction of Achilles, on which see Sistakou 2008a, 163–176.
[26] The effect of framing in Theocritus' pastoral poetics is superbly analyzed by Goldhill 1991, 246–261.

The three vignettes constituting the *ekphrasis* of the κισσύβιον reflect, directly or indirectly, human emotions (1.32–54): the love triangle of the woman with the two suitors conveys feelings of frustration and contempt within an erotic context, the snapshot of the old fisherman his loneliness and misery, the picture of the little boy with the foxes zeal and contentment. The realism with which the figures are represented on the pastoral cup through their facial expressions and bodily gestures evokes naturalistic trends of Hellenistic art—yet these figures impart a dispassionate view of the real world.[27] The contrast between frame and framed is carried to extremes once the song of Thyrsis is performed. The passions of Daphnis (Δάφνιδος ἄλγεα) sung therein combine two extreme dramatic situations, namely the sorrows of love and the mourning for the death of a youth.[28] It is within this context that one of the rare Hellenistic occurrences of πάσχω and/or its derivative is found, in a phrase highlighting the passivity of Daphnis' emotional state (81 πάντες ἀνηρώτευν τι πάθοι κακόν, cf. 85 δύσερως, ἀμήχανος) and its concomitant physical symptoms (66 ἐτάκετο, 82 τι τυ τάκεαι); the involvement of nature in the unfolding drama seems to heighten the emotion of the scene. Yet, although the death scene evokes tragic emotions, the *boukoloi*, *qua* listeners, are seduced by the sweetness of its artistic representation (see esp. vv. 146–148);[29] the *locus amoenus* wherein the enigmatic ἀσυχία reigns renders this eutopic society of poets almost emotion-free. Similar effects follow Polyphemos' serenade to Galatea in *Idyll* 11 and the love songs of Simichidas and Lykidas in *Idyll* 7.

If Theocritus promotes aesthetic distance as a means of neutralizing emotion, his followers, by contrast, further emotionalize poetry in both bucolic and non-bucolic contexts.[30] Love becomes almost a 'textual' emotion, in the sense that it reproduces the Theocritean prototype with all its formalistic conventions. But there are significant modifications in the handling of this emotion, which resonate with modern conceptions such as sentimentality and melodrama. From the ps.-Theocritea I shall point out two telling examples: the naive

---

[27] On the naturalistic depiction of πάθος and ἦθος in Hellenistic *ekphrases* and art criticism, see Prioux 2011.
[28] The key term in both is ἄλγος, which points to physical pain and corporeal sensation not to emotion proper; on this point, see Konstan 2006, 244–248.
[29] Bernsdorff 2006, 191–192 notes that Theocritean realism, the crude, obscene sexuality of his herdsmen, stands in stark contrast to the impassionate emotions implied by the content of their love songs: I suspect that this is another 'filter' through which emotional effect is blocked in Theocritus.
[30] Bernsdorff 2006, 188–201 argues that emotionalization, i.e. representation of emotions, increases in post-Theocritean bucolic poetry. For love as the emotion *par excellence* in the imitators of Theocritus, see Fantuzzi/Hunter 2004, 170–190.

cowherd who engages in a self-indulgent monologue on love in *Idyll* 20 *Boukoliskos* 'The Young Cowherd' and the sensational story of a young man, who overcome by erotic frustration, hangs himself at the door of his cruel lover in *Idyll* 23 *Erastes* 'The Lover'. Other variations, such as the mourning for (or *with*) ἔρως, as exemplified by the two epitaphs on Bion and Adonis from the bucolic corpus, further heighten the πάθος of post-Theocritean mannerism rather than connect to Aristotelian conceptions of cognitive emotions.[31] The all-importance of love in emotional excess is evident in the numerous poems dedicated to the god Eros by Bion and Moschus, as also in the later collection of *Erotika Pathemata* by Parthenius, all of which foreground the individualized, subjective experience of love as reflected in epigram and Roman elegy.[32]

Nothing to do with Aristotle, then.[33] With the exception, perhaps, of one Hellenistic heroine who represents a fine blend of epic and tragic emotion: Callimachus' Hekale.[34] And yet. Though Hekale appears to be a reincarnation, or even a phantom, of Aristotelian figures such as Eumaios (evoking the low character-type) or Hekabe (a tragic mother combining grief and vengefulness), she is remembered, in my view at least, for a particularly non-classical, non-Aristotelian emotion. This is loneliness, a psychological state that has only recently acquired the status of an emotion.[35] The opening line, portraying a desolate woman in a desolate setting (fr. 1 H. Ἀκταίη τις ἔναιεν Ἐρεχθέος ἔν ποτε γουνῷ 'Once, in the uplands of Erechtheus, lived an Attic woman...'), sets the tone for the entire epyllion. Loneliness is reflected in Theseus' critical question]γρηῦς ἐ[ρη]μαίη ἔνι ναίεις 'why you live, an old woman, in an isolated country...?' (fr. 40.5 H.). More intensely in the fact that Hekale lives only through her memories, that she awaits for strangers to engage in conversation and, of course, that she even-

---

[31] A concomitant of this πάθος is seen in the emotional interaction between human and nature, a device known as pathetic fallacy (Bernsdorff 2006, 195–197).
[32] Cf. Fantuzzi/Hunter 2004, 190 who conclude that "the combination of Bion's erotic values and the coincidence between *persona loquens* and author, which had existed in archaic lyric poetry and in epigram, would render more credible and immediate the exclusive, eternal faithfulness to the beloved and to love poetry which is claimed by Latin elegists".
[33] Despite admitting the significant influence of Aristotle in philological matters in Alexandria, Mori 1995, 220–223 seriously doubts whether Hellenistic poets likewise accepted Aristotelian views on emotion (e.g. in p. 220 "I would not want to claim that Apollonius himself was wholeheartedly Aristotelian in either his philosophical beliefs or his aesthetic tastes"); nevertheless, he argues that like Aristotle, Hellenistic poets, and especially Apollonius, were concerned with the appropriateness of speeches and actions to particular character-types.
[34] For Hekale as an epic hero professing κλέος, see McNelis 2003; as a tragic heroine, the equivalent of Hekabe, see Hutchinson 1988, 56–59 and Fantuzzi/Hunter 2004, 198–200.
[35] Loneliness, along with jealousy, are new emotions according to Konstan 2006, 219–221.

tually dies alone. This loneliness is inconceivable by Aristotelian standards: it lacks moral motivation and does not reflect social status—and it obviously cannot be construed as a response to another individual's action. It is rather a result of accidental events, such as, in the case of miserable Hekale, the collapse of family and the loss of wealth. As has been succinctly explained "we may particularly note the absence from Aristotle's inventory of such sentiments as sadness, loneliness, or grief, which may result from circumstances beyond anyone's control rather than from a hostile intention on the part of others. Such responses to natural loss, as opposed to morally charged social interactions and struggles for status and advantage, are not part of the core set of emotions in the classical period".[36]

What the example of Hekale teaches us about the evolution of emotion in Hellenistic poetry is the idea of modernization. Loneliness is not confined to Hekale, but may also evoke the romantic soliloquy of Berenike's Lock (*Aet.* fr. 110 Pf.) or the wanderings of lovesick Akontios in the country (*Aet.* fr. 72–73 Pf.). Through these emotional snapshots, Callimachus introduces novel emotions, among which melancholy is most prominent.[37] Along the lines of modernization we may also consider another Hellenistic emotion *par excellence*, namely ἀμηχανίη. Ἀμηχανίη 'helplessness' is coined already in Homer (denoting e.g. the helplessness of Odysseus and his comrades in *Od.* 9.295) and is recurrent in tragedy, yet it is the basic emotion that renders the character of Jason in the *Argonautica* consistent and intelligible. Some scholars have seen helplessness as a symptom of Jason's melancholy and depression, others as a concomitant of his depiction as a lover, but all agree that ἀμηχανίη is an emblem of the modern hero.[38] Helplessness, in effect, goes hand in hand with the inability of Jason to produce heroic speech and action thoughout the *Argonautica*. Moreover, Jason's helplessness is characterized by inwardness, passivity, pensiveness and an inclination to depression (1.460–461): ἔνθ' αὖτ' Αἰσονίδης μὲν ἀμήχανος εἶν ἑοῖ αὐτῷ / πορφύρεσκεν ἕκαστα, κατηφιόωντι ἐοικώς 'there, however, the son of Aison pondered upon everything helpless and absorbed, like a man in despair' (cf. 1.1286–1289). It is extremely interesting that Jason's melancholic

---

[36] Konstan 2006, 40, who, however, notes that emotions in the Hellenistic period diverge from Aristotle's scheme.
[37] On melancholy in ancient literature, see Toohey 2004.
[38] This view is first supported by Lawall 1966, 148–169 and further refined by Vian 1978; Jackson 1992 defends helplessness as a positive trait, characteristic of Jason as a human being. For the depiction of Jason as a depressive melancholic, see Toohey 2004, 42–45.

ἀμηχανίη reflects attitudes of a life dedicated to introspection, an intellectual or aesthetic stance that was to become so characteristic of the Romantic era.[39]

Modernization, along with the previously discussed stategies, dramatically alters classical conceptions of character and emotion. New genres, new aesthetics require a different approach to emotion—this is what I have termed 'sensation' and to which I shall now turn my attention.

2. The making of sensation

> Brooding music, faint and far-off,
> like the mood of the moonlight made audible.
> E. O'Neill, *Moon of Caribbees* (1919)

To emphasize the initial stimulus of an emotion, the sensory motivation over its logical procession, the affective experience that causes reactions beyond reason or value judgment holds a great fascination for Hellenistic poets. Not depending on generic conventions or complying with the logic of plot and character, sensations are autonomous as they are omnipresent in post-classical poetry. A noticeable example of an emotion developed into sensation is love—the idea of love at first sight is at least as old as Sapphic lyricism yet fully exploited in Hellenistic times. How does Jason seduce Hypsipyle in Book 1 of the *Argonautica*? Not by his eloquence but by his appearance, his ὄψις. Lemnian women and their queen fall in love *upon viewing* the hero (1.774–780): *He went towards the city like the bright star* (φαεινῷ ἀστέρι) *whose rising is admired* (θηήσαντο) *by young brides, shut up in their new-built chambers. Its red brilliance* (καλὸν ἐρευθόμενος) *through the dark air* (κυανέοιο δι' ἠέρος) *bewitches their eyes* (ὄμματα θέλγει), *and the virgin, too, rejoices* (γάνυται) *in her desire* (ἱμείρουσα) *for the young man who lives in a distant city.* Here love is inspired by visual perception, in which colour plays a prominent role.[40] Vision is of primary importance also in the case of the hapless Peisidike, who falls in love with Achilles while his ἀριστεία on the battlefield unfolds in front of her eyes in the *Lesbou ktisis* (fr. 12.6–9 CA).[41] And vision is im-

---

39 Cf. the apposite remark by Toohey 2004, 45: "Jason's depression, however, is extremely interesting in another way...His persistently depressive response to adversity suggests a disposition that is prone to melancholia. We might say that—whether or not he is certifiable as a melancholic—he has the signs of an individual who is prone to sorrow without cause".
40 Colour perception has a special importance for Hellenistic aesthetics, but has not been treated systematically by scholars; exceptions include the discussions of colour terminology in Nicander (Papadopoulou 2009) and Bion (Fountoulakis 2004).
41 For a visual reading of the Peisidike story, see Sistakou 2008b, 331–336.

mediately transformed into infatuation once Simaitha is struck by the image of the glistening Delphis (2.78–82): *I saw Delphis and Eudamippos walking together. More golden than helichryse were their beards* (ξανθοτέρα μὲν ἐλιχρύσοιο γενειάς), *and their breasts brighter* (στήθεα δὲ στίλβοντα) *than you, O Moon…I saw, and madness seized me* (χὡς ἴδον ὡς ἐμάνην), *and my hapless heart was aflame.*

Love, in Hellenistic poetry at least, is an emotion grounded in sight perception; to be more precise, though, what is explored in the abovementioned passages is desire not love proper.[42] Fear is also explored in similar terms. The only 'true' literary heroes in Hellenistic poetry, Jason and Medea in the *Argonautica*, often express fear. Jason's feigned speech on fear before the passage through the Symplegades (2.622–637) and Medea's nightmare fears in Books 3 and 4 are well-known paradigms; in both cases the emotion connects either to logical reasoning or moral dilemma. Yet not all Hellenistic depictions of fear have this Aristotelian touch. Immediacy of perception and impulsive reaction characterize fear, or rather terror, in numerous other passages. An extraordinary sight of supernatural provenance, accompanied occasionally by dreadful sounds, strikes terror into the hearts of the beholders: of the Argonauts, once they view the cliffs and listen to the roaring of the Symplegades (2.552 πολλὸν δὲ φόβῳ προτέρωσε νέοντο), the fire-breathing bulls of Aietes (3.1293 ἔδδεισαν δ' ἥρωες, ὅπως ἴδον) or Talos, the bronze automaton (4.1649–1650 αἶψ' ἀπὸ χέρσου / νῆα περιδδείσαντες ἀνακρούεσκον ἐρετμοῖς); of women who behold Theseus dragging the bull of Marathon (Callimachus, *Hek.* fr. 69.2 H. ὡς ἴδον, ὦ[ς] ἅμα πάντες ὑπέτρεσαν) or Kerberos carried alive from Hades by Herakles (Euphorion fr. 51.15 CA ταρβαλέαι σὺν παισὶν ἐθηήσαντο γυναῖκες); of Alkmene in the memorable scene from Theocritus' *Little Herakles* when the godsent serpents invade her house (24.35 'ἐμὲ γὰρ δέος ἴσχει ὀκνηρόν'). Formulaic as they may sound,[43] these passages highlight the importance of the sense stimulus for the generation of a sensation—in this case, terror.

Both paradigms treated above, desire and terror, point to the distinction, albeit blurred at times, between sensations and emotions, and demonstrate that the narrow criteria by which Aristotle defines and classifies the latter may not

---

[42] For the distinction between classical φιλία, that comprises comradeship, familiarity and kinship, and Romantic conceptions of love, see Konstan 2006, 169–184; for a thorough review of this, sexually motivated, love (ἔρως) as a passion, see Konstan 1994.
[43] The passages exploit a common Homeric formula suggesting the simultaneity of sense-stimulus and emotion (e.g. in *Il.* 12.208 Τρῶες δ' ἐρρίγησαν ὅπως ἴδον αἰόλον ὄφιν, 14.294 ὡς δ' ἴδεν, ὥς μιν ἔρως πυκινὰς φρένας ἀμφεκάλυψεν): on the device, see Gow 1950, 2.51–52.

be easily applied to the former.⁴⁴ Thus, it is explicable why only these primeval emotions can be rendered as sensations, and not more complex ones, such as shame or gratitude, emotions presupposing some kind of intellectual involvement on the part of the agent. In the passages discussed the motivation of desire and terror is real, 'visible', not vague or imaginary; and the response to it is immediate, instinctive, hence its result does not deserve to be called a genuine emotion.⁴⁵ It should be clear by now that the process of emotion has affective and psychological implications that are non-rational, and I believe that Hellenistic poets tend to concentrate on them rather than on the cognitive aspects of emotion. To demonstrate this I shall first discuss the physical manifestation of emotional states, then the irrational emotions and finally the concepts of *feeling* and *mood*; in each of these cases sense and sensation play a dominant role.

An important contribution of modern psychology to the study of emotion is the emphasis placed on bodily expressions which convey specific emotional properties: tears indicate grief, laughter joy, shudder fear and so on.⁴⁶ A notable contrast between classical and Hellenistic aesthetics, especially if we consider art, is the detached idealism vs. the violent realism of expression as reflected on statues; obviously the latter artistic vogue marks a turn towards individual sensibility.⁴⁷ A fully-fledged study on emotions triggering a series of bodily changes is offered by Apollonius in the portrayal of Medea in the *Argonautica*. Books 3 and 4 monitor the fluctuations of Medea's heart as somatic experiences. At the beginning Eros struck Medea, and *at one moment her soft cheeks were drained of colour, at another they blushed red, the control of her mind now gone* (3.297–298). Anguish overcame her as she lay on her bed with *both of her cheeks scratched in mourning* and *her eyes confused with tears* (3.672–673). Reflecting

---

44 Aristotle's list of emotions comprises anger, satisfaction, shame, envy, indignation, fear, gratitude, love, hatred, pity, jealousy and grief, a scheme followed by Konstan 2006 in his monograph on ancient Greek emotion.
45 The closest parallel to this notion is the Stoic conception of *preliminary passions* (προπάθειαι) or *emotional movements* (παθητικαὶ κινήσεις) which denote affective reactions beyond the voluntary control of the agent, and hence beyond reason—e.g. trembling or paleness as a result of a sudden fearful experience: on this psychological phenomenon, see Inwood 1985, 175–181.
46 For an overview of the psychology of emotion from Darwin onwards, see Konstan 2006, 7–29.
47 Konstan 2006, 29–30 points out this distinction and superbly links this turn to Romantic aesthetics (p. 29): "The emphasis on expression corresponds, then, not only to an interest in the communicative function of the emotions but to a Romantic conception of the self as an internal and private locus of feeling, which is exposed particularly in moments of intense passion—a view of the self that was receptive as well to the hermeneutics of Freudian depth psychology".

her inner struggle between shame and desire, *Medea's cheeks grew red and words rose to the very tip of her tongue, but they flew back again deep into her chest* (3.681–684). Upon deciding to help Jason, *Medea's heart within her leapt for joy, her beautiful face grew flushed, and a mist descended over her in the warmth of her delight* (3.724–726). During the night anguish seized her, and *often her heart fluttered wildly in her breast* and *from her eyes flowed tears of pity* (3.752–761). In her meeting with Jason she became sick with desire upon viewing him—*her heart within her breast dropped, her eyes grew misty, and a hot flush seized her cheeks, and she had no strength at all to move her legs, but her feet were held fast beneath her* (3.962–965). While fleeing the house of the father, Hera instilled fear into her heart: *fire filled her eyes, and in her ears was a terrible roaring, and often she felt her throat, often she screamed in pain and lamentation, pulling her hair out by its roots* (4.16–19). Medea—and the reader, we might add—senses the emotional distress with every inch of her body.[48]

Like these emotive states that are translated into physical symptoms, dream emotion can hardly be explained in terms of reason and cognition;[49] irrational emotions, mostly negative feelings stemming from nightmares or hallucinations, are richly explored by Hellenistic poets. Their sense connection is evident in the fact that they involve strong visual sensations. An obvious example is the figure of Kassandra, whose prophetic mania is both irrational and sensational. Hallucinations, rendered as visual impressions, form her psychological profile both in Aeschylus' tragedy and in Lycophron's *Alexandra*. In the latter sense-perception is reinforced by words suggesting vision (λεύσσω is the most common of these vv. 52, 86, 216 etc.) but particularly by the flood of horror images that are visualized for over 1400 verses.[50] Other senses are also involved, as in the following passage in which Alexandra's horror is stimulated by images *and* sounds of the conquered city (vv. 251–257): *all the land lies ravaged before my eyes* (προὐμ-

---

[48] Toohey 2004, 59–103 argues that the physical symptoms of emotional disorder in Apollonius' Medea resemble those of melancholy as a result of manic lovesickness and erotic trauma. On the psychological profile of Medea in Book 3, see Barkhuizen 1979.
[49] The idea is expressly stated, among others, by Plato (*R*. 571c.3–7): τὰς περὶ τὸν ὕπνον, ἦν δ' ἐγώ, ἐγειρομένας, ὅταν τὸ μὲν ἄλλο τῆς ψυχῆς εὕδῃ, ὅσον λογιστικὸν καὶ ἥμερον καὶ ἄρχον ἐκείνου, τὸ δὲ θηριῶδές τε καὶ ἄγριον, ἢ σίτων ἢ μέθης πλησθέν, σκιρτᾷ τε καὶ ἀπωσάμενον τὸν ὕπνον ζητῇ ἰέναι καὶ ἀποπιμπλάναι τὰ αὑτοῦ ἤθη.
[50] For a reading of the *Alexandra* as a *phantasmagoria*, in which however visuality does not have the status of sense-perception but rather of an imaginary vision, see Sistakou 2012, 133–145. But emotion may be generated either by immediate perception or by representation of a perception in memory; this is the notion given to φαντασία by Aristotle, which may also be a source of pleasure (e.g. in *Rh*. 1370a.27–29 ἐπεὶ δ' ἐστὶ τὸ ἥδεσθαι ἐν τῷ αἰσθάνεσθαί τινος πάθους, ἡ δὲ φαντασία ἐστὶν αἴσθησίς τις ἀσθενής).

μάτων)...*and in my ears seems a voice of lamentation* (οἰμωγὴ δέ μοι ἐν ὠσὶ) *from the top of the towers*... Sight and hearing are also combined in another Hellenistic dream scene—the nightmare of Medea in the *Argonautica* (3.616–644). Although Medea's dream has setting, characters and plot, i.e. has its own logical structure and scenario, it is the sudden cry of the parents, implying sense-perception, that precipitates her into fear (3.631–633): *her parents were seized by unbearable grief* (ἀμέγαρτον ἄχος) *and cried aloud in their anger* (ἐκ δ' ἐβόησαν χωόμενοι); *with their scream* (κλαγγῇ) *sleep left her, and she sprang up, quaking with fear* (παλλομένη δ' ἀνόρουσε φόβῳ)... Sensation beyond reason here too.[51]

A third example derives from the celebrated dream of Europa in Moschus' epyllion. In the opening lines, the heroine has a strange dream where two women fight over her; Moschus' innovation in the treatment of Europa's psychology lies in the depiction of her conflicting emotions. At first the dream has a sweet timbre (1–5) but once it is over Europa finds herself in the grip of fear (16–19); a vivid visual impression, sensed as an actual sight, generates this emotion—*but she still had both women before her wide open eyes* (19 εἰσέτι πεπταμένοισιν ἐν ὄμμασιν). Before realizing the meaning of the dream, Europa is overwhelmed by yet another sensation (25–27)—desire for the mysterious woman (ὥς μ' ἔλαβε κραδίην κείνης πόθος) with which she has an intimate contact (ὥς με καὶ αὐτή ἀσπασίως ὑπέδεκτο).[52] It is almost as if her senses (not only vision but also touch!) delude her into feeling desire instead of fear, whereas a logical interpretation of her dream would have suggested quite the opposite.[53] Sense is so powerful in Europa's vision, as it is in the entire epyllion, that it annihilates reason and brings primitive emotion to the fore.[54]

---

[51] The subjective feeling and the unconscious emotionality of Medea's dream as a reflection of her inner desire is superbly explored by Fusillo 1994.
[52] Cf. ἀνεπτοίησαν ὄνειροι in v. 23 with its sexual undertones: see Campbell 1991 on v. 23.
[53] Dream sensation in Moschus runs counter Aristotle's principle according to which men in the state of dreaming are incapable of experiencing true sensations (*On Dreams* 459b.19–21 ἀδυνατεῖ δὲ πάντα μύοντα καὶ καθεύδοντα ὁρᾶν, ὁμοίως δὲ καὶ ἐπὶ τῶν λοιπῶν, δῆλον ὅτι οὐκ αἰσθανόμεθα οὐδὲν ἐν τοῖς ὕπνοις· οὐκ ἄρα γε τῇ αἰσθήσει τὸ ἐνύπνιον αἰσθανόμεθα) but are only subject to φαντασία 'imagination'.
[54] The dichotomy between reason and emotion is modern, mainly introduced by Descartes' theory of the passions as stemming primarily from body perceptions (*The Passions of the Soul*, 1649), continued by Rousseau's stress on the superiority of feeling over reason and further refined by Romantic thinkers and Freudian depth psychology.

Moschus' *Europa* is a great starting point for approaching sensations in Hellenistic poetry;[55] Moschus, as well as Bion, to whom I will briefly refer, the later imitators of Theocritus, exaggerate the features of his poetry and provide telling examples of how emotion is transformed into sensation in Hellenistic times. The key lies in the very definition of *feeling* as denoting initially the physical sensibility of touch and then, by extension, the subjective experience of emotion, especially associated with pain and pleasure. Sense stimuli participate in the formation of feelings, and it is the emphasis on the sensual aspects of human passions that constitutes the quintessense of bucolic poetics.[56] Thus, starting from the end of the bucolic tradition, we can clearly observe the wealth of sensations which pervade this poetry. Two examples suffice to illustrate the point. The arrival of Zeus disguised as a bull at the idyllic meadow in Moschus' *Europa* kindles desire into the hearts of the girls—expressed in terms of touch and smell. *So came he into that meadow without affraying those maidens; and they were straightway taken with a desire* (ἔρως γένετ') *to come near and touch the lovely ox* (ψαῦσαί θ' ἱμερτοῖο βοὸς), *whose divine fragrance* (ἄμβροτος ὀδμή) *came so far and outdid even the delightsome odour of that breathing meadow* (89–92). In what follows Europa immerses herself in the sensation of the moment during her erotic encounter with the bull. *There went he then and stood before the spotless maiden Europa, and for to cast his spell upon her began to lick her pretty neck* (οἱ λιχμάζεσκε δέρην). *Whereat she fell to touching and toying* (ἣ δέ μιν ἀμφαφάασκε), *and wiped gently away the foam that was thick upon his mouth* (ἠρέμα χείρεσιν ἀφρὸν πολλὸν ἀπὸ στομάτων ἀπομόργνυτο), *until at last she kissed* (κύσε) *the bull* (93–96).[57] Europa translates erotic passion for the bull into tangible feeling, and so does Aphrodite when she describes desire as a process of kissing in Bion's *Epitaph for Adonis* (45–50). *Awake Adonis, awake for a little while, and give me one last kiss; kiss me all so long as ever the kiss be alive* (τοσσοῦτόν με φίλησον ὅσον ζώει τὸ φίλημα), *until you give up your breath into my mouth* (ἄχρις ἀποψύχῃς ἐς ἐμὸν στόμα) *and your spirit pass into my heart* (κεὶς

---

[55] "The *Europa* is an unusually sensual poem" remarks Schmiel 1981, 270–272, who rightly observes that the appeal to the senses (vision, touch, sound, even smell and taste) are prominent throughout the poem.

[56] By the term *bucolic* I refer to the poets of the bucolic corpus in general, and not to the poems which are explicitly set against a pastoral background: love poetry, mythological epyllia and mimes share a similar view on sensations with those idylls which have a strictly bucolic scenario. For a brilliant analysis of the bucolic terminology which embraced, especially for the imitators of Theocritus, love poetry in general, see Gutzwiller 2006.

[57] According to Campbell 1991, on vv. 95–96 ἀφρόν ἀπομόργνυτο is a double entendre suggesting that Europa is wiping off Zeus' semen from her body: the sexual connotation further heightens the impact of sensation in this passage.

ἐμὸν ἧπαρ πνεῦμα τεὸν ῥεύσῃ), *until I have drawn up all your charm* (τὸ δὲ σευ γλυκὺ φίλτρον ἀμέλξω) *and drunk your love* (ἐκ δὲ πίω τὸν ἔρωτα); *and that kiss of Adonis I will keep as it were he that gave it, now that you fly me, poor miserable...* Here the emotion, ἔρως, can be felt by the senses—it is drinkable, sweet to taste, of material nature, with a life of its own.[58]

Sensualism, sweetness, the arrest of the moment. This is what the bucolic ideal amounts to, and this is how emotions emerge not as moral entities or social values but as pure senses. As seen, Moschus and Bion render sensations as individualized feelings; love and mourning, desire and grief merge in a panorama of the senses. Theocritus, on the other hand, especially but not exclusively in those idylls that are based on a bucolic scenario, represents sets of sensations that pervade not only the songs and their characters but the entire cosmos. Indeed, Theocritus' *boukoloi* perceive the eutopia through the operation of all senses. Not just personified but at moments animated the bucolic world offers a plethora of sensuous experiences. At the beginning of *Idyll* 1 ἡδύτης 'sweetness' results from a combination of the five senses: hearing (1 ψιθύρισμα, 12 ἁ πίτυς μελίσδεται, 7–8 τὸ καταχὲς ὕδωρ), sight (8 ἀπὸ τῆς πέτρας καταλείβεται ὑψόθεν ὕδωρ, 13 τὸ κάταντες γεώλοφον), taste (6 χιμάρῳ δὲ καλὸν κρέας, cf. 58 τυρόεντα μέγαν λευκοῖο γάλακτος), smell (28 ἔτι γλυφάνοιο ποτόσδον) and touch (6 ἔστε κ' ἀμέλξῃς, 25 ἐς τρὶς ἀμέλξαι). As the poem develops, sensuality is reinforced by viewing, touching and smelling the ivy-cup and listening to Thyrsis' song; by the end of the idyll sweetness reaches its climax in an orgy of sensual and synesthetic experiences—Thyrsis' mouth is full of honey, his song more sweet-sounding than the voice of the cicada, the ivy-cup gives off a rich fragrance for those beholding it, the young animals are eager to be milked, the goats are about to be aroused...

Idyll 1 stands out as an extraordinary example of how emotion gives its place to sensation, and this, in turn, to a pervading *mood*, an atmosphere that conveys an overwhelming feeling—in this case, enigmatic sweetness. Mood tends to be dominant in non-mimetic contexts, in descriptions and lyrical passages, sometimes even in didactic, all of which are vital to Hellenistic aesthetics;[59] moreover,

---

[58] Bonelli 1979, 35–42 brilliantly points out the 'carnal' quality of love and death, and of Adonis' kiss in this epitaph which resonates with Romantic and Decadent tones.

[59] Mood becomes evident in passages dense with sensations. Apart from the Hellenistic *ekphrases*, sensational descriptions include the tempest scene and the awakening of the city from Callimachus' *Hekale* (fr. 18 H. and fr. 74.22–28 H. respectively) and lyrical passages from Theocritus such as the abduction of Hylas in *Idyll* 13 and the song for Adonis in *Idyll* 15. Didactic may be associated with sensation and the creation of specific moods such as horror and disgust

it turns the spotlight from dramatized to aesthetic emotion, and hence to sense impressions as aesthetic phenomena.[60]

3. Poetry, emotion, and the senses

> Be always searching for new sensations.
> Be afraid of nothing... A new Hedonism—
> that is what our century wants.
> O. Wilde, *The Picture of Dorian Gray* (1890)

Scattered over different genres, poets and periods, the passages discussed above only partially reflect the deconstruction of emotions in Hellenistic literature. Various parameters should be reckoned with in a systematic account: that, for example, Callimachus' intellectual and Theocritus' sensual approach to emotion are worlds apart; that Apollonius in the *Argonautica* is bound to engage in an intertextual dialogue with epic and tragic emotion; that Lycophron explores sensational discourse through visualization; that Parthenius is a unique case where emotions are thematized—but from a melodramatic point of view; that sensationalism is pursued in non-mimetic contexts such as Nicander's didactic; that genuine emotion, such as the grief for the deceased and unrequited love, is reserved for the miniature narratives of the epigram. Yet, despite the heterogeneity of the Hellenistic material, we perceive a change in attitude towards the emotions which are moderated, trivialized, ironized and, as a rule, replaced by sensations.[61]

It is not easy to offer a sole explanation for this dramatic turn. A possible direction points towards philosophy. If the classical era is marked by the moral contextualization of emotion and the denouncement of the lower sensations and desires by Plato and Aristotle, philosophical trends of the Hellenistic period carry these views to extremes. Stoics and Epicureans reject human emotions, striving either for apathy or pleasure, the absence of pain. Viewing emotions from such novel perspectives must have exerted some influence upon Hel-

---

in Nicander's poems on reptiles and their antidotes: on this reading of Nicander, see Sistakou 2012, 193–233.

60 On this basis it is expicable why Bonelli 1979 draws a parallel between Hellenistic and 19th century Aestheticism.

61 A fine analysis of the process in Johnson 2007, who, however, highlights erotic passion as *the* emotion of neoteric poetics.

lenistic poets; however, the extent of this influence still remains obscure.⁶² And yet, the Stoic rendering of emotions as passions (in the modern sense of the word) or the emphasis on their irrational nature may account for conceptions of emotion in Apollonius, Lycophron and Parthenius; the pursue of mental ἡδονή combined with ἀταραξία and ἀπονία by Epicureanism can elucidate the bucolic ideal of sweetness; and the notion, widespread in Hellenistic ethics, that passions could and should be healed finds its most telling parallel in Theocritus' conception of song as therapy for love.⁶³

But philosophy is not the only mechanism behind this process. Poetics also provides a sound basis for explaining the deconstruction of literary emotion. The dynamics of emotion and action, and, in literary terms, of character and plot, which are indispensable to classical genres, are not valid anymore.⁶⁴ Emotions like heroic μῆνις or φιλία or αἰδώς become a grand thing of the past, suitable only for the elevated genres of epic and tragedy. Jason's unepic responses to anger in the *Argonautica* and the less than tragic grief of Hekale prove the point.⁶⁵ The fragmented narratives of the Hellenistic poets cannot host believable characters with fully-fledged emotions. Sensation claims its independence from character and action, and it is therefore more functional in the new contexts. The coherent πρᾶξις dissolves and along with it the tragic passions, whereas ellipsis of plot, descriptions and impressions favour fleeting sensations. Eventually, breaking Aristotle's rules means to block out the final phase of his scheme

---

62 On the Hellenistic theories of the emotions, see Engberg-Pedersen/Sihvola 1998; the therapeutic use of Hellenistic philosophy to cure human passions is brilliantly discussed by Nussbaum 1994.
63 A philological field still unexplored. Some hints as to how Hellenistic ἔρως connects to the various philosophical trends of the era in Fantuzzi/Hunter 2004, 341–342. Less is said about the philosophical undertones of Jason's anger in the *Argonautica* again in Fantuzzi/Hunter 2004, 109–114; more systematically but not convincingly Jason is treated as a Stoic sage by Williams 1996. That Epicureanism forms the core of bucolic poetry is an old idea, already in Rosenmeyer 1969.
64 See the fine analysis by Halliwell 1998, 138–167, who rightly contrasts Aristotle's moral conception of character with the psychological complexity of characters in, say, modern novel.
65 The way the neoterics of Alexandria negotiate their relationship with the grand emotion of the past is aptly described by Johnson 2007, 180: "Callimachus' own time was, to be sure, vital, was sufficiently varied and fascinating enough to engender poetry plentifully, but he and his contemporaries could hardly be unaware that, though they clearly knew more—about almost everything—than Homer or Sophocles knew or could have known, they felt less, or rather felt big things more feebly, than had the poets of those heroic ages (but small, ephemeral, ordinary, trivial things they felt exquisitely): grandeur, in short, had somehow leaked out of existence as Callimachus and his contemporaries and their successors experienced it."

—namely *katharsis*. The audience cannot be emotionally purged by sensation: on the contrary, it is infected by the sensual.

This brings us to a critical question: how does sensation connect to the new role of poetry? Whereas archaic song aims at γοητεία 'enchantment' and classical poetry is perceived as διδασκαλία, primarily denoting moral teaching or the acquisition of knowledge, neoteric poetics opts for ψυχαγωγία. Pleasure addressed to the soul of the reader may be variously interpreted. The type of pleasure aroused in those perceiving the sensational discourse may be inferred from those Hellenistic poems that represent fictitious viewers or listeners. These include the Argonauts and the women of Lemnos in Apollonius' epic, the *boukoloi* in Theocritus' pastorals and the Adoniazousai in his urban *Idyll 15*, the women beholding Theseus in *Hekale*, the girls accompanying Europa in Moschus' epyllion—all these instances during which a poetic scene is perceived as a work of art or an aesthetic impression. The most persistent reactions to these instances are θάμβος 'amazement' (a primitive psychological state, a kind of collective pre-emotion) or ἡδονή, delight and pleasure stemming from sensual affect.[66] Such a hedonistic take on aesthetic emotion questions classical beliefs about the apocalyptic mission of poetry and its ontological status as the bearer of truth or the emphasis on cognitive pleasures.[67] Hellenistic aesthetics opposes exactly these beliefs.

Sensuality and, consequently, hedonism become emblematic of Hellenistic aesthetics then. I have attempted to support this assumption by focusing on elements of content, i.e. the depiction of emotions in Hellenistic poetry; one might well prove the same thesis by referring to formalistic aspects—verbal, sound or visual effects of the verse that stimulate the senses of the audience. A concluding remark about the nature of aesthetic thought and practice during the Hellenistic

---

66 Both aesthetic emotions have been associated to the sublime. Not primarily by [Longinus] who, despite recognizing the role of feeling and amazement, maintains that sublimity echoes first and foremost 'greatness of spirit'. But especially by modern theorists, starting with Edmund Burke who represents the sensationist and affectivist position on the sublime. Not coincidentally, his treatise *On the Sublime and Beautiful* (1756) begins with a definition of amazement in front of novelty ("The first and the simplest emotion which we discover in the human mind is curiosity. By curiosity, I mean whatever desire we have for, or whatever pleasure we take in, novelty") and continues by examining the duo of pleasure and pain.

67 The core of Platonic idealism lies in the philosopher's attack against hedonism in art, e.g. in the *Republic* 476b: Οἱ μέν πού, ἦν δ' ἐγώ, φιλήκοοι καὶ φιλοθεάμονες τάς τε καλὰς φωνὰς ἀσπάζονται καὶ χρόας καὶ σχήματα καὶ πάντα τὰ ἐκ τῶν τοιούτων δημιουργούμενα, αὐτοῦ δὲ τοῦ καλοῦ ἀδύνατος αὐτῶν ἡ διάνοια τὴν φύσιν ἰδεῖν τε καὶ ἀσπάσασθαι. On the radical empiricism defended by those who rejected Plato's views on the idealism of art and Aristotle's strict formalism and promoted, at the same time, the sensuous and the material, see Porter 2010, passim.

era may further strengthen the argument about the sensuous goal of poetry. Being neither the idealists Plato would favour or the 'philosophical' poets Aristotle would have liked, the neoterics of Alexandria and their followers are culturally defined by two interrelated developments. The first derives from an altered sense of the self, a new individuality, grounded in the 'here and now' of everyday life; to focus on human experience of the private sphere in alternative narratives and small-scale snapshots means to liberate emotion from communal good and illuminate its psychological, affective and subjective aspects.[68] The other development is marked by aesthetic materialism, a trend inherited from the archaic era, essentialy anti-Platonic and anti-Aristotelian, which highlights art as a primarily sensuous experience; regarding sensuality as a salient feature of Hellenistic aesthetics explains both the transition from emotion to sensation and the apprehension of the visual, audio or tactile implications of art.[69]

These new sensibilities capture the intensity of the *aesthetic moment*,[70] the art's direct appeal to the senses of the individual. Many centuries later, Walter Pater, the father of European Aestheticism, will vigorously defend the same view in his philosophical novel *Marius the Epicurean* (ch. 8):

> But our own impressions!—The light and heat of that blue veil
> over our heads, the heavens spread out, perhaps not like a curtain
> over anything!—How reassuring, after so long a debate about the
> rival criteria of truth, to fall back upon direct sensation, to limit
> one's aspirations after knowledge to that! In an age still materially
> so brilliant, so expert in the artistic handling of material things,
> with sensible capacities still in undiminished vigour, with the
> whole world of classic art and poetry outspread before it, and
> where there was more than eye or ear could well take in—how
> natural the determination to rely exclusively upon the phenomena
> of the senses, which certainly never deceive us about themselves,
> about which alone we can never deceive ourselves!

---

[68] For the concentration on the human psyche as the defining parameter of neoteric emotion, see Johnson 2007, 186–188.
[69] This is the core argument of Porter's 2010 monograph on pre- and post-Platonic materialist aesthetics. In commenting upon Hellenistic aesthetics, Porter 2010, 481–490 calls this tendency 'the materialist urges', which he regrettably restricts to the apotheosis of materials and objects in the epigram and does not expand to other areas of Hellenistic poetics.
[70] I borrow the term from Wolfgang Iser's study on the Aestheticism of Walter Pater. Here is how Pater himself defines this moment in the much-influential conclusion of his treatise on *The Renaissance:* "Of this wisdom, the poetic passion, the desire of beauty, the love of art for art's sake, has most; for art comes to you professing frankly to give nothing but the highest quality to your moments as they pass, and simply for those moments' sake."

Or, to rephrase Oscar Wilde's quotation from the *Picture of Dorian Gray: Hellenistic poets were always searching for new sensations...A new Hedonism, that is what their century wanted!*

Filippomaria Pontani
"Your first commitments tangible again" - Alexandrianism as an aesthetic category?

0. Introduction

> Alexandre le Grand, il parlait comme un livre
> Avec Aristote comme maître cela n'a rien d'étonnant
> On lui reproche fort d'avoir été—une fois—ivre
> C'est bien la peine de gagner tant de batailles pour être à la fin condamné moralement
>
> Arrivé au bout du monde ses soldats ne voulurent plus le suivre
> Pourtant après les Indes il y avait la Chine et le Japon et le Nouveau Continent
> Seulement ils ne savaient pas la géographie peut-être même manquaient-ils de vivres
> La plupart d'entre eux rentrèrent à pied et quelques-uns par le golfe d'Oman[1]

Raymond Queneau's hilarious 1958 sonnet entitled *L'Alexandrinisme des origines à nos jours* tackles the same issue that will keep us busy in this paper, albeit from a different angle. My attempt is to suggest a broader and at the same time more exact definition of the cultural and literary prerogatives of what we moderns call "Alexandrianism", as well as to investigate the dialectical relationship of this concept with our recent acquisitions in the study of Hellenistic poetry. Is it by sheer coincidence that one of the most important recent books on Hellenistic influence in Roman poetry alludes both in its general title and in its first section to the well-known *incipit* of Ezra Pound's *Hommage to Sextus Propertius* (1917)?[2]

Before even starting such an inquiry two preliminary assumptions should be clarified. First of all, I still believe (*cum grano salis*) in the Hegelian idea that most ages of Western culture are marked by characteristic genres or styles which coin or influence their *horizon d'attente*, their "spazio letterario"[3]. While confining myself to literature—for lack of confidence in a more wide-ranging as-

---

[1] Queneau 1965, 191–92. The second part is devoted to the pun between the Macedonian king and the famous French line named—however indirectly—after him (on the same topic see also Roubaud 1988).
[2] "Shades of Callimachus, Coan ghosts of Philetas, / it is in your grove I would walk...": see Hunter 2006.
[3] Mazzoni 2005, 9 and 17.

sessment of Hellenistic "mentality"[4], or of expertise in the very controversial issue of Alexandrian art[5]—I hasten to declare that the case of Hellenistic poetry is particularly difficult, due to the scanty data and information; however, if we focus on the early Ptolemaic age (3rd century BC), we are to a certain extent entitled to apply the criterion of "cultural hegemony", which must have led to the survival of some texts rather than others, and to the sometimes remarkable attention paid to these texts by political and cultural institutions[6].

A second preliminary need is to allow for the radical and perhaps unbridgeable difference between ancient and modern literature, or—to be more precise— between pre-Romantic and post-Romantic poetry in terms of production, communication, and system of genres, a difference that hampers any thorough comparison, and continuously calls for caution. For one thing, no poetry today can be understood without taking into account the preminence of "autobiographical empiric lyric" over *Gesellschaftslyrik* or similar typologies—and of course this trend starts from an overt reaction to ancient classical models[7]. Nonetheless, affinities between our own times and Hellenism in terms of politics, taste and mentality, have been evoked by too many scholars and critics for them to be entirely misplaced. As early as 1910 J.W. Mackail notoriously wrote about "decentralisation" (globalisation?) as a key phenomenon to understand (and estimate) Alexandrian poetry[8]; and it might be surprising to find a consistent consideration of the inherent link between Alexandrian poetry and our own *civilisation* in an otherwise largely disparaging appreciation of Hellenism as an epigonal age—Felix Jacoby's 1924 lecture deserves a longer quotation:[9]

> Wir finden uns selbst wieder in dieser hellenistischen Poesie, mit unseren komplizierten Seelenleben; mit dem unbedingt großstädtischen Charakter unserer Zivilisation, der eine starke Sehnsucht nach der Natur und die damit wohl unzertrennlich verbundene Idealisierung dieser Natur, ihre idyllische Verklärung erzeugt; in der Antinomie zwischen der Lebensmüdigkeit des einzelnen und dem stark bewegten Leben des Staates; in der Überbil-

---

[4] Onians 1979. See Hutchinson 1989, 8 on Alexandrian times as a period "so heterogeneous and, one might think, so unconscious of itself"; Hopkinson 1988.
[5] Grimm 1981; Elvira Barba 1981; Stewart 2003 (rather more "pessimistic" than Grimm). Tackling Alexandrianism in art would open up a series of interesting questions concerning the place of poetry and the visual arts in modern aesthetics and in the contemporary system of artistic production.
[6] See e.g. Weber 1993.
[7] Mazzoni 2005, 100–119.
[8] Mackail 1910, 182–89.
[9] Jacoby 1961 (1924), under some aspects a more lucid analysis than the more popular Trypanis 1947, who also resorts to the idea that "The Alexandrians, weak, infirm of purpose, lost in their aspirations and their dreams, appear much nearer to us".

dung und Überfeinerung der Kunst; in dem Interesse an allen technischen Problemen und an der Wissenschaft, wenn sie in populärer Form elegant geboten wird, neben einem tiefen Mißtrauen gegen den Wert aller Wissenschaft; in dem Widerstreit von Persönlichkeitsbewußtsein und sozialer Einstellung; in der seltsamen Mischung von Glauben und Skepsis, von philosophischer Aufgeklärtheit und dem immer wachsenden Drang nach religiösem Erleben.

1. Features and judgments

Jacoby's list of *Merkmale* of Hellenistic poetry is one of the many such lists produced by scholars over the decades. B.H. Fowler, devoting in 1989 an entire book to *Hellenistic Aesthetic*,[10] stated that modern poetry owed Alexandria several elements such as e.g. pathos, burlesque, grotesque, a certain kind of realism (pets, babies, women), an interest for nature and even the root of romantic love; but Fowler's reduction of the essence of Alexandrian aesthetic to a polymorphic *joie de vivre* may leave us unsatisfied. Nina Otto's more recent decalogue of commonly recognised features of Hellenism as a *geistige Epoche* commands greater admiration[11], but in its conventional nature it will necessarily leave room for other scholars to stress different aspects: J.K. Newman insists on emotions, unity of tone and feeling, scepticism, attention to the detail[12]; Theodore Papanghelis, shifting the focus to Propertius' Hellenistic heritage, mentions antiquarian interest, fascination with urban centres, magic and dreams, self-imitation, lack of drama or narrative[13]; and Michael Silk has his own twelve features to suggest[14].

These unstable lists, whether devoted to "Hellenistic" or "Alexandrian" aesthetic (for the sake of brevity, I shall not draw here a sharp distinction)[15], show amongst other things how the last few decades have added to our chart of this

---

10 Fowler 1989.
11 Otto 2009, 13–14: Loslösung der Kunst vom "Volk" und Selbstzweckhaftigkeit der Kunst; Gelehrsamkeit und Intertextualität; ausgehöhlte Religiosität; Hang zum Spielerischen; formale Ausarbeitung; abgelegene Mythen; Interesse am Detail; Realismus; Psychologisierung; Erotisches.
12 Newman 1986, 20–21.
13 Papanghelis 1987, 202–4.
14 Silk 2004, 356: metrical experiment, mixing of genres, anti-heroism, realism, eroticism, miniature forms, off-centring, unorthodox material, atmospheric vignettes, ecphrasis, foregrounding of technique, Homeric allusion.
15 On the issue see e.g. Otto 2009, 11; Kassel 1987; the distinction remains fundamental for Cameron 1995, 25.

poetic territory, urging us to abandon the old-fashioned dichotomy "between a content-laden and socially engaged poetry of the archaic and classical periods, on the one hand, and Hellenistic poetry which is only concerned with an appropriately sophisticated style in which to express things of little importance, on the other".[16] But to what extent did this evolution shape our perception of "Alexandrianism" as a literary phenomenon?

Philip Hardie has recently argued that the dialogue between scholarly practice and literary criticism has been hitherto inadequate in this respect[17]: needless to say, this is largely due to the weight of tradition. Over the centuries the place of a thorough terminological exam has been taken by a more simplifying pejorative bias, relying on the identification between Alexandrianism and "motionless academicism" proposed by Clement Greenberg in his pathbreaking 1939 essay on *Avant-garde and kitsch*[18], and ultimately going back to Theodore Mommsen's dismissal of Roman Alexandrianism[19], and to Friedrich Nietzsche's use of the adjective as a synonym of "theoretical, socratic, learned"—in a word, the librarian's attitude to art, the very root of the epigonal status of Renaissance and modern culture as opposed to the true idea of *Hellenenthum*.[20] Hence, for example, the *OED* definition of "Alexandrian": "silver age, derivative, imitative, artificial, addicted to recondite learning"[21]; hence also an indifferentiated use stretching down to Sartre's *Nausée*[22] and criticised by Marguerite Yourcenar[23]. Warburg's often quoted motto "Athen will immer neu aus Alexandrien zurückerobert werden" emerged from his study of Renaissance magic and divination: but in a

---

[16] Hunter 2006, 2.
[17] Hardie 2010, 32: "Many uses of the term predate (or are oblivious to) classical scholars' recent positive revaluation of the quality and interest of Alexandrian literature". Newman 1990, 4: "How narrowly Alexandrianism has been understood!" (with examples). A most interesting move towards a transhistorical literary reading of Alexandrian poetry is now offered by Sistakou 2012.
[18] Greenberg 1985, 49: "An academicism in which the really important issues are left untouched because they involve controversy, and in which creative activity dwindles to virtuosity in the small detail of form, all larger questions being decided by the precedent of the old masters": this is precisely what avant-garde, by refusing "art for art's sake" and by turning its attention to the contents rather than to the form, seeks to overcome.
[19] Hardie 2010, 32.
[20] Nietzsche 1872, § 18, on the Alexandrian man "der im Grunde Bibliothekar und Corrector ist und an Bücherstaub und Druckfehlern elend erblindet": Hartmann 1999, 73–74.
[21] Ricks 2004, 337–40, also for a history of the word since the 19th century.
[22] Sartre 2002 (1938), 196: "Voilà donc revenues ces discussions alexandrines...".
[23] Yourcenar 1958, 21: "... c'est par méprise qu'alexandrinisme fut longtemps tenu chez nous pour synonyme de décadence".

wider sense, it was applied to the struggle for a *Denkraum der Besonnenheit* between scholars and the object(s) of their study[24].

2. Directions of literary Alexandrianism

And yet, if we look more deeply into literary criticism, we might be surprised to find out that the term has been applied, whether in a negative or a simply descriptive tone, to rather different authors and works[25], indeed so different that one might feel inclined to accept Oscar Wilde's 1891 appraisal (complementary, though not alternative, to Nietzsche's): "There is really not a single form that art now uses that does not come to us from the critical spirit of Alexandria, where these forms were either stereotyped or invented or made perfect"[26].

According to this view Alexandrianism, being disseminated almost everywhere, would amount to little specific; but Wilde's immediately following words yield a more precise notion: "I say Alexandria, not merely because it was there that the Greek spirit became most self-conscious, and indeed ultimately expired in scepticism and theology, but because it was to that city, and not to Athens, that Rome turned for her models". Alexandria thus amounts to more than a metonymy for "academic": it becomes a crucial stage in the evolution of Western culture, an avatar of a new *Weltanschauung*, elaborated under precise historical and philosophical conditions.

2a. The earliest systematic adoption of "Alexandrian" in terms of literary criticism has to do with the French *Parnassiens*,[27] and with late symbolist or decadent poets from Samain to Pierre Louys, from Mallarmé to Valéry[28]. Late 19th-century "pure poetry" was (and still is) considered as quintessentially Alexandrian in view of its precious and elaborated form, its long preparatory linguistic chiselling (the metaphors of the narrow path, the water-drinking poet etc.), its predilection for the shorter genres[29], its allusivity and obscurity[30], its lack of a

---

[24] Warburg 1920, 70. Despite Hartmann 1999, 75, I could not find any reference to this motto in the Eliot-Curtius correspondence discussed by Godman 1989.
[25] See the encyclopedia articles: Newman 1993; Hartmann 1999; Hardie 2010.
[26] Quoted and discussed in Silk 2004, 353–54.
[27] Desonay 1928, esp. 331 and 405.
[28] Not only in France: the Greek Kostìs Palamàs refers to Ioannis Gryparis as νεοαλεξαντρινός in a positive sense: Ricks 2004, 340.
[29] "No very long poem will ever be popular any more" wrote E.A. Poe in 1850 (*The Poetic Principle*).

political dimension, its sentimental-erudite approach to myth, its circulation in small milieus[31]. E.A. Poe's theories, preaching as a supreme goal the "pure elevation of soul" and the rebuttal of any narrative dimension[32], offer an inviting parallel with the Callimachean programme in epigr. 28 Pf. and in the prologue of the *Aitia*, as opposed to other literary experiments such as e.g. Hugo's or Tennyson's works. In its exclusive narcissism directed to the *happy few*[33], in its extenuated aestheticism, this kind of "Alexandrianism" has often merged with the other keyword "Byzantinism" in the frame of a rather vague (and deliberately vague) constellation of cultural ingredients to 19th-century decadentism. To be sure, Alexandria is in this frame at best a by-product of Byzantium, for it but partially shares in the depth of the latter's *parfum de corruption*, of that "goût d'humanité que l'on sent, plutôt que de le comprendre en entier"[34]; however, according to the aforementioned Clement Greenberg, W.B. Yeats' *Sailing to Byzantium* proved particularly iconic precisely because "Byzantium is very close to Alexandria"[35].

It was this idea of decadent Alexandrianism that José Ortega y Gasset had in mind when he spoke in 1925 of the *Deshumanización del Arte*, thereby implying that contemporary art would have to rely on its aesthetic value, on its stylistic and linguistic originality, and would be directed to the few who have the knowledge and critical spirit to appreciate it, to the exclusion of all other audiences[36]: this claim could be (and was) easily presented as Callimachus' direct spiritual heritage.

2b. In the very same years, "Alexandrianism" was chosen by other critics as a label for a rather different poetical trend, namely early modernist American poetry, above all the work of T.S. Eliot and Ezra Pound. The great mentor of Eliot's identification as a "new Callimachus" is none less than Ernst Robert Curtius, in a

---

[30] Mallarmé writes in 1891 (*Sur l'évolution littéraire:* see Howald 1948, 42–43): "nommer un objet, c'est supprimer les trois quarts de la jouissance du poème qui est fait du bonheur de deviner peu à peu; le suggérer, voilà le but".

[31] See Howald 1948 and Bonelli 1989, with Papanghelis 1987, 210–14.

[32] "The Iliad is based on an imperfect sense of art" (quoted by Howald 1948, 40); no less harsh judgments about Milton's *Paradise Lost*.

[33] Mazzoni 2005, 198.

[34] See Citti 1987, 244; David-de Palacio 2001; Pontani 2002–2003.

[35] Greenberg 1985, 51.

[36] Ortega y Gasset 1925: his main example is Mallarmé, but Baudelaire is also evoked. See Bonelli 1989, 63–68 and 117.

crucial essay published in 1927[37]. By way of partial analogy with the decadent poets, the accent was put here on Eliot's wide-ranging erudition[38], on the role of ecphrasis and miniature forms[39], on the gloomy historical context, fraught with decreasing ethnic identity and fading religious faith: indeed, Curtius even rhetorically asks about his own time: "Und wenn es wirklich eine Epoche des Hellenismus wäre?"[40]. Of course, the most relevant elements of comparison were Eliot's allusiveness and learning, his militant re-use of previous literature, and his approach to intertextuality as "a determinative compositional principle"[41], a pivotal element towards the understanding of the poems' structure and contents.

This poetry, born as an artificial and necessarily obscure philological mosaic, is best intelligible to connoisseurs; fully aware of the process, and of the critical problems posed by the texts he quotes (Eliot was a ποιητὴς ἅμα καὶ κριτικός like Philetas or Callimachus)[42], the poet builds upon the tradition he has studied, digested and inherited through great labor (one is reminded here of Callimachus' *Pinakes*, but also of the philologists in the Museum)[43], thus bringing to the extreme consequences some features that essentially mark every literary act as such[44]. Tradition is for him myth, not as a sum of antiquarian details or of literary predecessors (this is the "bad" sense of Alexandrianism as pure style detached from life, rejected and condemned by Eliot himself in 1921[45]), but as a container of shifting values, conflicting ethical directions, multiple facets of heroism, and a plurality of stylistic trends. "Only now do we have a poetry whose whole rationale involves such a reconstitution of, and realignment towards, other poetry that it simply cannot be read intelligently (or, often, intelligibly) without that reference being, in turn, subjected to critical reconstruction".[46]

---

37 Curtius 1963 (1927), 318–19. Also useful, though perhaps less convincing in some details, is Newman 1967, 433–43.
38 An "atmosphere conductive to pedantry" according to MacKendrick 1953, 7.
39 Silk 2004, 356.
40 Curtius 1963, 318.
41 Silk 2004, 363.
42 Curtius 1963, 318. Silk 2004, 355–56.
43 The "thin trickle of tradition evoking the ghosts of our dead past": MacKendrick 1953. "Tradition cannot be inherited, and if you want it you must obtain it by great labour" writes Eliot 1920, 49 (in: *Tradition and the Individual Talent*).
44 Curtius 1963 (1927), 317–29.
45 Eliot 2005, 164 (*Prose and verse*): "The real decadence in literature occurs when both verse and prose cease their effort: Alexandrianism, or more truly Georgianism, is present when verse becomes a language, a set of feelings, a style quite remote from life".
46 Silk 2004, 364.

2c. Again in the early 20th century, almost simultaneously with the rise of an Alexandrian pedigree for American modernism, a third, influential strand of tradition saw the light, almost unexpectedly. The Greek poet Constantine Cavafy, an Alexandrian by birth, quickly became an eccentric literary phenomenon attracting the gaze of critics worldwide: he was combining in himself several of the characters featuring in the lists mentioned above § 1, from realism to meta-poetry, from eroticism to allusivity. In short, he became a sort of *Idealtypus* of Alexandrianism, and E.M. Forster, in a memorable essay published in *Athenaeum* in 1919, resolutely consecrated him as the follower of one only "literary ancestor", namely Callimachus.[47] While wrong in expecting that a poet like Cavafy "can never be popular", Forster acutely spotted one of the reasons of his success ("he flies both too slowly and too high"), and in 1924 he had the great merit of recommending *Ithaca* to his friend T.S. Eliot for publication in the magazine *Criterion*[48].

Since then, one facet of Alexandrianism has been linked with the unmistakable tone of Cavafy's poetic voice, perhaps the most recognizable one in the entire 20th century, as is demonstrated by his direct or indirect heirs (Auden, Seferis, Montale, Milosz, Brodskij etc.) and by the sheer number of imitations, parodies and rewritings it has received[49]. In a thoughtful essay on Cavafy's Alexandrianism, David Ricks has tried to unbundle the myth of the city (ancient and contemporary Alexandria, with its flavour of sordid lanes, ambiguous bars and secret homosexual pleasure[50]) from the more distinctly aesthetic categories embodied by the same name[51]. Ricks is of course right to stress Cavafy's elitism, his rebuttal of long forms, his own biographical *lathe biosas*, though Mary Depew's analysis has partly questioned this sort of analogy with Callimachus, and Acos-

---

47 Forster 1923, 94: "Alexandria, his birthplace, came into being just when Public School Greece decayed ; kings, emperors, patriarchs have trodden the ground between his office and his flat ; his literary ancestor, if he has one, is Callimachus". This judgment was satirised ten years later by the old Kostìs Palamàs: Daskalòpoulos-Stasinopoulou 2002, 139–40. See also Yourcenar 1958, 12; 35–36; 53.
48 Forster 1923, 96–97.
49 Vayenas 2000, 16–20.
50 See Green 1996 and Ghoneim 1996; Keeley 1996 on its literary transfiguration by and after Cavafy. L. Durrell (quoted in Ghoneim 1996, 293–95) opened *Justine* as follows: "Capitally, what is this city of ours? What is resumed in the word Alexandria? In a flash my mind's eye shows me a thousand dust-tormented streets. Flies and beggars own it today—and those who enjoy an intermediate existence between either". A radical overlap between the city, its history, and an aesthetic category, is proposed by Caygill 2003 especially on the basis of texts by Ungaretti and Cavafy.
51 Those especially praised by texts such as Mackail 1910: see Ricks 2004, 340–42.

ta-Hughes has rightly reminded how different Callimachus' *oeuvre* looked like in the days of Cavafy[52]. But to our ends one must remark that his poetry, at least since the early 1900 s, implies a radical turn away from the excess of Parnassian symbolism[53], and seeks refuge in Hellenistic, imperial and Byzantine texts and history not for merely decorative reasons *à la* Huysmans, but because, for all their anachronistic *facies*, they conjured up a universe of deeper erotic and sentimental freedom, of syncretism and openness, of spontaneity and pleasure, of shrewdness and treachery, of multitude and solitude[54].

Predictably, one of the crucial genres for this literary *Stimmung* is Hellenistic and imperial epigram: no wonder that this is also the background to understand the *Alexandrian Songs* by the Russian poet Michail Kuzmin, probably the only modern sylloge entirely set in Ptolemaic Alexandria, and the only one to declare overtly its debt to Callimachus as a literary ancestor[55].

3. Features reconsidered

Schematically, we have seen so far that "Alexandrianism" has been employed to classify three poets as remarkably different as Mallarmé, Eliot and Cavafy: this polysemy (if I can say so) belongs by now to the history of literary criticism, though it inevitably casts some doubts on the very interpretive value of the entire category: to its tentative refinement we shall now briefly turn.

For one thing, I think we should respect historically, but operatively reject as unfruitful or misleading the equation of Alexandrianism with "learned" poetry *tout court*. We may agree with Neil Hopkinson that the great novelty of Hellenistic poetics consists in "the degree of self-consciousness, cleverness, subtleness or 'wit' which Hellenistic poems display in their learning"[56], but many ages have produced subtle, witty and self-conscious poetry, and indeed it would be hard not to appreciate the learning and subtleness of Keats, Foscolo or even Ronsard. The dangers of analogies based on this kind of arguments is apparent from the

---

[52] See Depew 2003; Acosta-Hughes 2003, 19–20.
[53] Cavafy overtly declared his debt and admiration to Verlaine and other symbolistic poets: see e.g. Haas 1982, 59.
[54] It is thanks to Cavafy that "Alexandria, and the world of Hellenism that encircled it, so anticipated the prevailing aura of today that they now constitute a metaphor for it, in particular for the ironic scepticism about the games of nations and parties played so ruthlessly by the mighty and the not-so-mighty in recent decades": Keeley 1996, 150.
[55] Ilinskaja 2004, 45–60; de Haard 1998, defining more exactly the chronological span and the mythical dimension of Kuzmin's Alexandria.
[56] Hopkinson 1988, 8.

fact that some of Ernst Howald's parallels between Horace and Mallarmé, Propertius and Valéry are more convincing than others.[57] To be sure, even post-modernism (whether this movement lives down to our time or not, indeed whether it exists at all or not) has been regarded on good grounds as no more than a "cheap version of Alexandrianism"[58], a stage in the Alexandrianization of art due to its denial of depth for the sake of irony, parodic quotation and an empty facade.[59]

Much in the same way, if the element of exclusiveness and Barthesian *clôture* is chosen, then full right to Alexandrian citizenship might be boasted not only by the poets wishing to "donner un sens plus pur aux mots de la tribu",[60] but even by our own times, when high-brow poetry *tout court* (as opposed e.g. to narrative or to song) is all but a popular genre, and writers often fit in with the anthropological (or psycho-pathological) pattern of the man of letters humorously described by Valéry Larbaud.[61]

Allusion, erudition and to some extent exclusiveness are of course vital elements in Hellenistic poetry[62], and it is true that their use as a *Stilprinzip*, a step that only a book-minded culture can afford, marks most of post-Hellenistic poetry down to the present day: in this respect Nietzsche was right, and Timon of Phlius was perhaps the first to satirise this state of affairs with his famous epigram against the βυβλιακοὶ χαρακῖται (*SH* 786)[63]. Indeed, intertextuality (I do not dwell here on terminological distinctions with respect to "allusion"[64]) has been vastly recognised as a hallmark of Alexandrian poetry[65], and even outside of Classical studies the modern theory of intertextuality clings back to Alexandria and to its library as a standard paradigm[66]. But in order to assess the persistence of this feature over the centuries, it must be judged with respect to its causes and

---

57 Howald 1948, with Papanghelis 1987, 212.
58 Castoriadis 1991.
59 Kuspit 2000: "in Alexandrianism, a known art is reduced to a linguistic facade, which is reified into a copy that is appropriated as a look, and as such stripped of its aesthetic and expressive implications".
60 Mallarmé in his sonnet to E.A. Poe, quoted by Howald 1948, 35.
61 Larbaud 1936, 17: "Mais il a passé la grande épreuve éliminatoire. Il sait maintenant qu'un poète comme Callimaque, avec six cents lecteurs dans l'Europe entière, est plus célèbre et plus assuré de le rester que ce contemporain dont les livres se tirent à cent mille exemplaires".
62 For recent overviews see e.g. Gutzwiller 2007; Pretagostini 2000. Hutchinson 1988 may be too radical in denying even an erudite stance in Hellenistic literature.
63 Silk 2004, 354–60.
64 Summarised recently e.g. by van Tress 2004, 7–21.
65 E. g. Cusset 1999; Harder 2002; Acosta-Hughes 2010a.
66 Orr 2003, 56–57.

context, whereby it might prove somewhat limiting to reduce everything to the concept of "art's artificiality", as E.-R. Schwinge puts it in his analysis of metaliterary passages in Hellenistic poetry.

Schwinge is convinced that erudition, "pure poetry", and aesthetic value represent a sort of refuge against the impossibility of political writing[67]. He thus clearly brings to the extreme consequences the thesis linking the nature of Alexandrian art with the sense of political crisis entailed in the Greek world by the fall of Athenian democracy[68]. On another view, 3rd-century Alexandrian culture was shaped by a deeper crisis due to a sense of cultural isolation, to the citizens' displacement away from the Greek homeland, into a place endowed with a different, century-old tradition, and into a cultural horizon where the ideal of Pan-hellenism did not make any more sense[69]. Though partly criticised and nuanced by Alan Cameron[70], these two states of crisis may well subsist alongside each other, and they may help us conjure up an historical image of Alexandrianism as "the poetry resulting from conscious calculation by artists uneasy with their world and profoundly aware of the past"[71], as the artificial product of a multi-cultural society in a city with no past and lots of alibis[72], as "an archive of shared images, of evolving traditions" structured by the poet as an artificer of culture[73].

Uneasiness with the present, political change, or cultural displacement, do not necessarily result in "pure poetry": indeed, recent reappraisals have shown that, while deeply bookish, inward-looking and intertextual, Hellenistic culture did not give pride of place to the ludic and the intellectualistic element: metrical experimentalism was confined to some—if representative—authors (Sotades, Cercidas, Philicus, the *technopaignia*), while the three major poets of the 3rd century

---

67 Schwinge 1986, 44–47.
68 Jacoby 1924; Pfeiffer 1955; Bonelli 1989, 5–9 ("Come l'ellenismo nasce dall'impossibilità per l'uomo greco di integrare se stesso nell'universo della polis, così il decadentismo scaturisce dall'incapacità di aderire al sistema di idee e alle forme di vita in cui le classi colte si erano, pochi decenni prima, riconosciute": a Marxist approach according to Papanghelis 1987, 214–15); Goldhill 1991, 223–24 ("a deliberate, self-conscious turning away from the public poetry of the 5th century, a gesture of withdrawal from the persona of the public *sophos*, who speaks out to the citizen body").
69 Zanker 1987; Bing 1988; Stephens 2002.
70 Cameron 1995, esp. 25 ff.
71 Newman 1986, 516.
72 Selden 1998, 406: "The construction of Alexandria, both on a material and a social plane, constitutes a poetic act, a purposively ordered creative articulation of the world... in its own cultural imaginary, the world of Alexandria is ordered like a Callimachean text".
73 Acosta-Hughes/Stephens 2012, 202–3.

BC hardly ever resorted to something else than hexameter or elegiac distich[74]. As Fantuzzi-Hunter[75], Sistakou[76], Bing, and others have stressed, what Alexandrian "modernism" wants to do is something much more ambitious than to device an acrostich or a *figuratum carmen:* it is an entire re-structuring (from within) of the system of genres, displaying an intimate knowledge of (and an obsessive dialogue with) the literature of the past, as well as the wish to exploit these references in order to secure a link across the cultural rift: this self-conscious bridge-building activity is a sort of compensation for the authors' "perceived epigonality and artistic disjunction"[77].

One may argue that the invention of a different world, and the creation of a direct link with the past, is a characteristic of many literary acts; and yet the transformation of literary convention to this end—rather than e.g. to the effect of cautious imitation, of parody, or of a general subversion of the social or intellectual horizon—is not an obvious choice.

Jacoby, as we have seen above in the introduction, was perhaps the first to see an analogy between the period of historical and identitarian crisis represented by Hellenism and the beginning of the "short century".[78] This analogy of context also extends to a broader movement of renewal of poetic forms, rejecting the more extreme stances of avant-garde, but paving the way to a close critical dialogue with the literature of the past[79]: a dialogue that involves primarily the forms of poetry, and particularly those of archaic poetry. If the challenge to the old-fashioned view of Hellenistic poetry as something static[80] has to be taken seriously, and if we accept the (broadly speaking) "political" purport of Callimachus, Apollonius and Theocritus both in their encomiastic dimension and in the definition of a Greco-Egyptian universe[81], we might then well ask if there may be something similar going on in the cultural context(s) of the 20th century, and especially among the poets whom critics have already defined—if on different grounds—as "Alexandrians".

The answer to this question is surely too complex for the scope of the present paper, and would require a close scrutiny of many different poets and literary

---

74 Fantuzzi/Hunter 2002, 29–40.
75 Fantuzzi/Hunter 2002, 3–60.
76 Sistakou 2008a, 6–10.
77 Bing 1988, 74–75. See also, in a more distinctly cross-cultural frame, Stephens 2002, 257–62.
78 "A society of displaced persons" (Selden 1998, 289): I think this analogy is more fruitful than that with the 19th-century post-positivistic age posited by Bonelli 1989.
79 "Il ne suffit pas de faire pour créer, il faut aussi refaire d'une certaine manière ce qui était déjà là" (Cusset 1999, 378). See also Hunter 2006; Acosta-Hughes 2010a.
80 Greenberg 1985, 51: "the avant-garde moves, while Alexandrianism stands still".
81 Mori 2010, 6–27 (with further bibliography) and Stephens 2002 respectively.

movements; it is also somewhat impaired by the impossibility of taking into account linguistic matters, for the background of the literary languages to each author (Greek, English or French) is so dramatically different. Under this point of view, however, we might draw a line between the tradition stretching from Poe to Mallarmé to Symbolism, and that including Eliot and Cavafy: the former made a point of purifying and refining language through a long and patient *labor limae*, a conscious and fossilised archaism, whereas the latter openly rejected the received poetical idiom, ending up in a language "neutral and merciless" (as in Cavafy), or in an "everyday" idiom suitable to express the spontaneity of the self and to avoid "worn-out poetical fashion" (as in Eliot).[82]

Other features are also difficult to compare, for example the relationship with science, which we clearly detect in certain Hellenistic poets, though in a rather different way than in early 20th-century avant-garde (Oswald Spengler described the past century as "the century of scientific-critical Alexandrianism"[83]); or the role of irony, a hallmark of Cavafy's poetry according to Vayenas[84], certainly not unknown to Eliot, but almost absent from Decadentism: irony is indeed present in Hellenistic poetry[85], though it seems difficult to follow Effe in seeing it behind the conspicuous phenomenon of Hellenistic realism, which is best explained, with Zanker, as the trigger enabling the assimilation or appropriation of mythical *exempla* into contemporary reality[86].

4. History, myth, and poetry: a new Alexandrianism?

Precisely the issue of the references to myth, history and reality—in a word, the deeper substance of intertextuality, what Curtius identified as the main common ground between Eliot and the Alexandrians[87], what M. Silk calls "instrumental poetics"—may prove crucial in order to approach a definition of Alexandrian aesthetics. To put it bluntly, my question is: do readers need footnotes to read poetry? how many? and to which (performative or simply cultural) end?

---

82 See Vayenas 2000, 20; Silk 2004, 362.
83 See Hardie 2010, 32–33.
84 Vayenas 2000, 21–25.
85 In the "piquant combination of, or the delicate hovering between, the serious and the unserious, the grand and the less grand": Hutchinson 1988, 9.
86 Otto 2009, 19–29 for an overview of the polemic.
87 Curtius 1963, 321. The German critic relied on Jacoby's image of Alexandrian poetry: see Curtius 1963 (1949), 348.

This question invests the much-debated issue of obscurity, which needs some refinement at this point. The Italian poet and critic Franco Fortini has proposed an invaluable distinction between "difficult" and "obscure" poetry, the former implying enigmatic and learned allusions, feats of erudition ultimately explicable through footnotes (or, in the Hellenistic fashion, *hypomnemata*)[88], the latter accumulating references to autobiographical experiences or feelings, by definition non-accessible to readers beyond the writing subject.[89] In this sense, Mallarmé is obscure rather than difficult, whereas Cavafy and Eliot—albeit in different degrees—are rather difficult than obscure, as is—again in varying degrees—most of Hellenistic poetry, above all Callimachus[90].

In other words, difficult poetry may be demanding, but it is still anchored to a shared horizon, however remote from the audience's expectations and competence—potentially, it appeals to some readers more than others. This fact proves decisive when we come to assess the use of myth, a notorious hallmark of Hellenistic poetry, which often conceals—to put it with Reinhold Merkelbach—a direct reference to the archaic *mythische Denkformen*[91]. Myth—be it recondite myth—is offered to the reader not only as a self-contained display of erudition to be admired, but also as a way of alluding to old stories and old truths that can now be studied afresh and fruitfully compared, more or less directly, with contemporary reality. I just need to recall here Peter Bing's picture of the *Aitia* as a compendium of tales attempting to explain the peculiarities of the present by reference to their "causes" in the distant past, or Fantuzzi and Hunter's depiction of Alexandrian poetry as an art deeply engaged with the present, or Acosta-Hughes' and Stephens' recent attempt to vindicate the "causes of Alexandria" against the charge of pedantism[92]. Of course, this is nothing one could expect to find in Mallarmé, and this is to my mind an important obstacle to the consideration of late Symbolism and Decadentism as the genuine heirs to Alexandrian poetics[93]; but what about Eliot and Cavafy?

In a groundbreaking 1946 lecture entitled "Cavafy and Eliot: parallels", the poet George Seferis subverted the current image of Cavafy in an almost irrever-

---

[88] Some footnotes, as is well-known, were added by T.S. Eliot and by other authors (such as David Jones, on whom more below) to their own poems.
[89] Fortini 1991.
[90] See Fuhrmann 1966; Montanari 1991. Curtius 1963, 319 traced Eliot's "difficulty" back to prototypes such as (precisely) Hellenistic poetry, the medieval *trobar clus*, Dante and Mallarmé himself.
[91] Merkelbach 1981, 31–32 sees here an opposition with the rational thought of the Classical age.
[92] Bing 1988; Fantuzzi/Hunter 2002; Acosta-Hughes/Stephens 2012.
[93] Bonelli 1989, 88–95, with examples from Leconte de Lisle etc.

sible way: Nasos Vayenàs has shown that Seferis' idea was by no means unprecedented in the Greek tradition, indeed that it was even anticipated by other poets such as Papatsonis and Elytis[94]. Seferis identified the sentiment of time and history as a common root between the two otherwise so distant poets (it must be stressed that Seferis takes into account only *The Waste Land*, for the later mystical trends of Eliot's poetry hardly lend themselves to this sort of analysis): in Seferis' view, they both envisaged "the entire European literature as a simultaneous category" (Eliot), and above all mythical and historical events as parts of our consciousness and our emotion through the mechanism known as the "objective correlative", whereby things from life and things from books pulse and react in the same manner, in the same sensual rhythm[95].

This hermetic approach to poetry resonates differently in each of the two authors, for the American has conquered tradition through great labour, whereas the Alexandrian has simply digested the huge heritage of his kin. Yet, in both of them this approach proceeds less from vacuous erudition than from an implicit identification of the *then* with the *now*, not intending to evoke, but rather to presentify mythological or historical characters, or to glean from them some meaning and understanding for what has gone lost or destroyed in the present: it is the well-known "mythic method", first defined by Eliot himself in an essay about James Joyce's *Ulysses*[96]. Much like Eliot's Tiresias in the *Waste Land*, fruitfully compared by Michael Silk with his Callimachean counterpart[97], mythical or historical figures represent for Cavafy an opportunity to give a fresh look on a world beyond time, to construct the bookish but at the same time dramatically pulsing world that can be perceived in *The God Abandoning Antony*, *Myris* etc. The mythic method, in other words, gives sense to tradition, and brings it beyond the mere imitation of consecrated ancient prototypes (such as, say, the epigrams of the *Greek Anthology*, or scenes in Shakespeare): it is by rethinking tradition, by evoking that "archive of shared images", that both Eliot and Cavafy envisage a way out from (much less, a self-conscious way in) the waste land of our times, or the merciless setback of human condition, respectively.

---

[94] Elytis writes, also in 1946: "Just like Eliot, Kavafis *mythologises* the historical past and collocates within it his analogous sentimental conditions": see Vayenas 1994, esp. 266.
[95] Seferis 1974, esp. 347–48 and 360–63. See some developments of this idea in Savvidis 1994 (1977) and Maronitis 1994 (1970), and—about the "Byzantine" Cavafy—in Hirst 1998, esp. 113–17. On Seferis' modernism see most recently the lucid analysis by Yannoulopoulos 2011.
[96] "It is simply a way of controlling, of ordering, of giving a shape and a significance to the immense panorama of futility and anarchy which is contemporary history".
[97] Silk 2004, 367–70.

Comparing Callimachus and Cavafy in a fundamental essay on poetic memory, Benjamin Acosta-Hughes has identified a common trait in their "interactive relationship to the past", in the way they "refashion an earlier Hellenic experience into something novel, something that consciously calls attention to its similarity and difference".[98] Precisely this technique I suggest to regard as a modified trace of the old, Alexandrian lesson. For sure, Eliot and Cavafy remain two very different poets; but on balance we might recall that they are both quite remote from the "mainstream" picture of contemporary poetry, with its allergy to narrative and to erudition, its taste for autobiographical experience and obscure personal associations, its display of social marginality and at the same time its unruly proliferation in all quarters of society (the reason why there are nowadays so many people who write poetry, and so few people who read it)[99]. For sure, subjectivism represented a necessary fuel even for Eliot and Cavafy, though in different measures, and in a way that is of course inconceivable before the Romantic revolution. But the idea of myth, history and tradition lingering behind these two poets might really have something to do with the evolution of certain genres in Alexandrian literature.

To make things clearer, in my conclusion I shall try to give some examples, articulated by genre (bucolic, epic, aetiological poetry). These examples will involve more poets than those hitherto mentioned, in order to explore the possible boundaries of "Alexandrianism" as a general aesthetic category: my approach will be bold, at times provocative, but I hope not entirely unfruitful.

5. Some examples

5a. Pastoral poetry had deep implications with the modern Classical tradition since the Renaissance, both in terms of settings and in terms of literary content—for one thing, it represented the genre *par excellence* of meta-poetic speculation: one need just think of the 18th-century Italian academy named Arcadia, but it is no wonder that Theocritus (a poet Cavafy annotated heavily[100]) also appears in Cavafy's most openly meta-poetic piece, namely *The First Step*. The bucolic genre was then less than popular from the Romantic age onwards, and especially since the late 19th century, though of course it appealed, in the terms of an extenuated and calligraphic perfection, to Parnassian poets such as Leconte

---

98 Acosta-Hughes 2003, 21.
99 Mazzoni 2005, 40 and 199–204.
100 Peridis 1948, 77.

de Lisle, who often drew inspiration from Theocritus, indeed sometimes translated him *verbatim* within his own poems[101].

One author who paid a special attention to bucolic poetry, not reviving it as such, but conjugating in a new perspective the peculiar attention to nature and the literary creation of a separate poetical world, was the Italian Giovanni Pascoli. Pascoli, who in 1891 entitled his first sylloge *Myricae* (an open tribute to Vergil's *Eclogues*), numbers among the most influential authors in the development of contemporary Italian literature. Starting from "pure poetry" and from a cold and monumental Parnassian character, he soon renovated his style, opening the way to a more personal conception of ancient prototypes: his rural landscape, the names of rare flowers or plants, his dialogue with nature, are neither the hallmarks of a belated Romanticism, nor decorative elements of a longed-for simplicity or antiquity, but rather the correlatives of personal stories and feelings, often read and interpreted through the lens of the ancient models: theorists of allusive art such as Conte and Barchiesi, in the wake of Traina, have seen in Pascoli the new element of a "parificazione fra testi e mondo dell'esperienza come fonte di ispirazione"[102].

Now, it is well-known that the *locus amoenus* described by Theocritus at the end of *Idyll* 7 (esp. ll. 135–43 πολλαὶ δ' ἁμὶν ὕπερθε κατὰ κρατὸς δονέοντο / αἴγειροι πτελέαι τε etc.) represents an idealised homeland of the bucolic poet, of the urban citizen enthusiastically projected into a rural universe: Fantuzzi and Hunter compare in particular the cicadas, the river and the bucolic setting of *Phaedrus* 230b-d[103].

Leconte de Lisle opened one of his poems, entitled *Midi* (1852: "Midi, roi des étés, épandu sur la plaine, / Tombe en nappes d'argent des hauteurs du ciel bleu…" etc.), with a cameo patently reminiscent of the Greek *locus amoenus:* this is pure Parnassian style, evolving in the second half of the poem towards a Panic sentiment of *natura naturans*. In a poem of 1894, by the title *Estate*, Pascoli takes a slightly different path:

Sogno d'un dì d'estate.

Quanto scampanellare
tremulo di cicale!
stridule pel filare
moveva il maestrale
le foglie accartocciate.

---

[101] Bonelli 1989, 88–95.
[102] Conte-Barchiesi 1989, 89.
[103] Fantuzzi/Hunter 2002, 191–94. See also Hunter 1999, 192–93.

> Scendea tra li olmi il sole
> in fascie polverose:
> erano in ciel due sole
> nuvole, tenui, róse:
> due bianche spennellate
>
> in tutto il ciel turchino.
>
> Siepi di melograno,
> fratte di tamerice,
> il palpito lontano
> d'una trebbiatrice,
> l'angelus argentino...
>
> dov'ero? le campane
> mi dissero dov'ero,
> piangendo, mentre un cane
> latrava al forestiero,
> che andava a capo chino.

We have here several elements of the *locus amoenus* in a summer landscape (the cicadas, the wind, the sun, the trees, the clouds, the noise); but the twist of this almost idyllic setting leads in the last strophe to a radically different interior horizon, marked by the sound of bells, a sad passer-by, and a dog. This empathy with nature, where each element, though proceeding from a long-standing literary tradition, becomes an objective correlative for the poet's feelings, is so deep that in the fourth edition of *Myricae* (1897) the same poem will eventually change its title, and become *Patria:* Pascoli's homeland abides in this literary *locus amoenus* and in its inevitable sadness.[104] This is something more learned than romantic *Naturgefühl*, and something deeper than decadent classicistic re-writing. It is something one might well compare, as Stephen Harrison kindly suggests me, to the meaning of pastoral settings and style in the poems of Robert Frost[105].

In 1881, Pascoli had dedicated to a newly married couple an epithalamion built around the myth of Adonis[106], where the explicit references to Theocritus' *Adoniazousai* (15.100–44, particularly important in the god's resurrection[107])

---

[104] Pascoli 2002, I, 999–1001.
[105] Faggen 2001.
[106] It carries the Greek title Ὦ τὸν Ἄδωνιν.
[107] See esp. 119–22: χλωραὶ δὲ σκιάδες μαλακῷ βρίθοντες ἀνήθῳ / δέδμανθ'· οἱ δέ τε κῶροι ὑπερπωτῶνται Ἔρωτες, / οἷοι ἀηδονιδῆες ἀεξομένων ἐπὶ δένδρων / πωτῶνται πτερύγων πειρώμενοι ὄσδον ἀπ' ὄσδω. Pascoli's poem, ll. 49–52: "Amico, e tu riconducesti al cuore / I vaghi sogni che n'usciano in bando, / Quasi colombi che dal nido fuore / Volan rombando".

and to Bion's *Lament*[108], are coupled with an extended reference to Sappho fr. 1 V[109], thereby realising (and in a sense critically re-writing) the same intertextual contact between Hellenistic poetry and archaic lyric so carefully described in Theocritus' *Idylls* by Benjamin Acosta-Hughes in his recent book on *Arion's Lyre*.[110] Again, an erudite combination with a practical, historical goal.

An erudite and a professor, Giovanni Pascoli is of course no modernist poet. However, besides introducing lots of decisive technical novelties and experimental features in Italian metre and genre system, he based most of his activity on the re-interpretation and re-reading of tradition, with Classical literature and Dante in the foreground: of course Latin literature, especially Virgil and Horace (whom he studied and partly translated), played for him a paramount role of mediation. It is no wonder that his greatest achievements, namely the immensely learned and yet remarkably fresh and spontaneous Latin *Poëmata*, each devoted to a single character or episode of late republican, imperial or early Christian Rome, leave no reader with the taste of a magniloquent and dusty versification of things past, but rather indicate in virtues and vices, in glories and misdemeanours, in philosophies and everyday life of ancient times, a human and humanistic correlative to a growingly interlaced and changing world. No surprise, then, that Pascoli devoted two of his *Poemi conviviali* to the character of Alexander the Great and to his utterly human, melancholic reaction in front of an incommensurable world; and no surprise that his most attentive modern critic, who has showed once and for all how Pascoli's bookish universe found in the Latin language and in the classical world the only safe harbour for his complex personality, pronounced on him the clear-cut verdict: "un poeta per definizione alessandrino"[111].

5b. Upon the decline of narrative poetry since the late 19th century, the genre of large-scale epic has been largely neglected to the benefit of prose-writing, and novel in particular. In an age when brevity and density of lyrical expression are paramount, it is of course difficult to conceive and fashion an entire epic

---

108 Bion, *epit. Adon.* 19; 27–28 καὶ νύμφαι κλαίουσιν Ὀρειάδες... / στήθεα δ' ἐκ μηρῶν φοινίσσετο, τοὶ δ' ὑπὸ μαζοί / χιόνεοι τὸ πάροιθεν Ἀδώνιδι πορφύροντο. Cfr. Pascoli's poem, ll. 17–20 "Date a la terra le sue bianche spalle / Giace Adon sanguinoso. Ulula forte / De le piangenti Najadi la valle / Per la sua morte".
109 Esp. 7–10 ...πάτρος δὲ δόμον λίποισα / χρύσιον ἦλθες / ἄρμ' ὑπασδεύξαισα, κάλοι δέ σ' ἆγον / ὤκεες στροῦθοι... See Pascoli's poem, ll. 12–16: "Lenta Afrodite, // Lascia, Afrodite, de l'Olimpo i dumi: / Aggioga al cocchio i passeri, i veloci / Passeri, e scendi; urlano a te de' fiumi / Gonfi le foci".
110 Pascoli 2002, I, 369–76. See Acosta-Hughes 2010a, 16–39.
111 C. Garboli, in Pascoli 2002, I, 70.

poem, if not by sheer and conscious contradiction to the *horizon d'attente* of the prospective audience.

How problematic such a choice can prove is made clear by the meta-poetic opening of book one of Vikram Seth's *Golden Gate*, perhaps one of the most remarkable novels in verse of the past century. Irony, satire and estrangement are constant elements in Seth's poem, which employs Pushkinian metre to describe yuppiedom in the San Francisco Bay Area during the Reagan age: while I shall not argue that this is in itself an Alexandrian poem (for one thing, Seth's story does not rely on a pre-existing myth or legend, but represents an *ex novo* invention), I should like to draw attention to a couple of possible, non-intertextual parallels with Apollonius' *Argonautica* (the Golden Gate and the Golden Fleece, as it were).

The poem opens with an invocation to the Muse (1.1–5):

> To make a start more swift than weighty,
> Hail Muse. Dear Reader, once upon
> A time, say, circa 1980,
> There lived a man. His name was John.

Besides the very Callimachean tone of l. 1 (*Aitia* fr. 1.11–2), l. 2 encapsulates a reference to what turns out to be a decisive formal and contextual model for whole parts of the *Golden Gate*, namely G.G. Byron's *Don Juan*, and more precisely the incipit of *Canto the third:*

> Hail Muse! et cetera. We left Juan sleeping,
> Pillowed upon a fair and happy breast[112].

This is not just a tribute to a literary predecessor, for those lines in Byron refer to one of the typical moments of romantic love in don Juan's career; and precisely romantic love is the ubiquitous, latent term of comparison for Vikram Seth's protagonist John. John's first, blind dating with Liz is memorably described in book 2 by way of affinity and contradiction with respect to the canons of "traditional" encounters between lovers. Of course, then, the partly ironical partly reflexive allusion in the poem's opening is not only a matter of literary representations of love, but it affects the very message Seth wants to send us, an intelligent critique of the yuppy era.

How "Alexandrian" is all this? Let us turn to the opening of Apollonius Rhodius' book 3:

---

[112] I am very much indebted to Edvenson Thjømøe 2008, 14–16.

Εἰ δ'ἄγε νῦν, Ἐρατώ, παρά θ' ἵστασο, καί μοι ἔνισπε,
ἔνθεν ὅπως ἐς Ἰωλκὸν ἀνήγαγε κῶας Ἰήσων
Μηδείης ὑπ' ἔρωτι· σὺ γὰρ καὶ Κύπριδος αἶσαν
ἔμμορες, ἀδμῆτας δὲ τεοῖς μελεδήμασι θέλγεις
παρθενικάς· τῶ καί τοι ἐπήρατον οὔνομ' ἀνῆπται.

Come now, Erato, stand beside me and relate to me how it was that Jason brought the fleece from Colchis to Iolkos through the power of Medea's love. I invoke you because you also have been allotted a share of Kypris' power, and young girls, not yet mated, are bewitched by the cares you bring; for this reason a lovely name has been attached to you (transl. R. Hunter)

Here the invocation to the Muse Erato is very specific, for book 3 is going to be devoted to the love affair between Medea and Jason. But (here too) l. 2 presents the reader with a literary reference to an author of the past, in this case—as the ancient scholia duly inform us—Mimnermus (fr. 11 West), incidentally the same author praised by Callimachus for his "swift" Muse in the aforementioned prologue of the *Aitia*. It has been remarked that this choice is not merely an erudite *Spiel*, but introduces the reader in the literary horizon of this book, where epic is seasoned by massive intersections of other genres, chiefly drama and lyric poetry, and where love poetry of the past, and love conventions of the past, are picked up in the frame of an entirely new (for many critics, a radically modern) physiology of love[113]. In both Apollonius and Seth, then, literary allusion, whether relating to a mythical or a contemporary background, works as a marker of deeper meaning, and as a link to "historical" reflexion.

Some critics have viewed the character of Idas, "ein Don Quijote unter den Argonauten"[114], as the foil for the wiser, less simplistic and more "Aristotelian" behaviour of Jason, especially when Idas' defense of force and violence perverts some noble Homeric *mots d'ordre*, as in his famous and impious exclamation in *Arg.* 1.461–70[115]. Here, the allusion to the ethical paradigm of the ancient epic world substantiates Apollonius' own philosophical, or more precisely ethical (in Mori's terms, even cosmological) stance. Along a similar line, the pacifist Vikram Seth employs a subtle allusion to an earlier literary depiction of evil when condemning—in the words of one of his characters, a priest—the proliferation of nuclear weapons in the United States (one of the key topics of the *Golden Gate*): lines 7.28–29[116] refer to Hannah Arendt's well-known essay on the Nuremberg

---

113 Hunter 1989, xvi.
114 Fränkel 1960a.
115 Fantuzzi/Hunter 2002, 146–50; Mori 2010, 74–82.
116 7.28–37: Indeed, it's said that the banality / Of evil is its greatest shock. / It jokes, it punches its time clock, / Plays with its kids. The triviality / Of slaughtering millions can't

trial, and represent a direct hint to the Holocaust. Thus, through an undeclared comparison fuelled by literary material, Seth's reader is brought to approve of an ethical pattern (anti-militarism) which is at least as familiar to him as Aristotle's ideal of *metriotes* was to the reader of Apollonius.

Let's choose a different angle. If recent research on the *Argonautica* has put so much effort in enucleating its political aspect and its unceasing quest for identity[117], then a comparison is in order with another poem describing a long journey, and entirely devoted to the problematic definition of a post-colonial identity by way of analogy and contradiction with respect to the archaic Greek tradition: I mean Derek Walcott's *Omeros*[118]. Due to all its innovations in structure and facies, and due to its very attempt to challenge the most obvious tenets of epic as genre[119], *Omeros* has been ranged by J. Farrell in the same evolutive scheme to which belongs "Greek poetry of the Hellenistic period"[120]: Walcott himself says to Homer (56.3) 'Master, I was the freshest of all your readers'. To be sure, the ingenuity and the overt cultural critique on which this poem is based would by no means tolerate the definition of "Alexandrianism" in the usual sense. And yet.

Walcott's insistence on names[121] and particularly on etymologies, recalls the very Alexandrian practice of analysing words in (to our mind) irrational ways in order to glean from this operation special meanings or unusual connections. For example, when at the beginning of the poem Walcott derives the very name of "Omeros" from *O-mer-os* (2.3.9), this is part of his appropriation of Greek tradition in a Caribbean key. But etymology is a very common practice in Apollonius' *Argonautica* as well: the alleged derivation of Erato from ἔραμαι in 3.1–5 serves to highlight the element of love in the book that is about to start, whereas the implicit etymology of Achilles from ἄχος in *Arg.* 4.866–68 stresses the centrality of sorrow in Peleus' attitude to Thetis after her admonition[122].

---

impinge / Upon its peace, or make it cringe. // Killing is dying. This equation / Carries no mystical import. / It is the literal truth. Our nation / Has long believed war was a sport.
117 Mori 2010.
118 5.3.88–92: 'It wasn't Aegean. They climbed no Parthenon / to be laurelled. The depot faced their arena, / the sea's amphitheatre. When one wore a crown—/ victor ludorum—no one knew what it meant, or / cared to be told'. It is particularly in the last section of the poem that Greek and Greekness in ideals and architecture become more distinctly the signs of oppression.
119 On the problematic status of *Omeros* as "epic" see e.g. van Sickle 1999 and Henriksen 2006.
120 Farrell 1997, 283.
121 29.2.11–12 "His name / is what he's out looking for, his name and his soul".
122 More cases of etymology in 2.382; 4.812 etc.: see O'Hara 1996.

On a more structural niveau, the character of Walcott's Helen, who is both a waitress and a symbol for the island itself[123], is constructed in a very complex manner, by way of intertwined references to literary prototypes: book 29 of *Omeros* presents her longing for Hector as "Not Helen now, but Penelope, / in whom a single noon was as long as ten years" (29.1.16–17), but a few lines later, during her affair with Achille, Helen becomes Circe (29.3.16–18):

> I felt her sobbing, then small shoulders slacken
> to her body's smile. "Oh, God, I drank too much wine
> at dinner last night". Then Circe embraced her swine.

Walcott thus insists not only on Helen's literary ancestors or the multiplicity of her attitudes, but chiefly on her role as the crossroads of different longings and tensions, of conflicting heritages and powers. Any reader familiar with Apollonius Rhodius' book III will spot here an analogy with the construction of Medea[124], whose literary *persona*, as close lexical and intertextual scrutiny has shown, owes as much to πολυφάρμακος Circe[125] as to unfaithful Helen[126] as (paradoxically) to temperant Penelope[127].

Let me give one more example: the killing of Talos on the island of Crete in *Argonautica* book 4 is clearly reminiscent of Achilles' death (he is also vulnerable on the heel: 4.1646–47), and at the same time it represents a symbol for the severing of the last link with the race of the demigods, for Talos was the last survivor of the bronze age[128]. This is why Medea's successful attempt to kill him, clad in an Achillean tone, has been regarded as a metaphor for the perilous and almost impious severing of the Argonauts' links (and Medea's links in particular) with the cultural horizon of their ancestors and of earlier ages[129]. Now, at the beginning of *Omeros* book 4 the character of Philoctetes wanders in a logwood grove in the island of St. Lucia, an abandoned place with

> huge rusted cauldrons, vats for boiling the sugar
> and blackened pillars. These are the only ruins
> left here by history, if history is what they are (4.1.6–8).

---

123 See Kaufman 2006.
124 Hunter 1989, 164.
125 3.27 and 645 (cf. κ 230, 256, 276, 312).
126 3.641 ἔμπα γε μήν, θεμένη κύνεον κέαρ: cf. *Il.* 3.180, *Od.* 4.145.
127 3.616–18 (cf. σ 188–89, τ 509–34: Reddoch 2010).
128 4.1641–42: τὸν μὲν χαλκείης μελιηγενέων ἀνθρώπων / ῥίζης λοιπὸν ἐόντα μετ' ἀνδράσιν ἡμιθέοισι.
129 Clauss 2000, 20, with earlier bibliography.

At a certain point, after seeing the priest and remembering the offensive attitude to the natives by the white colonists, Philoctetes decides to cut down some yam-trees, and distinctly evokes the killing of Achilles in the following way[130]:

> He stretched out the foot. / He edged the razor-sharp steel / through pleading finger and thumb. The yam leaves recoiled / in a cold sweat. He hacked every root at the heel. / He hacked them at the heel, noticing how they curled, / head-down without their roots. He cursed the yams: "*Salope!* / You all see what it's like without roots in this world?" / Then sobbed, his face down in the slaughtered leaves. A sap / trickled from their gaping stems like his own sorrow (4.1.34–41).

The severing of roots (and the white bleeding) is of course *the* most important theme in the whole of *Omeros:* its literary *senhal* here corresponds remarkably to the botanic imagery adopted by Apollonius in introducing and developing the similitude for Talos' death (4.1679–88).

5c. In a very complicated, and much-debated, dialogical frame[131], fr. 43 Pf. = 50 Mass. of Callimachus *Aitia* book II explains (ll. 29–83) why the sacrifice to the founder in the city of Messina remains anonymous and introduces the answer to this question through a long catalogue of other, different rites celebrated in various Sicilian cities. While an opportunity to display Callimachus' expertise in one of his favourite subjects (foundations of cities) and an important specimen of Callimachus' art and of his way to organise aetiology[132], this list also visualises a link between the newly founded city of Alexandria and Southern Italy (a land peculiarly dear to the poet) as a venerable repository of Hellenic wisdom and cultic practices. More importantly, according to Susan Stephens, the list of once prosperous towns in Sicily might allude, by way of antithesis, to the present prosperity of early Ptolemaic Egypt—a sort of *translatio fortunae* for which other parallels can be found in Callimachus' fragments[133].

When T.S. Eliot devotes an entire section of *What the thunder said* (*Waste Land,* ll. 359–76)[134] to the reminiscence of an Antarctic expedition named *Endur-*

---

[130] More on the resonances of Achilles' heel in van Sickle 1999, 24.
[131] Hunter 1996a, with earlier bibliography.
[132] Fantuzzi/Hunter 2002, 101–103. Weber 1993, 364–68 insists, though with due caution, on the "political" and "historical" dimension of Callimachean references to the "griechische Oikumene".
[133] Acosta-Hughes/Stephens 2012, 141–44.
[134] "Who is the third who walks always beside you? / When I count, there are only you and I together / But when I look ahead up the white road / There is always another one walking beside you / Gliding wrapt in a brown mantle, hooded / I do not know whether a man or a woman /— But who is that on the other side of you? / What is that sound high in the air / Murmur of

ance (the allusion is not declared in the text, but it emerges from the author's footnotes), he blends two elements, one historical and one "religious", namely the hallucination of the "third man" appearing to the explorers on the flat antarctic horizon and the epiphany of the resurrected Christ to the two disciples in the *Gospel of Luke* (24.13–31): in this context, the interplay of myth and history is rounded off precisely by a catalogue of cities, the "falling towers" of the centres of Western civilisation in decay, among them Alexandria (a few lines later Eliot will famously speak of the "empty cisterns and exhausted wells", l. 384).

Cavafy, in a poem of 1931 (*In 200 BC*), tackles an aetiology exactly like Callimachus: starting from a text by Plutarch (*Life of Alexander* 16.17), he sets out to explain another absence, namely the absence of the Spartans from Alexander's inscriptions celebrating his victories; he resorts to the myth of Sparta's pride and fierce refusal of Macedonian rule—seen however from a distance, in a world where that pride and that refusal have been entirely superseded by a new order of things, once more represented by a catalogue of cities: in that context, the Spartans' gesture borders on ridiculous[135]. Once more, a myth (an entirely historical myth, this time) triggers an issue of identity that does not subsist in the mere realm of erudition or riddling, but reaches down to the present[136].

It would be idle to insist, after M. Silk, on the parallelism between Eliot's Tiresias and Callimachus' (in the *Hymn to Apollo*), or to remark after so many others that part IV of the *Waste Land* (*Death by water*, the epitaph of Phlebas the Phoenician) is shaped like a Hellenistic funerary epigram (much like Callimachus epigr. 18 Pf., or Cavafy's *Lanis* or *Iasis*), perhaps augmented by a hidden reference to a ritual of regeneration like those of Adonis or Osiris[137]. More to the point of aesthetics, one might add that the *Aitia* sometimes declare their erudite sources within the verse composition, most famously with Xenomedes at the end of the story of Acontius and Cydippe (III, fr. 75 Pf., 53–55)[138]. Rather than distancing the author from the story he is telling, this device lends to the story both authority and factual support, and it triggers a subtle interplay between the histor-

---

maternal lamentation / Who are those hooded hordes swarming / Over endless plains, stumbling in cracked earth / Ringed by the flat horizon only / What is the city over the mountains / Cracks and reforms and bursts in the violet air / Falling towers / Jerusalem Athens Alexandria / Vienna London / Unreal".
135 See Seferis' note (Seferis 1974, 511), where he suggests Cavafy may have identified the contemporary Greek government behind the Spartans.
136 See for another similar case Winder 2003.
137 See Eliot 1982, 112–13. Hunter 2006, 50–67.
138 Κεῖε, τεόν δ' ἡμεῖς ἵμερον ἐκλύομεν / τόνδε παρ' ἀρχαίου Ξενομήδεος, ὅς ποτε πᾶσαν / νῆσον ἐνὶ μνήμῃ κάτθετο μυθολόγῳ. But the same happened in other passages as well, e.g. fr. 92.2 Pf. See Fantuzzi-Hunter 2002, 85–88.

ical source and the poetical *reprise:* something similar happens in such a historically laden poetry as Cavafy's (see for example *Come, King of the Lacedaemonians*)[139], but also in Anglosaxon modernism—not openly in the *Waste Land*, though, but regularly in Pound's *Cantos*, and e.g. in a passage of an English poem written in 1952:

> Wot sort o'Jute-land lingo's that / or is it Goidel for—Mortuum Mare? / or did old Gaius Pliny —get his Pytheas wrong / or had the travelled diarist—gravelled his philology / in Cronos-meer?[140].

This philological discussion on the geography of Jutland is by no means ironical: it rather builds an integral part of what could turn out to be the only poetical work of the 20th century to bear as a title a neuter plural Greek noun, and to be entirely devoted (more organically than Pound's *Cantos*) to a learned and multi-faceted analysis of Europe's and especially England's historical heritage and identity. I am referring to David Jones' *Anathemata*, one of the most conspicuous results of the "second wave" of modernist poetry, described by one critic as the ciphered fruit of a "mythological mind"[141], and by another one as the embodiment of Joyce's allusive method in the wake of Eliot's conception of tradition[142]. Fully equipped with footnotes by their author (who remains skeptical about common knowledge of cultural terms of reference), and not entirely coherent in their partially fragmentary structure, the *Anathemata* derive their name— the author tells us—from the "devoted things", from the holiness of objects "laid up from other things"[143]. Jones' attempt to build a learned aetiology of our world starts from pre-historic times and ends up in the cultic and religious environment of Medieval Wales, pairing overt references to classical and to more obscure medieval writers.

In some cases, as in the lines devoted to the fall of Troy (pp. 84–85) the poet's difficulty, due to various forms of periphrastic indirectness and to unexpected associations, rivals that of Lycophron (a comparison with *Alexandra* 258–68 might be instructive): no wonder that Lycophron has been evoked as a term of comparison for Eliot too[144]. But once more, Jones uses the Homeric

---

139 ll. 8–11: πῆρε τὸν υἱό της στὸν ναὸ τοῦ Ποσειδῶνος, / καὶ μόνοι σὰν βρεθῆκαν τὸν ἀγκάλιασε / καὶ τὸν ἀσπάζονταν, "διαλγοῦντα", λέγει / ὁ Πλούταρχος, "καὶ συντεταραγμένον".
140 Jones 1952, 171. On the "mythic method" see above.
141 *Times Literary Supplement,* Friday 14.11.1952.
142 Raine 1952.
143 Jones 1952, 27–28. On the importance of *anathemata* in Callimachus and Cavafy see Acosta-Hughes 2003, 22–25.
144 R. Jarrell in 1942: see Hardie 2010, 33.

myth to signify something else (Hector's dragging and physical torment is in fact, we read in the footnotes, a prefiguration of the Passion of Christ), whereas the same scene evoked by Cavafy in his famous poem *Trojans* (ll. 15–21) is but the hallmark of the hopeless inadequacy and setback of human condition before the tremendous power of fate.

Once more, the connection with Callimachus, or with Alexandria, is not the fruit of the critic's imagination: the key statement in David Jones' dense introduction is that poetry is still occupied with the embodiment and expression of the mythus "even in our present civilizational phase, even in our hyper-Alexandrian and megalopolitan situation"[145]. Ζούμε μια νέα Αλεξανδρινή περίοδο, said 25 years ago the late Theo Anghelopoulos, thereby meaning that ours was the age of libraries, of bibliographies, a sort of "silence of new proposals and revision of the old ones"[146]. It could be perhaps a nice hommage to him, to Alexandria, and to Europe überhaupt, if we could see some Alexandrianism (in the sense we have tried to define) even in some of Theo's creations, which number among the most convincing, elaborated and historically meaningful re-readings of ancient Greek history and myth in our times. After all, the title of his last film, *Another sea*, is but an Alexandrian allusion to Seferis' version of the Alexandrian myth of the Argonauts (*Mythistorima* IV), and thus indirectly to the first line of the poem *The City* by Cavafy the Alexandrian. As in Seferis' text, it is through Socrates' admonition in the *First Alcibiades* (133b) that the "other sea" invites us to gaze at ourselves through the eyes of another soul.

---

[145] Jones 1952, 19.
[146] Anghelopoulos 1988, 727.

Évelyne Prioux
The Jewels and the Dolls: Late Hellenistic Ecphrastic Epigrams as Metapoetic Texts*

The idea that poetry can be regarded as a kind of painting is deeply rooted in ancient culture[1] and comparisons between poetry or rhetoric and the visual arts were apparently common in ancient literary criticism. Double *synkriseis* comparing a series of painters or sculptors with a series of poets or rhetors were used in order to suggest an evolution, a miniature history of the *tekhnai*, and to translate the characteristics of the various writers into visual metaphors[2]. The Hellenistic scholar-poets were of course aware of such comparisons and we can therefore suspect that when they included the description of a work of art in their poems it was, at least in some cases, a means to express and promote their own literary-aesthetic views: some of the ancient descriptions of works of art were likely meant as metaphors or even, in specific cases, as allegories of the poet's work[3]. In Hellenistic poetry, a good example is Theocritus' depiction of the goatherd's cup. Segal, Cairns and Faber have shown how it encapsulates a literary programme that the reader can identify through the presence of metaphors and hints in the entire *Idyll*[4]. The goatherd's cup is simultaneously a small, elaborate and carved reworking of the huge wooden bowl of Polyphemus

---

* I wish to thank the colleagues who read earlier versions of this paper and commented on it: Kathryn Gutzwiller and Michael Squire. All errors are of course my own. I am also grateful to Peter Roan and to the Trustees of the British Museum for their generosity in sharing their photographs.
1 For the famous aphorism by Simonides, see Plu. *Moralia*, 346 f-347a.
2 On sculptors, see the miniature history of sculpture alluded to by Cic. *Brut.* 70 and Quint. *Inst.* 12.10. These *synkriseis* are to be compared with shorter passages on similar topics: e. g. D.H. *Isoc.* 3.5 – 7, a passage based on a double *synkrisis* opposing two orators (Isocrates vs. Lysias) and two groups of artists (Polyclitus and Phidias vs. Callimachus and Calamis); *Is.* 4.1: on both passages, see Calcante, forthcoming. On painters, see Arist. *Po.* 1448 A on the various types of mimesis (three painters—Polygnotus, Dionysius of Colophon, Pauson—are opposed to four poets —Homer, Cleophon and a pair formed by Hegemon and Nicochares): Polygnotus and Homer represent men better then they are, Dionysius of Colophon and Cleophon represent them as they really are, Pauson, Hegemon and Nicochares produce caricatural representations. See also Plu. *Tim.* 36, a passage opposing two poets (Antimachus vs. Homer) and two painters (Dionysius of Colophon vs. Nicomachus): Prioux, forthcoming, suggests that this *synkrisis* may derive from Duris of Samos.
3 See Prioux 2012 (with bibliography).
4 Segal 1981, 27; Cairns 1984; Faber 1995, 412 – 414; Männlein-Robert 2007, 303 – 305.

in the *Odyssey*, a richer version of the poor drinking vessel of Eumaeus, the Homeric swineherd, and a wooden and αἰπολικόν ("suitable for a goatherd") reworking of Achilles' shield[5]. It is therefore probable that this cup encompasses a reflection on combinations of the grand with the humble, the epic and the pastoral and possibly on the middle style[6].

The ecphrastic epigrams of Posidippus have provided us with further examples: if Theocritus invented an imaginary artwork in order to present his readers with a programmatic allegory, Posidippus rather used references to existing artworks in order to promote his own views on poetry. The clearest example is Hecataeus' portrait of Philitas (63 A.-B.): Posidippus suggests that this portrait is a kind of visual image of Philitas' poetic style, of his λεπτότης and his ἀκρίβεια[7]. Other examples would be the gem carved by Theodorus that represented a literary symbol (9 A.-B.): the lyre of a poet, possibly Anacreon, the archaic forerunner of Alexandrian epigrammatists[8]. Another possible example would be the epigram on *Kairos* which is deprived of its original context (*APl* 275). That an epigrammatist would write on occasion is certainly no coincidence! Posidippus inspired himself of an artwork that was most likely already conceived of as programmatic by its sculptor[9]. I have argued, elsewhere[10], that Posidippus described the allegory of Lysippus' art in order to provide his reader with an allegory of his own poetry. The topic of his epigram is indeed occasion turned into a statue, which is an apt way to describe the paradoxical relationship between the occasion that justified the writing of an epigram and the perennial quality of the text.

It has been suggested that similar examples of programmatic ecphraseis can be found in the epigrams of the imperial period: for instance, Philips's epigram

---

5 Dubel 2010.
6 Prioux 2012, 198–199.
7 Prioux 2007a, 19–74; 2007b; 2008a, 217–221; 2008b; 2012, 195–197. Tsantsanoglou 2012 is most certainly wrong in proposing to identify the portrait of Philitas with the Old Singer type (known especially through the Ny Carlsberg Glyptothek exemplary, inv. nr. 1563): apart from sharing very few features with the possible replica of Hecataeus' Philitas in Lyon (a second century CE inscribed bust), the Copenhagen Old Singer is a typical retrospective portrait of an archaic poet insisting on *pathos* rather than *ethos*. It was designed in a period in which the true features of the poet it represents had for long been forgotten and had to be reinvented, whereas the Philitas portrait is most certainly a "real" portrait designed for viewers who potentially knew or were able to remember the real features of Philitas. For the seminal distinction between retrospective and real portraits, see Zanker 1995, 146–149.
8 On this epigram as a mise en abyme, see e.g. Bing 2005, 121; Gutzwiller 2005b, 314.
9 Prioux 2007a, 214–234.
10 Prioux 2007a, 228–234; Prioux 2012, 191–195.

on the *Eurotas* by Eutychides has been interpreted as a literary allegory[11]. Philip uses a critical terminology that could apply to a literary work: the very topic of the ecphrasis (the image of a river god) fits nicely with what we know about the most frequent programmatic metaphors used by ancient poets[12]. The same applies to the topics of many of Posidippus' ecphrastic epigrams: a mantle of bronze (69 A.-B.), images of chariots[13] or bridles (8, 15 and 67 A.-B.), gems[14] and stones (1–20 A.-B.), a rainbow[15] (6 A.-B.) and the image of one of the Graces (11 A.-B., and possibly 12 A.-B. which seems to engage with the same topic)[16].

The aim of my paper is to ask if this use of ecphrastic epigrams that we perceive in early Hellenistic epigrams and in Imperial epigrams can also be suspected in productions of the second and first centuries BCE, and if it can also be traced back beyond the canon of epigrammatists, in authors that we do not know as well as Posidippus or Philip, authors for which an original context is, at the moment, impossible to reconstruct. From a literary point of view, this work is only possible because of the previous studies on the topic by K. Gutzwiller[17] and because of the amazing material provided by the discovery of the New Posidippus. My aim is indeed to suggest the possibility of a clearer theoretical background and literary significance for several ecphrastic epigrams that have mostly been studied by art historians as *testimonia* on lost masterpieces[18]. By studying these epigrams, I also want to raise the question of the evolution of ecphrastic epigrams and of the way in which Hellenistic epigrammatists reacted to contemporary art. I intend to read these epigrams as the results of complex interactions between a precise cultural context and the knowledge of previous programmatic uses of ecphrastic epigram: I would like to show that at least some of

---

11 Männlein-Robert 2004.
12 See for instance Galand-Hallyn 1994, 122–124 and Worman 2009.
13 On the chariot as a metapoetic symbol, see esp. Simpson 1969 and Henderson 1970.
14 For gems as a metapoetic symbol, see Graver 1998; Hutchinson 2002; Petrain 2005 and esp. Philodemus in *P. Herc.* 1676 (= *Tract. tert.* col. XVI, 3–23 Sbordone). As M. Squire suggested to me after reading a previous version of this paper, carved stones and intaglios may also interest epigrammatists (especially the ones operating within the tradition of epigrammatic variation, which—I believe—is somehow already the case with Posidippus, a frequent imitator of Asclepiades), because seals are, by their very nature, embedded in ideas of representation at a second remove and embody a kind of *mise en abyme* of replication. For seals as the very image of replication, but also as a metaphor of sense perception and as an image widely used in ancient epistemology, see Platt 2006.
15 For the rainbow as a metapoetic symbol, see e.g. Barchiesi 1994, 247.
16 Prioux 2012, 209–210.
17 See esp. Gutzwiller 1998; 2002; 2011.
18 E. g. Benndorf 1862; Schwarz 1971.

these epigrams illustrate a change in the conception of imagery as much as in poetry[19].

Among the many possible examples, I have chosen to focus on three case studies in which the relationship of late Hellenistic epigrams with the earlier tradition of ecphrastic epigrams appears very clearly: 1. Antipater of Sidon's ecphrastic epigrams (with two sub-categories, namely the epigrams on funerary *symbola* and the epigrams on some fourth century CE *opera nobilia*) 2. the late Hellenistic poems on gems and intaglios 3. the image of dolls in a stream as a poetic *sphragis*.

1. Antipater of Sidon and ecphrasis

1.1. Inventing funerary reliefs

First, I would like to make a few remarks on Meleager and Antipater. Meleager 122 G.-P. is a *pastiche* of Antipater's funerary epigrams. Antipater indeed composed a series of epitaphs conceived as visual riddles: the epigrams describe the symbols represented on a tomb and represent a viewer in the process of decrypting their significance and understanding what the *sēmata* carved on the *sēma* are supposed to tell us about the deceased (28–32 G.-P.)[20]. H. von Hesberg has shown how this use of ecphrastic epigrams fits nicely with visual objects designed in the second century BCE: it is not unfrequent, indeed, to observe that sets of images dating back to the second century BCE are conceived as a juxtaposition of signs or objects scattered on a surface[21]. The meaning of the image derives from the ability to set them all together in a coherent interpretation. Examples in funerary art would be the Amyntas stele in the Louvre (from Smyrna)[22], and the

---

[19] The major change to which I am refering is the problem of the so-called *reuixit ars* in the middle of the second century BCE: see of instance Tanner 2006, 288–295 ("Art after art history"). On neo-Attic art, see *infra* p. 191. Interestingly, the late Hellenistic period is marked by the creation of multiple miniature replicas of the *opera nobilia*, with many different ways of copying and relating the copy to the archetype—sometimes meta-artistically (see Bartman 1992). The early Imperial period would see the creation, although as a very limited phenomenon, of objects combining meta-art and meta-poetry, such as the *Tabulae Iliacae:* see Squire 2011.
[20] On these epigrams, see Goldhill 1994, 197–210; Gutzwiller 1998, 265–276; Prioux 2007, 244–290.
[21] von Hesberg 1988.
[22] Paris, Musée du Louvre, Département des Antiquités grecques, étrusques et romaines, inv. nr. MA 3202. See Prioux 2007a, 284–285 and fig. 7.1.

Menophila stele (from Sardis)[23]. Examples in the major masterpieces would be the probable Attalid archetype of the image of Hercules discovering Telephus in Herculaneum[24], or the Attalid archetype of the *asorotos oikos* mosaics[25]. These examples tend to show that Antipater has an eye to the new and to contemporary art. His epigrams prove his sensibility to contemporary artworks, as well as his interest in the possibility of using ecphrastic epigrams as a means to convey a literary programme. This could be the meaning of Meleager's ironic homage to him:

Ἁ στάλα, σύνθημα τί σοι γοργωπὸς ἀλέκτωρ
 ἕστα, καλλαΐνᾳ σκαπτοφόρος πτέρυγι,
ποσσὶν ὑφαρπάζων Νίκας κλάδον· ἄκρα δ' ἐπ' αὐτᾶς
 βαθμῖδος προπεσὼν κέκλιται ἀστράγαλος
ἦ ῥά γε νικάεντα μάχᾳ σκαπτοῦχον ἄνακτα
 κρύπτεις; ἀλλὰ τί σοι παίγνιον ἀστράγαλος;
πρὸς δέ, τί λιτὸς ὁ τύμβος; ἐπιπρέπει ἀνδρὶ πενιχρῷ,
 ὄρνιθος κλαγγαῖς νυκτὸς ἀνεγρομένῳ.
οὐ δοκέω· σκᾶπτρον γὰρ ἀναίνεται. ἀλλὰ σὺ κεύθεις
 ἀθλοφόρον, νίκαν ποσσὶν ἀειράμενον.
οὐ ψαύω καὶ τῇδε· τί γὰρ ταχὺς εἴκελος ἀνὴρ
 ἀστραγάλῳ; νῦν δὴ τὠτρεκὲς ἐφρασάμαν·
φοῖνιξ οὐ νίκαν ἐνέπει, πάτραν δὲ μεγαυχῆ
 ματέρα Φοινίκων, τὰν πολύπαιδα Τύρον·
ὄρνις δ', ὅττι γεγωνὸς ἀνήρ, καί που περὶ Κύπριν
 πρᾶτος κἠν Μούσαις ποικίλος ὑμνοθέτας.
σκᾶπτρα δ' ἔχει σύνθημα λόγου· θνάσκειν δὲ πεσόντα
 οἰνοβρεχῆ, προπετὴς ἐννέπει ἀστράγαλος.
καὶ δὴ σύμβολα ταῦτα· τὸ δ'οὔνομα πέτρος ἀείδει,
 Ἀντίπατρον, προγόνων φύντ' ἀπ' ἐρισθενέων.

Tell me, thou stone, why does this bright-eyed cock stand on thee as an emblem, bearing a sceptre in his lustred wing and seizing in his claws the branch of victory, while cast at the very edge of the base lies a die? Dost thou cover some sceptred king victorious in battle? But why the die thy plaything? And besides, why is the tomb so simple? It would suit a poor man woke up o'nights by the crowing of the cock. But I do not think that is right, for the sceptre tells against it. Then you cover an athlete, a winner in the foot-race? No, I do not hit it off so either, for what resemblance does a swift-footed man bear to a die?

---

23 Istanbul, İstanbul Arkeoloji Müzeleri, inv. nr. 4033 (with an epigram much in the style of Antipater: *GVI* 1881 = *SEG* XXIX, 1798 = *SEG* XXX, 1396 = *SEG* XXXVIII, 1962 = *SEG* XXXIX, 1782 = *SEG* XLI, 1769 = *SEG* XLV, 2222 = *SEG* XLVI, 2304 = *SGOst* 04/02/11). See Prioux 2007a, 286–290 and fig. 7.3.
24 Naples, MANN, inv. nr. 9008 (found in Herculaneum, "Basilica" and thought to derive from an Attalid archetype).
25 See Plin. *HN* 36.60 (on Sosus, the mosaist who designed the *asarōton* of Pergamon).

Now I have it: the palm does not mean victory, but prolific Tyre, the proud mother of palms, was the dead man's birthplace; the cock signifies that he was a man who made himself heard, a champion too I suppose in love matters and a versatile songster. The sceptre he holds is emblematic of his speech and the die cast wide means that in his cups he fell and died. Well, these are symbols, but the stone tells us his name, Antipater, descended from most puissant ancestors. (Meleagr. 122 G.-P. = *AP* 7.428, transl. W. R. Paton)

Fig. 1: Paris, Musée du Louvre, inv. nr. MA 3202. Stèle d'Amyntas (prov.: Smyrna). © Cliché É. Prioux

Meleager invents two strange emblems to represent his own tomb and the one of Antipater, insisting on his drunkenness and the prolific and exuberant character of his poetry (Antipater is shown as an *oinopotēs*): he links Antipater to the concept of *poikilia*, here reinforced by the mention of the *kallaina* ("turquoise") wing of the rooster[26]. The sound of Antipater's poems is possibly assimilated to a rooster crowing at the crack of dawn, that is to say to a somehow violent and resounding sound). The fleeting references to Antipater as an athlete, a swift-footed man, an agonistic winner and an *astragalizōn* could ironically refer to his ability to improvise as if lines were running and flowing from his lips, an ability praised by Crassus in Cicero's *De oratore* [27]. Does this epitaph also tell us something about Antipater's programmatic use of ecphrastic epigram? It is quite possible if we consider the surviving pieces: a good example is the series of epigrams Antipater wrote on Myron's cow, that M. Squire has recently interpreted as a clever way of reflecting on μίμησις (imitation of nature in art, but also imitation of a model in epigram with the infinite possibilities of variation)[28]. The herd formed by all the *uaccae Myronis* composed by Antipater would also be a self reflexive image of the multiple epigrams that the poet assembled in his book[29]. For instance, M. Squire notes the frequent references to the fact of counting the cattle. Could it be, also, that reproducing the *opera nobilia* in many copies was already familiar to Antipater? He was a contemporary of the beginnings of neo-Attic art, and went to Rome in the late second cent. BCE, a few years before the *acmē* of Pasiteles, the author of books on *opera nobilia*, and one of the most influential sculptors of the late Hellenistic period who based his art on copying and setting together models[30].

---

26 Prioux 2007, 277.
27 Cic. *De orat*. 3.194. For the parallel between Meleager's and Cicero's *testimonia* see Benedetto 2004, 222 and n. 138.
28 Squire 2010.
29 See for instance Artemidorus of Tarsus' image of the herd of cows to represent an edition of bucolic poems (*AP* 9.205): Squire 2010, n. 133.
30 Pasiteles, a sculptor from South Italy, was a contemporary of Pompey (106–48 BCE). He settled in Rome in the first half of the first cent. BCE and was greatly admired by Varro as we learn from Plin. *HN* 35.156; 36.39. He had made a portrait of the orator Roscius as a child which also helps dating his activity (Cic. *De div.* 1.36). The students of Pasiteles, active around the middle of the first cent. BCE and in the second half of the first cent. BCE) are known through several testimonies both literary and epigraphic: Stephanus (Plin. *HN* 36.33 and *IG* XIV 1261 = Moretti, *IGUR* IV, 1584), Menelaos (*IGUR* IV, 1575), and the phantomatic and problematic Colotes (sometimes considered as a fifth century artist) who made the chryselephantine table for the temple of Zeus in Olympia (Paus. 5.20.2).

1.2. Replicating the *opera nobilia*: writing ecphrastic epigrams in the wake of the *reuixit ars*?

K. Gutzwiller has recently reconsidered the testimonia on Apelles' *Anadyomene*: she shows that, in the painter's view, this image embodied the quality of χάρις that was central to his art[31]. All later viewers were supposed to connect the painting with this concept. When Antipater celebrates the *Anadyomene*, he certainly knows of this and possibly expects the reader to connect the epigram itself and his poetic style with χάρις, a much wanted quality of Hellenistic poetry. Antipater closely imitates a third century epigram by Leonidas of Tarentum (*APl* 183 = 23 G.-P.). He borrows from Leonidas' epigram the idea of connecting the *Anadyomene*—Aphrodite rising from the sea—with the idea of a judgement: the Judgement of Paris that consists in giving the prize to Aphrodite's beauty and grace and in opposing it to other forms of beauty (Athena and Hera). In Antipater's epigram, the goddesses themselves confess that they are defeated once they have seen Apelles' depiction of their rival.

> Τὰν ἀναδυομέναν ἀπὸ μάτερος ἄρτι θαλάσσας
>   Κύπριν, Ἀπελλείου μόχθον, ὅρα, γραφίδος,
> ὡς χερὶ συμμάρψασα διάβροχον ὕδατι χαίταν
>   ἐκθλίβει νοτερῶν ἀφρὸν ἀπὸ πλοκάμων.
> αὐταὶ νῦν ἐρέουσιν Ἀθηναίη τε καὶ Ἥρη·
>   "Οὐκέτι σοὶ μορφᾶς εἰς ἔριν ἐρχόμεθα."

Look on the work of Apelles' pencil: Cypris, just rising from the sea, her mother; how, grasping her dripping hair with her hand, she wrings the foam from the wet locks. Athena and Hera themselves will now say, "No longer do we enter the contest of beauty with thee."
(Antipater of Sidon 45 G.-P. = *APl* 178, transl. W.R. Paton)

By celebrating the *Anadyomene*, Antipater is not only imitating the 3rd century epigram: he is also following the taste of his contemporaries that results in several sculpted versions of Apelles' painting. The iconographical scheme of the *Anadyomene* was indeed translated in other media, including marble statues, in the course of the second century BCE[32]. The *Anadyomene* was most probably

---

[31] Gutzwiller 2011. On the *Anadyomene* as a symbol of artistic and creative genesis, see Platt 2002.
[32] The chronology of the various translations of the Anadyomene in a three-dimensional medium is quite problematic. For instance Havelock 1995, 86 sets the problem quite differently than I would be inclined to do: in her view, Pliny's testimony (*HN* 35.91) according to which Apelles' *Anadyomene* was eclipsed by the Greek epigrams celebrating it would suggest that the renewed artistic interest in the *Anadyomene* was provoked by its many occurrences in Greek epigrams. I

considered, in the late second cent. BCE, as an *opus nobile* that deserved to be frequently imitated by sculptors.

But the *Anadyomene* was not the only 4th century representation of Aphrodite that interested Antipater: he also praised Praxiteles' *Cnidian Aphrodite*—another *opus nobile* reproduced in Antiquity in more than 200 surviving exemplaries[33]. I would like to suggest that he designed an epigram on the *Cnidian* in

---

would on the contrary be tempted to think that the *Anadyomene* was continuously known by erudites and cultivated people (both for its visual form and its celebrations in epigram) but that the process reached a climax after the *reuixit ars* and in the late Hellenistic period, when copying and recreating an *opus nobile* became one of the central activities of Greek sculptors—a process closely linked to the specific demands of Roman viewers and owners. Antipater's epigrams and, a maybe a few years later Archias' own variants on the theme are, I believe, a reaction to a new conception of art, both sculptural and epigrammatic. Their epigrams imitate earlier poetic models, through little variations, just as the neo-Attic sculptors imitate *opera nobilia*.

Havelock's views on the *Anadyomene* stand in strong contrast with Moreno 1994, I, 239–240 who argues that the creation of the first translation in sculpture of the *Anadyomene* may have been connected to the foundation of Laodicea on the Lycus, in Phrygia (the *Anadyomene* is indeed represented on the imperial coinage of this city) in the middle of the third century BCE. The movement of the arms was apparently derived, with an inversion, from the *Diadumenus* of Polyclitus. According to Moreno, the earliest copies that we know and that enable us to reconstruct the type, are the ones preserved in Rome, in the Museo Nazionale Nazionale Romano and in Palazzo Colonna (Moreno 1994, II, fig. 877).

The subsequent evolutions and reworkings of the type (possibly in an Alexandrian context, and in the course of the second century BCE—according to Moreno) were many: one can mention the group involving the *Anadyomene* and a Triton (Moreno 1994, II, 711–714 and fig. 878: Dresde, Albertinum), the Cyrene Aphrodite—fig. 2 (Moreno 1994, II, 714 and fig. 879–880: formerly in Rome, Museo Nazionale Romano), a crouching Aphrodite, fig. 3, that results from a contamination between the *Anadyomene* and the Doidalsas Aphrodite (Moreno 1994, II, 715–718 and fig. 883: Rhodes, Archaeological museum). In the first cent. BCE, the combination between the figure of Aphrodite and the posture of Polyclitus' *Diadumenus* was again reworked to create the Esquiline Venus (for which Moreno suggests an identification as Cleopatra: Moreno 1994, II, 746–752 and fig. 915–918, Rome, Musei Capitolini, Palazzo dei Conservatori). This last work shows many similarities with the work of Stephanus—one of Pasiteles' students, and therefore a specialist in copying *opera nobilia*.

Of course, the Anadyomene was also reproduced in miniature exemplaries: see for instance the late Ptolemaic or early Imperial terracotta in the British Museum (Terracotta 3348, registration nr. 1926,0930.47—first century BCE or first century CE). See also the bronze statuette (25.4 cm high) in the British Museum (this work is presented as a second century BCE bronze by the BM, fig. 4 in this paper): in this type known as the *Aphrodite pselioumene*, the position of the arms has been slightly reworked so that Aphrodite is no longer wringing her hair but fastening a necklace (London, British Museum, bronze 1084; registration number 1865.0103.37).

33 The chronology of the many variants inspired by the *Cnidian* is very complex and is an object of scientific debate: if some scholars believe that the *Cnidian* was already an important model for sculptors in the third cent. BCE, others tend, following Havelock 1995, to consider that the

Fig. 2: Cyrene Aphrodite. Roman replica (2nd cent. CE), after a Hellenistic original inspired by the *Anadyomene*. Discovered in 1913, restituted to Libya in 2008.
© Alinari archives, Florence/Dist. RMN Grand Palais/Anderson.

---

tradition of replicating the Cnidian and inventing variations on the Praxitelean archetype only started in the late second cent. BCE. Anyhow, it seems that the process at least underwent an acceleration around the time in which Antipater was active.

Among the replicas that we know, the ones generally considered as the most faithful to the original are two imperial exemplaries: the Venus Colonna (Vatican, Museo Pio Clementino, inv. nr. 812) and the Belvedere Venus (Vatican, Museo Pio Clementino, inv. nr. 812). The idea of reproducing with small variations the image of the Cnidian on a small scale which seems to emerge from the series of epigrams celebrating this image somehow echoes what really happened in the visual arts. Workshops in Myrina indeed specialized in reproducing this type on a small scale—see for instance the following terracotta statuettes: Paris, Musée du Louvre, inv. nr.

Fig. 3: Rhodes, Archaeological museum: crouching *Anadyomene*.
© Wikimedia commons/Jebulon.

Myr 19 et Myr 20 (between 50 BCE and 50 CE). See Prioux/Linant de Bellefonds, Text n° 736 in *CALLYTHEA* [En ligne]; http://www.cn-telma.fr/callythea/extrait736/.

Fig. 4: *Aphrodite pselioumene* (prov.: Peloponnese), second century BCE bronze statuette. © The Trustees of the British Museum (AN3405003).

order to respond to an epigram by Hermodorus and to an anonymous poet[34], and that he did so with the intent to promote his own aesthetic ideas. As a matter of fact, two epigrams from the *Garland* of Meleager establish a contrast between the

---

34 The date of the two epigrams is of course unknown. Corso 1988, 47–48, apparently considers both epigrams to predate the one by Antipater.

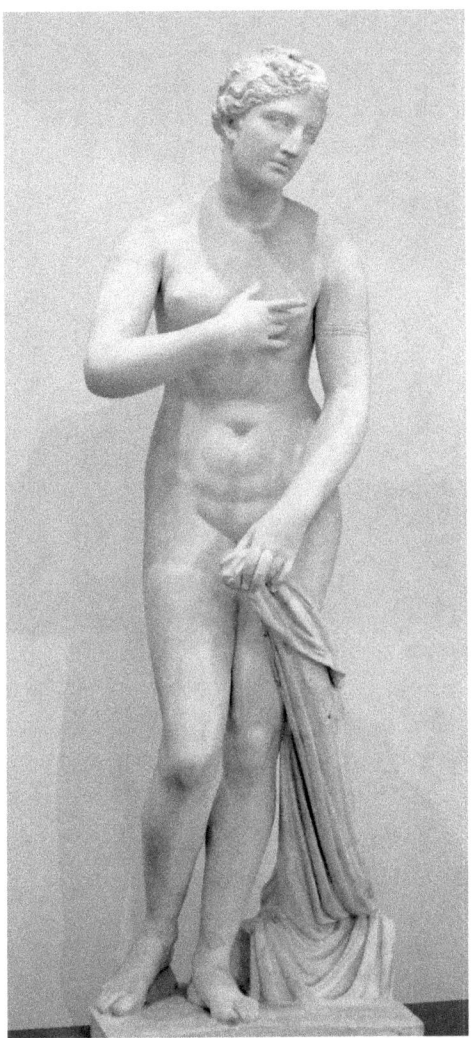

Fig. 5: Rome, Museo Nazionale Romano: Roman copy by Menophantos of the late Hellenistic "Troad Aphrodite", a work inspired by the Cnidian Aphrodite.
© Wikimedia commons/Marie-Lan Nguyen.

Cnidian by Praxiteles and a Phidian Athena, that art historians have tried to identify precisely[35] but that could be the Promachos, the Parthenos or the Lemnian since all three had a spear and could be seen in Athens. The works of Phi-

---

35 See Schwarz 1971 (*ad loc.*).

Fig. 6: Athens, Archeological Museum: Aphrodite, Pan and Eros—a work inspired by the Cnidian Aphrodite (Delos, Establishment of the Poseidoniasts). © Wikimedia commons/Sailko.

dias and the Cnidian were obviously the object of a lot of attention on the part of the sculptors of the middle and late second century BCE, and they inspired new works of art: variations on the archetype of the Cnidian Aphrodite (works *à la manière de Praxitèle*)[36] or pastiches of the works of Phidias (works *à la manière*

---

36 See for instance the work that was known in Antiquity as the "Troad Aphrodite", a late

Fig. 7: Venice, Museo archeologico: colossal head of Athena, by Demochares (second half of the second cent. BCE)—a work of Phidiac inspiration. © Alinari archives, Florence/Dist. RMN Grand Palais/Pietro Fiorentini.

de Phidias)[37]. For instance, a portrait of Cornelia, the mother of the Gracchi brothers, was designed by Tisicrates in a form that imitated the Aphrodite by Phidias that was apparently transferred to Rome and set in the same building[38]. Cornelia's portrait was arguably one of the first female portraits set in public in Rome (or maybe even the first)[39]—a small revolution that happened in the period of Antipater's visit to the city. Moreover, Timocles and Timarchides II, the exact contemporaries of Antipater, and the sons of Polycles, an artist considered as the major figure of the *reuixit ars*, designed the cult statue of Athena Kranaia (in Ela-

---

Hellenistic reelaboration of the *Cnidian* that we know through a Roman copy by Menophantus, fig. 5 (Rome, Museo Nazionale Romano: Moreno 1994, II, 664–665 and fig. 797); the dancing Artemis from Perge (Antalya, Museum), a colossal statue inspired by the Cnidian (Moreno 1994, II, 666–669 and fig. 801); the Aphrodite of the late Hellenistic Pan, Eros and Aphrodite Group found in the Establishment of the Poseidoniasts in Delos, fig. 6 (Athens, Archeological Museum; Moreno 1994, II, 680–682 and fig. 827).
37 See for instance the Athena by Democrates, fig. 7 (found in Crete, at Hierapetra and now in Venice, Museo archeologico: Moreno 1994, II, 545 and fig. 669) and the Athena attributed to Eubulides III, fig. 8 (Athens, National archaeological museum: Moreno 1994, II, 553–554 and fig. 668).
38 See Coarelli 1978.
39 Plin. *HN*, 34.31.

Fig. 8: Athens, Archaeological museum: colossal head of Athena attributed to Eubulides III (second half of the second cent. BCE)—a work of Phidiac inspiration.
© Wikimedia commons/Giovanni Dall'Orto.

teia) by combining features of two Athenas by Phidias, the Promachos and the Parthenos (Paus. 10.34.8)[40].

Τὰν Κνιδίαν Κυθέρειαν ἰδών, ξένε, τοῦτό κεν εἴποις·
   "Αὐτὰ καὶ θνατῶν ἄρχε καὶ ἀθανάτων."
τὰν δ' ἐνὶ Κεκροπίδαις δορυθαρσέα Παλλάδα λεύσσων
   αὐδάσεις· "Ὄντως βουκόλος ἦν ὁ Πάρις."

When you see, stranger, the Cnidian Cytherea, you would say this "Rule alone over mortals and immortals", but when you look at Pallas in the city of Cecrops boldly brandishing her spear you will exclaim, "Paris was really a bumpkin."

(Hermodorus 1 G.-P. = *APl* 170, transl. W.R. Paton)

---

40 Moreno 1994, II, 541–543.

Ἀφρογενοῦς Παφίης ζάθεον περιδέρκεο κάλλος,
καὶ λέξεις· Αἰνῶ τὸν Φρύγα τῆς κρίσεως·
Ἀτθίδα δερκόμενος πάλι Παλλάδα, τοῦτο βοήσεις·
"Ὡς βούτης ὁ Πάρις τήνδε παρετρόχασεν."

Gaze from every side at the divine beauty of the foam-born Paphian and you will say, "I applaud the Phrygian's judgment." Again when you look at the Attic Pallas you will cry out, "it was just like a neatherd for Paris to pass her by".

(Anonymous = *APl* 169, transl. W.R. Paton)

Both epigrams praise Praxiteles' Cnidian, but then reject it by reverting the topos of Paris' Judgement (the κρίσις) to express a preference for Phidias' Athena. They thus establish a contrast between two visual models, and possibly between two ethical models, the Cnidian, known for provoking *agalmatophilia*[41] and possibly praised at the beginning of the third century BCE in a treatise of Posidippus[42], and the majestuous and warlike character of a Phidian Athena[43]. The term κρίσις is of course appropriate for the Judgement of Paris, but it also suggests the idea of an aesthetic judgement. The anonymous epigram translates this opposition between two aesthetic models through the opposition between Asia and Greece, between the taste of Paris, the Phrygian *boutēs*, and the reader's preference for the Attic work. I would argue that Antipater picked up this detail from the anonymous epigram when he stated that Praxiteles had set two "dangerous" pictures on two different continents: the Cnidian Aphrodite in Asia, the Thespian Eros in Greece.

Φάσεις, τὰν μὲν Κύπριν ἀνὰ κραναὰν Κνίδον ἀθρῶν,
ἄδε που ὡς φλέξει καὶ λίθος εὖσα λίθον·
τὸν δ' ἐνὶ Θεσπιάδαις γλυκὺν Ἵμερον, οὐχ ὅτι πέτρον,
ἀλλ' ὅτι κἢν ψυχρῷ πῦρ ἀδάμαντι βαλεῖ.
τοίους Πραξιτέλης κάμε δαίμονας, ἄλλον ἐπ' ἄλλας
γᾶς, ἵνα μὴ δισσῷ πάντα θέροιτο πυρί.

You will say, when you look on Cypris on rocky Cnidus, that she, though of stone, may set a stone on fire; but when you see the sweet Love in Thespiae you will say that he will not only set fire to a stone, but to cold adamant. Such were the gods Praxiteles made, each in a different continent, that everything should not be burnt up by the double fire.

(Antipater of Sidon 44 G.-P. = *APl* 167, transl. W.R. Paton)

---

41 Robert 1992.
42 *SH* 706 = Posidippus 147 A.-B. = Clem. Al. *Protr.* 53.5.
43 Aphrodite's careful and elaborate *ornatus*, care of her locks, and use of complex perfumes (which poets such as Antipater may have wanted to use metapoetically) can thus be contrasted with the attitude of Hera and Athena, who, according to Callimachus (*Fifth Hymn: the Bath of Pallas*, 13–22) did not use a mirror before the Judgement of Paris.

It seems that Antipater has deliberately omitted mention of Phidias, and that he chose to focus on Praxiteles, the model that was rejected on second thoughts or downplayed by his probable predecessors. Antipater, who multiplies the images of the *uacca Myronis*[44], seems rather proud to have the taste of a βουκόλος! I suspect that these elements, the Geographic refences to Asia vs. Attica, and the reference to the βουκόλος as opposed to the suitors of the δορυθαρσέα Παλλάδα would make better sense if understood as meta-literary thoughts and as reactions to a contemporary context of double *synkriseis* between artists and poets or rhetors. Could it be that these epigrams provide us with a very early hint at the opposition between asianism and atticism? Was Antipater's famous ability to improvise a sign of his possible preference for asianism?

Interestingly, this is not the only testimony on a valorisation by Antipater of Praxiteles and his contemporaries. Argentieri and I have supposed, on the basis of different arguments, that an epigram on Nikias' *Nekuia* generally ascribed to Antipater of Thessalonica by Setti had in fact been written by the Sidonian[45]. It is interesting to note that this epigram praises a painter known for having worked with Praxiteles and added color to his sculptures[46], and that it praises him for being the first to have represented an *Nekuia* truly derived from Homer. This draws another implicit opposition between fifth century and fourth century art, since the most famous *Nekuia* was the one painted by Polygnotus, who introduced an Athenian background in his representation of the Underworld by adding in Theseus, a figure that the Homeric Odysseus had not encountered[47]. What Antipater praises is thus an artwork painted by the major collaborator of Praxiteles, in which he sees an exact representation of the Homeric poem—a feature often used to praise the works of Phidias.

Many elements enable us to think that Antipater is reworking and rethinking ideas and views he may have found in Posidippus[48]: this is the case for his epi-

---

44 See Squire 2010. Six poems of the *Anthology* are ascribed to "Antipater", five of which are explicitly labelled as being from the Sidonian (*AP* 9.720–724). The attribution of the sixth poem (*AP* 9.728) is debated: see Squire 2010, n. 28 (with earlier bibliography).
45 *AP* 9.792 = Antip. 85 G.-P. For the attribution to Antip. Thess., see Setti 1890, 109–110 (followed by all scholars until 2003). For the attribution to Antip. Sid., see Argentieri 2003, 144–145; Prioux 2008a, 134–136.
46 Plin. *HN* 35.133.
47 Paus. 10.29.9–10 describes Polygnotus' representation of Theseus in the Underworld (Delphi, Lesche) and notes that Homer's Odysseus regrets he was not able to see Theseus.
48 For instance, Benedetto 2004 has built an impressive case for allusions to Posidippus in Antipater's funerary epigrams.

grams on colossal buildings[49] and for the epigrams praising Antimachus' σεμνότης along with Erinna's λεπτότης[50]. His interest in Praxiteles' Cnidian may well have had a forerunner in Posidippus' work on Cnidus. One may also note that the *uacca Myronis* happens to be the central piece of the *andriantopoiika*[51].

2. The Poetic "Gems" of the *Garlands* of Meleager and Philip

This possible influence of Posidippus and his contemporaries also appears in other Hellenistic poems whose original context is very difficult to reconstruct. I would like to take a few examples of epigrams that bear a strong similarity to Posidippus' *lithika:* the poetic "gems" of the Garlands of Meleager and Philip, sometimes written by authors who were the contemporaries or near contemporaries of Maecenas, whose poetic style was connected with gems and drunkenness by Augustus[52].

We are ignorant of both the dating and the author of *AP* 9.325, an epigram that was in Meleager's *Garland*, perhaps in a separate section that included ecphrastic epigrams[53]:

> Πρὶν μὲν ἁλικλύστου πέτρας ἐνὶ βένθεσιν ἦμαν
> εὐαλδὲς πόντου φῦκος ἐπεννυμένα·
> νῦν δέ μοι ἱμερόεις κόλπων ἔντοσθεν ἰαύει
> λάτρις ἐϋστεφάνου Κύπριδος ἁβρὸς Ἔρως.

Of old I dwelt in the depths on a sea-washed rock clothed in luxuriant seaweed, but now in my bosom sleeps the delightful child, tender Love, the servant of diademed Cypris.
(Anonymous 55 G.-P. = *AP* 9.325, transl. W.R. Paton)

This epigram describes a figure of Eros carved in a sea-shell and thus recalls the theme of the two central epigrams of the *lithika* in which Posidippus (11–12 A.-B.) describes one or less likely two objects that come from the sea but deserves,

---

[49] See *AP* 7.748 and 9.58 (with an interest for the colossal and the wonders of the Ancient world).
[50] *AP* 7.713 and 7.409 (epigrams by Antipater of Sidon on Erinna and Antimachus) are modelled on another pair of companion pieces by Asclepiades of Samos (*AP* 7.11 and 9.63), whose views Posidippus apparently shared. See Prioux 2007a, 89–90, n. 33.
[51] Posidipp. 66 A.-B.
[52] See Sen. *Ep.* 114 and Graver 1998.
[53] On this epigram, see Prioux 2012, 210–211.

nevertheless, to be considered as a gem. The poem indicates that the image of one of the Graces—Aglaia[54]—has been carved inside the seashell : as a *Charis*, this figure can be read both as a ethical or political symbol and as the personification of a privileged aesthetic principle. The aesthetic interpretation is reinforced by the choice of the Grace represented on the seashell : being Aglaia, she is connected with splendid beauty. When reading Posidippus with an eye for metapoetic elements, we see that the structure of the central pieces of the *lithika*, the two descriptions of shells, replicates, as a literary diptych, the form of the bivalve. The central line of the *lithika* section ends with the word τέχνης[55]: the *tekhnē* applied to a product of the sea transforms it into a *pyxis* and into the equivalent of a gem, that is to say into the very symbols of *ornatus*. Of course, similar objects really existed in Posidippus' times[56], but the point of an allegory is precisely to describe something that is coherent and persuasive on a surface level and that may, at the same time, serve as a metaphor describing something else. In this poem, Posidippus is praising the miniature work of craftmanship that one can also observe in objects initially derived from the sea. But is he also thinking of the miniature details of, let's say, a small passage in Homer, a poet compared to the ocean and praised for his ability to combine the grand style and miniature details[57]? If the question is bound to remain open about the *lithika*, what should we say about the now isolated epigram of Meleager's *Garland*? The seashell, whether real or imaginary, was seemingly turned into a *pyxis* (a cosmetic box) for an elegant lady. There is a clever pun on the φῦκος, the red seaweed that used to drape the shell in the sea, and the φῦκος, the make-up that is now stored in this beautiful shell. Does this description have

---

54 Although the text is fragmentary, the reconstruction involving Aglaia, the Charis, seems the most probable one. For a complete apparatus, see version 12.1 (2011) of the "New Poems Attributed to Posidippus: An Electronic Text-in progress" in *Classics@*, 1 (http://chs.harvard.edu/).
55 Prioux 2008a, 171.
56 Sea-shells and boxes in the shape of sea-shells were used as cosmetic boxes. Tombs of the Egyptian and of the Graeco-Roman world have provided examples, as well houses in Pompeii: see for instance Bardiès-Fronty/Walter/Bimbenet Privat 2009, 138–139, cat. Cl. 65 (with seashells used as palettes for mixing pigments and/or as containers). Ornated examples are known: see for instance McFadden 1946, pl. 48.140 and De Juliis 1984, cat. nr. 318, with silver decorations (Taranto, *Museo archeologico nazionale*, inv. 50.686).
57 One may think of the possible importance, as a model for these poems, of *Il.* 18.400–405: Hephaistus, while still a child and long before he would forge the shield of Achilles, practiced a lighter type of craftmanship in a grotto with smooth walls on an island surrounded by the Ocean. There, in the company of Thetis and Eurynome, the mother of the Charites, he wrought jewels, rings and *kalykes* (cups or ornaments in the shape of flowers?) for the godesses. This passage was admired by Eustathius for its λειότης.

a metaliterary meaning[58]? Is there a recusatio in the πρὶν μὲν... νῦν δέ antithesis, and in the contrast between, on one hand the sea and the former purple mantle of the shell, and on the other the luxurious make-up which it now contains and its current erotic function? Without Posidippus 11 and 12 A.–B., and without the probable metaliterary significance of his *lithika*, this question would probably never have been raised; and because this epigram lacks context, it cannot be answered satisfactorily. What can be noted is also that Posidippus, Antipater and the unknown author of this epigram are all providing us, through their ecphrastic epigrams, with images of grace or love and refined **ornatus** emerging from the sea, possibly playing for some of them on the image of the sea of love, and, for others, or even the same texts, on the image of a literary sea.

A similar theme is to be found in Addaeus' epigram on Galene:

Ἰνδὴν βήρυλλόν με Τρύφων ἀνέπεισε Γαλήνην
 εἶναι, καὶ μαλακαῖς χερσὶν ἀνῆκε κόμας·
ἠνίδε καὶ χείλη νοτερὴν λειοῦντα θάλασσαν,
 καὶ μαστούς, τοῖσιν θέλγω ἀνηνεμίην.
ἢν δέ μοι ἡ φθονερὴ νεύσῃ λίθος, ὡς ἐν ἑτοίμῳ
 ὥρμημαι, γνώσῃ καὶ τάχα νηχομένην.

Tryphon coaxed me, the Indian beryl, to be Galene, the goddess of Calm, and with his soft hands let down my hair. Look at my lips smoothing the liquid sea, and my breasts with which I charm the windless waves. Did the envious stone but consent, you would soon see me swimming, as I am longing to do. (Ad(d)aeus 9 G.-P. = *AP* 9.544, transl. W.R. Paton.)

---

[58] Certain fifth century authors, such as Plato and Thucydides, used "ornaments" (κόσμοι) and coloring (ἐπιχρωματίζειν) as metaphors to denounce the stylistic devices used by the poets (see Wiseman 1979b). In Rome, the "makeup" (*fucus*) and the *color* were to become well attested metaphors for literary/rhetorical style and carried, in most contexts, a pejorative or ironic connotation (see e.g. Quint. 8.3.6). They are playfully employed by Cicero to refer to his own use of Isocratean and Aristotelian theories of rhetoric to provide ornamentation to a *commentarius* or ὑπόμνημα: see Wiseman 1979a, 5–6 and Cic. *Att.* 2.1.1–2, in which the author states that he has used up Isocrates' entire perfume-cabinet (*myrothecium*) and Aristotle' *rouge* (*pigmenta*). As far as poetry is concerned, it seems to me quite telling that Ovid, a poet earlier known for his deep interest in makeup and cosmetics (see *Ars amatoria* 3.199–209 and the fragmentary *Medicamina faciei feminae*, with Rosati 1985, 20–35 and Prioux 2009a and 2009b), insists on the poor quality of his *Tristia*, a book lacking *fucus*, that is to say the decoration of purple dye, but also stylistic embellishment. See Ov. *Trist.* 1.1.5 and Williams 1992, 184–185. Ovid's position on make-up is to be contrasted, for instance with Prop. *El.* 1.2. When confronted with Posidippus 11–12 A.B. we may wonder if there were Alexandrian antecedents in which makeup was used as a metaphor for poetry with positive connotations of refinement. This would fit nicely with what we know of of Arsinoe II's and Berenice II's interest for perfumes and cosmetics: see Apollonius Mys, *apud* Ath. 16.688f–689a, Holmes 1992 on the perfumes in Callimachus' *Coma*, Jackson 2001 and Prioux 2009b.

Fig. 9: New York, Metropolitan Museum of Art, accession nr. 17.194.28, blue glass oval of the second or first cent BCE depicting the bust of a Nereid. © Peter Roan.

Fig. 10: Boston, Museum of fine Arts (accession nr. 99.101 "Marlborough gem"). © Boston, MfA.

Unfortunately the Addaeus who wrote this epigram is most certainly not the third century Addaeus who was both an author of treatises on the visual arts and on literary composition[59]. This particular epigram indeed comes from one of the

---

59 For details, see Prioux, Text n° 25223 in *CALLYTHEA* [En ligne]; http://www.cn-telma.fr/callythea/extrait252231/.

well identified blocks of Philip's *Garland*[60]. Nothing is known about its author, but there are elements that could enable us to date it more precisely. First, I would like to point out that the description has most certainly nothing to do with the gems of the so-called "Galene" type[61], where the figure's lips have nothing extraordinary and whose breast is not shown[62]. These gems are based on an iconography that already existed around 72 BCE (as can be seen on Roman coins depicting Amphitrite). Further evidence comes from gems scattered in different collections that do bear the signature of Tryphon: almost all of these signatures are modern forgeries, but one of them is peculiarly interesting. The "Marlborough gem"[63] that depicts the wedding of Eros and Psyche, discovered in the fifteenth century, has the following inscription: ΤΡΥΦΩΝ ΕΠΟΙΕΙ. L. Stephani[64] and most scholars of the second half of the nineteenth century and the twentieth century considered this inscription to be a modern forgery inspired by Addaeus' epigram. More recently, Vollenweider and Boardman have argued that the inscription has some similarities with other products of the late Hellenistic or early Imperial period and tend to consider it as genuine[65], even if Boardman remains uncertain about the inscription's authenticity and states that the Addaeus epigram may have induced a Renaissance falsarius to add a signature on an ancient cameo. We now know, thanks to a fifteenth century letter, rediscovered recently, that the gem was found in Sentinum around 1490[66] and that it already had its inscription in the late fifteenth century. This letter narrows down the possibilities for a forgery: either the inscription is genuine or it was made around the time of the discovery. I would add that, in my view, the epigram in fact proves the inscription to be genuine: the nineteenth century scholars who studied the gem simply forgot that Addaeus' epigram was only known through the *Palatine anthology* and not through the *Planudean anthology*. Inscribing ΤΡΥΦΩΝ ΕΠΟΙΕΙ on a gem could not make sense for the fifteenth century frauds and their public: by that time, nobody knew that Tryphon was a famous gem-cutter of the late Hellenistic or early Imperial times since there was no other testimony on this artist. The viewers were to discover this additional fact only in the seventeenth century.

---

60 An alphabetic series indeed runs from *AP* 9.541 to *AP* 9.562, with the only exception of 9.547.
61 See for instance, New York, MET, accession nr. 17.194.28 (presented by the Museum's indications as a blue glass oval depicting the "bust of the nereid Galene"), here fig. 10.
62 See Boardman 1968, 32 and Vollenweider 1966, 11 and 26.
63 Boston, Museum of fine Arts (accession nr. 99.101 "Marlborough gem"):
[http://www.mfa.org/collections/object/cameo-with-the-wedding-of-cupid-and-psyche-or-an-initiation-rite-155692]
64 Stephani 1851, 4.
65 Vollenweider 1966, 36–37 and Boardman 2009, cat. nr. 1.
66 Micheli 2008.

This said, we now know that there really was a gem-cutter called Tryphon and that he wrought cameos, and that stylistic comparisons based on the Marlborough gem and other cameos show that he was probably a close collaborator of Sostratos, a gem-cutter who worked for Mark Antony[67]. Both gem-cutters apparently have an Alexandrian background and worked on images of force (Hercules) subdued by love, possibly as allegoric representations of Mark Antony himself[68].

In his epigram, Addaeus describes a gem cut by Tryphon, which the "Marlborough gem" proves to be a real gem-cutter. Addaeus probably composed this poem while Tryphon was still famous, which possibly means somewhere in the third quarter of the first century BCE. The beryl and the Indian provenance of the gem, as well as the swimming Nereid, recall Posidippus[69]. Addaeus praises the soft hands of the carver and his representation of the hair of Galene (hair and locks are a symbol of precision in art, but can also remind us of an important metaliterary metaphor). Tryphon and Galene are both experts in making things λεῖα (smooth to the touch/with a smooth worked surface/gentle/uniform), as was possibly the epigrammatist, who uses terms that can remind us of a critical terminology linked to the concept of λεπτότης[70] as well as of images of swiftness

---

[67] Squire 2011, 297–300 discusses the many cases in which gems are signed with artist names which are likely to be pseudepigraphic signatures ("Phidias", "Scopas", etc.), rather than the actual names of the gem-cutters who carved these objects. This is of course a wide-spread phenomenon, but, unlike Squire 2011, 298, n. 165, I do not believe that the Tryphon gem in Boston (the "Marlborough gem") belongs to this category of pseudepigraphic documents. It is indeed a cameo of extraordinary quality and may thus well be the work of a gem cutter who was famous enough to be celebrated in an epigram. Moreover, there seems to be a coherent context linking Tryphon to Mark Antony and epigrammatists such as Addaeus (and most interestingly Crinagoras, whose epigram on the *Hecale* was possibly paired with the Galene epigram—see below) to Cleopatra Selene. Interestingly, another example of early Imperial "satellite" king linked to epigrams, gems and Mark Antony is known to us: "King Polemo" (who could either be Polemo I who married the grand-daughter of Mark Antony—or his son Polemo II) is the author of two epigrams on gems (*AP* 9.746 and *AP* 11.38).

[68] For the Marlborough gem as the creation of a gem-cutter working for Mark Antony, see Vollenweider 1966, 36–37 and Micheli 2008.

[69] For the special relevance that the motive of the seal or intaglio may have had for poets operating in the tradition of epigrammatic variations and for the role of the seal as a possible symbol of the very process of replication, see *supra* n. 14. On reading an earlier version of this paper, M. Squire suggested to me that the image of the Nereid ready to jump into the sea may refer to the way in which Galene's image was to be pressed on liquid wax. If so, the point in describing a Nereid about to swim may have been to emphasize the very fact that this artifact and the epigram were conceived as a *sphragis*.

[70] Even if λεῖον and λεπτόν are not connected by etymology, ancient critics may have felt both words to be connected by their sonorities. Both terms have a possible equivalent in the latin

and readiness. He plays on several models, including the epigrams on athletes or on Myron's cow who are tied to their bases but longing to move; he applies this topos to the context of the gem (and produces, by doing so, a miniature image of the topos). Was this poetic gem originally part of a cycle? Was it a metapoetic symbol? Was this one of the very reasons for which Philip selected this epigram for his *Garland*? It is possible but not certain. Supposing that Addaeus 9 G.-P. was really followed by the epigram of the *Garland* of Philip that now follows it in the *Anthology*, we would have a nice context dealing with λεπτότης. The following poem is indeed the epigram by Crinagoras on Callimachus' *Hecale* (*AP* 9.545). We thus have, in a row, two epigrams on λεπτότης by two authors connected somehow to Mark Antony or his family: Addaeus wrote an epigram on a famous gem cutter working for Mark Antony, and Crinagoras wrote epigrams for Cleopatra Selene, the daughter of Mark Antony and Cleopatra VII, who may have tried to imitate the first Lagid queens, Arsinoe Philadelphus or Berenice II, both of whom are good candidates for the *anassa* addressed by Posidippus in the *lithika*. A similar pair formed by a literary symbol and a work of art can be found in the remnants of Philip's *Garland*: Philip's epigram on Eutychides' statue of the Eurotas (*AP* 7.709) was possibly paired with Tullius Geminus' epigram on the fertile waters of the Strymon, a new and better Nile (*AP* 7.707). This epigram, which is very close to the Eurotas epigram in the alphabetical order, was probably apt to please Philip by its celebration of a stream that could symbolize the fertility of a new generation of poets coming from Macedonia.

3. Little Dolls in a Clear Stream

Even in Philip's *Garland* there may thus have been traces of a confrontation between certain ecphrastic epigrams and other possible metaphors and images of poetry. What about Meleager's *Garland* in which there was apparently a repeated presence of statues and images depicting Eros or Aphrodite forming a kind of sequence if we follow the reconstruction suggested by K. Gutzwiller[71]? I believe that Meleager selected and set together (or at least at a short distance from each other) epigrams that contained metapoetic symbols. This is probably the case with his series of statues of the nymphs in a river or source. Of course, all these epigrams recall more or less the setting of Plato's *Phaedrus*: the descrip-

---

leue, a seminal notion for Ovid, for instance: see Klein 2008. For λειότης as a critical notion, see for instance D. H. Περὶ μιμήσεως (epitomy), 2.3, where it describes a *synthesis* producing an impression of smoothness.
71 Gutzwiller 1998, 315–321.

tion by Plato of this *locus amoenus* was considered by ancient critics to be an example of charm and grace. Dionysius of Halicarnassus even echoes the words of this description when describing Plato's style, as if the landscape was a reflexive metaphor of the author's style[72]. Meleager builds up a series by setting together several epigrams that represent the images of multiple dolls and statuettes:

Πέτρης ἐκ δισσῆς ψυχρὸν καταπάλμενον ὕδωρ,
χαίροις, καὶ Νυμφέων ποιμενικὰ ξόανα,
πίστραι τε κρηνέων, καὶ ἐν ὕδασι κόσμια ταῦτα
    ὑμέων, ὦ κοῦραι, μυρία τεγγόμενα,
χαίρετ'· Ἀριστοκλέης δ' ὅδ' ὁδοιπόρος, ᾧπερ ἀπῶσα
    δίψαν βαψάμενος τοῦτο δίδωμι γέρας.

Hail, thou cold stream that leapest down from the cloven rock, and ye images of the Nymphs carved by a shepherd's hand! Hail, ye drinking troughs and your thousand little dolls, ye Maidens of the spring, that lie drenched in its water! All hail! And I, Aristocles, the wayfarer, give you this cup which I dipped in your stream to quench my thirst.
(Leonidas of Tarentum G.-P. = AP 9.326, transl. W.R. Paton.)

Νύμφαι ἐφυδριάδες, ταῖς Ἑρμοκρέων τάδε δῶρα
    εἵσατο, καλλινάου πίδακος ἀντιτυχών,
χαίρετε, καὶ στείβοιτ' ἐρατοῖς ποσὶν ὑδατόεντα
    τόνδε δόμον, καθαροῦ πιμπλάμεναι πόματος.

Ye Nymphs of the water, to whom Hermocreon set up these gifts when he had lighted on your delightful fountain, all hail! And may ye ever, full of pure drink, tread with you lovely feet the floor of this your watery home. (Hermocreon G.-P. = AP 9.327, transl. W.R. Paton.)

Νύμφαι Νηϊάδες, καλλίροον αἵ τόδε νᾶμα
    χεῖτε κατ' οὐρείου πρωνὸς ἀπειρέσιον,
ὕμμιν ταῦτα πόρεν Δαμόστρατος Ἀντίλα υἱὸς
    ξέσματα, καὶ δοιῶν ῥινὰ κάπρων λάσια.

Ye Naiad Nymphs, who shed from the mountain cliff this fair stream in inexhaustible volume, Damostratus, the son of Antilas, gave you these wooden images and the two hairy boar-skins. (Damostratus 1 G.-P. = AP 9.328, transl. W.R. Paton.)

Νύμφαι ἐφυδριάδες, Δώρου γένος, ἀρδεύοιτε
    τοῦτον Τιμοκλέους κᾶπον ἐπεσσύμεναι·
καὶ γὰρ Τιμοκλέης ὕμμιν, κόραι, αἰὲν ὁ καπεὺς
    κάπων ἐκ τούτων ὥρια δωροφορεῖ.

Ye water Nymphs, children of Dorus, water diligently this garden of Timocles, for to you, Maidens, doth the gardener Timocles bring ever in their season gifts from this garden.
(Leonidas of Tarentum 6 G.-P. = AP 9.329, transl. W.R. Paton.)

---

72 Galand-Hallyn 1994, 122–123; Hunter 2012, chap. 4.

These epigrams are sometimes the only or rare testimonies that we have on an epigrammatist, as if Meleager repeatedly chose to summarize the production of an author by selecting, in his works, an image of the multiple, and especially the representation of multiple statuettes assembled together in one and the same stream. Gow and Page suspect Damostratus to be a ghost because we know nothing else from him. They note that the epigrammatist's name could have well been inferred from the epigram. And yet, the epigram by Hermocreon, who is indeed named as the author of another epigram (*APl* 11), shows that this may well be the *sphragis* of an epigrammatist of whose production we now completely ignorant[73]. It could be interesting to note the precise differences in the way in which the streams are described: the Callimachean pure drink of Hermocreon differs from the inexhaustible volume of the mountain waterfall imagined by Damostratus.

The earliest examples of the series are very interesting and have a clear metapoetic intent. In their commentary on Leonidas 6 G.-P., Gow and Page refute far-fetched speculations on the identity of Dorus as an equivalent of the stream Echedorus or as the eponym hero of the city of Dora[74]; they suspect that Dorus is here the eponym of the Dorians[75]. I would add that his presence makes better sense if the garden described by Leonidas is some kind of metaphor for the poet's work. The water that irrigates the garden may remind us of one of the passages most discussed and criticized in Homer's *Iliad:* the metaphor of the water-adduction system of a garden used for describing the Scamander in *Iliad* 21.257 ff., a passage in which excessive minuteness was felt to prevent the reader from visualizing the Scamander as he should[76]. One can also note Leonidas' mention of the fruit that celebrates the concept of *Horae*, the Seasons, but also beauty. The mention of Dorus, eponym of the Dorians, as the father of the water nymphs can be explained by the Dorian dialect of Leonidas, and by his Tarentine origin, since Taranto was very proud and aware of its Dorian origins. Dorus gives birth to the poetry of Leonidas, although many if not most of his known epigrams are not in Doric, including those spoken in his own per-

---

73 Gow/Page, *HE* II, 305.
74 Gow/Page, *HE* II, 315.
75 On Dorus as the founder of Dora, see *LIMC* III/1, 666–667, s.v. "Doros" (R. Vollkommer). It is unclear whether this Dorus, son of Poseidon, is, or not, the Dorus considered to be the eponym of the Dorians (Servius, *ad Aen.* 2.27 apparently considers them as one and the same). The Dorus who became the eponym of the Dorians is rather supposed to be the son of Hellen and the brother of Aiolus and Xuthus (Hesiod, fr. 9 Merkelbach/West): see *LIMC* VIII/1, 614–615, s.v. "Hellen" (A. Kossatz-Deissmann) and *LIMC* V/1, 702–705, s.v. "Ion" (E. Simon).
76 Duris fr. 89 Jacoby = *Scholia gen. in Homeri Iliadem* Φ 257.

son[77]. Once again, the visual culture helps us in understanding the context of the poem: this interest in a now poorly known mythological character that descended from Hellen has a parallel in Apulian vase painting, since the Underworld painter depicted, in the second part of the fourth century BCE, the rare Boeotos, a figure that interested Euripides in his two tragedies on *Melanippe* and that made sense in a South Italian context because of his role at the court of king Metapontos[78]. A few decades later, Euphorion, a poet coming from Chalcis—that is to say an Euboean city close to the Boeotian coast—, would also write about Boeotos, the eponym of the Boeotians[79]. The presence of his great uncle Dorus in Leonidas testifies the same interest in the origins of peoples, cities, and colonies as a means to define one's cultural (and maybe poetic) identity.

To sum up briefly this paper, I would say that the epigrams of the lesser-known epigrammatists of the Hellenistic period or of the major epigrammatists of the late Hellenistic period provide us with a good amount of material that leads us to suspect ecphrastic epigrams often had a metapoetic role, and some of them were possibly used as *sphragides* or set at key places in the poetry books. The influence of contemporary art and of the contemporary artistic context can be seen, if not through direct references to new masterpieces, at least in the choice of the *opera nobilia* that will be both copied by artists and celebrated by the poets.

---

[77] See Gutzwiller in this volume.
[78] Emory University, Michael C. Carlos Museum, volute-krater attributed to the Underworld Painter, accession number 1994.001.
[79] Euph. fr. 96 Powell = 125 a-b Cusset/Acosta Hughes.

IV. **Scholarship**

Marco Fantuzzi
Tragic smiles: When tragedy gets too comic for Aristotle and later Hellenistic readers

The corpora of tragic scholia are an amalgam of remarks that makes it difficult to determine authorial identities and their chronology, or at least more consistently difficult than, e.g., in the scholia to the *Iliad*. Their abridgement has toned down the interpretive peculiarities of their original authors and eliminated almost all those critical or approving references to other individual scholars which, in the case of the Iliadic scholia, make it easier to assess the scholia's relative chronology. The result is that the fairly clear-cut definition of classes of scholia which we are accustomed to finding in the Homeric scholia is severely impaired in the case of the scholia to the tragedians.

In an attempt at bringing some structure to the variant ideas amassed in the scholia to Euripides and contextualizing them among other texts of ancient literary criticism, this paper will investigate the views of some ancient critics concerning the failure of tragic sublimity or, as it is frequently put, the intrusion of "comic" or "excessively comic" features upon tragic action and heroes in Euripides.[1] The vast majority of these remarks focus on a character's ethics or actions, and they either descend from or are in tune with Aristotle's idea that it is comedy, as opposed to tragedy, that should be concerned with "baser but not wholly vicious characters"[2] (φαυλοτέρων μέν, οὐ μέντοι κατὰ πᾶσαν κακίαν, *Poet*. 1449a32), a concept already evinced in, e.g., Aristophanes' *Frogs*.[3] However, a coherent subset of the relevant scholia addresses a specific structural issue instead. They point to the "excessively comic" (or "excessively satyric") character of tragedies that do not end in a catastrophe. These remarks come mainly from hypotheseis ascribed to Aristophanes of Byzantium, and they seem distinct from the Aristotelian concept of a perfect tragedy; I will argue that they are possibly

---
[1] I will not even touch upon any other parameters that are often arbitrarily applied by ancient as well as by modern scholars to determine Euripides' "comicity". For a review of this issue in modern scholarship, see in particular Gregory 1999–2000. Nor will I deal with the task of assessing how frequently Aeschylean trilogies may have had "happy" vs sad endings; neither will I re-assess the long-standing question of what might have been the emotional impact on the audience by the satyr plays following all 5th cent. tragic trilogies. See Wise 2008 for an attempt at de-tragicizing the closures of 5th cent. tragedy (and tragic trilogies), which must be read alongside the qualifications by Hanink 2011.
[2] All translations from Aristotle's *Poetics* are by S. Halliwell (Loeb Class. Libr.).
[3] See now Schironi 2009, 290–7 and Cadoni 2010.

rooted in a specifically Hellenistic stance on the points of contact between Euripides' tragedy and new comedy, as well as on the Menandrean contamination of comedy and tragedy.

* * *

In the past century and a half, studies in ancient philology and hermeneutics have consistently emphasized that the ancient literary criticism of Homer shares a terminology and key-ideas with that of the three Tragedians, and that many of these two genres' central ideas are also found in the critical approaches documented in Aristotle (especially the *Poetics*, of course). I say "documented in Aristotle" because some of Aristotle' principles and terms may have been more widely shared within the 4th cent.'s philology in statu nascenti, and not all of them may originate with Aristotle.⁴

Aristotle considered the non-dramatic genre of epic akin to tragedy, in that both focus on "elevated matters/characters." Comedy and tragedy, on the other hand, he considered opposites, at least in subject matter, even though they are both dramatic genres: see *Poet.* 1448a11–7 "Homer represented superior people ... This very distinction separates tragedy from comedy: the latter tends to represent people inferior, the former superior, to existing humans" (ἡ τραγῳδία πρὸς τὴν κωμῳδίαν διέστηκεν· ἡ μὲν γὰρ χείρους ἡ δὲ βελτίους μιμεῖσθαι βούλεται τῶν νῦν) and 1449b8–9 "epic matches tragedy to the extent of being mimesis of elevated matters (or characters) in metrical language" (ἡ μὲν οὖν ἐποποιία τῇ τραγῳδίᾳ μέχρι μὲν τοῦ μετὰ μέτρου λόγῳ μίμησις εἶναι σπουδαίων ἠκολούθησεν). Theophrastus appears to have simply contributed a new emphasis on the social component of this "seriousness" of tragedy and epic. He opposed tragedy as "crisis in the hero's fortune" (ἡρωικῆς τύχης περίστασις) and comedy as "tale of private affairs involving no danger" (ἰδιωτικῶν πραγμάτων ἀκίνδυνος περίστασις) and belonging not to heroes and kings, like tragedy, but to humbler people.⁵ Though we do not know his opinions about the points of contact between epic and tragedy, he stresses that tragic characters are "heroes" of the mythological age, and he thereby implicitly equated the characters of epic and tragedy.

However Aristotle also specified, at 1449b16–20, that "epic and tragedy have some components (μέρη) in common, but others are peculiar to tragedy. So who-

---

4 The fact that most of Aristotle's investigative tools apply to both tragedy and epic should come as no surprise: see most recently Schironi 2009, 281–2. The idea that Homer was the "first tragedian" must have been relatively widespread between the 5th and 4th cent. It was shared by both Aristotle (*Poetics*: the *Iliad* as first tragedy) and Plato (*Resp.* 10.595b–c, 10.607a; *Theaet.* 152e).

5 Fr. 708 Fortenbaugh, ap. Diom. *Ars gramm.* 3. Cf. Seidensticker 1982, 250–1.

ever knows about good and bad tragedy knows the same about epic, as epic's resources belong to tragedy, but tragedy's ones are not all to be found in epic" (ἃ μὲν γὰρ ἐποποιία ἔχει, ὑπάρχει τῇ τραγῳδίᾳ, ἃ δὲ αὐτῇ, οὐ πάντα ἐν τῇ ἐποποιίᾳ). At 1452b.9–13, he lists three μέρη that belong to the specific μῦθος by which tragedy ψυχαγωγεῖ "draws out the souls of the audience"—πάθος, ἀναγνώρισις "recognition", and περιπέτεια "reversal". Tragic πάθος is here defined as "an act involving destruction or pain, for example deaths on stage and physical agonies and woundings and so on" (πρᾶξις φθαρτικὴ ἢ ὀδυνηρά, οἷον οἵ τε ἐν τῷ φανερῷ θάνατοι καὶ αἱ περιωδυνίαι καὶ τρώσεις καὶ ὅσα τοιαῦτα). Aristotle's exemplification thus preliminarily points to πάθη which have a visual impact, in partial contradiction to his statement that creating πάθος by visual means is an inferior device of the playwrights;[6] but he does use the idea of visuality "as a foil to his own theoretical principle that the most direct experience of tragic emotions can and should be generated by the 'action' itself, i.e. by the dramatically shaped structure of events". The other kinds of πάθος which do not rely on visual means are produced by specific features and actions of the characters, in tune with the principle that "feeling emotions in the right way towards the right things is an intrinsically ethical issue within Aristotelian philosophy".[7]

As regards what kinds of plots are most effective in producing fear and pity, Aristotle argues at *Poetics* 13 (1452b.30–53a39):

ἐπειδὴ οὖν δεῖ τὴν σύνθεσιν εἶναι τῆς καλλίστης τραγῳδίας μὴ ἁπλῆν ἀλλὰ πεπλεγμένην καὶ ταύτην φοβερῶν καὶ ἐλεεινῶν εἶναι μιμητικήν ... πρῶτον μὲν δῆλον ὅτι οὔτε τοὺς ἐπιεικεῖς ἄνδρας δεῖ μεταβάλλοντας φαίνεσθαι ἐξ εὐτυχίας εἰς δυστυχίαν, οὐ γὰρ φοβερὸν οὐδὲ ἐλεεινὸν τοῦτο ἀλλὰ μιαρόν ἐστιν· οὔτε τοὺς μοχθηροὺς ἐξ ἀτυχίας εἰς εὐτυχίαν, ἀτραγῳδότατον γὰρ τοῦτ' ἐστὶ πάντων, οὐδὲν γὰρ ἔχει ὧν δεῖ, οὔτε γὰρ φιλάνθρωπον οὔτε ἐλεεινὸν οὔτε φοβερόν ἐστιν· οὐδ' αὖ τὸν σφόδρα πονηρὸν ἐξ εὐτυχίας εἰς δυστυχίαν μεταπίπτειν· τὸ μὲν γὰρ φιλάνθρωπον ἔχοι ἂν ἡ τοιαύτη σύστασις ἀλλ' οὔτε ἔλεον οὔτε φόβον, ὁ μὲν γὰρ περὶ τὸν ἀνάξιόν ἐστιν δυστυχοῦντα, ὁ δὲ περὶ τὸν ὅμοιον, ἔλεος μὲν περὶ τὸν ἀνάξιον, φόβος δὲ περὶ τὸν ὅμοιον, ὥστε οὔτε ἐλεεινὸν οὔτε φοβερὸν ἔσται τὸ συμβαῖνον. ὁ μεταξὺ ἄρα τούτων λοιπός. ἔστι δὲ τοιοῦτος ὁ μήτε ἀρετῇ διαφέρων καὶ δικαιοσύνῃ μήτε διὰ κακίαν καὶ μοχθηρίαν μεταβάλλων εἰς τὴν δυστυχίαν ἀλλὰ δι' ἁμαρτίαν τινά, τῶν ἐν μεγάλῃ δόξῃ ὄντων καὶ εὐτυχίᾳ, οἷον Οἰδίπους καὶ Θυέστης καὶ οἱ ἐκ τῶν τοιούτων γενῶν ἐπιφανεῖς ἄνδρες ... διὸ καὶ οἱ Εὐριπίδῃ ἐγκαλοῦντες τὸ αὐτὸ ἁμαρτάνουσιν ὅτι τοῦτο δρᾷ ἐν ταῖς τραγῳδίαις καὶ (αἱ) πολλαὶ αὐτοῦ εἰς δυστυχίαν τελευτῶσιν. τοῦτο γάρ ἐστιν ὥσπερ εἴρηται ὀρθόν· σημεῖον δὲ μέγιστον· ἐπὶ γὰρ τῶν σκηνῶν καὶ τῶν ἀγώνων τραγικώταται αἱ τοιαῦται φαίνονται, ἂν κατορθωθῶσιν, καὶ ὁ Εὐριπίδης, εἰ καὶ τὰ ἄλλα μὴ εὖ οἰκονομεῖ, ἀλλὰ τραγι-

---

6 53b1–8. As remarked by Meijering 1987, 210, after Eggerking 1912, 44–5; Lucas 1968, 135.
7 The two quotations are from Halliwell 2012, 226 and 254 respectively. See also Munteanou 2012, 76–103.

κώτατός γε τῶν ποιητῶν φαίνεται. δευτέρα δ' ἡ πρώτη λεγομένη ὑπό τινῶν ἐστιν σύστασις, ἡ διπλῆν τε τὴν σύστασιν ἔχουσα καθάπερ ἡ 'Οδύσσεια καὶ τελευτῶσα ἐξ ἐναντίας τοῖς βελτίοσι καὶ χείροσιν. δοκεῖ δὲ εἶναι πρώτη διὰ τὴν τῶν θεάτρων ἀσθένειαν· ἀκολουθοῦσι γὰρ οἱ ποιηταὶ κατ' εὐχὴν ποιοῦντες τοῖς θεαταῖς. ἔστιν δὲ οὐχ αὕτη ἀπὸ τραγῳδίας ἡδονὴ ἀλλὰ μᾶλλον τῆς κωμῳδίας οἰκεία· ἐκεῖ γὰρ οἳ ἂν ἔχθιστοι ὦσιν ἐν τῷ μύθῳ, οἷον 'Ορέστης καὶ Αἴγισθος, φίλοι γενόμενοι ἐπὶ τελευτῆς ἐξέρχονται, καὶ ἀποθνήσκει οὐδεὶς ὑπ' οὐδενός.

Since the structure of the finest tragedy should be complex, not simple[8], as well as representing fearful and pitiable events ... it is, to begin with, clear that neither should decent men be shown changing from prosperity to adversity, as this is not fearful nor yet pitiable but repugnant, nor the depraved changing from adversity to prosperity, because this is the least tragic of all, possessing none of the necessary qualities, as it arouses neither fellow-feeling nor pity nor fear. Nor, again, should tragedy show the very wicked person falling from prosperity to adversity; such a pattern might arouse fellow-feeling, but not pity or fear, since the one is felt for the undeserving victim of adversity, the other for one like ourselves (pity for the undeserving, fear for one like ourselves); so the outcome will be neither pitiable nor fearful. This leaves, then, the person in-between these cases. Such a person is someone not preeminent in virtue and justice, and one who falls into adversity not through evil and depravity, but through some kind of error; and one belonging to the class of those who enjoy great renown and prosperity, such as Oedipus, Thyestes, and eminent men from such lineages. ... Which is why the same mistake is made by those who complain that Euripides does this in his tragedies and that most (or "many") of his tragedies end in adversity. For this, as explained, is the right way. And the greatest indication of this is that in theatrical contests such plays are found the most tragic, if successfully managed; and Euripides, even if he does not arrange other details well, is at least found the most tragic of the poets. The double structures which end with opposite outcomes for good and bad characters, like the *Odyssey*, are the result of the author's attempt at following the weakness of the spectators and pandering to their tastes, yet this is not the pleasure to expect from tragedy, but is more appropriate to comedy, where those who are deadliest enemies in the plot, such as Orestes and Aegisthus, exit at the end as new friends, and no one dies at anyone's hands.

This passage, or at least an 'Aristotelian' outlook on proper tragic ἦθος, probably explains the manner in which the scholiasts appreciate or criticize Sophocles' or Euripides' characters, and it determines whether or not they consider these personages' ἦθος conducive to producing tragic πάθος. In particular, they develop an articulated categorization of what a good tragic hero should and should not be, in terms which, though they cannot be demonstrated to derive from Aristotle, certainly are in tune with Aristotle's ideas.

There are two principles that guide many of the scholiasts' remarks about the quality of the tragic hero. 1) The greater the hero is, the greater is his potential for πάθος; but 2) he must have some faults, because if he is flawless and disgraceful, the audience sympathizes with him too much and considers his dis-

---

[8] Meaning that it should include reversal or/and recognition.

grace something repugnant. Comments to this end can be considered a practical application of principles already found in *Poetics* 13. A few examples will suffice.[9] In Soph. *OT* 33–34 Oedipus is presented as "the first of men, both in the incidents of life and in dealing with the higher powers". Σ ad loc. comments: ἐκ τούτου δὲ παθητικωτέραν τὴν τραγῳδίαν ποιεῖ ὅταν ὁ τοιοῦτος εἶναι νομιζόμενος φανῇ καινοῖς μύσεσιν ἔνοχος "in this way Sophocles makes the tragedy more pathetic if the one who has this reputation turns out to be defiled with unprecedented sins". The fact that everyone perceives Oedipus' character to be especially positive and upright at the beginning of the play increases the shock when this reputation is reversed, i.e., when he turns out to be affected by unseen sins. In *Aj.* 421 Ajax celebrates himself as a superior warrior, and Σ ad loc. comments: καὶ γίνεται ἐπίτασις τοῦ πάθους, ὁπόταν ὁ τοιοῦτος διαφθείρηται "it adds to the intensity of the pathos when it is such a man who is being destroyed". In Eur. *Hipp.* 656 indignant Hippolytus tells the nurse: "it is my pity that saves you"; the Σ comments: ἢ τάχα προτραγῳδεῖ τὸ πάθος, <τὸν> τοιοῦτον μικρὸν ὕστερον ἐπὶ καταγνώσει μοιχείας ποιῶν κατηγορούμενον "perhaps Euripides is already preparing the forthcoming tragic pathos, seeing it is a man like this whom he will soon make the victim of a charge of adultery". At the same time, the tragic hero must be good but cannot be irreproachably good and thus provoke the indignant surprise of the spectators at his undeserved destiny. Σ *Aj.* 112a, about Ajax' insubordination against Athena, comments: ὑπεροπτικὸν δὲ τὸ ἦθος αὐτοῦ ἐντεῦθεν ἐνδείκνυται ὁ ποιητής, ἐπεὶ πάνυ πρόσκειται ὁ ἀκροατὴς τῷ Αἴαντι διὰ τὴν συμφορὰν καὶ μονονουχὶ χαλεπαίνει τῶι ποιητῇ, ἵνα δόξῃ ἀξιοπαθεῖν ὁ Αἴας μὴ ὑποτεταγμένος τῇ δαίμονι "in this passage the poets exhibits Ajax's disdainful character. His motivation is that the audience is quite partial to Ajax through witnessing his sufferings and almost angry with the poet, and thus he now ensures that Ajax seems to deserve his misery, as he is not submitting to the goddess"; likewise, when the messenger observes Ajax's tendency to boast at *Aj.* 762a, the Σ comments: παρατήρει κἀνθάδε τὴν προσθήκην τοῦ ποιητοῦ, ὅτι προσῆψε τῶι Αἴαντι γλωσσαλγίαν, μονονουχὶ θεραπεύων τὸν θεατὴν μὴ ἄχθεσθαι ἐπὶ τῇ συμφορᾷ τοῦ Αἴαντος. προσῳκειωμένοι γὰρ ἤδη τῇ ἀρετῇ αὐτοῦ σχεδὸν καὶ τῷ ποιητῇ ὀργίζονται "acknowledge here as well the qualification that Sophocles has supplied to the character of Ajax in ascribing to him the trend to boast. In doing so the poet almost conciliates the spectator so that he will not be indignant over the sad fate of Ajax. In fact the spectators are so far strongly sympathetic with the qualities of Ajax and almost angry with the poet".

---

9 Some of these were already collated by Eggerking 1912, 47–8.

So much for the successful production of tragic pathos. But what if the attempt fails? If the tragic character does not manage to attract the pity and fear of the audience, the ancient commentators often maintain, then the tragic play gives rise to unwanted comicity. These kinds of remarks occur most often in the corpus of the scholia to Euripides, which are notorious for their derogatory outlook on the author[10], but can also be found in the Sophoclean scholia—the difference being that Euripides is criticized for quasi-comic blunders, whereas Sophocles is usually described as avoiding such slips down into comedy. As we have seen above, these latter remarks apply with particular frequency to Sophocles' *Ajax*, a tragedy where the pathos level is particularly high, and thus difficult to preserve; accordingly, the scholiasts are keen on defending Sophocles in the moments when he may seem to lapse into the less-than sublime. At *Aj.* 74, for instance, the scholiast suggests an interpretation which saves the text from giving this impression: παραιτεῖται ὁ 'Οδυσσεὺς οὐχ ὡς κωμῳδοῦντος τοῦ ποιητοῦ δειλίαν τοῦ ἥρωος (οὕτω γὰρ <ἂν> ἀφαιρεθείη τὸ τῆς τραγῳδίας ἀξίωμα), ἀλλὰ τὸ εὐλαβὲς ἐνδείκνυται "Odysseus begs (scil. Athena for a favor), not because the poet thinks of mocking his cowardice (in this way the sublimity of tragedy would be lost), but he shows caution". The Σ intervene to defend the tragicity of Sophocles again at *Ant.* 328, where the guard is ordered to examine who paid attention to the corpse of Polynikes. He promises to comply, but also never to return to Creon's presence; Σ ad loc. comments: ἀπιὼν ὁ θεράπων καθ' ἑαυτὸν ταῦτά φησιν· οὐ γὰρ δυνατὸν ἐπὶ τοῦ Κρέοντος ταῦτα λέγεσθαι ὡς καὶ ἐν τοῖς κωμικοῖς "the servant utters these words while he leaves, aside; in fact it is not possible that he says this in the presence of Creon, as it happens with the comic poets". At *Aj.* 1123 the Σ similarly tries to defend a drop in tragic pathos as a purposeful relaxation of tension: when Teucer boasts in dialogue with Menelaus: "with no shield I could deal with you fully armed!", Σ comments τὰ τοιαῦτα σοφίσματα οὐκ οἰκεῖα τραγῳδίας. μετὰ γὰρ τὴν ἀναίρεσιν ἐπεκτεῖναι τὸ δρᾶμα θελήσας ἐψυχρεύσατο καὶ ἔλυσε τὸ τραγικὸν πάθος "these kinds of arguments are not appropriate to tragedy. After the suicide, the poet, who wanted to prolong the play, let it grow cold and relaxed the tragic πάθος".[11] In the case of Soph. *El.* 62, however, where Orestes alludes to a 'modern' sage (perhaps Pythagoras), Σ can only (somewhat helplessly) defend Sophocles by maintaining that hints of comedy are frequent in tragedy and should not be reprimanded: καὶ μὴ τῶν θαυμαστῶν εἶναι δόξῃ, <εἰ> ἐν τραγῳδίᾳ καὶ μύθῳ παλαιῷ τετόλμηκέ τι κακόηθες εἰπεῖν καὶ προσκρουστικὸν εἰς τοὺς καθ' ἑαυτόν,

---

10 Evidence collected, e.g., by Elsperger 1908.
11 Römer 1906, 61–62; LaCourse Munteanu 2012, 199–200.

ὃ μᾶλλον ἥρμοζε κωμῳδίᾳ "no one has to be surprised if a tragedy, and within a tale belonging to the past, he should venture a malicious and offensive stab against his contemporaries, which would be more appropriate to comedy". And at *OT* 264, where Oedipus notes (more truthfully than he is aware) that he has completely replaced Laius in his family and city "as though he had been my father", the Σ observe that Sophocles makes use of such sensationalist phrases less frequently than Euripides: αἱ τοιαῦται ἔννοιαι οὐκ ἔχονται μὲν τοῦ σεμνοῦ, κινητικαὶ δέ εἰσι τοῦ θεάτρου· αἷς καὶ πλεονάζει Εὐριπίδης, ὁ δὲ Σοφοκλῆς πρὸς βραχὺ μόνον αὐτῶν ἅπτεται πρὸς τὸ κινῆσαι τὸ θέατρον "thoughts of this kind do not partake in sublimity; there are many of them in Euripides, whereas Sophocles makes use of them only scarcely in order to stir the theater". At *Aj.* 1127, where Menelaus defines Ajax as "the one who has killed me", and Teucer objects: "You have said a strange thing, if you have died but are alive", the Σ cannot find an excuse and plainly remarks: τὸ δὲ τοιοῦτον κωμῳδίας μᾶλλον ἢ τραγῳδίας "this is typical of comedy more than of tragedy".

The commentators' stance on the tragicity of Euripides is far less forgiving. We can find isolated defenses of this author's tragicity,[12] but these remarks are few and far between, and the commentators prefer to intervene to point out Euripides' descents onto a less-than-tragic level.[13] The play that attracted the scholiasts' greatest scorn is *Orestes*; in fact, as the hypothesis ascribed to Aristophanes of Byzantium preliminarily acknowledges, τὸ δρᾶμα τῶν ἐπὶ σκηνῆς εὐδοκιμούντων, χείριστον δὲ τοῖς ἤθεσι. πλὴν γὰρ Πυλάδου πάντες φαῦλοι ἦσαν "the play is one of those which are quite appreciated when they are performed, but it is very bad in terms of characters. In fact, Pylades apart, they all are flimsy". The ethical inconsistency of the characters and their actions is restated again and again, and at least when discussing Menelaus, Orestes' antagonist, the scholia seem about to downgrade this tragedy to a comedy. From his first appearance on stage, the hostility Menelaus displays toward Orestes for the killing of Clytemnaestra strikes the scholiasts as an incoherent, and therefore comically un-heroic, delay in taking revenge on the killers of his brother Agamemnon. This inability of Menelaus' to harm his "real enemies" is traced back to his Iliadic behavior toward the spared enemy Adrastus, despite the fact that it is a common epic motif for a defeated warrior to ransom himself,[14] and despite

---

12 At *Hec.* 342, Polyxena begins the speech in which she reveals her willingness to die (and thus to die free), and the Σ comment: ἐνταῦθα ἐφύλαξεν ὁ Εὐριπίδης τὸ ἡρωικὸν ἦθος· οὐ γὰρ ταπεινὸν αὐτὸ μεμίμηται, ἀλλὰ παρρησιαστικόν "here Euripides has preserved the heroic ethos; in fact he has presented this (speech) not as abased, but as outspoken".
13 For a detailed review, cf. Elsperger 1908, 33–54.
14 See Wilson 2002.

the fact that Menelaus' behavior with Adrastus was differently considered by the Σ *Il.* 6.62 as positive evidence of his moderation and lack of irascibility.[15] See Σ *Or.* 356 ἀπὸ πρώτης παρόδου σημειοῦται τὸ κακόηθες τῆς γνώμης Μενελάου. καὶ γὰρ οὐδὲ εἰς Σπάρτην ἀνήχθη, ἀλλὰ πρότερον εἰς Ἄργος ὡς ἐξελάσων Ὀρέστην, ὡς ἐν τοῖς ἑξῆς δῆλός ἐστι. καίτοι παρὰ τῷ ποιητῇ εὑρίσκεται τῶν πάλαι πολεμίων φειδόμενος· ἐν γὰρ τῇ Ζ ῥαψῳδίᾳ κωμῳδεῖται συγχωρῶν ζῆν τὸν Ἄδραστον δόσιν χρημάτων ἐπαγγειλάμενον "from his entrance at the beginning, the malignity of Menelaus' disposition is made clear. For in fact he did not set sail straight to Sparta, but went before to Argos to exile Orestes, as it is clear from what follows. And indeed in Homer he is found to spare inveterate enemies: in Book 6 (37–65) he is ridiculed as sparing the life of Adrastus, when Adrastus promises to give him money". See also Σ 371 ὕπουλα πάντα τὰ ῥήματα Μενελάου, ἀφ' οὗ ὁ ποιητὴς τὸ ἄστατον τῆς Λακεδαιμονίων γνώμης κωμῳδεῖ, ὡς καὶ ἐν Ἀνδρομάχῃ "what Menelaus says is unsound; hence the poet ridicules the instability of the disposition of the Lacedaemonians, as he also does in *Andromache* (445–6)".[16] Ancient commentators are also understandably tough on the "tragic inappropriateness" of the scene involving Helen's Phrygian slave. On the slave's entrance at line 1369 Σ comments: ἐντεῦθεν ἐξέστη τοῦ ἰδίου ἤθους ὁ Εὐριπίδης ἀνοίκεια ἑαυτῷ λέγων "at this point Euripides transgressed from the appropriate characterization, and said things that are inopportune to himself"; see also Σ 1512 ἀνάξια καὶ τραγῳδίας καὶ τῆς Ὀρέστου συμφορᾶς τὰ λεγόμενα "these words are not worthy of tragedy and of the disaster of Orestes" and Σ 1521 ταῦτα κωμικώτερά ἐστι καὶ πεζά "these things are a bit too comic and pedestrian". Apollodorus of Cyrene, a scholar of uncertain chronology[17], could even suggest that a phrase pointing in line 1384 to a specific melodic form (ἁρμάτειον μέλος) "is a stage instruction like the one in the comic plays (παρεπιγραφὴν εἶναι ὡς εἰς τὰ κωμικὰ δράματα)"—of course it is irrelevant for my discussion whether the phrase transmitted by the MSS. as Euripides' text was originally a stage instruction or (more probably) not.[18] What is relevant is that some ancient scholars could conceive of finding an explicit stage direction in *Orestes*, despite the fact that stage directions are typical of comedy and hardly

---

[15] This contrasts with the "cruelty" (θηριότης) of Agamemnon, who intervenes and kills Adrastus: Σ *Il.* 6.58–9.
[16] A detailed analysis of Menelaus' negative characterization in the Euripidean scholia can be found in Elsperger 1908, 37–41.
[17] Fragments collected by Dyck 1981.
[18] Taplin 1977, 125 denies the plausibility of Apollodorus' suggestion. On the other hand, Dawe 1978, 129 takes it for granted that it is correct.

ever to be found in our tragic texts.[19] This observation is all the more significant since nothing in the text makes it necessary or even probable that the phrase is, in fact, a stage direction.

To sum up, the scholia to the tragedians frequently point to elements that strike them as inadequate to the standards of sublimity or consistency customary in tragic characters. In the case of Euripides, they discuss these features' inadequacy; in the case of Sophocles, they tend to explain them away. In both cases, they often speak explicitly of comic intrusions into the tragic plot. This is an Aristotelian concept and yet, at the same time, it is not. Aristotle only once envisages that comic can interact with tragedy: in *Rhet.* 3.1408a he presents the tragic poet Cleophon as incapable of mastering the proper balance between style and subject matter, noting that by treating trifling matters within the sublime style of tragedy, Cleophon creates an "impression of comedy".[20] The scholiasts' ethical remarks on the "seriousness" required of tragic characters and action are substantially in tune with Aristotle's observations here. But apart from this one instance where Aristotle comments on stylistic shortcomings (notably not structural defects, see below), he never notes that tragedy may be contaminated with comedy. The idea seems, therefore, not to have been central to his teachings. What is more, it seems hardly compatible with the poetological ideas of his day. 5th and 4th cent. culture appears not to have readily accepted the idea that a single author could write both tragedies and comedies. This is clear from several pieces of evidence: the Atomists, for example, pointed to the dichotomy of tragedy and comedy, which are opposed to each other though the form of their names includes almost the same letters, as an example of the fact that things can be radically opposite to each other also if they are constituded of the same atomic substance;[21] Plato, *Resp.* 3.395a explicitly denies that the same person can be both tragic poet/actor and comic poet/actor; and both the tragic poet Agathon and the comic poet Aristophanes are reluctant to accept Socrates' suggestion in *Symp.* 223d that a professional playwright can master both

---

[19] Together with Taplin 1977, also see Holzinger 1883, 25; Falkner 2002, 358–9; Revermann 2006, 320–5.
[20] Τὸ δὲ πρέπον ἕξει ἡ λέξις ... τοῖς ὑποκειμένοις πράγμασιν ἀνάλογον. τὸ δ' ἀνάλογόν ἐστιν ἐὰν μήτε περὶ εὐόγκων αὐτοκαβδάλως λέγηται μήτε περὶ εὐτελῶν σεμνῶς, μηδ' ἐπὶ τῷ εὐτελεῖ ὀνόματι ἐπῇ κόσμος· εἰ δὲ μή, κωμῳδία φαίνεται, οἷον ποιεῖ Κλεοφῶν· ὁμοίως γὰρ ἔνια ἔλεγε καὶ εἰ εἴπειεν [ἂν] 'πότνια συκῆ' "propriety of style will be obtained ... by proportion to the subject matter. Style is proportionate to the subject matter when neither weighty matters are treated offhand, nor trifling matters with dignity, and no embellishment is attached to an ordinary word; otherwise there is an appearance of comedy, as in the poetry of Cleophon, who used certain expressions that reminded one of saying 'madame fig'."
[21] Cf. Aristot. *gen. et corr.* 315b = VS 67 A9; Kalphas 2011, 47.

tragic and comic compositions.²² Aristotle's comments on Cleophon may therefore simply constitute a reference "to the commonplace that a tragedy is more serious than a comedy in content and tone,"²³ and no connection between his statement and the scholiasts' discussions needs to exist.

In any case these analogies of orientation between Aristotle (or Aristotelian-Peripapetic thought) and the scholiasts on the ethical dimensions of the (good) tragic character and plot coexist with at least one evident difference in the evaluation of the *catastrophe*. Aristotle's thought, or at least a part of it, is at variance with some of the later views on 'tragedies of interrupted catastrophe.' In fact, at 1453a24–30, as we have seen above, Aristotle mentions Euripides as a "most tragic" (τραγικώτατος) dramatist who adopts sad endings in many (or most) of his tragedies, and defends Euripides' special taste for unhappy ends from the objections of some critics who had disapproved of his too sad ends (after all Aristotle clearly states at *Poet.* 1452a3 that tragedy is mimesis of "fearful and pitiable matters" (καὶ φοβερῶν καὶ ἐλεεινῶν)). In other words, he addresses a criticism of Euripides that focuses on the sadness of his unhappy endings, whereas he does not have anything to say about his more or less happy endings without final catastrophe. Aristotle never states that these sad endings are necessary features of tragedy, nor does he ever assert that the catastrophe has to occur at the end of the play. He does, however, emphasize that the 'good' tragedy has a catastrophe somewhere (namely is a "complex", not "simple" plot: 1452b31–2 quoted above). As has been correctly commented, according to *Poetics* 13 "the 'most tragic' plays ... end unhappily, but these unhappy-ending plays are only a subset of 'the finest tragedies': provided a story involves some serious misfortune, whether actual and ultimate or only prospective, it can end happily or sadly".²⁴ Aristotle in fact more than once envisages that a successful tragedy may depict not only the change from good luck to misfortune but also its reverse.²⁵ The idea that specifically the change of fortune from good to bad defines the *best* tragic plots may however be lurking in *Poetics* 13, 1453a12–4, where Sophocles' *OT* seems to be pointed out as the best tragedy: ἀνάγκη ἄρα τὸν καλῶς ἔχοντα μῦθον ἁπλοῦν εἶναι μᾶλλον ἢ διπλοῦν, ὥσπερ τινές φασι, καὶ

---

22 Socrates is here possibly advertising the poetics of the *Symposium*, where he seems to be endowed with both the seriousness of a tragic character and the irony belonging to comic characters: Clay 1975; see also Mader 1977, 58–79; Seidensticker 1982, 14–16. As remarked by Knox 1979 (=1970), 251, "only Socrates could have proposed such a paradox; for the fifth-century Athenian, tragedy was tragedy and comedy comedy, and never the twain should meet".
23 Meijering 1987, 219.
24 White 1992, 231.
25 See at least 1451a13–15, 1452a31, 1455b28.

μεταβάλλειν οὐκ εἰς εὐτυχίαν ἐκ δυστυχίας ἀλλὰ τοὐναντίον ἐξ εὐτυχίας εἰς δυστυχίαν "the well-made plot, then, ought to be single rather than double, as some maintain, with a change not to prosperity from adversity, but on the contrary from prosperity to adversity". Aristotle here also criticizes the tragedies which have a "double structure" (διπλῆ σύστασις), namely the ones that have a good outcome for good and a bad one for bad characters. It is hard to be sure which concrete tragedy he was thinking of. Perhaps revenge tragedies such as Aeschylus' *Choephoroi;* and Sophocles' *Electra* should come to mind.[26] In any case the fact that Aristotle compares the "double structure" tragedy to the *Odyssey*, which he considers a proto-*comedy*, leads us to surmise that he considered comic elements a possible component of this kind of tragedy. Besides, Aristotle explicitly says that these tragedies are widely thought to be the best because they panders to the taste of the spectators, though he personally believes that the pleasure they provide is more appropriate to comedy than to tragedy.

In chap. 14 Aristotle seems to completely abandon this view that the best tragedies involve a turn for the worse, preferably near their end. Here, the plot most effective in arousing pity and fear is described as the one in which τὸ μέλλοντα ποιεῖν τι τῶν ἀνηκέστων δι' ἄγνοιαν ἀναγνωρίσαι πρὶν ποιῆσαι "the person is on the point of unwittingly committing something irremediable, but recognizes it before doing so" (1453b34–6)—this plot is presented as more effective than the one where the agents actually commit the "incurable deed" in ignorance, and only afterwards realize what they have done, as in the *OT* (1453b29–31). To exemplify this supposedly best kind of tragic plot, Aristotle provides three examples, two of which are Euripidean plays of interrupted catastrophe, *Cresphontes* (Merope identifies Cresphontes as her son just when she is close to killing him in his sleep) and *Iphigenia in Tauris* (Orestes comes close to killing his sister, but recognizes her in time, and happily escapes with her back to Greece): 1454a4–8.

It goes without saying that the "double structure" tragedy described in *Poetics* 13 with some hostility is not the same as the tragedy of interrupted catastrophe exemplified by Euripides and quoted with approval by Aristotle in *Poetics* 14: in narratives like the *Odyssey* a reversal from good luck to misfortune (for the bad suitors) mirrors another from misfortune to good luck (for Odysseus), whereas in the tragedy of interrupted catastrophe a "single structure" plot focuses primarily on the fate of the good character. Thus, it may include a radically happy ending. But it is also true that the "double structure" tragedy and the tragedy of interrupted catastrophe both save those character(s) from failure or destruction

---

26 Lucas 1968, 148.

who attract(s) the sympathy of the audience, and both contrast with what we might call the most common modern perception of the tragic. Therefore modern scholars usually acknowledge some level of contradiction in Aristotle's statements on "bad reversals of fortune for good characters": this particular reversal of fortunes seems preferable in *Poetics* 13 (where in fact the "double structure" plays are seen with diffidence), but should be rejected according to *Poetics* 14. Different explanations have been proposed to account for this contradiction, the most agreeable of all being that the immediacy of the impending "incurable deed" is powerful enough, in Aristotle's view, to produce *proleptic* fear and pity: "the action forces us to imagine the evils, to recognize and hence respond emotionally to their implication; and it is this imagination, not the physical actuality of the 'incurable', which Aristotle now appears to identify as sufficient for the experience of tragedy". Aristotle's taste for the tragedy of interrupted catastrophe may thus reflect an eagerness to avoid the "starkest tragedy", i.e., a tragedy with the dark and sad ending that according to Aristotle (*Poetics* 13 quoted above) some of his contemporaries criticized.[27]

To sum up, Aristotle records the criticisms raised against the endings of Euripides' plays as excessively sad and 'catastrophic', and defends them as properly tragic. But he also presents Euripides' tragedies of interrupted catastrophe as an at least equally admissible kind of tragedy. As a matter of fact, in *Poetics* 14 they are discussed as the fear and pity-inducing tragedies par excellence, and we therefore have to surmise that Aristotle actually considered them superior to their 'catastrophic' counterparts.

* * *

In contrast, Euripidean hypotheseis ascribed to Aristophanes of Byzantium, as well as multiple scholia to Euripides, criticize Euripides for deviating from the tragic paradigm and allowing his protagonist to avoid the final catastrophe. The catastrophe is considered essential to tragedy, and without it, tragedy appears to turn 'comic'. As we will see, according to this view of the tragic genre, a tragedy with occasional downfalls into comedy may well remain a tragedy, but a happy ending of necessity impairs the tragedy's 'purity.' It may, in fact, transform the tragedy into a play that is more comedy than tragedy. Not surprisingly, the two tragedies for which the ancient hypotheseis & scholia to Euripides observe

---

[27] Halliwell 1998, 180–2 and 222–37 is fundamental for the complex dynamics between *Poetics* 13 and 14 (hence my quotations). But see also Else 1957, 450–2 and Donini 2004, 87–106.

that they have spoiled their tragicity with a comic final are two of Euripides' tragedies of interrupted catastrophe: *Orestes* and *Alcestis*.[28]

The hypothesis to *Orestes* ascribed by the MSS. to Aristophanes of Byzantium[29] includes the concise but categoric statement: τὸ δρᾶμα κωμικωτέραν ἔχει τὴν καταστροφήν "the play has the conclusion a bit too comic". In the hypothesis to *Alcestis*, also ascribed to Aristophanes, we find another very similar observation, though the label adopted to classify this play is "too satyrical" rather than "too comic"[30]. It is precisely because these plots start with disastrous situations and end happily (as opposed to the other way around) that they are considered closer to comedy or satyr play than to tragedy: τὸ δὲ δρᾶμά ἐστι σατυρικώτερον ὅτι εἰς χαρὰν καὶ ἡδονὴν καταστρέφει [παρὰ τοῖς τραγικοῖς] <καὶ> ἐκβάλλεται ὡς ἀνοίκεια τῆς τραγικῆς ποιήσεως ὅ τε Ὀρέστης καὶ ἡ Ἄλκηστις, ὡς ἐκ συμφορᾶς μὲν ἀρχόμενα, εἰς εὐδαιμονίαν <δὲ> καὶ χαρὰν λήξαντα, <ἅ> ἐστι μᾶλλον κωμῳδίας ἐχόμενα. <πολλὰ δὲ τοιαῦτα παρὰ τοῖς τραγικοῖς>[31] "this drama is a bit too satyric, because it develops towards a conclusion of joy and pleasure; *Orestes* and *Alcestis* exceed the boundaries of tragedy as incongruous with it, since they start from misfortunes, but end in happiness and joy, which rather pertain to comedy. <This kind of things are frequent in tragedy>".[32]

This idea is not limited to the *Orestes* and *Alcestis* hypotheseis. There seems, rather, to have been a debate on the nature and limits of comicity within tragedy

---

28 These, of course, are the only two Euripidean tragedies of this kind that came down to us provided with scholia.
29 Even though the ancient MSS. ascribe wrongly many *hypotheseis* to Aristophanes, there is widespread agreement that at least those prefacing *Alcestis*, *Orestes* and *Bacchae* substantially go back to him: cf. Brown 1987, 428; van Rossum-Steenbeek 1998, 32–3.
30 On the "satyrical" features of Euripides' *Alcestis* (and also the points of contact between comedy and satyr-drama) see Burnett 1971, 31, 33, 44, 71–2, 186; Sutton 1973; Seidensticker 1982, 129–52; Marshall 2000.
31 The last phrase has been added to the end of the hypothesis by Schwartz, coll. Σ *Or.* 1691 (see below). But the remark in our *Alcestis* hypothesis, like the parallel one in the hypothesis of *Orestes*, does not have the epologetic stance that Σ *Or.* 1361 has about the tragicity of *Orestes*, and therefore I think that this defensive observation should not be added at the end of the *Alcestis* hypothesis.
32 Aristophanes' structural distinction of genres had a long afterlife. With some slight differences (Sophocles' *Electra* is added to the 'canon' of faulty plays, and the definition "too satyric" ends up displacing the label "too comic"), Tzetzes develops it in his *Prolegomena* to comedy, as well as in one of his notes to his poem περὶ διαφορᾶς ποιητῶν (p. 30–31 and 90 Koster). Tzetzes also quotes and criticizes a source (left anonymous) where Euripides' *Or.* and *Alc.*, and also Sophocles' *El.*, were labeled "satyric plays" (see, from the *Prolegom.*, *Proem.* I pp. 30.150–31.156 Koster).

among the commentators of Euripides. Toward the end of *Orestes*, in Σ *Or.* 1691, we find a comment which reports—and ultimately rejects—a fuller version of Aristophanes' thought than the skeletal remarks in his hypotheseis:

> ἡ κατάληξις τῆς τραγῳδίας ἢ εἰς θρῆνον ἢ εἰς πάθος καταλύει, ἡ δὲ τῆς κωμῳδίας εἰς σπονδὰς καὶ διαλλαγάς. ὅθεν ὁρᾶται τόδε τὸ δρᾶμα κωμικῇ καταλήξει χρησάμενον· διαλλαγαὶ γὰρ πρὸς Μενέλαον καὶ Ὀρέστην. ἀλλὰ καὶ ἐν τῇ Ἀλκήστιδι ἐκ συμφορῶν εἰς εὐφροσύνην καὶ ἀναβιοτήν. ὁμοίως καὶ ἐν Τυροῖ Σοφοκλέους ἀναγνωρισμὸς κατὰ τὸ τέλος γίνεται, καὶ ἁπλῶς εἰπεῖν πολλὰ τοιαῦτα ἐν τῇ τραγῳδίᾳ εὑρίσκεται.

> Tragedy ends either in a lament or in pathos, comedy in peace and reconciliation. This leads us to conclude that the present drama has a comic ending, as Menelaus and Orestes are reconciled. However, in the *Alcestis* too the plot develops from misfortune to joy and revival, and likewise in the *Tyro* of Sophocles [*TrGF* p. 463] a recognition takes place at the end, and, to speak in general terms, this kind of things are frequent in tragedy.

It is relatively simple to map out the similarities and differences between Aristotle's views and those summed up in the beginning of Σ *Or.* 1691. Aristotle too spoke of reconciliation between enemies as an appropriate end for comedy rather than tragedy (at the end of *Poetics* 13, where he mentions Euripides to defend his sad endings). Yet not all happy endings are impermissible to Aristotle: in *Poetics* 14 he mentions Euripides again, this time for what he considers the perfect tragic plot of *IT*, where the catastrophe is avoided and Orestes "recognizes" that Iphigeneia is his sister in time not to kill her. The two kinds of happy endings (one criticized as comic and one approved as perfectly tragic in the two contiguous chapters 13 and 14) differ in that one is prefaced by a "reconciliation", the other by an "anagnorisis" (these two types if scenes are also mentioned by Σ *Or.* 1691, see above). Add to this that the unexpected reconciliation of Orestes and Aegisthus criticized in *Poetics* 13 closely parallels the idea, reported by Σ *Or.* 1691, that final "reconciliations" (διαλλαγαί) between ex-enemies like Orestes and Menelaus err on the side of comedy; but the Aristotelian friendship between Orestes and Aegisthus is a much more extreme case of reconciliation, as it involves two figures who in traditional myth were most drastically opposed to each other (a father's killer and that father's son) than the opponents in Eur. *Orestes*; their appeasement reverses the psychology consistently ascribed to these two tragic characters and transgresses into a properly comic παρατραγῳδία; it is almost a comic adynaton. Aristotle not only criticizes this kind of tragedy, but does not even deem it worthy to mention one by name. Instead, the *Odyssey* and an unknown comic or farcical drama (it may also be an exemplum fictum) serve as examples. As a result, the reader is left with the impression that Aristotle presents this tragedy more in theory than in practice. Differently, Σ *Or.* 1691 and the *Orestes* hypothesis of Aristophanes present a thesis about the boundaries between tragedy and comedy according to which Euripides' *Orestes* is an actual contamination of tragedy and comedy, namely a tragedy that incorporates as its end a scene of comic reconciliation between enemy characters.

The influence of Aristotle or his school of thought on Hellenistic culture, and particularly Hellenistic scholarship, was widely discussed in the previous century.[33] Without assuming a direct reliance of Aristophanes of Byzantium on Aristotle, Aristophanes' idea of the "comicity" inherent in a tragedy without final catastrophe, at least in the form it is presented and softly criticized in Σ 1691, *may* be a radical re-thinking of *Poetics* 13 and 14 that condenses elements from both chapters (or from Peripatetic thought descending from *Poetics* 13 and 14). The "double structure" tragedy of *Poetics* 13, which Aristotle had left un-exemplified, would then have been replaced by the tragedy of interrupted catastrophe of chap. 14. The idea of final reconciliations as preface to happy endings, that Aristotle had used about the "double structure" tragedy, is also set by Σ *Or.* 1691 side by side with the idea of "recognition" as preface to happy ending, which Aristotle had also used in chap. 14. There is a substantial difference, however. Σ *Or.* 1691 radicalizes the opinion (already prospected in *Poetics* 13) that the final catastrophe is an opportune ending for a tragedy to be tragic. The scholion can only redeem the tragedies that lack this sad ending by pointing out that they are not uncommon. But there is no trace in it of the Aristotelian point (chap. 14) that a tragedy of reversed catastrophe can be an especially good tragedy. *If* Aristophanes of Byzantium started his classification of "comic tragedy" from *Poetics* 13 and 14 or from Peripatetic reconsiderations of the thought expressed in *Poetics* 13 and 14, then either Aristophanes or Aristotle's school came to prefer opinions voiced in *Poetics* 13 to those of *Poetics* 14.

In Σ Eur. *Andr.* 32 the principle of the special comicity and anti-tragicity of a happy ending undergoes a further specification. It seems that this Σ, as well as Σ *Or.* 1691, presents Aristophanes' thought in an expanded form. According to Andromache, Hermione (Neoptolemus' wife) has been accusing her, war slave and mother of a son to Neoptolemus, of trying to poison Hermione in order to get rid of the rival. The Σ comment: "the superficial commentators accuse Euripides, saying that he has arranged a comedy with tragic characters (οἱ φαύλως ὑπομνηματισάμενοι ἐγκαλοῦσι τῷ Εὐριπίδῃ φάσκοντες ἐπὶ τραγικοῖς προσώποις κωμῳδίαν αὐτὸν διατεθεῖσθαι): the diffidence, the jealousy and the

---

33 The most authoritative scepticism was expressed by Pfeiffer 1968; but see Montanari 1993, 262–4 and 2012, 348–56; Schironi 2009; Cadoni 2010. On Aristotle' relevance for the Σ to Euripides, Eggerking 1912, 42–56; the opposite thesis had been argued most spiritedly by Lord 1908, 66–81.

abuses of women against each other and other things like these that contribute to comedy (ἄλλα ὅσα εἰς κωμῳδίαν συντελεῖ), all of them are supposedly included in this play. They do not understand. What in fact contributes to tragedy is what happens at the end of the play: the death of Neoptolemus and the mourning of Peleus, these are tragic matters (ὅσα γὰρ εἰς τραγῳδίαν συντελεῖ, ταῦτα περιέχει ἐν τέλει, τὸν θάνατον τοῦ Νεοπτολέμου καὶ θρῆνον Πηλέως, ἅπερ ἐστὶ τραγικά)".

The first part of the Σ reports the objections (possibly by Didymus) to the prologue of *Andromache* as dominated by jealous rivalries between women in love with the same man. Some critics considered these too comic for tragedy. The second part does not deny that there are comic aspects to the prologue; the commentator simply seems to maintain that it is relatively unimportant if an initial scene is too comic. He observes that what makes a tragedy tragic (a killing or a mourning) is found *in the end*.[34] If it is in particular the "comic in the end" that ruins a tragedy, then this nullifies all objections to comic elements at its start. Our Σ can thus also afford to dismiss all objections to Euripides' characters as flimsy or base or laughably comic (a criticism otherwise quite dominant in the scholia to Euripides, as we have seen above) as unwarranted as long as comic elements occur over the course of the play. Only a too comic element in the end qualifies the tragedy as "too comic".

* * *

To summarize the main differences between Aristotle's idea of "inadequate tragedy" and later critics' (particularly Aristophanes') opinions on tragedies that are "too comic". Aristotle had considered "serious" (χρηστόν) behavior a minimum requirement in tragic character and action. Following in the footsteps of this non-structural approach to ethical evaluation many scholia labeled the actions of various characters as "comic" or "too comic". Aristotle however did not speak of a tragedy that is "more comic than tragic". Such a category of plays was never explicitly envisaged in his speculation: he viewed the *IT*, one of Euripides' tragedies of 'catastrophe survived', in quite positive terms, and he never labeled these tragedies "(too) comic." He only spoke of "double structure" plays as producing a "weak" pleasure that resembled the pleasure of comedy (and in fact exemplified them from a comic or farcical play and from the *Odyssey*). One century or so after him, Aristophanes of Byzantium developed an approach that was

---

34 The criticism may be by Didymus, and the justification by a commentator who worked after Didymus and is used to defending Euripides from past criticism—he has been called the "defensor Euripidis", and was investigated by Trendelenburg 1867, 54–67; see also Moore 1901, 296–7; Römer 1906, 50–61.

new, though not in total contrast with at least a part of Aristotle's theories (see in fact *Poetics* 13). His idea was that the absence of a final catastrophe produces a tragedy with "too comic" a conclusion. Such supposedly inappropriate endings make the entire tragedy seem too comic or too satyric. And from several additional comments either defending or attacking Aristophanes, we can understand that his views triggered a rather heated discussion.

It is impossible to ascertain when and why this shift in scholarly discourse took place. But some conjectures can be suggested. The Hellenistic poets' practice of blurring the borders between genres—Callimachus' indignant rejection of genre-borders in, e.g., his statement of *Iamb.* 13, 31–3, should suffice as an example—may have been instrumental in creating the idea that a tragedy can be "too comic." It may have led the critics to consider the problem of purity or combinations of genres, and the limits of these combinations. Besides, the great Hellenistic success of tragedies like Euripides' *Orestes*[35] may have led the early Hellenistic scholars to re-evaluate the generic nature of tragedies of interrupted catastrophe, which Aristotle had left undistinguished, and to see them as prototypal contaminations of genres.

It is compatible with our insights into Aristophanic tastes that the tragedy *Rhesus*, probably a new piece of the 4th cent.[36], involved scenes that the audience could understand as comic (the buffoonish disguise of Athena as Aphrodite, most of all) or that seemed much better paralleled in comedy than in tragedy (the hectic-chaotic behavior of the chorus in both *parodos* and *epiparodos*, or the guessing game between Dolon and Hector).[37] However, the *Rhesus* had a very bathetic end, with the Muse mourning at length and most intensely for her son. But what was the origin of such a play that allowed for so many smiles without compromising its tragic identity?[38]

Considering parallel literary developments, a tragedy like *Rhesus* may have been interpreted as the tragic-comic pendant to the comic-tragic hybrid represented by Menander's comedy. Both Menandrian comedy and the *Rhesus* tragedy

---

35 Of the about 50 papyri of Euripides in Pack (2nd ed.), a dozen are from *Orestes*.
36 But this play was already ascribed to Euripides in the *Didascaliai* compiled by Aristotle or his school (cf. hypothesis b Diggle), and certainly the text was known to Aristophanes of Byzantium in the version which came down to us (we have a hypothesis of the *Rhesus* under the name of Aristophanes of Byzantium (c Diggle).
37 See Fantuzzi forthcoming and, specifically on Dolon and Hector, Fantuzzi and Konstan.
38 "Are Smiles Allowed?" is the title of Burnett 1985, a paper that I consider one of the finest literary interpretations of the *Rhesus*, though I cannot agree with the thesis that the *Rhesus* would have been felt by the ancients as a satyrical drama like *Alcestis*, more than a tragedy. Maybe it could seem an *Alcestis*-like drama to *some* of the ancients, but for Aristophanes of Byzantium, because of its sad conclusion, it would have been a "normal" tragedy.

play with generic boundaries but reassert their original affiliations *via* appropriate endings. Besides, Menander may have helped the Hellenistic critics (in particular the source of Σ *Or.* 1691) to relabel "reconciliation" and "anagnorisis" as typical closures for comedy, rather than tragedy. Aristotle had not labeled Orestes' recognition of his sister in *IT* as comic, and he appreciated this play as a tragedy, despite its happy ending. In fact recognition scenes could still be felt as tragic scenes in the 5th cent., and as such triggered the παρατραγῳδία of the Old Comic playwright Aristophanes (Eurip. *Helen* in the *Thesmophoriazousae* and Aesch. *Choephoroe* in the *Clouds*). But the very frequent use of recognition scenes in Menander may have greatly helped to identify this scene, because of its efficacy in happily resolving the dramatic action, as a feature typical of comedy—Menander himself pointed to this efficacy in a phrase that easily ring metaliterary: *Epitrep.* 1121–2 νυνὶ δ' ἀναγνωρισμὸς αὐτοῖς γέγονε καὶ ἅπαντ' ἀγαθά "now they have recognized each other and everything is fine". "Reconciliations" had already concluded some 5th cent. comedies (Aristoph. *Lysistrata*, *Thesmoph.*, and *Plutus*), but Menander had more regularly ended his comedies with διαλλαγαί, and he had also emphasized the structural effectiveness of these scenes as λύσεις … τῶν κακῶν: καὶ νῦν μὲν ὁρμῶντ' ἐπὶ πονηρὸν πρᾶγμά σε / ταὐτόματον ἀποσέσωκε, καὶ καταλαμβάνεις / διαλλαγὰς λύσεις τ' ἐκείνων τῶν κακῶν "and now, when you were bent on mischief, chance has intervened to save you, and you find reconciliations and those knots of troubles untied" (*Epitrep.* 1106–9).[39] Last but not least, the radical contamination of tragic and comic elements in the comedies of Menander[40] (that Aristotle could not have known yet) may have led post-Aristotelian critics to discuss analytic approaches to the "recognizability of tragedy" despite comic contamination, and to reconsider in this light in particular Euripides, the tragic author who was closest to Menander's practice. Fittingly, Aristophanes of Byzantium, who focuses on a clear structural definition of the borders between tragedy and comedy in the case of *Orestes* and *Alcestis*, was also probably an editor of Menander[41], and

---

39 See also *Periceir.* 1006. On both the kaleidoscope of tragic origins and comic appropriation of the motif of *anagnorisis* by Menander's tragic comedy, and the metaliterary awareness with which Menander deals with the motif of final reconciliation, cf. Hunter 1983, 27 n. 1 and 1985, 130–6.
40 On the overlappings of tragedy and comedy in the 5th cent., after Seidensticker 1982, see most recently Medda, Mirto, and Pattoni 2006 (in particular Goldhill's contribution); for the 4th cent., Xanthakis-Karamanou 1980. On Menander and tragedy, see now above all Petridis forthcoming.
41 On the papyrus of the *Dyscolos* as evidence that Aristophanes edited at least some of Menander's comedies, cf. Pfeiffer 1968, 191–2.

we know that he specifically wrote on the models of Menander.[42] Re-reading Euripides, and in particular his happy-ending dramas, through the lens of Menander could have been much easier for the ancients than it might seem to our historicist viewpoint. For instance, the 3rd cent. Peripatetic[43] scholar (and roughly contemporary of Aristophanes) Satyrus certainly did reread Euripides from a panchronic perspective that resulted in what we perceive of anachronisms: he went so far as to present Euripides as the author who "brought to perfection" some of the typical motifs of New Comedy (from what remains in the papyrus, these motifs seem to be precisely our "reversal of situations" and "recognition"), "after Homer being the starting point in this and in the colloquial arrangement of verses".[44]

It was possibly after Menander, then, and in the context of a Hellenistic debate on the function and identity of literary genres, that critics assumed the task of demarcating Euripides' happy-ending tragedy from Menander's tragically infused comedy. This may have become a very intriguing and hot subject, one that Aristotle had almost ignored.[45]

---

42 From Euseb. *Praep. Evang.* 10.3.
43 Cf. West 1974.
44 ταῦτα γάρ ἐστι δήπου τὰ συνέχοντα τὴν νεωτέραν κωμῳδίαν, ἃ πρὸς ἄκρον ἤγαγεν Εὐριπίδης, Ὁμήρου ὄντος ἀρχῆς καὶ στίχων γε συντάξεως λεκτικῆς (*POxy.* 1176, 39.vii, pp. 59–60 Arrighetti).
45 This paper profited from suggestions by Stephen Halliwell and Richard Hunter; its English form was revised by Mathias Hanses.

Andrew Faulkner
Philo Senior and the Waters of Jerusalem[1]

It was not unthinkable a century ago to suggest that Greek Hellenistic poets of the third century BC were influenced by the Septuagint translation of Hebrew scripture. Correspondences in language and imagery (comparisons to celestial bodies and horses) raised the possibility of links between Theocritus' epithalamium for Helen (*Idyll* 18) and the *Song of Songs*, the account of Apollo's expected epiphany at the outset of Callimachus' second hymn (6–7, αὐτοὶ νῦν κατοχῆες ἀνακλίνασθε πυλάων, | αὐταὶ δὲ κληῖδες· ὁ γὰρ θεὸς οὐκέτι μακρήν) was compared to Psalm 23: 7 (ἄρατε πύλας, οἱ ἄρχοντες ὑμῶν, | καὶ ἐπάρθητε πύλαι αἰώνιοι, | καὶ εἰσελεύσεται ὁ βασιλεὺς τῆς δόξης), while particular similarities were noted also between Callimachus *Ep.* 55 ("Εσπερε, πῶς ἔπεσες) and *Isaiah* 14: 12 (πῶς ἐξέπεσεν ἐκ τοῦ οὐρανοῦ ὁ Ἑωσφόρος ὁ πρωὶ ἀνατέλλων). None of these instances, the first two of which are quite general and have sufficient parallels elsewhere,[2] offers compelling evidence for direct influence of scripture on these poets.[3] Even in the case of Callimachus *Ep.* 55 ~ *Isaiah* 14: 12, where the language is particularly close, the notion of a star falling out of the sky goes back to Hesiod and cannot be considered unique.[4] Moreover, regardless of the controversies surrounding the famous letter of Pseudo-Aristeas,[5] which places the Greek translation of the Pentateuch in the reign of Ptolemy II Philadelphus (285–46 BC), there is no evidence to place the Septuagint versions of Psalms,

---

[1] A preliminary version of this paper was read at the 6th Trends in Classics conference held in Thessaloniki in May 2012. I am grateful to the organizers of the conference and to all those who offered helpful feedback on that occasion. For their insightful comments on subsequent versions, I should like to thank also Prof. William Furley, Dr Athanassios Vergados, and Dr Christos Simelidis.
[2] For parallels see Williams 1978 and Gow 1950, ad loc.
[3] Cf. Dorival 1987, 1988, 92, and on the *Song of Songs* see most recently Hunter 2005b. Fraser 1972, 714 n. 256, who provides a good swift review of the evidence together with earlier bibliography, discounts any direct influence of the Septuagint on Theocritus or Callimachus' second hymn, but thinks it probable that Callimachus 'was familiar with a Greek version of at least part of *Isaiah*'.
[4] *Op.* 618–19 Πληϊάδες... | ...πίπτωσιν ἐς ἠεροειδέα πόντον; cf. *Isaiah* 34: 4, and later in the New Testament *Marc.* 13:25, *Apoc.* 6:13, 8:10. On *Ep.* 55 (16) Gow/Page 1965, ad loc. speak of the 'oddly parallel LXX *Is.* 14.12'.
[5] For an overview of the voluminous scholarship on the Pseudo-Aristean letter, see Fernández Marco 2000, 35–52.

Isaiah, and *Song of Songs* prior to the early second century BC.⁶ To be sure, should Callimachus have had access to an early Greek version of *Isaiah*, one superficial verbal reminiscence amidst prevailing silence would be evidence more of general disregard than attentive appreciation.⁷

Should one feel obliged to suppose a direct link between Callimachus and LXX-*Isaiah*, it would be more reasonable to suggest that the poet has influenced the translator. Not only has the impact of Alexandrian Homeric scholarship on the production of the Septuagint versions of Hebrew scripture and Jewish exegesis been well demonstrated in recent scholarship,⁸ but it has been suggested, albeit not without controversy, that the author of the LXX-*Isaiah* demonstrates a particular affinity for intertextuality and identifies with the methods of the Hellenistic γραμματικοί.⁹ The surviving literature of the period attests to the education of Hellenized Jews in Greek poetry, philosophy, and history,¹⁰ whose language and forms they simultaneously embraced and adapted as part of a complex process of cultural rapprochement and recalibration. It is not unimaginable that learned translators of Hebrew scripture were to some extent familiar with the Greek poetic tradition. Indeed, to judge from the few extant fragments, Hellenized Jewish poets characteristically used Greek poetic forms to recount versions of the familiar narratives of Hebrew scripture: Ezechiel's tragic drama in iambic trimeters treats the popular story of Exodus,¹¹ Theodotus deals in hexameter verse with the lineage of Jacob and the rape of his daughter Dinah,¹² while another poet named Philo, also writing in hexameters, negotiates the

---

6 See Dorival 1988, 83–122: *Psalms* beginning of 2nd c. BC, *Isaiah* first half of 2nd c. BC, and *Song of Songs* first half of 1st c. AD.
7 On the general disregard of the Septuagint by Greek Hellenistic authors, cf. Momiligiano 1975, 91–2.
8 See e.g. Honigman 2003 and Niehoff 2011.
9 Troxel 2008, who points out that at *Isa*. 33:18 Hebrew סֹפֵר 'scribe', which elsewhere in the *Septuagint* is rendered by ὁ γραμματεύς, is uniquely translated as οἱ γραμματικοί. For reservations concerning Troxel's identification of the translator with the Alexandrian γραμματικοί, see Kooij 2009 and Hugo 2010.
10 See Collins 1999, 5, 'The Hellenistic Jews were not reluctant exiles. They were attracted by Hellenistic culture, eager to win the respect of the Greeks and to adapt their ways'.
11 The fragments of Ezechiel (prob. 2nd c. BC) have been edited by Lanfranchi 2006, Holladay 1983–6, 2. 301–529, and Jacobson 1983. See with further bibliography Davies 2008, Collins 1999, 224–30 and Gruen 1998, 129–33.
12 The surviving text of Theodotus (prob. 2nd c. BC) is edited among others by Lloyd-Jones/Parsons as *SH* 757–64, Holladay 1983–6, 2. 51–204, and now Kuhn 2012. See with further bibliography Collins 1999, 57–60, 1980, and Gruen 1998, 120–5.

story of Abraham, Isaac, and their descendents.[13] The *Third Sibylline Oracle*, much of which goes back to Hellenistic Jews, in its own way blends biblical prophecy and Jewish wisdom literature with the Greek hexameter tradition.[14]

It seems correct to assume with Collins that the audience of such literature included both Hellenized Jews and Greeks, for whom the expression of Jewish cultural heritage in Greek poetic forms enacted a two-sided process of cultural integration and redefinition: 'The expression of traditional Jewish material in Hellenistic forms, such as tragedy and epic, blurs the differences between the two traditions and serves to show that Judaism is not an alien body in the Hellenistic world.'[15] A tragedy such as Ezechiel's *Exagoge* is therefore, as Davies has argued, 'simultaneously Hellenistic and Alexandrian, but also fulfills the biblical command for remembrance and replication of the construction of sacrificial ritual … not only is tragedy—and the propriety of tragic diction—the perfect form in which to retell a story in the Greek city of Alexandria but, because of tragedy's ritualistic connotations, the *Exagoge* becomes essential to Jewish Hellenistic religious regeneration.'[16]

In what follows, I will consider in further detail the surviving twenty four hexameter lines of Philo's Περὶ Ἱεροσόλυμα,[17] mentioned briefly above. These fragments are preserved in Eusebius' quotations of Alexander Polyhistor (1st century BC), who initially excerpted the passages of the poem. The poetry of Philo has been said to 'receive expression in tortured language, enveloped in studied obscurity, the vocabulary riddled with *hapax legomena* and a variety of arcane allusions as if to compete with or outdo the opacity of a Lycophron.'[18] These qualities make worthwhile a close reexamination of the transmitted text, not only with respect to certain points of textual criticism, but also Philo's engagement with Greek literary tradition, including the aesthetics and imagery of Hel-

---

13 Often identified with Philo the Elder mentioned by Josephus *Ap.* 1.23. The extant text of Philo (prob. 2nd c. BC) is edited among others by Lloyd-Jones/Parsons as *SH* 681–6, Holladay 1983–6, 2. 205–99, and now Kuhn 2012. See further with bibliography Collins 1999, 55–7 and Gruen 1998, 125–7.
14 On the *Third Sibylline Oracle*, see with further bibliography Lightfoot 2007, Buitenwerf 2003, and Gruen 1998, 268–90.
15 Collins 1999, 14–16, who, rather than insisting on strict divisions between Jewish and non-Jewish audiences, speaks universally of reducing cultural dissonance. Gruen 1998 instead argues that the principal audience for such literature would have been Hellenized Jews, not Greeks.
16 Davies 2008, 414–15, who argues that the *Exagoge* serves as a replacement for Temple-based sacrificial cult amongst the Jewish Diaspora.
17 This is the title given in Eusebius' quotations of Alexander Polyhistor (1st c. BC), who initially excerpted the surviving passages of the poem. See further Holladay 1983–96, 2. 205–6.
18 Gruen 1998, 126.

lenistic poetics. Apart from his apparently hyperbolic interest in recherché vocabulary and expression, which prompts a superficial comparison with Hellenistic authors such as Lycophron, it has been noted how Philo's particular interest in Jerusalem links his poem to the widespread interest of Hellenistic authors in geography and foundation narratives.[19] Beyond these general observations, I will consider how some details of Philo's poetic fragments recall common metaphors of poetic composition in Greek literature, which may suggest a more sophisticated engagement with the Greek poetic tradition than merely the selection of unusual language and foundation narratives.

Fragments 681–2 *SH*

fr. 681

ἔκλυον ἀρχεγόνοισι τὸ μυρίον ὥς ποτε θεσμοῖς
<   >
Ἀβραὰμ κλυτοηχές, ὑπέρτερον ἅμματι δεσμῶν
παμφαές, ἐπλήμμυρε μεγαυχήτοισι λογισμοῖς
θειοφιλῆ θέλγηθρα. λιπόντι γὰρ ἀγλαὸν ἕρκος
αἰνοφύτων ἔκκαυμα βριήπυος αἰνετὸς ἴσχων
ἀθάνατον ποίησεν ἐὴν φάτιν· ἐξέτι κείνου
ἔκγονος αἰνογόνοιο πολύμνιον ἔλλαχε κῦδος

μυρίον codd.: μηρίον Mras ὑπέρτερον codd.: ὑπερτέρῳ Mras ἅμματι codd.: αἵματι Philippson: ἅμμα τι Ludwich ἐπλήμμυρε N: πλήμμυρε BIO ἕρκος codd.: ἔρνος Séguier αἰνοφύτων codd.: αὐτοφύτων Séguier: αἰοφύτων Mras ἐξέτι Lloyd-Jones/Parsons: ἐξότε ON: ἐξ' ὅτ' BI[20]

I have heard in the ancestral laws how once your love of God caused the infinite [glory of your family line], O renowned Abraham, glory pre-eminently bright in the binding [of Isaac], to flow forth by means of your glorious reasoning. For to you, when you had abandoned the shining bulwark of your celebrated offspring, the loud-shouting and praiseworthy messenger, preventing the sacrifice, made his divine pronouncement. From that time, the descendants of your praised child received much-hymned glory.

The very first line of this fragment has given rise to significant confusion. Against the suggestion of Mras that ἔκλυον be derived from ἐκλύω 'to release',[21] the form

---

[19] See Collins 1999, 54, Holladay 1983–96, 2.206, and Gutman 1954, 60–3. The fragments of Theodotus' epic poem suggest a similar interest in cities, in his case Schechem: cf. Holladay 1983–96, 2. 135, Collins 1980, 93 n. 5.
[20] The apparatus underneath the fragments in this paper indicate noteworthy variants and conjectures but are not exhaustive.
[21] This and subsequent references to Mras 1954–6, ad loc. For the form, cf. *Cert.* 107–8. See further discussion in Holladay 1983–96, 2. 247–8.

is more plausibly taken by others as the first-person aorist of κλύω 'I have heard'.[22] Mras's reading is justified only by his further conjecture τὸ μηρίον 'thigh' for τὸ μυρίον 'constantly' or 'the endless [something]'—an awkward singular ('they loosed the thigh...'), which he takes as a reference to circumcision. There seems, however, little reason to assume a specific mention of circumcision in the passage, which serves principally to introduce the story of the immolation of Isaac (line 4 ἔκκαυμα) treated in detail in the next fragment.

Further difficulty here lies in how one understands ἀρχεγόνοισι θεσμοῖς. Mras again creates unnecessary complication by taking ἀρχεγόνοισι as a substantive adjective separated from the noun, thus giving a meaning along the lines of 'for our ancestors, as once according to the laws...'.[23] The relatively rare adjective ἀρχέγονος in fact goes most naturally with θεσμός, as twice later in Nonnus' *Paraphrase of St John's Gospel* ἀρχεγόνῳ τινὶ θεσμῷ (7.83, 16.46).[24] The first Nonnian parallel (7.83) appears in the context of Jesus rebuking the Jews for condemning his healing of a man on the Sabbath, when they themselves perform circumcision on the Sabbath according to Moses' (or rather, as Jesus specifies, the Patriarchs') law.[25] With its mention of circumcision, this could support Mras' conjecture of τὸ μηρίον, discussed above. But the second (16.46) Nonnian parallel is more generalized: it does not in fact correspond to any mention of ancestral law in the New Testament passage, which reads simply πάντα ὅσα ἔχει ὁ πατὴρ ἐμά ἐστιν (Jo. 16: 15, paraphrased by Nonnus καὶ ἀρχεγόνῳ τινὶ θεσμῷ | κλῆρος ἐμὸς πέλε πάντα, πατὴρ ἐμὸς ὅσσα κομίζει), but may be an example of the influence of biblical exegesis on Nonnus' paraphrase. It is well established that Nonnus was influenced in his paraphrase by St Cyril of Alexandria's commentary on St John's Gospel.[26] St Cyril does not draw a particular link between Christ's words and the Old Testament, but St John Chrysostom notably connects the New Testament verse to the words of God given to Moses in *Exodus*.[27] Nonnus may have been thinking of this or something similar in introducing ἀρχεγόνῳ τινὶ θεσμῷ.

---

22 Cf. perhaps A. R. 3.597–8 ὥς ποτε βάξιν | λευγαλέην οὗ πατρὸς ἐπέκλυεν Ἠελίοιο, of Aeetes hearing a prophecy from his father Helios.
23 Cf. Holladay 1983–96, 248–9.
24 Cf. also in the 12th century Theodoros Prodromos *Carm. Hist.* 2.89 θεσμοῖσιν γὰρ ὑπείκαθον ἀρχεγόνοισι θεοῖο.
25 *Jo.* 7: 22 διὰ τοῦτο Μωϋσῆς δέδωκεν ὑμῖν τὴν περιτομήν—οὐχ ὅτι ἐκ τοῦ Μωϋσέως ἐστὶν ἀλλ' ἐκ τῶν πατέρων—καὶ ἐν σαββάτῳ περιτέμνετε ἄνθρωπον.
26 See *inter alia* Livrea 1989, 25, 2000, 85–92 and Agosti 2003, 52–70.
27 *Trin.* (PG 48, p. 1089) Πάντα ὅσα ἔχει ὁ Πατὴρ ἐμά ἐστιν, εἶπεν ὁ μονογενὴς Θεός, ὁ ὢν εἰς τὸν κόλπον τοῦ Πατρός. Μωϋσῆς λέγει· Ὁ ὢν ἀπέσταλκέν με (*Ex.* 3: 14). Ὁ ὢν ἐστιν ὁ Πατήρ, ὁ ὢν ἐστιν ὁ Υἱός, ὁ ὢν πρὸς τὸν ὄντα, ἀνάρχως καὶ ἀχρόνως γεγεννημένος. Πάντα ἔχει ὁ Πατήρ,

Returning to Philo's own mention of the ancestral laws, it could well be that this is a reference not to a set of ancestral laws as such, but to the Pentateuch as a whole, including its narrative sections in which the story of Abraham and Isaac is recounted. The Hebrew term *Torah* 'instruction, advice, law' carries this inclusive sense by the second century BC, as does νόμος in the prologue to the second-century BC Greek translation of Sirach by Jesus Ben Sira's grandson.[28] Philo would in this case be appealing quite pointedly to his own reading and/or hearing of Jewish literary narrative.

Philippson, followed by Parsons and Lloyd-Jones, supposed a lacuna after the first line, in which case τὸ μυρίον can be taken as a descriptor of a now lost noun rather than as an adverb, 'incessantly' or 'constantly'.[29] The adverbial sense is not impossible ('I have heard often how once...'), but assuming a lacuna after the first line has the distinct advantage of accounting for an object in the sentence (see below). A missing phrase concerning the glory of Abraham's lineage, corresponding to the last line of the fragment, would be particularly appropriate: Parsons and Lloyd-Jones point not only to the tantalizing parallel at Theocritus *Ep.* 21.2 οὗ τὸ μυρίον κλέος, of the glory of Archilochus, but also the fittingness of the subsequent adjective ὑπέρτερον, as in the Homeric collocation ὑπέρτερον κῦδος.[30] It might also be noted that μυρίος not uncommonly describes flowing liquids: in Homer of grief (ἄχος), imagined as a liquid that pours over the eyes, and then later of the flowing stream (ῥεῦμα) of the river Tanais in the third book of the *Sibylline Oracles*.[31] A similar semantic range is found in the adjective ἀέναος, used frequently of rivers and streams but also κλέος and τιμή.[32] The figure of ever-flowing glory would correspond with the verb ἐπλήμμυρε in line

---

ἀληθῶς ζωή, καὶ ἀθανασία, καὶ φῶς, καὶ παντοδύναμος, καὶ Θεός, καὶ Κύριος· ἅπερ ἔχει καὶ ὁ Υἱός. On Nonnus underlining the prophetic weight of Old Testament scripture at *Pa.* 19.129–32 (*Jo.* 19: 24), see Faulkner (forthcoming).

28 Sir. prol. 1.8, also later in 2 and 4 Maccabees. See Muraoka 2009, ad loc. 4. On νόμος as a canonical term for the Pentateuch in the prologue to Ben Sira, cf. Orlinsky 1991. On the term *Torah* see Crüsemann 1996, 331.

29 For the adverbial use Parsons and Lloyd-Jones compare Antiphilus *AP* 9.73.5 θαμβῶ σε τὸ μυρίον.

30 *Il.* 12.437, 15.491, 644. Cf. Ibycus fr. S176. 12 SLG and later Nonnus *Pa.* 11.17 ἀλλὰ Θεοῦ τόδε κῦδος ὑπέρτερον, who uses the expression to render ὑπὲρ τῆς δόξης τοῦ Θεοῦ in the New Testament story of Lazarus (*Jo.* 11: 4). If παμφαές in line three is taken as an adjective attached to the supposed κλέος (see below), the neuter ὑπέρτερον is best here taken adverbially 'preeminently'.

31 *Il.* 20.282 ἄχος οἱ χύτο μυρίον ὀφθαλμοῖσι, *Orac. Sib.* 3.340 τὸ δὲ ῥεῦμα τὸ μυρίον; cf. D.P. 166 ἐκ τῆς γὰρ Πόντοιο τὸ μυρίον ἕλκεται ὕδωρ.

32 See LSJ ad loc. For κλέος Simon. fr. 26. 9 PMG, Heraclit. fr. 29 DK.

three,[33] and with the imagery of flowing water prominent in the description of Jerusalem in subsequent fragments.

The phrase ἅμματι δεσμῶν in line two is taken by Holladay as a pleonastic expression 'by the knot of bonds', of the covenant between God and Abraham (cf. Gen. 17). Philippson preferred to emend the text to αἵματι δεσμῶν 'the blood of bonds',[34] but the pleonasm is not so troubling: at least, Parmenides makes use of the very similar ἐν πείρασι δεσμῶν.[35] In any case, the phrase most naturally refers to the binding of Isaac. Given the ensuing context of his immolation in fr. 682, it is also worth noting that the lexicographer Hesychius later glosses ἐν ἅμματι as ἐν φλογί, and ἅμμα is used of kindling by Philo of Alexandria.[36] The meaning could thus be 'in the fire of bonds', with reference to the sacrificial binding of Isaac.[37] In Gen. 22: 9 Abraham is said explicitly to bind his son to the sacrificial altar: the Hebrew verb עָקַד 'to bind',[38] unique in the Old Testament, is translated in the Septuagint by the Greek verb συμποδίζω.[39] Fire and wood are also important in the biblical account. Abraham does not actually reach the point of burning Isaac, but the fact that he brings fire and wood for what is intended to be a whole burnt offering (Heb. עֹלָה *'olah* or 'that which as-

---

33 For the association of κλέος with flowing water, cf. e.g. Pi. *N.* 7.62–3 ὕδατος ὧτε ῥοὰς φίλον ἐς ἄνδρ' ἄγων | κλέος ἐτήτυμον αἰνέσω.
34 See Holladay 1983–96, 2.250–1. Parsons and Lloyd-Jones compare the similar ἅμματι χειρῶν, which occurs five times at line-end in Nonnus *Dionysiaca* (37.560, 570, 41.212, 45.266, 48.142). Ludwich alternatively proposed reading the accusative ἅμμα τι together with ὑπέρτερον, but it is hard to see how τι would function here.
35 Parm. B 8. 26; cf. also B 8. 31 πείρατος ἐν δεσμοῖσιν. I am grateful to Prof. David Sider for this reference.
36 Hsch. ad loc., Ph. *Aet.* 88. ἅμμα is presumably in these instances thought to come from the meaning of ἅπτω 'to light a fire'.
37 One might perhaps also consider the possibility that δεσμός refers to the bonds between parent and child, although the expression would be awkward. Cf. Ph. *Spec. leg.* 137 μέρη γὰρ διαιρετὰ γονέων παῖδές εἰσιν, εἰ δὲ δεῖ τἀληθὲς εἰπεῖν, ἀδιαίρετα, συγγενικῷ αἵματι καὶ λόγοις προγόνων, ἀοράτοις εἴδεσιν, εἰς ἐκγόνους διήκουσι φίλτροις τε ἐνωτικῆς εὐνοίας καὶ <u>φύσεως δεσμοῖς ἀλύτοις</u> ἡρμοσμένοι.
38 In later Hebrew tradition the sacrifice of Isaac became known as the Akedah (עֲקֵדָה) or 'binding', a noun connected to the verb in the biblical passage. The use of the noun itself, elsewhere linked to the sacrificial binding of the Tamid Lamb, as a description of the sacrifice of Isaac in *Genesis* 22 is certainly attested only in the late second century AD: see Davies-Chilton 1978, 533–6. Philo may nonetheless be picking up on the particular mention of binding in the biblical passage.
39 Cf. Parsons/Lloyd-Jones '*famam sublimiorem habuit Abraham e vinculis, id est* συμποδίσας Ἰσαὰκ τὸν υἱὸν αὐτοῦ ἐπέθηκεν αὐτὸν ἐπὶ τὸ θυσιαστήριον ἐπάνω τῶν ξύλων'. On the Hebrew עָקַד, with the specific implication of 'tying fast the shank of an animal at the upper thigh' for sacrifice, see Koehler/Baumgarten/Stamm 1994–2000, ad loc.

cends' and LXX ὁλοκάρπωσις) is repeated several times across Gen. 22: 2–9.⁴⁰ The particular mention of the sacrificial fire here would fit with παμφαές in the next line—the adjective is elsewhere used of shining in the light of fire,⁴¹ and is appropriate also as a descriptor of glory.⁴² The mention of fire here would also prepare for the statement three lines later that God prevented the burning (ἔκκαυμα ἴσχων), where the rare word ἔκκαυμα refers to the wood of fires.⁴³

The form ἐπλήμμυρε in line three is transmitted by N, where the other manuscripts have πλήμμυρε. The latter has been taken as a vocative form,⁴⁴ but it seems preferable to read the imperfect of πλημμύρω, assuming that a finite verb did not stand in the supposed lacuna. The sense of this verb is often intransitive 'to overflow/fill', but it is also used transitively with the accusative 'to make flow'.⁴⁵ The verb can therefore take an object, which would here most naturally be Abraham's glory with θειοφιλῆ θέλγηθρα as subject.

The *hapax* form θέλγηθρα, paralleled in morphology by δέρκηθρον in Philo fr. 683. 2, has been understood variously as 'charms/gestures pleasing to God', 'inspired ecstasy', or even 'prayers'.⁴⁶ Another possibility is that θέλγηθρα was intended to signify 'love of God', based on the semantic range of φίλτρον, which like θέλγηθρον means 'spell/charm' but also has the additional and well-attested sense of 'love': it is used notably by Euripides in the plural of the love of the gods for Troy (*Tr.* 857–8, τὰ θεῶν δέ | φίλτρα φροῦδα Τροίαι) and is employed later by Nonnus of the love of Christ for the disciples in his paraphrase of St John's Gospel (16.400–6).⁴⁷ Taking this as the subject of the verb

---

40 Another possibility is that δεσμῶν is the genitive of δέσμη, used of bundles of plants and wood: thus 'in the fire of wood', again with reference to the frequent mention of these items in *Genesis*. In the Septuagint, the word is used of the bundle of hyssop employed to spread blood above the doors (*Ex.* 12: 22; cf. Ezechiel *Ex.* 185). See Aesop. *Prov.* 53 ῥάβδων δέσμην and later Athen. *Deip.* 700a φανὸν δέ τινές φασι τὴν ἐκ ξύλων τετμημένων δέσμην.
41 See S. *Ph.* 728 [ἀνὴρ = Heracles] πυρὶ παμφαής.
42 Cf. A. R. 4.1749 ἀγλαὸν ἔμμορε κῦδος.
43 See S. fr. 225 TrGF (Ἡρακλῆς Σατυρικός) συνέλεγον τὰ ξύλ', ὡς ἐκκαυμάτων | μή μοι μεταξὺ προσδεήσειεν. Cf. Ph. *Spec. leg.* 2.251 οὐδὲ τὰ πυρὸς ἐκκαύματα συλλέγειν.
44 See Holladay 1983–96, 2. 251.
45 See LSJ ad loc. For the transitive sense, cf. Ph. *Op.* 38 διὸ φλέβας μαστοῖς ἐοικυίας ἐπλημμύρει (of causing rivers to flow throughout earth), Orph. A. 493–4 ἔνθα δὲ νύμφαι κρήνῃ ὑπ' Ἀρτακίῃ καλὰ νάματα πλημμύρουσιν.
46 See Holladay 1983–96, 2. 252–3.
47 *Pa.* 16.400–6 ὑψιμέδων γὰρ | ἀντίτυπον πόθον ἁγνὸν <u>ἐμοῖς φίλτροισι</u> φυλάσσων | ὑμέας αὐτοκέλευστος ἐμὸς γενέτης ἀγαπάζει, | ὅττι θεοῦ λόγον υἷα σοφῷ καὶ ὁμόφρονι δεσμῷ | θέσκελον εἰς ἐμὲ φίλτρον ἐπιστώσασθε καὶ ὑμεῖς | ἤθεσιν ἀπλανέεσσιν· ἐπεφράσσασθε δὲ θυμῷ, | ὅττι φερεζώοιο θεοῦ παρὰ πατρὸς ἱκάνω, paraphrasing *Jo.* 16.27–8 αὐτὸς γὰρ ὁ πατὴρ φιλεῖ

ἐπλήμμυρε (understood transitively as above) would give the meaning '...love of God caused the glory of Abraham's race to flow forth through [Abraham's] glorious reasoning'.[48] This could mean the love of God for Abraham, but is perhaps best taken as Abraham's love for God. This corresponds with Abraham's particular demonstration of love for God in the biblical account, which takes priority over even his beloved son (Gen. 22: 2 λαβὲ τὸν υἱόν σου τὸν ἀγαπητὸν ὃν ἠγάπησας, 16 τοῦ υἱοῦ σου τοῦ ἀγαπητοῦ).

In keeping with this interpretation, it seems fitting, with Attridge, to connect μεγαυχήτοισι λογισμοῖς ('glorious reckonings') to Abraham's obedience of God's commands,[49] which is again emphasized in the angel's report of God's words to Abraham at Gen. 22: 17– 18 (ἦ μὴν εὐλογῶν εὐλογήσω σε καὶ πληθύνων πληθυνῶ τὸ σπέρμα σου ὡς τοὺς ἀστέρας τοῦ οὐρανοῦ καὶ ὡς τὴν ἄμμον τὴν παρὰ τὸ χεῖλος τῆς θαλάσσης καὶ κληρονομήσει τὸ σπέρμα σου τὰς πόλεις τῶν ὑπεναντίων καὶ ἐνευλογηθήσονται ἐν τῷ σπέρματί σου πάντα τὰ ἔθνη τῆς γῆς <u>ἀνθ' ὧν ὑπήκουσας τῆς ἐμῆς φωνῆς</u>): all the nations of the earth are in future blessed through Abraham's lineage because Abraham obeys God, just as the future glory of Abraham's offspring is presented as the consequence of his actions in the final two lines of the fragment. The γάρ in the next sentence indicates how God's actions are a response to Abraham's faith and love.

I see no reason to suppose in the *hapax* αἰνοφύτων of line five any reference to a race of giants, specifically the men of Babel, as have some.[50] The word, according to the standard meaning of the prefix αἰνο- in compounds, should mean 'dread/awesome' plants or offspring, although we might not rule out entirely an intended meaning of praiseworthy, as if the prefix derives from αἶνος.[51] On either reading of the prefix, αἰνοφύτων will most probably mean offspring rather than

---

ὑμᾶς, ὅτι ὑμεῖς ἐμὲ πεφιλήκατε καὶ πεπιστεύκατε ὅτι ἐγὼ παρὰ τοῦ θεοῦ ἐξῆλθον. ἐξῆλθον ἐκ τοῦ πατρὸς καὶ ἐλήλυθα εἰς τὸν κόσμον· πάλιν ἀφίημι τὸν κόσμον καὶ πορεύομαι πρὸς τὸν πατέρα. See further examples in LSJ ad loc.

48 Philo of Alexandria uses the adjective θεοφιλής of Abraham, Isaac, and Jacob in the context of their virtues and love for God at *Spec. leg.* 50 καὶ πάντας φιλοθέους ὁμοῦ καὶ θεοφιλεῖς, ἀγαπήσαντας τὸν ἀληθῆ θεὸν καὶ ἀνταγαπηθέντας ὑπ' αὐτοῦ.
49 Attridge 1985, 783. Cf. Holladay 1983– 96, 2. 251– 2, who rightly, together with Collins 1999, 55– 7, rejects any mystical notions in the rare adjective μεγαύχητος.
50 See the discussion of such interpretations in Holladay 1983– 96, 2. 254– 6.
51 So *LSJ* ad loc. 'plants of praise' and similarly ad αἰνογόνοιο below in line 7 'child of praise'. Cf. αἰνόφρων, provided as a gloss for ἀγανόφρων by Hsch. The adjective αἰνετός 'praiseworthy' appears in the same line and the passage as a whole is focused upon glory.

plants: there would be no clear referent for dread or praiseworthy plants in this context,[52] and the word seems linked to αἰνογόνοιο two lines below.

Relevant to construing αἰνοφύτων is the problem of how one understands ἀγλαὸν ἕρκος in the previous line. The unique collocation recalls ἀγλαὸν ἔρνος or even at line end Homeric ἀγλαὸν υἱόν.[53] A reference to offspring, specifically Isaac, would indeed make good sense here in relation to the narrative of Genesis 22, where God, through his messenger angel, stops the sacrifice of Isaac. The dative λιπόντι in line five, while awkward at sentence beginning, can only refer to Abraham: to him who has left something behind (λιπόντι), a loud-shouting praiseworthy one, having prevented the sacrifice (ἔκκαυμα ἴσχων), made a divine pronouncement. Previously, ἕρκος has been taken to mean an enclosure of some type, a garden or even Babel. Without resorting to emendation of the text, ἕρκος could instead, especially given the similarity to expressions indicating a glorious offspring noted above, be a unique manner in which to refer to Isaac. The concept of children acting as a bulwark for parents was established at least by the fifth century BC: Jason refers to his royal children as the bulwark of the house in Euripides' *Medea* 597 ([θέλων] φῦσαι τυράννους παῖδας, ἔρυμα δώμασιν).[54] Taking λιπόντι in the sense of 'to leave behind/forsake',[55] Abraham would therefore abandon his son Isaac to God. The reference to Isaac as the bulwark of Abraham's children underlines the enormity of the father's sacrifice.

The adjective βριήπυος perhaps suggests that the subject of the sentence is the angel of God, again in keeping with the biblical account. The word is rare, attested in poetry only three other times: in Homer (*Il.* 13.521) and pseudo-Hesiod (fr. 10a. 69 M-W) it is applied to Ares, but then it is notably used later of a messenger in the poetry of Gregory of Nazianzus (II. 1. 13.116 κῆρυξ μὲν δὲ τοῖα βριήπυος). If, as Parsons and Lloyd-Jones point out, αἰνετός is frequently used of God himself in the Septuagint (2 Reg. 22. 4 αἰνετὸν ἐπικαλέσομαι κύριον, etc.), that adjective is more common and widely applicable. Should the angel be envisioned here as the one staying the hand of Abraham on behalf of God, it would

---

52 Holladay 1983–96, 2. 256 suggests that the reference could in this case be to the dread plants from which the sacrificial firewood (intended for a dread purpose) derived, but this seems an awkward transposition of the quality of the wood's purpose.
53 For ἀγλαὸν ἔρνος, to which Seguier emended the text, cf. Macedonius, *Paean ad Apollinem et Aesculapium* 4 CA, IC IV 323.5, SEG 23.126.6. The combination ἀγλαὸν υἱόν at line end is common in Homer, *Il.* 5.843, 15.445 etc. For instances of ἕρκος in hymns, see Furley-Bremer (2001) ii. 418.
54 The particular term ἕρκος is of course also used of Homeric warriors (Ajax *Il.* 3.229 or Achilles *Il.* 1.284 etc.).
55 See LSJ ad loc. 3.

make sense, again following the biblical account, for the loud-shouting angel to be said to announce the prophecy of God. The phrase ἀθάνατον ποίησεν ἐὴν φάτιν, in which φάτις will naturally refer to the oracular pronouncement of God concerning the future of Abraham's lineage, is best interpreted thus.[56] Idiomatically, one would expect the middle form of ποιέω with φάτιν to give the meaning 'the loud-shouting praise-worthy one uttered the divine pronouncement',[57] but the active can here be understood similarly to mean that the angel 'brought about' or 'revealed' to Abraham the divine command of God.

Furthermore, if I am right that the angel is here described as the mouthpiece of God, the particular choice of language could carry apposite metapoetic weight. The term φάτις is linked closely to poetic production in Aristophanes' *Birds*, when a hapless poet aligned with traditional poetics comes on stage and speaks, concerning his poetic inspiration, of τις ὠκεῖα Μουσάων φάτις | οἷάπερ ἵππων ἀμαρυγά (924–5). This recalls the common associations of poet, Muse, and prophet, a link notable in the term προφήτης ('interpreter') in Pindar and Bacchylides.[58] In Hellenistic poetry a similar association of prophecy, poetry and the Muses is present in the related terms ὑποφήτης and ὑποφήτωρ, used prominently by both Theocritus and Apollonius.[59] Turning back to Philo, the verb ποιέω is also intrinsically linked to poetry: it is commonly employed in the active of poetic composition, including the rendering of prose into verse.[60] The phrase ποίησεν φάτιν therefore applies on one level to the angel, the prophetic mouthpiece of God's promise of future glory for Abraham's race, but on another level suggests an association between the angel and the poet Philo, the versifier and poetic mouthpiece of God's word in scripture. This association is particularly apt: God's divine message, paraphrased in the next sentence, announces future glory (κῦδος) for Abraham's lineage, a benefit which Greek poet-

---

[56] The version of Holladay 1983–96, 2. 256 'he [God] made his own voice immortal', who following Walter and Atwell-Hanson takes ἀθάνατον as predicate, makes little sense. For φάτις of divine pronouncement, see LSJ ad loc. I.
[57] See LSJ ad loc. 5. It would be an easy change to ἀθάνατον ποίησετ' ἐὴν φάτιν.
[58] See P. *Pae.* 6.6 ἀοίδιμον Πιερίδων προφάταν, 8.1ff. Κλυτοὶ μάντι[ες] Ἀπόλλωνος (prophets associated with the Muses), fr. 150 μαντεύεο, Μοῖσα, προφατεύσω δ' ἐγώ, B. 9.3 Μουσᾶν γε ἰοβλεφάρων θεῖος προφ[άτ]ας. As Rutherford 2001, 174 notes, the prominence of the link in the vestiges of Pindar's *Paeans* suggests that the theme was a prominent one. Cf. Plato *Phdr.* 262d Μουσῶν προφῆται.
[59] Theoc. *Id.* 16.29, 17.115, 22.116, A. R. 1.22. On the close connection of the term to prophecy and the revelation of divine knowledge, see González 2000. The association of prophets and poets is also well established in Hebrew tradition: cf. West 1997, 606.
[60] See LSJ ad loc. 4. See Pl. *Phd.* 61b οὓς προχείρους εἶχον μύθους καὶ ἠπιστάμην τοὺς Αἰσώπου, τούτων ἐποίησα οἷς πρώτοις ἐνέτυχον.

ry famously confers upon its subjects from Homer right down to the Hellenistic period,[61] and with which, to judge from fr. 681 as a whole, Philo seems particularly concerned.

Philo thus potentially does far more in this fragment than draw bluntly on obscure language to Hellenize superficially a Jewish message. Rather, having at the outset appealed in a typically Hellenistic fashion to preceding literary tradition (but in this case Jewish literary tradition, which serves as the basis for his account of the offering of Isaac), he appropriates the well-known Hellenic trope of the Muses, whose traditional role within poetic inspiration is usurped by the Hebrew Yaweh. Through association with the angel, Philo further implies his own function as the poetic mouthpiece of God, who, once again subverting a trope of the Greek poetic tradition, plays a role in conveying divine glory to Abraham and his descendants. The substitution of God's inspiration for that of the Muses will notably, several centuries later, become a common tactic of Christian classicizing poets, for whom Christ or the Holy Spirit takes the place of the Muses.[62]

fr. 682

ἄρτι χερὸς θηκτῷ ξίφεϊ φθόρον ἐντύνοντος
λήμματι καὶ σφαράγοιο παρακλιδὸν ἀθροισθέντος·
ἀλλ' ὁ μὲν ἐν χείρεσσι κερασφόρον ὤπασε κριόν.

ἄρτι χερὸς ON: ἄρτι χειρός I: ἀρτίχερος Séguier θηκτῷ ξίφεϊ φθόρον Faulkner: θηκτοῖο ξιφηφόρον I: θνητοῖο ξιφηφόρον ON λήμματι codd.: λήματι Mras

...presently [Abraham] was preparing death by the sharp sword of his hand according to the commission [of God], and [Isaac's] throat was gathered sidelong [under the blade]. But God delivered a horn-bearing ram in his hands.

Polyhistor (Eus. *PE* 9.20.1) indicates that this fragment came just after the preceding verses (οἷς μετ' ὀλίγα ἐπιφέρει). It seems clear that the lines describe Abraham preparing to sacrifice his son, only to have God intervene to stop him with the provision of a ram as an alternative sacrifice, once again a paraphrase of the

---

61 Within Hellenistic literature, the κλέος conferred by poets is a prominent theme in Theoc. *Ids.* 16 and 17, both of which also reflect upon the poet as the interpreter of the Muses (see above n. 59). On the continued but altered significance of κλέος in the literary and allusive epic of Apollonius Rhodius, see Hunter/Fantuzzi 2005, 93–4.
62 E.g. in Latin Juv. 1.25–7, Sedul. 1.85, Arat. 2.577–8 with Green 2006, 21–2, 300–2. In Greek, Greg. Naz. *Arc.* 1.22, *Met. Pr.* 1–2, 109–10. See further Shorrock 2011, 22–33.

narrative known in Genesis 22.⁶³ The precise language and meaning of its first two lines have nonetheless proved elusive, to the extent that Parsons and Lloyd-Jones placed much of the first line between *cruces*. Progress can, I think, be made on previous attempts.

The first line is transmitted by manuscripts ON as ἄρτι χειρὸς θνητοῖο ξιφηφόρον ἐντύνοντος and by manuscript I as ἄρτι χειρὸς θηκτοῖο ξιφηφόρον ἐντύνοντος. There are several problems: ἐντύνοντος must function as a genitive absolute of the subject Abraham, but should one read θνητοῖο or θηκτοῖο, to what should either of these adjectives be attached, and how does the accusative adjective ξιφηφόρον function on its own? Moreover, both θνητοῖο ξιφηφόρον and θηκτοῖο ξιφηφόρον are unmetrical, unless we admit an irregularity in the treatment of ξ.⁶⁴

The lack of metre and sense prompted Ludwich to emend the line to θηκτοῦ ξίφεος φόρον. This is ultimately unsatisfactory, for φόρος 'tribute/payment' is awkwardly applied to Isaac as a blood sacrifice to God. It nonetheless seems to me a step in the right direction. The non-Homeric adjective θηκτός, used several times in Aeschylus and Euripides of swords, but relatively rare,⁶⁵ should be retained as the clear *lectio difficilior* over the common θνητός: the same variant θνητῷ for θηκτῷ is, for example, found in a fragment of Euripides' *Cresphontes* (fr. 453.12). It is also possible to explain how the problematic ξιφηφόρον could have replaced the original reading: the non-canonical 4 *Maccabees* 16.20 describes Abraham's hand as ξιφηφόρος at the moment it moves to kill Isaac (ὁ πατὴρ ἡμῶν Ἀβραὰμ ἔσπευδεν τὸν ἐθνοπάτορα υἱὸν σφαγιάσαι Ἰσαάκ, καὶ [ὁ Ἰσαὰκ] τὴν πατρῴαν χεῖρα ξιφηφόρον καταφερομένην ἐπ' αὐτὸν ὁρῶν οὐκ ἔπτηξεν). The fifth-century AD Basil of Seleucia also uses the adjective of Abraham in this context (*Or.* 7). Such examples could have suggested substitution of ξιφηφόρος to a scribe, who may have been further influenced by the similar κερασφόρον two lines below.

I suggest emending the first line to read ἄρτι χερὸς θηκτῷ ξίφεϊ φθόρον ἐντύνοντος, which both provides good sense and leaves the transmitted text relatively undisturbed. A Byzantine scribe could easily have mistaken the graphically similar ξίφεϊ φθόρον for the more familiar ξιφηφόρον (note also the identical pronunciation of the diphthong ει and η, should the diacritic have been

---

[63] There is no justification for Mras' suggestion that the lines describe God outfitting his angel with a sword. Cf. Holladay 1983–96, 2. 262–3 citing the objections of Walter.
[64] Cf. Parsons/Lloyd-Jones, 'sed Philonem -ὄ ξ- ausum esse quis credit, ad exemplum etiam litterarum ζ-, σκ- apud Homerum'.
[65] See with ξίφος E. *Ion* 1064, *Rh.* 669, φάσγανον E. *Med.* 40, 379, and σίδαρος A. *Th.* 944, E. *Phoen.* 68, fr. 453. 12 (*Cresphontes*).

missing or ignored). The corruption of the dative θηκτῷ to the genitive, and indeed subsequently to θνητοῖο, is then easily explained by the ensuing difficulty in construing the original case. The masculine φθόρος, a rare equivalent for ἡ φθορά 'death/destruction', is found elsewhere in Hellenistic poetry at Call. *Iamb.* 7.25 (Kerkhecker) and Theoc. *Id.* 15.18, and accords with the recherché style of Philo. For preparing death, here expressed with the verb ἐντύνω 'to prepare/make ready', one can compare παρασκευάζω used of preparing both θάνατος and φθορά.⁶⁶ The meaning of the line therefore becomes, '...presently Abraham was preparing death by the sharp sword of his hand.' Many editors have preferred to join ἄρτι and χειρός to form the rare adjective ἀρτίχειρ, found once earlier in Plato (*Lg.* 795d), thus 'strong handed Abraham....', which may be correct. The expression 'with the sword of his hand' is awkward. On the other hand, the adversative ἀλλ' ὁ at the outset of line three signals the abrupt halt to Abraham's sacrifice brought about by God *in media res*, an element of the narrative in Genesis 22 here signalled by ἄρτι.

At the beginning of line two, λήμματι, whose basic sense is 'something received' often 'gain', has also caused unnecessary trouble to editors. Mras emended the word to λήματι 'will/desire', while Ludwich put forward the laboured λῆμμά τι, understood as 'gain [for God]' in apposition to his conjectured φόρον 'offering [to God]'. Holladay follows Mras, rendering λήματι 'with firm resolve' and commenting that λῆμμα 'is more difficult to translate'.⁶⁷ In the Septuagint, however, λῆμμα has the particular meaning 'commission received', 'burden', or 'prophecy' of God.⁶⁸ The dative therefore provides in this context the perfectly comprehensible meaning 'according to the commission of God', which corresponds directly to the burden laid upon Abraham by God at the beginning of Genesis 22.

Familiarity with the language of the Septuagint also, I think, offers the solution to the disputed meaning of σφαράγοιο ἀθροισθέντος in line two. The rare noun σφάραγος is glossed by Hesychius as 'throat' or 'neck' (βρόγχος, τράχηλος, λαιμός), or alternatively as 'noise' (ψόφος), its basic sense contained in the verb σφαραγέομαι 'to make noise' or 'crackle'. According to Photius, Apion explained the word's meaning 'throat' (φάρυγξ) by the association of noise with throats. Some editors have taken σφάραγος in Philo to refer to an uncertain rustling

---

66 See Antiphon *Or.* 1.28 οὐ γὰρ δή που μαρτύρων γ' ἐναντίον οἱ ἐπιβουλεύοντες τοὺς θανάτους τοῖς πέλας μηχανῶνταί τε καὶ παρασκευάζουσιν and Philo Mech. Παρασκευαστικὰ καὶ Πολιορκητικὰ 2.54 Diels-Schramm ἵνα φόβον καὶ φθορὰν ταχεῖαν παρασκευάζῃ.
67 Holladay 1983–96, 2.263.
68 Cf. LXX *Je.* 23.33–4 λῆμμα κυρίου, for Hebrew מַשָּׂא *massa'* 'burden' or 'utterance' of God. See LSJ ad loc. IV.

sound, or the crackling noise of the sacrificial fire and wood, in accordance with the use of the verb σφαραγέομαι in Homer to describe the sounds of burning.[69] A reference to the neck of Isaac, however, seems far more likely, following as it does upon the mention of a knife in Abraham's hand. This echoes the context of the Homeric *hapax* ἀσφάραγος at *Il.* 22.328, where Achilles' fatal cast of the spear is said remarkably not to cut the windpipe of Hector, such that Hector can still speak as he dies (οὐδ' ἄρ' ἀπ' ἀσφάραγον μελίη τάμε χαλκοβάρεια). Parsons and Lloyd-Jones, who render the phrase '*collo in obliquum contracto*', also compare E. *Or.* 1471 ὤμοις ἀριστεροῖσιν ἀνακλάσας δέρην, | παίειν λαιμῶν ἔμελ|λεν εἴσω μέλαν ξίφος. This interpretation is in my mind further confirmed by the attested range of the verb ἀθροίζω 'to gather together'. The verb does not naturally describe sound 'becoming concentrated' or 'gathering strength',[70] but it does in the Septuagint have the meaning to be placed under the sword. At *Jeremiah* 18. 21 the prophet Jeremiah, as he foretells the destruction of the sinful people of Judah and Jerusalem, exclaims 'give their sons over to famine and gather them under hands of the sword' (δὸς τοὺς υἱοὺς αὐτῶν εἰς λιμὸν καὶ ἄθροισον αὐτοὺς εἰς χεῖρας μαχαίρας). In the light of such an expression, the use of ἀθροίζω to describe the gathering of Isaac's neck under the sword of Abraham's hand becomes explicable.

Fragments 683–6 SH

Three (683–5) of the four remaining fragments of Philo's poem describe the waters of Jerusalem. These waters cannot be identified with certainty,[71] a problem with which I do not propose to deal here. My interpretative aims below are more literary. A final fragment (686) deals with the descendants of Abraham and Isaac, Jacob and Joseph.

fr. 683

νισσόμενος δ' ἐφύπερθε τὸ θαμβηέστατον ἄλλο
δερκηθρόν. συναοιδὰ μεγιστούχοιο λοετροῖς
ῥεύματος ἐμπίπλησι βαθὺν ῥόον ἐξανιείσης

νισσόμενος Séguier: νηχόμενος codd.: νηχομένοις Lloyd-Jones/Parsons συναοιδὰ Gifford: σὺν ἀοιδᾷ ION

---

[69] *Od.* 9.390 of the burning roots of Polyphemus' eye σφαραγεῦντο δέ οἱ πυρὶ ῥίζαι, and 9.440 οὔθατα γὰρ σφαραγεῦντο. For a summary of previous views, see Holladay 1983–96, 2.263–5.
[70] Holladay 1983–96, 2.264–5 can point only to Mras's appeal to Xen. *Cyr.* 5.2.34, where the verb describes fear (φόβος) gaining strength.
[71] For a summary of possibilities, see Holladay 1983–96, 2.273–8.

...and flowing from above is the other most marvellous sight. In harmony with the baths of the ruler it fills with its flow the deep stream [of a spring] gushing forth ...

The transmitted νηχόμενος 'swimming' is emended by Lloyd-Jones/Parsons to the dative νηχομένοις; accordingly, τὸ θαμβηέστατον ἄλλο δερκηθρόν provides the subject, with reference presumably to a flow of water, a sight for swimmers in the baths (λοετροῖς). The nominative νηχόμενος would instead focus the viewing through the eyes of a single swimmer, with δερκηθρόν the grammatical object and a verb of sight understood from the lost lines preceding. Either of these readings is possible, but one might doubt altogether whether Philo chose to focalize his description through the eyes of a swimmer. The verb νηχόμενος has alternatively been taken to mean 'flowing', with appeal to the adjective νήχυτος, used in Hellenistic poetry of flowing water.[72]

A relatively neglected but distinct possibility is Vossius' emendation of the text to νισσόμενος—accepted by Seguier in the notes accompanying his nineteenth century French translation of Eusebius' *Preparatio*, but not recorded in the apparatus of the *SH* by Parsons/Lloyd-Jones.[73] I will below suggest that Philo in this fragment alludes to a description of the Rhône and Po rivers at Apollonius Rhodius' *Argonautica* 4.627–9, where the particular expression βαθὺς ῥόος first occurs, and there also in the context of waters mixing together. If this is correct, it is notable that the movement of the Rhône is described in Apollonius with the verb μετανίσεται (628). Parallel to the description in Philo of water descending from above is also *Argonautica* 2.975–6 μία δ' οἴη ἐτήτυμος | ἔπλετο πηγή· | ἡ μέν τ' ἐξ ὀρέων κατανίσεται.

This also has the advantage of providing the inferred subject for the next sentence beginning with adverbial συναοιδά: the moving water, a sight to see, in harmony with the baths of the king, fills with its flow the deep stream of the [spring] gushing forth'. It is reasonable to follow previous editors in taking the feminine participle ἐξανιείσης with an unexpressed or missing κρήνης.[74] One might compare the verb of the Achelous bursting forth from the earth at A. R. 4.293 ὑμετέρης γαίης Ἀχελώιος ἐξανίησιν. The description in Philo is one of the water from above mixing with a water source that comes from below out of the ground. Prof. W. D. Furley also suggests to me the possibility of emending to ναόμενος 'flowing'.

---

72 A.R. 3.530 νήχυτον ὕδωρ.
73 For discussion see Holladay 1983–96, 2. 281.
74 Most recently Lloyd-Jones/Parsons. See discussion at Holladay 1983–96, 2.285–7, who instead tries somehow to link ῥεύματος and ἐξανιείσης, despite the grammatical discord. A κρήνη is mentioned in fr. 684. 3, but one might also supply πηγῆς.

fr. 684

ῥεῦμα γὰρ ὑψιφάεινον, ἐν ὑετίοις νιφετοῖσιν
ἱέμενον πολυγηθές, ὑπαὶ πύργοις συνόροισιν
στρωφᾶται, καὶ ξηρὰ πέδῳ κεκονιμένα κρήνης
τηλεφαῇ δείκνυσιν, ὑπέρτατα θάμβεα λαῶν

ὑψιφάεινον ON: ὑψιφάεννον BI ὑετίοις νιφετοῖσιν codd.: ὑετίοις νιφετοῖς τε Lloyd-Jones/Parsons ὑπαὶ Viger: ὑπὲρ codd. πύργοις συνόροισιν Gifford: πύργοισιν ὅροισιν codd.: πύργοισιν ὀρεινοῖς Viger πέδῳ codd.: πέδου Lloyd-Jones/Parsons

...for the high-shining flow, rushing forth joyfully in wet rains, winds its way under the neighbouring towers, and makes the dry dust of the bed of the spring far-shining, a glorious wonder of the people.

We cannot be sure exactly what distance separated this fragment from the previous one, but the two are closely connected. Eusebius reports Polyhistor as saying that Philo, at some point below, adds to fr. 683 this further description of the filling waters (οἷς πάλιν ὑποβὰς περὶ τῆς πληρώσεως ἐπιλέγει). The implication of ὑψιφάεινον is that the ῥεῦμα here flows down from a high source before turning under the neighbouring towers (ὑπαὶ πύργοις συνόροισιν).[75] Of water, one can compare the later use of the adjective by Nonnus to describe the rain of Zeus at *D.* 21.335 ὑψιφανὴς Διὸς ὄμβρος.

The collocation ὑετίοις νιφετοῖσιν provides uncertain sense. It has often been taken to mean 'rainy snow', but νιφετός is better understood here as 'rain'. Significant in this respect is the use of νιφετός to mean rain at *Deut.* 32: 2.[76] I argue below that Philo may be alluding to this specific passage, in which water is used as a metaphor for the song of Moses. If correct, this would explain the unusual combination of ὑέτιος and νιφετός, which will have a sense similar to 'wet rains' or 'rain showers'.[77]

The phrase ξηρὰ πέδῳ κεκονιμένα κρήνης must mean 'the dry dust on the bed of the spring'. Lloyd-Jones and Parsons, whose conjecture πέδου for πέδῳ would provide more comfortable syntax, rightly link the dry πέδον to the spring rather than a plain outside Jerusalem, as others have done.[78] As they point out,

---

[75] The clever conjecture of Gifford ὑπαὶ πύργοις συνόροισιν (with ὑπαί adopted from Viger) is recommended by the very slight change required from the transmitted ὑπὲρ πύργοισιν ὅροισιν, which is clearly corrupt—ὑπέρ is very rarely joined with the dative and the two nouns πύργος and ὄρος cannot be construed together.

[76] Cf. *Dan.* 3:68. This use of νιφετός in the Septuagint is noted also by Holladay 1983–96, 2. 289, who summarizes previous discussion.

[77] Also possible here would be Lloyd-Jones/Parsons' suggestion ὑετίοις νιφετοῖς τε 'in rains and showers' in *SH* ad loc.

[78] See Holladay 1983–96, 2.292–4 on this interpretation by Mras and Walter.

Polyhistor's introduction to his citation of fr. 683 specifies that Philo describes a spring drying up in the winter and filling in the summer (φησὶ δὲ ὁ Φίλων ἐν τοῖς περὶ Ἱεροσολύμων κρήνην εἶναι, ταύτην δὲ ἐν μὲν τῷ χειμῶνι ξηραίνεσθαι, ἐν δὲ τῷ θέρει πληροῦσθαι). The subject of δείκνυσι is most naturally the ῥεῦμα of the beginning of the fragment, with τηλεφαῆ attached to ξηρὰ κεκονιμένα: not only is there a fitting parallelism in a ῥεῦμα ὑψιφάεινον making the dry bed of a spring τηλεφαῆ, but it is notable that the rare form τηλεφαής describes the κόνις of a burial mound in a third-century B.C. funerary epigram for Hermias found in Smyrna (Peek *GV* I 1745). Thus: 'And [the high-shining flow makes the dry dust of the bed of the fountain far-shining, a preeminent marvel of the people'.[79]

fr. 685

αἰπὺ δ' ἄρ' ἐκπτύουσι διὰ χθονὸς ὑδροχόοισι
σωλῆνες

ὑδροχόοισι codd.: ὑδροχύτοιο Faulkner

... and through the earth, pipes in flowing channels spit out precipitously...

Polyhistor reports that this is part of Philo's description of the draining of the archpriest's fountain (εἶτα πάλιν περὶ τῆς τοῦ ἀρχιερέως κρήνης καὶ τῆς ἀποχετεύσεως διέξεισιν οὕτως). It is difficult to construe ὑδροχόοισι within the quoted text. In the context of draining liquid, the pipes (σωλῆνες) presumably spit out water,[80] just as the verb on other occasions describes bodies of water spitting out liquid.[81] Elsewhere, ὑδροχόος means 'water-pourer', appearing most commonly as the name of the constellation Aquarius. Here, it would mean something through which water flows, and has plausibly been taken to signify 'in channels' or 'in conduits'.[82] The reading is perhaps suspect, although there is little to go on in such a short fragment. Given Philo's penchant for rare or unique vocabulary, one might consider emending to something such as ὑδροχύτοιο, a *hapax legomenon* found in Euripides' *Cyclops* of springs gushing with water (κρήναις παρ' ὑδροχύτοις, 66), with the corresponding form of κρήνη understood. The sense would then be something like: 'pipes through

---

[79] Cf. Lloyd-Jones/Parsons *SH* ad loc., 'sicca ista et pulverulenta alvei fontani conspicua reddit'.
[80] *Pace* Holladay 1983–96, 2.297, who takes the verb to describe the pipes jutting out.
[81] See LSJ s.v. πτύω 2, and for the compound of a body of water spitting something forth, see the third-century B.C. epigrammatist Theodoridas σκολιὸς δ' ἐξέπτυσε πορθμός (*AP* 6.224.5). On the metaphorical use of the verb, see below n. 90.
[82] See Holladay 1983–96, 2. 298.

the ground spit out [water] precipitously from the gushing [spring].' Compare Herodotus' description of the Samian tunnel through which water is carried in pipes to the city (δι' οὗ τὸ ὕδωρ ὀχετευόμενον διὰ σωλήνων παραγίνεται ἐς τὴν πόλιν ἀγόμενον ἀπὸ μεγάλης πηγῆς, 3. 60).[83]

> fr. 686
>
> τοῖσιν ἕδος μακαριστὸν ὅλης μέγας ἔκτισεν ἄκτωρ
> ὕψιστος καὶ πρόσθεν ἀπ' Ἀβραάμοιο καὶ Ἰσάκ
> Ἰακὼβ εὐτέκνοιο, τόθεν Ἰωσήφ, ὃς ὀνείρων
> θεσπιστὴς σκηπτούχῳ ἐν Αἰγύπτοιο θρόνοισιν
> δινεύσας λαθραῖα χρόνου πλημμυρίδι μοίρης.
>
> ὅλης ION: ὅλως B: ὅλου Ludwich λαθραῖα Stephanus: λατραῖα codd.
>
> ...and for them the great leader, the most-high, fashioned the most blessed seat of the whole [earth], even early on from the time of Abraham and Isaac, and of Jacob rich in children, from whom came Joseph, who was an interpreter of dreams for the king upon the thrones of Egypt, spinning the secrets of time in the current of fate...

This fragment, separated by an unknown distance from the previous description of the waters of Jerusalem,[84] traces the lineage of Abraham down to Joseph, on whom Philo expands as the dream interpreter of Pharaoh (cf. Genesis 37–50). The identity of the μέγας ἄκτωρ in the first line is, while disputed, most probably God. This is strongly suggested by the epithet at the outset of line two, which in the Septuagint is used only of God.[85] The conjecture σκηπτούχῳ of Lloyd-Jones and Parsons for the transmitted σκηπτοῦχος in line four also seems preferable. While it is not impossible that Joseph, who was given extraordinary powers in Egypt, is described as scepter-bearer on the throne of Egypt, this explicitly contradicts the limit of his powers given by Pharaoh in Genesis 41: 40 (πλὴν τὸν θρόνον ὑπερέξω σου ἐγώ). [86] The specific expression ἐν Αἰγύπτοιο θρόνοισι strongly suggests Pharaoh.

---

83 For a body of water flowing διὰ χθονός see Q.S. 6. 466–7 Παρθενίου, ὅς τ' εἰσὶ διὰ χθονὸς ἠΰτ' ἔλαιον | πόντον ἐς Εὔξεινον προχέων καλλίρροον ὕδωρ.

84 On the vexed question of whether this fragment formed part of a fourteenth book of Philo's poem, as the transmitted commentary in Eusebius indicates, or came in the first or fourth book of a shorter poem, see the summary of scholarship in Kuhn 2012, 72. It is not inconceivable that the poem extended to fourteen books.

85 See Kuhn 2012, 46–7 and for a list of parallels Holladay 1983–96, 2.268. Others have suggested less plausibly that Philo refers here to Joseph or Pharaoh.

86 Kuhn 2012, 48, in defence of the nominative, appeals unconvincingly to the comments concerning Joseph which immediately precede Polyhistor's quotation of this fragment (Eus. PE 9.23): neither συσταθέντα βασιλεῖ nor τῆς Αἰγύπτου δεσπότης (the first certainly and the second

The Symbolism of Jerusalem's Waters

Springs, rivers and streams, as well as the thirst and dryness brought about by their absence, are well established poetological metaphors in the Greek poetic tradition from the archaic period onward. In Hellenistic poetry, an interest in rivers and springs is pronounced: Callimachus' interest in rivers (on which he wrote a prose treatise) and water metaphors linked to poetry is well known, while rivers are intimately tied to the foundation narratives and poetic structures of both Callimachus' poetry and Apollonius' *Argonautica*.[87] It is notable therefore that, to judge from these fragments, waters seem to have played a role in Philo's own Hellenistic foundation narrative of Jerusalem.

Certain points of the language and imagery associated with springs, founts, and streams in the surviving fragments of Philo suggest a metaphorical association of song and water that goes beyond the *realia* of the description. Most striking in this respect is fr. 683. 2–3: as discussed above, the text is difficult to construe with any precision, but we can at the very least say that a description of gushing streams of water (ῥεύματος ἐμπίπλησι βαθὺν ῥόον ἐξανιείσης) and a bath/pool (λοετροῖς) begins in line two with what the manuscripts transmit as σὺν ἀοιδᾷ ('with song'). At the beginning of the last century, Gifford, in his edition of Eusebius, cleverly suggested emending this to the rare adjective συναοιδά. The contracted form συνῳδός can be used metaphorically in non-acoustic contexts to mean 'according to' or 'in harmony with',[88] such that the adverbial form here can indicate water flowing 'in harmony with the baths'. On another level, however, the choice of vocabulary hints at an equivalence of water and poetry. The poetic form συναοιδός is attested only once elsewhere, in Euripides *HF* 785–9:

> σὺν τ' Ἀσωπιάδες κόραι
> πατρὸς ὕδωρ βᾶτε λιποῦσαι συναοιδοί
> Νύμφαι τὸν Ἡρακλέους
> καλλίνικον ἀγῶνα.

One cannot, of course, be certain that Philo was thinking of this particular passage in his choice of vocabulary, but it should be noted that the context of Euri-

---

probably drawn from the historian Artapanus) justify the description of Joseph as sceptre-bearer on the throne of Egypt.

87 Cf. *Hy.* 2.105–10 and *Ep.* 28. See e.g. Depew 2007, Cameron 1995, 403–7, Williams 1978, 85–9. For poetry and water imagery, see also Powell *CA Lyrica Adespota* 20 Μνημοσύνη (pp. 191–2).
88 See LSJ ad loc. II. For the neuter plural used adverbially cf. Ar. *Av.* 635 ἐμοὶ φρονῶν ξυνῳδά.

pides' use of the word is particularly apposite should Philo be hinting at singing waters: the lyric chorus call upon the water nymphs, daughters of Asopus, to come and sing with them, having just called also upon the water nymph Dirce to dance with them.

One other point of language in this fragment recalls Hellenistic literary waters. Prior to Quintus Smyrnaeus, the combination βαθὺς ῥόος is attested elsewhere only once, and at the same *sedes* of the line, in Apollonius Rhodius' *Argonautica* 4.627–9: the Argonauts are there said to enter the deep stream of Rhodanus (Rhône), at the point where it mixes with the river Eridanos (Po) in a churning of waters (ἐκ δὲ τόθεν Ῥοδανοῖο βαθὺν ῥόον εἰσεπέρησαν | ὅς τε εἰς Ἠριδανὸν μετανίσεται, ἄμμιγα δ' ὕδωρ | ἐν ξυνοχῇ βέβρυχε κυκώμενον). As in the Philo fragment, the phrase is used in the context of mixing waters, although for Philo the union is harmonious (συναοιδά), whereas in Apollonius the waters come together in confusion (ἄμμιγα). It has furthermore been noted that the confluence of rivers in the Apollonian passage may have metapoetic significance. The Argonauts at this point in their journey first take a wrong turn up a river (apparently the Rhine), a mistake which Apollonius says would have brought them to an ἀεικελίη ἄτη (4.637), due to the fact that the river exits into Ocean, had Hera not turned them back: Romm and Jones have both argued that this redirection away from Ocean signals symbolically a departure from Homeric poetics towards an Alexandrian aesthetic.[89]

In fr. 684 the vocabulary again recalls a passage in which water is employed as a metaphor for poetry, but this time the text in question is not of the tradition of Greek poetry but a well-known passage of Jewish scripture. In the Septuagint translation of Deut. 32: 1–2, Moses memorably begins his ode to the people of Israel by comparing his song to various forms of water:

> πρόσεχε, οὐρανέ, καὶ λαλήσω,
> καὶ ἀκουέτω γῆ ῥήματα ἐκ στόματός μου.
> προσδοκάσθω ὡς ὑετὸς τὸ ἀπόφθεγμά μου,
> καὶ καταβήτω ὡς δρόσος τὰ ῥήματά μου,
> ὡσεὶ ὄμβρος ἐπ' ἄγρωστιν
> καὶ ὡσεὶ νιφετὸς ἐπὶ χόρτον.

The unusual combination ὑετίοις νιφετοῖσι in the first line of Philo fr. 684, discussed above, combines the first and the last of Moses' comparisons, ὑετός and νιφετός, both of which refer to rain. Could the awkwardly tautologous expression therefore have a particular allusive function, which evokes the associations

---

[89] See Romm 1992, 195–6 and Jones 2005, 79–80.

of water and song in Jewish tradition? It is perhaps also worth noting in this respect the adjective πολυγηθής, employed here uniquely of flowing water. Used in Homer of the seasons (*Il.* 21.450) and elsewhere of Dionysus (e.g. Hes. *Th.* 941), in the first lines of the second book of *Sibylline Oracles* (1–3) it describes the prophetic voice of divine words given by God to the Sibyl, who is said, like Moses, to sing an ode:

ἦμος δὴ κατέπαυσε θεὸς πολυπάνσοφον ᾠδήν,
πολλὰ λιταζομένης, καί μοι πάλιν ἐν στήθεσσιν
ἔνθετο θεσπεσίων ἐπέων πολυγηθέα φωνήν.

Such traces as these are, I think, tantalizing, despite the uncertainty inherent in the fragmentary nature of the poem,[90] and suggest that Philo deserves more credit as a poet than scholars have thus far afforded him. Let me close with one final observation. Beyond the three fragments which describe the waters of Jerusalem (683–5), it is striking that Philo makes metaphorical use of language associated with water on two other occasions in the limited remains of his poem. In line five of fr. 686, we hear of the prophet Joseph 'spinning the secrets of time in the current of fate' (δινεύσας λαθραῖα χρόνου πλημμυρίδι μοίρης), a description which suggests the practice of hydromancy, an unusual choice for Joseph in and of itself. We have also seen above that the imagery of flowing makes an appearance in line three of fr. 682 in the word ἐπλήμμυρε: if, as I have argued there, this verb has as its grammatical subject the glory of Abraham's race, in the context of a passage that seems to reflect upon literary tradition and poetic inspiration, we may begin to glimpse the larger significance of Philo's waters of Jerusalem, in which Jewish and Hellenic poetics flow together συναοιδά.

---

90 Despite the brevity of the fragment, one might also consider whether the verb ἐκπτύω in fr. 685, seemingly used of spring water emitting from pipes, could also have metapoetic resonances. In a Hellenistic lyric fragment, Homer is described spitting out poetry like the sea, *CA* 10 τήν τ' ἀπὸ Μουσῶν ἄφθιτον αὐδήν / ἣν σὺ μερίμναις ταῖσιν ἀτρύτοις / καθυφηνάμενος πόντος τις ὅπως ἔπτυσας ἄλ[λο]ις. For ἐκπτύω of the sea spitting out water, cf. the Hellenistic epigrammatist Theodoridas (quoted above in n. 81).

V. Contexts

Annette Harder
Spiders in the Greek Wide Web?

1. Introduction

When one reads the works of Callimachus, particularly the *Aetia*, one is struck by the many different places that are mentioned and by the way in which the reader is constantly carried through the Greek world in all directions. In recent studies on Callimachus these geographical aspects of his work have been a subject of investigation and it has been plausibly suggested that all these references to Greek locations must have helped to create a sense of Greek identity[1]. One could, however, try to get a little further with this kind of research and to form a clearer picture of the *kind* of Greek world Callimachus presents in his work and how this fits in with his position as a poet connected with the Ptolemaic court in Alexandria. The starting point for this investigation are recent publications by John Ma and Irad Malkin. In an article of 2003 and in his monograph on the "small Greek world" of 2011[2] Malkin studies the Greek world as a "decentralized network" of Greek cities and colonies in the archaic period until V BC. He observes what he calls a "new Greek convergence", stimulated by the fact that because of the process of colonization the Greeks came to live far apart and sought a "virtual center"[3], based on a combination of connecting elements such as a mythic framework, genealogy, festivals and religion (with a strong focus on Delphi and Apollo) and the ties between colony and mother city. Within this network there is no hierarchy of "Greece" (as overlapping with modern Greece) as centre and the colonies as periphery, which one could describe as "tree and branches": on the contrary, "Hellas functioned more as an abstract term that covered the wide, fragmented Greek horizons of the islands and coasts of the Black Sea and the Mediterranean" (Malkin 2011, 51). So, there seems to have been a kind of network of participants of equal status connected by the sea on which most of them were bordering. The new towns and colonies were

---

[1] See on these issues within the framework of Ptolemaic politics Harder 2003 (particularly on the temporal dimensions); Männlein-Robert 2010, 178 (about the geographical dimension of *Aetia* fr.1) and Asper 2011 (on the 'geopoetics' and 'chronopoetics' of Callimachus' works, particularly the *Aetia* and the *Iambi*, and the way in which Callimachus used space and time to offer his readers a sense of ethnic unity and identity in spite of an apparently disorderly presentation).
[2] See the bibliography.
[3] See Malkin 2011, 54.

all part of a "small Greek world" and participated in a sense of Greekness and shared an awareness of "sameness". Thus "the result was a civilization that was undeniably Greek"[4]. This perception was made more concrete by an emphasis on foundation myths, cults of founders, connections with the mother city, links with the oracle at Delphi (which often sanctioned the foundation of colonies), taking part in the Panhellenic games and in the cults of the Panhellenic gods, particularly Apollo[5].

Malkin's work applies to the archaic period and invites the question: what happened afterwards and what became of the web in the course of time? Was it a permanent feature of the ancient world? Did the fact that ca. 500 BC certain "zones of influence" were developing[6] and subsequently the rise of the Hellenistic kingdoms lead to fundamental changes? These questions have been dealt with by historians, such as Jonn Ma, who have, in fact, observed that in spite of the new political constellation also in the Hellenistic age "there existed a strong network of self-governing, articulate, ideologically confident *poleis*, which covered much of the Hellenistic world and was crucial in determining the texture of this world"[7]. Thus, while Malkin's focus is on the archaic age, Ma shows that this state of affairs was in fact continued throughout the Hellenistic age, when, in spite of the rule of the Ptolemaic kings in large capitals, the network of Greek *poleis*, which functioned on the basis of "peer polity interaction" was continued and flourished on a local level.

This article will address the question whether aspects of this general sense of Greekness and a network of Greek city-states can also be found in the Greek world as presented in the poetry of the Hellenistic period in III BC. Was the sense of a Greek Wide Web still alive in the work of poets such as Callimachus, Apollonius Rhodius and Lycophron, who worked within the framework of the new Hellenistic kingdoms? Can one see traces of a different attitude in which the new kingdoms with their flourishing capitals formed the centre and the other parts of the Greek world became the periphery? All three authors are relevant and interesting in this respect, because their works encompass large areas of the world in a geographical as well as in a historical sense and may suggest specific ways of looking at this world.

---

[4] Malkin 2011, 24.
[5] On the role of myth and ritual in a network context see in general also e.g. Kowalzig 2007.
[6] See Malkin 2011, 40–41 on the "centralization process" and "concentration on major hubs" that developed in the course of time.
[7] See Ma 2003b, 13, with references to older literature on the subject, and his conclusion on p. 34 that the archaic world with its networks of *poleis* is in fact "closely related to that of Hellenistic peer polity interaction".

A strong dimension of space and time is visible in Callimachus' *Aetia*, which begins with the early history of the human race in the generation of Minos and the other pre-Homeric heroes, such as Heracles and the Argonauts, and ends with the story of the lock of Berenice in the poet's own time. Geographically the *Aetia* covers most of the known world, from Sicily to Asia Minor and from Egypt to Thracia. In a similar way Apollonius Rhodius in his *Argonautica* covers the world as travelled by the Argonauts, from Greece to Colchis at the end of the Black Sea and back with big detours in the West and in Libya. The temporal dimension in this work is present through the notion of the Argonauts "leaving traces even in our time" by the foundation of cults and monuments. In a different way also Lycophron's *Alexandra* covers a large part of the world and its history, but here these are viewed from the Trojan perspective. The work covers the period of the Trojan War and its aftermath through the return of the various heroes and their histories as well as the history of West and East in later days. Geographically this includes most of the Greek world, including (Rome and) the Western areas[8].

2. Callimachus: traces of a Greek network in the *Aetia*

2.1 General observations

For the purpose of this article I will first focus on Callimachus' *Aetia*[9] for a more detailed investigation. On a general level it is striking that Callimachus in his *Aetia* presents a Greek world, surrounding the Mediterranean, very much like the archaic world described as a network of Greek towns and islands by Malkin and the world of "peer polity interaction" as described by Ma. Both the timespan of the stories and the geographical dimensions fit in with that picture. The presentation of the stories seems to underline the notion of a network without hierarchy, as we have no systematic chronological ordering of the stories, but only a rough chronological line from Minos to Berenice II[10]. The towns and islands may

---

[8] It would be interesting to explore Lycophron further from this point of view, but for reasons of space I will largely leave him out of account in this article.
[9] For similar approaches of the *Aetia* and its importance for the establishment of a Greek cultural identity in Ptolemaic Alexandria see e.g. Asper 2001, Selden 1998, Männlein-Robert 2010, 166–83.
[10] See Harder 2003; 2012, 1, 18–20 and in relation to networks Malkin 2011, 11.

be connected in a variety of ways, often of an associative nature, as e.g. the links between the first stories of the *Aetia*, where the story of the scurrilous ritual at Anaphe seems to inspire that of the scurrilous ritual for Heracles at Lindos, which because of the killing of an ox seems to lead on to the story of Heracles and Thiodamas[11]. Thus the organisation of the *Aetia* seems to mirror the idea of a network of Greek settlements of equal status and shows no indications of centre and periphery.

2.2 The Panhellenic dimension

If one looks through all the stories in the *Aetia* systematically it is striking that the stories are often of a very *local* nature, such as could be found in the work of local historians, and thus seem to reflect the ongoing importance of such traditions. Examples are Xenomedes of Ceos, from whose work Callimachus derived the love story of Acontius, the ancestor of the ruling family on Ceos, as he tells us in fr. 75,53–77, or the work of the Argive Hagias and Dercylus, who are mentioned as a source in an ancient commentary on the story about the sacrifices to the Graces on Paros (fr. 7a,15–16). Even so, these local stories are related to *Panhellenic* gods and characters. To stay with the examples just mentioned: in the story of Acontius there is a strong element of Panhellenic Greek cult. Acontius meets his beloved Cydippe, whom he eventually marries, at Delos, at a Panhellenic festival for Apollo, where people from all over Greece converge, among them the young Acontius from Ceos and the girl Cydippe from Naxos (fr. 67). Other Panhellenic elements are found throughout the story. Thus the goddess Artemis plays a central part, because she takes care that Cydippe fulfils the oath she had unwittingly sworn to marry Acontius. Her Panhellenic character is brought to the reader's attention because before mentioning her sojourn at Delos Apollo first mentions a number of places across the Greek world where she could also be: he tells that she was not fighting the Cimmerians and Lygdamis in Asia Minor nor plaiting rushes in Sparta nor washing herself in the river Parthenius in Paphlagonia, South of the Black Sea (fr. 75,23–25). Other passages evoke Zeus, who caused the blowing of the Etesian winds to bring some relief to Ceos from the heat of summer (fr. 75,32–37); an oracle of Apollo consulted by Cydippe's father when his daughter keeps falling ill (fr. 75,21–38); and the early history of Ceos, when the Olympian gods destroyed the island because of the evil behaviour of its inhabitants (fr. 75,64–69). Thus we get the impression of a local love story, explain-

---

[11] See fr. 7c-25d. The fragments are quoted from Harder 2012.

ing the rule of a local family on Ceos, but at the same time firmly embedded in the Greek tradition. It becomes clear that the relatively small island attracts the interest and attention of a number of Panhellenic gods and thus shares in the larger history and religious and mythical framework of the Greek world on an equal footing and as part of an extensive network.

The same can be said about the other example mentioned above, the story of the Graces at Paros (fr.3–7b), where we have the explanation of a local ritual: at Paros the sacrifice to the Graces takes place without garlands and music. Here too the explanation involves Panhellenic characters: when Minos, who had extended his sea power from Crete over the Greek islands, was sacrificing to the Graces at Paros he was told that his son Androgeos had died in Athens. He then went on with the sacrifice, but refrained from garlands and music. Thus again the explanation of a local ritual on a small island is closely connected with Greek myth in general and its mainstream heroes and places.

If we read through the remains of the *Aetia* this kind of connection between local traditions and mainstream Greek cults and heroes can be observed in most of its aetiological stories[12]. All kinds of small towns or islands are presented in a way that shows that they are part of a larger network of Greek settlements. In some examples we can even observe a general tendency, also mentioned by Malkin, to reduce the local elements of stories in favour of more Panhellenic versions. Thus in the story of the anonymous founder ritual at Zancle in fr. 43–43a, we see how the original founders, Crataemenes (from Chalcis) and Perieres (from Cumae, which was founded from Chalcis), disqualify themselves by quarrelling about the town's name and are then banished from the town's cult by the oracle of Apollo, who orders that the cult will be anonymous[13]. This fits in with Malkin's observations about a tendency to adapt the foundation myths in the course of time. At first the new colonies seem to be proud of their "real" historical founders, who appear in stories and are honoured with special cults. Then, gradually, there is a shift of focus, as in e.g. Croton, where the original local founding hero Myscellus is replaced by Heracles, so that the colony becomes part of Panhellenic history and seems to have a long history, reaching far back into the heroic past, just like its mother city[14]. Thus the effect of the colonization was that it led to a world filled by Greeks and that this Greekness was

---

[12] Only rarely there seems to be no Panhellenic connection, as in e.g. the scapegoat ritual at Abdera in fr. 90–90b, but in these few cases we cannot exclude that this is due to the fragmentary state of our evidence.
[13] See on the these aspects of the foundation of Zancle also Malkin 2011, 56–57.
[14] See Malkin 2011, 120–21.

stimulated and made visible by a number of means, creating a "Greek Wide Web".

2.3 Co-operation and interaction

An interesting aspect of the stories of the *Aetia* is also that they present a world in which there was a great deal of interaction between the towns and islands, all on a basis of apparent equality. One reads that they all send embassies to Panhellenic events, as in the story of Acontius and Cydippe, or that they are connected by bonds of marriage, like Naxos and Ceos in the same story. In other instances we can observe that towns co-operate in the fulfilment of religious duties for Panhellenic gods. A good example of this kind of co-operation is the story of the sacrifices of the Hyperboreans in fr. 186. When the girls who used to bring these sacrifices from the far North to Apollo at Delos were raped, a new system was invented in which the various peoples along the route brought the sacrifices from their borders to the next border, where their neighbours took over, so that eventually the sacrifices were handed down through a range of peoples until they reached Delos. Also in other stories there is a great deal of peaceful movement related to religious events, such as the bringing of wreaths to Apollo in Delphi from the Tempe valley (fr. 86–89a), or we get a picture of the movements of athletes as in fr. 84–85a (Euthycles) and 98–99b (Euthymus) [15]. In this respect the world of the *Aetia* also closely resembles the Hellenistic world as described by Ma 2003b, which was characterized by a large amount of "peer polity interaction" between the various *poleis*.

There are also stories where Panhellenic heroes or Panhellenic religious traditions help to establish order between peoples. Thus there is much attention for the travels of Heracles, performing his various tasks and playing his part in civilizing the world by the destruction of monsters and villains and the elimination of disorder. A particularly interesting example in this respect is his treatment of the uncivilized Dryopians, a people of robbers and brigands, whose king Thiodamas refuses to feed Heracles' starving son Hyllus in fr. 24–25d. The scholia on Apollonius Rhodius tell us that after defeating these people in a battle Heracles transported them to the Peloponnese, where they mixed with other people and because of this gradually lost their evil state of mind (fr. 25b). Another example

---

[15] For the notion of human connectors in the network of Greek towns see also Malkin 2011, 27–31, where he discusses a.o. the way in which specialists arrive in the newfound colony in Aristophanes' *Birds*.

concerns the war between two towns in Asia Minor. In the love story of Phrygius and Pieria (fr. 80–83b) we hear how Myus and Miletus had long been at war and only suspended the fighting during a festival for Artemis at Miletus, to which the people of Myus could come without being harmed. At this festival Phrygius, the king of Miletus, fell in love with Pieria, a girl from Myus and offered her a present. The girl chose peace between their towns and thus the war was ended. This is an interesting case of shared Greek religious values, which first inspire a first step towards the relaxing of the war and are then followed by the more general human impulses of love and gratitude which lead to a civilized solution and bring the end of the war.

As we may see particularly in these last few examples, but elsewhere too, the interaction often has moral overtones: wars end in peace, as in the case of Miletus and Myus, human sacrife at Tenedos ends when Orestes comes to the island (fr. 92a), the love of Acontius and Cydippe leads to a new and stable dynasty of rulers on Ceos after a turbulent history during which the gods' anger had almost destroyed the whole population of the island, and the people of Isindus, who maltreat strangers, are excluded from the festival of the Panionia (fr. 78–78c). It looks as if, in the *Aetia*, a general sense of Greekness and shared Greek values helps to create a better world—or at least that Callimachus wanted to present such a picture to his readers and hint that this was the way the world should work, ideally. Thus the world of the *Aetia* seems a generally peaceful network, where occasional disturbances and misdemeanour are corrected.

2.4 The role of Alexandria

This leads to the question: what about Alexandria, which was the political and cultural centre of Callimachus' world? Does the *Aetia* not reflect this position and does it not give signs of a new kind of hierarchy in the Greek world with Ptolemaic Alexandria as its centre?

In our remains of the *Aetia* the town appears three times, although it is not mentioned explicitly. In fr. 178 it probably is the setting of a symposium at the home of the Athenian Pollis, who, though in Egypt, still celebrates the Anthesteria. At this symposium the narrator, "Callimachus", hears the story of Peleus' death at Icus from Theogenes, a stranger from Icus who is on business in Egypt. Here we see Alexandria as part of the wider Greek world embedded in a circuit of business travel and migration, attracting people from Athens and Icus. Through the story of Peleus, the father of Achilles, the Greek cultural inheritance of the *Iliad* comes into the picture too and, to cap it all, Callimachus has phrased his text in a way which makes it strongly reminiscent of the part of the *Odyssey* where Odysseus tells his story at the symposium of the Phaeacian king Alcinous[16]. So here we really have "network Greekness" at its most intricate and Alexandria seems to be at the centre of it, attracting people from various Greek places and providing a setting for an Athenian festival and poetry in the Panhellenic tradition.

The other appearances of Alexandria in the *Aetia* are in the poems for Berenice II, which frame books 3 and 4 and were probably added to a second edition of the work[17]. The first reference is in fr. 54,4–6, where at the beginning of the *Victory of Berenice* we read that the message of Berenice's victory came to Alexandria. Here the message's arrival at the town is described in a way which relates it closely to the Greek mythical tradition, as the phrasing εἰς Ἑλένη[ς νησῖδ]α καὶ εἰς Παλληνέα μά[ντιν] | ποιμένα [φωκάων] ("to Helen's island and the Pallenean seer, the sealherd") evokes scenes from Greek literature by means of a technique similar to that used in fr. 178[18]. Also the fact that a message comes from Nemea, the location of the Panhellenic Nemean Games, helps to relate the town to the Greek world outside Egypt. The second reference to Alexandria is at the end of book 4 in the *Lock of Berenice* (fr. 110–110f). Here the town is the setting of the appearance of the new constellation, the Coma Berenices, and of the only aetiological story that refers to the present and future and not to the past. In this poem the Alexandrian queen Berenice II is prominent and forms the centre of attention. Here, at the end of the *Aetia*, we may observe a certain contrast with the preceding books and in fact also with the first edition of the first two books of the *Aetia*, in which the poems about Berenice were not yet there. Although the Panhellenic goddess Aphrodite plays a part in the apotheosis of the lock she is in fr. 110,54–58 explicitly associated with the deified Arsinoe-Zephyritis, who had a sanctuary on cape Zephyrium near Alexandria. It is rather emphatically in this *local* role as Aphrodite-Arsinoe-Zephyritis living on the coast at Canopus that the goddess is responsible for the lock's promotion and its entering the realms of the gods. Thus after all the pictures of a Greek world full of towns and islands sharing in Greekness on an equal footing the picture of Alexandria presented in de *Lock of Berenice* suddenly stands out and may supplement the earlier picture of fr. 178 (which was probably from the beginning of book 2) and the *Victory of Berenice*. The setting of the apotheosis of the lock,

---

16 For details see Harder 2012, ad loc.
17 See e.g. Harder 2012, 1.2–12 (with further references).
18 The "island of Helen" later became part of the mainland, east of Alexandria, where the harbour Canobus was and was connected with the story that Helen tried to cure Canobus, the helmsman of Menelaus.; the "Pallenean seer" is Proteus on Pharos, visited by Menelaus. For details see Harder 2012, ad loc.

which foreshadows the later deification of Berenice and generally looks to the future rather than to the shared Greek past, is very much Alexandria and even the Panhellenic goddess is given a local dimension and appears in the guise of an Alexandrian queen. This seems to give the town a special standing, somewhat like Berenice's lock appearing as ἐν ἀρχαίοις ἄστρον ... νέον "a new star among the old ones" (fr. 110,64, if the supplement is right), and to invite looking back at what preceded from a different angle[19].

2.5 A Greek Wide Web?

In conclusion one can say about Callimachus that his *Aetia* presented the world still very much as the Greek Wide Web as sketched for the archaic period by Malkin. It also fits in with what seems to have been the reality of contemporary *polis* life on a local level as described by Ma 2003a, who summarizes the situation as follows: "This network of relations is a striking feature of the third century, which was also the age when the Hellenistic kings were at their most powerful and determined the high politics of the period. Yet the kings passed, and the *poleis* abided"[20]. However, two aspects of Callimachus' treatment deserve special attention. On the one hand there are the strong moral overtones and the emphasis on the network of towns and islands as a positive force. On the other hand there is the last minute emphasis on Alexandria, which seems to stand out from the Greek Wide Web on its own, self-contained and with an eye on the future. These moral overtones and the Alexandrian point of view may suggest a new perspective on the whole network of Greek communities[21]. It can be made to fit in with recent studies on the role of Hellenistic poetry in relation to the interests of the Ptolemaic court, such as e. g. Rolf Strootman's article on "literature and the kings"[22]. Strootman argues that the notion of an orderly, wealthy and peaceful world under Ptolemaic rule was an important aspect of the Ptolemaic "poetics of power". This notion is found quite explicitly in e. g. Callimachus' *Hymn to Zeus*, where Ptolemy as the king following Zeus' divine example on earth rules in a wealthy and orderly world. On the other hand the idealized picture may be effectively contrasted with the practice of the many wars carried out

---

19 As Ivana Petrovic observes, the picture presented by Callimachus may mirror what happened in the Library, where the efforts to collect most of Greek literature also suggest a Panhellenic effort centred in Alexandria.
20 See Ma 2003b, 36–37.
21 On the importance of the Alexandrian perspective, see also Asper 2011, 164–7.
22 Strootman 2010.

by the Ptolemies in order to achieve and maintain their position: it could serve as an antidote and encouragement.

3. The perspective of Apollonius

A brief glance at Apollonius Rhodius may help to put Callimachus' presentation of the Greek world into a contemporary perspective and suggest interesting possibilities for further study of these issues[23]. In contrast with the *Aetia* Apollonius Rhodius in his *Argonautica* presents a picture of the world that is conceived as consisting of "Hellas" as the home of the Argonauts, largely overlapping with mainland Greece, and a strange and often hostile and exotic world of others outside this area into which the Argonauts are venturing. There are several ways in which Apollonius underlines this view of the world.

It first of all appears in the catalogue of the Argonauts in AR 1.23–227. The Argonauts are mostly from mainland Greece[24], which is thus appearing as "the" Greek world. This state of affairs is underlined by the fact that genealogically most of the Argonauts are connected as descendants of the daughters of Minyas[25] and is reflected in the use of the term Hellas, which is reserved for mainland Greece, to which the Argonauts hope to return at the end of their journey[26], in contrast with its use in the archaic period, when it could even cover parts of Italy[27].

Secondly, the Black Sea as well as parts of the Mediterranean, which already in the archaic period as well as in the world of the *Aetia* are part of the Greek

---

[23] Other authors, such as Posidippus, would also be worth studying in this respect, as their work too has geopoetic dimensions; see e.g. Bing 2005 and the article of Ivana Petrovic in this volume. In Latin literature we find a similar approach in a forthcoming article of Damien Nelis: "Poetry and Politics in Vergil's Georgics", who explores the many references to Italy and the Greek world in the *Georgics*, which, while much in debt to Callimachus' *Aetia*, show an Italocentric picture of the world against a shared cultural heritage and history.

[24] The Argonauts are said to come from Pieria and Thessalia, Locris, Euboea, Attica, Boeotia, the Peoloponnese, Ionia (with Samos and Miletus), Aetolia, Phocis, Thracia. For further discussion of the geography of the catalogue, which is intertextually connected with that of the catalogue of ships in the *Iliad*, see Delage 1930, 38–49; Scherer 2006, 125–34.

[25] Cf. AR 1.228–33.

[26] For (mainland) Hellas mentioned as point of departure and return of the Argonauts cf. e.g. AR 2.1141 ἀφ' Ἑλλάδος and 1164; 2.414 ἐс Ἑλλάδα, 637 and 1192.

[27] See Malkin 2011, 214. It is intriguing in this respect that the word Πανελλάδος is found in Call.*Aet.* fr. 106 from the story about the Roman Gaius, but for lack of context the impact of the word there is not clear.

world, here are often exotic and strange. The people the Argonauts meet or pass are often described as very different from the Greeks: they can be hostile or strange; there are hardly any connections between them and if there are, they are rather in terms of war and hostility; sometimes the Argonauts help to improve the world a little, but the reader is not told about any permanent effects for a better and more connected world because of this. Thus the first stop at Lemnos (AR 1.609–909) seems to set the tone for what is going to follow: a story about war, adultery and criminal and violent revenge, as the men have been involved in wars with the Thracians, from where they abducted captive girls with whom they began adulterous affairs (AR 1.612–14) and the women of Lemnos in revenge killed not only their husbands, but all the men on the island (AR 1.617–19). After Lemnos things only get worse: the Doliones at Cyzicus are neighbours of fearful sons of the earth with six hands (AR 1.942–7), who later attack the Argonauts and are destroyed by them (AR 1.989–1011). A little later they meet the Bebrycian king Amycus, who, blatantly ignoring the conventions of hospitality usual among the Greeks, forces strangers to a boxing match and is ultimately defeated and killed by Polydeuces, after which the Argonauts drive the Bebrycians away and the neighbouring Mariandyni destroy their country (AR 2.1–153). Then they sail through the Black Sea, where they pass a range of strange and exotic peoples, such as the Amazones, Chalybes and Mossynoeci and finally arrive at Colchis, ruled by the hostile Aeetes. The dangers of this part of the world are described in AR 2.627–30, when Jason is making trial of the Argonauts:

> νῦν δὲ περισσὸν δεῖμα καὶ ἀτλήτους μελεδῶνας
> ἄγκειμαι, στυγέων μὲν ἁλὸς κρυόεντα κέλευθα
> νηὶ διαπλώειν, στυγέων δ' ὅτ' ἐπ' ἠπείροιο
> βαίνωμεν, πάντη γὰρ ἀνάρσιοι ἄνδρες ἔασιν.

> But now I am given over to excessive fear and unbearable worries,
> dreading to sail over the chilling paths of the sea in a ship,
> and dreading the time when we set foot on land,
> for everywhere are hostile men.[28]

The Argonauts react in a courageous manner and thus also encourage Jason, who states that they are ἔμπεδοι ἀργαλέοις ἐνὶ δείμασιν ("steadfast in terrible dangers"). Only rarely the Argonauts meet people who seem to adhere to Greek values, such as Cyzicus, who gives them a warn welcome in AR 1.961–84 or the hospitable and friendly Lycus, the king of the Mariandyni (AR 2.751–814), but they too are surrounded by enemies and involved in wars—and ironi-

---

[28] All translations of Apollonius are by Race 2008.

cally it is his former guest Jason who eventually kills Cyzicus (AR 1.1032–5), when the Doliones mistake the Argonauts for enemies and start a battle. The fate of Cyzicus seems to illustrate the futility of adhering to Greek conventions in the grim world beyond Hellas.

While the Argonauts travel to Colchis and back they leave traces everywhere[29]: they establish cults and rituals, found monuments, build tombs, and leave objects in many far away places. All these Argonautic traces are said "to be still there in our time". Still, though they contain elements of Greekness[30], there is no sense of a *network* or of interaction between all these Argonautic remains. Each monument stands on its own, with its individual Greek past, but there is no sense of a coherent Greek world as a result of the Argonauts' journey. Accordingly, monuments may loose their original status in the course of time, like the tomb of Idmon, which later becomes the place of a cult for the local hero Agamestor (AR 2.849–50)[31].

So in Apollonius Rhodius there is some kind of Greek expansion[32], but no sense of a Greek network as in the *Aetia*[33]. There is a clear contrast between Hellas, which largely overlaps with mainland Greece, and the strange and dangerous world outside, full of wars and crimes, monsters and exotic peoples, of which the Argonauts get a first taste already at Lemnos[34].

---

29 See e.g. Harder 1994.
30 Often the Greekness consists only in a name, as in e.g. AR 1.988 Ἰηςονίη ... ὁδός; 1019; 2,296–7; 686–7; 929.
31 See Σ AR 2.849–50b τὸν τάφον τοῦ Ἀγαμήςτοροc λέγουcί τινοc ἥρωοc ἐπιχωρίου.
32 See on this aspect of the *Argonautica* also Hunter 1993b, 159–62; Meyer 2011, 233–5. For an optimistic view of the achievements of the Argonauts in clearing the world "of primordial monsters and brutes that impeded travel and cultural exchanges" and creating possibilites for travel and contact between West and East see Clauss 2000, 26.
33 As Silvia Barbantani remarks, it would be interesting to see whether Apollonius approached these issues from a different angle in his *Ktiseis* (fr. 4–12 Powell). Although the evidence is scanty it may be worth noticing that the fragments as we have them show a certain focus on Asia Minor and the islands in the eastern part of the Aegean Sea (Caunos, Rhodos, Cnidos, Lesbos) and on Egypt (Alexandria and Naucratis). On Apollonius' foundation poems see further Krevans 2000.
34 For a similar view see Sistakou 2012, 100–30, who argues that the world through which the Argonauts are travelling is presented as a fantasy world full of horrors contrasted with the civilized town of Iolcus with its well-built streets, which they leave behind in AR 1.317–8.

4. Conclusion

In the previous chapters two rather different pictures of the Greek world have emerged[35]. On the one hand, there is Apollonius with his focus on mainland Greece as Hellas and the occasional fragmented and faded Greekness on the edges of the Greek world, where everything is grim and exotic. Here in spite of the repeated claims that traces of the Argonauts are still there we do not get any signs of a living and flourishing network of Greek communities. On the other hand, the picture of the Greek world in the archaic and Hellenistic age, as a network of towns and islands sharing in Greekness, appears in Callimachus' *Aetia*, where it acquires moral connotations and at the end of the work seems to be combined with a new strongly Alexandrian perspective on the future, which in view of Ptolemaic claims suggests that the old world may be able to survive in a new setting with new guarantees of riches, peace and order.

Now it should be emphasized that all these views are ultimately the views of *poets* on the Greek world, given in the increasingly important medium of books. In the *Aetia*, which seems to be closest to the picture sketched by Malkin and Ma, we see that the Greek network of towns and islands which appears as a living and working organism in the real world, has become a "bookish" network: a Greek Wide Web that can be shaped and modified by the poet as he sees fit to suit his own poetic and ideological agenda as well as the political claims of the rulers at Alexandria. In the *Argonautica* the notion of a web is altogether absent and seems to be, in fact, contradicted in favour of a world-view that presents mainland Greece as Hellas and the rest of the world as a dangerous area into which the Greeks are venturing. The spiders that to a large extent rule the web or decide on the lack of it are the poets working in the environment of the Ptolemaic court. The fact that they take such different positions should be taken into consideration in further studies on the interaction and differences between the two poets.

---

35 Lycophron's *Alexandra* again shows a different perspective. Here too large parts of the Greek world and its history come into the picture, but the perspective is that of the Trojan princess Cassandra, who predicts the future: the Trojan War, its aftermath and the return of the Greeks heroes, and the later course of history with its recurring conflicts between East and West. Here the overruling emphasis is that on the enmity between the Greek world and the East, as befits the speaker's perspective: we get a picture of the Greek world in lasting conflict with the East and the energy of this world seems to be directed towards external conflict rather than towards internal networking. Even so it would be worth exploring how this Greek world is organized: which towns and islands does it include, how do they work together, are there signs of centre and periphery or rather of a network on the basis of equality, which elements are used to describe this world?

Ivana Petrovic
Posidippus and Achaemenid royal propaganda*

Most scholars now agree that the collection of 112 epigrams from the Milan Papyrus, which was written toward the end of the 3rd century BC and published about a decade ago, is probably the work of Posidippus of Pella. A remarkable feature of the papyrus is the division of text into sequences: At the start of our papyrus, the final letters of a heading "ka" have been interpreted as λιθικά "stones". Other headings are better preserved: We have οἰωνοσκοπικά "bird omens", ἀναθεματικά "dedications", ἀνδριαντοποιικά "statues", ἱππικά, "horse racing", ναυαγικά "shipwrecks", ἰαματικά "thanksgiving for cures", τρόποι "characters".[1] The subtitle of the third sequence, [ἐπιτύμβια] "epitaphs" has been completely restored. The headings testify to Posidippus' debt to the traditional genres of inscriptional epigrams and to his interest in exploring the literary dimension of the inscribed text. By molding his collection after the form of inscriptional genres, such as dedicatory inscriptions and epitaphs, Posidippus invited readers to negotiate different levels and forms of epigrammatic contextualization.

The sequence of epigrams on stones—Lithika—comes at the head of the collection and is programmatic in many ways. As is often the case with Hellenistic poetry, poetological interpretations of the poems are prominent. Scholars have compared the epigrammatic genre with the stones Posidippus describes, and the fine art of the engravers (Posidippus mentioned several by name) with the subtle art of the epigrammatic poet. Astute observations have been made on the way Posidippus plays with the origins of the genre itself. Epigram, the first Greek literary genre, and one that originated as epi-gramma, "in-scription", became so refined and sophisticated in the hands of Posidippus that it could be attached to precious rubies and glittering crystals. It was also versatile enough

---

* I am grateful to Markus Asper, Paola Ceccarelli, Barney Chesterton, Johannes Haubold, Lloyd Llewellyn-Jones, Susan Stephens, and Mark Woolmer for comments on drafts of this essay. Earlier versions were presented at conferences in Thessaloniki and Exeter, and as research papers in Florence and Reading, where I also benefited from helpful feedback.
Posidippus' text is quoted after: *New Poems Attributed to Posidippus: An Electronic Text-in progress*, Revised and periodically updated by Benjamin Acosta-Hughes, Elizabeth Kosmetatou, Martine Cuypers, and Francesca Angiò, version 12.1 Newly revised and updated, August 2011. http://chs.harvard.edu/wa/pageR?tn=ArticleWrapper&bdc=12&mn=3990 accessed on 5.2.2012.
1 On the papyrus, see Stephens/Obbink 2004.

to be imagined on both minuscule gems and gigantic rocks serving as divine weapons of mass destruction.

The Milan papyrus is a poetic book, with epigrams carefully arranged by the author himself, or by a later compiler.[2] Scholars have argued that the opening section, Lithika, highlights and announces the main motifs of the collection. The Lithika section not only cleverly hints at the material origins of the genre itself,[3] it announces the sections which are to follow and highlights the leitmotifs of the entire collection: Ptolemaic rule and patronage, royal power and luxury, gifts and exchange, artistic craft, geopoetics.[4] The Lithika also refer to the contexts of the early Greek epigram, such as dedications and grave inscriptions, and performance at symposia. Furthermore, they make references to chariots and horses, omens, and statues, and thus serve as a directory or table of contents of the entire collection.

It has been noted, most prominently by Peter Bing (2005), Ann Kuttner (2005), and Susan Stephens (2004a), that one of the basic themes of the Lithika is poetry in the service of the Ptolemies. As Peter Bing remarked, "The stones exemplify, in their geographical distribution and social construction, both the territorial and cultural/artistic aims of the Ptolemies and their poet, Posidippus ... the section on Stones explores and maps out a political landscape reflecting certain aspirations of sovereignty that set the tone for the whole work".[5]

In this paper, I, too, will investigate the geopoetics of the Lithika. My aim is to explore and trace the origins of the specific way Posidippus represents a Ptolemaic political landscape. If there is indeed a higher unity of poetry and geography in the Lithika,[6] and if the places mentioned in the poems are meant to provide a blueprint for the scope of Ptolemaic royal power, where can we seek the origins of this type of royal propaganda?

It has been noted that the vision of the Ptolemaic Empire that stretches from the East to the West, encompassing the entire known world, is not only prominent in Posidippus' poetry, but is a recurring motif in Alexandrian court poetry. In his *Idyll* 17, Theocritus envisages the scope of Ptolemy Philadelphus' reign as

---

[2] Höschele 2010, 152–156 with an overview of earlier scholarship.
[3] Hunter 2004b.
[4] Stephens 2004a; Bing 2005, 119–120.
[5] Bing 2005, 119–120. See also Stephens 2004a, 170–171.
[6] White 1992, 174 defined geopoetics as a "higher unity of poetry and geography". In his Gray Lectures on "Virgilian Geopoetics" (delivered in Cambridge 2001), Alessandro Barchiesi introduced the term into classical studies. For a recent excellent discussion of geopoetics in Callimachus, see Asper 2011.

encompassing "*all the sea and the land and the crashing rivers*".[7] In a similar vein, Callimachus presents Ptolemy Philadelphus as the future ruler of "*both continents and the lands which are set in the sea, as far as where the end of the earth is and again whence his swift horses carry the sun.*"[8]

In his commentary on Theocritus 17, Richard Hunter noted that the striking claim to universal rule of Ptolemy Philadelphus emulates the image of Zeus in the *Iliad* (12.241–42) and Apollo in the *Homeric Hymn to Apollo* (22–24). Closer to home—chronologically, genealogically and geographically—he sees it as an echo of the prophecy of the Siwa oracle to Alexander.[9] Such claims were a commonplace of Hellenistic royal propaganda, and could also be found in Pharaonic Egyptian texts.[10]

However, Posidippus does not merely mention places which outline the territorial claims of the Ptolemies; he presents the riches and wonders of the world as moving from their places of origin towards Ptolemaic Egypt. His representation of the centre of the empire pulling its resources towards it, like a gigantic magnet, is more akin to a text which has not been discussed in this context: Herodas' first Mime. In this poem, Herodas presents a conversation of two female characters, young and old, with the older trying to persuade the younger woman to renounce her lover, who has left for Egypt months ago, and to take a new one. In this poem, Alexandria is presented as so attractive that it irresistibly pulls resources and manpower from everywhere towards it. Alexandria is depicted as a paradise of luxury and a showpiece of conspicuous consumption, a city to satisfy all tastes and urges—intellectual, material, or sexual:

ἀλλ' ὦ τέκνον, κόσον τιν' ἤδη χηραίνεις
χρόνον μόνη τρύχουσα τὴν μίαν κοίτην;
ἐξ εὖ γὰρ εἰς Αἴγυπτον ἐστάλη Μάνδρις
δέκ' εἰσὶ μῆνες, κοὐδὲ γράμμα σοι πέμπει,
ἀλλ' ἐκλέλησται καὶ πέπωκεν ἐκ καινῆς. (25)
κεῖ δ' ἐστὶν οἶκος τῆς θεοῦ· τὰ γὰρ πάντα,
ὅσσ' ἔστι κου καὶ γίνετ', ἔστ' ἐν Αἰγύπτωι·
πλοῦτος, παλαίστρη, δύναμι[ς], εὐδίη, δόξα,
θέαι, φιλόσοφοι, χρυσίον, νεηνίσκοι,
θεῶν ἀδελφῶν τέμενος, ὁ βασιλεὺς χρηστός, (30)

---

[7] Theocritus, *Idyll* 17.91–2, Translation: Hunter 2003. See on this motif Hunter 2003, 167–168 and Bing 2005, 120–121.
[8] Callimachus, *Hymn to Delos* 168–170. Translation: Mair, Loeb 1921. See on this motif Bing 2005, 120–121.
[9] According to Curtius Rufus 4.7.26, Siwa issued an oracle to Alexander foretelling that he will rule the entire inhabited world.
[10] Hunter 2003, 167–168.

Μουσῆιον, οἶνος, ἀγαθὰ πάντ' ὅσ' ἂν χρήιζηι,
γυναῖκες, ὀκόσους οὐ μὰ τὴν Ἄιδεω Κούρην
ἀστέρας ἐνεγκεῖν οὐραν[ὸ]ς κεκαύχηται.

Come on, child, how long are you going to put up with the separation,
Wearing out your solitary bed on your own?
It's ten months since Mandris went off to Egypt,
And he doesn't send you even a word,
But has forgotten all about you and has drunk out of a new cup.
The Goddess has her own house there. Everything
You can find anywhere else is there in Egypt –
Wealth, the wrestling-club, power, the peaceful life, reputation,
Shows, philosophers, money, young lads,
The temple of the brother and sister gods, the King is good
There's the Museum, wine, all the good things he could want,
Women, so many of them that the sky can't boast it's got as many stars.[11]

In Herodas' poem, Ptolemy is not represented as merely ruling the entire *oecumene*, he is the centre of the world, a benevolent ruler who has created a metropolis to stimulate and satisfy all tastes and urges. Consumption plays an important role in this passage. The impression conveyed is that of luxury, plentitude, and conspicuous *truphe*. The seemingly disorderly sequence in a list: wealth, wrestling-club, power, peace, reputation, philosophers, show, money, young lads, Museum, wine—all the things one could want – creates an impression of irresistible pull, almost a yearning to drop everything and immediately rush to this fabulous place of plenty. Alexandria gathers and attracts everyone who is anyone—be it a beautiful woman, handsome lad, or a sage philosopher. It offers all kinds of attractions, from good wine to a rare book-roll. It is not simply the seat of the master of the empire, but presents a certain way of life, which enables its citizens to enjoy what the entire world has to offer without ever leaving their doorstep. All citizens have the opportunity to partake in the collective act of consumption. The world becomes a vast buffet, and the Alexandrians demonstrate their mastery over the world by tasting and experiencing all it has to offer.

What connects this passage with Posidippus' Lithika is the image of the centre of the empire pulling everything towards it, and nature's riches and wonders responding to the pull. Furthermore, in Posidippus' Lithika, the motif of consumption and utilization plays a prominent role. These stones are not gathering dust in a treasure-chest, they are used as jewelry, adorning the breasts and hands of sensuous women and handsome men, they are utilized as perfume-bottles, and carved into pieces of sympotic furniture and equipment. On the one hand, the

---

[11] Herodas, *Mime* 1.21–33. Text and translation: Zanker 2009.

stones are represented as a product of masterful *techne*, carved with astonishing skill, and, on the other hand, their owners are represented as using them with gusto, cherishing their value, since they are sophisticated and cultured people, worthy of such objects, and fully deserving them. Rather than presenting the king as conquering the *oecumene*, Posidippus paints a picture of an assembly of connoisseurs, fully equipped to rule, and of the countries of the world as willing subjects, eager to be valued and appreciated by the Alexandrian elite. Finally, the reader, too, partakes in the collective act of consumption, since (s)he is able to value and appreciate Posidippus' sophisticated poetry, which was also composed in order to be consumed at court. By reading the collection, the reader is invited to partake in the court culture, to catch a glimpse of a lavish symposium, to admire and desire the elegant ladies and cultured and powerful men. To Greek audiences, the collection must have conveyed a sense of empowerment. Not everyone could possess precious jewels, but surely objects such as rock crystal and Persian shells were more widely available and did circulate amongst the population more freely.[12] Finally, the sympotic setting, which features prominently in the Lithika, was a cultural space all Greeks could share and partake in.

Whereas the passages from Theocritus 17 and Callimachus' *Hymn to Delos* discussed above convey an image of one ruler subjecting many lands and areas, Herodas' first Mime and Posidippus' Lithika paint a picture of the universe willingly subjecting itself to the connoisseurship of the elite, rushing towards them, eager to place itself under their sway. From the readers' perspective, Posidippus and Herodas are far more inclusive than Theocritus and Callimachus, since the latter paint a picture of one man ruling the world, while the former focus on the collective act of consumption. This is not to say that the underlying ideology of Lithika is cosmopolitanism: on the contrary, the world exists in order to provide for the Greeks. Possession and utilization of the treasures of the world implies domination. What Herodas and Posidippus accomplish with their poems is an impression that the elite circles of Alexandria can be expanded to include all who feel and behave like Greeks. As in Herodas, so in Posidippus, too, consumption and *truphe* demonstrate cultural and political domination of the centre over the periphery. Where does this motif come from?

Susan Stephens (2004a, 170 – 173) was among the first to note that geographic movement is one of the main topics of Posidippus' collection. She posited (2004a, 170): "The roll opens with epigrams on gemstones that have been finely carved to

---

[12] In Epigram 16, the virtues of the grey rock crystal are extolled and it is specifically mentioned that it is radiant and transparent, but not expensive, since the rock is not rare. On the circulation of shells as containers for perfume and cosmetics, Kuttner 2005, 140 – 150.

epigrams on larger, uncarved stones and ostraca to a vast boulder hurled up on the beach. The stones seem to migrate from their original locations on periphery of empire—India, Persia, the Caucasus—to their position as jewel, signet, or ostracon moving ever closer to Ptolemaic Egypt. The first section concludes with a prayer for the well-being of the Ptolemies, while the second epigram in the Oionoskopika features a ship's journey embarking upon "The Egyptian sea"."[13] Figure 1 represents a schematic overview of the types of stones Posidippus mentions, with information about their provenance and movement, engraving or other special characteristic and the name of the engraver (when mentioned). This table should illustrate the importance and prominence of motion as a motif in the Lithika. Every stone is either moving itself, travelling by changing hands and settings, or at least it has the ability to move. Finally, some stones represent and thematize motion. I will first discuss the political implications of the motif of movement in the Lithika, and will then discuss the origins of this motif, tracing it back to Near Eastern royal ideology, as represented in the Aechaemenid inscriptions and visual art.

The initial 16 poems thematize the journey of the stones from exotic, faraway places to the bracelets, necklaces, drinking cups and treasure chests of the Greeks. The first poem is in tatters, yet the word "Hydaspes" is legible, which immediately recalls the outer edge of Alexander's empire and the final point in his quest towards the East. The second poem tells the story of an Indian stone engraved by the famous Kronios, being used at a symposium in some way. The third is probably on a blazing ruby engraved with an image of a cup, presented at a symposium as a gift to a noble lady.

Ann Kuttner (2005), 151 compared poems four, five, six and seven to a *daktuliotheke*, the gem-jewelry museum. Poems four and five are placed in a Persian context: Poem four is on a Persian stone which was first set in Darius' ring, then into a bracelet, in order to be given to a woman named Mandane. Poem five is on a Persian gem, lapis lazuli, which was given to a Greek, Nikaea from Cos, in exchange for a kiss. If poem six really centres on a beryllion (the text is fragmentary) it is noteworthy that Pliny stated that this stone is very seldom found outside of India,[14] which would make Nikonoe's pendant a travelling stone, too. Lucky Nikonoe is also the owner of the seventh stone. Movement is a prominent motif of this poem, too, as the stone is depicted as "rolling down Arabian mountains to the sea, swept by the storm-swollen river."[15] Engraved by Kronios, the stone was set in gold and now sparkles on Nikonoe's breast.

---

13 See also Gutzwiller 2005b; Höschele 2010, 156–163.
14 *Nat. Hist.* 37.76–77.
15 I 30–31.

[Λιθ]ικά

	Stone	Origin of stone	Journey	Setting of the stone	Engraving or special characteristic	Engraver	Setting of the epigram
1	?	Indian Hydaspes	The place of Alexander's battle against Porus evokes Alexander's victorious journey to the eastern edges of the world.	?	?	?	?
2	amethyst (?)	India (?)		A rhyton made of precious stone (Kosmetatou 2004b; Kuttner 2005) or ...	...a stone engraved with an image of a drinking horn (Kanthak forthcoming).	Kronios	sympotic (?) (Kanthak forthcoming)
3	ruby (?)	?	Given as a present to a noble lady / goddess (l 13: πότνια).	Not specified	Engraved with an image of a drinking cup (phiale) with flowers with triple tendrils traced in gold.	?	sympotic (Kanthak forthcoming)
4	blue Persian stone	Persia	Previously set in a ring of Darius, then set in gold and given to Mandane to wear as a bracelet.	First a ring worn by a man, then set in gold to adorn a female arm.	Shines like the moon (l 16: ἀντισέληνον).	?	? Kuttner 2005: erotic Kanthak forthcoming: sympotic
5	lapis lazuli	Persia	Carved as a gift for Demylis, then given to Coan Nicaea in exchange for a kiss; demonstrative pronoun suggests nearness to the	Gift for a lady.	Sparkles like a star, (l 20: ἀστερόεντα); flecked with gold pyrites (l 21: χρυσίτην); semi-precious stone (l 21: ἡμίλιθος).	Timanthes	erotic

	Stone	Origin of stone	Journey	Setting of the stone	Engraving or special characteristic	Engraver	Setting of the epigram
			speaker / reader (l 21: τόνδε)				
6	beryllion (?) or "beryl projecting the image of a rainbow" (Gutzwiller 2003, Kuttner 2005)	(?) Kanthak forthcoming: India	Admired by Heros (?); now adorns a female breast as a pendant. Demonstrative pronoun suggests nearness to the speaker / reader (l 24: τῶιδε).	First connected to a certain Heros, now set in a golden necklace, lies on Niconoe's breast.	Carved with an image of Iris.	? ("Kronios" restored by AB)	erotic
7	?	Arabia	Movement strongly suggested, l 30–31: "rolling in the storm-swollen river from Arabian mountains to the sea", now in a necklace.	Set in a golden necklace, lies on Nicnoe's breast.	Engraved; like honey in colour (l 32: τὸν μέλιτι χροιήν), sparkles like honey (l 35: ευϋλλάμπει λευκῶι χρωτί μελιχρὰ φάη)	Kronios	erotic
8	cornelian (τὸ σάρδιον)	The name suggests Sardes in Lydia	Movement first strongly denied (l. l 36: οὔτ' αὐχρὴν ἐφόρηςε); but then attributed to the very picture within it (ll. l 38–39: Δαρεῖον φορέων ὁ καλὸ[ς] λίθος ἅρμα δ' ὑπ' αὐτὸν γλυφθέν ἐπὶ σπιθαμήν μῆκεος ἐκτέταται); a chariot suggests movement.	? large-scale cameo (Kosmetatou 2003) / a royal pectoral necklace taken by Ptolemy after Alexander's victory over Darius (Kuttner 2005).	Carved with an image of Darius in a chariot, a span in length, and three spans around; illuminated from below. Brighter than Indian rubies. The stone is not discoloured.	x	?
9	Not specified. (Hdt 3.41.1, Paus. 8.14.8 claim	?	Movement of the ring is not specified, but it is the point of the famous story: the	Not specified. Hdt 3.41.1: emerald set in gold. Pliny NH	Lyre (?)	Not specified. According to Hdt. 3.41. 1 it	?

Posidippus and Achaemenid royal propaganda — 281

	Stone	Origin of stone	Journey	Setting of the stone	Engraving or special characteristic	Engraver	Setting of the epigram
	that Polycrates' ring bore an emerald, whereas Pliny *NH* 37.2: claims it was a sardonyx.)		ring is tossed into the sea and returns to Polycrates in the belly of a big fish. Direct address of Polycrates (II 3) might imply some sort of proximity.	37.2: placed in a golden horn in the temple of Concordia at Rome. Polycrates used the ring as a seal (l. II, 3: ϲφρηγῖδα).		was engraved by Theodoros, Pliny, 37.4: *intacta inlibataque* (!) Kuttner (2005) remarks that emeralds were almost impossible to carve.	
10	?	?	"Nabataean ... king of Arabian cavalrymen" mentioned (ll. II 15–16)	Cylinder (II 7: κ[ύ]λινδρον) is a typical Near Eastern form.	? Near Eastern seal cylinders were usually engraved with an image and/or text. (Klengel-Brandt 1997.)	?	?
11	No stone, but mother-of-pearl (II 19: μαργαρῖτιϲ)	Persia	From the shores of the Persian sea (II 17–19)	Kuttner 2005: perfume vessel	Representation of Aglaia with a wax film on the surface	?	? Kuttner 2005: erotic
12	Sea-shell	Persia	From the sea	Perhaps set in gold and emerald? Kuttner 2005: perfume vessel	Some sort of engraving is mentioned (II 28: γλύμμα)	?	? Kuttner 2005: erotic
13	tricky stone II 29: κ[ερδα]λέη λίθοϲ	Persia	Demonstrative pronoun suggests nearness to the speaker / reader (II 29: ἥδε)	?	It looks different when oiled.	?	?
14	jasper	?	Motion is the topic of the engraving: Bellerophon has	?	Stone is like the wind (II 33 ἠερόεϲϲαν) and	Name not mentioned, but	?

Stone	Origin of stone	Journey	Setting of the stone	Engraving or special characteristic	Engraver	Setting of the epigram
		fallen to Cilicia's Aleian Plain, Pegasus ascends in the air.		ethereal (II 38: αἰθερίῳ), with an engraving featuring Pegasus without a rider.	skill abundantly praised (II 33–34: εὖ ... / χεῖρά τε καὶ κατὰ νοῦν ἔγλυφ᾽ ὁ χειροτέχνης: Lynceus	?
15 dracontias	"Not from a river, but from a bearded serpent's head." (II 39–III1)	?	?	Minuscule chariot engraved in a stone which, according to Pliny, NH 37.54 was impossible to engrave.		?
16 grey rock crystal	Arabia	"Torn from the Arabian mountains, washed by the torrent endlessly down to the beach" (III 8–10).	?	Radiant, but massive and thus not precious, since it is not rare.	x	?
17 magnet	Mysian Olympus.	"Torn from the roots of Mysian Olympus." (III 14). σκέψαι ... τόνδε λίθον (III 14–15) implies vicinity of the object. The stone itself possesses the agency to move objects towards it or away.	?	It attracts and repels.	x	?

Stone	Origin of stone	Journey	Setting of the stone	Engraving or special characteristic	Engraver	Setting of the epigram
18	?	Motion towards the object implied – it invites nine men to recline on it. δεῦτ' ἐπ' ἔμ', ἐννέα φῶτες, ἀνακλίνθητε (III 20).	Bing 2009d : sympotic kline or table, AB: krater	Precise dimensions specified.	x	sympotic
19–20	Sea	Poseidon broke off a massive stone from the Capherean main and tossed it towards the cities on the shore. Mentioning Polyphemus, Helike, Eleusis, Geraestus brings to mind the entire Western Mediterranean. At the end, the land of Ptolemy is focalised (νήσων μέτα τὴν Πτολεμαίου/ γαῖαν ἀκινήτην ὥσχε καὶ αἰγιαλούς.) Motion strongly implied – as a threat and source of destruction.	Destructive and formidable missile	Huge size (50 feet across) and destructive potential (scarier than the door-bar of Polypmehus' cave)	x	Hymn to Poseidon ending with a prayer.

| Stone | Origin of stone | Journey | Setting of the stone | Engraving or special characteristic | Engraver | Setting of the epigram |

Figure 1: Λιθικά

Thus ends the sequence of stones as gifts for the ladies. Men take centre stage now, two famous rulers, Darius (in poem eight) and Polycrates of Samos (in poem nine).

The central poem in the collection suitably mentions the most famous ring of the ancient world. According to a well-known story, the tyrant Polycrates was so fortunate that he was advised to part with his most prized possession, in order to avert the vengeance of the gods. He chose his signet ring and tossed it into the sea, only to find it again in the belly of a fish at a feast. Did Posidippus tell the story of the ring's journey? He didn't have to, for the journey is at the core of the legend anyway and the mere mention of the ring implies it.

The motion of the ring from the depths of the sea back to Polycrates can be interpreted as a symbol of his thalassocracy. The Ptolemies, too, commanded a great maritime empire, and it has been suggested that the mention of Polycrates in the Lithika was intended to link the two great maritime empires, and their rulers as famous patrons of the arts.[16]

Epigram ten is yet another kingly poem. "Nabataean ... king of Arabian cavalrymen" is legible in line 10 (II 15–16), but the context is tantalizingly fragmentary. The shape of the object (κ]ύλινδρον, II, 7), however, is highly significant. Cylinder was a distinctly Near Eastern form, and Near Eastern cylinder seals were usually engraved with an image and a text.[17] These objects were small and portable, and the Greeks were familiar with them as dedications in sanctuaries or through cultural and economic contact with Eastern nations.

The three central poems in the collection (8, 9, 10) are frustratingly fragmentary. Any attempt at interpretations seems hazardous. Yet, I wonder if the sequence of previous great kings—Darius, the last ruler of Persia, who was defeated and succeeded by Alexander, and Polycrates, the famous Samian tyrant, who was perceived as the most powerful ruler of the seas of his time[18] who had failed so spectacularly after fortune turned its back on him[19]—suggests the topic of transition of power. The thalassocracy of Polycrates is symbolized in his ring, one that miraculously returns from the depths of the sea to its master.[20]

Darius in a chariot as a motif of poem eight could evoke the huge span of the Persian Empire, and the king's control over this vast land. The motif of size is

---

[16] Fuqua 2008, 10.
[17] Porada 1993; Klengel-Brandt 1997.
[18] Hdt. 3.39; Thuc. 1.13; Str. 14.1.16.
[19] For Herodotus, Polycrates is an exemplary tyrant, famous for his lavish lifestyle and *truphe* and for his sudden and violent death (he was ambushed and crucified by the Persian governor Oroites: Hdt. 3.120–125).
[20] The legend is first attested in Herodotus (3.40–43).

prominent in the eighth poem, since the dimensions of the chariot (it is 22 cm long) and the stone itself (its perimeter measures 66 cm) are provided.

Both rulers evoke the power which the Ptolemies now claim and suggest the transition of power and a certain line of succession which ends—or perhaps culminates—in the reign of the Ptolemies.

Perhaps it is significant that both rulers were famous for their court and kingly lifestyle. For the Greeks, the kings of Persia were perceived as the embodiment of *truphe*. They were even credited as the first men in history to become notorious for *truphe* and luxury.[21] Polycrates, too, was famous both as a patron of the arts and sciences and as a lover of luxury. In fact, Herodotus singles him out as famous for magnificence (*megaloprepreie*).[22] Briant argues that Polycrates epitomized the characteristics the Greeks commonly attributed to oriental kings, and credits him with creating a genuine court at Samos, which even boasted a park populated with plants and animals from afar, modeled upon *paradeisoi* in the Persian capitals.[23] Following these similarities between the Persian king and the Greek tyrant, poems eight and nine (and perhaps also ten) highlight the motif of the royal court, which, as I shall argue, plays a prominent role in the ideology of Lithika.

The next two poems, eleven and twelve, depict vessels made of Persian shells. There is a strong emphasis on the provenance of the material in both poems. Poem thirteen probably also focuses on a Persian stone. The stone in poem fourteen, similarly to that in poem eight which features a representation of Darius in a chariot, is not described as moving itself, but depicts movement. It is a jasper stone engraved with an image of Pegasus, who ascends to Olympus. Poem fifteen is on a fabulous stone from a serpent's head whose engraving implies motion (a chariot); sixteen thematizes motion of the stone itself, as it features a massive grey rock crystal, which was "torn from the Arabian mountains, washed by the torrent endlessly down to the beach".[24] Poem seventeen is on a magnet with a power to both attract and repel. Here it is the stone itself which is invested with the power to move. This motif is taken up in poem eighteen: here, too, we encounter a massive stone (the dimensions are specified) that was carved into a piece of sympotic furniture. The stone invites the reader to approach it, so, like the magnet, the object has the power to attract.

Finally, poems nineteen and twenty feature a formidable stone which places all poems firmly in the context of Ptolemaic Egypt: It tells of the power of Pos-

---

21 Athenaeus 12.513f.
22 Hdt 3.125.
23 Briant 2002, 83. On the Persian *paradeisoi*, Briant 2002, 442–444.
24 III 8–10.

eidon to break off a massive rock from the raging sea with his trident and to destroy an entire island with it (yet another rock!), or an entire city, as he did in the case of Helike. Posidippus prays to the god to spare the lands of Ptolemy and keep its shores and lands unshaken. With this prayer, the deictics from all previous poems in the Lithika become firmly localized. The prayer to Poseidon at the end of Lithika places all stones previously mentioned right before the reader's eyes: in Egypt.

The urge of nature's riches to become a part of the Ptolemaic Empire corresponds to the royal propaganda of universal rule. The lands are represented through their symbols, the stones. They come from far and wide: mentioned are the Indian border, Lydia, Arabia, Persia, Mysia, but also the Greek islands and mainland. From the depths of the sea, evoked in poem eight on Polycrates' ring, to the uppermost ether (mentioned in poem fourteen), all levels of the world are represented as, and united in, belonging to the realm of the Ptolemies. The tiny precious gems, sea-shells, mother-of-pearl are joined by nature's wonders such as magnets, legendary dracontias and massive rock crystals; they travel from far-away mountains and rivers to find their place on the noble breast of a lady, on a drinking cup, or to be carved into a sympotic *kline*, to be used and treasured by the ruling elite in Alexandria.

The ideology of universal rule represented here, just like the empire that Ptolemies claimed, has a history. Before Alexander, Persia was the dominant empire in the Mediterranean and its emperor was the king of kings. Indeed, when Greek writers mention *basileus* in the time before Alexander, this is who they mean—the ruler of Persia. I propose that the ideology of universal rule, as presented in Callimachus, Theocritus, Herodas and Posidippus, can be traced as far back as Achaemenid royal propaganda. Achaemenid royal inscriptions and visual art provide numerous testimonies to the idea that the empire is represented by the materials that come together to form the space of the king, and the skill of the empire's craftsmen in shaping the material according to the king's wishes.

The Persian royal inscriptions are texts inscribed by order of the kings of the Achaemenid dynasty in two scripts and in three different languages: Old Persian, language of the empire's rulers; Elamite, already an ancient language in the time of the Achaemenids, once spoken in southwestern Iran; and Akkadian, the ancient language of Babylonia and Assyria. Old Persian used its own script, whereas Akkadian and Elamite used two versions of the same cuneiform script. A few Achaemenid inscriptions also provide versions in Egyptian. The great majority of these inscriptions were conspicuously displayed at the royal palaces and tombs at Pasargadae, Persepolis, Naqš-i Rustam, Susa, and Babylon. The texts are often prefaced by sentences like "the King declares" and represent instances of royal propaganda which are strikingly direct and powerful. They did not attempt to narrate historical events,[25] but were dedicated to exalting the king as a guarantee of order in the empire. They were often accompanied by reliefs which conveyed the written message visually. The texts usually reiterated their message in three or four languages of the empire, and were published multiple times and on a variety of materials at the same site. A striking example of Achaemenid royal propaganda is Darius' building inscription from Susa, the royal residence in Elam.

Susa, as one of the Achaemenid royal residences since the reign of Darius I (522–486 BC), boasted a magnificent royal palace. Its building inscription tells how Darius I had it constructed using materials and craftsmen from all over his empire. The text is preserved in many fragments (13 in Old Persian, 27 in Babylonian, and 12 in Elamite) of marble, clay, or glazed tiles. The fragments were discovered in the Apadana (audience palace), but also other places on the hill. There are parallel texts with the same or slightly abridged content in three languages of the empire: DSaa (in Babylonian), DSz (in Elamite) and DSf (in Old Persian). All are remarkably similar to the type of royal propaganda we have encountered in Posidippus' Lithika. The narrative regarding the building of the palace translated from Old Persian is the following:

7. This palace, which I built in Susa, its materials were brought from far away; downwards, the earth was dug, until I reached the rock in the earth. When it had been dug, and the rubble packed—on one side its depth was 40 cubits, on the other, its depth was 20 cubits, on this rubble, the palace was set.
8. And that the earth was dug downwards and the rubble packed and the bricks moulded, the Babylonian people did it.
9. The cedarwood was brought from a mountain called Lebanon; the Assyrian people brought it as far as Babylon; from Babylon, the Carians and Ionians brought it as far as Susa; the yaka-wood was brought from Gandara and Carmania.
10. The gold which was worked here was brought from Lydia (Sardis) and Bactria; the lapis lazuli and the carnelian which was worked here was brought from Sogdiana; the turquoise which was worked here was brought from Chorasmia.
11. The silver and the ebony were brought from Egypt; the decoration, with which the walls were ornamented, was brought from Ionia; the ivory which was worked here was brought from Nubia, India and Arachosia.
12. The stone columns which were worked here were brought from a village called Abiradu in Elam; the masons who crafted the stone were Ionians and Sardians.
13. The goldsmiths who worked the gold were Medes and Egyptians; the men who worked the wood were Sardians and Egyptians; the men who crafted the bricks were the Babylonians; the men who decorated the wall were Medes and Egyptians.

---

25 One exception is the trilingual inscription, carved on the cliffs at Bisutun between 520 and 518 BC on the order of Darius I which describes the events preceding his accession to power.

14. King Darius proclaims: At Susa much that was excellent was commanded (to be done), much that was excellent was done. Me may Auramazda protect, and my father Hystaspes and my people.[26]

DSf 7–14

The entire empire is represented by its products and riches, which come together in order to compose a palace for its living embodiment, Darius. The palace is the kingdom *en miniature*, just like scholars have argued for Posidippus' Lithika. Darius reiterates this point in Old Persian, Babylonian and Elamite, stating again and again that *"With the protection of Auramazda, the materials of the decoration of the palace were brought from far away."*[27]

Pierre Briant comments on this and other similar inscriptions, noting that it is the detail "from afar" that is key to the logic of the discourse.[28] He argues that these documents "eloquently attest to the royal desire to depict every country and every people of the Empire united in harmonious cooperation organized by and surrounding the king."[29] The phrase "from afar" is also present in the royal titulature: Darius I is called "King in this great earth far and wide".[30]

The inscription from Susa has many visual and textual parallels from all over the Persian Empire.[31] One striking example of image and text working together to convey the same idea is a statue of Darius, found near a monumental gate at Susa.[32] The statue represents the king as a Persian, dressed in the Persian robe, but the posture (one foot advancing, the arm folded against the breast) and the stone (metamorphic sandstone from Wadi Hammamat near the Red Sea) are Egyptian. The base of the statue has the Egyptian symbol of the union of Upper and Lower Egypt on the front and the back. On the sides of the base, representations of the countries of the Empire are depicted: Each country is identified by a figure in national costume, and by a name inscribed in a cartouche.

The folds of Darius' dress are inscribed in three cuneiform languages of the empire and in hieroglyphics. This is the cuneiform version of the text (DSab 2):

This is the statue of stone, which Darius the king ordered to be made in Egypt, so that whoever sees it in time to come will know that the Persian man holds Egypt.

---

26 All translations of Achaemenid royal inscriptions are from Kuhrt 2007.
27 DSaa 5 (Babylonian); DSz 6 (Elamite).
28 Briant 2002, 165–203.
29 Briant 2002, 178.
30 DNa.
31 For a list of all parallels, Briant 2002, 172–173.
32 On the statue, Razmjou 2002.

As is frequently the case with Persian royal art, visual representation is interpreted and explained in the inscription. The inscription tells us that the provenance of the stone and the local craftsmanship symbolize the king's dominion over Egypt. In this case, too, it is the origin of the stone and the specific, local *techne* that is placed at the king's disposal. The king demonstrates his sway over Egypt by using the material resources and skills of the region. Having entered and conquered Egypt, Darius commemorates this moment by infusing a symbolic representative of the Egyptian soil with his image, shaping it to the contours of his body. Darius impresses his royal iconography upon local material, and at the same time the king incorporates the material and its country of origin into his realm. The local material assumes the shape of Darius' body, so we can argue that Darius inhabits the local material. This is a gesture similar to the way his royal palace consists of materials from various localities. Individual regions form the place wherein the king dwells. Consumption is again used as an expression of dominance.

I find it particularly interesting that the inscription envisages its reception in very broad terms: Darius addresses a man from any land, from any point in the future, who is imagined as inspecting the form and the material of this extraordinary statue (this is one of the very rare examples of Achaemenid sculpture in the round), seeking an explanation of its meaning. Is it not tempting to presume that, when Alexander the Great captured Susa in mid-November 331BC, he, too, was drawn to the statue and had someone interpret the inscription? This very city was also the setting of the famous mass-marriage ceremony in April 324, when Alexander and his ninety *philoi* took prominent Persian brides. On this occasion, Alexander also distributed gifts to 10,000 soldiers who had taken wives from amongst Asian women. The wedding was a five-day spectacle, the event of the decade, described in many sources and attended by a veritable who's who of the ancient world.[33] It is plausible to assume that the gathered guests would take up the opportunity to see the royal city and admire its lavish decorations. The wedding was probably celebrated in the palace complex itself. The Greeks had a rich and prolific inscriptional culture, and Alexander was deeply interested in Persian royal propaganda and the Persian way of life.[34] He had numerous interpreters at his disposal. The monumental building inscription at Susa, as well as the statue of Darius which was probably placed at the gates to the palace, must have made an impression on the Greeks, and I would argue that they

---

33 Heckel/Yardley 2004, 182–184 provide an overview of sources. Chares provided a detailed description of the festivities (FGrH 125 F 4 = Athenaeus 12.538b-539a) and a catalogue of famous Greek and Barbarian artists who performed at the wedding.
34 Petrovic, forthcoming, with bibliography.

must have enlisted an interpreter to read the inscriptions to them. Among Alexander's generals, and present at Susa, was also Ptolemy, who on this occasion took Artacama, daughter of Artabazus for a wife.[35] He was later to found a ruling dynasty in Egypt and was also the author of one of the Histories of Alexander's conquest. The royal complex must have made an impression on this man, who later faced the task of erecting a court for his own needs in Alexandria. Other Greeks gathered in Susa in order to attend the wedding ceremony could have displayed interest in the royal inscriptions as well, and some could have committed them to writing. After all, the Greeks were so fascinated with Persian customs and the King's way of life that every generation had one or several writers of Persian history (*Persika*) since the beginning of the 5th century.[36]

In the section below, I will address the question of the possible channels that conveyed Achaemenid royal ideology to the Greeks, but for now let it be said that in the case of Alexander and his generals, direct contact with Persian art and an interest in royal inscriptions, easily accessible via a translator, must be taken into account.

Another striking instance of Achaemenid royal propaganda is the building complex at Persepolis. There, the idea of material as a representation of the extent of royal power, the king's sway over the empire, is reiterated on a much grander scale. The city was founded by Darius I in 518 BC. It contained a sequence of ceremonial palaces, a residential quarter, treasury and a chain of fortifications. Darius' successors, Xerxes (486–466 BC) and Artaxerxes I (466–424 BC) each added to the complex. Alexander the Great reached the city early in February 330 and spent several months in the residence, before it was burned and looted. The booty from the city was enormous—according to Greek historians, Persepolis was "the richest city under the sun".[37]

While residing in Persepolis, Alexander held games in honor of his victories, entertained friends bountifully and performed sacrifices to the gods.[38] He probably also visited the tombs of Achaemenid kings nearby.[39] There are six finished

---

35 Arrian 7.4.6. According to Plutarch, *Eumenes* 1.3, Ptolemy's bride was named Apame.
36 See on this below, p. 299–302.
37 Diodorus Siculus 17.70.1. Diodorus 17.70–72 provides a detailed description of the city and the royal quarters derived from accounts of Alexander's historians.
38 DS 17.72.1.
39 Greek historians single out Alexander's visit and restoration of Cyrus' tomb in Pasargadae, and, following the report on this event, they also provide an abridged version of the inscription on Darius' tomb. (Plutarch, *Alexander* 69; Strabo 15.3.7; Arrian 6.29.9–11). See on this Bosworth 1988, 46–55; Schmitt 1988. Alexander must have been aware of the existence of Achaemenid royal tombs in Persepolis and Naqš-i Rustam nearby and probably saw them. At any rate, Greek

Achaemenid royal tombs: Four have been discovered at Naqš-i Rustam (5 km NW of Persepolis) and two at Persepolis. They all look the same since they are probably all copies of the tomb of Darius the Great: The relief on the upper part of the tomb shows the king sacrificing to the eternal, sacred fire and Auramazda. The king is standing on a platform that is carried by people wearing national dress, who each represent a territory of the Persian Empire. Such depictions of the people of the empire as the throne-bearers of the Great King are frequent in Persian art:[40] there are 30 known instances, all very similar, executed in high-relief. Peoples of the empire as throne-bearers adorn all royal tombs, several royal residences, Darius' statue at Susa and the stelae of the Suez Canal, dug by Darius. The reliefs are very impressive and executed on a grand scale—on the royal tombs, each throne-bearer is one meter tall. The inscriptions accompanying reliefs on the tomb of Darius I at Naqš-i Rustam and that of Artaxerxes I at Persepolis identify each figure as a representative of its land: "This is the Persian; This is the Mede", etc. Similarly to the inscription on Darius' statue at Susa, the one on his grave provides instructions for the viewing of the visual representations:

> 2. I (am) Darius the great king, king of kings, king of countries containing all kinds of men, king on this great earth far and wide, son of Hystaspes, an Achaemenid, a Persian, son of a Persian, an Aryan, having Aryan lineage.
> 3. Darius the king proclaims: By the favour of Auramazda these are the countries which I seized outside Persia; I ruled over them; they bore me tribute; what was said to them by me, that they did; my law—that held them (firm): Media, Elam, Parthia, Areia, Bactria, Sogdiana, Chorasmia, Drangiana, Arachosia, Sattagydia, Gandara, India, Saca who drink hauma, Saca with pointed hats, Babylonia, Assyria, Arabia, Egypt, Armenia, Cappadocia, Sardis, Ionia, Scythians who are across the sea, Thrace, petasos-wearing Ionians, Libya, Nubia, Maka, Caria.
> 4. Darius the king proclaims: Auramazda, when he saw this earth in commotion, thereafter bestowed it upon me, made me king; I am king. By the favour of Auramazda I put it in its proper place; what I said to them, that they did, as was my desire. If now you should think: "How many are the countries which King Darius held?", look at the sculptures (of those) who bear the throne, then shall you know, then shall it become known to you: the spear of the Persian men has gone forth far; then shall it become known to you: the Persian man has delivered battle far indeed from Persia.
> DNa 2–4

Here, too, we have an implied reader from the future, wishing to learn about Darius and the Persian Empire on the basis of the reliefs and texts displayed on the

---

historians are aware of their existence and describe the tombs and offer translations of the inscriptions n them (in abridged form).
40 Briant 2002, 173–175.

tomb. (S)he is instructed to read the relief as a symbol of the Empire, and the act of bearing the throne as subordination. The lands are represented by a human figure in national dress, and they all come together in order to elevate the Persian king and bring him closer to the Eternal fire and Auramazda.

The royal residence in Persepolis also boasted a building inscription at its gates. In the inscription, Darius enumerates all countries which were subject to him and brought tribute as a sign of subordination.[41] The diversity of Persia's imperial realm, represented in the materials and in the participation of imperial subjects in the building of the palace, is stressed in the inscription from the south side of the Persepolis terrace wall:

> A great (god is) Auramazda, who is the greatest among all the gods, who created heaven and earth, created mankind, who gave all well-being to mankind who dwell therein, who made Darius king, and bestowed on Darius the king kingship over this wide earth, in which there are many lands: Persia, Media and the other lands of other tongues, of mountains and plains, from this side of the sea to that side of the sea, from this side of the desert to that side of the desert.
>
> Darius the King speaks: With the protection of Auramazda, these (are) the lands, who did this, who gathered here: Persia, Media, the lands of other tongues, of mountains and plains, from this side of the sea to that side of the sea, from this side of the desert to that side of the desert, as I commanded them. All that I did, I did with the protection of Auramazda. May Auramazda, together with all the gods, protect me, me and all I love.[42]

Darius' palace in Persepolis represents the vast realm of his empire, just like the palace in Susa. And there is more: On the magnificent relief that dominates the façade of the Apadana in Persepolis, 23 subject nations of the Persian king are represented as gift-bearing delegations, each in its own national dress. The "treasure reliefs" depict delegations that bring animals (cattle, horses, camels, lions, a giraffe, an antelope), vessels made of precious metals, clothes, armour, jewellery, and various raw materials (wool, leather etc.).

The Apadana at Persepolis was the largest and most imposing structure in the city. It could accommodate 10,000 guests. The tribute-bearing delegations are represented on its left wing. The right wing shows three superimposed registers of guards, staff-bearers and dignitaries. In the central part of the Apadana

---

41 DPe 2 (Old Persian): *King Darius proclaims: By the favour of Auramazda, these (are) the countries of which I took possession together with these Persian people; these feared me (and) brought me tribute: Elam, Media, Babylonia, Arabia, Assyria, Egypt, Armenia, Cappadocia, Lydia (Sardis), Ionians of the mainland and (those) by the sea, and the countries beyond the sea, Sagartia, Parthia, Drangiana, Areia, Bactria, Sogdiana, Chorasmia, Sattagydia, Arachosia, India, Gandara, Scythians (Saca), Maka.*
42 DPg (Babylonian).

façade, the enthroned king is represented as greeting the dignitaries and the tribute-bearing delegations. A rectangular area in the centre was covered with inscriptions of Xerxes in the three languages of the empire. The inscriptions stress the Persian king's claim to universal rule.[43]

Specialists in Persian history have argued that this relief is a representation of a procession which really did take place annually and that the delegations symbolize their subordinate position by bringing products of their native land.[44] It has been suggested that the festival was organized as a celebration of the New Year in March. Significantly, numerous Greek writers from Herodotus onwards offer testimonies about the processions and sacrifices organized at Persepolis, and about the importance of gift-giving as a sign of subordination to the Persian King, whether he was residing in one of the capital cities or was passing through a specific region, with the whole court on the move.[45] Whether the occasion depicted was one particular festival, or simply a ritual which repeated itself whenever the King passed through his land or received delegations, symbolic gift-giving had a prominent role in Persian court ceremonial and was universally seen (also by the Greeks!) as a gesture of subordination.[46] It is significant for my argument to stress that the Greeks were well-acquainted with the importance and with the symbolic potential of gift-giving in the Persian Empire since the 5th century BC. Not only do numerous Greek writers describe the ritual, but it is also important to mention that Alexander the Great actually re-enacted this ceremony in Babylon in 324 BC. Diodorus provides an important account of this occasion, demonstrating that Alexander and those around him knew full well the meaning and symbolic potential of gift-giving as a sign of subordination.

From practically all the inhabited world came envoys on various missions, some congratulating Alexander on his victories, some bringing him crowns, others concluding treaties of friendship and alliance, many bringing handsome presents, and some prepared to defend themselves against accusations. Apart from the tribes and cities as well as the local rulers of Asia, many of their coun-

---

43 XPb.
44 Fundamental on the reliefs: Walser 1966, who provides a detailed discussion and parallels for tribute-bearing representations in other cultures of the ancient Orient. See also Briant 2002, 174–189 (with bibliography).
45 On gifts in Persian empire, Sancisi-Weerdenburg 1989. Briant 2002, 184–195 offers an overview and discussion of Greek sources.
46 Briant 2002, 194 suggest that, instead of trying to pinpoint a specific New Year celebration as a model for the friezes, we should rather see an idealized depiction of a festival exalting the imperial power.

terparts in Europe and Libya put in an appearance; from Libya, Carthaginians and Libyphoenicians and all those who inhabit the coast as far as the Pillars of Heracles; from Europe, the Greek cities and the Macedonians also sent embassies, as well as the Illyrians and most of those who dwell about the Adriatic Sea, the Thracian peoples and even those of their neighbours the Gauls, whose people become known then first in the Greek world.[47]

Arrian provides an interpretation of the event:

> It was then more than ever that both in his own estimation and in that of his entourage Alexander appeared to be master of every land and sea.[48]

A display of power such as this may have influenced the Athenian festival in which the representatives of the cities united as the Delian league presented their revenues in a procession.[49] After Alexander, such processions became popular and are attested all over the Hellenistic world. The most direct influence is evident in the case of the grand procession of Ptolemy II, where the link between the territorial claims and tributes was clearly established.[50] According to Kallixenos' list of the participants in this procession, it included birds and animals from all over the world, tame and wild, examples of flowers and trees from everywhere, tribute-bearers from Ethiopia carrying vast quantities of tusks, ebony, gold, and silver; vast quantities of spices from all over the world,[51] and even carts with scenes depicting "barbarian countries, and women from India and elsewhere sat on them dressed like war-captives"[52]. It is evident that Ptolemy II was well aware of the symbolic potential of royal festivals and processions, and had put this awareness to good use. Finally, through Hellenistic influence, this Persian custom influenced the Roman triumph, too.[53]

Bringing the symbolic products of a region to the centre of the empire, in order to be given to the king, is a gesture which highlights the fact that all the empire belongs to the King, that he is the uniting factor of all its regions, far

---

47 Diodorus 17.113.1–2 (Translation: C. Bradford Welles, Loeb). See also Justin 12.13.1–2; Arrian 7.15. 4–6; 19.1–2; Cleitarchus FGrH 137 F 31.
48 Anabasis 7.15.5.
49 Briant 2002, 199.
50 Kallixenos of Rhodes (FGrH 627 F 2) described the procession, relying in part on official records; Athenaeus 5.196–203 offers lengthy excerpts. Rice 1983 discusses the political meanings of the processional imagery and Dunand 1981, 24–25 provides a link with Achaemenid festivals.
51 Athenaeus 5.200e-201c.
52 Athenaeus 5.201a.
53 Köhler 1996.

and wide. The image of a procession on the walls of Apadana tells, in the language of the visual arts, the same story that the building inscriptions from Susa and Persepolis advertise to its readers: the empire comes together at its centre, and the king embodies it. The king's body, dress, food, drink, way of life, houses and palace-complex all represent the empire. Even the food he ate and his everyday pursuits had symbolic potential—one that was clear to the Greeks, too. For instance, the lavish table of the king was, in fact, also his kingdom on display:

> They used to set on the king's table all the delicacies produced by the country over which the king ruled, the choice first-fruits of each. For Xerxes did not think that the princes should use any foreign food or drink, this is why a custom forbidding such use arose later.[54]
>
> The king used to relax in the royal paradises, hunting preserves populated by animals from all over his empire, and featuring plants from everywhere.[55] Even his sexual life was loaded with symbolic potential, since the harem of the Great King consisted of the most beautiful girls from the various regions of his empire![56]

The king is the uniting factor of the multi-national Persian Empire, and, since he is a true king, chosen by and supported by Auramazda, the lands subordinate themselves willingly. The lands, in the form of the material and craft employed to make his palaces; the symbolic gifts of food and drink; the plants and animals in his garden, and beautiful women and men; all are consumed, used by the king, or stored in his treasuries, united in his body and palace. What was previously disparate, separate and regional becomes a union in King's body and palace-complex. This type of propaganda, strikingly similar to Posidippus' Lithika or Herodas' first Mime, was understood well by the Greeks. Xenophon, who provides an image of an ideal ruler in the person of Cyrus, wrote:

> People were so devoted to him, that those of every nation thought they did themselves injury if they did not send to Cyrus the most valuable productions of their own country, whether the fruits of the earth, or animals bred there, or manufacturers of their own arts, and every city did the same.[57]

---

54 Dinon FGrH 690 F 12a = Athenaeus 14.652b – c. On the Persian royal table, Briant 2002, 200 – 201 (with bibliography)
55 Briant 2002, 201– 203, with important remarks on the way Greeks from Polycrates onwards adopted elements of the Persian royal lifestyle.
56 Briant 2002, 203.
57 *Cyropaedia* 8.6.23.

Here, too, we have the motif of a union of products and craftsmanship as representatives of each region sent to the king to enjoy.

Dinon even offers a sophisticated interpretation of the items stored in the King's treasury: *"The Persian king had water fetched from the Nile and the Danube, which they laid up in their treasuries as a sort of testimony of the greatness of their power and universal empire."*[58]

The final question that needs to be tackled is how Posidippus (and other Hellenistic writers) found out about Persian royal propaganda.

In the Ptolemaic kingdom, the eye-witness account of Ptolemy, who followed Alexander and wrote a history of his conquests, must have been of significant importance. Having seen the Persian royal capitals and tombs, having experienced the court ritual first-hand, Ptolemy must have adopted some models of behaviour and representation of majesty. After all, it is evident that he knew full well about the significance of the king's body, having snatched the corpse of Alexander in order to bury it in Alexandria. The famous Museum could also be seen as an attempt to encompass the entire Greek world through symbolic representatives: its literature. The Museum also gathered living scholars and scientists from all over the Greek world in an intellectual *paradeisos* of sorts. The political and propagandistic implications of this institution cannot be overlooked. Such measures could not have been lost on the poets living at the court. Equally, since Greeks in Asia were not only the subjects of the Persian king, but had collaborated in the major building projects, sending material and craftsmen to the Persian royal capitals, they, too must have been aware of Persian royal propaganda.

Another important source of Achaemenid royal propaganda were the Persian histories written in Greek. Starting with Dionysius of Miletus in the early fifth century BC,[59] each generation of Greeks had their own *Persika*, books dedicated to Persian history and the royal way of life.[60] Other known writers of *Persika* are Charon of Lampsacus (second half of 5th century BC)[61]; Hellanicus of Lesbos (480–407 BC)[62]; Ctesias of Cnidus (born ca. 441 BC)[63]; Dinon (fl. approximately

---

[58] Dinon FGrH 690 F 23b = Plutarch, *Alexander* 36.4.
[59] Schmitt 1995; Lenfant 2007, 201.
[60] On the genre, Drews 1973; Lenfant 2007; Llewellyn-Jones/Robson 2010, 45–55.
[61] Schmitt 1991; Lenfant 2007, 201.
[62] Drews 1973, 22–24; Wiesehöfer 2003a; Lenfant 2007, 201–2.
[63] By far the most influential Greek historian of Persia, Ctesias was a doctor at court and offers numerous and often salacious details about the royal way of life. Apart from *Persika*, Ctesias also wrote a book *"On the tributes in Asia"*. Quotes from this work in Athenaeus (2.67a and 10.442b) are lists of food products conveyed to the court from various places of the empire with ethno-

360–330 BC)[64]; Heracleides of Cyme (mid-fourth century BC)[65]; and in the Hellenistic period writers whom we know by name and title of work only: Diogenes, Diocles, Baton of Sinope, and Criton of Pieria.[66] To this list should be added the *Histories* of Herodotus, since books 1–5.27 offer a history of Persian expansion, and Xenophon's *Cyropaedia*. This book is admittedly a largely fictionalized biography of Cyrus the Great, but it does contain valuable information about life at court and the Persian Empire in general. Theopompus (late 4th century BC) wrote an epitome of Herodotus' *Histories* and used Ctesias as his source as well.[67] Ephorus (late 4th century BC) wrote a *Universal History* with books 8–9 dedicated to the history of Media, Lydia and Persia.[68]

Of these authors, Ctesias claims to have used Persian official documents (he mentions "royal parchments" or "royal leather record books")[69]. Heracleides of Cumae[70] offers a description of the ceremony of the king's dinner which is universally accepted as credible, and, according to Lenfant 2007, 207 is "factual,

---

graphical details of regions mentioned. On Ctesias, Schmitt 1993, Lenfant 2007, 202–205, Llewellyn-Jones/Robson 2010, 1–87; Stronk 2010, 2–59.

64 Held in high esteem by Cornelius Nepos and considered more reliable than Ctesias by Plutarch, Dinon had a special interest in court hierarchy and royal majesty. On Dinon, Felix 1995, Lenfant 2007, 206.

65 Based on transmitted fragments, his *Persika* in five books offered the most exhaustive information about royal life and courtly ceremonial. Lenfant 2007, 207 credits him with "long and highly precise descriptions of the palace practices, especially the care of the king, his staff (concubines, guards, cooks, bedmakers, etc.) and court etiquette. (…) F 2, which described the king's dinner—its organization, the hierarchy among his guests, and the graded distribution of the dishes to them,—has especially interested modern historians as a valuable document on court institutions." See also Lewis 1997; Wiesehöfer 2003b; Sancisi-Weerdenburg 1993.

66 FGrH 692, 693, and app. to 693.

67 Drews 1973, 121.

68 Drews 1973, 121–122.

69 Ctesias claimed that one of his main sources of information were the royal archives, which he refers to as "royal parchments" βασιλικαὶ ἀναγραφαί (Diodorus 2.22.5) or "royal leather record books" (βασιλικαὶ διφθέραι, Diodorus 2.32.4). It appears that Ctesias did not consult these records himself, for the facts in question are said to be "given in the royal records according to what the barbarians say" (ἐν ταῖς βασιλικαῖς ἀναγραφαῖς ἱστορεῖσθαί φασιν οἱ βάρβαροι, Diodorus, 2.22.5). Scholars are still divided on the historicity of these claims. Drews 1973, 111 provides an overview of scholars who thought that Ctesias was credible on this matter, but he himself is sceptical. Recently, both Llewellyn-Jones/Robson 2010, 58–65 and Stronk 2004–5, 101–122 and 2010, 15–30 (with bibliographies and discussion of previous scholarship) deem Ctesias' claims credible. They both conclude that Ctesias drew on a variety of written and oral sources that came from inside Persia.

70 FGrH 689 F 2 = Athenaeus 4.145b-146a.

precise, and reasoned, (and) tallied with Near Eastern documents such as the Persepolis tablets ... and suggests that Heracleides was well informed."[71]

The very existence of a genre such as *Persika* testifies to the lively interest of Greeks in the Persians' history and way of life. Based on the transmitted fragments of *Persika*, one gains the impression that large portions of these books were dedicated to the depiction of royal lifestyle and court intrigues. Some writers of Persian histories claim access to the royal documents, some quote Persian inscriptions. Already Herodotus features several Persian inscriptions: the Bosporus-Inscriptions of Darius I (4.87.1), an equestrian Statue of Darius I (3.88.3), and the Tearos-Stelae (4.91.1–2). Historians vary in their assessment of their historicity,[72] but, genuine or not, Herodotus' Persian (or "Persian") inscriptions testify to the interest of Greek audiences in reading Persian inscriptions. If anything, Herodotus raised awareness of inscriptions as a possible source of information about the Persian way of life. It is thus not surprising to see that all historians of Alexander portray him as a careful reader of inscriptions.[73]

Especially interesting is the episode related by Polyaenus: Alexander found the list of foodstuffs for the Persian king's breakfast and dinner inscribed on a bronze pillar in the royal palace. Polyaenus provides the full list,[74] which, ac-

---

[71] See also Lewis 1997.

[72] Bibliography on Herodotus' use of Persian material is vast. Rollinger 2003 provides an overview.

[73] On Alexander and the tomb of Cyrus at Pasargadae: Plutarch, *Alexander* 69.2–3 who features Alexander reading the inscription and ordering it to be repeated in Greek letters; Aristobulos FGrH 139 F 51b = Strabo 15.3.8 has Alexander visit the tomb and offers a transcript of the inscription; Onesicritus FGrH 134 F 34 = Strabo 15. 3. 7 adds the (drastically abbreviated!) grave inscription of Darius to the episode; Aristos of Salamis (FGrH 143 F 1 = Strabo 15.3.8) adds that there was one Greek and one Persian inscription on Cyrus' tomb.

[74] Strat. 4.3.31–2. *"Of fine wheat flour four hundred artabae (a Median artaba is an Attic bushel). Of second flour three hundred artabae, and of third flour the same: in the whole one thousand artabae of wheat flour for supper. Of the finest barley flour two hundred artabae, of the second four hundred, and four hundred of the third: in all one thousand artabae of barley flour. Of oatmeal two hundred artabae. Of paste mixed for pastry of different kinds ten artabae. Of cresses chopped small, and sifted, and formed into a kind of ptisan, ten artabae. Of mustard-seed the third of an artabae. Male sheep four hundred. Oxen a hundred. Horses thirty. Fat geese four hundred. Three hundred turtles. Small birds of different kinds six hundred. Lambs three hundred. Goslings a hundred. Thirty head of deer. Of new milk ten marises (a maris contains ten attic choas). Of milk whey sweetened ten marises. Of garlick a talent's worth. Of strong onions half a talent's worth. Of knot grass an artaba. Of the juice of benzoin two minae. Of cumin an artaba. Of benzoin a talent worth. Of rich cider the fourth of an artaba. Of millet seed three talents worth. Of anise flowers three minae. Of coriander seed the third of an artaba. Of melon seed two capises. Of parsnips ten artabae. Of sweet wine five marises. Of salted gongylis five marises. Of pickled capers five marises. Of salt ten artabae. Of Ethiopian [Aethiopian] cumin six capises (a capise is an attic chaenix). Of*

cording to the current *communis opinio*, reflects Persian practices and is based on a genuine Persian document.[75]

In the *Alexander Romance*, the king is also portrayed as inspecting and engaging with all sorts of barbarian documents.[76]

I posit that Posidippus, as the first poet attested as ἐπιγραμματοποιός,[77] a professional who composed inscribed epigrams, and as a court poet, may have been interested in literature about the Persian court. He could even have consulted the Greek translations of the Persian royal inscriptions.

Even though neither the Ptolemies nor the Seleucids presented themselves as direct heirs of the Achaemenids—quite the contrary!—they were kings and had adopted the propaganda and the modes of representation of kingship from the Achaemenids. Excellent studies have been dedicated to the way Hellenistic rulers adopted the royal propaganda of Pharaonic Egypt,[78] but it is worth reflecting on the fact that Egypt was part of the Persian Empire when Alexander conquered it. This paper does not intend to shift the focus away from the study of Egyptian influence, but offers an additional perspective on the sources of royal propaganda in the Hellenistic period. The King of Persia had been, in the eyes of the Greeks, the king of kings for generations. There must have been some Achae-

---

dried anise thirty minae. Of parsley feed four capises. Oil of Sisamin ten marises. Cream five marises. Oil of cinnamon five marises. Oil of acanthus five marises. Oil of sweet almonds three marises. Of dried sweet almonds three artabae. Of wine five hundred marises. (And if he supped at Babylon or Susa, one half was palm wine, and the other half wine expressed from grapes). Two hundred load of dry wood, and one hundred load of green. Of fluid honey a hundred square palathae, containing the weight of about ten minae. When he was in Media, there were added—of bastard saffron feed three artabae: of saffron two minae. This was the appointment for dinner and supper. He also expended in largesses five hundred artabae of fine wheat flour. Of fine barely flour a thousand artabae: and of other kinds of flour a thousand artabae. Of rice five hundred artabae. Of corn five hundred marises. Of corn for the horses twenty thousand artabae. Of straw ten thousand load. Of vetches five thousand load. Of oil of Sisamin two hundred marises. Of vinegar a hundred marises. Of cresses chopped small thirty artabae. All, that is here enumerated, was distributed among the forces, that attended him. In dinner, and supper, and in largessess, the above was the king's daily expenditure." Translation obtained here: http://www.attalus.org/translate/polyaenus4 A.html (adapted from *Shepherd* (1793), accessed 15.2.2013).

75 Lewis 1997 thinks that the document is genuine and argues for Ctesias as possible source.
76 Monuments in the *Alexander Romance*: tomb of Cyrus (rec. α 2.18); tomb of Xerxes (recc. B, L 2.18, γ 2.17); Alexander and the statue of Nectanebo (rec. γ 2.27); Alexander and the statue of Sesonchosis (rec. γ 2.31). In a similar tradition is the epitaph of Sardanapalus (Arr. *Anab.* 2.5.3–4). Further inscriptions on the decadence of Sardanapalus: Plut. *De Alex. Fort.* 330F; 336C-d; Dio Chr. 4.135; Athen. 12.529d-530. On the monuments in the *Alexander Romance*, Stoneman 1995 and Zadorojnyi forthcoming.
77 IG IX 1² I, 17 A = T 3 AB, ca 263–2 BC. See also Bing 2009b, 183–5.
78 Stephens 2003 is a classic.

menid influence on the way Greeks imagined the Empire in the age of Alexander. One needn't assume that, in order to fashion their kingdoms after a Persian model, the Diadochs had to present themselves as the heirs of the Achaemenids. After all, propaganda travels well and can be adopted and adapted to individual needs. In taking a leaf from the Persian book, the Macedonian kings did the same thing the Persians had done for centuries before them. As Lloyd Llewellyn-Jones argues in his recent monograph on the king and court in Persia, "as the Persian Empire expanded its territory, the ruling dynasty came into contact with pre-existing court structures: Ancient Egyptian, Neo-Assyrian, Babylonian, Urartian, Levantine, and Anatolian courts all provided the Achaemenids with blueprints for constructing a courtly identity, and, as with all forms of art and architecture, the Persians readily took from these mature royal societies the elements which they found most appealing or meaningful."[79]

For centuries, the Greeks were fascinated with the Great King of Persia, with luxury, expenditure, royal gifts and the Persian way of life. Greeks in Asia, as subjects of the Great King, knew first-hand about royal propaganda. Those who encountered the Persians in the course of Alexander's conquests were also fascinated with the royal palaces, ceremonial, harems and tombs. Greeks knew well about tribute and gifts as symbols of subordination, and they even provided symbolic interpretations of the things stored in the Persian treasuries. It is this type of royal propaganda that the Ptolemies adopted and adapted for their own purposes and which, directly or indirectly, found its way into Posidippus' epigrammatic collection.

If this assumption is correct, the central poems of the Lithika (8, 9, and 10) could be interpreted as programmatic in yet another way: These epigrams thematize a Greek engraved signet-ring (9), a Near Eastern cylinder (10) and a vast ornamental Persian stone (8) that Kuttner has identified as an Achaemenid royal pectoral necklace.[80] Three kings and three distinct—and kingly—forms of stones might represent Posidippus' merger of the Greek and Near-Eastern inscriptional traditions in forming a new one, fit for the rulers of the Ptolemaic kingdom.

---

[79] Llewellyn-Jones 2013, 8. For general remarks on the way all Hellenistic kingdoms adopted Achaemenid propaganda, Ma 2003a.
[80] Kuttner 2005, 153 and plate 14.

Silvia Barbantani
"Déjà la pierre pense où votre nom s'inscrit"

Identity in context in verse epitaphs for Hellenistic soldiers

As Louis Aragon puts it in bitter, sharp words, when young men leave to go to war, "Déjà la pierre pense où [leur] nom s'inscrit" ("the stone is already thinking where [their] name will be inscribed").[1] These words sounds even optimistic if we consider the mass graves and innumerable unknown soldiers buried in unmarked spots in the same trenches and fields where they fell during the first World War—just to name one. Today, soldiers' epitaphs tend to be extremely laconic: you can hardly find more than the name, the rank and a couple of dates recorded on the stone. However, it is not the words but the context wherein the tomb is placed that is meant to carry across a message: modern military cemeteries around the world (e.g. Arlington in the U.S., Longueval-Somme and Colleville, in France), with the endless repetition of almost identical headstones, seem to abolish individuality and give the impression of a tight, emotionally and ideologically compact social body united for a higher purpose even in death: the body of an army. In the monumental, essential geometry of Redipuglia, the voice of the dead is repeated as a silent echo engraved in the grey stone as they ideally reply, with a depersonalized, identical answer ("Presente!"), to an imaginary roll-call of their individual names[2]. Before the birth of modern nations, such ideological purpose was fulfilled by the *polyandria*, common burials paid for by the community, and accompanied by dry but carefully elaborated epigrams, often commissioned to professional poets (like Simonides), expressing the moral values of the deceased.[3] I have no intention to linger on such epigrams

---

[1] Precisely, *Déjà la pierre pense où votre nom s'inscrit*, beginning of the last strophe of *La guerre et ce qui s'en suivit* (on the fallen of the First World War), in *Le roman inachevé*, 1956. The poem has been made into a song (*Tu n'en reviendras pas*) by Leo Ferré (*Les Chansons d'Aragon*, 1961).
[2] The widest Italian military cemetery, for the dead of 1915–1918, was built in 1938, and is an interesting example of the political use made by Mussolini of the memories of the Great War. It is located at Fogliano Redipuglia, Gorizia.
[3] Sometimes even among the deceased of a common grave a single man stands out, thanks to a simple, individual epigram, like Thibron (Peek *GVTh*, nr. 24 = *IG* IX,2 nr. 251), but this is a rare occurrence. Exclusively military necropoles comparable to modern military cemeteries are quite rare or non-existent in antiquity, and in any case the single graves are distinctively individually marked, e.g. with painting or reliefs representing the deceased; see Launey 1949, 791–794 (Sidon; Hadra).

for common graves, most of which have been already studied in depth, from the philological and historical point of view. My curiosity is rather focused on verse epitaphs for individual soldiers, whether they happened to die in a war or just peacefully at home after a life-long and successful career in the army: this contribution, which stems from a wide research project still *in fieri* on epigrams of military subject, is meant to offer some examples on how revealing on the history and identity of the deceased soldiers funerary headstones can be. My aim in gathering a *corpus* of thematically homogeneous epigrams such as "Hellenistic military epitaphs" is to investigate, beyond their poetic value and celebratory intention, something of the context that contributed to produce them. Here I must necessarily present a random choice of some of the most interesting issues one could deal with when confronted with this kind of material.

In the Hellenistic world, when the armies—either organized by *poleis* and *koina* or by monarchies—were a composite lot of local professionals, foreign mercenaries and common citizens, exclusively military cemeteries did not exist yet. There is no such sub-genre of epigram as "*the* military epitaph", but rather "epitaphs for soldiers or ex-soldiers", each one of them unique, and sometimes wildly individual, in spite of some recurrent rhetorical motives and poetic *formulae*. In the military lists found in papyri from Ptolemaic Egypt soldiers are asked to qualify themselves, for administrative and fiscal purposes, with name, patronymic, city or country of origin (*patris*), military unit and *epiphorai* (income, equivalent to rank);[4] in the epitaphs, of course, such a rigid format is never followed, and many of these data are missing. Even the name, surprisingly, is sometimes lacking in the epigram, and could have been supplied occasionally by a prose inscription on the stele, above the poem; in any case the name itself is rarely the first thing stated in epitymbian verses.

1. Language

I take into consideration only poetic epitaphs in Greek, although the composition of the Hellenistic armies was certainly ethnically complex. The Ptolemaic army is the best known of this period. The high officials were all Macedonian and Greek, and most of the Egyptians serving in the lower ranks did not speak Greek; some of them, however, could learn the language in the hope of climbing the social ladder and gaining access to court, royal administration and higher ranks in

---

[4] See Thompson 2001. As for the homeland, in the list where ethnics are missing, all the soldiers are generally considered Greeks, but see Fraser 2007 for a variety of examples.

the army:⁵ it is the case of Tearoos and his brother, members of the royal guard as ἡγεμόνες τῶν περὶ αὐ<λ>ὴν ἐπιλέκτων μαχίμων (*OGIS* II 731, Alexandria, 204–194/3 BC), and of Petesouchos son of Chrysippus, one of the ἐγλελοχισμένοι μαχαιροφό(ροι) βα(σιλικοί) (*SB* I 4206.239 and 245 = Bernand 1999, nr. 5; Hermoupolis Magna, 80/79 BC)⁶. Members of the army we consider to be ethnically *Hellenes*, on the other hand, could be only half-Greek; already in the second generation of military settlers (*klerouchoi*) one could count a good number of mixed marriages with local women, and although these individual generally styled themselves as Greek, we could confidently assume that they could at least speak and understand also the Egyptian language: it is the case of the *katochos* of the Memphite Serapeum Ptolemy and of his younger brother Apollonius, sons of Glaucias (both the father and Apollonius followed a military career)⁷.

There is at least one case of military man provided with double epitaph, in Greek and in Egyptian (the latter in prose). Apollonius, son of Ptolemy, member of a notable priestly family of Apollonopolis Magna- Edfu, who probably died in the War of the Sceptres (103–101 BC),⁸ had his epitaph composed by the professional poet Herodes (Bernand 1969, 57–58, nr. 5, pl. LVI):

[πατρ]ίδ' ἐμὴν συγγνοὺς καὶ τίς τίνος εἰμὶ προσελθώ[ν],   1
   [ξ]εῖνε, σὺν εὐτυχίῃ στεῖχε δι' ἀτραπιτοῦ
εἰμὶ γὰρ εὐκλειοῦς Ἀπολλώνιος ὁ Πτολεμαίου
   κοῦρος, ὃν Εὐέρκται μίτρᾳ ἐπηγλάισαν,
συγγενικῆς δόξης ἱερὸν γέρας· εὔνοια γάρ μιν   5
   βαῖνε καὶ εἴσω γᾶς ἄχρι καὶ ὠκεανόν.
τοὔνεκα κἀμὲ πατρὸς καλὸν κλέος εἰσορόωντα
   τῆς αὐτῆς ψαύειν θυμὸς ἔθηγ' ἀρετῆς,
καὶ πατρίδος καλῆς τὸν ἐπάξιον ἐσμὸν ἑλέσθαι,

---

5 See Thompson 2001, 273 ff.; Peremans 1983; Fischer-Bovet 2014, ch. 1.2 (Egyptian soldiers), ch. 2 (Ethnic composition of the Ptolemaic army).
6 See Peremans 1983, 275.
7 See Clarysse 2010; Legras 2011; Thompson 2011, 197–246. Apollonius son of Glaucias describes himself as "Macedonian" but records his dreams in Demotic (Thompson 2001, 314; see Nardelli 1987 and 1988 for his literary choices, focusing on the theme of "Greek among Barbarians"). Fraser 2007, analyzing two inscriptions from Hermoupolis Magna dating 73/2 BC, with about a thousand names of soldiers, shows that many beginning with "Apollo-" are theophoric names referring to the local god Kos; as proven by Clarysse 1985, 57 and Yoyotte 1969, soldiers could use both a Greek and a Demotic name according to their needs and the circumstances; the Greek anthroponym is generally a translation, sometimes a rough transliteration of the Egyptian one.
8 See Van't Dack/Clarysse/Cohen/Quaegebeur/Winnicki 1989, 84–88, with the suggestion to read in the epitaph a reference to the Syrian campaign of 103/102 BC.

αἰπείας Φοίβου τῆσδ' ἱερᾶς πόλεως,   10
πατρὸς ἐμοῦ γνωτοῖσι συνεκπλεύσαντα φέριστε
    ξεῖνε, ὅτε σκάπτρων ἤλυθ' Ἄρης Συρίην.
καὶ γενόμην εὔνους, γλυκερὰν τηρῶν ἅμα πίστιν
    καὶ δορὶ καὶ τόλμᾳ πάντας ἐνεγκάμενος.
ὡς δ' ἐμὲ Μοῖρ' ἐδάμασσε βιοκλώστειρα, τί σὲ χρὴ   15
    τοῦτο μαθεῖν, νόστου μνησάμενον γλυκείου
ἡλικίης ἀκόρητον, ὅτ' οὐδὲ φίλων ἐνέπλησα
    θυμὸν ἐμῶν τέκνων, ὧν λίπον ἐν θαλάμοις;
ταῦτα μαθών, ὦ ξεῖνε, λέγοις πατρὶ τῷ κτερίσαντι,
    "σαυτὸν μὴ τρύχειν μνησάμενον βιότου"   20
καὶ σοὶ δ' εὐοδίης τρίβον ὄλβιον εὔχομαι εἶναι
    πρός γ' ἔτι καὶ τέκνοις σοῖσι φιλοφροσύνοις.
    Ἀπολλώνιε χρηστέ, χαῖρε.
    Ἡρώδου.

Having learned of my homeland, of my identity and of my father, / o stranger, proceed further on your path with good fortune. / For I am Apollonius son of the illustrious Ptolemy / whom the Euergetai honored with a diadem, / sacred prerogative of the glory of the "Relatives". His goodwill / made him proceed inland, and as far as the Ocean. / Therefore, looking to the noble glory of my father, / I was seized by the desire of attaining the same virtue, / and of choosing the worthy swarm of my beautiful homeland: / this high, sacred city of Phoebus;/ and sailed out together with the acquaintances of my father, o excellent stranger, / when Ares of the scepters came to Syria. / And I was benevolent, preserving sweet loyalty, and, at the same time / surpassing all with my spear and my boldness. / How Moira, who spins human destinies, tamed me, why / should you learn this? I was remembering the sweet homecoming, / still hungry for my youth, without fulfilling my desire to see my children, / whom I had left in their chambers. Having learned these things, stranger, / I hope you can say to my father, who buried me: / "Do not torture yourself, remember the human destiny", / and I pray that you can tread a prosperous path of good fortune, / and with you your loving children.
Noble Apollonius, greetings!
(Composed by) Herodes.

His Greek epitaph, like those of his relatives,[9] is complemented by a near-by hieroglyphic stele, praising him in Egyptian style (Kamal 1905, nr. 22018, pl. VII); in the Egyptian headstone Apollonius bears the name of "Pashai" son of "Pamenches"; while his military and administrative activities at the service of the

---

[9] In the necropolis of Hassaia (Apollinopolis Magna, near Edfu/Bakhthis) the aristocratic family of Apollonius had long Greek funerary epitaphs in elegiac couplets commissioned to a local professional poet, Herodes, engraved on their *stelae* (Bernand 1969, nos 5, 6, 7, 35; cf. Garulli 2008, 633–637; Santin 2009, 171–186; Mosino 2001; Boyaval 2004b, 147–149; Clarysse 2001, 14–17) and, nearby, traditional Egyptian headstones written in hieroglypic, celebrating them as members of a noble priestly family (see Yoyotte 1969; Kamal 1905, nos 22018–22021).

king are dutifully listed ("grand général et commandant[10], ami unique, chef de la cavalerie, vaillant dans la bataille, premier lieutenant de Sa Majesté, dont il accomplit les décisions dans le territoire du Sud"),[11] sometimes in terms quite similar to those of the Greek epigram,[12] he is also defined "third prophet", "second prophet", and "prophet" of various Egyptian deities (Osiris, Ammon, Harsomtous son of Hathor, Min, and Horus of Edfu). In the Greek stele there is no mention of his Egyptian priestly engagements—certainly an important element in his life outside the army—let alone any hints of his ability to shift at ease between the two cultures. A striking common feature of the two epitaphs, apart from the military rank, however, is the aulic titulature, which Pashai shares with his father Ptolemy (in the epitaph for his wife, Bernand 1969, nr. 35, ll. 8–10, Ptolemy is qualified as βουλᾷ καὶ δορὶ θαρσαλέος/ καὶ στρατιᾷ Φοίβου δ[ε]ικνὺς σέλας αἰὲν ἄμωμον / συγγενικῆς τε φορῶν δόξαν ἰσουρανίαν) and his homonym grandfather Pahsai: this key-role at court is defined in Egyptian as *sn-nswt*, "brother of the king", in the Greek epitaph as "συγγενής of the king"; the diadem or μίτρα (Bernand 1969, nr. 5, l. 4), which has been granted to him as sign of συγγενικῆς δόξης (l. 5), finds a correspondence in the Egyptian "golden band" mentioned in documents for other Egyptian *strategoi* and "brothers of the King", and represented in their statues.[13] Apollonius, with his notable double epitaph, is just the most prominent example among many other bicultural members of the Ptolemaic ruling class, composed by royal *philoi*, bureaucrats and courtiers, whose double identity has come to evidence since, in the last few decades, papyrologists and philologists, Egyptologists and archeologists started to collaborate comparing prosopographical data in different languages (Egyptian, Greek, Latin): in the multifaceted panorama of the Ptolemaic court, the cultivated priest Manetho, perfectly mastering his native language and that of the conquerors,[14]

---

10 *Mr mš' wr*, in Demotic *p', srtks* (στρατηγός) designates the "stratèges indigènes" in the sense of ἡγημόνες, military commanders of Egyptian troops, according to Yoyotte 1969, 135.
11 I use here the translation of Yoyotte 1969, 134. For the interpretation and translation of the Egyptian inscription see Yoyotte 1969, esp. 134–135, 138 and Thompson 2001, 315–316.
12 See the detailed comparison in Yoyotte 1969, 138–139. If the cartonnage published by Maspero 1886, 3–4 belongs to the same Pashai or a member of the same family, as Yoyotte believes, this would offer a further Egyptian version of Apollonius/Pashai Greek military encomium.
13 See Yoyotte 1969, 129 with notes 1 and 2.
14 Since the use of different languages is reserved for specific and sometimes separate domains, it will be more correct to call the phenomenon "diglossia": see Mairs 2012a; on the use of interpreters whitin a bilingual environment see Mairs 2012b. Until now there are no hints that Alexandrian Greek scholars could speak or understand also Egyptian; there must have been ways, however, for them to grasp some of the main features of the local culture, as stressed by

appears no more an isolated case.¹⁵ Non-Greek royal officials bearing Greek names and able to move at ease in both worlds, being perfectly bilingual, bi-literate and, at a different degrees, culturally bifunctional were also present in the Seleucid empire (e.g. Berossus): one could expect that also in the Greek and Aramaic/Babylonian speaking area bilingual epitaphs would be produced, although until now nothing comparable to the majestic Apollonius double epitaph has been found.

2. Ethnic and cultural identity

Even when we are reading epitaphs in Greek, then, this does not mean that we are always dealing with "ethnic" Greeks, but only that these individuals chose to present themselves, on given occasions or most of the time, as *culturally* Greek. Identity, ultimately, is a matter of negotiation between different cultural and ethnic components of an individual: that is, a matter choice, much more than a matter of genes.¹⁶ Probably the most paradoxical case it that of the epitaph, found in Maronea, of the famous Galatian mercenary chief Briccon, native of the Phrygian Apamea (Moretti 1975, 115–118, nr. 115):¹⁷

---

some pioneers in the field of the intercultural intepretation of Alexandrian literature like Selden 1998 and Stephens 2003.
15 See Thompson 1992, 44–45; Quaegebeur 1980, esp. 78–79; Klotz 2009; Collombert 2000; Pfeiffer 2004, 4; Bingen 2007. A good example is that of Nectanebo, of Egyptian royal descent, official in the army and in administration under the reign of Ptolemy I Soter: a stele in Hieroglyphic, Demotic and Greek, from Denderah (ca. 12 BC), documents his activities and those of his father Panas, son of Psenobastis (see La'da 1994; de Meulenaere 1963, 90–93): like Apollonious, Ptolemy, on top of being στρατηγός and a συγγενής of the king, is also a high representative of the local clergy. Cf. also *OGIS* 111.14–20 (2ⁿᵈ BC): Heroides, son of Demophon of Pergamum (Thompson 2001, 319, n. 56).
16 See Barth 1969; Jones 1997, 84–85; Goudriaan 1992, 76–77; Herring 2009; Mairs 2010a and Mairs 2010b. There is always an interplay between different identities in any individual, based on elements such as gender, age, ethnicity, class, level of education. Shared language is one of the strongest ties marking identity within a community ("*barbaroi*" are those excluded from verbal communication within a certain group), cf. Østergård 1992, 36–37.
17 On this text see also *SEG* 24 (1969), 213, nr. 637; *SEG* 38 (1991), 21, nr. 731; Daux 1968, 924–925 with fig. 11 and 12. Welles 1970 contextualized the epigram in the period of the Chremonidean War (the Galatian would serve under Antigonos Gonatas), while Grandjean 1971, after a paleographic study of the inscription (end 3ʳᵈ-beginning 2ⁿᵈ BC), placed the death of Briccon at the time of Antiochus III's campain in Greece (195–4 BC); cf. also Heinen 1972, 170–172; Masson 1982; Chamoux 1988, 499–500. Apamea could be the Bithynian (Grandjean 1971, 293 n. 52), or better the city on the Meander (Welles 1970; Chamoux 1988; Moretti 1975).

πατρὸς Ἀτευρίστου Βρίκκων ὅδε τῆδ' ὑπὸ γαίῃ
κεῖμαι, Ἀπαμείας πατρίδος ἐκ προμολῶν·
ἦλθον δ' ἡγήτωρ Γαλατῶν καὶ μοῦνος <ἐ>ν αἰχμᾷ
δάϊον ἐμ προμάχοις Ἄρεα μαρνάμενος
λείπομαι· εὐσεβέων δὲ τὸ μυρίον ἵξομαι ἄστυ,
εἴ τι καὶ εἰν Ἀΐδῃ τίμιόν ἐστι βροτοῖς.

I, Briccon, son of Ateuristos, under this earth / I am resting, coming from my hometown Apamea; / I came as a commander of the Galatians and I succumbed in the battle / fighting in the first line against hostile Ares. / I shall go to the vast city of the Blessed, / if also in Hades there is some reward for the mortals.

Mercenary service flourished in the Hellenistic era,[18] yet the social consideration and moral evaluation of a professional soldier still included some elements of ambiguity. The two faces of the same coin have been well intepreted by two poignant modern epigrams on the same subject (the men of the "British Expeditionary Force" fallen in the Great War in 1914), penned by Housman and MacDiarmid:

> These, in the day when heaven was falling,
>   The hour when Earth's foundations fled,
> Followed their mercenary calling
>   And took their wages and are dead.
> Their shoulders held the sky suspended;
>   They stood, and earth's foundations stay;
> What God abandoned, these defended,
>   And saved the sum of things for pay
>   A.E. Housman, *Epitaph on an Army of Mercenaries* (1922)

> It is a God-damned lie to say that these
> Saved, or knew, anything worth a man's pride.
> They were professional murderers and they took
> Their blood money and impious risks and died.
> In spite of all their kind some elements of worth
> With difficulty persist here and there on earth.
>   H. MacDiarmid, *Another Epitaph on an Army of Mercenaries* (1935).

Mercenaries could save the day, yet their loyalty was perceived as shaky, and their origin was often questionable. For a "barbarian" mercenary (as well as for a Greek one) the only solution in order to improve the perception of his liability among the Hellenes, at least after death, was to let Greek poetry speak in

---

[18] On Hellenistic mercenaries see Griffith 1935; Krasilnikoff 1992; Baker 1999; Landucci 2001 and 2002; Chaniotis 2005, 78–88, 99–100.

defense of his own *areté*, making it comparable to those of the epic heroes and of the hoplites who defeated the Persians in the 5th century BC. Although belonging to the most vilified barbarian *ethne* of the time, presented by all the rulers and by mainland Greeks as the arch-enemy of the civilized (i.e. Hellenic) world,[19] Galatian mercenaries soon managed to earn some place as useful supporters of the official armies in many kingdoms. Judging from his epitaph, the smart commander Briccon was a model of cultural blending in—certainly also when he was alive. His epitaph displays the main *topoi* used in Greek epic and praise poetry over deceased warriors since Homer and Tyrtaeus, so that a military chief belonging to a nation presented by the Greeks as totally antiphrastic to their culture suddenly becomes the equivalent of the perfect Hellenic hero. In the first couplet he presents himself proudly in the first person, and in Greek, but flaunting as first identitarian elements his very non-Hellenic patronymic ("son of Ateuristos"), name ("Briccon") and *patris* (Apamea). The second couplet portrays fiercely his valor and steadiness under attack (he died ἐμ προμάχοις), on the consequence of which he expects, with some degree of self-assuredness, to find his place in the Greek heaven among the pious (εὐσεβέων; cf. *SGO* IV, 17/17/01, l. 8):[20] his self-portrait is therefore the opposite of the *cliché*, disseminated in Greek propaganda and historical narratives, of the indisciplined and mindlessly audacious Galatians, the most impious creatures on Earth, the New Titans (Call. *Hymn*. 4.165–188; *SH* 958.9: ὑβρισταί τε καὶ ἄφρονες).[21] In spite of the episode of the revolt described by Callimachus *Hymn* 4 (cf. *schol. ad* vv. 175–187) and Pausanias 1.7.2, Galatian mercenaries settled quite well in Egypt and even advertised after death their identity, and their complete integration into the Alexandrian society, with beautifully painted *stelae* (see e.g. those preserved in the Metropolitan Museum in New York and in the Louvre).[22]

---

19 On Galatians in the Hellenistic historical and literary context see Hannestad 1993; Barbantani 2001; Mitchell 2007; Strootman 2005; Kistler 2009.
20 The "citadel of the pious" is variation on the classical *topos* of the "Island/Land/Meadows of the Blessed", to be found in many epitaphs (not only of military men), e.g. in Peek, *GVI* 943.1; *SGO* IV, 17/17/01, l. 8 (cf. below pp. 330 and 321); Bernand 1969 nr. 66,3: κέκλιμαι εὐσεβέων λειμώνια νῦν ὑπὸ βένθη (for the soldier Philonides); Bernand 1969, nr. 64,18; *CIRB* 131.11= *IosPE* II 298 (1st BC-1st AD): εὐσεβέων ναίοις ἱερὸν δόμον; *IC* III iv 37 (Crete, 1st BC); *IGR* IV 1579 (Teos); Kaibel 648 (Rome) and 338 (Cyzicus).
21 On the two passages see Barbantani 2001, 116–179; 188–203.
22 Metropolitan: http://www.metmuseum.org/toah/works-of-art/04.17.6; http://www.metmuseum.org/toah/works-of-art/04.17.4; http://www.metmuseum.org/toah/works-of-art/04.17.5; Louvre: Rouveret 2004, 29–91, with tables; cf. also Pagenstecher 1919, 47 nr. 30, 53 nr. 52, 60 nr. 75.

Another mercenary chief, Diazelmis, coming from the Bithynian Apamea, speaks loud and clear with a Greek voice, in spite of his Thracian name, from his tomb in Terenuthis (31 BC; Peek *GVI* 1153 = Bernand 1969, nr. 10):[23]

ὁ πρὶν ἐγὼ κατὰ δῆριν ἐν[όπ]λιον ὄρχαμος ἀνδρῶν	1
φῦλα δαϊξάνδρῳ χειρὶ τροπωσάμενος,	
ἀσκηθὴς ἐν νευσὶ καὶ ἀστυφέλικτος ἐπ' αἴῃ,	
πείθ[ων α]ἱμοχαρῆ κῶ[μ]ον Ἐνυαλίου,	
Ἀσίδο[ς] ἐν γυάλ[ο]ις ἤ[μο]ς [λ]ῃστῆρας ἀλαλκὼν	5
σκῦλα δοριδμήιτ[ων ἔ]πραθον ἐνδαπίων,	
στείχων Αἰγύπτο[υ] κλεινὴν σταχυμήτορα τύρσιν,	
κοιρανίδαις ζαμενῆ πίστιν ἐνεγκάμενος·	
νῦν δὲ καθ' ὀγδο[ά]δη[ς δ]εκ[άδος] στείχοντα κέλευθον	
Ἄδας ὀρφ<ν>αίο<ι>ς ἐγγ[υ]άλιξε μυ<χ>ο<ῖ>ς,	10
τέκνων οὐ κατ[ιδόντ'] α[ἰνὸν] μόρον, ἀλλὰ κ[αὶ] παίδων	
παῖδας ἐφ' ὑστατίῳ τέρματι γηροκόμους.	
πάτρη γάρ μ' ἐλόχευσεν Ἀπάμεα, γαῖα δ' ἔθρεψεν	
Αἰγύπτου θνατο<ῖ>ς πᾶσι γεγῶτα φίλον,	
Διάζελμιν, βασιλεῦσι τετειμένον· ὦ παροδῖτα,	15
"χαῖρε", λέγοις, "κούφη δ' ἀμφιπέλοιτο κόνις".	

Once, in the clash of the weapons, I was commander of men / and with my murderous hand I routed tribes (of enemies), well experienced on the sea and unshaken on the ground, giving orders to the bloodlusting company of Enyalios, / when in the valleys of Asia, repelling marauders, / I took the spoils of the locals tamed by my spear. / Moving to the glorious fortress of Egypt, mother of ears,/ I brought to her rulers my strong loyalty. / Now, while I was following the path of the eight decade,/ Hades grabbed me in his obscure depths; /I did not witness the death of my children, but (I had) / the children of my children taking care of me in the extreme term of my old age. / The homeland who gave me birth is Apamea, but the land who nurtured me/ was Egypt: I was dear to everyone, /I, Diazelmis, honored by the kings; passerby, / may you say "I salute you, may the ground be light on you".

Diazelmis pleads, vigorously, allegiance (ζαμενῆ πίστιν, l. 8) to his latest employers, the Ptolemies, by whom he was honored (l. 15): so far goes his loyalty as to

---

[23] See also *SEG* 54 (2008), 639, nr. 1759; Launey 1949, 808–809; Boyaval 2004a, 72–73; Boyaval 2005, 163–164. Peek dated the epigram to the 2nd-1st century BC, but it may well be complementary to the funerary stele with an inscription in prose, dated 31 BC, published by El Nassery-Wagner-Abdul-Al 1978, 236–237, nr. 2 = *SEG* 28 (1982), nr. 1492: Διάζελμι / χρηστὲ χρῆσι/με ἄλυπε, χαῖ/ρε (ἔτους) κβ' τοῦ καὶ ζ'/Φαῶφι κα'. Diazelmis' Thracian name suggests that he could come from the Bythinian Apamea, on the Propontis (so Bernand 1969, 79, following L. Robert and J. Zingerle); Boyaval 2005 places his activities against the bandits in the area of Pisidia, Isauria, Cilicia, Pamphylia; a couple of centuries before, also the high-ranking Ptolemaic commander Neoptolemus had to face multiethnic bands of marauders in the same region (see Barbantani 2007).

declare Egypt his second homeland, since it "supported/nurtured him", while Apamea just "gave him birth" (ll. 13–14; for the multiple homelands, all cherished for different reasons and listed in a funerary epigram cf. the fictitious self-epitaph of Meleager, *A.P.* 7.417–419). The relevant place given to the key-value of loyalty in this epigram makes the mercenary Diazelmis no different from the Graeco-Egyptian high ranking officer and notable priest Apollonius, who also, in spite of representing the third generation of a family in the service of the Ptolemies, still felt the need of emphasizing his πίστις (l. 13) to them, while boasting his bravery as a military man. Military prowess and loyalty are universal values for soldiers, and overcome any possible other cultural and ethnic difference once they earn them the benevolence of the kings and /or the fellow citizens: another case from the Ptolemaic world is the epitaph of Gaza (201 BC) for Charmadas son of Taskomenes, a Cretan from Anopolis serving under the Ptolemies in Coele Syria, and for his Etolian son-in-law Machaios (Peek *GVI* 1508; *SGO* IV, 21/05/01)[24]: ἦ μὴν ἀμφοτέρους γε παλαίπλουτοι βασιλῆες / Αἰγύπτου χρυσέαις ἠγλάισαν χάρισιν (ll. 9–10), "sure, the kings of Egypt of ancient wealth glorified both of them with golden favors". The individual worth of the soldier is clearly enhanced by the importance of the ruler for whom it is displayed, and, as we have seen in funerary poems from the Ptolemaic area, the name of the "employer" is carefully advertised in the epitaph: a further example is the epigram for Praxagoras (Peek *GVI* 1076, Cyprus, Kition/Larnaka, 3rd BC). In four lines this Cretan officer, admirable for his synthesis, a trademark of his country,[25] conveys to the passerby his main anagraphic data, in the following order: homeland, name of the parents, his own name (honorably spent), rank (ἡγεμών) and employer; the key expression Λαγείδας κοίρανος stands up right in the centre of the last pentameter, just before the military title the king granted to the proud Praxagoras.

Κρήτα μὲν πατρίς μου, ὁδοιπόρε, τίκτε δὲ μάτηρ
   Νικώ, Σωσιάναξ δ' ἦ[ε]ν ἐμὸς γενέτας·
Πραξαγόρας δ' ὄνομ' ἔσχον ἐπικλεές, ὃν πρὶν ἐπ' ἀνδρῶν
   θήκατο Λαγείδας κοίρανος ἀγεμόνα.

Creta was my homeland, passer-by, my mother Niko, Sosianax my father. My name was Praxagoras, and I bore it with glory, once the Lagid king establised me as a commander of men.

---

24 See *SEG* 8 (1937), nr. 269; Roussel 1933; Tod 1933; Vincent 1937; Launey 1949, 807–808; Chaniotis 2002, 111–112; Chaniotis 2006, 102; inscr. nr. 1 in the Appendix of Glucker 1987.
25 Cf. Call. *Ep.* XI Pfeiffer = *A.P.* 7.447; Posid. *Ep.* 102 Austin/Bastianini. See Gronewald 1993; Celentano 1995.

A Seleucid instance for this topic is the epigram for two Milesian members of the family of Menestheus (left anonymous in the poem, but probably named on a nearby stone),[26] ὑψηλοὺς... ἀγεμόνας, "high commanders" serving under Demetrius I Soter (162–150 BC), son of Seleucus IV Philopator (Peek *GVI* 1286 = *SGO* I, 01/20/35); the positive connotation of "fortunate, affluent" (l. 3), possibly not apt enough to Demetrius' troubled career, is even less realistic if attributed to his father, and must be taken as a rhetoric device to enhance the prestige of the Milesian officers.

> σῆμα μὲν ἴσθ' ὅτι τοῦτο Μενεσθειδᾶν ἐπὶ δισσοῖς   1
> κίοσιν ὠνκώθη, ξεῖνε, καταφθιμένοις·
> εἴ τινας εὐόλβου μεγάλας παρὰ παιδὶ Σελεύκου
> Ἀσίδος ὑψηλοὺς ἔκλυες ἀγεμόνας.

> Stranger, you must know that this funerary monument stands on the two columns of the sons of Menestheus, deceased, if you have ever heard of the high commanders of great Asia who served under the son of fortunate Seleukos.

The *topos* of the good official, who is able to earn the confidence of his direct superiors and of the kings as well, will be repeated in epitaphs of the Roman empire: see e.g. *SGO* IV, 21/23/01 (Gerasa, Syria, 150–200 AD), an epigram for the *centurio* Germanus, ἡγεμόνων ὑπάτων χρησάμενος φιλίαις (l. 4). Although it was advisable to market this quality effectively when operating in the competitive and relatively restricted circle of a court, the value of loyalty was not exclusive of soldiers serving under Hellenistic kings or Roman emperors: it is celebrated also as a civic virtue, for example, in the epitaph for a citizen of Lokris Opous, the commander of cavalry Nikasichorus (*IG* IX,1 270 = Kaibel 855 = Posidippus *Dubia* nr. 33 Fernández-Galiano; dated either between 265–245 or after 229 BC):[27] πίστις ... πάντων κοίρανος ἁγνοτάτα, "loyalty is the purest leader of all", the antidote of corruption, and one of the pillars of Eunomia.

We have seen above that "barbarian" or half-Greek soldiers could use poetry in order to state their own sense of belonging to the Hellenic culture and therefore to enhance their reputation or promote their status, at least after death. Con-

---

[26] They could be identified with the Menestheus and Meleager sons of Apollonius (adoptive father), who helped Demetrius in his escape from Rome in 162 BC, see Polyb. 27.19.1; 28.1.6–9 and 22.2; 31.13; cf. also *SGO* I 157–158, Hermann 1987, 175–179, Gera 1998, 261–267 for a biographic essay; *SEG* 37 (1990), nr. 991.

[27] See Moretti 1975, 38–40, nr. 84; Woodhouse 1897, 286; Wilhelm 1911, 192–193; Quaß 1993, 116; Garulli 2013. For a combination of loyalty and military valor see also the laconic epitaph for Callias of Tegea, from Pherai (3rd BC; Peek *GVI* 1460 = *IG* IX,2 nr. 430): σώιζων μὲν πίστιν, τιμῶν δὲ ἀρε[τὰν] / θάνες ὧδε, Κα<λ>(λ)ία Σ<τ>ασαγόρα / πατρίδος ἐκ Τεγέας.

versely, in Hellenistic and Roman epitaphs for Greek soldiers killed in battle against non-Greek enemies, identity is heavily defined in a contrastive way, the heroism of the deceased being boosted by the mention of the ethnicity of its adversary, the barbarian, perceived as a frightening and devastating entity. The main model were, obviously, the epitymbian epigrams for the fallen of the Persian Wars. The first occurrence of the *topos* in the Hellenistic era appears in the dedicatory epigram accompanying the shield offered to Zeus Eleutherios (*FGE* Anon. CXL, from Paus. 10.21.5) once belonging to the young Cydias, who died at the Thermopylae (279 BC) fighting in battle for the first time, against the Galatians:

ἧμαι δὴ ποθέουσα νέαν ἔτι Κυδίου ἥβην
ἀσπὶς ἀριζήλου φωτός, ἄγαλμα Διί,
ἇς διὰ δὴ πρώτας λαιὸν τότε πῆχυν ἔτεινεν,
εὖτ' ἐπὶ τὸν Γαλάταν ἤκμασε θοῦρος Ἄρης.

"Here hang I, yearning for the still youthful bloom of Cydias, / The shield of a glorious man, an offering to Zeus. / I was the very first through which at this battle he thrust his left arm, / When the battle raged furiously against the Gaul".[28]

The examples are numerous, even from the most remote regions touched by Greek colonization: see e.g. the 1st century BC epitaph from Pantikapaion (Kerch, Tauric Chersonnesos),[29] for an Apollonius son of Apollonius, presented as a model of heroic valor (l. 9: ὁ τῆς γὰρ ἀρετῆς μοῦνος ἐκλάσθης κανών; ll. 12–13: <ν>ῦν οὐ κελαινὸς οἶκος, ἡρώων δὲ σὲ / ἕξουσι σηκοί), fallen against an unspecified barbarian enemy (l. 11: πρὸς δεινὸν ἔγχος βαρβάρων νενευκότα), or the 2nd-1st century BC epitaph for Lysimachos son of Psycharion, also from Pantikapaion, killed by "Nomads" (l. 5: Νομάδων ἔκτανε θοῦρος Ἄρης).[30]

---

28 I report here the translation by W.H.S. Jones from Pausanias, *Description of Greece*, Cambridge, MA-London 1918. Another interesting document of the wars against Celtic tribes is the Mysian epitaph for a certain Sotas, killed by Galatians in the 2nd century BC (Peek *GVI* 754 = *SGO* I 06/01/01, Elaia = Kaibel 242a); see Robert 1938, 206–209.
29 Peek *GVI* 1471; *CIRB* 119; *SGDI* 5558; see *SEG* 55 (2009), nr. 866 and Gavrilov 2005 for a commentary.
30 Peek *GVI* 843; Kaibel 251; *CIRB* 120; *IosPE* 2.171; the epitaph insists, more than the previously cited one, on the mourning of the young warrior deceased. Many other examples come from the same region.

When the soldier is both ethnically and culturally Greek,[31] it is not always possible to assess his precise geographic origin from his epitaph, as the information is often, but not always given; it is rarely missing in the case of a burial in a foreign land, see e.g. the epitaph for Nikolaos of Miletus (Bernand 1969, nr. 65 = Peek *GVI* 557, Alexandria, 1st-2nd BC), where homeland and name of the father are stated clearly in the first verse, even before the name of the fallen:[32] πατρίδος ἐγ Μιλήτου ἐσθλὸν γόνον ὧδε τὸ Σώσου / γῆ ἱερὰ Λιβύης τόνδε Νικόλαον ἔχει (ll. 1–2). Some of the Ptolemaic soldiers, exactly like their rulers (e.g. in Posidippus' *Hippika*),[33] are proudly declaring their Macedonian origin: this is the case of Archippus, whose epitaph (Alexandria, 2nd BC; Bernand 1969, nr. 9; *SEG* 8 (1937), nr. 370) opens with an unambiguous and detailed geographic statement (ll. 1–2): "Μυγδονία γαῖ' ἐστι Μακη[δονίας – —] / πάτρη σεῦ," "Your homeland is Mygdonia, (region) of Macedonia".

3. Military Rank

In Hellenistic epitaphs the actual rank of the deceased is rarely stated with precision. The lack of this information may be justified by the fact that technical terms defining military rank are sometimes unfitting metrical requirements, or simply perceived as not poetic enough to appear in a verse epitaph; accompanying lines of prose, however, may have filled up this gap. On the contrary, the use of a specific, technical terminology is more common in Greek epitaphs from the Roman empire, where we can frequently find Latin military vocabulary transliterated into Greek: see e.g. the epitaph for the soldier Alexander, from Krateia/Flaviopolis (Gerede), Bithynia (*SGO* II 09/10/01, 2nd century AD?): πρώτης οὐρβανῆς στρατιῆς (l. 2) = *cohors prima urbana*; the epitaph for the prematurely deceased Menianus, dedicated to him by his father Aquila, a *signifer* of the *legio I Italica* (σίγνων θεράπων λεγιῶνος / Ἰταλικῆς {τε} πρώτης, ll. 3–4), from Temenothyrai, Phrygia (Peek *GVI* 849 = *SGO* III 16/08/03, 1st century AD); the epitaph for the soldier Conon, from Aralleia, Lycaonia (Eastern Phygia/Sourthen Galatia), dedicated to him by his father Sambatios, ὀρδινάριος ὀβρίμων λανκιαρίων (*SGO* III 14/

---

[31] The *patris*, as we have seen above, was important for fiscal as well as for tactical reasons: under Ptolemy III, e.g., some new hipparchies were denominated from the ethnicity of their first components: Thracians, Macedonians, Thessalians, Mysians, Persians (Thompson 2001, 306).
[32] See Boyaval 2004b, 162–164 (*Les emplois funéraires de chrestos*).
[33] On the use of this ethnic see Criscuolo 2003, 312–313; Stephens 2004, 65–66 and 2005, 231–243; Barbantani 2005, 149. On the pseudo-ethnic designations (included "Macedon") used in the army see Fischer-Bovet 2014, ch. 2.2.1.1.

05/02 = *MAMA* 1, 306, 1. 5); and the epitaph for the *decurio* Amandus, from Tiberias (*SGO* IV, 21/06/01, 3rd century AD): ἐνδόξως στρατιᾶς ἄρξας δεκαταρχίδι τειμῇ (l. 3). In the Hellenistic period poetic words are preferred to express the rank of the deceased: even a mercenary chief like Diazelmis takes care of recalling, with an epic formula, his position as ὄρχαμος ἀνδρῶν (Bernand 1969, nr. 10.1), while the Galatian Briccon reminds us, using another Homeric word, that he came to Maronea as ἡγήτωρ Γαλατῶν (Moretti 1975, nr. 115.3). Another mercenary chief, the Arcadian Botrichus, who fell in Sparta in the 2nd century BC (*ante* 189 BC), is presented as ....πολλὸν ἄριστον / ἀνδρῶν αἰχματᾶν .... ἀγεμόνα (Peek *GVI* 903.1–2).[34] The qualification ἡγεμών is one of the most frequent: it is a very generic term, as it could designate different ranks, like φρούραρχος or commander of a garrison, commander of a σύνταγμα ("regiment"), or it could even be the equivalent to the role of the ἱππάρχος in cavalry. In a world where military career could be a matter of social prestige, however, stating the rank, even in poetic, nonspecific words, could be extremely relevant: in Bernand 1969, nr. 4 = Peek *GVI* 1149 (3rd-1st BC), ἀγεμόνα Πτολεμαῖον are the first words of the first line of the epitaph for Ptolemy of Coptus; at l. 6 the concept is repeated, while at l. 10 is added the specification of his role in times of peace, that of gymnasiarch; the poet shows similar care in pointing out the role in the army of his son Menodorus, who died in the same battle as a courageous warrior and a flag-bearer (l. 4):

> ἀγεμόνα Πτολεμαῖον, ὀδοιπόρε, τῇιδέ με κεύθει   1
> τύμβος, ἀνὰ κρατερήν φυλόπιδα φθίμενον,
> παῖδά τε Μηνοόδωρον ἐνὶ πτολέμοισιν ἀταρβῆ
> καὶ θρασὺν αἰχμητὴν σημοφόρωι κάμακι,
> εὖτ' ἐπὶ δυσμενέεσσι Μακηδόνι σὺν στρατιώτῃ,   5
> τοῖο τόθ' ἀγεμόνων, θούριον ἄγον Ἄρη·
> δήϊα δ' ἐν προμάχοισι καὶ ἄσπετα φῦλα κανόντας
> ἀμφοτέρους Ἀίδας ὠμὸς ἐληΐσατο.
> κλεινὰ δ' ὑπὲρ πάτρας θάνομεν θρεπτήρια δόντες,
> γυμνασιάρχος ἐν αἶ καὶ τὸ πάρος γενόμαν,   10
> πολλάκι τ' ἐμ πρυλέεσσιν ἀρήιος, ἔνθα δὲ βουλᾶς
> χρῆμα, τὸν ἐκ πραπίδων αἶνον ἐνεγκάμενος.
> [ἀλλ]ὰ σύ, καρτερέ, χαῖρε καὶ ἐμ φθιμένοις, Πτολεμαῖε·
> [ὅν τε προσ]αυδήσας, υἱό<ν>, ὁδῖτ', ἄπιθι.
> l.14 integr. Bernand

Here, o passer-by, the tomb encloses me, the commander Ptolemy:/ I died in a mighty battle; and there is also my son Menodorus, / never trembling in wars, courageous warrior holding the flag-bearing pole, / when against the enemies, with the Macedonian troops /

---

34 = Moretti 1967, 127–128, nr. 50; *IG* V,1 724; *SEG* 25 (1970), nr. 425.

of which I was then the commander, / I guided the furious Ares; / having killed innumerable enemies, while fighting in the front ranks, / cruel Hades took both of us. / We died after giving glorious gifts for our homeland / where previously I was also gymnasiarch, / often valiant among the infantry, and when it was time to give advice, / I received the praise for my wisdom. / O mighty Ptolemy, I salute you even among the dead; /speak to his son, passer-by, and then leave.

An anonymous soldier, probably a mercenary (l. 9 μισθο[φόρος; l. 8 πεζός, "infantry man"), buried in the necropolis of Hassaia (Apollonopolis Magna/Edfu) boasts εἰμὶ γὰρ ἡγεμόνος ἀνδρῶ[ν....] / ἶνις, "I am indeed the son of a commander" (ll. 5–6), using the present, as if the rank of his father could still be the most important qualification for the deceased (Bernand 1969, nr. 8).[35] The above mentioned epitaph for the sons of Menestheus, serving under a Seleucid king, also classifies them as Ἀσίδος ὑψηλοὺς ... ἀγεμόνας (Peek *GVI* 1286.4). The Byzantine Menas, who fell at Curupedion (3rd-2nd century BC),[36] presents himself as ἔξοχον ἡγέμονα (l. 8),[37] and fiercely underlines, with more than a pinch of pride for having proved himself at the same level of a rival military unit tradionally considered superior, how he fell fighting as an infantryman among the first ranks of cavalry (l. 3); his name, homeland and patronymic, information evidently perceived as secondary to his gallantry, are relegated at the end of both epitaphs appearing on his tomb.[38] His stele is embellished by an equally boastful relief showing two enemies succumbing to Menas (Peek *GVI* 1965 = *SGO* II 09/05/16, Nicaea, Bithynia):[39]

---

35 = Peek *GVI* 1302; see Santin 2009, 191–194.
36 It is not necessarily the famous battle of 281 BC. For a discussion on chronology see especially Bar-Kochva 1974 (discarding Bevan's contextualization of the epitaph in the war between Prusias I and Eumenes II, 188–183 BC, lowers the chronology to 159–154 BC, to the war between Prusias II and Attalos II), Post 2013 and Dumitru 2011, 367–372 (prefers a higher date, 3rd century BC).
37 Cf. συνμαχίας δ' ἔξοχον ἀγεμόνα (*IG* IV²,1 244.4) in the epigram accompanying to honorific statue of Telemnastos of Gortina (Epidauros, ca. 192 BC); see Moretti 1967, 125–127, nr. 49; *SEG* 25 (1970), nr. 419; [ἔξοχος ἡγε]μόνων Ἑλλάδος εὐρ[υχ]όρου in *FD* III1, 51.2; ἡγεμονῆος [...] ἐξόχου ἀνδρῶν in *IG* II² 5201.2–3 (267 AD).
38 Menas would have been a Bithynian *thureophoros*, member of the light infantry; while in the Hellenistic period this function was generally assigned to mercenaries (Post 2013, 10), Menas appears to be a citizien fighting for his homeland and family (see ll. 11–12: ἀμφί τε πάτρης,/ ἀμφί τε κυδαλίμων μαρνάμενον τοκέων).
39 An image of the relief is in Chaniotis 2005, 205 fig. 10,5. On the epigrams for Menas see Launey 1949, 370, 434, 438, 448, 807; Bevan 1966, 322–323; Bar-Kochva 1974; Cohen 1995, 399; Chaniotis 2005, 204–205; Fantuzzi 2008, 603–622; Dumitru 2011, 367–372 (with previous bibliography, at note 53); Post 2013, 9–10.

εἰ καὶ μεῦ δολιχὸς περιαίνυται ὅστεα τύμβος,
ξεῖνε, τὸ δυσμενέων γ' οὐχ ὑπέτρεσσα βάρος·
πεζομάχος δ' ἱππεῖας ἐνὶ προμάχοισιν ἔμεινα
ὁππότε περ Κούρου μαρνάμεθ' ἐμ πεδίωι·
[Θ]ρήϊκα δὲ προπάροιθε βαλὼν ἐνὶ τεύχεσιν ἄνδρα   5
[κ]αὶ Μυσόν, μεγάλας κάτθανον ἀμφ' ἀρετᾶς·
τῶι <τ>ις ἐπαινήσειε θοὸν Βιοήριος υἷα
Βιθυνὸν Μηνᾶν, ἔξοχον ἡγέμονα.
       ἄλλο·   8a
[δ]άκρυα μὲν δειλοῖς τις ἰὼν ἐπιτύμβια χ<ε>ύοι   9
[ν]ώνυμον ἐγ νούσων δεξαμένοις θάνατον·
αὐτὰρ ἐμὲ Φρυγίοιο πάρα ῥοόν, ἀμφί τε πάτρης,
ἀμφί τε κυδαλίμων μαρνάμενον τοκέων
εὐκλέα δέξατο γαῖα μετὰ προμάχοισι δαμέντα,
δυσμενέων πολλοὺς πρόσθε δαΐξάμενον·
Βιθυνὸν τῶι τις Βιοήριος υἱέα Μηνᾶν   15
αἰνήσαι με, ἀρετᾶς φέγγος ἀμειψάμενον.

Although a long tomb contains my bones, stranger, I did not shrink back in view of the heavy weight of the enemies. Although I fought on foot I stood my ground in front of riders among those who fought in the first line, when we battled in the plain of Kouros. After I had hit a Thracian in his armor and a Mysian, I died because of my great bravery. For this, may someone praise the swift Menas, the son of Bioeris, the Bithynian, an excellent officer.

Another (epigram)
One may come and pour tears on the tombs of cowards, who have died an inglorious death through illness. But earth has received me, who fought near the flow of the Phrygian river for my fatherland and for my parents, as a man who died while fighting with others in the first line, having first slain many enemies. For this, may someone praise the Bithynian Menas, the son of Bioeris, who exchanged light [life] with bravery.
(Translation by A. Chaniotis 2005, 204).

In the epigram for Nikasichorus, probably composed as a companion piece for a statue, his rank is stated in the second line (Βοιωτῶν ἀρχὸν), followed by a list of his military successes; the name of his father, evidently an already famed member of his community, is placed first, while the name of the deceased comes last, his glory justified by the deeds summarized in the short poem:[40]

πατρὸς ἀριζήλοιο Πολυκρίτου υἷα σὺν ἵππῳ
  δέρκεο, Βοιωτῶν ἀρχὸν ἀεθλοφόρων·
δὶς γὰρ ἐνὶ πτολέμοις ἁγήσατο τὰν ἀσάλευτον
  νίκαν ἐκ πατέρων τηλόθεν ἀρνύμενος,
καὶ τρίτον ἱππήων· Ὀπόεντα δὲ πολλάκι τάνδε   5
  καὶ χερὶ καὶ βουλᾶι θῆκε ὀνομαστοτέραν.

---

40 For reference and bibliography of this epigram see above, p. 313 note 27.

ἐν δὲ ἀρχαῖς ἀχάλινος ὑπ' ἀργύρου ἔπλετο πάσαις,
    ἀστῶν εὐνομίας θέσμια παρθεμένων·
τῷ καὶ ἀείμναστον Νικασιχόρῳ κλέος ἔσται,
    πίστις ἐπεὶ πάντων κοίρανος ἁγνοτάτα.

Watch the son of the noble Polykritus, mounted on horseback, leader of the victorious Boeotians; / twice in war he guided them, preserving, far away, the unshaken victory inherited from his fathers, / and a third time as a commander of cavalry. Often he made this city, Opous, more renowned with the work of his hand and of his mind. / In all his appointments he was never bridled by the greed of money, for his fellow citizens laid the foundations of Good Government. / Therefore the glory of Nikasichorus will be eternal, since loyalty is the purest leader of all.

One of the first details of the statue stressed by the epigram and submitted to the attention of the viewer/reader, in the tradition of the Hellenistic *ekphraseis* (l. 2: δέρκεο), is the horse: Nikasichorus in fact was twice commander of infantry (*Boiotarchos*) and once of cavalry, and as evidence of this latest, higher status he is portrayed in full equestrian gear. For vague that the epitymbian poems could be about the rank denomination, fighting on horseback, being a knight, was an important information to give in an epitaph, especially in the absence of an iconographic support, since this position immediately identified the fallen as a member of the upper class. Sometimes it was enough to state that the deceased had fought ἱππομαχο<ῦ>ντα, like in the epitaph of Neon son of Theokles, l. 5 (Peek *GVI* 1504, a stele from Oreos/Histiaia, Euboea, 3rd century BC?).[41] Without further specifying his rank, the epitaph for the suitably named Cretan warrior Thrasymachus (Peek *GVI* 1513 = *IC* I viii 33; Cnossos, Crete, 2nd century BC),[42] also reminds us that he was a horseman (ll. 5 and 7), and, like many others whose military career was a household tradition (cf. the above mentioned Nikasichoros), that he accomplished deeds worthy of his father Leontius. The unnamed versifier foresees that Thrasymachus' legendary endeavors would be a matter of epic song in the future; needless to say, the Cretan hero had to be contented with this bombastic epitaph:

Θαρσύμαχος Λεοντίω.
οὐδὲ θανὼν ἀρετᾶς ὄνυμ' ὤλεσας, ἀλλά σε φάμα
    κυδαίνουσ' ἀνάγει δώματος ἐξ Ἀΐδα,
Θαρσύμαχε· τρανὲς δὲ καὶ ὀψαγόνων τις ἀείσει
    μνωόμενος κείνας θού[ριδ]ος ἱπποσύνας,   5
Ἐρταίων ὅτε μοῦνος ἐπ' ἠ[νε]μόεντος Ἐλαίου

---

41 Cf. Peek *GVI Addenda* 177; Kaibel 209; *IG* XII,9 1195; Preuner 1920, 73.
42 He died in Messenia about 183/2 BC; see Launey 1949, 806–807; *SEG* 28 (1982), nr. 749; Chaniotis 2005, 204.

οὐλαμὸν ἱππείας ῥήξαο φοιλόπιδ<ο>ς,
ἄξια μὲν γενέταο Λεοντίου, ἄξια δ' ἐσθλῶν
ἔργα μεγαυχήτων μηδόμενος προγόνων.

Thrasymachos son of Leontius.
You have not lost the glory of your valor, not even after your death, but the fame which honors you brings you up from Hades' chambers, Thrasymachus. Someone of the later generations will sing about you, recalling that impetuous chivalry, when near windy Elaion you, alone among the Cretans, broke a squadron during the battle of the cavalry, in your effort to accomplish deeds worthy of your father Leontios.

(Translation by A. Chaniotis 2005, 204).

A (possibly fictitious and ironically intended) epitaph attributed to Peisandros of Rhodes (*A.P.* 7.304)[43] portrays a model of Hellenic social and moral aristocracy: the noble cavalryman Hippaemon is portrayed accompanied by the symbols of his status: a horse, a hound, and a servant:

Ἀνδρὶ μὲν Ἱππαίμων ὄνομ' ἦν, ἵππῳ δὲ Πόδαργος
καὶ κυνὶ Λήθαργος καὶ θεράποντι Βάβης·
Θεσσαλός, ἐκ Κρήτης, Μάγνης γένος, Αἵμονος υἱός·
ὤλετο δ' ἐν προμάχοις ὀξὺν Ἄρη συνάγων.

The man's name was Hippaemon, the horse's Podargos, the dog's Lethargos, and the serving-man's Babes, a Thessalian, from Crete, of Magnesian race, the son of Haemon. He perished fighting in the front ranks. (Translation by W. Paton)

As well shown by the last verse of this epigram, what is significant in Hellenistic epitymbian poetry, more than the actual rank, is the conduct of the soldier in battle, often epitomized in the capability to fight and to die "in the first line" (ἐμ προμάχοις), a frequently used expression which does not necessarily indicate the actual positioning of the soldier in the army (usually the actual first line at the beginning of the battle was assigned to light infantry, slingmen, and the likes), but generally his adherence to a classical model still perceived as suitable for different categories of fighters: for citizens of *poleis*, for mercenaries and for subjects/*philoi* of kings. Even two old Lycian veterans, Osses and Manossas, are compared to the very Hellenic hero Ajax Telamonius for their προστασίη,[44] that

---

43 Peek *GVI* 865; for a commentary see *FGE* 80–82. It is quoted by Nicolaos Damascenus, *FGrHist* II A 90 F 140; Dio Prus. 37.39, II 26 Arnim; Pollux 5.26. See also De Falco 1931, 7; Keydell 1935, 303.
44 Aiax' legendary προστασίη was still celebrated in the 5th century BC as one of his main characteristics, as shown by Antisthenes' fr. 14 Caizzi (Αἴαντος λόγος).

is the ability to hold the ground and wait for the enemy standing in the front line (*SGO* IV, 17/17/01, Choma, Lycia, 4th-3rd century BC):[45]

ἀσπίδα καὶ σιβύνην καὶ φάσγανον ἠδὲ κυνείην
σημε' ἀρήϊα ἐφέστα Ὄσσης Ὀσαβίμος υἱός
Ὄσσῃ πατρὸς πατρί καὶ τούτου πατρί Μανόσσᾳ
ἀνδράσι ἰφθίμοισι γέρας ἐπιτύμβιον εἶναι
σώφροσιν εὐκλεέσιν ἐτεόλβοις ἠνόρεσίν τε   5
προστασίῃ τε Αἴαντι ὁμωίοις Τελαμῶνος,
τοὺς καὶ δοιὼ δουπήσαντες ἔχει γεραιοὺς ὅδε τύμβος
ἀενάοιο δόμῳ Ἀίδος μακάρων ἐνὶ χώρῳ.

Παίων Μουσαίου Περγαῖος λαϊνοουργῶν
τέχνῃ κάλλιστος σήματα ἔτευξε τάδε.
ἄν τις βλάψῃ τι τῶν περὶ τὸν τάφ[ον, ἔ]σται ἁμαρτωλὸς θεοῖς πᾶσιν

Osses, son of Osabimis, set up the shield, spear, sword and helmet, emblems of war, to be an adornment of the tomb of Osses his grandfather and Manossas his great-grand-father, mighty men of good fame, prudent and brave, of honest wealth, champions equal to Ajax son of Telamon, both fallen in their old age, held by this tomb in the land of the Blessed, in the halls of eternal Hades.

Paeon, son of Musaeus, of Perge, supreme in the stone-cutter's art, worked these emblems. If anyone injures anything pertaining to this tomb, he shall be judged a sinner in the eyes of all the gods. (Adapted translation by Bean and Harrison 1967, 43).

On the other hand, there are also valiant soldiers for whom to fight in the first ranks and to be an efficient and trustworthy combatant are not a pretext to compare oneself too easily, like a *miles gloriosus*, with Homeric heroes; it is the case of Cretan archer Cimon son of Didymandros, a professional soldier who, after serenely reaching the old age in spite of his dangerous life, looks back with a mixture of pride and realistic modesty (he was no Ajax or Achilles) to his military career (Peek *GVI* 1811 = *IG* XII,3 47; Telos, 2nd century BC); again, the soldier's name, the name of his father and his homeland come last in the poem, while his specialty (good aim at archery—in modern times he will be a sniper) and his being "πιστὸς ἀεὶ προμάχεσθαι" come first as a main feature of his character:[46]

---

[45] Bean-Harrison 1967, 43–44, nr. 8, with plate V. The relief work of the self-celebrating Paion of Perge, with the representation of the weapons listed in the first line is lost.

[46] Rayet 1879, 43 judged him a mercenary. In fact πολυπλάγκτου δὲ Ἄρεος (Ares is generally a metaphor for "war" or "battle") could be a reference not just to the fray of the battle, uncertain in its confuse movement, but to the fact that Cimon had to travel in order to take part to many different conflicts.

[ο]ὐκ ἐπόνησα Αἴαντος ἐγὼ πλεῖον οὐδὲ Ἀχιλεῖο[ς],
οὐδὲ ἀρετὴν εἶσχον μείζονα τῶν πρότερον,
ξεῖνε. πολυπλάγκτου δὲ Ἄρεος ἐγραφόμαν
πιστὸς ἀεὶ προμάχεσθαι, ἐπεὶ ῥυτῆρά με τόξ[ων]
[α]ἴνεσε καὶ Κρῆτα πᾶσα κατ' εὐστοχίαν·   5
εὐκλειὲς δέ με γῆρας ἐδέξατο τὸν Διδυμάνδρο[υ]
παῖδα Κίμωνα· χρόνος δὲ εἷλέ με ὁ πανδαμάτω[ρ].

My toils were not superior to those of Aiax or Achilles, nor was my bravery greater than that of the ancients, o stranger. But, as a trusted man, I was always designated to fight in the first ranks in the ever-wandering Ares, since all Crete too praised me as a drawer of arrows for my precision. An honorable old age welcomed me, Cimon son of Didymandros; Time, the all-tamer, took me.

We shall come back to the topic of the "combat in the first ranks" later on. It is worth noticing that the tomb of the old Lycian warriors Osses and Manossas was decorated with a relief showing with great precision a variety of weapons and military attire they used, which feature prominently in the first line of the epigram accompanying their tomb. The epitaph of Cimon is also focusing on his weapon of election, the bow. Weapons, representing the profession of the deceased and to a certain extent also his rank, are frequently depicted on the gravestone (e. g. on *stelae* from Northern Greece and Macedonia). Verse epitaphs, on the contrary, do not mention them as often as one may think, and, again, the vocabulary used to define them is generally quite conventional, drawing mostly from Homer; the symbolic value of the weapon is often more important than its real use: as I have shown in a recent work,[47] the spear appears quite often both in encomiastic poems for living persons and in epitaphs, as a symbol of legitimate (and sometimes royal) power; for an example coming from a *polis*, see the epigram for a statue of Philopoimen of Tegea, celebrated, in the Homeric style, as αἰχμητής and δούρατος ἀγεμών.[48]

---

47 Barbantani 2007.
48 Quoted by Paus. 8.52.6 (= *FGE* anon. CLVII; 2nd BC): τοῦδ' ἀρετὰ καὶ δόξα καθ' Ἑλλάδα, πολλὰ μὲν ἀλκαῖς, / πολλὰ δὲ καὶ βουλαῖς ἔργα πονησαμένου, / Ἀρκάδος αἰχμητᾶ Φιλοποίμενος, ᾧ μέγα κῦδος / ἕσπετ' ἐνὶ πτολέμῳ δούρατος ἀγεμόνι. / μανύει δὲ τρόπαια τετυγμένα δισσὰ τυράννων / Σπάρτας· αὐξομέναν δ' ἄρατο δουλοσύναν. / ὧν ἕνεκεν Τεγέα μεγαλόφρονα Κραύγιδος υἱόν / στᾶσεν, ἀμωμήτου κράντορ' ἐλευθερίας. Throughout Greece are renowned the virtue and fame of this man, who /accomplished many deeds with his strength, and many with his wisdom, / the Arcadian warrior Philopoimen; great glory / followed him in war as a commander of the spear. / The evidence are two trophies obtained over the tyrants / of Sparta; he took away the growing slavery. / Therefore Tegea set up (the statue of) the magnanimous son of Craugis / who conquered blameless freedom."

4. Tones and imagery

As wisely remarked by Erasmus of Rotterdam in his *Adagia*, *bellum dulce imperitis*. But how is depicted war by those who had a taste of it? Reactions, now as in antiquity, vary—in our case depending more from the persons who commissioned the epitaph (family, fellow soldiers, the *polis*) than from the character of the deceased. It is surprising that, in spite of predominant the epic tradition, derogatory images of war are not so uncommon in military epitaphs, while an embellishing, aestheticism-oriented celebration of conflict or its ambiguous, exhilarating depiction dear to some writers of the XX century are rarer than we expect in private funerary epigrams. War is an odious necessity, seems to state with admirable synthesis the epitaph for Aristarchus (Peek *GVI* 1640 = *IG* IX,1 1064; Phocis, Anticyra; end of 3rd century BC), ll. 1–2: οἷς ἀρετῆς κατὰ πάντα μέλει βίον, οἱ δὲ τάχιστα / θνήσκουσι στυγερῶν ἐγ ξυνοχαῖς πολέμων· "Those who cultivated bravery for all their life, they are the first to die in the clashes of odious wars".[49] Yet, in an epitaph for a man who had fallen during a war or, in the luckiest instance, survived until old age after years of practicing the military profession, the commemoration of martial ἀρετή was a stringent cultural necessity like, in epitaphs for women, the celebration of the maternal role and of the faithful love towards their husbands. Gender' roles can be quite aggressively defined, in a contrastive way, e. g. in the epitaph for Antigenes (Peek *GVI* 943.9) where the soldier states, with an unusual litotes, "I did not march against the enemies like a female" (οὐ γὰρ ἔβην θῆλυς ἐπ' ἀντιπάλους).[50] But in most instances eulogy of valor is kept quite simple, and tones are more positive. Epitaphs for soldiers, first and foremost for reasons of space, are lacking detailed descriptions of the battle; either in the more elementary inscriptions or in the more elaborated epigrams, to praise the bravery of the deceased it is sometimes enough to state that the warrior fought and died "in the first ranks", following a *topos* well known since Homer (cf. e.g. Hom. *Il.* 3.31, 458; 4.252; 15,522; 17.590; 18.456; 19.414;

---

[49] Cf. already Homer, e.g. *Il.* 4.240; 6.330, and the fictitious dedicatory epigram by Hegesippos *A.P.* 6.178: Δέξαι μ', Ἡράκλεις, Ἀρχεστράτου ἱερὸν ὅπλον, / ὄφρα ποτὶ ξεστὰν παστάδα κεκλιμένα / γηραλέα τελέθοιμι χορῶν ἀίουσα καὶ ὕμνων· / ἀρκείτω στυγερὰ δῆρις Ἐνυαλίου. "Accept me, Heracles, the consecrated shield of Archestratus, so that, resting against thy polished porch I may grow old listening to song and dance. Enough of the hateful battle!" (Translation W. Paton). Cf. also ἐν π]ολέμωι στυγερῶι· l. 2 of the honorific inscription *SEG* 22 (1967) nr. 156; *SEG* 30 (1983) nr. 339; Manganaro 1959–60, 422–427 (Aegina, 2nd AD).
[50] From Demetrias, Thessaly, post 217 BC (for the archaeological contaxt see Helly 1992); Launey 1949, 808; Moretti 1975, nr. 107; *SEG* 42 (1995) nr. 498; Peek 1973, 69 attributed it tentatively to Theodoridas.

Od. 18.379; 24.526: ἐν δ' ἔπεσον προμάχοισ')[51] and Tyrtaeus (cf. e.g. fr. 10.1, 21, 30 West). Exemplar is the epitaph for the Acarnanian Timocritus, attributed to Posidippus (see esp. ll. 5, 7–8):[52]

> τὸμ Μούσαις, ὦ ξεῖνε, τετιμένον ἐνθάδε κρύπτει
> Τιμόκριτογ κόλπωι κυδιάνειρα κόνις·
> Αἰτωλῶν γὰρ παισὶ πάτρας ὕπερ εἰς ἔριν ἐλθὼν
> ὡγαθὸς ἢ νικᾶν ἤθελε ἢ τεθνάναι.
> πίπτει δ' ἐμ προμάχοισι λιπὼμ πατρὶ μυρίον ἄλγος,   5
> ἀλλὰ τὰ παιδείας οὐκ ἀπέκρυπτε καλά·
> Τυρταίου δὲ Λάκαιναν ἐνὶ στέρνοισι φυλάσσων
> ῥῆσιν τὰν ἀρετὰν εἵλετο πρόσθε βίου.

Stranger, here the dust conceals in its bosom Timocritus, honored by the Muses. /When he went to war against the sons of the Aetolians to defend his homeland, the brave chose to win or to die. / He falls in the first ranks leaving infinite grief to his father, but he did not keep secret his excellent education; / holding in his heart the Spartan saying of Tyrtaeus, he preferred valor to life.

Displaying the "Laconian virtue" of courage is de rigueur in other epitaphs from the Doric area of mainland Greece, like the one for Meletus, from Priene (Peek GVI 799 = SGO I 03/01/05; 3rd century BC):[53] this Messenian soldier, possibly a mercenary, honors his Dorian ancestry boasting to never have given his back to the enemy troops, and to have erected two trophies:

> [Ἀντιμάχου? μ'ἐσαθρε]ῖς Μεσσήνιον ὄντα Μέλητον,   1
> [πολλάκις εἰς δῆριν] δοράτων ἐλθόντα σὺν ὅπλοις·
> [ἀντιπάλων δ' οὐδεὶς κ]αυχήσεται ἐν δορὸς αἰχμῆι
> [ἐντροπαλιζομένοι]ο ἰδεῖν σάκος ἀμφ' ὤμοισιν·
> [πρόσθ' ἀγέλας δὲ νεκ]ρᾶς ἐχθρῶν στὰς δισσὰ τρόπαια   5
> [ἤγειρα· προγόνων δ' ἄ]ξια δρῶν ἔθανον.

You see me, the Messenian Meletus [son of....], / [who often] went armed [into the clash] of the spears. / [None of the enemies] will boast / of having seen, in heat of the battle, the shield on my shoulder [while I was running away], / [but....] standing firm against the enemy troops, two trophies / [I erected;] I died accomplishing deeds worthy [of the ancestors].

---

51 Among the archaic inscriptions see e.g. IG I³ 1240 (Attica c. 540–530 BC; Jeffery 1962, 143–144, nr. 57): στέθι : καὶ οἴκτιρον : Κροίσο παρὰ σέμα θανόντος : / hόν ποτ' ἐνὶ προμάχοις : ὄλεσε θōρος : Ἄρες.
52 From Thyrrheum, Acarnania: Peek GVI 749; Posidippus' *Dubia* 32, Fernández-Galiano; IG IX,1² 2 298; Friedländer 1942 (attributes it to Damagetus); Moretti 1975, 48–50, nr. 88; SEG 45 (1998), nr. 527; Garulli 2013; Criveller 2010, 431–435.
53 *Integravit* Peek 1980, 14, nr. 6; SEG 30 (1983), nr. 1363.

Another example is the epitaph of Aristagoras/Areimenes, by Damagetus (Ambracia, ca. 219 BC; *A.P.* 7.231 = *HE* IV; Peek *GVI* 1604): [54]

Ὧδ' ὑπὲρ Ἀμβρακίας ὁ βοαδρόμος ἀσπίδ' ἀείρας
τεθνάμεν ἢ φεύγειν εἵλετ' Ἀρισταγόρας,
υἱὸς ὁ Θευπόμπου. μὴ θαῦμ' ἔχε· Δωρικὸς ἀνὴρ
πατρίδος, οὐχ ἥβας ὀλλυμένας ἀλέγει.

Thus for Ambracia's sake the warrior Aristagoras, son of Theopompus, holding his shield on high, chose death rather than flight. Wonder not threat: a Dorian cares for his country, not for the loss of his young life.   (Translation by W. Paton)

The same principle can be applied to non-Laconian soldiers when fighting for Sparta: the already mentioned epitaph for the Arcadian mercenary chief Botrichus, who served in the Spartan army in the 2nd century BC, emphasizes that he was "nurtured" as an excellent commander by Sparta (ll. 1–2: Σπάρτα... ἔτρεφεν) and consequently he died κυδαίνοντ' ἀρετὰν Λακεδαίμονος, ἄν ποτ' ἐτίμα / ἀλκαῖς Ἑλλάνων ἔξοχα ῥυόμενος (Peek *GVI* 903, ll. 3–4). Praise of Doric martial tradition kept on being extolled in poetry even at a time when Sparta had lost most of its ancient power and autonomy. Thessalian warriors are also often "fallen in the first ranks", not because they were better than others, but most probably for the lack of creativity of the composers of their epigrams. The young Thessalian Ason son of Demokles περὶ πάτρας / μαρνάμενος πρῶτος δ' ἐμ προμάχοισι θάνεν (Peek *GVI* 425.1–2; *IG* IX.2 466; Crannon, 3rd BC); the remark "ο]ὐχὶ [κ]αταισχύνας πατρίδ' οὐδὲ γ[ο]ν[ῆ]ας ἑαυτοῦ" (l. 3) recalls the oath of the Athenian ephebes, "I shall not dishonor the sacred weapons" (οὐκ αἰσχυνῶ τὰ ἱερὰ ὅπλα οὐδὲ λείψω τὸν παραστάτην ὅπου ἂν στειχήσω, Arist. *Const. Ath.* 42). Thibron, also a Thessalian, died at Pharsalus fighting in the first line (l. 1): π]ρομάχοιο Θίβρωνος (Peek *GVTh*, 26–27, nr. 24 = *IG* IX,2 251), which earned him a common grave but an individual epitaph praising his valor. The same formula ἐν προμάχοις fits well a lacuna in Peek *GVI* 100.2 = Gonnoi II 211, a 3rd century BC epitaph for Demokrates, son of Aristokrates.[55]

As we have noticed before, the barbarian mercenary Briccon carefully followed the path of the Hellenic epic commonplace reminding the passer-by that he fell (ll. 3–4) ...μοῦνος <ἐ>ν αἰχμᾷ / δάϊον ἐμ προμάχοις Ἄρεα μαρνάμενος. The elementary

---

[54] For the name of the deceased see Gow/Page 1965, II, 225; see also Legrand, 1901, 185–186; Friedländer 1942, 80.
[55] τοῦτο τὸ Δαμοκράτους [μνημεῖον ἔτευξεν ὁ δῆμος] / πατρὸς Ἀριστοκράτο[υς, ἐν προμάχοις φθιμένου] / ὃς καὶ δυσμενέων ἀν[δρῶν πόλιν ἐξαλαπάξας] / πολλάκις ὤρθωσεν πατ[ρίδα μαρνάμενος].

image of the warrior looking for a glorious death in the front line could be enhanced with further descriptive touches, like in the epitaph from Canopus/Aboukir (3rd–2nd century BC)[56] for the soldier Lycus from Priene: οὐ γὰρ ἔτρεσσε φάλαγγος ἐπερχόμενομ μέγα [πλῆθος]/ [ἀνδ]ρῶν δυσμενέων. ἐμ προμάχοις δ' ἔθανεν, "He was not afraid of the great mass of the phalanx / of the enemies coming up against him, but he died in the front line" (integr. and transl. by Clarysse/Huys 2003, 148). A more elaborated description of the battle and of the circumstances of death is rare to be found: an example is the already mentioned Bernand 1969, nr. 4, for Ptolemy and Menodorus, which also repeats the old refrain ἐν προμάχοισι (l. 7). Another epitaph where the deceased speaks in the first person giving some information on his conduct in battle is the epitaph for Meletus, found in Priene (see above, p. 324). Menas from Byzantium specifies, also speaking in the first person, the circumstances in which he fell, heroically defying on foot enemies mounted on horseback (see above, p. 317–318). The attitude to defy danger and wait for the enemy in the front line, or προστασίη "to stand, to hold ground in the front of the army" (cf. l. 5 of the epitaph for Meletus, "standing firm", στὰς) is what made Osses and Manosses similar to Ajax Telamonius (see above, p. 321). In spite of their boldness, those two old warriors had the luck to reach a venerable age; standing on the front line, however, has generally produced opposite results, as remarked with bitter irony by Rudyard Kipling, in one of his famous, and lapidary *Epitaphs of War 1914–18* (ed. 1919):

> The Beginner
>
> On the first hour of my first day
> In the front trench I fell. [.....]

We are bound to imagine that epitaphs would tend to embellish in a poetic way more prosaic situations. But it is wrong to suppose that lies were consigned to the stone whenever death came in not such an heroic fashion. The epigram accompanying a statue for the Aetolian cavalry officer Scorpion, fallen near Tiethron (Posidippus' *Dubia* nr. 31 Fernández-Galiano; Aetolia, Thermos, ca. 284–281 BC)[57] does not conceal the miserable circumstances of his death, a vile ambush (ll. 1–3): ἄλσει ἐνὶ χρυσέῳ σε βοαδρομέοντα σὺν ἵππῳ / [Φ]ωκίσι Τείθρωνος κτεῖνεν ὑπὸ στεφάναις / δυσμενέων κρυφθεὶς ἄφατος λόχος [...]. The virtue of the deceased is however safe (ll. 3–4: ἄξια πάτρας, / ἄξια δ' Οἰνειδᾶν

---

[56] Bernand 2002; Clarysse/Huys 2003, 147–148; see also *SEG* 52 (2006), nr. 1782 for further commentary.
[57] = *IG* IX,1² 1 51 = Moretti 1975, 41–42, nr. 85; see also Garulli 2013; Cavalli 2010, esp. 410–414, 417, 420–421.

μησάμενον προγόνων), and the blame for the cowardly act rebounds on the enemy. Unsurprisingly, modesty is the key of the Alexandrian epitaph for a non professional soldier, a 25–year-old scribe (Bernand 1969, nr. 64; 1st -2nd century BC)[58], evidently more skilled with the *stilus* than with the sword, who died in battle: the classical formula ἐμ προμάχοις is cleverly avoided for a more generic στρατιᾶς ἄμμιγα, "within the army" (ll. 9–12).

Epitaphs insisting on the details of the battle, or on gory and aggressive imagery, are quite exceptional. Surprisingly, the few violent traits are to be found not in a specific category of epigrams, but are randomly scattered in epitaphs of professional mercenaries, of career soldiers faithful to one king, and of common citizens. At the core of the depiction of blood there is the ancestral idea that the gods of War (Ares, Enyo), and the weapons which are their instruments, are thirsty of blood, and demand human sacrifice. The concept is elaborated in numerous epigrams of the *Greek Anthology* for dedication of arms: shiny, clean weapons are not worthy offers for these gods (see here below Leonidas *A.P.* 9.322; Antipater Sidonius *A.P.* 9.323; Meleager *A.P.* 6.163);[59] spears, arrows, swords must be encrusted with blood of the enemy, as they literally drink it.

> Simonides, *A.P.* 6.2
> Τόξα τάδε πτολέμοιο πεπαυμένα δακρυόεντος
>   νηῷ Ἀθηναίης κεῖται ὑπωρόφια,
> πολλάκι δὴ στονόεντα κατὰ κλόνον ἐν δαΐ φωτῶν
>   <u>Περσῶν ἱππομάχων αἵματι λουσάμενα.</u>
>
> This bow, resting from tearful war, hangs here under the roof of Athene's temple. Often mid the roar of battle, in the struggle of men, <u>was it vashed in the blood of Persian cavaliers</u>. (Translation by W. Paton)
>
> Paul. Silent. *A.P.* 6.81
> Ἀσπίδα ταυρείην, ἔρυμα χροός, <u>ἀντιβίων τε</u>
>   <u>πολλάκις ἐγχείην γευσαμένην χολάδων</u>
> καὶ τὸν ἀλεξιβέλεμνον ἀπὸ στέρνοιο χιτῶνα
> καὶ κόρυν ἱππείαις θριξὶ δασυνομένην
> 5 ἄνθετο Λυσίμαχος γέρας Ἄρεϊ, γηραλέον νῦν
>   ἀντὶ πανοπλίης βάκτρον ἀμειψάμενος.
>
> Lysimachus, who has now exchanged his armour for an old man's staff, presents to Ares his oxhide shield, the protector of his body, <u>his spear that often tasted the entrails of his foes</u>, his coat of mail that

---

[58] *SEG* 15 (1958) 853; Boyaval 2005, 173–174.
[59] On the dedications of used weapons see Durbec 2013.

warded off missiles from his breast, and his helmet
with thick horse-hair plume.

(Translation by W. Paton)

Anyte, *A.P.* 6.123
Ἔσταθι τᾶδε, κράνεια βροτοκτόνε, <u>μηδ' ἔτι λυγρὸν
  χάλκεον ἀμφ' ὄνυχα στάζε φόνον δαΐων</u>·
ἀλλ' ἀνὰ μαρμάρεον δόμον ἡμένα αἰπὺν Ἀθάνας,
  ἄγγελλ' ἀνορέαν Κρητὸς Ἐχεκρατίδα.

Stand here, <u>thou murderous spear, no longer drip from thy brazen barb that dismal blood of foes</u>; but resting in the high marble house of Athene, announce the bravery of Cretan Echecratidas.

(Translation by W. Paton)

Leonidas *A.P.* 6.129
Ὀκτώ τοι θυρεούς, ὀκτὼ κράνη, ὀκτὼ ὑφαντοὺς
  θώρηκας, τόσσας δ' <u>αἱμαλέας κοπίδας</u>,
ταῦτ' ἀπὸ Λευκανῶν Κορυφασίᾳ ἔντε' Ἀθάνᾳ
  Ἅγνων Εὐάνθευς θῆχ' ὁ βιαιομάχος.

Eight shields, eight helmets, eight woven coats of mail and <u>as many blood-stained axes</u>, these are the arms, spoil of the Lucanians, that Hagnon, son of Euanthes, the doughty fighter, dedicated to Coryphasian Athene.

(Translation by W. Paton)

Meleager *A.P.* 6.163
Τίς τάδε μοι θνητῶν τὰ περὶ θριγκοῖσιν ἀνῆψεν
  σκῦλα, πανασχίστην τέρψιν Ἐνυαλίου;
οὔτε γὰρ αἰγανέαι περιαγέες οὔτε τι πῆληξ
  ἄλλοφος οὔτε <u>φόνῳ χρανθὲν</u> ἄρηρε σάκος,
ἀλλ' αὕτως γανόωντα καὶ ἀστυφέλικτα σιδάρῳ,
  οἷά περ οὐκ ἐνοπᾶς, ἀλλὰ χορῶν ἔναρα.
οἷς θάλαμον κοσμεῖτε γαμήλιον, <u>ὅπλα δὲ λύθρῳ
  λειβόμενα βροτέῳ σηκὸς Ἄρηος ἔχοι.</u>

What mortal hung there on the wall these spoils in which it were disgraceful for Ares to take delight? Here are set no jagged spears, no plumeless helmet, <u>no shield stained with blood</u>; but all are so polished, so undinted by the steel, as they were spoils of the dance and not of the battle. With these adorn a bridal chamber, <u>but let the precinct of Ares contain arms dripping with the blood of men</u>.

(Translation by W. Paton)

Leonidas *A.P.* 9.322
Οὐκ ἐμὰ ταῦτα λάφυρα. τίς ὁ θριγκοῖσιν ἀνάψας
  Ἄρηος ταύταν τὰν ἄχαριν χάριτα;
ἄκλαστοι μὲν κῶνοι, <u>ἀναίμακτοι</u> δὲ γανῶσαι
  ἀσπίδες, ἄκλαστοι δ' αἱ κλαδαραὶ κάμακες.
αἰδοῖ πάντα πρόσωπ' ἐρυθαίνομαι, ἐκ δὲ μετώπου   5
  ἱδρὼς πιδύων στῆθος ἐπισταλάει.
παστάδα τις τοιοῖσδε καὶ ἀνδρειῶνα καὶ αὐλὰν
  κοσμείτω καὶ τὸν νυμφίδιον θάλαμον·

Ἄρευς δ' αἱματόεντα διωξίπποιο λάφυρα
 νηὸν κοσμοίη· τοῖς γὰρ ἀρεσκόμεθα. 10

These spoils are not mine. Who hung this unwelcome gift on the walls of Ares? Unbruised are the helmets, <u>unstained by blood</u> the polished shields, and unbroken the frail spears. My whole face reddens with shame, and the sweat, gushing from my forehead, bedews my breast. Such ornaments are for a lady's bower, or a banqueting-hall, or a court, or a bridal chamber. <u>But blood-stained be the cavalier's spoils that deck the temple of Ares; in those I take delight.</u> (Translation by W. Paton)

Antipater Sidonius A.P. 9.323
Τίς θέτο μαρμαίροντα βοάγρια, τίς δ' ἀφόρυκτα
 δούρατα καὶ ταύτας ἀρραγέας κόρυθας
ἀγκρεμάσας Ἄρηι μιάστορι κόσμον ἄκοσμον;
 οὐκ ἀπ' ἐμῶν ῥίψει ταῦτά τις ὅπλα δόμων;
ἀπτολέμων τάδ' ἔοικεν ἐν οἰνοπλῆξι τεράμνοις 5
 πλάθειν, οὐ θριγκῶν ἐντὸς Ἐνυαλίου·
<u>σκῦλά μοι ἀμφίδρυπτα καὶ ὀλλυμένων ἄδε λύθρος
 ἀνδρῶν, εἴπερ ἔφυν ὁ βροτολοιγὸς Ἄρης.</u>

Who hung here these glittering shields, these unstained spears and unbroken helmets, dedicating to murderous Ares ornaments that are no ornaments? Will no one cast these weapons out of my house? Their place is in the wassailing halls of unwarlike men, not within the walls of Enyalius. I <u>delight in hacked trophies and the blood of dying men, if, indeed, I am Ares the Destroyer.</u> (Translation by W. Paton)

[Leonid. Alex.] A.P. 9.324
Πέμματα τίς λιπόωντα, τίς Ἄρεϊ τῷ πτολιπόρθῳ
 βότρυς, τίς δὲ ῥόδων θῆκεν ἐμοὶ κάλυκας;
Νύμφαις ταῦτα φέροι τις· <u>ἀναιμάκτους δὲ θυηλὰς
 οὐ δέχομαι βωμοῖς ὁ θρασύμητις Ἄρης.</u>

Who offered to me, Ares the sacker of cities, rich cakes, and grapes, and roses? Let them offer these to the Nymphs, but <u>I, bold Ares, accept not bloodless sacrifices on my altars.</u> (Translation by W. Paton)

A literary funerary epigram, not for a soldier but for a war-horse, attributed to the otherwise sweet poetess Anyte (A.P. 7.208 = Peek GVI 220), is worth mentioning in this section since it describes at length and in a disturbing way the agony of the poor animal:

Μνᾶμα τόδε φθιμένου μενεδαΐου εἴσατο Δᾶμις
 ἵππου, ἐπεὶ στέρνον τοῦδε δαφοινὸς Ἄρης
τύψε· μέλαν δέ οἱ αἷμα ταλαυρίνου διὰ χρωτὸς
 ζέσσ', ἐπὶ δ' ἀργαλέᾳ βῶλον ἔδευσε φονᾷ.

This tomb Damis built for his steadfast war-horse pierced through the breast by gory Ares. The black blood bubbled through his stubborn hide, and he drenched the earth in his sore death-pangs. (Transl. by W. Paton)

As for human beings, the epitaph for Antigenes Peek GVI 943 (see above, n. 50) takes care of reminding us that his body was pierced by spears (plural, probably not just a poetic one) and horrendously disfigured by "hot wounds in the brain", suggesting an synaestethic image of blood still warm flowing from his fractured skull (see ll. 2–3).

> Ἀντιγένης Σωτίμου·
> εἰς μακάρων νήσους με κατήγαγεν ἀγχόθι Μίνως,
>   θερμὰ κατ' ἐνκεφάλου τραύματα δεξάμενον
> καὶ δέμας ἐκ καμάκων πεπαλαγμένον, ἀνίκ' Ἐνυὼ
>   πεζὸν ἀπ' Αἰτωλῶν ἀμφορόθυνεν Ἄρη,   5
> Ἀντιγένη· Μάγνης δὲ δόμος καὶ πατρὶς ἔπολβος
>   ἡ Δημητριέων οὔ με κατωικτίσατο,
> υἱὸν Σωτίμου τὸν γνήσιον· οὐδέ με Σωσὼ
>   μήτηρ· οὐ γὰρ ἔβην θῆλυς ἐπ' ἀντιπάλους·
> ἀλλὰ τὸν ἡβητὴν σώιζων λόχον -ἵστορα τῶνδε -,   10
>   Ζῆνα καὶ ὁπλίτην αὐλὸν Ἐνυαλίου,
> καὶ τὸν Ἀλεξάνδρου χθόνιον τάφον, οὗ μέγα θάρσος,
>   ῥυόμενος, Θήβης ἀμφεκάλυψα κόνιν.

> Antigenes son of Sotimus.
> Minos, standing close, pushed me to the Island of the Blessed / as I received hot wounds to my head / and my body was pierced by spears, when Enyo / instigated the Ares of the Aetolian infantry; /me, Antigenes; but my house in Magnesia and my blessed homeland, / Demetrias, did not mourn me, / the noble son of Sotimos; nor did it Soso, / my mother; because I did not move as a female against the enemies; / but saving the battalion of the youths –a witness to these deeds– / and defending Zeus and the hoplitic flute of Enyalios/ and the grave of Alexander, whose bravery was great / I covered the dust of Thebes.

The same gloomy doom was met by Menodorus son of Apollonius of Sinope, who "after grabbing many blood-spattered spoils of the enemies / lies hit by a spear in the land of Bosporus" (πολλὰ δὲ δυσμενέων ἔναρα βροτόεντα δαΐξας (cf. Hom. Il. 6.480) / κεῖμαι δουριτυπὴς ἐν χθονὶ Βοσπορίδι).[60] When a soldier managed to avoid being stabbed to death by spears probably succeeded in performing the same act of butchery on the enemies: it is the case of another Apollonius, a Carian from Tymnus (Rhodian Peraia, now Bozburun), who "wielded many murderous spears, piercing the flesh of his adversaries" (Peek GVI 1260 = SGO I 01/02/ 01, l. 4),[61] cf. the epitaph of the soldier Philonides, from Naucratis, Peek GVI 944

---

[60] *CIRB* 131 = *IosPE* II 298; Black Sea, Pantikapaion/Kerch; 1st BC- 1st century AD.
[61] Ca. 250 BC. See for context and commentaries Bean/Fraser 1954, 41, no. 27a (l. 8); *SEG* 14 (1957) nr. 704; Bresson 1991, 105–106, nr. 95 (Apollonius' enemy would be the army of Philip V); Bresson 2001, 95; Ma 2004, 208–211; Chaniotis 2005, 25, 96; Barbantani 2007, 115–116.

= Bernand 1969, nr. 66.2; 2nd-1st century BC): στυγνά τ' ἐπ' ἀντιπάλοις δούρατ' ἐρεισάμενος.

ὦ ξένε, θάησαι, παριὼν ἰδὲ τόνδε δράκοντα,
    ἀνδρὸς ἐπὶ κρατεροῦ σάματι φαινόμενον·
ὅς ποκα ναυσὶ θοαῖς πάτρας ὕπερ ἄλκιμον ἦτορ
    δεικνύμενος πολλοὺς ὤλεσε δυσμενέων·
πολλὰ δ' ὅ γ' ἐν χέρσωι κατενήρατο φοίνια δοῦρα   5
    ἀνδρῶν ἀντιπάλων σάρκας ἐρειδόμενος.
νῦν δὲ θανὼν γηραιὸς ἐφ' αὑτῶι τόνδε δράκοντα
    εἵσατο, τοῦδε τάφου θοῦρον ἔμεν φύλακα,
ὃν καὶ ἐπὶ ἀσπίδος εἶχεν, ὅτ' Ἄρεος ἔργα ἐπονεῖτο,
    πολλὰ ἐπὶ δυσμενέσιν πήματα μαιόμενος.   10
τοὔνομα δ' εἴ κ' ἐθέλῃς αὐτοῦ καὶ πατρὸς ἀκοῦσαι,
    εἰδήσεις ἐτύμως τὰ κατώτατα γράμματ' ἀναγνούς.
    vacat
Ἀπολλώνιος Ἀθ[ην]ίωνος.   13

Stranger, while you are passing by, have a look at this snake / which appears on the tomb of a strong man. / Once, showing his mighty courage on the swift ships of his homeland, / destroyed a great number of enemies; / also on dry land he wielded many murderous spears, piercing the flesh of his adversaries. / Now that he has died in old age, he has placed above himself this snake / so that it could be a bold sentinel for his tomb. / He had it also on his shield, when he was toiling in the deeds of Ares, / inflicting many sufferings on his enemies. / If you want to hear his name and the name of his father, / you will truly know them reading the letters below: Apollonius son of At[hen]ion (or D[rak]on).

The epigram is remarkable for many reasons. First of all it is probably the best example of indulgence on violent tones among Hellenistic epitaphs. The most striking feature is that we are not in the presence of a wild, bloodthirsty mercenary, but simply of a citizen of Tymnus who enrolled in the civic army when he was needed to defend his homeland.[62] Epitaphs and funerary reliefs for citizens of Greek Anatolia rarely mention war: military values, although an important part of the Hellenic culture, were certainly present in Anatolia, but not advertised with particular emphasis, with the exception of some regions like Rhodes, Caria, Kibyratis and Pisidia.[63] Our epitaph confirms this view: Apollonius was a Carian, and Carians, since Homer (see *Il.* 16.90 and 835; 17.194), were famous in antiquity for their combative attitude and fighting abilities, so that they were always easily enrolled as mercenaries. Egypt was one of their main destinations and the place where many of them settled down as landowners after retirement, as they were

---

62 See Chaniotis 2005, 18–36.
63 See Ma 2004.

hired first by the Saïte pharaos (Hdt. 2.152–154; Diod. Sic. 1.66.12)[64] and then by the Ptolemies, who also controlled their region in the 3rd-2nd century BC (cf. Theocr. *Id.* 17,89).[65]

There is another interesting aspect to this epigram. According to Hdt. 1.171 (καὶ γὰρ ἐπὶ τὰ κράνεα λόφους ἐπιδέεσθαι Κᾶρές εἰσι οἱ καταδέξαντες καὶ ἐπὶ τὰς ἀσπίδας τὰ σημήια ποιέεσθαι, καὶ ὄχανα ἀσπίσι οὗτοί εἰσι οἱ ποιησάμενοι πρῶτοι; cf. Strab. 14.2.27; Plin. *N.H.* 7.200), it was the Carians that first created a special, fear-provoking military attire, fastening crests to their helmets and putting blazons on their shields. Whatever the actual role of Carians in launching this fashion, decorations on round shields probably were in use in Greece since the archaic period;[66] since the Peloponnesian war, or even before, most *poleis* introduced standard shield devices (ἐπισήματα ἀσπίδων), signifying the unity of the civic body in battle (e.g. Lambda for Sparta, the club of Herakles for Thebes, etc.),[67] even though particularly prominent individuals could still chose their own personal emblem (e.g. the Eros of Alcibiades: Plut. *Alc.* 16; Athen. 12.543e); the most famous poetic representation of individual shield insignia in the classical period is due to Aeschylus, in his *Seven against Thebes*, where, among other peculiar symbols, appear two common theriomorphic emblems, the lion of Polyneikes and the boar of Tydeus.[68] The snake was also one of the favorite blazons in the classical period: it is one of the most recurrent image on shields in vase-paintings,[69] and in literature and art is attributed to her-

---

[64] See Griffiths 1935, 236; Bettalli 1995, 63–69; Ray 1995 and Ray 1998; Moyer 2011, 55–58; Thompson 2012², 76–90; Fischer-Bovet 2014, ch. 1.1 (esp. 1.1.3.3: *Carians in Egypt*). In spite of their Hellenization, the Carians were regarded for long time by the Greeks as mainly barbarians (cf. Hom. *Il.* 2.867–869: Carian βαρβαρόφωνοι; see Hall 2002, 111–117; Barbantani 2013a, comm. to the *Foundation of Kaunos*); the reputation of professional soldiers also gained Carians a bad name in Greek proverbs and poetry: see Barbantani 2013b, commentary to F 3, with bibliography.

[65] Ptolemies controlled Caria in the '70s and '60s of the 3rd century BC, although the extent of their influence there depended from the sorts of the Syrian Wars. See Bagnall 1976, 89–102; Cohen 1995, 263–265, 270; Marquaille 2008, 46–47. On the Carian presence in the Hellenistic army see Launey 1949, 451–460.

[66] On the emblems on the Greek shields in general see Chase 1902; Snodgrass 1964; Spier 1990; Stephens 1991; Vaerst 1980; Berman 2007, 33–86.

[67] See Chase 1902, 77; Lacroix 1958; Berman 2007, 60–61.

[68] On Aesch. *Theb.* 387 ff. see Zeitlin 2009²; Bacon 1964, 27–38; Berman 2007, esp. 33–86 (*Decorating the Heroes: The Shield Blazons of the Seven*).

[69] See Chase 1902, 84–85, 119–120 (catalogue of vase-paintings showing a serpent as a shield device, more than 20 occurrences); Berman 2007, 67.

oes like Alcmeon/Alcman (Pind. *Pyth.* 8.44–47)[70] and Menelaus (in a painting by Polygnotus described by Paus. 10.26.3).[71] A famous historical snake/*drakon* emblem belongs to Neochorus, who killed Lysander (Plut. *Lys.* 29.5–6)[72]. For the Hellenistic period the documentation is not abundant; leaving aside pictorial representations on vases, it is quite difficult to assess which emblems were actually used as shield devices in the Hellenistic era: one could comb temple inventories, or hope for some lucky archaeological finds. The epigram for Apollonius is precious in this respect, because informs us that the snake guarding the tomb of the Carian soldier was also an emblem on his shield (l. 9), possibly also with reference to his patronymic.[73] The snake, or *drakon*, had been one of the most common motifs on shields since the Archaic period, first and foremost for his fearsome appearance. A close parallel to Apollonius' decorated headstone is suggested by Pausanias (8.11.8) who reports the presence of the image of a shield emblazoned with a snake on the tomb of the Epaminondas:

Paus. 8.11.8–9: τῷ τάφῳ δὲ κίων τε ἐφέστηκε καὶ ἀσπὶς ἐπ' αὐτῷ δράκοντα ἔχουσα ἐπειργασμένον· ὁ μὲν δὴ δράκων ἐθέλει σημαίνειν γένους τῶν Σπαρτῶν καλουμένων εἶναι τὸν Ἐπαμινώνδαν, στῆλαι δέ εἰσιν ἐπὶ τῷ μνήματι, ἡ μὲν ἀρχαία καὶ ἐπίγραμμα ἔχουσα Βοιώτιον, τὴν δὲ αὐτήν τε ἀνέθηκεν Ἀδριανὸς βασιλεὺς καὶ ἐποίησε τὸ ἐπίγραμμα τὸ ἐπ' αὐτῇ.

On the grave stands a pillar, and on it is a shield with a dragon in relief. The dragon means that Epaminondas belonged to the race of those called the Sparti, while there are slabs on

---

[70] Amphiaraus prophesizes: θαέομαι σαφές / δράκοντα ποικίλον αἴθας Ἀλκμᾶν' ἐπ' ἀσπίδος / νωμῶντα πρῶτον ἐν Κάδμου πύλαις. "I see clearly Alcman, wielding a dappled serpent on his gleaming shield, first at Cadmus' gate" (translation by Berman 2007, 37–38).
[71] Paus 10.26.3: Μενελάῳ δὲ ἀσπίδα ἔχοντι δράκων ἐπὶ τῇ ἀσπίδι ἐστὶν εἰργασμένος τοῦ ἐν Αὐλίδι φανέντος ἐπὶ τοῖς ἱερείοις τέρατος ἕνεκα. The snake/dragon was also a symbol of the Spartan Aegiads.
[72] ἦν γάρ, ὡς ἔοικε, τῷ Λυσάνδρῳ δεδομένος χρησμὸς οὕτως ἔχων· Ὁπλίτην κελάδοντα φυλάξασθαί σε κελεύω γῆς τε δράκονθ' υἱὸν δόλιον κατόπισθεν ἰόντα. τινὲς δὲ τὸν Ὁπλίτην οὐ πρὸς Ἁλιάρτῳ ῥεῖν λέγουσιν, ἀλλὰ πρὸς Κορώνειαν χειμάρρουν εἶναι τῷ Φιλάρῳ ποταμῷ συμφερόμενον παρὰ τὴν πόλιν, ὃν πάλαι μὲν Ὁπλίαν, νῦν δὲ Ἰσόμαντον προσαγορεύουσιν. ὁ δὲ ἀποκτείνας τὸν Λύσανδρον Ἁλιάρτιος ἀνὴρ ὄνομα Νεόχωρος ἐπίσημον εἶχε τῆς ἀσπίδος δράκοντα· καὶ τοῦτο σημαίνειν ὁ χρησμὸς εἰκάζετο. "For Lysander, as it appears, had received an oracle running thus: 'Be on thy guard, I bid thee, against a sounding Hoplites, And an earth born dragon craftily coming behind thee.' Some, however, say that the Hoplites does not flow before Haliartus, but is a winter torrent near Coroneia, which joins the Philarus and then flows past that city; in former times it was called Hoplias, but now Isomantus. Moreover, the man of Haliartus who killed Lysander, Neochorus by name, had a dragon as emblem on his shield, and to this, it was supposed, the oracle referred". (Translation by by B. Perrin).
[73] Bresson 1991, 161 fills the lacuna in the last line with Δ[ράκ]ωνος, while Ἀθ[ην]ίωνος is the integration by Peek.

the tomb, one old, with a Boeotian inscription, the other dedicated by the Emperor Hadrian, who wrote the inscription on it. (Transl. W.H.S. Jones).

However, the metrical epitaph of the Theban leader (*FGE anon*. CXXI in Paus. 9.15.6) does not mention a reptilean crest.[74] Until now I have found no other epigram describing a shield-device with such precision as the epitaph of the Carian Apollonius, with the exception of the literary epigram *A.P.* 6.126, by Dioscourides, focusing on the Gorgoneion shining on the shield of a Cretan soldier (Cretans had always been, like Carians, one of the ethnic groups more active in the professional military business):[75]

Σᾶμα τόδ' οὐχὶ μάταιον ἐπ' ἀσπίδι παῖς ὁ Πολύττου
 Ὕλλος ἀπὸ Κρήτας θοῦρος ἀνὴρ ἔθετο,
Γοργόνα τὰν λιθοεργὸν ὁμοῦ καὶ τριπλόα γοῦνα
 γραψάμενος· δῆοις τοῦτο δ' ἔοικε λέγειν·
"Ἀσπίδος ὦ κατ' ἐμᾶς πάλλων δόρυ, μὴ κατίδῃς με,
 ἢ φεῦγε τρισσοῖς τὸν ταχὺν ἄνδρα ποσίν. 5

Not idly did Hyllus the son of Polyttus, the stout Cretan warrior, blazon on his shield the Gorgon, that turns men to stone, and the three legs. This is what they seem to tell his foes: "O thou who brandishest thy spear against my shield, look not on me, and fly with three legs from the swift-footed man." (Translation by W. Paton)

The link between warriors and totemic animals embodying boldness, depicted both on their shields and on their graves is, however, confirmed by another epitaph, the one composed by Antipater of Sidon for the legendary Messenian king Aristomenes, *A.P.* 7.161, describing an eagle on his tomb:

Ὄρνι, Διὸς Κρονίδαο διάκτορε, τεῦ χάριν ἔστας
 γοργὸς ὑπὲρ μεγάλου τύμβον Ἀριστομένους; —
"Ἀγγέλλω μερόπεσσιν, ὁθούνεκεν, ὅσσον ἄριστος
 οἰωνῶν γενόμαν, τόσσον ὅδ' ἠιθέων.
δειλαί τοι δειλοῖσιν ἐφεδρήσσουσι πέλειαι, 5
 ἄμμες δ' ἀτρέστοις ἀνδράσι τερπόμεθα.

On Aristomenes, on whose Tomb stood an Eagle.
"Fleet-winged bird of Zeus, why dost thou stand in splendour on the tomb of great Aristomenes?" "I tell unto men that as I am chief among the birds, so was he among the youth. Timid doves watch over cowards, but we delight in dauntless men."
(Translation by W. Paton)

---

74 For the epigram see Gow/Page *FGE anon*. CXXI commentary *ad l.*; Vottéro 2002, 86.
75 Agamemnon bears the shield blazon of the Gorgoneion in Hom. *Il*. 11.36–37.

We are informed by Pausanias (4.16.7), who claims to have seen the item with his own eyes, that the spread eagle was also an emblem on Aristomenes' shield (ἐπίθημα δέ ἐστιν αὐτῆς ἀετὸς τὰ πτερὰ ἑκατέρωθεν ἐκτετακὼς ἐς ἄκραν τὴν ἴτυν).[76] As for the epitaph, we are certainly in the presence of a literary piece, of the Hellenistic type "enigmatic epitaph" (*A.P.* 7.37, 7.422–429),[77] which most probably was never inscribed on Aristomenes' tomb; already Gow/Page *HE* II, 49 took into account the possibility that Antipater may have composed a purely literary exercise without connection with the reliefs carved on the monument of the Messenian leader who lived many centuries before him. Since his tomb, given the importance of the character, must have been quite famous,[78] however, I rather suggest that Antipater elaborated his "fancy piece" (Gow/Page) starting from the symbol actually shining on Aristomenes' funerary pillar. Another literary epigram, an epitaph by the same Antipater Sidonius, *A.P.* 7.426, inspired by the Simonidean *A.P.* 7.344–344bis (epitaph for Leon), but probably composed for the sepulture of a contemporary of the poet, a prominent citizen of Cos,[79] suggests that the lion too, even when not used as a riddle for the name of the deceased, might have been a desirable subject for ornaments on a soldier's gravestone:

A. Εἰπέ, λέον, φθιμένοιο τίνος τάφον ἀμφιβέβηκας,
    βουφάγε; τίς τᾶς σᾶς ἄξιος ἦν ἀρετᾶς; —

---

[76] Paus. 4.16.7: "He recovered his shield also, going to Delphi and descending into the holy shrine of Trophonius at Lebadeia, as the Pythia bade. Afterwards he took the shield to Lebadeia and dedicated it, and I myself have seen it there among the offerings. The device on it is an eagle with both wings outspread to the rim. Now on his return from Boeotia having learnt of the shield at the shrine of Trophonius and recovered it, he at once engaged in greater deeds"; Paus. 4.18.5: "The rest of the Messenians were killed at once as they fell, but Aristomenes now as on other occasions was preserved by one of the gods. His panegyrists say that, when Aristomenes was thrown into the Ceadas, an eagle flew below him and supported him with its wings, bringing him to the bottom without any damage to his body and without wound. Even from here, as it seems, it was the will of heaven to show him a means of escape." (Translation by W.H.S. Jones).
[77] The passer-by engages in the game of interpreting the symbols on a tombstone; sometimes the animal or the object depicted is a riddle for the name of the deceased. On the epigram see Chirico 1978–1979; Argentieri 2003, 86; Fantuzzi/Hunter 2004, 328–338 (esp. 335).
[78] The body of Aristomenes was transferred from Rhodes, where he died (7th cent. BC), to Messene: his tomb was surmounted by a pillar (Paus. 4.24.3; 4.32.3), like the tomb of Epaminondas: we do not know if, like in the case of the Theban commander, the pillar carried a real shield or an image of a shield with the embossed eagle, or simply a sculpture of an eagle (cf. *A.P.* 7.62).
[79] Cf. the lion aptly located on the tomb of Leonidas in Hdt. 7.225.2. For the identification of the Teleutias of *A.P.* 7.426 see *HE* II 59; on the epigram see Gow 1954; Benedetto 2004, 192–193, 217; Fantuzzi/Hunter 2004, 333–335.

B. "Υἱὸς Θευδώροιο Τελευτίας, ὃς μέγα πάντων
    φέρτερος ἦν, θηρῶν ὅσσον ἐγὼ κέκριμαι.
οὐχὶ μάταν ἔστακα, φέρω δέ τι σύμβολον ἀλκᾶς   5
    ἀνέρος· ἦν γὰρ δὴ δυσμενέεσσι λέων."

A. "Tell, lion, thou slayer of kine, on whose tomb thou standest there and who was worthy of thy valour."

B. "Teleutias, the son of Theodorus, who was far the most valiant of men, as I am judged to be of beasts. Not in vain stand I here, but I emblem the prowess of the man, for he was indeed a lion to his enemies." (Translation by W. Paton)

Conclusion[80]

Many more topics featured in the military epitaphs I am exploring, like the bond between father and son, the depiction of war and peace, the reaction of the family to a death in a foreign land, the relationship between iconographic elements of the tomb and the epitaph. The comparison between epitaphs for citizens of independent *poleis* and epitaphs for men who served in the army of a king is particularly fruitful and may lead to unexpected results. I shall be able to offer a detailed analysis of such themes in forthcoming contributions on the subject, as my research on the corpus of military epitaphs makes progress. With the analysis of the epigrams here proposed I hope to have shown how promising this field is in terms of historical, cultural and archaeological information: definitely, a stone which covers a soldier's body may tell far more than his name.

---

80 I would like to thank Christelle Fischer-Bovet and Ruben Post for letting me read a provisional version of their work before publication.

Bibliography

Acosta-Hughes, B. (2003), 'The Poem Remembers: Conceptualization of Memory in the Poetry of Callimachus and Cavafy,' in: *Classical and Modern Literature* 23, 19–36.
Acosta-Hughes, B. (2010a), *Arion's Lyre: Archaic Lyric into Hellenistic Poetry*, Princeton.
Acosta-Hughes, B. (2010b), 'Reflections: Two Letters, and Two Poets,' in: *Dictynna* 7, 5–12.
Acosta-Hughes, B./Kosmetatou, E./Baumbach, M. (eds.) (2004), *Labored in Papyrus Leaves: Perspectives on an Epigram Collection Attributed to Posidippus (P.Mil.Vogl. VIII 309)*, Cambridge, Mass.
Acosta-Hughes, B./Stephens, S. (2012), *Callimachus in Context: From Plato to the Augustan Poets*, Cambridge.
Alden, M. (2005), 'Lions in Paradise: Lion Similes in the *Iliad* and the Lion Cubs of *Il.* 18.318–22,' in: *CQ* 55, 335–342.
Ambühl, A. (2004), 'Entertaining Theseus and Heracles: The *Hecale* and the *Victoria Berenices* as a Diptych,' in: Harder, M.A./Regtuit, R.F./Wakker, G.C. (eds.), *Callimachus II*, Leuven, 23–47.
Ambühl, A. (2005), *Kinder und junge Helden: Innovative Aspekte des Umgangs mit der literarischen Tradition bei Kallimachos*, Leuven.
Ambühl, A. (2010a), 'Narrative Hexameter Poetry,' in: Clauss/Cuypers 2010, 151–165.
Ambühl, A. (2010b), 'Sleepless Orpheus: Insomnia, Love, Death and Poetry from Antiquity to Contemporary Fiction,' in: Scioli, E./Walde, C. (eds.), *Sub Imagine Somni: Nighttime Phenomena in Greco-Roman Culture*, Pisa, 259–284.
Anghelopoulos, Th. (1988), 'Ζούμε μια νέα Αλεξανδρινή περίοδο,' in: *Η Λέξη* 78, 727–733.
Arenz, A. (2006), *Herakleides Kritikos "Über die Städte in Hellas". Eine Periegese Griechenlands am Vorabend des Chremonideischen Krieges* (Quellen und Forschungen zur Antiken Welt 49), Munich.
Argentieri, L. (2003), *Gli epigrammi degli Antipatri*, Bari.
Arkins, B. (1999), *An Interpretation of the Poems of Catullus*, Lewiston.
Asper, M. (2001), 'Gruppen und Dichter', *A&A* 47, 84–116.
Asper, M. (2007), *Griechische Wissenschaftstexte: Formen, Funktionen, Differenzierungsgeschichten*, Stuttgart.
Asper, M. (2011), 'Dimensions of Power: Callimachean Geopoetics and the Ptolemaic Empire,' in: Acosta-Hughes, B./Lehnus, L./Stephens, S. (eds.), *Brill's Companion to Callimachus*, Leiden 155–177.
Asquith, H. (2005), 'From Genealogy to Catalogue: the Hellenistic Adaptation of the Hesiodic Catalogue Form,' in: R. Hunter (ed.). *The Hesiodic Catalogue of Women. Constructions and Reconstructions*, Cambridge 2005, 266–286.
Atherton, C. (ed.) (1997), *Form and Content in Didactic Poetry*, Bari.
Attridge, H. (1985), 'Philo the Epic Poet,' in: J.H. Charlesworth (ed.), *The Old Testament Pseudepigrapha* Vol. 2, London, 781–784.
Austin, C./Bastianini, G. (2002), *Posidippi Pellaei quae supersunt omnia*, Milan.
Austin, N. (1967), 'Theocritus and Simonides,' in: *TAPhA* 98, 1–21.
Bacon, H. (1959), 'Socrates Crowned,' in: *Virginia Quarterly Review* 35, 414–430.
Bacon, H. (1964), 'The Shield of Eteocles,' in: *Arion* 3, 27–38.
Bagnall, R.S. (1976), *The Administration of the Ptolemaic Possessions outside Egypt*, Leiden.

Baker, P. (1999), 'Les mercenaires,' in F. Prost (ed.), *Armées et sociétés de la Grèce classique*, Paris, 240–255.
Bal, M. (2009), *Narratology: Introduction to the Theory of Narrative*, 3rd edition, Toronto.
Ballati, T. (2001), 'Nota al Περὶ τῶν ἐν τῇ Ἑλλάδι πόλεων di Eraclide Critico: Ellade e Peloponneso,' in: S. Bianchetti *et al.* (eds.), ΠΟΙΚΙΛΜΑ. *Studi in onore di Michele R. Cataudella in occasione del 60° compleanno*, 2 vols., La Spezia, 49–62.
Bar-Kochva, B. (1974), 'Menas' inscription and Curupedion,' in: *SCI* 1, 14–23.
Barbantani, S. (2001), Φάτις νικηφόρος, *Frammenti di elegia encomiastica nell età delle guerre galatiche: Supplementum Hellenisticum 958, 969*, Milan.
Barbantani, S. (2005), 'Goddess of Love and Mistress of the Sea. Notes on a Hellenistic Hymn to Arsinoe-Aphrodite (P. Lit.Goodsp. 2, I-IV)', in: *Ancient Society* 35, 133–163.
Barbantani, S. (2007), 'The Glory of the Spear. A Powerful Symbol in Hellenistic Poetry and Art. The Case of Neoptolemus "of Tlos" (and Other Ptolemaic Epigrams),' in: *SCO* 53, 67–138.
Barbantani, S. (2013a), edition and commentary on Apollonios Rhodios' *Ktiseis*, in: *Brill Jacoby Continuatus (Die Fragmente der griechischen Historiker* IV C part 2), ed. by D. Engels, Leiden.
Barbantani, S. (2013b), edition and commentary on Aristeides, 444, in: *Brill Jacoby Continuatus (Die Fragmente der griechischen Historiker* IV C part 2), ed. by D. Engels, Leiden.
Barchiesi, A. (1993), 'Future Reflexive: Two Modes of Allusion and Ovid's *Heroides*,' in: *HSCPh* 95, 333–365; reprinted in: A. Barchiesi (2001), *Speaking Volumes: Narrative and Intertext in Ovid and Latin Poets*, ed. and transl. by M. Fox/S. Marchesi, London, 105–127.
Barchiesi, A. (1994), *Il poeta e il principe*, Rome/Bari.
Bardiès-Fronty, I./Walter, Ph./Bimbenet Privat, M. (eds.) (2009) *Le Bain et le Miroir. Catalogue de l'exposition du Musée National du Moyen Âge et du Musée National de la Renaissance (mai-septembre 2009)*, Paris.
Barkhuizen, J.H. (1979), 'The Psychological Characterization of Medea in Apollonius of Rhodes, *Argonautica* 3, 744–824', in: *AClass* 22, 33–48.
Barrett, J. (2002), *Staged Narrative: Poetics and the Messenger in Greek Tragedy*. Berkeley/Los Angeles.
Bartels, A. (2004), *Vergleichende Studien zur Erzählkunst des römischen Epyllion*, Göttingen.
Barth, F. (ed.) (1969), *Ethnic Groups and Boundaries*, Boston.
Bartman, E. (1992), *Ancient Sculptural Copies in Miniature*, Leiden/New York/Cologne.
Bastianini, G./Galazzi, C., with Austin, C. (2001), *Posidippo di Pella: Epigrammi (P.Mil. Vogl. VIII 309), (Papiri dell'Università degli Studi di Milano 8)*, Milan.
Baumbach, M./Bär, S. (eds.) (2012a), *Brill's Companion to Greek and Latin Epyllion and Its Reception*, Leiden.
Baumbach, M./Bär, S. (2012b), 'A Short Introduction to the Ancient Epyllion,' in: Baumbach/Bär 2012a, ix–xvi.
Bean, G.E./Fraser, P.M. (eds.) (1954), *The Rhodian Peraea and Island*, London.
Bean, G.E./Harrison, R.M. (1967), 'Choma in Lycia,' in: *JRS* 57, 40–44.
Belfiore, E.S. (1992), *Tragic Pleasures. Aristotle on Plot and Emotion*, Princeton, NJ.
Bell, M. (2011), 'Agrarian Policy, Bucolic Poetry, and Figurative Art in Early Hellenistic Sicily,' in: R. Neudecker (ed.), *Krise und Wandel: Süditalien im 4. Und 3. Jahrhundert v. Chr.*, Wiesbaden, 193–211.

Benedetto, G. (2004), 'Su alcuni epigrammi di Antipatro di Sidone in relazione al nuovo Posidippo,' in: *Eikasmos* 15, 189–225.

Benndorf, O. (1862), *De Anthologiae Graecae epigrammatis quae ad artes spectant*, Diss. Bonn.

Berman, D.W. (2007), *Myth and Culture in Aeschylus' Seven Against Thebes*, (Filologia e critica 95), Rome.

Bernand, É. (1969), *Inscriptions métriques de l'Égypte gréco-romaine. Recherches sur la poésie épigrammatique des Grecs en Égypte*, (Annales littéraires de l'Université de Besançon 98), Paris.

Bernand, É. (1999), *Inscriptions grecques d'Hermoupolis Magna et de sa nécropole* (Institut Français d'Archéologie Orientale, Bibliothèque d'étude 123), Paris.

Bernand, É. (2002), 'Epitaphe d'un soldat-bouvier,' in: *ZPE* 140, 97–98.

Bernsdorff, H. (2006), 'The Idea of Bucolic in the Imitators of Theocritus, 3rd-1st century BC,' in: M. Fantuzzi/Th.D. Papanghelis (eds.), *Brill's Companion to Greek and Latin Pastoral*, Leiden, 188–201.

Bernsdorff, H. (2011), 'Der Schluss von Theokrits "Herakliskos" und Vergils vierte Ekloge,' in: *Archiv für Papyrusforschung* 57, 187–194.

Bettalli, M. (1995), *I mercenari nel mondo greco. I. Dalle origini alla fine del V sec. a.C.* (Studi e testi di storia antica 5), Pisa.

Bettini, M. (1999), *The Portrait of the Lover*, transl. from the Italian by L. Gibbs, Berkeley.

Bevan, E.R. (1966), *The House of Seleucus*, London.

Beye, C.R. (1982), *Epic and Romance in the* Argonautica *of Apollonius*, Carbondale/Edwardsville.

Bielohlawek, K. (1940), 'Gastmahls- und Symposienlehren bei griechischen Dichtern. (Von Homer bis zur Theognissammlung und Kritias),' in: *WS* 58, 11–30.

Bignone, E. (1929), 'Ennio ed Empedocle,' in: *RFIC* 57, 10–30.

Billault, A. (2008a), 'Théocrite et Platon: remarques sur l'*Idylle* VII,' in: *RÉG* 121, 497–514.

Billault, A. (2008b), 'La littérature dans les *Erotica Pathémata* de Parthénios,' in: Zucker 2008, 13–26.

Bing, P. (1988), *The Well-Read Muse. Present and Past in Callimachus and the Hellenistic Poets*, Göttingen.

Bing, P. (1995), '*Ergänzungsspiel* in the Epigrams of Callimachus,' in: *A&A* 41, 115–131; reprinted in: Bing 2009a, 85–105.

Bing, P. (2005), 'The Politics and Poetics of Geography in the Milan Posidippus, Section One: On Stones (AB 1–20),' in: Gutzwiller 2005a, 118–140; reprinted in: Bing 2009a, 253–272.

Bing, P. (2009a), *The Scroll and the Marble. Studies in Reading and Reception in Hellenistic poetry*, Ann Arbor.

Bing, P. (2009b), 'Reimagining Posidippus,' in: Bing 2009a, 177–193.

Bingen, J. (2007), 'PSAAthen. 9 +13 et le diecète Dioskuridès,' in: *CdÉ* 82, 207–217.

Biraud, M./Voisin, D./Zucker, A. (2008), with the collaboration of E. Delbey/K. Vanhaegendoren/F. Wendling/B. Charlet, *Parthénios de Nicée, Passions d'amour. Texte grec établi, traduit et commenté*, Grenoble.

Block, E. (1984), "Carmen 65 and the Arrangement of Catullus' Poetry,' in: *Ramus* 13, 48–59.

Boardman, J. (1968), *Engraved gems: the Ionides collection*, Northwestern University Press, Evanston IL.

Boardman, J. (2009), *The Marlborough Gems: Formerly at Blenheim Palace, Oxfordshire*, Oxford.
Bonelli, G. (1979), *Decadentismo antico e moderno. Un confronto fra l'estetismo alessandrino e l'esperienza poetica contemporanea*, Torino.
Bosworth, A.B. (1988), *From Arrian to Alexander*, Oxford.
Boyaval, B. (2004a), 'Cinque notes d'épigraphie grecque,' in: *CRIPEL* 24, 69–74.
Boyaval, B. (2004b), 'Notes Egyptiennes,' in: *Kentron* 20, 147–185.
Boyaval, B. (2005), 'Notes Egyptiennes,' in: *Kentron* 21, 161–178 (163–164: Les campagnes militaires de Diazelmis; 173–174: Les épitaphes métriques des militaires lagides).
Bramble, J.C. (1970), 'Structure and Ambiguity in Catullus LXIV,' in: *PCPhS* 16, 22–41.
Braswell, B.K. (1998), *A Commentary on Pindar Nemean Nine*, Berlin/New York.
Bresson, A. (1991), *Recueil des inscriptions de la Pérée Rhodienne (Pérée intégrée)*, Paris.
Bresson, A./Brun, P./Varinlioğlu, E. (2001), *Les Hautes terres de Carie*, (Institut Ausonius, Mémoires 4), Bordeaux (81–268: Ch. 5, Les inscriptions grecques et latines).
Briant, P. (2002), *From Cyrus to Alexander, A History of the Persian Empire*, Translated by P. T. Daniels, Eisenbrauns.
Brink, C.O. (1969), 'Horace and Empedocles' Temperature,' in: *Phoenix* 23, 138–142.
Brown, A.L. (1987), 'The Dramatic Synopses Attributed to Aristophanes of Byzantium,' in: *CQ* 37, 427–431.
Brunck, R. (ed.) (1772–1776), *Analecta veterum poetarum Graecorum*, 3 vols., Argentorati.
Bubeník, V. (1989), *Hellenistic and Roman Greece as a Sociolinguistic Area*, Amsterdam/Philadelphia.
Buck, C. (1913), 'The Interstate Use of the Greek Dialects,' *CPh* 8, 133–159.
Buck, C. (1923), 'A Question of Dialect Mixture in the Greek Epigram,' *ΑΝΤΙΔΩΡΟΝ: Festschrift Jacob Wackernagel*, Göttingen, 132–136.
Buck, C. (1955), *The Greek Dialects*, rev. ed., Chicago.
Buitenwerf, R. (2003), *Book III of the Sibylline Oracles and its Social Setting*, Leiden.
Bulloch, A.W. (1985), *Callimachus. The Fifth Hymn*, Cambridge.
Burnett, A.P. (1971), *Catastrophe Survived: Euripides' Plays of Mixed Reversal*, Oxford.
Burnett, A.P. (1985), 'Rhesus: Are Smiles Allowed?,' in: P. Burian (ed.), *Directions in Euripidean Criticism*, Durham, NC, 13–51.
Burstein, S. M. (1989), *Agatharchides of Cnidus, On the Erythraean Sea: Translated and Edited*, London.
Burton, J. (1995), *Theocritus's Urban Mimes*, Berkeley.
Burzacchini, G. (1995), 'Lirica arcaica (I). Elegia e giambo. Melica monodica e corale (dalle origini al VI secolo a.C.),' in: U. Mattioli (ed.), *Senectus. La vecchiaia nel mondo classico*, vol. 1, Bologna, 69–124.
Cadoni, N. (2010), 'Aristotele e l'omeristica antica: sondaggi su ἦθος,' in: F. Montana (ed.), *ANER POLYTROPOS. Ricerche di filologia greca antica dedicate dagli alievi a F. Montanari*, Rome, 3–39.
Cairns, F. (1984), 'Theocritus' First Idyll: The Literary Programme,' in: *WS* 18, 89–113.
Cairns, F. (1992), 'Theocritus, *Idyll* 26,' in: *PCPhS* 38, 1–38.
Caizzi, F.D. (1966), *Antisthenis fragmenta*, Milan.
Calcante, C.M. (forthcoming), 'The Verbal Icon: Rhetoric and the Visual Arts in the Stylistic Theory of Dionysius of Halicarnassus,' in: M. Cojannot-Le Blanc/C. Pouzadoux/É. Prioux (eds.) (forthcoming).
Cameron, A. (1995), *Callimachus and his Critics*, Princeton.

Campbell, M. (1991), *Moschus* Europa, Hildesheim-Zürich-New York.
Campbell, M. (1994), *A Commentary on Apollonius Rhodius Argonautica III 1–471*, Leiden-New York.
Casadio, V. (2007), 'La terra di Pelope e i "talenti" di Creso (Ps. Theocr. 8. 53ss.),' in: Pretagostini/Dettori 2007, 25–31.
Casali, S. (1996), 'Il letto celibe. "Mallio", Laodamia e l'unità di Catullo 68,' in: *RFIC* 124, 440–444.
Castoriadis, C. (1991), 'The Crisis of Culture and the State,' in: D. Ames Curtis (ed.), *Philosophy, Politics, Autonomy*, New York, 219–241.
Cavalli, E. (2010), 'ΩΣ ΑΓΑΘΩΝ ΟΥΚ ΑΠΟΛΩΛΕ ΑΡΕΤΑ. Storia e gloria nell'età dei Diadochi,' in: Antonetti, C. (ed.), *Lo spazio ionico e le comunità della Grecia nord-occidentale. Territorio, società, istituzioni. Atti del Convegno Internazionale (Venezia, 7–9 gennaio 2010)* (= *Diabaseis* 1), Pisa, 409–428.
Caygill, H. (2003), 'The Alexandrian Aesthetic,' in: J. J. Joughin, S. Malpas (eds.), *The New Aestheticism*, Manchester/New York, 99–118.
Celentano, M.S. (1995), 'L'elogio della brevità tra retorica e letteratura: Callimaco, ep. 11 Pf. = AP VII 447,' in: *QUCC* 49, 67–97.
Chamoux, F. (1988), 'Pergame et les Galates,' in: *REG* 101, 492–500.
Chandler, C. (2006), *Philodemus On Rhetoric, Books 1 and 2: Translation and Exegetical Essays*, New York/London.
Chaniotis, A. (2002), 'Foreign Soldiers—Native Girls? Constructing and Crossing Boundaries in Hellenistic Cities with Foreign Garrisons,' in: A. Chaniotis (ed.), *Army and Power in the Ancient World*, Stuttgart, 99–113.
Chaniotis, A. (2005), *War in the Hellenistic world: A Social and Cultural History*, Oxford.
Chaniotis, A. (2006), 'Die hellenistischen Kriege als Ursache von Migration: Das Beispiel Kreta,' in: E. Olshausen/H. Sonnabend, (eds.), *'Troianer sind wir gewesen"—Migrationen in der antiken Welt. Stuttgarter Kolloquium zur Historischen Geographie des Altertums 8, 2002*, Stuttgart, 98–103.
Chase, G.-H. (1902), 'The Shield Devices of the Greeks,' in: *HSCP* 13, 61–127.
Chiesa, I. (2009), 'L'elegia *In Magam et Berenicen* di Callimaco: *In Berenices nuptias?*,' in: *Acme* 62 (2), 227–234.
Chirico, M.L. (1978–1979), 'Topoi e imitazione in alcuni epigrammi di Antipatro Sidonio,' in: *AFLN* 9, 11–21.
CIRB = Struve, V. (ed.) (1965), *Corpus inscriptionum regni Bosporani*, Moscow.
Citti, P. (1987), *Contre la Décadence*, Paris.
Clare, R.J. (1996), 'Catullus 64 and the *Argonautica* of Apollonius Rhodius: Allusion and Exemplarity,' in: *PCPhS* 42, 60–88.
Clarke, J. (2008), 'Mourning and Memory in Catullus 65,' in: C. Deroux (ed.), *Studies in Latin Literature and Roman History* 14, Brussels, 131–143.
Clarysse, W. (1985), 'Greek and Egyptians in the Ptolemaic Army and Administration,' in: *Aegyptus* 65, 57.
Clarysse, W. (2001), *Het Griekse millennium: 500 v. Chr. Tot 500 n. Chr.*, Academiae analecta (Koninklijke Vlaamse Academie van België voor Wetenschappen en Kunsten nr. 7), Brussels.
Clarysse, W. (2010), 'Bilingual papyrological archives,' in: A. Papaconstantinou (ed.), *The Multilingual Experience in Egypt, from the Ptolemies to the Abassids*, Aldershot, 47–72.

Clarysse, W./Huys, M. (2003), 'A Soldier's Epitaph Rescued from the Sea,' in: *ZPE* 143, 147–148.
Clausen, W. (1970), 'Catullus and Callimachus,' in: *HSCPh* 74, 85–94.
Clauss, J.J. (1993), *The Best of the Argonauts*, Berkeley/Los Angeles.
Clauss, J.J. (1995), 'A Delicate Foot on the Well-Worn Threshold: Paradoxical Imagery in Catullus 68b,' in: *AJPh* 116, 237–253.
Clauss, J.J. (2000), 'Cosmos without Imperium,' in: M.A. Harder/R.F. Regtuit/G.C. Wakker, *Apollonius Rhodius*, Groningen, 11–32.
Clauss, J.J./Cuypers, M. (eds.) (2010), *A Companion to Hellenistic Literature*, Malden, Mass./Oxford.
Clay, D. (1975), 'The Tragic and Comic Poet of the *Symposium*,' in: *Arion* 2, 238–261.
Clay, J. S. (2009), '*Works and Days*: Tracing the Path to *Arete*,' in: F. Montanari et al. (eds.), *Brill's Companion to Hesiod*, Leiden, 71–90.
Coarelli, F. (1978), 'La statue de Cornélie, mère des Gracques et la crise politique à Rome au temps de Saturninus,' *Le dernier siècle de la République romaine et l'époque augustéenne. Journées d'étude*, Strasbourg, 13–28 [= F. Coarelli, *Revixit ars*, Rome 1996, 280–299].
Cohen, G.M. (1995), *The Hellenistic Settlements in Europe, the Islands, and Asia Minor*, (*Hellenistic Culture and Society* 17), Berkeley.
Cojannot-Le Blanc, M./Pouzadoux, C./Prioux, É. (eds.) (forthcoming), *L'Héroïque et le Champêtre. La théorie des styles appliquée aux arts et à leur histoire entre schème explicatif et modèle analytique*, Nanterre.
Colesanti, G. (2001), 'Dittografie e scambi simposiali nel *corpus* teognideo,' in: *Athenaeum* 89, 459–495.
Colesanti, G. (2007), 'Insegnamenti, maestri e allievi del *corpus* teognideo,' in: *SemRom* 10, 249–266.
Collins, J.J. (1980), 'The Epic of Theodotus and the Hellenisms of the Hasmoneans,' in: *HThR* 73, 91–104.
Collins, J.J. (1999), *Between Athens and Jerusalem: Jewish Identity in the Hellenistic Diaspora*, 2nd ed., Grand Rapids.
Collombert, P. (2000), 'Religion égyptienne et culture grecque: L'example de Διοσκουρίδης,' in: *CdÉ* 75, 47–63.
Conrad, S. (2004), *Die Grabstelen aus Moesia Inferior: Untersuchungen zu Chronologie, Typologie und Ikonografie*, Leipzig.
Conte, G.B./Barchiesi, A. (1989), 'Imitazione e arte allusiva,' in: *Lo spazio letterario di Roma antica*, I, Roma, 81–96.
Cooper, L. (1922), *An Aristotelian Theory of Comedy, With an Adaptation of the Poetics and a Translation of the 'Tractatus Coislianus,'* New York.
Corso, A. (1988), *Prassitele: Fonti epigrafiche e letterarie—Vita e opere*, t. I (*Xenia—Quaderni* 10), Rome.
Courtney, E. (ed.) (2003), *The Fragmentary Latin Poets*, Oxford.
Cribiore, R. (2001), *Gymnastics of the Mind: Greek Education in Hellenistic and Roman Egypt*, Princeton, NJ.
Criscuolo, L. (2003), 'Agoni e politica alla corte di Alessandria. Riflessioni su alcuni epigrammi di Posidippo,' in: *Chiron* 33, 311–334.
Criveller, E. (2010), 'Epigrammi funerary di Etolia e Acarnania tra III e II sec. a.C.,' in: C. Antonetti (ed.), *Lo spazio ionico e le comunità della Grecia nord-occidentale. Territorio,*

società, istituzioni. Atti del Convegno Internazionale (Venezia, 7–9 gennaio 2010) (Diabaseis 1), Pisa, 429–457.
Crowther, C./Facella, M. (2003), 'New Evidence for the Ruler Cult of Antiochus of Commagene from Zeugma,' in: Heedemann/Winter 2003, 41–80.
Crüsemann, F. (1996), *The Torah: Theology and Social History of Old Testament Law*, Edinburgh.
Curran, L.C. (1969), 'Catullus 64 and the Heroic Age,' in: *YClS* 21, 169–192.
Curtius, E.R. (1963³), *Kritische Essays zur europäischen Literatur*, München.
Cusset, C. (1999), *La Muse dans la bibliothèque*, Paris.
Cusset, C. (ed.) (2007), *Musa docta: Recherches sur la poesie scientifique dans l'Antiquité*, Paris.
Cusset, C. (2011), 'Le bestiaire de Lycophron: entre chien et loup,' in: *Anthropozoologica* 33–4, 61–72.
Cusset, C./Prioux, É. (2009), *Lycophron: éclats d'obscurité*, Saint-Etienne.
Cuypers, M. (2010), 'Historiography, Rhetoric, and Science: Rethinking a Few Assumptions on Hellenistic Prose,' in: Clauss/Cuypers 2010, 317–336.
D'Alessio, G.B. (1996, 2007⁴), *Callimaco. Inni, epigrammi e frammenti*, 2 vols., Milano.
D'Alessio, G.B. (2007), 'Note su PSI XIV 1391,' in: *Comunicazioni dell'Istituto Papirologico "G. Vitelli"* 7, 75–80.
Daskalòpoulos, D./Stasinopoulou, M. (2002), *Ο βίος και το έργο του Κ. Π. Καβάφη*, Athens.
Daux, G. (1968), 'Chronique des fouilles et découvertes archéologiques en Grèce en 1967,' in: *BCH* 92, 711–1135.
David de Palacio, M.-F. (2001), 'Les "nacres de la perle et de la pourriture": Byzance', in: A. Montandon (ed.), *Mythes de la décadence*, Clermont-Ferrand, 163–175.
Davies, P.R./Chilton, B.D. (1978), 'The Aqedah: A Revised Tradition History,' in: *The Catholic Biblical Quarterly* 40, 514–558.
Davies, R.B. (2008), 'Reading Ezekiel's *Exagoge*: Tragedy, Sacrificial Ritual, and the Midrashic Tradition,' in: *GRBS* 48, 393–415.
Dawe, R.D. (1978), *Studies on the Text of Sophocles*. vol. 3, Leiden.
DeBrohun, J. Blair (2007), 'Catullan Intertextuality: Apollonius and the Allusive Plot of Catullus 64,' in: Skinner 2007a, 293–313.
Dekker, R. (2002), 'Introduction,' in: R. Dekker (ed.), *Egodocuments and History: Autobiographical Writing in its Social Context since the Middle Ages* (Publicaties van de Faculteit der Historische en Kunstwetenschappen Maatschappijgeschiedenis 38), Hilversum, 7–20.
Delage, E. (1930), *La géographie dans les Argonautiques d'Apollonios de Rhodes*, Paris.
Depew, M. (2003), 'The Poetics of the Museum: Aesthetics in Callimachus and Cavafy,' in: *Classical and Modern Literature* 23, 2003, 37–50.
Depew, M. (2007), 'Springs, Nymphs, and Rivers: Models of Origination in Third-Century Alexandrian Poetry,' in: A. Bierl/R. Lämmle/K. Wesselmann (eds.), *Literatur und Religion 2: Wege zu einer mythisch-rituellen Poetik bei den Griechen,* Berlin/New York, 141–171.
Desonay, F. (1928), *Le rêve hellénique chez les poètes parnassiens*, Paris.
Dettori, E. (2004), 'Appunti sul "Banchetto di Pollis" (Call. fr. 178 Pf.),' in: R. Pretagostini/E. Dettori (eds.), *La cultura ellenistica. L'opera letteraria e l'esegesi antica*, Roma, 33–63.
Dillon, J. (2003), *The Heirs of Plato: A Study of the Old Academy*, Oxford.

Di Marco, M. (2010), 'Un *topos* rovesciato: sul fr. 380 Pf. di Callimaco,' in: *Eikasmos* 21, 197–216.
Döpp, S. (2005), '*Munera et Musarum et Veneris*. Catull c. 68 in der Entwicklungsgeschichte der römischen Elegie,' in: Tar 2005a, 5–19.
Dorandi, T. (2009), 'La tradizione papirologica di Eraclide Pontico,' in: Fortenbaugh/Pender 2009, 1–25.
Dorival, G. (1987), 'La Bible des Septante chez les auteurs païens (jusqu'au Pseudo-Longin),' in: *Lectures anciennes de la Bible* (*Cahiers de Biblia Patristica* 1), Paris, 9–26.
Dorival, G. (1988), 'L'achèvement de la Septante dans le judaïsme. De la faveur au rejet,' in: G. Dorival/M. Harl/O. Munnich (eds.), *La Bible Grecque des Septante. Du judaïsme hellénistique au christianisme ancien*, Paris, 83–122.
Drews, R. (1973), *The Greek Accounts of Eastern History*, Washington.
Dreyer, B. (2011), *Polybios. Leben und Werk im Banne Roms*, Hildesheim/Zurich/New York.
Du Quesnay, I. (2012), 'Three Problems in Poem 66,' in: Du Quesnay/Woodman 2012, 153–183.
Du Quesnay, I./Woodman, T. (eds.) (2012), *Catullus: Poems, Books, Readers*, Cambridge.
Dubel, S. (2010), 'Aphrodite se mirant au bouclier d'Arès: Transpositions homériques et jeux de matière dans l'*epos* hellénistique,' in: É. Prioux/A. Rouveret (eds.), *Métamorphoses du regard ancien*, Nanterre, 13–28.
Dumitru, A. (2011), 'Les Séleucides et les Balkans (III-II siècles av. J.Chr.),' in: *Le Symposium International Le Livre. La Roumanie. L'Europe. Troisième édition—20 à 24 Septembre 2010*, t. IV,4: *Latinité Orientale*, Bucarest, 349–376.
Dunand, F. (1981), 'Fête et propagande à Alexandrie sous les Lagides,' in: F. Dunand, *La fête. Pratique et discours d'Alexandrie hellénistique à la Mission de Besançon*, Paris, 13–41.
Durbec, Y. (2006), 'Lycophron et la poétique de Callimaque: le prologue de l'*Alexandra*,' in: *ARF* 8, 81–83 = *Essais sur l'Alexandra de Lycophron*, Amsterdam, 2011, 12–16.
Durbec, Y. (forthcoming), 'Usages des traditions homériques dans les épigrammes de dédicaces d'armes de guerre: la vieillesse des armes et des hommes,' in: Acts of the conference 'Traditions épiques et poésie épigrammatique. Présence des épopées archaïques dans les épigrammes grecques et latines,' Aix-en-Provence 7–9 Novembre 2012.
Dyck, A.R. (1981), 'On Apollodorus of Cyrene,' in: *HSCPh* 85, 101–106.
Edmonds, J.M. (1912), *The Greek Bucolic Poets*, Cambridge, Mass.
Edvenson Thjømøe, J. (2008), *Poetic Technique in Vikram Seth's* The Golden Gate, Diss. Oslo.
Edwards, M. (1991), *The Iliad: A Commentary, Volume V: Books 17–20*, Cambridge.
Effe, B. (1977), *Dichtung und Lehre: Untersuchungen zur Typologie des antiken Lehrgedichts*. (*Zetemata* 69), Munich.
Effe, B. (2005), 'Typologie und literarhistorischer Kontext: zur Gattungsgeschichte des griechischen Lehrgedichts,' in: Horster/Reitz 2005, 27–44.
Eggerking, G. (1912), *De Graeca artis tragicae doctrina, imprimis de affectibus tragicis*, Diss. Berlin.
El-Nassey, S.A.A./Wagner, G./Hafeez Abdul-Al, A. (eds.) (1978), 'Nouvelles stèles de Kôm Abou Bellou," in: *BIFAO* 78, 231–258.
Eliot, T.S. (1920), *The Sacred Wood*, London.
Eliot, T.S. (1982), *La terra desolata* (crit. ed. A. Serpieri), Milan.
Eliot, T.S. (2005), *The Annotated Waste-Land with Eliot's Contemporary Prose*, ed. L. Rainey, Yale.

Else, G.F. (1957), *Aristotle's Poetics: The Argument*, Cambridge Mass.
Elsperger, W. (1908), *Reste und Spuren antiker Kritik gegen Euripides, gesammelt aus den Euripidesscholien* (Philologus Supp. 11), Leipzig.
Elvira Barba, M.A. (1981), *El Alejandrinismo*, Madrid.
Engberg-Pedersen, T./Sihvola, J. (eds.) (1998), *The Emotions in Hellenistic Philosophy*, Dordrecht.
Erbì, M. (2009), 'Il retore e la città nella polemica di Filodemo verso Diogene di Babilonia (PHerc. 1004, coll. 64–70),' in: *Cronache Ercolanesi* 39, 119–140.
Erbì, M. (2010), 'Eraclito e l'inganno della retorica in Filodemo (PHerc. 1004, coll. 57–63),' in: *Cronache Ercolanesi* 40, 65–74.
Erren, M. (1986), *Untersuchungen zum antiken Lehrgedicht*, Diss. Freiburg.
Everson, S. (1997), *Aristotle on Perception*, Oxford.
Faber, R. (1995), 'Vergil *Eclogue* 3.37, Theocritus 1 and Hellenistic Ekphrasis,' in: *AJPh* 116, 411–417.
Fabiano, G. (1971), 'Fluctuation in Theocritus' Style,' in: *GRBS* 12, 517–537.
Fabre-Serris, J. (2004), 'Tibulle 1,4 : l'élégie et la tradition de la poésie didactique,' in: *Dictynna* 1: http://halmaipel.recherche.univlille3.fr/Dictynna/Articles/1Articlespdf/fabre-serris.pdf.
Faggen, R. (2001), 'Frost and the Questions of Pastoral,' in: R. Faggen (ed.), *The Cambridge Companion to Robert Frost*, Cambridge, 49–74.
Fakas, C. (2001), *Der hellenistische Hesiod: Arats Phainomena und die Tradition der antiken Lehrepik*, Wiesbaden.
Falco, V. de (1931), 'L'epigramma attribuito a Pisandro, in: *RIGI* 15, 57–60.
Falkner, T. (2002), 'Scholars Versus Actors: Text and Performance in the Greek Tragic Scholia,' in: P. Easterling/E. Hall (eds.), *Greek and Roman Actors: Aspects of an Ancient Profession*, Cambridge, 342–361.
Fantuzzi, M. (2000), 'Theocritus and the "Demythologizing" of Poetry,' in: M. Depew/D. Obbink (eds.), *Matrices of Genre: Authors, Canons, and Society*, Cambridge, Mass., 135–51.
Fantuzzi, M. (2008), 'La doppia gloria di Menas,' in: A.M. Morelli (ed.), *Epigramma longum. Da Marziale alla tarda antichità. From Martial to late Antiquity*. Atti del convegno internazionale, Cassino, 29–31 maggio 2006, II, Cassino, 603–622.
Fantuzzi, M. (forthcoming), 'On the Bastardy of the *Rhesus*: Orphan of Unknown Paternity or Child of Many Genres?,' in: M. Formisano/C.S. Kraus (eds.), Proceedings of the Conference 'Marginality, Canonicity, Passion' (Yale Univ., March 2012), Cambridge.
Fantuzzi, M./Hunter, R. (2002), *Muse e modelli*, Rome/Bari.
Fantuzzi, M./Hunter, R. (2004), *Tradition and Innovation in Hellenistic Poetry*, Cambridge.
Fantuzzi, M./Konstan, D. (2013), 'From Achilles' Horses to a Cheese-seller Shop: on the History of the Guessing Game in Greek Drama,' in: E. Bakola/L. Prauscello/M. Telò (eds.), *Comic Interactions: Genres in Comedy and Comedy in Genres*, Cambridge, 256–274.
Faraone, C.A. (2008), *The Stanzaic Architecture of Early Greek Elegy*, Oxford.
Farrell, J. (1997), 'Walcott's *Omeros* : The Classical Epic in a Postmodern World,' in: M. Beissinger/J. Tylus/S. Wofford (eds.), *Epic Traditions in the Contemporary World*, Berkeley/Los Angeles/London, 270–296.
Farrell, J. (2008), 'The Six Books of Lucretius' *De rerum natura:* Antecedents and Influence,' in: *Dictynna* 5: http://dictynna.revues.org/385.

Faulkner, A. (2014), 'Faith and Fidelity in Biblical Epic: the *Metaphrasis Psalmorum*, Nonnus, and the Theory of Translation,' in: K. Spanoudakis (ed.), *Nonnus*, Berlin, 195–210.
FD = *Fouilles de Delphes, III. Épigraphie*, Paris 1929 ff.
Feeney, D. (1992), '*Shall I Compare Thee ...?*: Catullus 68B and the Limits of Analogy,' in: Woodman, T./Powell, J. (eds.), *Author and Audience in Latin Literature*, Cambridge, 33–44, 220–224; reprinted in: Gaisser 2007, 429–446.
Felix, W. (1995), 'Dinon,' *Encyclopaedia Iranica*, vol. VII, Fasc. 4, 419–420.
Fernandelli, M. (2008), 'Miti, miti in miniatura, miti senza racconto: Note a quattro epilli (Mosch. *Eur.* 58–62, Catull. 64,89–90, Verg. *georg.* IV 507–515, Ov. *met.* XI 751–795),' in: *CentoPagine* 2, 12–27.
Fernandelli, M. (2012), *Catullo e la rinascita dell'epos. Dal carme 64 all'Eneide*, Hildesheim.
Fernández Marco, N. (2000), *The Septuagint in Context: Introduction to the Greek Version of the Bible*, Leiden.
Fernández-Galiano, E. (1987), *Posidipo de Pela*, (*Manuales y anejos de Emerita* 36), Madrid.
Ferrari, F. (1987), 'Sulla ricezione dell'elegia arcaica nella silloge teognidea: il problema delle varianti,' in: *Maia* 39, 177–197.
FGE = Page, D.L. (ed.) (1981), *Further Greek Epigrams. Epigrams before A.D. 50 from the Greek Anthology and other sources not included in* Hellenistic Anthology *or* Garland of Philip, Cambridge.
Fischer-Bovet, C. (2014), *Army and Society in Ptolemaic Egypt (330–30 BC)*, Cambridge.
Fitzgerald, J.T. (2008), 'The Passions and Moral Progress: An Introduction,' in: J.T. Fitzgerald (ed.), *Passions and Moral Progress in Graeco-Roman Poetry*, London/New York, 1–25.
Fögen, T. (2004), 'Zur Transformation griechischer Wissensbestände durch römische Fachschriftsteller: Aspekte des Fachübersetzens in der Antike,' in: G. Hassler/G. Volkmann (eds.), *History of linguistics in texts and concepts. Geschichte der Sprachwissenschaft in Texten und Konzepten*, Münster, 433-454.
Fögen, T. (2005), 'The Transformation of Greek Scientific Knowledge by Roman Technical Writers: On the Translation of Technical Texts in Antiquity,' in: J. Althoff, B. Herzhoff, and G. Wöhrle (eds.), (*Antike Naturwissenschaft und ihre Rezeption* 15), Trier, 91–114.
Fordyce, C.J. (ed.) (1961), *Catullus. A Commentary*, Oxford.
Formicola, C. (2003), 'Il pomo della concordia (Catull. 65, Callimaco e l'elegia latina),' in: *Vichiana* 4a ser. 5, 183–205.
Forster, E.M. (1923), 'The Poetry of C.P. Cavafy,' in: E.M. Forster, *Pharos and Pharillon*, Richmond Surrey, 91–97 (1st ed. 1919).
Fortenbaugh, W.W. (2002), *Aristotle on Emotion*, London (1st ed. 1975).
Fortenbaugh, W.W./Pender, E. (eds.) (2009), *Heraclides of Pontus: Discussion* (*Rutgers University Studies in Classical Humanities* 15), New Brunswick/London.
Fortini, F. (1991), 'Oscurità e difficoltà,' in: *L'Asino d'oro* 2, 84–89.
Fountoulakis, A. (2004), 'The Colours of Desire and Death. Colour Terms in Bion's *Epitaph on Adonis*,' in: L. Cleland/K. Stears/G. Davies (eds.), *Colour in the Ancient Mediterranean World*, Oxford, 110–116.
Fowler, A. (2003), 'The Formation of Genres in the Renaissance and after,' in: *New Literary History* 34, 185–200.
Fowler, B.H. (1989), *The Hellenistic Aesthetic*, Madison.
Fowler, D. (2000a), 'The Didactic Plot,' in: M. Depew/D. Obbink (eds.), *Matrices of Genre: Authors, Canons, and Society*, Washington, 205–219.

Fowler, D. (2000b), 'The Ruin of Time: Monuments and Survival at Rome,' in: D. Fowler, *Roman Constructions. Readings in Postmodern Latin*, Oxford, 193–217.
Fowler, R.L. (2000), *Early Greek Mythography* I: *The Texts*, Oxford.
Fox, M. (2009), 'Heraclides of Pontus and the Philosophical Dialogue,' in: Fortenbaugh/Pender 2009, 41–67.
Fränkel, H. (1960a), 'Ein Don Quijote unter den Argonauten,' in: *MH* 17, 1–20.
Fränkel, H. (1960b), *Wege und Formen frühgriechischen Denkens*, 2nd ed., Munich.
Fraser, P.M. (1972), *Ptolemaic Alexandria*, Oxford.
Fraser, P.M. (2007), 'The Ptolemaic Garrison of Hermoupolis Magna,' in: E. Matthews (ed.), *Old and New Worlds in Greek Onomastics*, Oxford, 69–85.
Fréchet, C. (2006), '*Les Remèdes à l'amour* d'Ovide,' in: Cusset 2007, 193–214.
Friedländer, P. (1942), 'A New Epigram by Damagetus,' in: *AJPh* 63, 78–82.
Fuhrer, T. (1992), *Die Auseinandersetzung mit den Chorlyrikern in den Epinikien des Kallimachos*, Basel/Kassel.
Fuhrmann, M. (1966), 'Obscuritas. Das Problem der Dunkelheit in der rhetorischen und literarästhetischen Theorie der Antike,' in: W. Iser (ed.), *Immanente Ästhetik, ästhetische Reflexion*, Munich, 47–72.
Fulbrook, M./Rublack, U. (2010), 'In Relation: the "Social Self" and Ego-documents', in: *German History* 28, 263–272.
Fuqua, C. (2008), 'An Internal Ring Composition in Posidippus' Lithika,' *CW* 102, 3–12.
Furley, W./Bremer, J. (2001), *Greek Hymns*, vols. 2, Tübingen.
Fusillo, M. (1984), 'L'*Alessandra* di Licofrone: racconto epico e discorso drammatico,' in: *ASNP* 14, 495–525.
Fusillo, M. (1994), 'El sueño de Medea," in: *Revista de Occidente* 158/159, 92–102.
Gaisser, J.H. (1995), 'Threads in the Labyrinth: Competing Views and Voices in Catullus 64,' in: *AJPh* 116, 579–616; reprinted in: Gaisser 2007, 217–260.
Gaisser, J.H. (ed.) (2007), *Catullus. Oxford Readings in Classical Studies*, Oxford.
Gaisser, J.H. (2009), *Catullus*, Chichester.
Galand-Hallyn, P. (1994), *Le Reflet des fleurs: Description et métalangage poétique d'Homère à la Renaissance*, Genève.
Gale, M.R. (ed.) (2004), *Latin Epic and Didactic Poetry: Genre, Tradition and Individuality*, Swansea.
Gale, M.R. (2012), 'Putting on the Yoke of Necessity: Myth, Intertextuality and Moral Agency in Catullus 68,' in: Du Quesnay/Woodman 2012, 184–211.
García J.F. (2002), 'Symbolic Action in the Homeric Hymns: the Theme of Recognition,' in: *CA* 21, 5–39.
Garulli, V. (2008), '*L'*epigramma longum *nella tradizione epigrafica sepolcrale greca*,' in: A.M. Morelli, (ed.), *Epigramma longum. Da Marziale alla tarda antichità. From Martial to late Antiquity.* Atti del convegno internazionale, Cassino, 29–31 maggio 2006, II, Cassino, 623–662.
Garulli, V. (2013), '*Posidippo epigrafico*,' in: *L'Épigramme dans tous ses états, épigraphiques, littéraires, historiques, jeudi 3 et vendredi 4 juin 2010*, ENS Lyon.
Gavins, J. (2007), *Text World Theory: An Introduction*, Edinburgh.
Gavrilov, A.K. (2005), 'Боспорский воин Аполлоний и его поэт [Der Bosporaner Apollonius und sein Dichter" (CIRB 119)]," in: *Hyberboreus* 11, 60–85, and *Hyberboreus* 12, 215–241.
Genette, G. (1980), *Narrative Discourse*, transl. by J.E. Lewin, foreword by J. Culler, Oxford.

Gera, D. (1998), *Judaea and Mediterranean Politics. 219–161 B.C.E.* (Brill's Series in Jewish Studies 8), Leiden/New York/Cologne.

Gerber, D.E. (1999), *Greek Elegiac Poetry from the Seventh to the Fifth Centuries BC*, Cambridge, Mass./London.

Ghoneim, M. (1996), 'Alexandrian Culture in Modern Times: Egyptian Identity and Cosmopolitan Aspects,' in: Walsh/Reese 1996, 285–301.

Glei, R. (2008), 'Outlines of Apollonian Scholarship 1955–1999,' in: Th.D. Papanghelis/A. Rengakos (eds.), *Brill's Companion to Apollonius Rhodius*, Second, Revised Edition, Leiden/Boston, 1–28.

Glucker, C.A.M. (1987), *The City of Gaza in the Roman and Byzantine Periods* (BAR International Series, 325), Oxford; 'Appendix: The Inscriptions of Gaza,' 115–163.

Godman, P. (1989), 'T.S. Eliot e E.R.Curtius: Una collaborazione europea,' in: *Liber* 1, 5–6.

Godwin, J. (ed.) (1995), *Catullus: Poems 61–68*, with introduction, translation and commentary, Warminster.

Goldhill, S. (1991), *The Poet's Voice. Essays on Poetics and Greek Literature*, Cambridge.

Goldhill, S. (1994), 'The Naive and Knowing Eye: Ecphrasis and the Culture of Viewing in the Hellenistic World,' in: S. Goldhill/R. Osborne (eds.), *Art and Text in Ancient Greek Culture*, Cambridge, 197–223.

Gonnoi II = Helly, B. (1973), *Gonnoi*, vol. 2. *Les Inscriptions*, Amsterdam.

González, J. M. (2000), 'Musai Hypophetores: Apollonius of Rhodes on Inspiration and Interpretation,' in: *HSCPh* 100, 268–92.

González, J.M. (2010), 'Theokritos' *Idyll* 16. The Χάριτες and Civic Poetry,' in: *HSCPh* 105, 65–116.

Gottschalk, H.B. (1980), *Heraclides of Pontus*, Oxford.

Goudriaan, K. (1988), *Ethnicity in Ptolemaic Egypt*, (*Dutch monographs on ancient history and archaeology* 5), Amsterdam.

Gow, A.S.F. (1950), *Theocritus: Edited with a Translation and Commentary*, 2 vols., Cambridge.

Gow, A.S.F. (1954), 'Antipater of Sidon: Notes and Queries,' in: *CR* N.S. 4, 1–6.

Gow, A.S.F./Page, D.L. (1965), *The Greek Anthology: Hellenistic Epigrams*, 2 vols., Cambridge.

Gowing, A.M. (2010), 'From Polybius to Dionysius: the Decline and Fall of Hellenistic Historiography,' in: Clauss/Cuypers 2010, 384–394.

GP = Gow, A.S.F./Page, D.L. (eds.), (1968), *The Greek Anthology. The Garland of Philip*, 2 vols., Cambridge.

Grandjean, Y. (1971), 'Note sur une épigramme de Maronée,' in: *BCH* 95, 283–294.

Graver, M. (1998), 'The Manhandling of Maecenas: Senecan Abstractions of Masculinity,' in: *AJPh* 119, 607–632.

Green, P. (1996), 'Alexander's Alexandria,' in: Walsh/Reese 1996, 3–25.

Green, P. (2005), *The Poems of Catullus*. A bilingual edition, translated, with commentary, Berkeley.

Greenberg, C. (1985), 'Avant-garde and Kitsch (1939),' in: F. Frascina (ed.), *Pollock and After*, London, 48–59.

Gregory, J. (1999–2000), 'Comic Elements in Euripides,' in: *ICS* 24–25, 59–74.

Griffith, G.T. (1935), *The Mercenaries of the Hellenistic World*, Cambridge.

Griffiths, F.T. (1979), *Theocritus at Court*, Leiden.

Grimm, G. (1981), 'Orient und Okzident in der Kunst Alexandriens,' in: Hinske 1981, 13–25.

Gronewald, M. (1993), 'Der neue Poseidippos und Kallimachos, Epigramm 35,' in: *ZPE* 99, 28–29.
Gruen, E. (1998), *Heritage and Hellenism: The Reinvention of Jewish Tradition*, Berkeley.
Guichard, L. (2005), 'Dialecto y género literario en los epigramas de Posidipo (PMil.Vogl. VIII 309', in: *Actos del XI Congreso Español de estudios clásicos* 2, 311–320.
Günther, W. (1971), *Das Orakel von Didyma in hellenistischer Zeit. Eine Interpretation von Stein-Urkunden*, (*Istanbuler Mitteilungen Beiheft* 4), Tübingen.
Gutman, Y. (1954), 'Philo the Epic Poet,' in: *Scripta Hierosolymitana* 1, 36–63.
Gutzwiller, K. (1983), 'Charites or Hiero: Theocritus' *Idyll* 16,' in: *RhM* 126, 212–238.
Gutzwiller, K. (1997), 'The Poetics of Editing in Meleager's *Garland*,' in: *TAPhA* 127, 169–200.
Gutzwiller, K. (1998), *Poetic Garlands: Hellenistic Epigrams in Context*, Berkeley/Los Angeles/London.
Gutzwiller, K. (2002), 'Art's Echo: The Tradition of Hellenistic Ecphrastic Epigram,' in: M.A. Harder/R.F. Regtuit/G.C. Wakker (eds.), *Hellenistic Epigrams*, Leuven, 85–112.
Gutzwiller, K. (2003), 'Nikonoe's Rainbow (Posidippus 6 Austin-Bastianini),' in: *ZPE* 145, 44–46.
Gutzwiller, K. (ed.) (2005a), *The New Posidippus. A Hellenistic Poetry Book*, Oxford.
Gutzwiller, K. (2005b), 'The Literariness of the Milan Papyrus, or 'What Difference a Book?",' in: Gutzwiller 2005a, 287–319.
Gutzwiller, K. (2006), 'The Bucolic Problem,' in: *CPh* 101, 380–404.
Gutzwiller, K. (2007), *A Guide to Hellenistic Literature*, London.
Gutzwiller, K. (2009 [2011]), 'Apelles and the Painting of Language,' in: *Revue de Philologie* 83, 39–63.
Gutzwiller, K. (2010), 'Literary criticism', in: Clauss/Cuypers 2010, 337–365.
Gutzwiller K. (2013), 'Genre and Ethnicity in the Epigrams of Meleager,' in: S. Ager/F. Riemer (eds.), *Belonging and Isolation in the Hellenistic World*, (*Phoenix Supplementary Volume* 51), Toronto, 47–69.
Haard, E. de (1998), 'Kuzmin's Alexandria,' in: *Neo-Formalist-Papers*, Amsterdam, 181–200.
Haas, D. (1982), 'Cavafy's Reading Notes on Gibbon's *Decline and Fall*,' in: *Folia Neohellenica* 4, 25–96.
Halliwell, S. (1998), *Aristotle's* Poetics, Chicago (1st ed. 1986).
Halliwell, S. (2011), *Between Ecstasy and Truth: Interpretations of Greek Poetics from Homer to Longinus*, Oxford.
Hanink, J. 2011. 'Aristotle and Tragic Theater: A Response to J. Wise', *Arethusa* 44, 310–28.
Hannestad, L. (1993), 'Greeks and Celts: the Creation of a Myth,' in: P. Bilde *et al.* (eds.), *Centre and Periphery in the Hellenistic World*, Aarhus, 16–38.
Harder, A. (1990), '*Untrodden Paths:* Where Do They Lead?,' in: *HSCPh* 93, 287–309.
Harder, A. (1994), 'Travel Descriptions in the *Argonautica* of Apollonius Rhodius,' in: Z. von Martels (ed.), *Travel Fact and Travel Fiction*, Leiden, 16–29.
Harder, A. (1998), '"Generic Games" in Callimachus' *Aetia*,' in: A. Harder *et al.* (eds.), *Genre in Hellenistic Poetry*, Leuven, 95–113.
Harder, A. (2002), 'Intertextuality in Callimachus' *Aetia*,' in: F. Montanari/L. Lehnus (eds.), *Callimaque*, Vandoeuvres-Genève, 189–233.
Harder, M.A. (2003), 'The Invention of Past, Present and Future in Callimachus' *Aetia*,' in: *Hermes* 131, 290–306.
Harder, A. (2005), 'Catullus 63: A 'Hellenistic Poem'?,' in: Nauta/Harder 2005, 574–595.

Harder, A. (2007a), 'To Teach or not to Teach?,' in: A. Harder et al. (eds.), *Calliope's Classroom*, Leuven, 23–48.
Harder, A. (2007b), 'Callimachus,' in: de Jong/Nünlist 2007, 81–96.
Harder, A. (2011), 'More Facts from Fragments?,' in: D. Obbink/R. Rutherford (eds.), *Culture in Pieces: Essays on Ancient Texts in Honour of Peter Parsons*, Oxford, 174–187.
Harder, A. (2012), *Callimachus, Aetia: Introduction, Text, Translation, and Commentary*, 2 vols., Oxford.
Harder, A./Regtuit, R.F./Wakker, G.C. (eds.) (1998), *Genre in Hellenistic Poetry*, Groningen.
Hardie, P. (1993), *The Epic Successors of Virgil*, Cambridge.
Hardie, P. (1995), 'The Speech of Pythagoras in Ovid *Metamorphoses* 15: Empedoclean Epos,' in: *CQ* 45, 204–214.
Hardie, P. (2002), *Ovid's Poetics of Illusion*, Cambridge.
Hardie, P. (2010), art. 'Alexandrianism,' in: A. Grafton/G.W. Most/S. Settis (eds.), *The Classical Tradition*, Cambridge, Mass., 32–34.
Harrison, S.J. (2005), 'Altering Attis: Ethnicity, Gender and Genre in Catullus 63,' in: Nauta/Harder 2005, 520–533.
Harrison, S.J. (2001), 'Picturing the Future: The Proleptic Ekphrasis from Homer to Virgil,' in: S.J. Harrison (ed.), *Texts, Ideas, and the Classics: Scholarship, Theory, and Classical Literature*, Oxford, 70–92.
Hartmann, J. (1999), art. 'Alexandrinismus,' in: *Der Neue Pauly* 13, Rezeption, Stuttgart/Weimar, 73–75.
Haslam, M.W. (1983), '**3544**. Philosophical dialogue (Heraclides Ponticus, περὶ ἀρχῆc?) (addendum to **664**)', in: A.K. Bowman et al. (eds.), *The Oxyrhynchus Papyri* L, (*Graeco-Roman Memoirs* 70), London, 93–99.
Haslam, M.W. (1992), 'Heraclides Ponticus 1: *De imperio* (?),' in: F. Adorno et al. (eds.), *Corpus dei papiri filosofici greci e latini. Testi e lessico nei papiri di cultura greca e latina. Parte* I: *Autori Noti. Vol.* 1**, Florence, 199–214.
Havelock, Chr. (1995), *The Aphrodite of Knidos and Her Successors: A Historical Review of the Female Nude in Greek Art*, Ann Arbor.
HE = Gow, A.S.F./Page, D.L. (eds.), (1965), *The Greek Anthology. Hellenistic Epigrams*, 2 vols., Cambridge.
Headlam, W. (1901), 'τοκέων "A Parent" and the Kindred Forms,' in: *CR* 15, 401–404.
Heath, M. (1985), 'Hesiod's Didactic Poetry,' in: *CQ* 35, 245–263.
Heath, M. (2009), 'Cognition in Aristotle's *Poetics*,' in: *Mnemosyne* 62, 51–75.
Heckel, W./Yardley, J.C (ed.) (2004), *Alexander the Great. Historical sources in translation*, Malden, Mass.
Heedemann, G./Winter, E. (eds.) (2003), *Neue Forschungen zur Religionsgeschichte Kleinasiens, Elmar Schwertheim zum 60. Geburtstag gewidmet* (*Asia Minor Studien* 49), Bonn.
Heinen, H. (1972), *Untersuchungen zur Hellenistischen Geschichte des 3. Jahrhunderts v. Chr. Zur Geschichte der Zeit des Ptolemaios Keraunos und zum Chremonideischen Kieg*, (*Historia Einzelschriften* 20), Wiesbaden.
Helly, B. (1992), 'Steles funéraires de Démetrias, Recherches sur la chronologie des remparts et des nécropoles méridionales de la ville,' in: *Diethnes Sunedrio gia tin Archaia Thessalia sti mnimi tou Dimitri R. Theochari [International Congress for Ancient Thessaly. In the memory of D.R. Theocharis]*, Athens, 349–365.

Henderson, A.A.R. (1970), 'Insignem conscendere currum (Lucretius 6.47),' in: *Latomus* 29, 739–743.
Henriksen, L. (2006), *Ambition and Anxiety: Ezra Pound's* Cantos *and Derek Walcott's* Omeros, Amsterdam/New York.
Henry, W. B. (2009a), *Philodemus,* On Death: *Translated with an Introduction and Notes (Society of Biblical Literature, Writings from the Greco-Roman World* 29), Atlanta.
Henry, W. B. (2009b), 'New Light on Philodemus, *On Death*,' in: *Cronache Ercolanesi* 39, 89–102.
Herring, E. (2009), 'Ethnicity and Culture,' in: A. Erskine (ed.), *A Companion to Ancient History*, Oxford, 123–133.
Herrmann, P. (1987), 'Milesier am Seleukidenhof. Prosopographische Beiträge zur Geschichte Milets im 2. Jhdt. v. Chr.,' in: *Chiron* 17, 183–190.
Hesberg, H. von (1988), 'Bildsyntax und Erzählweise in der hellenistischen Flächenkunst,' in: *JDAI* 103, 309–365.
Hinds, S. (1998), *Allusion and Intertext: Dynamics of Appropriation in Roman Poetry*, Cambridge.
Hinske, N. (ed.) (1981), *Alexandrien. Kulturbegegnungen dreier Jahrtausende im Schmelztiegel einer mediterranen Großstadt*, Mainz am Rhein.
Hirst, A. (1998), 'Two Cheers for Byzantium: Equivocal Attitudes in the Poetry of Palamas and Cavafy,' in: D. Ricks/P. Magdalino (eds.), *Byzantium and the Modern Greek Identity*, Aldershot, 105–117.
Hirst, A./Silk, M. (eds.) (2004), *Alexandria: Real and Imagined*, Aldershot.
Holladay, C.R. (1983–1996), *Fragments from Hellenistic Jewish Authors*, 4 vols., Atlanta.
Hollis, A.S. (2007), *Fragments of Roman Poetry c.60 BC–AD 20: Edited with an Introduction, Translation, and Commentary*, Oxford.
Holmes, L. (1992), 'Myrrh and Unguents in the *Coma Berenices*,' in: *CPh* 87, 47–50.
Holzberg, N. (2002), *Catull: Der Dichter und sein erotisches Werk*, Munich.
Holzinger, von. K.R. (1883), *Über die Parepigraphae zu Aristophanes. Eine Scholienstudie*, Vienna.
Honigman, S. (2003), *The Septuagint and Homeric Scholarship in Alexandria: A Study in the Narrative of the* Letter of Aristeas, London.
Hopkinson, N. (1988), *A Hellenistic Anthology*, Cambridge.
Horrocks, G. (2010), *Greek: A History of the Language and its Speakers*, 2nd ed., Oxford/Malden, MA.
Horster, M./Reitz, C. (eds.) (2003), *Antike Fachschriftsteller: Literarischer Diskurs und sozialer Kontext*, Stuttgart.
Horster, M./Reitz, C. (eds.) (2005), *Wissensvermittlung in dichterischer Gestalt (Palingenesia* 85), Stuttgart.
Horstmann, A.E.-A. (1976), *Ironie und Humor bei Theokrit*, Meisenheim am Glan.
Höschele, R. (2009a), 'Catullus' Callimachean Hair-itage and the Erotics of Translation,' in: *RFIC* 137, 118–152.
Höschele, R. (2009b), 'Meleager and Heliodora: A Love Story in Bits and Pieces?,' in: I. Nilsson (ed.), *Plotting with Eros: Essays on the Poetics of Love and the Erotics of Reading*, Copenhagen, 99–134.
Höschele, R. (2010), *Die blütenlesende Muse: Poetik und Textualität antiker Epigrammsammlungen*, (*Classica Monacensia* 37), Tübingen.
Howald, E. (1948), *Das Wesen der lateinischen Dichtung*, Zürich.

Hubbard, T.K. (1984), 'Catullus 68: The Text as Self-Demystification,' in: *Arethusa* 17, 29–49.
Hugo, P. (2010), 'Review of Troxel (2008),' in: *Journal of Hebrew Scriptures* 10 (http://www.arts.ualberta.ca/JHS/reviews/reviews_new/review468.htm).
Hunter, R. (1983), *Eubulus. The Fragments*, Cambridge.
Hunter, R. (1985), *The New Comedy of Greece and Rome*, Cambridge.
Hunter, R. (1989), *Apollonius of Rhodes. Argonautica book III*, Cambridge.
Hunter, R. (1993), 'Callimachean Echoes in Catullus 65,' in: *ZPE* 96, 179–182; reprinted in: Hunter 2008b, i.206–211.
Hunter, R. (1993a), *Apollonius of Rhodes. Jason and the Golden Fleece*, Oxford.
Hunter, R. (1993b), *The Argonautica of Apollonius: Literary Studies*, Cambridge.
Hunter, R. (1996a), 'Callimachus Swings (Frr. 178 and 43 Pf.),' in: *Ramus* 25, 17–26; reprinted in: Hunter 2008b, i.278–289.
Hunter, R. (1996b), *Theocritus and the Archaeology of Greek Poetry*, Cambridge.
Hunter, R. (1998), 'Before and After Epic: Theocritus (?), *Idyll* 25,' in: Harder, M.A./Regtuit, R. F./Wakker, G.C. (eds.), *Genre in Hellenistic Poetry*, Groningen, 115–132; reprinted in: Hunter 2008b, i.290–310.
Hunter, R. (1999), *Theocritus, a Selection: Idylls 1, 3, 4, 6, 7, 11 and 13*, Cambridge.
Hunter, R. (2003), *Theocritus. Encomium of Ptolemy Philadelphus, Text and Translation, Introduction and Commentary*, Berkeley.
Hunter, R. (2004a), 'Notes on the *Lithika* of Posidippus,' in: Acosta-Hughes/Kosmetatou/Baumbach 2004, 94–104.
Hunter, R. (2004b), 'Theocritus and Moschus,' in: de Jong/Nünlist/Bowie 2004, 83–97.
Hunter, R. (2005a), 'The Hesiodic *Catalogue* and Hellenistic Poetry,' in: R. Hunter (ed.), *The Hesiodic Catalogue of Women. Constructions and Reconstructions*, Cambridge, 239–265; reprinted in: Hunter 2008b, i.470–502.
Hunter, R. (2005b), '"Sweet Talk": *Song of Songs* and the Traditions of Greek Poetry,' in: A.C. Hagedorn (ed.), *Perspectives on the Song of Songs*, Berlin, 228–244.
Hunter, R. (2005c), 'Speaking in *Glossai*: Dialect Choice and Cultural Politics in Hellenistic Poetry,' in: W. Bloomer (ed.), *The Contest of Language: Before and Beyond Nationalism*, Notre Dame, 187–206.
Hunter, R. (2006), *The Shadow of Callimachus: Studies in the Reception of Hellenistic Poetry at Rome*, Cambridge.
Hunter, R. (2008a), 'Written in the Stars: Poetry and Philosophy in the *Phainomena* of Aratus', in: Hunter 2008b, i.153–188.
Hunter, R. (2008b), *On Coming After. Studies in Post-Classical Greek Literature and Its Reception*, 2 vols., Berlin/New York.
Hunter, R. (2009a), *Critical Moments in Classical Literature*, Cambridge.
Hunter, R. (2009b), 'Hesiod's Style: Towards an Ancient Analysis,' in: F. Montanari *et al.* (eds.), *Brill's Companion to Hesiod*, Leiden, 253–270.
Hunter, R. (2012), *Plato and the Traditions of Ancient Literature. The Silent Stream*, Cambridge/New York.
Hutchinson, G.O. (1988), *Hellenistic Poetry*, Oxford.
Hutchinson, G.O. (1995), 'Rhythm, Style, and Meaning in Cicero's Prose,' in: *CQ* 45, 485–499.
Hutchinson, G.O. (2002), 'The New Posidippus and Latin Poetry,' in: *ZPE* 138, 1–10.
Hutchinson, G.O. (2008a), *Talking Books: Readings in Hellenistic and Roman Books of Poetry*, Oxford.

Hutchinson, G.O. (2008b), 'Structuring Instruction: Didactic Poetry and Didactic Prose', in: *Talking Books: Readings in Hellenistic and Roman Books of Poetry*, Oxford, 228–250.
Hutchinson, G.O. (2009), 'Read the Instructions: Didactic Poetry and Didactic Prose,' in: *CQ* 59, 175–190.
Hutchinson, G.O. (2012), 'Booking Lovers: Desire and Design in Catullus,' in: Du Quesnay/Woodman 2012, 48–78.
Hutchinson, G.O. (2013), *Greek to Latin: Frameworks and Contexts for Intertextuality*, Oxford.
IC = Guarducci, M. (ed.) (1935–1950), *Inscriptiones Creticae*, 4 vols., Rome.
IG = *Inscriptiones Graecae*, Berolini 1873 ff.
IGR = Cagnat, R. et al. (eds.), (1901–1927), *Inscriptiones graecae ad res romanas pertinentes*, 3 vols., Paris. Reprint: Chicago 1975.
Ilinskaja, S. (2004), *Ο Κ. Π. Καβάφης και η Ρωσική ποίηση του αργυρού αιώνα*, Athens.
Inwood, B. (1985), *Ethics and Human Action in Early Stoicism*, Oxford.
IosPE = Latyshev, V. (1885–1901), *Inscriptiones antiquae orae septentrionalis Ponti Euxini graecae et latinae*, 3 vols., St. Petersburg. (vol. 1, *Inscriptiones Tyriae, Olbiae, Chersonesi Tauricae*, St. Petersburg 1916²).
Isager, S./P. Pedersen (2004), *The Salmacis Inscription and Hellenistic Halikarnassos*. Odense.
Iser, W. (1994), *Der Akt des Lesens: Theorie ästhetischer Wirkung*, 4th ed., Munich.
Jackson, S. (1992), 'Apollonius' Jason: Human Being in an Epic Scenario,' in: *G&R* 39, 155–162.
Jackson, S. (2001), '*Coma Berenices*: Origins,' in: *Mnemosyne* 54, 1–9.
Jacobs, F. (ed.) (1794–1814), *Anthologia Graeca sive poetarum graecorum lusus ex recensione Brunckii*, 13 vols., Leipzig.
Jacobson, H. (1974), *Ovid's Heroides*, Princeton.
Jacobson, H. (1983), *The Exagoge of Ezekiel*, Cambridge.
Jacoby, F. (1930), *Die Fragmente der griechischen Historiker. 2. Teil: Zeitgeschichte. D Kommentar zu Nr. 106–153*, Berlin.
Jacoby, F. (1961), 'Die griechische Moderne,' in: F. Jacoby, *Kleine philologische Schriften*, II, Berlin, 285–300 (1st ed. Kiel 1924).
Janan, M. (1994), *"When the Lamp is Shattered": Desire and Narrative in Catullus*, Carbondale.
Janko, R. (1984), *Aristotle on Comedy: Towards a Reconstruction of Poetics II*, London/Berkeley.
Janko, R. (1992), *The Iliad: A Commentary, Volume IV: Books 13–16*, Cambridge.
Jeffery, L.H. (1962), 'The Inscribed Grave-stones of Archaic Attica,' in: *BSA* 57, 115–153.
Joachim, H. (1922), *Aristotle on Coming-to-be and Passing-away (De generatione et corruptione)*, Oxford.
Johnson, W.R. (2007), 'Neoteric Poetics,' in: M.B. Skinner (ed.), *A Companion to Catullus*, Malden, MA, 175–189.
Johnston, P.A. (1983), 'An Echo of Sappho in Catullus,' in: *Latomus* 42, 388–394.
Jones, D. (1952), *The Anathemata*, London.
Jones, P. (2005), *Reading Rivers in Roman Literature and Culture*, Lanham.
Jones, S. (1997), The *Archaeology of Ethnicity. Constructing Identities in the Past and Present*, London/New York.
Jong, I.J.F. de (1991), *Narrative in Drama: The Art of the Euripidean Messenger Speech*, Leiden.

Jong, I.J.F. de (ed.) (2012), *Space in Ancient Greek Literature*, (*Studies in Ancient Greek Narrative* 3), Leiden/Boston.
Jong, I.J.F. de/Nünlist, R. (eds.) (2007), *Time in Ancient Greek Literature*, (*Studies in Ancient Greek Narrative* 2), Leiden/Boston.
Jong, I.J.F. de/Nünlist, R./Bowie, A.M. (eds.) (2004), *Narrators, Narratees, and Narratives in Ancient Greek Literature*, (*Studies in Ancient Greek Narrative* 1), Leiden/Boston.
Jouanna, J. (1975), *Hippocrate*, La Nature de l'homme. *Édité, traduit, et commenté*, (*CMG* I.1.3), Berlin.
Juliis, E.M. de (1984), *Gli Ori di Taranto in Età Ellenistica*, Milan.
Kaczko, S. (2009), 'From Stone to Parchment: Epigraphic and Literary Transmission of Some Greek Epigrams,' in: *Trends in Classics* 1, 90–117.
Kaesser, C. (2005), 'The Poet and the "Polis". The *Aetia* as Didactic Poem,' in: Horster/Reitz 2005, 95–114.
Kaibel, G. (1878), *Epigrammata Graeca ex lapidibus conlecta*, Berlin.
Kalphas, B. (2011), Ἀριστοτέλης, Ἔργα. vii: Περὶ γενέσεως καὶ φθορᾶς, Athens.
Kamal, A.B. (1905), *Stèles Ptolemaiques et Romaines, Catalogie Général des Antiquités Egyptiennes du Musée du Caire*, Cairo.
Kanthak, M. (forthcoming), *Kommentar zu Posidippus' "Lithika"*, Darmstadt.
Kassel, R. (1987), *Die Abgrenzung des Hellenismus in der griechischen Literaturgeschichte*, Berlin.
Kaufmann, H. (2006), 'Decolonizing the Postcolonial Colonizers: Helen in Derek Walcott's Omeros,' in: C. Martindale/R.F. Thomas, *Classics and the Uses of Reception*, Oxford, 192–203.
Keeley, E. (1996), *Cavafy's Alexandria*, Princeton.
Kennedy, D.F. (1999), '"Cf.": Analogies, Relationships and Catullus 68,' in: S.M. Braund/R.G. Mayer (eds.), *Amor, Roma: Love & Latin Literature*, Cambridge, 30–43.
Kenney, E. J. (1979), 'The Typology of Didactic' [rev. of B. Effe, *Dichtung und Lehre*], in: *CR* 29, 71–73.
Kerkhecker, A. (1999), *Callimachus' Book of* Iambi, Oxford.
Keydell, R. (1935), 'Die Dichter mit Namen Peisandros,' in: *Hermes* 70, 301–311.
King, J.K. (1988), 'Catullus' Callimachean *Carmina*, cc. 65–116,' in: *CW* 81, 383–392.
Kistler, E. (2009), *Funktionalisierte Keltenbilder. Die Indienstnahme der Kelten zur Vermittlung von Normen und Werten in der hellenistischen Welt*, Berlin.
Klein, F. (2008), *La leuitas dans l'œuvre ovidienne. Étude d'une catégorie poétique dans le système littéraire de la Rome augustéenne*, Diss. Université Lille 3.
Klengel-Brandt, E. (ed.) (1997), *Mit Sieben Sieglen versehen. Das Siegel in Wirtschaft und Kunst des Alten Orients*, Mainz.
Klooster, J.J.H. (2007a), 'Apollonius of Rhodes,' in: de Jong/Nünlist 2007, 63–80.
Klooster, J.J.H. (2007b), 'Theocritus,' in: de Jong/Nünlist 2007, 97–111.
Klotz, D. (2009), 'The Statue of the *dioiketes* Harchebi/*Archibios*. Nelson-Atkins Museum of Art 47–12,' in: *BIFAO* 109, 281–310.
Knöbl, R. (2010), 'Talking about Euripides: *Paramimesis* and Satyrus' *Bios Euripidou*,' in: *Phrasis* 51, 37–58.
Knox, B. (1979), 'Euripidean Comedy' (1970), in: B. Knox, *Word and Action: Essays on the Ancient Theater*, Baltimore.
Knox, P.E., (2007), 'Catullus and Callimachus,' in: Skinner 2007a, 151–171.
Knox, P. E. (2011), 'Cicero as a Hellenistic Poet,' in: *CQ* 61, 186–191.

Koehler, L./Baumgartner, W./Stamm, J. (1994–2000), *The Hebrew and Aramaic Lexicon of the Old Testament*, vols. 1–5, English version edited by M.E.J. Richardson, Leiden.
Köhler, J. (1996), *Pompai. Untersuchungen zur hellenistischen Festkultur*, Frankfurt am Mein.
Konstan, D. (1994), *Sexual Symmetry. Love in the Ancient Novel and Related Genres*, Princeton, NJ.
Konstan, D. (2006), *The Emotions of the Ancient Greeks. Studies in Aristotle and Classical Literature*, Toronto/Buffalo/London.
Kooij, A. van der (2009), 'Review of Troxel (2008),' in: *The Bulletin of the International Organization of Septuagint and Cognate Studies* 42, 147–152.
Kopidakis, M. Z. (1987), *Τὸ Γ Μακκαβαίων καὶ ὁ Αἰσχύλος*, Herakleion.
Kosmetatou, E. (2003), 'Posidippus, Epigr. 8 AB and Early Ptolomaic Cameos,' in: *ZPE* 142, 35–42.
Kosmetatou, E. (2004a), '"Persian" Objects in Classical and Early Hellenistic Inventory Lists,' in: *MH* 61, 139–170.
Kosmetatou, E. (2004b), 'On Large Gemstones,' in: *ZPE* 146, 81–84.
Koster, W. J. W. (1975), *Prolegomena de Comoedia. Scholia in Archarnenses, Equites, Nubes.* Fasc. I A, *Prolegomena de Comoedia*, Groningen.
Kowalzig, B. (2007), *Singing for the Gods*, Oxford.
Krasilnikoff, J.A. (1992), 'Aegean Mercenaries in the Fourth to Second Centuries BC,' in: *C&M* 43, 23–36.
Krevans, N. (2000), 'On the Margins of Epic: The Foundation-Poems of Apollonius,' in: M.A. Harder/R.F. Regtuit/G.C. Wakker (ed.), *Apollonius Rhodius*, Leuven/Paris/Sterling, Virginia, 69–84.
Kroll, W. (1925), 'Lehrgedicht,' in: *RE* 12, 1842–1857.
Kroll, W. (ed.) (1968), *C. Valerius Catullus*, herausgegeben und erklärt, fünfte durch neue Zusätze vermehrte Auflage, Stuttgart.
Kruschwitz, P.,/M. Schumacher (2005), *Das vorklassische Lehrgedicht der Römer*, Heidelberg.
Kuhn, T. (2012), *Die jüdisch-hellenistischen Epiker Theodot und Philon. Literarische Untersuchungen, kritische Edition und Übersetzung der Fragmente*, Göttingen.
Kuhrt, A. (2007), *The Persian Empire. A Corpus of Sources from the Achaemenid Period*, London.
Kurke, L. (1990), 'Pindar's Sixth Pythian and the Tradition of Advice Poetry,' in: *TAPhA* 120, 85–107.
Kuspit, D. (2000), *The Semiotic Anti-Subject*, http://www.artnet.com/Magazine/features/kuspit/kuspit4-20-01.asp
Kuttner, A.L. (2005), 'Cabinet Fit for a Queen: The *Lithika* as Posidippus' Gem Museum,' in: Gutzwiller 2005a, 141–163.
Kyriakou, P. (2004), 'κλέος and Poetry in Simonides fr. 11 W and Theocritus, Idyll 16,' in: *RhM* 147, 221–246.
La'da, C. (1994), 'One Stone: Two Messages (CG 50044),' in: A. Bülow-Jacobsen, *Proceedings of the 20th International Conference of Papyrologists, Copenhagen, 23–29 August 1992*, Copenhagen, 160–164.
Lacroix, L. (1958), 'Les "Blasons" des villes grecques,' in: *Extraits des Etudes d'Archéologie Classique* 1, 1955–1956, Paris, 89–115.
Lanfranchi, P. (2006), *L'Exagoge d'Ezéchiel le Tragique: Introduction, texte, traduction et commentaire*, Leiden.
Larbaud, V. (1936), *Ce vice impuni, la lecture. Domaine anglais*, Paris.

Launey, M. (1949), *Recherches sur les Armées Hellenistiques*, Paris.
Laursen, S. (1989), 'The Apple of Catullus 65: A Love Pledge of Callimachus,' in: *C&M* 40, 161–169.
Lawall, G. (1966), 'Apollonius' *Argonautica*: Jason as Anti-Hero,' in: *YCS* 19, 121–169.
Lee, D.J.N. (1964), *The Similes of the Iliad and the Odyssey Compared*, Melbourne.
Lefèvre, E. (1991), 'Was hatte Catull in der Kapsel, die er von Rom nach Verona mitnahm? Zu Aufbau und Aussage der Allius-Elegie,' in: *RhM* 134, 311–326.
Legrand, P.E. (1901), 'Sur quelques epigrammes du troisième siècle,' in: *REA* 1, 185–195.
Legras, B. (2011), *Les reclus grecs du Sarapeion de Memphis (Studia Hellenistica 49)*, Leuven.
Leighton, S.R. (1982), 'Aristotle and the Emotions,' in: *Phronesis* 27, 144–173. (Revised in: A. Rorty (ed.) (1996), *Essays on Aristotle's Rhetoric*, Berkeley, 206–237).
Lelli, E. (2005), *Callimaco, Giambi XIV-XVII. Introduzione, testo critico, traduzione e commento (Lyricorum Graecorum quae exstant 14)*, Rome.
Lelli, E. (2006), *Volpe e leone. Il proverbio nella poesia greca (Alceo, Cratino, Callimaco)*, Rome.
Lenfant, D. (2007), 'Greek Historians of Persia,' in: J. Marincola (ed.), *A Companion to Greek and Roman Historiography*, Malden, MA/Oxford, 200–209.
Levine, D.B. (1985), 'Symposium and the Polis,' in: T.J. Figueira/G. Nagy (eds.), *Theognis of Megara. Poetry and the Polis*, Baltimore/London, 176–196.
Lewis, D. (1997), 'The King's Dinner,' (first published in 1987) in: D. Lewis, *Selected Papers in Greek and Near Eastern History*, Cambridge, 332–341.
Lieberg, G. (1958), 'L'ordinamento ed i reciproci rapporti dei carmi maggiori di Catullo,' in: *RFIC* 86, 23–47.
Lieberg, G. (1962), *Puella divina: Die Gestalt der göttlichen Geliebten bei Catull im Zusammenhang der antiken Dichtung*, Amsterdam.
Lightfoot, J. (1999), *Parthenius of Nicaea, the Poetical Fragments and the Ἐρωτικὰ Παθήματα: Edited with Introduction and Commentaries*, Oxford.
Lightfoot, J. (2007), *The Sibylline Oracles*, Oxford.
Littlewood, A.R. (1968), 'The Symbolism of the Apple in Greek and Roman Literature,' in: *HSCPh* 72, 147–181.
Liveley, G./Salzman-Mitchell, P. (eds.) (2008), *Latin Elegy and Narratology: Fragments of Story*, Columbus.
Llewellyn-Jones, L. (2013), *King and Court in Ancient Persia (559–331 BCE)*, Edinburgh.
Llewellyn-Jones, L./Robson, J. (2010), *Ctesias' History of Persia. Tales of the Orient*, New York.
Lloyd-Jones, H. (1968), 'Again Meleager's Epigram on Heraclitus,' in: *CR* n.s. 18, 21.
Longo Auricchio, F. (1977), Φιλοδήμου Περὶ ῥητορικῆς *libros primum et secundum edidit . . . (Ricerche sui papiri ercolanesi* 3), Naples.
Longo Auricchio, F. (1985), 'Testimonianze dalla *Retorica* di Filodemo sulla concezione dell'oratoria nei primi maestri epicurei,' in: *Cronache Ercolanesi* 15, 31–61.
Lord, L.E. (1908), *Literary Criticism of Euripides in the Earlier Scholia and the Relation of This Criticism to Aristotle's Poetics and to Aristophanes*, Diss. Yale, Göttingen.
Loukopoulou, L.D./Zournatzi, A./Parissaki, M. G./Psoma, S. (2005), Ἐπιγραφὲς τῆς Θράκης τοῦ Αἰγαίου μεταξὺ τῶν ποταμῶν Νέστου καὶ Ἕβρου (Νομοὶ Ξάνθης, Ῥοδόπης καὶ Ἕβρου)/*Inscriptiones antiquae partis Thraciae quae ad ora maris Aegaei sita est (Praefecturae Xanthes, Rhodopes et Hebri) ediderunt et commentariis sermone graeco conscriptis instruxerunt* . . . , Athens.
Lowrie, M. (2006), '*Hic* and Absence in Catullus 68,' in: *CPh* 101, 115–132.

Lucas, D.W. (1968), *Aristotle. Poetics*, Oxford.
Luz, C. (2010), *Technopaignia. Formspiele in der griechischen Dichtung*, Leiden.
Luz, C. (2012), 'Pindaric Narrative Technique in the Hellenistic Epyllion,' in: Baumbach/Bär 2012a, 201–219.
Lyne, R.O.A.M. (1980), *The Latin Love Poets: From Catullus to Horace*, Oxford.
Lyne, R.O.A.M. (1998), 'Love and Death: Laodamia and Protesilaus in Catullus, Propertius, and Others,' in: *CQ* 48, 200–212.
Ma, J. (2003a), 'Kings,' in: Erskine, A. (ed.), *A Companion to the Hellenistic World*, Malden, MA/Oxford, 177–195.
Ma, J. (2003b), 'Peer Polity Interaction in the Hellenistic Age,' in: *Past and Present* 180, 9–39.
Ma, J. (2004), 'Une culture militaire en Asie Mineur hellénistique?,' in: J.C. Couvenhes/H.-L. Fernoux, *Les cités grecques et la guerre en Asie Mineur à l'époque hellénistique*, Tours, 199–220.
MacKail, J.W. (1910), *Lectures on Greek Poetry*, London/New York.
MacKendrick, P. (1953), 'T.S. Eliot and the Alexandrians,' in: *CJ* 49, 7–12.
MacLeod, C.W. (1974), 'A Use of Myth in Ancient Poetry,' in: *CQ* 24, 82–93.
Mader, M. (1977), *Das Problem des Lachens und der Komödie bei Platon*, Tübingen.
Mairs, R. (2010a), 'Intersecting Identities in Hellenistic and Roman Egypt,' in: R.J. Dann/D.K. Exell (eds.), *Approaching Ancient Egypt*, New York.
Mairs, R. (2010b), 'An "Identity Crisis"? Identity and its Discontents in Hellenistic Studies,' in: M. Dalla Riva (eds.), *Meetings between Cultures in the Ancient Mediterranean. Proceedings of the 17th International Congress of Classical Archaeology, Rome 22–26 sept. 2008*, Rome.
Mairs, R. (2012a), 'Bilingualism,' in: R.S. Bagnall/K. Brodersen/C.B. Champion/ A. Erskine/S. R. Huebner (eds.), *The Encyclopedia of Ancient History*, Malden, MA/Oxford.
Mairs, R. (2012b), 'Interpreters and Translators in Hellenistic and Roman Egypt,' in: P. Schubert (eds.), *Actes du 26e Congrès international de papyrologie (Genève 2010). (Recherches et Rencontres: Publications de la Faculté des Lettres de l'Université de Genève 30)*, Geneva, 457–462.
Malkin, I. (2003), 'Networks and the Emergence of Greek Identity,' in: *MHR* 18, 56–74.
Malkin, I. (2011), *A Small Greek World: Networks in the Ancient Mediterranean*, Oxford.
MAMA = Monumenta Asiae Minoris Antiqua, Manchester, 1928–
Manakidou, F. (1998), 'Χόλος, μῆνις, νεῖκος in den *Argonautika* des Apollonios Rhodios,' in: *Philologus* 142, 241–260.
Manganaro, G. (1959/60), 'Due epigrafi rinvenute ad Egina,' in: *ASAtene* 37/38, 421–428.
Mangoni, C. (1988), 'Prosa e poesia nel V libro della *Poetica* di Filodemo,' *Cronache Ercolanesi* 18, 127–138.
Mangoni, C. (1993), *Filodemo, il quinto libro della Poetica (PHerc. 1425 e 1538). Edizione, traduzione e commento (La Scuola di Epicuro 14)*, Naples.
Männlein-Robert, I. (2004), 'Griechische Kunst und römischer Stil. Zum Eurotas-Epigramm des Philipp von Thessalonike (AP IX 709 = GP I 63),' in: *Würzburger Jahrbücher für die Altertumswissenschaft* 28a (= L. Braun/M. Erler (eds.), *Festschrift für Udo W. Scholz*), 35–48.
Männlein-Robert, I. (2007), *Stimme, Schrift und Bild. Zur Verhältnis der Künste in der hellenistischen Dichtung*, Heidelberg.

Männlein-Robert, I. (2010), 'Zwischen Musen und Museion oder die poetische (Er-) Findung Griechenlands in den "Aitien" des Kallimachos,' in: G. Weber (ed.), *Alexandreia und das ptolemäische Ägypten*, Berlin, 160–186.
Maronitis, D. (1994), 'Υπεροψία και μέθη' (1970), in: M. Pieris (ed.), *Εισαγωγή στην ποίηση του Καβάφη*, Rethymno, 269–287.
Marquaille, C. (2008), 'The Foreign Policy of Ptolemy II,' in: P. McKechnie/P. Guillaume (eds.), *Ptolemy II Philadelphus and his World* (Mnemosyne Suppl. 300), Leiden/Boston/Tokyo, 39–64.
Marshall, C.W. (2000), '*Alcestis* and the Problem of Prosatyric Drama,' in: *CJ* 95, 229–238.
Maspero, G. (1886), 'Notes sur quelques points de grammaire et d'histoire,' in: *ZÄS* 23, 3–13.
Massimilla, G. (1996), *Callimaco. Aitia, libri primo e secondo. Introduzione, testo critico, traduzione e commento*, (Biblioteca di studi antichi 77), Pisa.
Massimilla, G. (2010), *Callimaco. Aitia, libro terzo e quarto. Introduzione, testo critico, traduzione e commento* (Biblioteca di studi antichi 92), Pisa/Rome.
Masson, O. (1982), 'Quelques noms celtiques en Grèce et en Asie Mineure,' in: *Études Celtiques* 19, 129–135.
Mastronarde, D. 1999–2000. 'Euripidean Tragedy and Genre: The Terminology and Its Problems', *ICS* 24–25: 23–39.
Matteo, R. (2007), *Apollonio Rodio:* Argonautiche *Libro II. Introduzione e commento* (Satura 6), Lecce.
Mazzoni, G. (2005), *Sulla poesia moderna*, Bologna.
McCall, M.H. (1969), *Ancient Rhetorical Theories of Similes and Comparison*, Cambridge Mass.
McFadden, G.H. (1946), 'A Tomb of the Necropolis of Ayios Ermoyenis at Kourion,' in: *AJPh* 50, 449–489.
McGing, B. (2010), *Polybius' Histories*, Oxford.
McNelis, C. (2003), 'Mourning Glory: Callimachus' *Hecale* and Heroic Honors,' in: *MD* 50, 155–161.
McNelis, C./Sens, A. (2011), 'Trojan Glory: *kleos* and the Survival of Troy in Lycophron's *Alexandra*,' in: *Trends in Classics* 3, 54–82.
Medda, E./Mirto, M.S./Pattoni, M.P. (eds.) (2006), *Komodotragodia. Intersezioni del tragico e del comico nel teatro del V secolo a.C.*, Pisa.
Meijering, R. (1987), *Literary and Rhetorical Theories in Greek Scholia*, Groningen.
Meincke, W. (1965), *Untersuchungen zu den enkomiastischen Gedichten Theokrits*, Diss. Kiel.
Merkelbach, R. (1981), 'Das Königtum der Ptolemäer und die hellenistischen Dichter,' in: Hinske 1981, 27–35.
Merkelbach, R./Stauber, J. (eds.), (1998–2004), *Steinepigramme aus dem griechischen Osten*, 5 vols., Stuttgart.
Meulenaere, H. de (1963), 'La famille royale des Nectanébo,' in: *ZÄS* 90, 90–93.
Meyer, D. (1993), 'Die Einbeziehung des Lesers in den Epigrammen des Kallimachos,' in: M.A. Harder/R.F. Regtuit/G.C. Wakker (eds.), *Callimachus*, Groningen, 161–175.
Meyer, D. (2001), 'Apollonius as a Hellenistic Geographer,' in: T.D. Papanghelis/A. Rengakos (eds.), *A Companion to Apollonius Rhodius*, Leiden/Boston/Köln, 217–235.
Meyer, D. (2005), *Inszeniertes Lesevergnügen: Das inschriftliche Epigramm und seine Rezeption bei Kallimachos*, Stuttgart.
Meyer, J. (2009), 'Heraclides' Intellectual Context,' in: Fortenbaugh/Pender 2009, 27–40.

Micheli, M.E. (2008), 'Tryphon a Sentinum?,' in: M. Medri (ed.), *Sentinum 295 a.C. Sassoferrato 2006. 2003 anni dopo la battaglia. Una città romana tra storia e archeologia (Studia archaelogica* 163, *Sentinum III)*, Rome, 127–139 and pl. XXIX–XXXIII.
Mickey, K. (1981), 'Dialect Consciousness and Literary Language: An Example from Ancient Greek,' in: *TPhS* 79, 35–66.
Migliori, M. (1976), *Aristotele. La generazione e la corruzione*, Naples.
Miller, P.A. (2004), *Subjecting Verses: Latin Love Elegy and the Emergence of the Real*, Princeton.
Miller, P.A. (2007), 'Catullus and Roman Love Elegy,' in: Skinner 2007a, 399–417.
Mineur, W.H. (1984), *Callimachus*, Hymn to Delos: *Introduction and Commentary* (*Mnemosyne Suppl.* 83), Leiden.
Mitchell, S. (2007), 'The Galatians: Representation and Reality,' in: A. Erskine (ed.), *Companion to the Hellenistic World*, Malden, MA/Oxford, 280–292.
Molinos Tejada, T. (1990), *Los Dorismos del Corpus Bucolicorum*, Amsterdam.
Momigliano, A. (1975), *Alien Wisdom: The Limits of Hellenization*, Cambridge.
Montanari, F. (1991), 'Appunti per lo studio dell'oscurità nella poesia classica,' in: *L'Asino d'oro* 2, 31–52.
Montanari, F. (1993), 'L'erudizione, la filologia e la grammatica,' in: G. Cambiano/L. Canfora/D. Lanza (eds.), *Lo spazio letterario della Grecia antica*. i.2 *La produzione e la circolazione del testo*, Rome, 235–281.
Montanari, F. (2012), 'The Peripatos on Literature. Interpretation, Use and Abuse,' in: A. Martano/E. Matelli/D. Mirhady (eds.), *Praxiphanes of Mytilene and Chamaeleon of Heraclea. Text, Translation, and Discussion*, New Brunswick, 339–358.
Moore, C.H. (1901), 'Notes on the Tragic Hypotheses,' in: *HSCPh* 12, 287–298.
Moretti, L. (1967), *Iscrizioni storiche ellenistiche* I, (*Biblioteca di studi superiori* vol. l), Florence.
Moretti, L. (1975), *Iscrizioni storiche ellenistiche* II, Florence.
Mori, A. (2005), 'Jason's Reconciliation with Telamon: A Moral Exemplar in Apollonius' Argonautica (1.1286–1344),' in: *AJPh* 126, 209–236.
Mori, A. (2010), *The Politics of Apollonius Rhodius'* Argonautica, Cambridge.
Morpurgo Davies, A. (2000), 'Greek Personal Names and Linguistic Continuity,' in: S. Hornblower/E. Matthews (eds.), *Greek Personal Names: Their Value as Evidence*, (*Proceedings of the British Academy* 104), Oxford, 15–39.
Morrison, A.D. (2007), *The Narrator in Archaic Greek and Hellenistic Poetry*, Cambridge.
Mosino, F. (2001), 'Ospizio di poeti antichi sommersi,' in: *Epigraphica* 63, 283–287.
Most, G.W. (1981), 'On the Arrangement of Catullus' *Carmina Maiora*,' in: *Philologus* 125, 109–125.
Most, G.W. (1985), *The Measures of Praise*, Göttingen.
Moyer, I.S. (2011), *Egypt and the Limits of Hellenism*, Cambridge.
Mras, K. (1954–6), *Die Praeparatio Evangelica. Eusebius Werke*, vol. 8, 2 vols., Berlin.
Munteanu, D. LaCourse (ed.) (2011), *Emotion, Genre and Gender in Classical Antiquity*, London.
Munteanu, D. LaCourse (2012), *Tragic Pathos. Pity and Fear in Greek Philosophy and Tragedy*, Cambridge.
Muraoka, T. (2009), *A Greek-English Lexicon of the Septuagint*, Leuven.
Mynors, R.A.B. (ed.) (1958), *C. Valerii Catulli Carmina*, Oxford.

Nardelli, M.L. (1987), 'Ancora sulla Biblioteca di Tolomeo: frammenti di un discorso ai margini della papirologia,' in: *Aegyptus* 67, 13–25.
Nardelli, M.L. (1988), 'Testi letterari dall'archivio del Serapeo di Memfi: ipotesi di una biblioteca,' in: B. Mandilaras, *Proceedings of the XVIIIth International Congress of Papyrology, Athens 25–31 May 1986*, II, Athens, 179–188.
Nauta, R.R./Harder, A. (eds.) (2005), *Catullus' Poem on Attis: Text and Contexts*, Leiden.
Nelis, D.P. (2004), '*Georgics* 2.458–542: Virgil, Aratus and Empedocles,' *Dictynna* 1: http://dictynna.revues.org/161.
Nelis, D.P. (2012), 'Callimachus in Verona: Catullus and Alexandrian Poetry,' in: Du Quesnay/Woodman 2012, 1–28.
Nelson, S.A. (1998), *God and the Land: The Metaphysics of Farming in Hesiod and Vergil*. New York.
Netz, R. (2004), *The Works of Archimedes Translated into English, together with Eustochius' Commentaries, with Commentary, and Critical Edition of the Diagrams*. I: *The Two Books On the Sphere and the Cylinder*, Cambridge.
Netz, R. (2009), *Ludic Proof: Greek Mathematics and the Alexandrian Aesthetic*, Cambridge.
Netz, R./Noel, W./Tchernetska, N./Wilson, N. (eds.) (2011), *The Archimedes Palimpsest*, 2 vols., Cambridge.
Newman, J.K. (1967), *Augustus and the New Poetry*, Brussels.
Newman, J.K. (1986), *The Classical Epic Tradition*, Madison Wisc.
Newman, J.K. (1990), *Roman Catullus and the Modification of the Alexandrian Sensibility*, Hildesheim.
Newman, J.K. (1993), art. 'Alexandrianism,' in: *The New Princeton Encyclopedia of Poetry and Poetics*, Princeton, 28–30.
Niehoff, M. R. (2011), *Jewish Exegesis and Homeric Scholarship in Alexandria*, Cambridge.
Nightingale, A. W. (1995), *Genres in Dialogue: Plato and the Construct of Philosophy*, Cambridge.
Nisetich, F. (2001), *The Poems of Callimachus*, Oxford.
Noussia-Fantuzzi, M. (2010), *Solon the Athenian, the Poetic Fragments*, Leiden/Boston.
Nünlist, R. (1998), *Poetologische Bildersprache in der frühgriechischen Dichtung*, Stuttgart/Leipzig.
Nünlist, R. (2009), *The Ancient Critic at Work*, Cambridge.
Nussbaum, M.C. (1994), *The Therapy of Desire. Theory and Practice in Hellenistic Ethics*, Princeton, NJ.
Nussbaum, M.C. (1996), 'Aristotle on Emotions and Rational Persuasion,' in: A. Rorty (ed.), *Essays on Aristotle's Rhetoric*, Berkeley, 303–323.
O'Hara, J.J. (1996), *Vergil and the Alexandrian Tradition of Etymological Wordplay*, Ann Arbor.
O'Hara, J.J. (2007), *Inconsistency in Roman Epic: Studies in Catullus, Lucretius, Vergil, Ovid and Lucan*, Cambridge.
OGIS = Dittenberger, W. (ed.) (1903–1905), *Orientis Graeci Inscriptiones Selectae. Supplementum Sylloges Inscriptionum Graecarum*, I-II, Lipsiae.
Öhrman, M. (2009), 'The Potential of Passion: The Laodamia Myth in Catullus 68b,' in: I. Nilsson (ed.), *Plotting with Eros: Essays on the Poetics of Love and the Erotics of Reading*, Copenhagen, 45–57.
Olson, S.D. (1998), *Aristophanes: Peace*, Oxford.
Olson, S.D./Sens, A. (2000), *Archestratos of Gela: Greek Culture and Cuisine in the Fourth Century BCE: Text, Translation, and Commentary*, Oxford.

Onians, J. (1979), *Art and Thought in the Hellenistic Age. The Greek World View 350–50BC*, London.
Orlinksy, H.M. (1991), 'Some Terms in the Prologue to Ben Sira and the Hebrew Canon,' in: *JBL* 110, 483–490.
Ormand, K. (2012), *A Companion to Sophocles*, Malden, MA.
Orr, M. (2003), *Intertextuality: Debates and Contexts*, Cambridge.
Ortega y Gasset, J. (1925), *La deshumanización del arte*, Madrid.
Østergård, U. (1992), 'What is National and Ethnic Identity?,' in: P. Bilde/T. Engberg-Pedersen/L. Hannestad/J. Zahle (eds.), *Ethnicity in Hellenistic Egypt* (Studies in Hellenistic Civilization), Aarhus, 16–38.
Otto, N. (2009), *Enargeia. Untersuchung zur Charakteristik alexandrinischer Dichtung*, Stuttgart.
Ouvré, H. (1894), *Méléagre de Gadara*, Paris.
Pagenstecher, R. (1919), *Nekropolis. Untersuchungen über Gestalt und Entwicklung der alexandrinischen Grabanlagen und ihrer Malereien*, Leipzig.
Papadopoulou, M. (2009), 'Scientific Knowledge and Poetic Skill: Colour Words in Nicander's *Theriaca* and *Alexipharmaca*,' in: M.A. Harder/R.F. Regtuit/G.C. Wakker (eds.), *Nature and Science in Hellenistic Poetry*, Leuven/Paris/Walpole, MA, 95–119.
Papanghelis, Th. (1987), *Propertius: A Hellenistic Poet on Love and Death*, Cambridge.
Papanikolaou, D. (2009), 'The Aretalogy of Isis from Maroneia and the Question of Hellenistic "Asianism",' in: *ZPE* 168, 59–70.
Parker, R.C.T. (2005), *Polytheism and Society at Athens*, Oxford.
Pascal, C. (1902), 'L'imitazione de Empedocle nelle *Metamorfosi* di Ovidio,' in: *RAN* 61–85.
Pascoli, G. (2002), *Poesie e prose scelte*, ed. C. Garboli (with A. Oldcorn/G. Leonelli/F. Pontani), Milan.
Payne, M. (2007), *Theocritus and the Invention of Fiction*, Cambridge.
Peek, W. (1932), 'Zu griechischen Epigrammen,' in: *Philologus* 87, 229–241.
Peek GVI = Peek, W. (ed.) (1955), Griechische Vers-Inschriften I, Grab-epigramme, Berlin.Peek, W. (1973), 'Ein Weihgedicht des Theodoridas,' in: *Philologus* 117, 66–69.
Peek, GVTh = Peek, W. (ed.) (1974), Griechische Versinschriften aus Thessalien, Sitzungsberichte der Heidelberger Akademie, Heidelberg.
Peek, W. (1980), *Griechische Versinschriften aus Kleinasien* (TAM Suppl. 8; Denkschrift der Österreichischen Akademie der Wissenschaften, Philosophisch–Historische Klasse 143), Vienna.
Pelliccia, H. (2010/2011), 'Unlocking *Aeneid* 6.460: Plautus' *Amphitryon*, Euripides' *Protesilaus* and the Referents of Callimachus' *Coma*,' in: *CJ* 106, 149–219.
Peremans, W. (1983), 'Les Égyptiens dans l'armée de terre des Lagides,' in: H. Heinen (ed.), *Althistorische Studien H. Bengtson zum 70. Geburtstag dargebracht von Kollegen und Schülern*, (Historia Einzelschriften 40), Wiesbaden, 92–102.
Peridis, M. (1948), *Ο βίος και το έργο του Κωνσταντίνου Καβάφη*, Athens.
Perrotta, G. (1925), 'Studi di poesia ellenistica,' in: *SIFC* 4, 5–68.
Petrain, D. (2005), 'Gems, Metapoetics, and Value : Greek and Roman Responses to a Third-Century Discourse on Precious Stones,' in: *TAPhA* 135, 329–357.
Petrain, D. (2006), 'Moschus' *Europa* and the Narratology of Ecphrasis,' in: M.A. Harder/R.F. Regtuit/G.C. Wakker (eds.), *Beyond the Canon*, Leuven, 249–269.
Petrides, A. (forthcoming), *Menander, New Comedy and the Visual*, Cambridge.

Petrovic, I. (forthcoming), 'Ptolemaic court in Hellenistic Poetry,' in: A. Erskine/L. Llewellyn-Jones/S. Wallace (eds.), *The Hellenistic Court*, Swansea.
Pfeiffer, R. (1949), *Callimachus*, vol. 1, Oxford.
Pfeiffer, R. (1968), *History of Classical Scholarship, from the Beginnings to the End of the Hellenistic Age*, Oxford.
Pfeiffer, S. (2004), *Das Dekret von Kanopos (238 v. Chr.). Kommentar und historische Auswertung eines dreisprachigen Synodaldekretes der ägyptischen Priester zu Ehren Ptolemaios' III. und seiner Familie*, (APF Beiheft 18), Munich/Leipzig.
Pfister, F. (1951), *Die Reisebilder des Herakleides. Einleitung, Text, Übersetzung und Kommentar. Mit einer Übersicht über die Geschichte der griechischen Volkskunde*, Vienna.
Pfuhl, E./Möbius, H. (1977–1979), *Die ostgriechischen Grabreliefs*. 2 vols., Mainz am Rhein.
Platt, V. (2002), 'Evasive Epiphanies in Ekphrastic Epigram,' in: *Ramus* 1, 33–50 (= V. Platt, *Facing the Gods: Epiphany and Representation in Graeco-Roman Art, Literature and Religion*, Cambridge 2011, 180 ff.).
Platt, V. (2006), 'Making an Impression: Replication and the Ontology of the Graeco-Roman Seal Stone,' in: *Art History* 29.2, 233–257.
PMG = Page, D. (ed.) (1962), *Poetae melici Graeci*, Oxford.
Poliakoff, M. (1985), 'Clumsy and Clever Spiders on Hermann's Bridge: Catullus 68.49–50 and *Culex* 1–3,' in: *Glotta* 63, 248–250.
Pontani, A. (2002–2003), 'A margine di *Bisanzio e la décadence*,' in: *Bollettino della Badia greca di Grottaferrata*, n.s. 56–57, 285–307.
Porada, E. (1993), 'Cylinder Seals,' in: *Encyclopaedia Iranica*, vol. VI, Fasc. 5, 479–505.
Porro, A. (2007), 'Archiloco e gli Alessandrini,' in: Pretagostini/Dettori 2007, 209–222.
Porter, J.I. (2010), *The Origins of Aesthetic Thought in Ancient Greece: Matter, Sensation, and Experience*, Cambridge.
Porter, J.I. (2011), 'Against *leptotes*: Rethinking Hellenistic Aesthetics,' in: A. Erskine/Ll. Llewellyn-Jones/E.D. Carney (eds.), *Creating a Hellenistic World*, Swansea, 271–312.
Post, R. (forthcoming), *The Bithynian Army in the Hellenistic Period*, in: *Phoenix*.
Prato, C. (1968), *Tyrtaeus*, Rome.
Prato, C. (1973), 'Nota a Tyrt. 9, 4,' in: *Paideia* 28, 45–46; reprinted in: P. Giannini/S. Delle Donne (eds.), *Carlo Prato. Scritti minori*, Galatina 2009, 15–16.
Pretagostini, R. (2000), 'Spunti per una riflessione sulla letteratura ellenistica,' in: R. Pretagostini (ed.), *La letteratura ellenistica*, Rome, 3–19.
Pretagostini, R./Dettori, E. (eds.) (2007), *La cultura letteraria ellenistica. Persistenza, innovazione, trasmissione*, Rome.
Preuner, E. (1920), 'Archäologisch-Epigraphisches,' in: *JdI* 35, 59–82.
Prince, C.K. (2003), *The Rhetoric of Instruction in Archaic Greek Didactic Poetry*, Diss. Stanford.
Prioux, É. (2007a), *Regards alexandrins. Histoire et théorie des arts dans l'épigramme hellénistique (Hellenistica Groningana 12)*, Leuven.
Prioux, É. (2007b), 'Entre critique littéraire et critique d'art: l'épigramme de Posidippe sur le portrait de Philitas de Cos (*P. Mil. Vogl.* VIII, 309, col. X, 16–25),' in: G. Sauron/F.-H. Massa-Pairault (eds.), *Images et modernité hellénistiques. Appropriation et représentation du monde d'Alexandre à César* (CEFR 390), Rome, 233–245.
Prioux, É. (2008a), *Petits musées en vers. Épigramme et discours sur les collections antiques (L'Art et l'Essai* 5), Paris.

Prioux, É. (2008b), 'Le portrait perdu et retrouvé du poète Philitas de Cos: Posidippe 63 A.-B. et *IG* XIV, 2486,' in: *ZPE* 166, 66–72.
Prioux, É. (2009a), 'Fards et cosmétiques dans les sources littéraires antiques,' in: Bardiès-Fronty/Walter/Bimbenet Privat 2009, 35–40.
Prioux, É. (2009b), 'Ovide, *De Medicamine faciei*,' in: Bardiès-Fronty/Walter/Bimbenet Privat 2009, 231–233.
Prioux, É. (2011), 'Emotions in Ecphrasis and Art Criticism,' in: D. LaCourse Munteanu (ed.), *Emotion, Genre and Gender in Classical Antiquity*, London, 135–174.
Prioux, É. (2012), 'Hellenistic Ekphraseis as Programmatic Allegories,' in: F. Cairns (ed.), *Papers of the Langford Latin Seminar (PLLS)*, 15th Volume, ARCA, Cambridge, 191–222.
Prioux, É. (forthcoming), 'Douris et Posidippe: similitudes et dissemblances de quelques éléments de critique d'art et de critique littéraire,' in: V. Naas/M. Simon (eds.), *De Samos à Rome: personnalité et influence de Douris*, Nanterre.
Puelma, M. (1982), 'Die *Aitien* des Kallimachos als Vorbild der römischen Amores-Elegie,' in: *MH* 39, 221–246, 285–304; reprinted in: M. Puelma, *Labor et Lima. Kleine Schriften und Nachträge*, Basel 1995, 360–414.
Putnam, M.C.J. (1961), 'The Art of Catullus 64,' in: *HSCPh* 65, 165–205.
Quaegebeur, J. (1980), *The Genealogy of the Memphite High Priest Family in the Hellenistic Period*, (Studia Hellenistica 24), Leuven, 43–89.
Quaß, F. (1993), *Die Honoratiorenschicht in den Städten des griechischen Ostens. Untersuchungen zur politischen und sozialen Entwicklung in hellenistischer und römischer Zeit*, Stuttgart.
Queneau, R. (1965), *Le chien à la mandoline*, Paris.
Race, W.H. (1982), *The Classical Priamel from Homer to Boethius*, Leiden.
Race, W.H. (1997), *Pindar. Olympian Odes, Pythian Odes*, Cambridge, Mass./London.
Race, W.H. (2008), *Apollonius Rhodius* Argonautica, Cambridge, Mass./London.
Radermacher, L. (1951), *Artium scriptores (Reste der voraristotelischen Rhetorik)*, (Österreichische Akademie der Wissenschaften, Phil.-hist. Klasse, SB 27.3), Vienna.
Raine, K. (1952), rev. of D. Jones, *Anathemata*, in: *The New Statesman and Nation*, Nov. 22, 607–608.
Ray, J.D. (1995), 'Soldiers to Pharaoh: the Carians of Southwest Anatolia,' in: J.M. Sasson (ed.), *Civilizations of the Ancient Near East* II, New York, 1185–1194.
Ray, J.D. (1998), 'Aegypto-Carica,' in: *Kadmos* 37, 125–136.
Rayet O. (1879), 'Inscriptions métriques de Télos,' in: *BCH* 3, 42–45.
Razmjou, S. (2002), 'Assessing the Damage: Notes on the Life and Demise of the Statue of Darius from Susa,' *Ars Orientalis* 32, 81–104.
Reddoch, M.J. (2010), 'Conflict and Emotion in Medea's "Irrational" Dream (A.R. 3.616–35),' in: *AC* 53, 49–67.
Reinsch-Werner, H. (1976), *Callimachus Hesiodicus. Die Rezeption der hesiodischen Dichtung durch Kallimachos von Kyrene*, Berlin.
Reitz, C. (2003), 'Dichtung und Wissenschaft,' in: Horster/Reitz 2003, 61–71.
Rengakos, A. 1994. 'Lykophron als Homererklärer,' in: *ZPE* 102, 111–130.
Revermann, M. (2006), *Comic Business: Theatricality, Dramatic Technique, and Performance Contexts of Aristophanic Comedy*, Oxford.
Rey-Coquais, J.-P. (2006), *Inscriptions Grecques et Latines de Tyr*, Beirut.
Rice, E.E. (1983), *The Grand Procession of Ptolemy Philadelphus*, Oxford.

Richardson, N. J. (1980), 'Literary Criticism in the Exegetical Scholia to the *Iliad:* A Sketch,' in: *CQ* 30, 265–287.
Ricks, D. (2004), 'Cavafy's Alexandrianism,' in: Hirst/Silk 2004, 337–351.
Robert, L. (1938), *Études épigraphiques et philologiques,* (*Bibliothèque de l'École des Hautes Études, Sciences Historiques et Philologiques* 72), Paris.
Robert, R. (1992), '*Ars regenda amore.* Séduction érotique et plaisir esthétique de Praxitèle à Ovide,' in: *MEFRA* 104–1, 373–437.
Rohde, E. (1960), *Der Griechische Roman und seine Vorläufer,* Darmstadt.
Rollinger, R. (2003), 'Herodotus,' *Encyclopaedia Iranica,* vol. XII, Fasc. 3, 254–288.
Römer, A. (1906), 'Zur Würdigung und Kritik der Tragikerscholien,' in: *Philologus* 65, 24–90.
Romm, J. S. (1992), *The Edges of the Earth in Ancient Thought: Geography, Exploration, and Fiction,* Princeton.
Rosenmeyer, P.A. (1996), 'Love Letters in Callimachus, Ovid and Aristaenetus or the Sad Fate of a Mailorder Bride,' in: *MD* 36, 9–31.
Rosenmeyer, Th.G. (1969), *The Green Cabinet. Theocritus and European Pastoral Lyric,* Berkeley/Los Angeles.
Rosenmeyer, Th.G. (2006), 'Ancient Literary Genres: A Mirage?,' in: A. Laird (ed.), *Oxford Readings in Classical Studies: Ancient Literary Criticism,* Oxford, 421–439.
Roubaud, J. (1988), *La vieillesse d'Alexandre,* Paris.
Rousseau, P. (1996), 'Instruire Persès: Notes sur l'ouverture des *Travaux* d'Hésiode,' in: P. Judet de la Combe/P. Rousseau (eds.), *Le Métier du mythe: Lectures d'Hésiode,* Lille, 83–91.
Roussel, P. (1933), 'Epitaphe de Gaza commémorant deux officiers de la garnison ptolémaique,' in: *Aegyptus* 13, 145–151.
Rouveret, A. (ed.) (2004), *Peintures grecques antiques. La collection hellénistique du musée du Louvre,* avec la collaboration de Philippe Walter, Paris.
Russell, D.A. (1983), *Greek Declamation,* Cambridge.
Russell, D.A./Wilson, N.G. (1981), *Menander Rhetor: Edited with Translation and Commentary,* Oxford.
Rutherford, I. (2001), *Pindar's Paeans,* Oxford.
Rutherford, R.B. (2007), 'Tragedy and History,' in: J. Marincola (ed.), *A Companion to Greek and Roman Historiography,* 2 vols., Malden, MA/Oxford, ii.504–514.
Salzman-Mitchell, P. (2008), "Snapshots of a Love Affair: *Amores* 1.5 and the Program of Elegiac Narrative,' in: Liveley/Salzman-Mitchell 2008, 34–47.
Sancisi-Weerdenburg, H. (1989), 'Gifts in the Persian Empire,' in: P. Briant/C. Herrenschmidt (eds.), *Le tribut dans l'empire Perse. Actes de la table ronde de Paris,* Paris, 129–146.
Sancisi-Weerdenburg, H. (1993), 'Persian Food: Stereotypes and Political Identity,' in: J. Wilkins (ed.), *Food in Antiquity,* Exeter, 286–301.
Sarkissian, J. (1983), *Catullus 68: An Interpretation,* Leiden.
Sartre, J.-P. (2002), *La Nausée,* Paris (1st ed. 1938).
Savvidis, G.P. (1994), 'Η πολιτική αίσθηση στον Καβάφη' (1977), in: M. Pieris (ed.), *Εισαγωγή στην ποίηση του Καβάφη,* Rethymno, 249–268.
SB = *Sammelbuch griechischer Urkunden aus Ägypten,* I, Straßburg-Berlin 1913–1915; II-III, Berlin -Leipzig 1918–1927; IV-V, Heidelberg 1931–1955; VI – , Wiesbaden 1958 -
Sbardella, L. (1997), 'Il poeta e il bifolco,' in: *MD* 38, 127–141.
Sbardella, L. (2004), 'Teocrito pindarico. Il κέρδος, la fama e la poesia omerica in *Nemea* 7.17–31 e nell'*Idillio* XVI,' in: *Seminari Romani* 7, 65–83.

Schepens, G. (2005), 'Polybius' criticism of Phylarchus,' in: Schepens/Bollansée 2005, 141–164.
Schepens, G./Bollansée, J. (2005), *The Shadow of Polybius: Intertextuality as a Research Tool in Greek Historiography. Proceedings of the International Colloqium, Leuven, 21–22 September 2001* (*Studia Hellenistica* 42), Leuven.
Scherer, B. (2006), *Mythos, Katalog und Prophezeiung. Studien zu den* Argonautika *des Apollonios Rhodios*, Stuttgart.
Schiesaro, A./J.S. Clay/P. Mitsis (1993) (eds.), *Mega Nepios: Il destinario nell'epos didascalico* = *MD* 31.
Schironi, F. (2009), 'Theory into Practice: Aristotelian Principles in Aristarchean Philology,' in: *CPh* 104, 279–316.
Schmale, M. (2004), *Bilderreigen und Erzähllabyrinth: Catulls Carmen 64*, Munich/Leipzig.
Schmidt, E.A. (1985), *Catull*, Heidelberg.
Schmidt, M. (2002), 'The Homer of the Scholia: What is Explained to the Reader,' in: F. Montanari (ed.), *Omero tremila anni dopo. Atti del congresso di Genova 6–8 luglio 2000. Con la collaborazione di Paola Ascheri*, (*Storia e Letteratura* 210), Rome, 159–183.
Schmiel, R. (1981), 'Moschus' *Europa*,' in: *CPh* 76, 261–272.
Schmitt, R. (1988) 'Achaimenideninschriften in griechischer literarischer Überlieferung,' in: *A Green Leaf, Papers in Honour of Professor Jes P. Asmussen*, Leiden, 17–38.
Schmitt, R. (1991), 'Charon of Lampsacus,' in: *Encyclopaedia Iranica*, vol. V, Fasc. 4, 388–389.
Schmitt, R. (1993), 'Ctesias,' in: *Encyclopaedia Iranica*, vol. VI, Fasc. 4, 441–446.
Schmitt, R. (1995), 'Dionysius,' in: *Encyclopaedia Iranica*, vol. VII, Fasc. 4, 423.
Schmitz, Th.A. (2012), 'Herakles in Bits and Pieces: *Id.* 25 in the *Corpus Theocriteum*,' in: Baumbach/Bär 2012a, 259–282.
Schorn, St. (2004), *Satyros aus Kallatis. Sammlung der Fragmente mit Kommentar*, Basel.
Schütrumpf, E./Stork, P./Ophuijsen, J. van/Prince, S. (2008), *Heraclides of Pontus: Texts and Translation* (*Rutgers University Studies in Classical Humanities* 14), New Brunswick/London.
Schwartz, J. (1960), *Pseudo-Hesiodeia. Recherches sur la composition, la diffusion et la disparition ancienne d'oeuvres attribuées à Hésiode*, Leiden.
Schwarz, G. (1971), *Die griechische Kunst des 5. und 4. Jahrhunderts v.Chr. im Spiegel der Anthologia Graeca*, Diss. Vienna.
Schwinge, E.-R. (1986), *Künstlichkeit von Kunst*, Munich.
Scott, W.C. (1974), *The Oral Nature of the Homeric Simile*, Leiden.
Sedley, D. N. (2003), *Lucretius and the Transformation of Greek Wisdom*, Cambridge.
Seferis, G. (1974), 'Καβάφης – Ἔλιοτ. Παραλληλισμοί' (1946), in: G. Seferis, Δοκιμές, I, Athens, 324–363 (= G. Seferis, *Le parole e i marmi*, ed. F.M. Pontani, Milan 1965, 117–140).
SEG = *Supplementum Epigraphicum Graecum*.
Segal, C. (1962), 'Gorgias and the Psychology of the Logos,' in: *HSCPh* 66, 99–155.
Segal, C. (1981), *Poetry and Myth in Ancient Pastoral. Essays on Theocritus and Virgil*, Princeton.
Seidensticker, B. (1982), *Palintonos harmonia: Studien zu komischen Elementen in der griechischen Tragödie*, Göttingen.
Selden, D.L. (1998), 'Alibis,' in: *CA* 17, 289–415.

Sens, A. (2004), 'Doricisms in the New and Old Posidippus,' in: B. Acosta-Hughes/E. Kosmetatou/M. Baumbach (eds.), *Labored in Papyrus Leaves: Perspectives on an Epigram Collection Attributed to Posidippus (P.Mil.Vogl. VIII 309)*, Cambridge, Mass., 65–83.

Sens, A. (2011), *Asclepiades of Samos: Epigrams and Fragments*, Oxford.

Sens, A. (forthcoming), 'Dialect in the *Anacreontea*', in: M. Baumbach/N. Dümmler (eds.), *Imitate Anacreon! Mimesis, Poiesis and the Poetic Inspiration in the Carmina Anacreontea*, Berlin, 97–112.

Seth, V. (1986), *The Golden Gate: A Novel in Verse*, New York.

Setti, G. (1890), *Studi sulla antologia greca—gli epigrammi degli Antipatri*, Turin.

SGDI = Collitz, H./Bechtel F. et al. (eds.) (1884–1915), *Sammlung der griechischen Dialekt-Inschriften*, Göttingen.

SGO = Merkelbach, R./Stauber, J. (eds.) (1998–2004), *Steinepigramme aus dem griechischen Osten*, 5 vols., Stuttgart/Leipzig/Munich.

SH = Parsons, P.J./Lloyd-Jones, H. (eds.) (1983), *Supplementum Hellenisticum*, (*Texte und Kommentare* 11), Berlin/New York.

Shapiro, K. (1945), *Essay on Rime*, New York.

Sherwin-White, S. (1978), *Ancient Cos: An Historical Study from the Dorian Settlement to the Imperial Period*, Göttingen.

Sherwin-White, S./Kuhrt, A. (1993), *From Samarkhand to Sardis. A New Approach to the Seleucid Empire*, (*Hellenistic Culture and Society* 13), London.

Shorrock, R. (2011), *The Myth of Paganism: Nonnus, Dionysus and the World of Late Antiquity*, London.

Sider, D. (2004), 'How to Commit Philosophy Obliquely: Philodemus' Epigrams in the Light of his *Peri Parrhesias*,' in: J.T. Fitzgerald/D. Obbink/G. Holland (eds.), *Philodemus and the New Testament World*, Leiden, 85–101.

Sider, D. (2005), 'Posidippus on Weather Signs and the Tradition of Didactic Poetry,' in: K. Gutzwiller (ed.), *The New Posidippus: A Hellenistic Poetry Book*, Oxford, 158–176.

Sider, D./Brunschön, W. (2007), *Theophrastus of Eresus: On Weather Signs*, Leiden.

Sider, D. (1977/2012), 'Plato's Early Aesthetics: The *Hippias Major*,' in: *Journal of Aesthetics and Art Criticism* 35 (1977), 465-470. Reprinted in A. Denham (ed.) (2007), *Plato on Art and Beauty*, London, 75–83.

Sider, D. (forthcoming), 'Homer Ethicus'.

Silk, M.S. (2004), 'Alexandrian Poetry from Callimachus to Eliot,' in: Hirst/Silk 2004, 353–372.

Silk, M.S. (2006), *Interaction in Poetic Imagery: With Special Reference to Early Greek Poetry*, Cambridge/New York.

Simpson, M. (1969), 'The Chariot and the Bow as Metaphors for Poetry in Pindar's *Odes*', in: *TAPhA* 100, 437–447.

Sistakou, E. (2008a), *Reconstructing the Epic: Cross-Readings of the Trojan Myth in Hellenistic Poetry*, Leuven/Paris/Dudley, MA.

Sistakou, E. (2008b), 'Beyond the *Argonautica*: In Search of Apollonius' *Ktisis* Poems,' in: Th. D. Papanghelis/A. Rengakos (eds.), *Brill's Companion to Apollonius Rhodius*, Second, Revised Edition, Leiden/Boston, 311–340.

Sistakou, E. (2009a), '"Snapshots" of Myth: The Notion of Time in Hellenistic Epyllion,' in: J. Grethlein/A. Rengakos (eds.), *Narratology and Interpretation: The Content of Narrative Form in Ancient Literature*, Berlin/New York, 293–319.

Sistakou, E. (2009b), 'Poeticizing Natural Phenomena: The Case of Callimachus,' in: M.A. Harder/R.F. Retguit/G.C. Wakker (eds.). *Nature and Science in Hellenistic Poetry*, Leuven, 177–99.
Sistakou, E. (2012), *The Aesthetics of Darkness. A Study of Hellenistic Romanticism in Apollonius, Lycophron and Nicander*, Leuven/Paris/Walpole, MA.
Skinner, M.B. (1984), 'Rhamnusia Virgo,' in: *ClAnt* 3, 134–141.
Skinner, M.B. (2003), *Catullus in Verona: A Reading of the Elegiac Libellus, Poems 65–116*, Columbus.
Skinner, M.B. (ed.) (2007a), *A Companion to Catullus*, Malden, MA.
Skinner, M.B. (2007b), 'Authorial Arrangement of the Collection: Debate Past and Present,' in: Skinner 2007a, 35–53.
Snipes, K. (1988), 'Literary Interpretation in the Homeric Scholia: The Similes of the *Iliad*,' in: *AJP* 109, 196–222.
Snodgrass, A.M. (1964), 'Carian Armourers: The Growth of a Tradition,' in: *JHS* 84, 107–118.
Spatafora, G. (2008), 'Les *Erotica Pathémata* de Parthénios et la récriture en format abrégé,' in: Zucker 2008, 27–38.
Spawforth, A. J. S. (2012), *Greece and the Augustan Cultural Revolution*, Cambridge.
Spier, J. (1990), 'Emblems in Archaic Greece,' in: *BICS* 37, 107–129.
Squire, M. (2010), 'Making Myron's Cow Moo? Ecphrastic Epigram and the Poetics of Simulation,' in: *AJPh* 131, 589–634.
Squire, M. (2011), *The* Iliad *in a Nutshell. Visualizing Epic on the* Tabulae Iliacae, Oxford.
Stephani L. (1851), *Über einige angebliche Steinschneider des Altherthums*, Saint Petersburg.
Stephens, M.H. (1991), *Shield Devices of the Greeks*, University of California, Diss. Berkeley.
Stephens, S. (2003), *Seeing Double: Intercultural Poetics in Ptolemaic Alexandria*, Berkeley.
Stephens, S. (2004a). '"For you, Arsinoe",' in: Acosta-Hughes/Kosmetatou/Baumbach 2004, 161–176.
Stephens, S. (2004b), 'Posidippus' Poetry Book. Where Macedon Meets Egypt,' in: W.V. Harris/G.R. Ruffini (eds.), *Ancient Alexandria between Egypt and Greece*, (*Columbia Studies in the Classical Tradition* 26), Leiden, 63–86.
Stephens, S./Obbink, D. (2004) 'The Manuscript,' in: Acosta-Hughes/Kosmetatou/Baumbach, 2004, 9–16.
Stephens, S. (2005), 'Battle of the Books,' in: K. Gutzwiller (ed.), *The New Posidippus. A Hellenistic Poetry Book*, Oxford, 229–248.
Stewart, A. (1996), 'The Alexandrian Style: a Mirage?,' in: Walsh/Reese 1996, 231–241.
Stockt, L. van der (2005), 'Πολυβιάcαcθαι? Plutarch on Timaeus and "Tragic History",' in: Schepens/Bollansée 2005, 271–305.
Stoevesandt, M. (1994/1995), 'Catull 64 und die Ilias: Das Peleus-Thetis-Epyllion im Lichte der neueren Homer-Forschung,' in: *WJA* 20, 167–205.
Stoneman, R. (1995), 'Riddles in Bronze and Stone. Monuments and their Interpretation in the Alexander Romance,' in: *Groningen Colloquia on the Novel* 6, 159–170.
Stronk, J.P. (2004/5), 'Ctesias of Cnidus. From Physician to Author,' in: *Talanta* 36–7, 101–122.
Stronk, J.P. (2010), *Ctesias' Persian History. Part I: Introduction, Text, and Translation*, Düsseldorf.
Strootman, R. (2005), 'Kings against Celts. Deliverance from Barbarians as a Theme in Hellenistic Royal Propaganda – from the Soteria of Delphi to the Great Altar of Pergamon,' in:

K. Enenkel/I.L. Pfeijffer (eds.), *The Manipulative Mode: Political Propaganda in Antiquity*, Leiden, 101–141.
Strootman, R. (2010), 'Literature and the Kings,' in: Clauss/Cuypers 2010, 30–45.
Sutton, D.F. (1973), 'Satyric Elements in the *Alcestis*,' in: *RSC* 21, 384–391.
Swales, J.M. (1990), *Genre Analysis: English in Academic and Research Settings*, Cambridge.
Sweet, D.R. (2006), 'Catullus 65: Grief and Poetry,' in: C. Deroux (ed.), *Studies in Latin Literature and Roman History* 13, Bruxelles, 87–96.
Syndikus, H.P. (2001), *Catull: Eine Interpretation. Zweiter Teil: Die großen Gedichte (61–68)*, Darmstadt.
Tanner J. (2006), *The Invention of Art History in Ancient Greece: Religion, Society and Artistic Rationalisation*, Cambridge.
Taplin, O. (1977), 'Did Greek Dramatists Write Stage Instructions?,' in: *PCPhS* 203, 121–132.
Tar, I. (2005a) (ed.), *Studia Catulliana in memoriam Stephani Caroli Horvath (1931–1966)*, Szeged.
Tar, I. (2005b), 'Vergleich als vollständiges Gedicht? (Catull c. 2a),' in: Tar 2005a, 39–43.
Theodorakopoulos, E. (2000), 'Catullus, 64: Footprints in the Labyrinth,' in: A. Sharrock/H. Morales (eds.), *Intratextuality: Greek and Roman Textual Relations*, Oxford, 115–141.
Theodorakopoulos, E. (2007), 'Poem 68: Love and Death, and the Gifts of Venus and the Muses,' in: Skinner 2007a, 314–332.
Thomas, R.F. (1982), 'Catullus and the Polemics of Poetic Reference (Poem 64.1–18),' in: *AJPh* 103, 144–164; reprinted in: R.F. Thomas (1999), *Reading Virgil and His Texts: Studies in Intertextuality*, Ann Arbor, 12–32.
Thompson, D.J. (1992), 'Language and Literacy in Early Hellenistic Egypt,' in: P. Bilde *et al.* (eds.), *Ethnicity in Hellenistic Egypt (Studies in Hellenistic Civilization* 3), Aarhus, 39–52.
Thompson, D.J. (2001), 'Hellenistic Hellenes: the Case of Ptolemaic Egypt,' in: I. Malkin (ed.), *Ancient Perceptions of Greek Ethnicity*, Washington DC, 301–322.
Thompson, D.J. (2012²), *Memphis under the Ptolemies*, Princeton.
Thompson, D.W (1895), *A Glossary of Greek Birds*. Oxford.
Tod, M.N. (1933), 'A Greek Epigram from Gaza,' in: *Aegyptus* 13, 152–158.
Toohey, P. (1996), *Epic lessons: An Introduction to Ancient Didactic Poetry*, London.
Toohey, P. (2004), *Melancholy, Love, and Time. Boundaries of the Self in Ancient Literature*, Ann Arbor.
Toohey, P. (2005), 'Periodization and Didactic Poetry,' in: Hörster/Reitz 2005, 15–26.
Tosi, R. (2010), *Dictionnaire des sentences latines et grecques* (transl. by R. Lenoir), Grenoble.
Townend, G.B. (1983), 'The Unstated Climax of Catullus 64,' in: *G&R* 30, 21–30.
Trendelenburg, A. (1867), *Grammaticorum Graecorum de arte tragics iudiciorum reliquiae*, Bonn.
Trimble, G. (2012), 'Catullus 64: The Perfect Epyllion?,' in: Baumbach/Bär 2012a, 55–79.
Troxel, R.L. (2008), *LXXX-Isaiah as Translation and Interpretation: The Strategies of the Translator of the Septuagint of Isaiah*, Leiden.
Trypanis, C.A. (1947), 'The Character of Alexandrian Poetry,' in: *G&R* 16, 1–7.
Trypanis, C.A. (1958, 1978²), *Callimachus. Aetia, Iambi, Hecale and Other Fragments*, Cambridge, Mass./London.
Tsantsanoglou K. (2012), 'The Statue of Philitas,' in: *ZPE* 180, 104–116.
Ukleja, K. (2005), *Der Delos-Hymnus des Kallimachos innerhalb seines Hymnensextetts*, Münster.

Vaerst, A. (1980), *Griechische Schildzeichen vom 8. bis zum ausgehenden 6. Jh.*, Diss. Salzburg.
van Groningen, B.A. (1966), *Theognis. Le premier livre*, Amsterdam.
van Rossum-Steenbeek, M. (1997), *Greek Reader's Digest? Studies on a Selection of Subliterary Papyri*, Leiden.
van Sickle, J. (1999), 'The Design of Derek Walcott's *Omeros*,' in: *CW* 93, 7–27.
van Tress, H. (2004), *Poetic Memory. Allusion in the Poetry of Callimachus and the Metamorphoses of Ovid*, Leiden/Boston.
Van't Dack, E./Clarysse, W./Cohen, G./Quaegebeur, J./Winnicki, J.K. (eds.) (1989), *The Judean-Syrian-Egyptian Conflict of 103–101 B.C. A Multilingual Dossier Concerning a "War of Sceptres"*, Brussels.
Vannini, L. (2007), 'Un commentario a Pindaro: PSI XIV 1391 con nuovi frammenti,' in: *Comunicazioni dell'Istituto Papirologico "G. Vitelli"* 7, 29–73.
Vayenas, N. (1994), *Η ειρωνική γλώσσα*, Athens.
Vayenas, N. (ed.) (2000), *Συνομιλώντας με τον Καβάφη· ανθολογία ξένων καβαφογενών ποιημάτων*, Thessaloniki.
Vessey, D. W. T. (1976), 'Philaenis,' in: *RBPh* 54, 78–83.
Vian, F. (1978), 'ΙΗΣΩΝ ΑΜΗΧΑΝΕΩΝ,' in: E. Livrea/G.A. Privitera (eds.), *Studi in onore di Anthos Ardizzoni*, Rome, 2.1025–1041.
Vian, F./Delage, É. (2002³), *Apollonios de Rhodes*: Argonautiques. Tome I : Chants I-II, Paris.
Vincent, L.H. (1937), 'Une épitaphe métrique de Gaza,' in: *Mélanges Maspero II: Orient grec, romain et byzantin*, Cairo, 41–52.
Volk, K. (2002), *The Poetics of Latin Didactic: Lucretius, Vergil, Ovid, Manilius*, Oxford.
Vollenweider, M.L. (1966), *Die Schneidekunst und ihre Künstler in spätrepublikanischer und augusteischer Zeit*, Baden-Baden.
Vottéro, G. (2002), "Boeotica Epigrammata,' in: J. Dion (ed.), *L'épigramme de l'antiquité au XVIIe siècle. Du ciseau à la pointe*, Nancy, 69–122.
Vox, O. (2002), 'ἀγαθὸν κλέος: poeta e committente nelle *Cariti* (Theocr. 16),' in: *Kleos* 7, 193–209.
Wagner, J./Petzl, G. (2003), 'Relief- und Inschriftfragmente des kommagenischen Herrscherkultes aus Ancoz,' in: Heedemann/Winter 2003, 85–96.
Walbank, F. W. (1957–79), *A Historical Commentary on Polybius*, 3 vols., Oxford.
Walcott, D. (1990), *Omeros*, New York 1990 (It. ed. with facing text, ed. A. Molesini, Milan 2003).
Walser, G (1966), *Die Völkerschaften auf den Reliefs von Persepolis: Historische Studien über den sogenannten Tributzug an der Apadanatreppe*, Berlin.
Walsh, J.J./Reese, T.F. (eds.) (1996), *Alexandria and Alexandrianism*, Malibu.
Warburg, A. (1920), *Heidnisch-antike Weissagung in Wort und Bild zu Luthers Zeiten*, Heidelberg 1920 (= A. Warburg, *Ausgewählte Schriften*, ed. D. Wuttke, Baden-Baden 1992, 199–268).
Weber, C. (1983), 'Two Chronological Contradictions in Catullus 64,' in: *TAPhA* 113, 263–271.
Weber, G. (1993), *Dichtung und höfische Gesellschaft*, Stuttgart.
Weber, G. (2011), 'Poet and Court,' in: B. Acosta-Hughes/L. Lehnus/S. Stephens (eds.), *Brill's Companion to Callimachus*, Leiden/Boston, 225–244.
Wehrli, Fr. (1968), *Die Schule des Aristoteles. Texte und Kommentar. VII: Herakleides Pontikos²*, Basel/Stuttgart.

Wehrli, Fr. (1978), *Die Schule des Aristoteles. Texte und Kommentar. Supplementband* II: *Sotion*, Basel/Stuttgart.
Welles, B. (1970), 'Gallic Mercenaries in the Chremonidean War,' in: *Klio* 52, 477–490.
Wendel, C. (ed.) (1914), *Scholia in Theocritum vetera*, Leipzig.
Wender D. (1979), 'From Hesiod to Homer by Way of Rome,' in: *Ramus* 7, 59–64.
Werth, P. (1999), *Text Worlds: Representing Conceptual Space in Discourse*, Harlow.
West, M.L. (1967), 'An Epigram on Heraclitus,' in: *CR* n.s. 17, 127–128.
West, M.L. (1970), Review of Prato (1968), in: *CR* 84, 149–151.
West, M.L. (1974), *Studies in Greek Elegy and Iambus*, Berlin/New York.
West, M.L. (1997), *The East Face of Helicon*, Oxford.
West, S. (1974), 'Satyrus: Peripatetic or Alexandrian,' in: *GRBS* 15, 279–286.
West, S. (1984), 'Lycophron Italicised,' in: *JHS* 104, 127–151.
White, K. (1992), 'Elements of Geopoetics," in: *Edinburgh Review* 88, 163–181.
White, S.A. (1992), 'Aristotle's Favorite Tragedies,' in: A. Oksenberg Rorty (ed.), *Essays on Aristotle's* Poetics, Princeton, 221–240.
Whitmarsh, T. (2010), 'Prose Fiction,' in: Clauss/Cuypers 2010, 395–411.
Wiesehöfer, J. (2003a), 'Hellanicus of Lesbos,' in: *Encyclopaedia Iranica*, vol. XII, Fasc. 2, 156.
Wiesehöfer, J. (2003b), 'Heracleides of Cyme,' in: *Encyclopaedia Iranica*, vol. XII, Fasc. 2, 201.
Wilamowitz-Moellendorff, U. von (1924), *Hellenistische Dichtung*, 2 vols., Berlin.
Wilhelm, A. (1911), 'Die lokrische Mädcheninschrift,' in: *OJ* 14,163–256.
Willi, A. (2004), 'Poétique au seuil de l'alexandrinisme: idylle 16 de Théocrite,' in: *AC* 73, 31–46.
Williams, F. (1978), *Callimachus:* Hymn to Apollo, Oxford.
Williams, G.D. (1992), 'Representations of the Book-Roll in Latin Poetry: Ovid, *Tr.* 1, 1, 3–14 and Related Texts,' in: *Mnemosyne* 45, 178–189.
Williams, M.F. (1996), 'Stoicism and the Character of Jason in the *Argonautica* of Apollonius Rhodius,' in: *Scholia* 5, 17–42.
Wilson, D.F. (2002), *Ransom, Revenge, and Heroic Identity in the* Iliad, Cambridge.
Winder, S. (2003), 'Secrets and Lies: The Circumscribed Voice in Callimachus and Cavafy,' in: *Classical and Modern Literature* 23, 2003, 51–65.
Winterbottom, M. (2011), 'On Ancient Prose Rhythm: The Story of the Dichoreus,' in: D. Obbink/R.B. Rutherford (eds.), *Culture in Pieces: Essays on Ancient Texts in Honour of Peter Parsons*, Oxford, 262–276.
Wirth, G. (1993), *Diodor und das Ende des Hellenismus. Mutmaßungen zu einem fast unbekannten Historiker (Österreichische Akademie der Wissenschaften, Phil.-hist. Klasse, SB* 600), Vienna.
Wise, J. 2008. 'Tragedy as an "Augury of Happy Life"', *Arethusa* 41, 381–410.
Wiseman, T.P. (1979a), *Clio's Cosmetics. Three Studies in Greco-Roman Literature*, Leicester.
Wiseman, T.P. (1979b), 'Fucatio,' in: T.P. Wiseman (1979a), 1–8.
Wisse, J. (1995), 'Greeks, Romans, and the Rise of Atticism,' in: J.G.J. Abbenes/S.R. Slings/I. Sluiter (eds.), *Greek Literary Theory after Aristotle: A Collection of Papers in Honour of D. M. Schenkeveld*, Amsterdam, 65–82.
Wöhrle, G. (1998), 'Bermerkungen zur lehrhaften Dichtung zwischen Empedokles und Arat,' in: W. Kullmann/J. Althoff/M. Asper (eds.), *Gattungen wissenschaftlicher Literatur in der Antike*, Tübingen, 279–286.
Woodhouse, W.J. (1897), *Aetolia: Its Geography, Topography, and Antiquities*, Oxford.
Woodman, T. (2012), 'A Covering Letter: Poem 65,' in: Du Quesnay/Woodman 2012, 130–152.

Worman, N. (2009), 'Bodies and Topographies in Ancient Stylistic Theory,' in: Th. Fögen/M.M. Lee (eds.), *Bodies and Boundaries in Graeco-Roman Antiquity*, Berlin, 45–62.
Xanthakis-Karamanos. G. (1980), *Studies in Fourth-Century Tragedy*, Athens.
Yannoulopoulos, G. (2011), *Ο μοντερνισμός και οι δοκιμές του Σεφέρη*, Athens.
Yourcenar, M. (1958), *Présentation critique de Constantin Cavafy*, Paris.
Yoyotte, J. (1969), 'Bakhthis: Réligion égyptienne et culture grecque à Edfou,' in: *Religions en Egypte hellénistique et romaine: colloque de Strasbourg 16–18 Mai 1967*, Paris, 127–141.
Zadorojnyi, A.V. (forthcoming), 'Shuffling Surfaces: Epigraphy, Power and Integrity in the Greco-Roman Narratives,' in: P. Liddel/P. Low (eds.), *Inscriptions and their Uses in Ancient Literature*, Oxford.
Zanker, G. (1987), *Realism in Alexandrian Poetry*, London.
Zanker, G. (1996), 'Pictorial Description as a Supplement for Narrative: The Labour of Augeas' Stables in *Heracles Leontophonos*,' in: *AJPh* 117, 411–423.
Zanker, G. (2004), *Modes of Viewing in Hellenistic Poetry and Art*, Madison.
Zanker, G. (2009), *Herodas, Mimiambs, Edited with a Translation, Introduction and Commentary*, Oxford.
Zanker, P. (1995), *The Mask of Socrates—The Image of the Intellectual in Antiquity*, transl. A. Shapiro, Berkeley/Los Angeles/Oxford.
Zanker, P. (2004), *The Heart of Achilles: Characterization and Personal Ethics in the* Iliad, Ann Arbor.
Zeitlin, F.I. (2009^2), *Under the Sign of the Shield: Semiotics and Aeschylus'* Seven Against Thebes, Lanham, MD (1st ed. 1982).
Zetzel, J.E.G. (1983), 'Catullus, Ennius, and the Poetics of Allusion,' in: *ICS* 8, 251–266; reprinted in: Gaisser 2007, 198–216.
Zucker, A. (ed.) (2008), *Littérature et érotisme dans les* Passions d'amour *de Parthénios de Nicée. Actes du colloque de Nice, 31 mai 2006*, Grenoble.

Notes on Contributors

Annemarie Ambühl has been teaching at various universities in Switzerland, Germany and the Netherlands, where she currently has a position as a lecturer in Latin language and literature at Leiden University. She completed her PhD on children and young heroes in Callimachus at the University of Basel (*Kinder und junge Helden: Innovative Aspekte des Umgangs mit der literarischen Tradition bei Kallimachos,* Leuven 2005) in 2002 and her habilitation on the reception of Greek literature in Lucan's *Bellum civile* at the University of Mainz in 2012. Her research interests focus on Greek and Roman epic and tragedy as well as on Hellenistic poetry and its reception at Rome. She has published articles in the *Brills Companion to Hellenistic Epigram* (eds. P. Bing/J.S. Bruss, Leiden 2007) and the *Blackwell Companion to Hellenistic Literature* (eds. J.J. Clauss/M. Cuypens, Malden, Mass./Oxford 2010).

Silvia Barbantani is researcher and Professor Aggregato at the Università Cattolica del Sacro Cuore in Milano and Brescia. She has published extensively on Hellenistic poetry and history and on literary papyrology, but her research interests include also the reception of archaic poetry, the definition of the literary genres, and military history. Among her publications are Φάτις νικηφόρος, *Frammenti di elegia encomiastica nell'età delle guerre galatiche: SH 958, 969* (Milano 2001) and *Three Burials. Facts and fiction on Lyric poets in Magna Graecia in the epigrams of the Greek Anthology* (Alessandria 2010). She is currently publishing fragments of *ktiseis* for Brill *Jacoby Continuatus* (*FGrHist*) and planning a monograph on military epitaphs from the Hellenistic and Roman periods.

Marco Fantuzzi, teaches Classics at the Universities of Macerata (Italy) and Columbia University, New York. He is the author of *Achilles in Love: An Intertextual Approach* (2012); *Tradition and Innovation in Hellenistic Poetry* (2 004, with R. Hunter); *Ricerche su Apollonio Rodio* (1988); *Bionis Smyrnaei "Adonidis epitaphium"* (1985). He co-edited (with T. Papanghelis) *Brill's Companion to Greek and Latin Pastoral* (2006), and (with R. Pretagostini) *Struttura e storia dell'esametro greco* (1995–6), and is now co-editing (with C. Tsagalis) *A Companion to the Epic Cycle*. He is a member of the board of *Bryn Mawr Classical Review, Materiali e Discussioni per l'analisi dei testi classici,* and *Seminari Romani di Cultura greca*. He is currently completing a commentary on the *Rhesus* ascribed to Euripides (CUP).

Andrew Faulkner is Associate Professor in the Department of Classical Studies, University of Waterloo. He has previously published a commentary on the Homeric Hymn to Aphrodite (Oxford, 2008), edited a volume of collected essays on the Homeric Hymns (Oxford, 2011), and published articles on Greek poetry of the Hellenistic period and Late Antiquity.

Kathryn Gutzwiller is Professor of Classics at the University of Cincinnati. Her books include *Theocritus' Pastoral Analogies: The Formation of a Genre; Poetic Garlands: Hellenistic Epigrams in Context,* which won the American Philological Association's Charles J. Goodwin Award of Merit; *The New Posidippus: A Hellenistic Poetry Book*; and *A Guide to Hellenistic Literature.* She has recently published an article on new mosaics illustrating comedies by Menander from ancient Antioch. She is currently working on a critical edition and commentary for the epigrams of Meleager, a project that has been supported by grants from the National Endowment for the Humanities, Institute for Advanced Studies at Princeton, American Council of Learned Societies, Loeb Classical Library Foundation, and All Souls College, Oxford.

Annette Harder is Professor of Ancient Greek Language and Literature at the University of Groningen (The Netherlands). She has written on Greek tragedy and published a number of mythographic papyri, but her main field of interest is Hellenistic Poetry. She has published various articles on this subject, organizes the biennial *Groningen Workshops on Hellenistic Poetry* and has edited several volumes of the series *Hellenistica Groningana*. She has also published a Dutch translation of a selection of Callimachus' poetry and her edition with introduction and commentary of Callimachus'*Aetia* has been publisehd by Oxford University Press in 2012.

Richard Hunter is Regius Professor of Greek at the University of Cambridge and a Fellow of Trinity College. His most recent books are *Critical Moments in Classical Literature* (Cambridge 2009), (with Donald Russell) *Plutarch, How to study poetry (De audiendis poetis)* (Cambridge 2011), *Plato and the Traditions of Ancient Literature: the silent stream* (Cambridge 2012) and *Hesiodic Voices: Studies in the Ancient Reception of Hesiod's Works and Days* (Cambridge 2014). Many of his essays have been collected in *On Coming After: Studies in Post-Classical Greek Literature and its Reception* (Berlin 2008).

G. O. Hutchinson is Professor of Greek and Latin Languages and Literature at the University of Oxford. He has written the following books: *Aeschylus,* Septem contra Thebas, *Edited with Introduction and Commentary* (Oxford, 1985); *Hellenistic*

Poetry (Oxford, 1988); *Latin Literature from Seneca to Juvenal: A Critical Study* (Oxford, 1993); *Cicero's Correspondence: A Literary Study* (Oxford, 1998); *Greek Lyric Poetry: A Commentary on Selected Larger Pieces* (Oxford, 2001); *Propertius: Elegies Book IV* (Cambridge, 2006); *Talking Books: Readings in Hellenistic and Roman Books of Poetry* (Oxford, 2008); *Greek to Latin: Frameworks and Contexts for Intertextuality* (Oxford, 2013).

Giulio Massimilla is Associate Professor of Greek Literature at the University of Naples "Federico II". He is the author of a two-volume critical edition, with commentary, of Callimachus' *Aetia* (1996, 2010). He has written on archaic Greek lyric, Hellenistic poetry, imperial Greek epic, ancient Greek novels, and Greek literary papyri.

Ivana Petrovic is Senior Lecturer at the Department of Classics and Ancient History at the University of Durham. She is the author of a monograph on the cult of Artemis in Callimachus and Theocritus (Brill 2007), which studies contemporary religion in Hellenistic poetry. She has co-edited volumes on Roman triumph (2008) and on Greek archaic epigram (2010), and published papers on Greek Archaic and Hellenistic poetry, Greek religion and magic.

Filippomaria Pontani is Associate Professor of Classical Philology at the University of Venice "Ca' Foscari". While primarily concerned with issues of manuscript transmission in the Byzantine and humanistic period (*inter alia* the edition of unpublished or little known exegetical or literary texts, from Isaac Porphyrogenitus to Maximus Planudes to Marcus Musurus), he is currently editing the scholia to Homer's *Odyssey* (two volumes so far, Rome 2007 and 2010; prolegomena: *Sguardi su Ulisse*, Rome 2005). He has published extensively on Greek and Latin texts (from Sappho's *Nachleben* to Callimachus' *Aitia*, from Aeschylus' *Choephori* to quotations in Demosthenes, from the rise of ancient grammar and scholarship to allegory and the literary *facies* of some ancient myths), as well as on Byzantine, Humanist and Modern Greek literature (*Poeti greci del Novecento*, Milan 2010).

Alexander Sens is the Markos and Eleni Tsakopoulos Kounalakis Chair of Hellenic Studies at Georgetown University. His research focus is on the literature of the late-Classical and Hellenistic periods, especially poetry. His most recent book is a critical edition of Asclepiades of Samos, with commentary (Oxford 2011). He is currently at work on commentary on select epigrams for the Cambridge "green and yellow" series and, with his colleague Charles McNelis, a literary study of Lycophron's *Alexandra*.

David Sider teaches at New York University and writes on Greek poetry and philosophy, especially when they overlap, such as in Empedocles, Parmenides, Plato, and Philodemus, and in didactic poetry in general. He has edited *The Fragments of Anaxagoras* (second edition, 2005), *The Epigrams of Philodemos* (1997), and *Theophrastus On Weather Signs* (2007).

Evina Sistakou is Associate Professor of Greek Literature at the Aristotle University of Thessaloniki. Her publications include: *The Aesthetics of Darkness. A Study of Hellenistic Romanticism in Apollonius, Lycophron and Nicander* (Leuven 2012), *Reconstructing the Epic. Cross-Readings of the Trojan Myth in Hellenistic Poetry* (Leuven 2008) and *The Geography of Callimachus and Hellenistic Avant-Garde Poetry* (Athens 2005, in Modern Greek). She has published articles on Apollonius, Callimachus, Lycophron, Euphorion, Greek epigram and Hellenistic poetics.

Index

Abraham   237, 240–241, 243–246, 249
Achaemenid royal propaganda   273–300
Achilles   66–71, 145, 179–180, 249
Addaeus   205–209
Aeschylus   109–110, 148, 225, 330
aesthetic materialism   155
aesthetic moment   155–156
Agamemnon   109–111
Agatharchides   35
Aglaia   204
Aiolus   212
Ajax   73–74, 101–102, 219–221, 318–319
Alexander the Great   175, 181, 275, 278, 286, 289–290, 293–294
Alexander Polyhistor   237, 246, 251–252
Alexandria   55, 159, 161–162, 164–166, 180–181, 183, 237, 265–267, 275–276
Alexandrianism   157–183
Anacreon   88, 102
Anadyomene (painting by Apelles) 192–196
Antipater of Sidon   83, 91, 188–203, 332–333
Anyte   327
Aphrodite   192–202, 210, 266
Aphrodite pselioumene   193, 196
Apollodorus of Cyrene   222
Apollonius of Rhodes
– *Argonautica*   31, 37–38, 47, 119, 140–141, 144–148, 176–180, 250, 254–255, 261, 268–270
– *Lesbou ktisis*   145
apple   118–131
Aragon, Louis   301
Aratus   22–23
– Hipparchus' treatment of   40
Archilochus   3, 102
Archimedes   43–44, 46–47
Aristarchus   105
Aristophanes   18–20, 232, 245
Aristophanes of Byzantium   105, 215, 221, 226–233
Aristotle   21–22, 49, 135–136, 138–139, 143, 216–218, 222–225, 228–231
art   185–212

Asclepiades   82
Asianism   34, 202
Athena   192, 197–202
Atticism   34, 202
author   17, 20, 39–49, 77, 215

Bacchylides   61
barbarian   307–308, 311–312, 323
Bion
– Epitaph for Adonis   150–151, 175
Boeotos   212
bucolic corpus   142–143
bucolic poetry   172–175

Callimachus   3–11, 25–26, 35, 44–48, 76, 94, 235–236, 254, 261
– *Acontius and Cydippe*   4–5, 47–48, 128–129, 181, 262, 265
– *Aetia*   3–11, 44, 47, 144, 180–182, 261–268
– *Bath of Pallas*   3
– *Hecale*   143–144
– *Hymns*   117
– *Hymn to Delos*   38–39
– *Hymn to Zeus*   45, 267
– *Iambi*   41–42
– *Ibis*   3–4
– *Lock of Berenice*   266
– *Victory of Berenice*   115–116, 266–267
– *Victory of Sosibius*   3, 7–8
– first person in   44–45, 46
– game in   47–48
– handling of polemic   41, 44–45
– imagination and metre   33–34
– knowledge in   47–48
– his poetry and prose   44–45
Calvus   34
cameo   203–210
Cassandra   97–111, 148–149
catastrophe   224, 228–229
Catullus   118–131
Cavafy, Constantine   164–165, 170–172, 181–183
Ceos   262–263

Cephalas 85
character 139–141, 215–219, 221, 225–226, 229–230
Cicero 34, 36
Clytemnestra 109–111
Cnidian Aphrodite (sculpture by Praxiteles) 193–203
comedy 216, 222–233
Cornelia 199
Cos 81, 83, 89–90, 95
cosmetics 205
Cow (sculpture by Myron) 191, 202–203

Damagetus 325
Daphnis 142
Darius 284–285, 287–292
decadence 162, 169
detachment 141–142
dialect
– Attic-Ionic 75, 82–83, 89–90, 92–94
– dialect mixture 76–78, 90
– Doric 75, 80–83, 86–90, 91, 94–95, 212
– epic-Ionic 77, 81, 88
– in epigram 75–95
dialogue in prose 45, 48–50
didactic poetry 13–29
– poetry as instruction 17–20
– and scientific prose 22–23
– 'teacher-student' constellation 16–17
Diodorus 31–32
Dionysius of Halicarnassus 65, 210
Dorus 211–212
'double structure' tragedy 225–226, 230

Echedorus 211
ecphrasis 115, 119–121
ecphrastic epigram 185–212
ego-language 39–42
Egypt 265–266, 275–276, 278, 285–291, 299–300, 302–306
elegy 3–11
– elegiac tradition 4–11
– gnomic element 7–9
– 'instructive banquet' theme 10–11
– Latin love elegy 124–125, 132
– military and paraenetic elements 4–6
– paederastic element 6–7

– proverbs 9
– sympotic conversation 9–10
– wine drinking 9–10
Eliot, T.S. 162–163, 170–172, 180–183
ellipsis 113, 120
emotion 135–156
– anger 140
– dislocation of 141
– in dreams 148–149
– fear 140, 146
– fossilization of 141
– helplessness 144–145
– loneliness 143–144
– love 141, 142–143, 145–146
– physical manifestation of 147–148
Empedocles 21–22
Ephesus 93–94
epic 25–26, 139–141, 175–180, 216
Epicurus 21, 25
epitaph 81, 83, 87, 91–94, 131, 143, 188, 273, 301–334
epyllion 118–131
Erinna 91
Eros 198–199, 201, 203–204, 207, 210
Eros of Thespiae (sculpture by Praxiteles) 201
Euphorion 212
Euripides 45, 125, 212, 215–233, 242, 244, 247, 252, 254–255
Europa 149–151
Eurotas (sculpture by Eutychides) 187, 209
Eusebius 237, 250–251
Eutychides 187, 209
exemplum 5, 169
extremity in poetry 35–39
Ezechiel 236

feeling 150–151
fiction
– in poetry 35, 39, 41, 42, 44
– in prose 48–50
fountain 210–212
'future reflexive' 117

Galen 40, 43–44
Galene 205–209
garden 211–212

gem 186–188, 203–210
genre 172–173
– and authorial language 39–40
– contamination of 232–233
– reconstruction of 168
geography 259–261, 274–275, 277
goatherd's cup 185–186
Gorgias 136–137
grandeur 35–36
Greek Anthology 325–327
Greek identity 306–313
Greekness 260, 263, 265–266, 270–271
'Greek Wide Web' 259–271
Greek world 259–271, 296

Hebrew 235–236, 241
Hecale 143–144
Hector 108–109, 183, 249, 255
Hedylus 82
Hegesias 33–39
– oratory 36
– style 33–34, 36, 37–38, 39
Heliodora 87–88, 91
Hellen 212
Hellenes 303, 307
Hellenistic aesthetics 135–156, 159–161
Hellenistic poetry and prose
– age in 49–50
– asyndeton in 38–39
– author in 39–48
– controversy in 40–46
– debate on relationship 33
– division and genre 33, 44
– ego-language in 39–48
– fiction in 35, 48–50
– mutual interest 31–33
– poetry 'translated' into prose 32
– prose changes appreciation of poetry 36, 38, 39, 50, 51
– prose rhythm and metre 33–34
– questions in 40–41
Hellenistic prose
– controversies in 34
– fiction in 48–50
– self-assertion in 40, 43
Hellenistic style 61–74
Hera 192, 201

Heracles 115–116, 140, 146, 261–264
Heraclides Creticus 43–44
Heraclides Ponticus 49–50
Heraclitus of Ephesus 92–94
Hermodorus 82
Herodas 39, 77, 275–276
Herodes 303–304
Herodotus 39, 103, 253, 285, 297–298
Hesiod 5, 13–14, 17, 19, 22, 25–28
Hesychius 248
Hipparchus of Athens 20
Hippolytus 219
Hipponax of Ephesus 93
history 170–171
Homer 19–22, 59–60, 64–71, 74, 110–111, 144, 202, 215–216, 240, 249, 256, 319–321
Homeric scholia 97–98, 104–106, 107–108
Homeric simile 98–101, 104–107, 109, 111
Homeric style 64–65
Horace 25
Hyperboreans 264

individuality 155
intaglio 186–188, 203–210
intertextuality 166–167
Ion 137
Isaac 237, 240–241, 244

Jacoby, Felix 158–159
Jason 144–145
Jerusalem 238, 252–253, 254–257
Jones, David 182–183
Judgement of Paris 192

Kairos (sculpture by Lysippus) 186
Kallixenos 294
katharsis 136, 154
Kuzmin, Michail 165

Laodamia 123–128
learned poetry 165–166
Leconte de Lisle, Charles 173–174
Lemnian Athena (sculpture by Phidias) 197
Leonidas of Tarentum 93, 94, 211–212
literary language 169

locus amoenus 142, 173–174, 210
Lord Byron 176
Lucretius 25
Lycophron 182–183, 237
– *Alexandra* 97–111, 148–149
lyrical 'I' 131–132
Lysippus 186

Mallarmé, Stéphane 161, 165–166, 170
Mark Antony 208–209
Marlborough gem 205–209
mathematics 44, 47–48
Medea 147–148, 149
Melanippe 212
Meleager 77–95, 188–191, 196, 203, 209–210
Menander 231–233
Menelaus 221–222
mercenary 306–310, 314–315, 318–319, 322–323, 325, 329
metamorphosis poetry 25–26
metaphor 97, 100, 103–104
metapoetics 127–131, 185–212
Metapontos 212
Miletus 265
Mimnermus 3, 177
miniature replicas of the *opera nobilia* 188, 194–195
modernization 144–145
mood 151–152
Moschus
– *Europa* 115, 149–151
Moses 239, 251, 255–256
Myron 191
myth 113–132, 169–171

narrative
– elliptical 114–132
– and simile 100–111
Nekuia (painting by Nikias) 202
neo-Attic art 188, 191–193
network 259–271
Nietzsche, Friedrich 160–161, 166
Nonnus 239, 242
Nossis 94

obscurity 170
Oedipus 219

oratory
– Attic 34, 36, 48
– Hellenistic 36
Orestes 109
ornatus 201, 204–205
Ortega y Gasset, José 162
Ovid 25–26, 28

Pan 198–199
Panhellenism 262–264
Paris 104–105, 192, 200–202
Parmenides 16–17
Parnassianism 161, 165, 172–173
Paros 263
Parthenius 32–33, 143
Parthenos Athena (sculpture by Phidias) 197, 200
Pascoli, Giovanni 173–175
pastoral poetry 172–175
Pater, Walter 155
patron 59–60, 72–74, 284–285
patronage 41, 55, 274
patronymic 82, 302, 308, 315, 331
Pausanias 331, 333
Peisandros of Rhodes 318
Persepolis 290–293
Persia 278, 285–300
Persian king 285, 292–293, 296, 298
Persika 296–298
Phidias 198–201
Philitas 3, 186
Philodemus 31–33, 40–42
Philo the Elder 235–257
Pindar 8, 58–59, 62–64, 72–73
places as people 35, 39
Plato 9, 21, 49, 137, 209–210, 223
poetic pleasure 138–139, 154
poetic voice 80–81
poetic worlds 39
poetry book 57, 117, 212
Polyaenus 298
polyandria 301
Polybius
– and authorial interventions 39, 40, 43–44
– and emotive writing 36–37
– handling of self 45–46

– religion in   45–46
– and self-assertion   40, 43–44
Polycrates   284–286
Posidippus   75, 82, 186–187, 203–205
– *Lithika*   273–300
Pound, Ezra   182
Praxiteles   193, 197, 201–203
Promachos Athena (sculpture by Phidias)
    197, 200
prose rhythm   33–34
Protesilaus   123–128
Pseudo-Aristeas   235
Psyche   207
Ptolemies   235, 267–268, 274–276, 278,
    284–286, 290, 294, 296, 299–300,
    302–305, 309–310, 313–315
'pure poetry'   161–162, 167–168
pyxis (cosmetic box)   204

reader
– imagined/actual   80–81
– supplementation/participation   113, 115–131
reuixit ars   192–203
Rhodes   89
Rutilius Lupus   36

Sappho   66
satyr play   227
Satyrus   45, 233
Seferis, George   170–171, 183
sensation   135–156
sense-perception   138
Septuagint   235–236, 241, 248, 253, 255
Seth, Vikram   176–178
shield   330–333
shield of Achilles   186, 204
Sibylline Oracles   237, 240, 256
simile   97–111, 122–123, 128
– and narrative   100–111
snake   330–331
Socrates   17
Solon   8–9, 18
Sophocles   111, 219–221
statuettes of the Nymphs   210–212

St Cyril of Alexandria   239
St John Chrysostom   239
structure as formal characteristic   57–61
Susa   287–292
synkrisis   185, 202

Talos   179–180
Theocritus   55–74, 81, 172–175
– *Idyll* 1   141–142, 151, 185–186
– *Idyll* 2   146
– *Idyll* 7   50, 173
– *Idyll* 14   68–72
– *Idyll* 16   41, 55–68, 72–74
– *Idyll* 17   274–275
– *Idyll* 25   116
– controversy in   41–42
– and post-Platonic dialogue   48–50
Theodoridas   82, 91
Theognidean corpus   7–8, 10–11
Theophrastus   216
Theseus   202
Tractatus Coislinianus   15–16
tragedy   215–233, 236–237
– comic features in   215–233
tragic pathos   217–221
tragic scholia   215–233
Trojan War   119, 121, 123
Tryphon   207–208
Tyre   90
Tyrtaeus   4–7

Varro   34
visuality   145–146, 148–149, 217
votive offerings   210–212

Walcott, Derek   178–180
water   210–212
Wilde, Oscar   156, 161
World War I   301

Xenomedes   48, 181, 262
Xerxes   290–291, 293
Xuthus   212

Zenophila   87–88, 91

www.ingramcontent.com/pod-product-compliance
Lightning Source LLC
Chambersburg PA
CBHW071810230426
43670CB00013B/2416